T0407227

Memory, Music, Manuscripts

STUDIES IN EAST ASIAN BUDDHISM 30

Memory, Music, Manuscripts

THE RITUAL DYNAMICS OF *KŌSHIKI* IN JAPANESE SŌTŌ ZEN

Michaela Mross

A KURODA INSTITUTE BOOK
University of Hawai'i Press
Honolulu

Printed in the United States of America

First printing, 2022

Library of Congress Cataloging-in-Publication Data

Names: Mross, Michaela, author.
Title: Memory, music, manuscripts : the ritual dynamics of Kōshiki in Japanese Sōtō Zen / Michaela Mross.
Other titles: Studies in East Asian Buddhism ; no. 30.
Description: Honolulu : University of Hawaiʻi Press, 2022. | Series: Studies in East Asian Buddhism ; 30 | "A Kuroda Institute book." | Includes bibliographical references and index.
Identifiers: LCCN 2021042972 | ISBN 9780824892739 (hardback) | ISBN 9780824892876 (adobe pdf) | ISBN 9780824892883 (epub) | ISBN 9780824892890 (kindle edition)
Subjects: LCSH: Sōtōshū—Rituals. | Buddhist hymns, Japanese—History and criticism. | Buddhist music—Japan—History and criticism.
Classification: LCC BQ9423.5.J3 M76 2022 | DDC 294.3/927—dc23
LC record available at https://lccn.loc.gov/2021042972

The Kuroda Institute for the Study of Buddhism is a nonprofit, educational corporation founded in 1976. One of its primary objectives is to promote scholarship on the historical, philosophical, and cultural ramifications of Buddhism. In association with the University of Hawaiʻi Press, the Institute also publishes Classics in East Asian Buddhism, a series devoted to the translation of significant texts in the East Asian Buddhist tradition.

University of Hawaiʻi Press books are printed on acid-free paper and meet the guidelines for permanence and durability of the Council on Library Resources.

Cover art: First page of the *Nehan kō kada narabini Shichisan,* a manuscript containing the verses of the *Nehan kōshiki* (1694). The verse shown here is the general obeisance. The lines in red ink indicate the melodic movements. Archive of Sōjiji Soin, Monzen. Photo by the author. Used with permission.

Contents

Preface ix

Abbreviations xv

Conventions xvii

Introduction 1

Aims of This Study 2

Liturgy and Music in Japanese Buddhism 6

Zen Liturgy 10

Methods and Sources 12

Overview of the Book 14

PART ONE *Development and Performance of* Kōshiki

Chapter 1. History of *Kōshiki* 19

Kōshiki *in Japanese Buddhism* 21

History of Kōshiki *in the Sōtō School* 31

Kōshiki *Practice in Contemporary Sōtō Zen* 51

From Manuscript to Print 54

Conclusions 58

Chapter 2. Ritual Structure of Sōtō *Kōshiki* 60

Modules and Frames: Theoretical Considerations 61

A Brief History of the Arhat Cult 63

Performance of the Rakan kōshiki *in Contemporary Japan* 68

Ritual Frames and the Structure of the Rakan kōshiki 93

Modules in the Rakan kōshiki 102

The Rakan kōshiki *on the Move* 107

Conclusions 114

Chapter 3. *Kōshiki* as Music Practice 116
The Music of Kōshiki 117
Musical Notation in the Realm of Oral Transmission 130
The Study and Transmission of Shōmyō 148
Kōshiki Shōmyō *as Zen Practice* 153
Conclusions 168

PART TWO Kōshiki *and Collective Memory: The Case of Keizan*

Chapter 4. Early Modern Lineage Divergences 173
Keizan's Temples: Yōkōji and Sōjiji 175
Memorial Service for Keizan at Sōjiji 178
Butsuji kōshiki 183
Differences between the Two Transmission Lineages 196
Conclusions 200

Chapter 5. Innovations in the Meiji Era 201
The Sōtō School in the Meiji Era 201
Hakugan's Revision of the Butsuji kōshiki 203
Tōjō dentō kōshiki: *A New* Hōon kōshiki *for Keizan* 210
Intertextuality of the Dentō kōshiki 226
Conclusions 227

Epilogue 232

Appendices: Kōshiki *Commemorating Keizan*
1. Extant Manuscripts of the Butsuji kōshiki 239
2. Shikimon *of the* Butsuji kōshiki *(Translation)* 243
3. Kohō Hakugan's Preface to the Taiso Butsuji kōshiki *(Translation)* 259
4. Azegami Baisen's Preface to the Tōjō dentō kōshiki *(Translation)* 261
5. Bukkan Bonjō's Postscript to the Tōjō dentō kōshiki *(Translation)* 263
6. Shikimon *of the* Tōjō dentō kōshiki *(Translation)* 265
7. Butsuji kōshiki *(ca. 1725): Yōkōji Manuscript (Facsimile)* 281
8. Kaisan Kokushi Butsuji kōshiki *(1806): Taineiji Manuscript (Facsimile)* 293
9. Tōjō dentō kōshiki *(1893) (Facsimile)* 303
Bibliography 317
Index 349

Online Supplemental Materials

Video excerpts of performances of the *Rakan kōshiki* and *Dentō kōshiki,* recorded at Sōjiji from 2004 to 2018, are available for viewing at the Stanford Digital Repository, https://searchworks.stanford.edu/view/dq109wp7548.

Preface

THE SEEDS for this project were sown many years ago when I first visited Japan to spend a summer at Hōkōji, a remote monastery of the Rinzai school in Shizuoka prefecture. Before coming to Japan, I had imagined that life at a Japanese Zen monastery would be relatively quiet, but to my surprise I encountered a rich soundscape. The sounds of various instruments regulated our schedule, and we chanted sacred texts at least twice a day. What especially caught my attention as a jazz musician was a ritual we performed every morning—a rolling reading of the *Great Sutra on the Perfection of Wisdom.* It started with a recitation of the *Heart Sutra* at a very fast tempo to dynamic drum playing. The sound of the energetic drum, which at points reminded me of a jazz improvisation, together with our loud voices, broke the silence of the morning.

I left Japan with a deep impression of the vivid soundscape that characterizes a Japanese monastery. As I approached the end of my MA program at the University of Hamburg, I decided to combine my interests in music, Japanese culture, and Buddhism in my master's thesis. With a declared interest in the aural landscape, I started a six-month field study in 2004 to explore the role of music in Japanese Buddhism. At that time, I was introduced to Sawada Atsuko, an ethnomusicologist working on Buddhist music, who in turn kindly introduced me to many temples and monks. Among the latter was Maekawa Bokushō, a well-known specialist in *shōmyō* (Buddhist chant) of the Sōtō school, who has taught at Sōjiji and Nittaiji Senmon Sōdō. Maekawa was very supportive and organized a research trip for me that inspired my study of Sōtō Zen rituals in the years to come.

First I visited Eiheiji, the place where Japanese Sōtō Zen originated and one of the two head temples of the Sōtō school, located deep in the mountains of Fukui prefecture. It was early October, and I fortunately arrived just a few days before the memorial day of Bodhidharma, the semi-legendary Indian monk who is said to have transmitted Chan from India to China. Hearing that I was interested in Buddhist music, a senior monk encouraged me to stay one day longer in order to witness the *Daruma kōshiki,* a ritual for Bodhidharma that was to be performed during the memorial service—it was, he assured me, one of the most musical observances of the Sōtō school. Thus, I stayed. And indeed the ritual truly impressed me: the novices sang elegant, solemn melodies in several distinctive styles, and all their movements were carefully choreographed.

I then left the green mountains of Fukui for the gray metropolis of Yokohama to visit Sōjiji, the other head temple of the Sōtō school. Again, I arrived just in time to see another *kōshiki,* this one performed in remembrance of Keizan Jōkin, the founder of Sōjiji. The monks warmly welcomed me, and thanks to their interest in my research—and to the introduction of Maekawa, who had taught at Sōjiji—I was able to attend several rehearsals that are usually closed to outsiders, especially a foreign woman. The monk in charge of the musical training of the novices was Akiba Tairyū, and I observed the meticulous care with which he taught them how to read the musical notation and sing the challenging melodies. Akiba's clear voice and elegant singing style invested the whole ritual with a special atmosphere. A month later, when I returned to Sōjiji, the monks were again performing a *kōshiki*—on this occasion, a *Rakan kōshiki,* a ritual for the Sixteen Arhats that had originally been performed by Dōgen, the founder of the Japanese Sōtō school, and subsequently by Keizan.

These encounters with the liturgical genre called *kōshiki,* which had been almost entirely overlooked in Western Zen studies, piqued my curiosity, and I decided to write my master's thesis on the *Rakan kōshiki.* In the course of that work, I came to realize that the genre's rich history in the Sōtō school had not yet been thoroughly studied, even by Japanese scholars: Zen scholarship revolved around Dōgen and his thought, while scholars of *kōshiki* focused on works associated with the earlier Nara schools. I therefore decided to explore the historical development of this genre in the Sōtō school in order to illuminate the vital role of music and ritual in Sōtō Zen. I spent six years in Japan, from 2007 to 2013, fully engaged in research on this topic, and after finishing my PhD in 2014, I have visited Japan once or twice a year to continue it. *Memory, Music, Manuscripts* represents the results of this long and intense period of work on *kōshiki.*

My research was possible because I was able to establish fruitful connections to Sōtō priests and institutions while living in Japan. First of all, Maekawa Bokushō aided my research in countless ways. He has a wide network, mainly of Sōjiji-affiliated priests, and he introduced me to many individuals and institutions. During my years in Japan, I was a visiting researcher at the Research Institute for Japanese Music Historiography at Ueno Gakuen University, where I was able to use the institute's large collection of manuscripts and woodblock prints. I was also a graduate student at Komazawa University in Tokyo, the flagship university of the Sōtō school. Being a student there offered me another network, as well as access to an excellent library with a good rare book collection. Komazawa University is also the home of the Sōtōshū Bunkazai Chōsa Iinkai (Committee for the study of cultural assets of the Sōtō school), which conducts archival work at Sōtō temples across Japan and has many facsimiles of premodern texts in its archive. The scholars of the Sōtōshū Bunkazai Chōsa Iinkai helped me gain access to other temples as well. For example, Itō Ryōkō introduced me to Tamamuro Fumio, who allowed me to join his research group in the archive of Sōjiji Soin for two subsequent summers. During that time, I had the rare privilege of unlimited access to all the texts in this archive, where I discovered many valuable manuscripts, including a *kōshiki* whose existence had been forgotten.

Although I established strong connections to Sōtō priests and institutions early on, I still needed to request formal permission both to do research in temple archives and to observe the rituals conducted at a particular temple. Usually a priest friend of mine would call the head priest of the temple to introduce me informally, and I would write a formal letter requesting permission whenever I set out to visit a temple for the first time. For subsequent visits, I again wrote a letter asking permission to see a certain text or ritual. When I planned to film a ritual or take photos of texts, I likewise requested permission, and in many cases I had to sign forms that detailed how the images were to be used. If I did not know anyone who could introduce me to the temple in question, I wrote a formal letter to the head priest, enclosing an article or two I had written in Japanese to demonstrate that I had worked in archives before, and to show my sincerity. Since articles on rituals rarely appear in Japanese scholarship on Zen, whereas many Sōtō priests are interested in the history of their ritual practice, they kindly permitted me access and supported my research.

A scholar doing fieldwork usually grows closer to her interlocutors over the years. This was also the case for me, and I naturally became friends with some of my informants. At the large Sōtō temple of Tōkōji, I twice had the honor of playing saxophone in a ceremony that we newly created combining elements of *shōmyō* and jazz. Shortly after, I helped organize a concert tour to Germany for the Sōtō priest choir Zen-Kūge Ryūgin Kai. Through these collaborations, my bonds with the Sōtō priests who participated in these events grew stronger and I was able to learn more about ritual practices than would have been possible otherwise.

In these ways and myriad others, my research has been indebted to the support and guidance of numerous people, foundations, and institutions, to whom I am deeply grateful. Klaus Vollmer, my dissertation supervisor at LMU Munich, provided unwavering guidance and insightful advice. I am also very grateful to Steven Heine, who has given me invaluable feedback and encouragement over the years since we first met in Japan. Niels Gülberg provided help on many occasions and openly shared his vast knowledge of *kōshiki* and his collection of manuscripts and woodblock prints with me. I would also like to express my gratitude to my early teachers at the University of Hamburg, especially Roland Schneider, Judit Árokay, and Jörg Quenzer.

In Japan, Satō Shūkō, my doctoral supervisor at Komazawa University, offered constant advice on rituals and manuscripts. At Komazawa University, Hareyama Shun'ei, Hirose Ryōkō, Ishii Kōsei, Ishii Seijun, Ishii Shūdō,

Matsuda Yōji, Ogawa Takashi, Okuno Mitsuyoshi, Takahashi Shūei, Tsunoda Tairyū, the late Yoshizu Yoshihide, and Yotsuya Kōdō provided counsel and encouragement. Matsuda Yōji, Itō Ryōkyū, and Tanaka Hiroshi of the Sōtōshū Bunkazai Chōsa Iinkai kindly offered access to their archive and valuable assistance. I also benefited from the expertise of the members of the Research Institute for Japanese Music Historiography of Ueno Gakuen University—first of all its director, Fukushima Kazuo, as well as Arai Kōjun, Iso Mizue, Steven Nelson, Sakurai Rika, and Tanaka Yukie. Ozaki Shōzen, Shimizu Yūshō, and Sawada Atsuko also provided selfless guidance on many occasions.

Many priests supported my research and generously shared their knowledge and ideas with me. As mentioned above, I am deeply indebted to Maekawa Bokushō. I also wish to express my gratitude to the late Akiba Tairyū, Baba Gijitsu, Imamura Genshō, Inoue Gishin, Kōya Keinin, Maekawa Shinshō, Matsumoto Jōtai, Munakata Gihō, Nozaki Taiyū, Suzuki Bunmei, Suzuki Eiichi, Taga Sōjun, and Terakura Shōyū, as well as to the members of the *shōmyō* choir Zen-Kūge Ryūgin Kai for helping me gain insight into the sounding world of Sōtō Zen. I would also like to thank Sōjiji, Sōjiji Soin, Yōkōji, Eiheiji, Eiheiji Betsuin in Tokyo, Eiheiji Betsuin in Nagoya, Nittaiji Senmon Sōdō, Tōkōji, Kasuisai, Kenchōji, Engakuji, and Tōfukuji for allowing me to pursue fieldwork and archival studies at their temples. Without their assistance, this research would never have been possible.

During the writing of this book, I benefited from the feedback of several colleagues. Carl Bielefeldt, Ronald Grimes, John Kieschnick, Richard Jaffe, and Jacqueline Stone kindly took the time to read a completed draft of this manuscript and provided important comments during a book manuscript workshop hosted by the Stanford Humanities Center. I am very grateful to two anonymous readers for their valuable and detailed responses, which helped immensely in my final revisions. Joshua Capitanio read chapters at different stages and gave detailed suggestions. Pamela Winfield and Tom Owens also read parts of my manuscript and provided helpful comments. Robert Buswell, director of the Kuroda Institute for the Study of Buddhism and Human Values, was very supportive in guiding me through the review process. I would also like to thank Stephanie Chun and Cheryl Loe of University of Hawai'i Press for their attentiveness during the publication process, Stuart Kiang for his thorough copyediting, and Mary Mortensen for preparing the index.

Many other colleagues and friends offered support, suggestions, and feedback, whether by helping me obtain resources or by championing me in other ways during my research and writing. Among them are Heidi Buck-Albulet, Barbara Ambros, Arai Ikkō, Marcus Bingenheimer, William Bodiford, Clara Böhme, James Ford, Griffith Foulk, Oliver Freiberger, Hanawa Kōmei, Martin Hanke, Paul Harrison, Hasegawa Keiichi, Xi He, Mack Horton, Ute Hüsken, Vanessa Kam, Kamata Mukan, Andreas Klein, Kobayashi Toyokazu, Kasai Kōyū, Sujung Kim, Kigensan Stephan Licha, Mark Lewis, Bryan Lowe, Michael Jametz, Lori Meeks, Martin Mellech, Mark MacWilliams, Chuck

Muller, Nagasaki Kiyonori, Nakano Shōzen, Nishizawa Mayumi, Justin Pehoski, Grace Ramswick, Heinz-Dieter Reese, Daniel Schley, Pia Schmitt, Takai Shōjū, Tahara Ryōhei, Tanaka Genjō, Luke Thompson, Robban Toleno, Katja Triplett, Wakayama Yūkō, Thorsten Wettich, Yamaguchi Seishō, and my *senpai* in Professor Satō's PhD course.

I was fortunate to spend two inspiring years as a Shinjō Itō postdoctoral fellow at the University of California, Berkeley, and wish to thank especially Mark Blum, Robert Sharf, and Alexander von Rospatt for their advocacy. During my stay, Mark Blum organized a conference on Buddhist music that not only provided a wonderful occasion to discuss the history, role, and performance practices of numerous traditions of Buddhist music, but also included performances by many groups.

At Stanford University, where I have taught since 2016, I have benefited from stimulating conversations with faculty and graduate students in the Department of Religious Studies. The Ho Center for Buddhist Studies has hosted numerous talks, workshops, and other events, creating a space for inspiring intellectual exchange. The Stanford Humanities Center (together with the Department of Religious Studies) supported a manuscript workshop that proved very helpful, and Regan Murphy Kao and the staff of the East Asia Library made precious resources available and provided superb service.

My research has received generous financial support from the Bukkyō Dendō Kyōkai, the Japanese Government (MEXT), the Japan Foundation, the German Academic Exchange Service (DAAD), Komazawa University, the University of Hamburg, the headquarters of the Sōtō school, and Sōjiji.

I would also like to express my gratitude to Sōjiji Soin, Yōkōji, Taineiji, Zenkyūin, Dairyūji, Niels Gülberg (Kadono Konzen Library Collection), the Sōtōshū Bunkazai Chōsa Iinkai, the Toyohashi City Museum of Art and History, and the Stanford East Asia Library for allowing me to reproduce rare manuscripts and woodblock prints in their possession. I am deeply grateful to the monks of Sōjiji who went above and beyond to provide photos of *kōshiki* performances and instruments for this book, and also to Eiheiji and Arai Ikkō for granting permission to reproduce photos. I am further indebted to the headquarters of the Sōtō school, Maekawa Bokushō, and Suzuki Bunmei for permission to publish images of musical notations and *kōshiki* texts. In addition, Ilona Mross provided incredible help with the editing of photos and facsimiles and with creating diagrams.

Last but not least, I would like to thank my family for supporting me during the many years of study and research.

Abbreviations

Bunkazai	*Sōtōshū bunkazai chōsa mokuroku kaidaishū*
DZO	*Dōgen zenji zenshū. 2 vols. 1969–1970.*
DZSK	*Dōgen zenji shinseki kankei shiryōshū*
DZSS	*Dōgen zenji shinpitsu shūsei*
DZZ	*Dōgen zenji zenshū. 7 vols. 1988–1993.*
JDZ	*Jōsai daishi zenshū*
K	*Shohon taikō Eihei kaizan Dōgen zenji gyōjō Kenzeiki*
Komonjo	*Sōtōshū komonjo*
KZ	*Keizan Zen*
Monzenshi 2	*Shinshū Monzenchō shi, Shiryōhen 2: Sōjiji*
MSS	*Myōe shōnin shiryō*
NKS	*Nihon kayō shūsei*
Shūhō	*Sōtōshū shūhō chōsa mokuroku kaidaishū*
SZ	*Sōtōshū zensho*
T	*Taishō shinshū daizōkyō*
X	*Shinsan Dai Nihon zoku zōkyō*
ZGD	*Zengaku daijiten (shinpan)*
ZSZ	*Zoku Sōtōshū zensho*

Conventions

JAPANESE IS TRANSCRIBED using a modified Hepburn system. Chinese names, terms, and titles are given in pinyin. Japanese and Chinese terms are generally written in lowercase letters. Only names and titles, including the titles of *shōmyō* pieces, are capitalized. Terms indicating a genre of liturgical texts, such as *hōon kōshiki* or *shikimon,* are not capitalized.

The romanization of premodern Japanese remains a question of critical debate. This is especially so in a work on *kōshiki,* because "traditional" readings, on the one hand, are preserved in liturgical texts and, on the other, the pronunciation of certain words differs according to the school or lineage. In my translations, I follow the reading indicated in the ritual handbooks, or, if no pronunciation is given, I provide the contemporary reading.

I observe the Japanese custom of giving surnames first, followed by given names.

For dates until Meiji 5 (1872), I provide the reign name and year followed by the corresponding year in the Gregorian calendar in parentheses. If applicable, it is followed by the month and day in the lunar calendar. On January 1, 1873, the Japanese government switched to using the Gregorian calendar. Therefore, for dates from 1873 onward, I only indicate the Gregorian calendar year.

Introduction

As THE CLEAR TONES of bells resound in the Hall of the Great Ancestors, monks file in. Once seated, they lift their voices in the exquisite and solemn melody of a Chinese chant while three monks circumambulate the hall. One of them scatters golden paper flowers, one sprinkles water, and another carries an incense vessel. Soon the fragrance of fine incense fills the air. A Sanskrit incantation praising the Four Wisdoms follows, creating a unique atmosphere. Each syllable is energetically sung several times on one pitch, with small melodic inflections incorporated now and again. At the beginning and end of this piece, two monks play on cymbals in fixed patterns of short and long strokes with carefully choreographed movements. Next, a monk recites a text in Japanese that praises Keizan Jōkin 瑩山紹瑾 (1264 / 68–1325), known as the great popularizer of Japanese Sōtō Zen, asking him to accept offerings placed on the altar with highly formalized gestures. Thereafter, the assembly sings a verse expressing their devotion to Keizan. Another monk intones a highly melismatic piece praising the Buddha. Its vocalization style, with a profusion of melismas on the single syllable "me," naturally forms a musical climax in the ritual. The following three liturgical pieces, each sung with a cheerful melody in an arresting, almost jazzy rhythm, stand in contrast to the preceding ones, all sung in free rhythm. Finally, the officiant reads the central text of the ceremony, which first narrates the transmission of the Dharma from the Buddha to the Chinese Chan patriarchs, and then to Japanese Zen masters, before detailing the biography and virtues of Keizan. The recitation of the officiant is interspersed with Chinese verses sung by the assembly to solemn melodies, followed by full prostrations, expressing veneration to Keizan. The ritual concludes with the singing of a verse to transfer the merit produced by the performance.

This scene describes a ritual annually performed on the evening of October 14 at Sōjiji 總持寺, one of the two head temples of the Sōtō school of Japanese Zen. It is the *Tōjō dentō kōshiki* 洞上傳燈講式 (*Kōshiki* on the transmission of the light in the Sōtō school), a ritual in the *kōshiki* 講式 genre that Sōjiji's monks perform to commemorate the founder of their temple, Keizan. This *kōshiki* is part of a larger ritual program performed during the joint memorial service for Keizan and Sōjiji's second abbot, Gasan Jōseki 峨山韶碩

(1276–1366), who are commemorated together from October 12 to 15 each year. I have attended this service many times, most recently in 2018. It is an occasion at which hundreds of Sōtō clerics from all over Japan gather to pay respect to their lineage founder Keizan and to perform a series of rituals in the Hall of the Great Ancestors from early morning to afternoon. Among them are several head priests from other Sōtō temples who serve as officiants during the sutra-chanting rituals. The *kōshiki* on the evening of October 14, however, differs from the other rituals. Most of them feature sutra chanting in a constant rhythm with very limited or no melodic inflections, whereas the *kōshiki* incorporates a wide range of styles, from solemn melodic verses in free rhythm to chants with a cheerful melody, to highly melismatic pieces. Additionally, only monks living at Sōjiji actively participate in the *kōshiki,* which takes place in the evening when the doors of the large hall are closed, preventing any lay devotee from seeing or hearing the ritual. It is thus a private remembrance of the temple founder, performed by Sōjiji's monastic congregation.

The *Tōjō dentō kōshiki* is one of eleven rituals in the *kōshiki* genre that Sōtō clerics still perform today. Although Sōtō monks have performed *kōshiki* since the thirteenth century, their significance as an important ritual form has been almost entirely overlooked in Western Zen studies so far.[1] *Memory, Music, Manuscripts* ventures into this terra incognita for the first time, exploring the intricate interplay of doctrine, devotion, music, literature, and ritual that characterizes this genre, and shedding new light on the practice of Zen Buddhism as a lived tradition.

Aims of This Study

For most of the twentieth century, Western publications described Zen as an iconoclastic school of meditation. This view developed from a narrow focus on certain textual genres, such as the collected sayings of Zen masters, with the result that scholars tended to overlook aspects of Zen Buddhism that receive little or no emphasis in doctrinal texts. Another reason was that Zen officials in the Meiji era (1868–1912) emphasized the iconoclastic discourse found in Song dynasty sources, imagining "a 'pure Zen' (*junsuizen*) relatively free of Buddhist rituals for dealing with spirits and meeting the religious needs of lay patrons."[2] In the 1990s, however, scholars began to move beyond a preoccupation with doctrine to explore what Zen monks actually did, and

1. Only two of the *kōshiki* performed in the Sōtō school have been previously studied by Western scholars: Paula Arai (2000, 2008) and Barbara Ambros (2016a, 2016b) have analyzed the *Anan kōshiki* (*Kōshiki* on Ānanda), a ritual specifically performed by Sōtō nuns, and Marinus Willem de Visser (1923) provided an abbreviated translation of the *Rakan kōshiki* (*Kōshiki* on the arhats).

2. Foulk 2008, 26. For a discussion of the image of "pure Zen" and the discourse concerning the importance of a "meditative experience" since the Meiji era, see also Sharf 1993 and 1995.

still do, in concrete times and places.[3] As a result, the study of rituals became a major research field in contemporary Zen studies, redefining our understanding of Zen by showing that Zen monks have continually been engaged in a wide range of ritual practices, including some not previously associated with the Zen tradition.[4]

Memory, Music, Manuscripts adds another vital dimension to the revaluation of Zen Buddhism by offering the first systematic study of the history and development of *kōshiki* in the Sōtō school.[5] It reveals how Zen monks created a ritual practice that expresses devotion, founder worship, and communal memory in a highly musical ceremony. The liturgical genre known as *kōshiki* was invented several centuries before the founding of independent Zen schools in Japan when most laypeople could not understand the content of the sutras chanted in Chinese during Buddhist ceremonies. In response, Japanese clerics in the tenth century began to reform their liturgy by creating ritual texts recited in Japanese. This reform signaled the beginning of new liturgical genres that soon contributed to the spread of Buddhism across different social strata. Among the new genres, the most important was *kōshiki*, and its invention proved a milestone in the development of a liturgy in the vernacular language. *Kōshiki* were composed and performed for a wide range of objects of veneration, including buddhas, bodhisattvas, *kami*, eminent monks, and even music and poetry. With the rapid spread of works in this genre throughout all Buddhist traditions during the early medieval period, it was perhaps inevitable that Sōtō clerics would also adopt this ritual genre. Yet, while *kōshiki* in other schools have received increasing scholarly attention

3. Without presuming to give a comprehensive overview of this trend, a few exemplary studies can be noted: William Bodiford's (1993) study of institutional development and practices such as ordinations and funerary services in medieval Sōtō Zen; Bernhard Faure's (1991, 1996) innovative use of postmodern theory to problematize the traditional Zen narrative, including a study of Keizan that illuminates the interplay of imagination, local cults, and dreams; Duncan Williams's (2005) monograph on Sōtō Zen in Tokugawa Japan, which explores pilgrimages, healing practices, and funerals; and the recent volume *Zen and Material Culture*, which highlights the intimate relations between doctrine, practice, and material culture (Winfield and Heine 2017).

4. For studies on the use of Chan portraits, icons, robes, and medicine in Zen rituals, see the essays in Faure 2003 and Heine and Wright 2008. Foulk (1987) and Yifa (2002) further demonstrate how Chan monastic codes were intimately related to ritual customs of Chinese Buddhism broadly considered. On the monastic codes known as "rules of purity" (*qinggui* 清規, J. *shingi*), see also Collcutt 1983 and Foulk 2004 and 2006. Borup (2008), Irizarry (2011), and Graf (2017), moreover, have detailed the role of rituals in contemporary Zen Buddhism. On rituals performed by Sōtō nuns, including the *Anan kōshiki* 阿難講式, see Arai P. 2008 and Ambros 2016a and 2016b. For a study of a contemporary Kannon festival celebrated once every thirty-three years, see Bodiford 1994. For a study of how the Rinzai monk Tōrei Enji 東嶺円慈 (1721–1792) believed sutra chanting would aid meditative concentration, provide protection from negative influences, and promote good health, see Joskovich 2019.

5. Nakano Tōzen (1984) offered a very brief overview of the history of Sōtō *kōshiki*. Since that publication, however, many new manuscripts and woodblock prints have been discovered that provide vital new information about the evolution of Sōtō *kōshiki*.

in recent years, *kōshiki* in the Zen schools, as well as their development, have eluded systematic study so far.[6]

Western scholars have frequently viewed Japanese Buddhism through a sectarian lens, rarely venturing to explore the relations among different schools. That constraint is in part due to the influence of Japanese Buddhist scholarship, which has largely reflected sectarian identities. Zen in particular has often been represented as though it is independent of other Japanese Buddhist traditions. Nevertheless, some Western scholars have analyzed Japanese Zen rituals against the backdrop of Chinese ritual practices and argued that Japanese Zen Buddhism has preserved many of the ritual forms that were originally transmitted from China to Japan.[7] In this study, I show that Japanese Zen clerics also practiced rituals that were invented in Japan, *kōshiki* chief among them, and used elements of a ritual repertoire widely shared in Japanese Buddhism. Indeed, by demonstrating how *kōshiki* are embedded in a ritual culture shared across Buddhist schools and lineages, this book not only challenges long-standing sectarian approaches to the study of Japanese Buddhism, but confirms that studying a shared ritual language is vital for understanding both the evolution of Japanese Buddhist rituals and the way Zen Buddhists came to develop a distinctive tradition of their own within the broad religious landscape of Japan.

While Sōtō *kōshiki* draw on elements from a shared ritual repertoire, the performance of particular *kōshiki*, as well as the performance practice, expresses the school's identity. By highlighting the role of rituals in community building, I argue that the performance of *kōshiki* is inherently an affirmation

6. Despite the fact that Marinus Willem de Visser's (1923) partial translation of the Sōtō *Rakan kōshiki* appeared nearly one hundred years ago, only in the last twenty years have Western scholars begun to acknowledge the importance of this liturgical genre. The first book-length publication on *kōshiki* in a European language was Niels Gülberg's (1999) study of the development of *kōshiki* and its influence on literature, which provides an overview of the history of *kōshiki* in all Buddhist schools. Gülberg also maintained an invaluable *kōshiki* database (1997–2019), and his innovative work was followed by a number of publications analyzing the content of specific *kōshiki*. Among them are James Ford's (2005, 2006a, 2006b) work on Jōkei's *Miroku kōshiki* 弥勒講式 (*Kōshiki* on Maitreya); David Quinter's (2006, 2011, 2016) studies of two *Monjū kōshiki* 文殊講式 (*Kōshiki* on Mañjuśrī) written by Jōkei 貞慶 (1155–1213) and Eison 叡尊 (1201–1290), and of Eison's *Shōtoku Taishi kōshiki* 聖徳太子講式 (*Kōshiki* on Shōtoku Taishi) (2014a, 2014b); and Lori Meeks's (2010) work on *kōshiki* at the Hokkeji 法華寺 convent in Nara and her study of the *kōshiki* on Rāhula (2016). In addition, Chris Callahan (2011, 2016) has studied the *Hōon kōshiki* 報恩講式 (*Kōshiki* to repay benevolence received) in commemoration of Shinran; and Paula Arai (2000, 2008) and Barbara Ambros (2016a, 2016b) the *Anan kōshiki* that is still performed by Sōtō nuns. The role of music in the *kōshiki* of the Shingon schools has been illuminated by Steven Nelson (2001b, 2009) and myself (Mross 2012c, 2016a). Recently, Chari Pradel (2016, chap. 4) has studied the *Taishi mandara kōshiki* 太子曼荼羅講式 (*Kōshiki* on the Taishi Mandala) in relation to the Tenjukoku Mandara 天寿国曼荼羅, and Matthew Hayes (2018) has studied Gahō's 我寶 (1239–1317) commentary on a *kōshiki* on relics composed by the Shingi Shingon branch founder Kakuban 覺鑁 (1095–1144). The *Japanese Journal of Religious Studies* also published a special issue on *kōshiki* (Ambros, Ford, and Mross 2016).

7. See, for example, Foulk 2008, 61.

of collective memory. Many of the *kōshiki* performed in the Sōtō school commemorate important Zen patriarchs by narrating their biographies. Through the performance, the performers are connected not only to the Zen patriarch who is being commemorated by the ritual, but also to earlier generations of clerics who performed the same ritual. Thus each performance connects them with their lineage and heritage, and regular communal performances help create a community of memory.

Importantly, however, I also show how monks revised liturgical texts when certain key stories in their communal memory or the biographic images of eminent monks changed. In this way, liturgical texts can be seen as fluid, and their fluidity is an aspect of ritual change. Although common definitions of the term "ritual" suggest that rituals are relatively invariant, it is often acknowledged that no single performance is like another.[8] In spite of that, few attempts have been made so far to track the development of a ritual genre over time through a combination of archival and ethnographic research. This book does so by highlighting the innovations that occurred in *kōshiki* composition and performance over centuries, and it demonstrates that such changes were often due to factors that lay outside the ritual context per se, involving institutional interests, evolving biographic images, and changes in cultural memory.

I understand rituals as multidimensional and multisensorial performances that comprise multiple registers or dimensions, such as places, texts, materials, actions, gestures, and sounds. Therefore, I approach *kōshiki* from a performative perspective and employ an interdisciplinary approach in the analysis of how these different dimensions work together in the performance of the ritual. This approach stands in contrast to that of previous *kōshiki* studies, which have focused chiefly on the content of ritual texts. The same tendency can be observed in Buddhist studies in general, since earlier generations of Buddhist studies scholars tended to examine the content of the texts and the ideas embedded in them rather than how those texts might have been performed or vocalized. Nonetheless, in order to fully understand rituals, we need to explore them as embodied practices and multidimensional performances.

A central feature of most rituals is the aural dimension—music and sounds. Curiously, scholars have rarely examined this facet of rituals.[9] Yet musical practice is central for many ritual specialists, precisely because the acquisition of ritual expertise is often a matter of learning the proper ways of vocalizing sacred texts and playing musical instruments. The liturgical texts of *kōshiki*, for example, are sung with melodies, and clerics spend many years

8. Roy Rappaport, for example, defines rituals as "the performance of more or less invariant sequences of formal acts and utterances not entirely encoded by the performers" (1999, 24) but allows for the possibility or necessity of "deliberate variation" on the part of the performers (36).

9. For detailed overviews and bibliographies of research on Buddhist music, see Greene et al. 2002, Szczepanski 2014, and Douglas 2015.

learning how to vocalize them. Additionally, musical instruments create a special soundscape that demarcates ritual time from non-ritual time. These musical aspects strongly contribute to the ritual's aesthetic quality and affective experience. Japanese Zen Buddhism, in particular, has often been depicted as a silent tradition despite the fact that sounds and chanting reverberate in Zen monasteries throughout the day.[10] Among the various Sōtō rituals, *kōshiki* are undoubtedly the most musical. By introducing Western readers to this vital aspect of Japanese Sōtō Zen, I argue that the sonic dimension of rituals is just as significant as the other, more intensively studied dimensions.

Further, by highlighting the importance of chanting and liturgical performance, I show that vocalization often plays a greater role in Buddhist cultivation than doctrinal study or introspective contemplation. Apart from studies focusing on chants of specific traditions, such as the *nenbutsu* (recitation of a buddha's name, often Amida Buddha's) or esoteric mantras, only scant attention has been paid so far to the importance of Buddhist vocal practice. This book therefore offers a corrective to our understanding of Zen, long represented as a tradition focused on silent contemplation, and shows it to be a bodily practice accompanied by a rich aural component.

Liturgy and Music in Japanese Buddhism

Musicologists use the term "music" to describe sounds that are organized by humans and differ from ordinary speech.[11] In the context of Japanese Buddhism, we find various styles of music that contemporary Japanese clerics and

10. Although the vocalization of Buddhist texts has played a vital role in the lives of Zen clerics, Japanese Buddhist chant has received very little scholarly attention in Western Zen studies so far. One exception is the work of the Austrian musicologists Franz Fördermayr and Werner Deutsch, who analyzed a recording of a *shōmyō* piece sung at Eiheiji in order to study biphonic vocal production (Fördermayr 1982; Fördermayr and Deutsch 1995). Nor has *shōmyō* received close attention in Japanese Zen studies. Japanese musicologists have studied the rich repertoires of *shōmyō* in the Tendai and Shingon schools instead, leaving the history of *shōmyō* in the Zen schools still to be written. There are, however, a few studies of Zen *shōmyō* from the standpoint of contemporary performance practice; see Yokoi 1967; Uemura 1979; Watarai and Sawada 1980, 1982; and Watarai and Tsukamoto 1983.

Musicologist Stephen Slottow, in his 2019 study of the Americanization of Zen chanting, highlights the fact that Zen Buddhism has its own music while distinguishing the great diversity of chanting styles adopted in American Zen practice. In this light, the lay practice of singing *eisanka* 詠讃歌 (Buddhist hymns) in a musical style quite different from that of *shōmyō* should be mentioned. The Sōtō clerics who invented this style of hymn chanting in the early 1950s based on the model of earlier practices in other Buddhist schools named it Baikaryū 梅花流 (lit., style of plum blossoms). This new chanting style quickly became popular, and today many Sōtō temples have choirs singing Buddhist hymns. For a detailed account of its history, see Baikaryū Eisanka Kenkyū Purojekuto 2019, and for an ethnographic study of the choir at Sōjiji, see Irizarry 2001, chap. 5.

11. See, for example, ethnomusicologist John Blacking's oft-cited definition that music "is

musicologists call "Buddhist music" (*bukkyō ongaku* 仏教音楽).[12] This rubric includes a wide range of different musical forms, and we can broadly distinguish between music within a ritual context and music outside it.[13] Most Buddhist rituals feature vocal music, with instruments often used solely to provide cues. This vocal music is called *shōmyō* 声明 (lit., bright voice), a term usually translated as "Japanese Buddhist chant." This term was originally a translation of the Sanskrit term *śabda vidyā,* which refers to the science of grammar and linguistics, one of the five sciences in ancient India. In Japan, *shōmyō* became the general term for Buddhist liturgical chant around the twelfth century. Prior to this, Buddhist chant was generally called *bonbai* 梵唄 (Ch. *fanbei;* lit. Sanskrit hymn, or pure hymn), a term still used in China and in the Ōbaku school of Japanese Zen.[14]

Over the centuries, many *shōmyō* lineages with distinct repertoires and performance practices developed, several of which have been handed down to the present day. Buddhist chant was first transmitted together with Buddhist ideas and practices from Korea and China; later Japanese clerics developed new liturgical genres. One of the earliest references to Buddhist music in Japan states that hundreds of monks recited sutras and sang the standard liturgical pieces *Praise of the Thus Come One* (*Nyoraibai* 如来唄), *Falling Flowers* (*Sange* 散華), *Sanskrit Sound* (*Bonnon* 梵音), and *Sounding Staff* (*Shakujō* 錫杖) during the Eye-Opening Ceremony of the Great Buddha of Tōdaiji 東大寺 (Nara) in Tenpyō 17 (752).[15] With the founding of the Shingon and Tendai schools in the Heian period (794–1185), many new liturgical pieces were introduced from China to Japan: Kūkai 空海 (774–835), the founder of the Shingon school, is said to have introduced the core repertoire of Shingon *shōmyō,* while Ennin 円仁 (794–864), a disciple of the Tendai school founder Saichō 最澄 (767–822), laid the foundation for Tendai *shōmyō*. Monks of these two schools have emphasized the importance of Buddhist chant. Over the centuries, they wrote many treatises on *shōmyō,* and some clerics made vital contributions to the development of musical

---

humanly organized sound" (1973, 10). For a discussion of the challenges faced in defining music, see Nettl 2015, chap. 2.

12. The vocalization of sacred texts has played an important role in Buddhism since its early times. The *Vinaya* originally prohibited certain musical forms, such as instrumental music and secular vocal music (see, for example, Liu 2018). However, in many cultures there was and still is a discrepancy between traditional precepts and the use of music in Buddhist rituals, as Li Wei (1992), for example, has pointed out.

13. There are many different forms of Buddhist music that are performed outside the ritual context. For instance, lay devotees or clerics sometimes sing popular hymns and songs such as *wasan* 和讃, *goeika* 御詠歌, and *imayō* 今様.

14. For more detailed historical overviews of *shōmyō* in English, see Demieville 1929–1930; Harich-Schneider 1973, chap. 10; Arai K. 1986, 1999; Nelson 2003, 2008a; and Sawada 2002. For a survey of Western-language publications on *shōmyō,* see Mross 2009.

15. *Todaiji yōroku,* 50.

notation systems.[16] Remarkably, the oldest dated printed musical notation in the world is a *shōmyō* notation of the Shingon school produced on Mt. Kōya 高野山 in Bunmei 4 (1472).[17]

The new Kamakura schools that emerged in the thirteenth century developed their own musical traditions, but most of them were influenced by Tendai *shōmyō* because all of those schools' founders had originally studied Tendai Buddhism. Although the new schools did not produce musical treatises to the same extent that monks of the Shingon or Tendai schools did, they were nonetheless engaged in the vocalization of Buddhist texts. For example, the chanting of Amida Buddha's name and the recitation of the title of the *Lotus Sutra* are part of the sounding world of Japanese Buddhism. The Zen schools founded during the Kamakura period remained part of this world, incorporating manifold sounds and *shōmyō*, as this book details. In the seventeenth century, new styles of Buddhist chant were again introduced when the Chinese monk Yinyuan Longqi 隠元隆琦 (J. Ingen Ryūki, 1592–1673) came to Japan and founded the Ōbaku school of Zen.

The Meiji era was a major turning point for Buddhist music, as well as for the Japanese music landscape in general. When Meiji officials began the modernization of Japan based on the adoption of Western models, Buddhist leaders also undertook to reform their religion. Some clerics enthusiastically embraced newly introduced Western musical styles and composed Buddhist songs using those styles, creating new musical forms for expressing Buddhist devotion. At the same time, Western music was being taught in schools and soon became popular throughout Japanese society. This development began to vitiate the status of traditional Japanese music, including *shōmyō*, and these styles were slowly rendered less familiar to many Japanese. In the twentieth century, clerics and musicologists became conservationists, researching *shōmyō* and preserving some of it through audio recordings and other means. Additionally, clerics began to perform *shōmyō* on the concert stage, both in Japan

16. Only a few studies on Shingon and Tendai *shōmyō* have been published in European languages. Walter Giesen (1977) offered a detailed study of medieval treatises on Tendai *shōmyō*. Arai Kōjun (1986, 1995, 1996) has studied the development of musical notation for *shōmyō*. Michael Monhart (1992–1993, 1994) has explored contemporary Shingon *shōmyō*. Steven Nelson (2001b, 2009) and I (Mross 2012c, 2016a) have further studied the vocalization of *kōshiki* in the Shingon schools. Ōuchi Fumi (2009) offered a fascinating study of the role of music in the *Lotus Repentance Ceremony* (*Hokke senbō* 法華懺法), a key ritual of the Tendai school, as performed in the Haguro lineage of contemporary Shugendō. She (2016) also published a book-length study in Japanese about medieval Tendai *shōmyō* from a soteriological perspective.

Japanese scholars and clerics have produced numerous studies of Shingon and Tendai *shōmyō*. On Shingon *shōmyō*, see, for example, Iwahara 1932 and Ōyama 1969. On Tendai *shōmyō*, see Kataoka 1981, Iwata 1999, and Amano 2000. The edited volume *Bukkyō ongaku* contains chapters on Japanese Buddhist chant as well as Buddhist music in Tibet (Tōyō Ongaku Gakkai 1972). In addition, vol. 84 of the *Taishō* canon contains ten *shōmyō* treatises, including the *Gyosan shōmyō shū* 魚山声明集 of the Tendai school (No. 2712) and the *Gyosan shishō* 魚山私鈔 of the Shingon school (No. 2713). Both works include musical notation.

17. *Shōmyōshū*, in the archive of the Research Institute for Japanese Music Historiography, Ueno Gakuen University. For a facsimile and detailed study, see Fukushima 1995, and Fukushima, Arai, and Nelson 2018.

and abroad. As a result, *shōmyō* came to be appreciated as a unique element of world music, a Buddhist counterpart to Gregorian chant.

Despite these developments, clerics continue to sing *shōmyō* at Buddhist temples, where laypeople can hear it. Each school of Buddhism has its own ritual repertoire with distinctive styles of vocalization and instrumentation. These styles have been transmitted from teacher to disciple over the centuries, primarily orally but often supplemented by musical notation. Traditional Buddhist chant occurs throughout a wide range of rituals, from daily services to diverse monthly and annual observations, to death-related rites. Among the yearly observances are the memorial service for the Buddha's passing, the *Lotus Repentance Ceremony* (*Hokke senbō* 法華懺法) in the Tendai school, the *Contemplation of the Rishu Sutra* (*Rishu zanmai* 理趣三昧) in the Shingon school, and the *Kannon Repentance Ceremony* (*Kannon senbō* 観音懺法) in the Zen schools. These annual ceremonies accommodate complex liturgical structures with elaborate chants, attracting numerous lay devotees and visitors in many cases. Both in premodern times and in the present, lay devotees sometimes participate in the vocalization of "simpler" chants, such as the recitation of Amida's name. *Shōmyō*, however, requires special training and is performed solely by clerics.

During the first centuries after Buddhism's introduction to Japan, clerics chanted texts written in either Chinese or Sanskrit. Then, in the tenth century, Japanese clerics started to invent new liturgical forms that were vocalized in Japanese, including *hyōbyaku* 表白 (pronouncement of intention), *saimon* 祭文 (offertory declaration), *wasan* 和讃 (Japanese hymns), and *kōshiki*. As a result, the *shōmyō* repertoire consists of liturgical pieces in three different languages—Sanskrit, Chinese, and Japanese—and most rituals include chants in at least two languages. In addition, most rituals contain a range of different styles of Buddhist music, which helps create an interesting soundscape throughout the ritual. The various genres of *shōmyō* can be categorized into song (*utau shōmyō* 歌う声明), recitation (*kataru shōmyō* 語る声明), and reading (*yomu shōmyō* 読む声明), depending on how many melodic inflections a genre or piece uses. These categories suggest that Buddhist ritual music includes styles ranging from highly melismatic pieces in free rhythm to more syllabic chanting of sutras in a fixed rhythm with one character per beat. When defining *shōmyō*, pieces on one pitch in fixed rhythm are sometimes excluded from this category because they lack melodies. This is typically done by Sōtō clerics who exclude the recitation of sutras from *shōmyō*.[18]

---

18. Although *gagaku* 雅楽 (court music), a broad category of classical styles with instrumental accompaniment, is today not considered to be Buddhist music, it shares a common history with *shōmyō*, since musicians sometimes performed *gagaku* during elaborate Buddhist ceremonies. Especially popular for highly festive rituals were formats that included dance pieces (*bugaku hōe* 舞楽法会). A ritual in this form, combining *shōmyō* and dance pieces, is still performed at Shitennōji in Osaka during the annual memorial service for the prince regent Shōtoku Taishi 聖徳太子 (574–622). For a detailed explanation of *gagaku*, including its relation to *shōmyō*, see Nelson 2008a and 2008b. Fabio Rambelli (2021) provides an overview of *gagaku* in Buddhist ceremonies and further shows how monastics, aristocrats, and professional musicians in medieval Japan interpreted instrumental music as a means leading to salvation.

The vocalization of sacred texts has long been an essential practice in many Buddhist schools, serving, on the one hand, as a way to reach soteriological goals, and, on the other hand, as an expression of devotion to buddhas, bodhisattvas, and other objects of veneration, or as a means to asking them for protection. Learning how to perform the vocal art of *shōmyō* has therefore been an essential component of monastic training, and it can take many years of devoted study. In addition, Buddhist music creates a social space that serves as a medium of interaction between laity and clergy. Rituals and the musical performances they contain offer entertainment and enjoyment to lay devotees, giving us insight into how practitioners engage their congregation through the aural senses in their practice. By focusing on some of these aspects in this book, I hope to inspire more scholars to engage in studying the sonic dimension of Buddhism.

Zen Liturgy

Since the advent of Japanese Zen Buddhism in the thirteenth century, Zen monks have performed a wide range of rituals that include the vocalization of sacred scriptures. These rituals play a major role in the liturgy of Zen monasteries,[19] and the transmission of ritual expertise constitutes a large part of the monastic curriculum. As many observers have noted, all activities in the monastery, from eating meals to taking a bath, are highly ritualized. Even practices that are described as expressions of "pure Zen," such as zazen, ascending the Dharma hall to preach, and Dharma combats, are highly stylized and can be considered rituals in themselves. Zazen in particular, especially as understood in the Sōtō school, has been interpreted as ritualized sitting.[20] The correct performance of all these activities is considered by Sōtō clerics to be an essential part of their practice.

Japanese Zen temples generally fall into two broad categories: training temples or monasteries and temples that mainly perform rituals for lay parishioners. In contemporary Japan, all young monks undergo an initiatory period at a monastery for a fixed period of time—usually one year, although a few novices elect to stay for several years—during which they engage in zazen and a wide range of ritualized activities. When they finish their training at a monastery, most novices return home to assist at and later take over their family temple, where they chiefly perform funeral and memorial services for

19. I understand liturgy as the entirety of all rituals performed at Sōtō temples, including daily, monthly, and annual observances, as well as the rituals performed only at special occasions.

20. See, for example, Leighton 2008 and Braak 2015 on zazen, Poceski 2008 on ascending the Dharma hall to preach, and Riggs 2008 on walking meditation. For an illuminating analysis of zazen and related forms of practice from a ritual studies perspective, see Grimes 2010, chaps. 6 and 7.

their parishioners. Ian Reader therefore described the life of monks at parishioner temples as "zazenless" Zen.[21]

The rituals at a training temple are usually categorized into daily, monthly, and annual observances. Within these categories, sutra-chanting services (*fugin* 諷経) are the most common. Several times a day, the assembly chants sutras. Every month, Sōtō clerics perform additional sutra-chanting services that are conducted for important patriarchs or deities on fixed days of the month. For example, a sutra-chanting service is performed on the first and fifteenth days of every month, first for the emperor and then for the tutelary deities (*chinju* 鎮守). Some monthly rituals can be more elaborate than a sutra-chanting service, such as the *Ryaku fusatsu* 略布薩 (Abbreviated repentance ritual), a simplified version of the *Grand Precepts Meeting*, held on the fifteenth of every month.

In addition to these observances, Sōtō clerics perform a number of special annual rituals at their monasteries: the New Year's celebration; the three rituals for the Buddha's birthday (4 / 8), enlightenment (12 / 8), and death (2 / 15); the other shore assemblies (*higane* 彼岸会) at the spring and autumn equinoxes; the O-Bon festival for feeding the hungry ghosts (*segaki* 施餓鬼 or *sejikie* 施食会) in summer; the *Grand Precepts Meeting* (*Daifusatsu bosatsu shiki* 大布薩菩薩式); the annual memorial services for the founder(s) and other influential Zen patriarchs; and the birthday celebrations of Dōgen 道元 (1200–1253) and Keizan, among others. Many of these annual observances consist of sutra-chanting services, but several feature more complex ritual forms. For example, during the New Year's celebration, which usually lasts three days, clerics perform a rolling reading (*tendoku* 転読) of the *Great Sutra on the Perfection of Wisdom* (*Mahāprajñāpāramitā Sūtra*), a highly theatrical ritual centered on the speed-reading of this lengthy sutra, which is thought to produce great merit. On that occasion, clerics at many monasteries also conduct the *Ceremony of Praising the Buddhas* (*Tanbutsue* 歎仏会), a very musical ritual, and monks at the head temple Eiheiji 永平寺 conduct a *kōshiki* on the *Great Sutra on the Perfection of Wisdom.*[22] Likewise, Eiheiji monks perform a *kōshiki* during the memorial service of Bodhidharma, the semi-legendary Indian monk who is said to have introduced Chan to China.

Additionally, many monasteries offer funerals and prayer rituals for lay devotees, sharing in that way some of the functions of smaller temples. One example is the head temple Sōjiji, which gained hundreds of new parishioners after its 1911 relocation to Yokohama from the remote village of Monzen

21. Reader 1986. The following overview focuses on rituals in contemporary Japan, but in earlier times the same core rituals were performed. See, for example, the detailed descriptions in the *Keizan shingi,* Ozaki Shōzen's 2010 comparison of monastic codes from different time periods, or my analysis of the rituals performed at Sōjiji in the Tokugawa period (Mross 2014a, 112–127). For a detailed description of the rituals performed in contemporary Zen temples, see Foulk 2008, 57–82.

22. For studies on the Ceremony of Praising the Buddhas, see Matsuura 1976 and Uemura 1979.

on the Noto peninsula. As a result, its novices are kept busy performing funeral and memorial services for lay parishioners, and this has led to the shortening of some of the traditional rituals, as well as the time for zazen. Other examples are the three great prayer temples of the Sōtō school—Daiyūzan Saijōji 大雄山最乗寺, Toyokawa Inari Myōgonji 豊川稲荷妙厳寺, and Zenpōji 善宝寺—where the novices spend a great deal of time performing prayer rituals for visiting lay devotees.[23]

It is important to note that the efficaciousness of these rituals, from the daily sutra-chanting services to special prayer rituals and funeral services, depends on the logic of merit. On this rationale, merit is produced by the performance of good deeds—in the case of rituals, by the chanting of sutras and the provision of offerings. At the end of the ritual, the merit is dedicated to patrons, ancestors, deities, or universally to all beings, and such a bestowal lies at the heart of the performance of many Buddhist rituals.[24]

The rituals just described are further characterized by a diverse soundscape. In the sutra-chanting services, sutras in Sino-Japanese are vocalized on one note, often in unison, to the beat of the wooden fish (*mokugyo* 木魚), a round hollow wooden drum. This is likely the soundscape most often associated with Zen rituals in Japan. But some of the special rituals that are performed as part of an annual observance, such as the *Grand Precepts Meeting* and the *Ceremony of Praising the Buddhas,* together with the various *kōshiki,* differ markedly from the sutra-chanting services in that musical chants with elaborate melodic inflections, most of them in free rhythm, are featured, and thus these rituals belong to the category of *shōmyō.* On this basis, we can say that *kōshiki* are the most musical rituals that Sōtō clerics perform, and if we overlook them, we miss the fact that Sōtō Zen possesses its own unique *shōmyō* tradition, one that deserves recognition as an important facet of the religious culture and practice of Zen.

Methods and Sources

The task of studying *kōshiki* requires an interdisciplinary approach combining historical-philological, anthropological, and musicological methods in order to grasp the various elements that comprise a *kōshiki.* In particular, I combined historical-philological work with ethnographic fieldwork.

Since only a few *kōshiki* are available in modern print editions, handwritten *kōshiki* manuscripts and woodblock prints served as my primary sources, with prefaces, postscripts, and colophons providing valuable information about *kōshiki* performance and transmission. I also examined monastic codes and official documents. The manuscripts and woodblock prints of Niels Gülberg (Kadono Konzen Library Collection), the Research Institute for Traditional Japanese Music Historiography at Ueno Gakuen University, and

23. For a detailed study of the prayer rituals at Kasuisai, see Graf 2017.

24. On the concept of merit, see also Foulk 2008, 62–64, and Kieschnick 2003, chap. 3.

the library of Komazawa University, as well as facsimiles available at the Sōtōshū Bunkazai Chōsai Iinkai, were vital for my study. Additionally, I conducted research in temple archives, including Sōjiji Soin 總持寺祖院 (Monzen, Noto), Sōjiji (Tsurumi, Yokohama), Yōkōji 永光寺 (Hakui, Noto), and Dairyūji 大隆寺 (Takayama).

To study the contemporary performance practices of *kōshiki*—in other words, the continuationof ritual practices established centuries ago—I conducted extensive fieldwork in Japan over a period of more than six years, observing and filming rituals as well as interviewing Sōtō clerics. My primary field site was the head temple Sōjiji in the Tsurumi ward of Yokohama. The choice to focus my research on Sōjiji sprang from its historical importance as one of the two head temples of the Sōtō school and the fact that it has had famous *shōmyō* teachers in the last decades. There were two other reasons for this decision as well. One was that I was based in Tokyo for around six years, so Sōjiji was nearby. The second and more important reason was that when I first started to work on Buddhist music, I was introduced to Maekawa Bokushō 前川睦生, a highly acclaimed *shōmyō* specialist who is affiliated with Sōjiji and has taught there. Since he has been a cornerstone of my fieldwork, it was comparatively easy to obtain permission to attend and film rituals at Sōjiji, as well as to interview monks there. Maekawa also taught at Nittaiji Senmon Sōdō 日泰寺専門僧堂 and invited me to visit this training temple. Furthermore, Suzuki Bunmei 鈴木文明, one of his former students, taught *shōmyō* at Kasuisai 可睡斎, where I was also warmly welcomed. Later, when I again visited Kasuisai, Haruki Shōshū 春木正秀, who had formerly taught at Eiheiji, now worked there, and I was able to learn about the *shōmyō* practice of a different lineage. I also visited other temples that regularly perform *kōshiki,* such as Eiheiji's satellite temples in Tokyo and Nagoya. In addition, monks at Eiheiji have performed many *kōshiki* over the centuries, so I visited Eiheiji a few times to attend rituals and interview priests. But since this head temple was located far away, and my close network did not include senior monks teaching there, my access to Eiheiji was limited. Nevertheless, through my extended fieldwork at Sōjiji and the contacts I developed, I was able to observe both ritual performances and rehearsals. Thanks to the support of my interlocutors, I was also able to acquire contemporary materials that Sōtō monks have produced for the study of rituals, such as audio and video recordings that are not available in regular bookstores. Thus I was able to gain insights into aspects of monastic life that are usually hidden to outsiders.

It is important to note that my research has focused on the historical development of rituals. My fieldwork centering on participant observation was originally done to supplement my textual work, in order to overcome the limitations of textual analysis when studying rituals. Fieldwork has allowed me to better understand the instructions in the ritual handbooks, as well as to develop a deeper understanding of ritual practice in general. In this way, my experience in the field was crucial, and this book introduces results from my long-term fieldwork in Japan.

Overview of the Book

This book is divided into two parts. Part I, consisting of chapters 1–3, explores Sōtō *kōshiki* in broad terms. Chapter 1 introduces the diverse worlds of *kōshiki* and analyzes their history in Japanese Buddhism in general and in the Sōtō school in particular. *Kōshiki* were performed in all Buddhist schools and can be considered a form of vernacular Buddhism as well as part of a shared ritual vocabulary within Japanese Buddhism. The historical development of *kōshiki* in the Sōtō school shows that it has played a vital role in Sōtō Zen liturgy since the time of the founder, Dōgen. Sōtō monks adopted *kōshiki* from other Buddhist traditions as well, including the Tendai, Hossō, and Kegon schools. The ritual tradition of the Japanese Sōtō school is therefore highly eclectic and needs to be approached with a broad understanding of Japanese Buddhist liturgy.

Chapter 2 examines the performance practice and ritual structure of *kōshiki* within the Sōtō school, showing how specially composed *kōshiki* texts were placed within a distinctive ritual frame. In other words, Sōtō monks used a more or less fixed ritual structure into which they inserted the central text of a *kōshiki*, either adopted from another tradition or newly composed. I show that this ritual structure consists not only of texts but also of acoustic, kinetic, and material components. Each of the schools, moreover, developed its own way of arranging liturgical modules, as can be seen in a comparison of the *Rakan kōshiki* 羅漢講式 in the Sōtō, Rinzai, and Shingon schools. Thus, although many of the liturgical elements and texts belonged to a shared tradition, the ritual structure actually used in performance was sectarian and contributed to reinforcing group identity.

The most important elements in the performance of a *kōshiki* are singing and reciting. The vocalization breathes life into the text, and only through its vocalization can the ritual text fulfill its function. Additionally, the transmission of ritual expertise is closely tied to instruction in vocal performance. Chapter 3 therefore studies the sonic dimension of *kōshiki*. After introducing the vocalization styles and instrumentation, as well as the musical notation that has been used for *kōshiki* since the sixteenth century, I analyze how contemporary Sōtō monks view their own ritual practice, based on essays they have written and my fieldwork in Japan. I demonstrate that many ritual specialists interpret their ritual practice in the same way they interpret zazen. For them, vocalizing texts and practicing zazen share the same soteriological foundation.

Part II, consisting of chapters 4 and 5, explores the narration of communal memory in the *kōshiki* composed and performed in remembrance of Keizan. I show how his biography was set into a ritual frame, and how the *kōshiki* thus created functioned not only to repay benevolence but also to form a community, to contest status, and to establish in the collective memory a foundation on which a particular temple or Sōtō lineage could thrive in the future. Chapter 4 first considers the differences between two transmission lineages of the *Butsuji kōshiki* 仏慈講式 (*Kōshiki* on Zen Master Butsuji) dating from the Tokugawa period (1603–1868) and performed at Sōjiji and Yōkōji on the Noto peninsula.

Chapter 5 then turns to the *Tōjō dentō kōshiki*, a *kōshiki* written in the Meiji era (1868–1912), to show how the development of a new biographic image of Keizan in the second half of the nineteenth century inspired monks at Sōjiji to compose a new *kōshiki* commemorating him. At the same time, the monks at Yōkōji, who were using the memory of Keizan to revive their temple, undertook their own revision of the *Butsuji kōshiki* to emphasize the position their temple had held in medieval Japan. The two chapters together illustrate how *kōshiki* have been used both to narrate and to enact the cultural memory of a particular lineage or temple community.

The epilogue synthesizes the findings of the previous chapters. The appendices provide additional materials related to the *kōshiki* performed in commemoration of Keizan, including translations and facsimiles of the central texts of the *Butsuji kōshiki* and the *Tōjō dentō kōshiki*.

An online supplement, viewable through the Stanford Digital Repository, makes available video recordings of *kōshiki* performed at contemporary Sōtō temples. These videos are intended to give readers an idea of how these rituals are performed. Hopefully, they can also help preserve the current state of *kōshiki* and *shōmyō* performance practice for future generations.

PART ONE

Development and Performance of Kōshiki

1

History of Kōshiki

> *Kōshiki,* as a cultural property of our school, are important ceremonies that express [our] feelings of making recompense for the benevolence we have received, and of longing for the buddhas and patriarchs of ancient times.
>
> —*Inoue Gishin*

IN 2002, the Sōtō school commemorated the 750th anniversary of the death of its founder, Dōgen. Throughout the year, a stream of Sōtō clerics and lay devotees visited the head temple Eiheiji in Fukui prefecture to pay their respects to Dōgen and to participate in the ceremonies honoring him. Among them, a group of clerics closely affiliated with Eiheiji's satellite temple in Nagoya performed a new *kōshiki* for Dōgen, a special ritual composed by one of their leaders, Inoue Gishin 井上義臣. That same year, another monk, Imamura Genshū 今村源宗, heavily revised the *kōshiki* that had been performed for Dōgen for over two centuries. It was then performed by the monks at Eiheiji's satellite temple in Tokyo during their commemoration of Dōgen's grand death anniversary, and a recording of the performance on compact disc was also produced.

Sōtō clerics have conducted *kōshiki* on other special occasions as well. In 1990, the Sōtō nuns' association performed a *kōshiki* for the bodhisattva Jizō 地蔵 to celebrate the inauguration of a hall for lay devotees at Sōjiji, the other head temple of the Sōtō school. Twenty-seven years later, when Eiheiji's satellite temple in Nagoya opened a new Dharma hall, the monks of that temple performed a *kōshiki* for Hakusan 白山 (White Mountain), the protector deity of a sacred mountain range on the borders of Fukui, Gifu, and Ishikawa prefectures. In all these instances, the *kōshiki* performances highlighted the importance of the occasion with the special qualities that render these rituals distinct from other Sōtō ceremonies, in which clerics chant sutras on a single pitch in a steady rhythm. *Kōshiki* are the most musical rituals the Sōtō school has to offer, creating a celebrative mode with chants set to elaborate melodies, mostly in free rhythm. Unlike sutra-chanting services, which do not require rehearsals, a *kōshiki* must be practiced intensively by the monks performing it. Indeed, the very act of preparing for the ceremony emphasizes the special character of the occasion.

The history of *kōshiki* spans more than one thousand years. First developed by Tendai monks in the late tenth century to express their devotion to Amida and his Pure Land, the genre spread to other Buddhist denominations, including the new Kamakura schools. In medieval Japan, *kōshiki* became very popular, and people from all strata of society were involved in their performance. One major reason for their ready acceptance was that the texts, although written in Chinese, were recited in Japanese, allowing audiences to follow the content. In rituals in the eighth and ninth centuries, by contrast, clerics mainly recited texts in Chinese, and few Japanese were able to understand what they heard. The invention of *kōshiki* was thus an important milestone in the development of ritual genres in the vernacular language.[1]

Monks of various traditions composed *kōshiki* for different objects of veneration, such as buddha(s), bodhisattvas, sutras, *kami,* and even music or poetry. Over time, works for the same object of worship were written, and thus *kōshiki* with the same title can actually be different ritual texts—we know of at least five different works titled *Kannon kōshiki* (*Kōshiki* on Kannon), for example. The comprehensive *Kōshiki database* compiled by Niels Gülberg lists 374 *kōshiki,* mostly written during the medieval period, but it is likely that well over four hundred works in this genre were composed, a number whose magnitude reflects the great popularity of *kōshiki* in premodern Japan.

The influence of *kōshiki* extended beyond the formal boundaries of Buddhist liturgy to a wide range of other cultural practices. In Japanese music, *kōshiki* belong to the repertoire of Japanese Buddhist chant (*shōmyō* 声明), and it is acknowledged that their distinctive recitation style strongly influenced other genres of traditional Japanese music, including *heikyoku* 平曲 (recitation of the *Heike monogatari* to the accompaniment of the *biwa*), *yōkyoku* 謡曲 (recitation in *nō* drama), and *jōruri* 浄瑠璃 (a musical genre of epic tales recited to the accompaniment of the *shamisen*). In Japanese literature, *kōshiki* texts, considered to be part of Buddhist preaching literature, influenced works in other literary genres such as *setsuwa* 説話 (tale literature), *monogatari* 物語 (epic tales), *enkyoku* 宴曲 (medieval songs), and *waka* 和歌 (poetry).[2]

This chapter traces the historical development of *kōshiki* in Japanese Buddhism in general and the Sōtō school in particular. I will show that the ritual tradition of the Sōtō school was very eclectic: Sōtō clerics did not simply import all their rituals from China; they also adopted liturgical forms unique to Japanese Buddhism, including *kōshiki.* To trace the trajectory of this development, the next section explains the term *kōshiki* and the significance of this genre in Japanese Buddhism; then I turn to exploring how Sōtō clerics adapted it to meet their own needs.

1. On the development of vernacular readings of literary Sinitic texts in East Asia, see Kornicki 2018, especially chaps. 6 and 8.

2. Gülberg, for example, has shown that Genshin's *Nijūgo zanmai shiki* and Yōkan's *Sanji nenbutsu kanmon shiki* were cited in literary works (1999, 101–209).

Kōshiki in Japanese Buddhism

Defining *Kōshiki*

Since there is no ritual similar to it in the Western tradition, I leave the term *kōshiki* untranslated in this book because any translation would be misleading. Instead, it is best to begin by explaining the term's meanings and then proceed to defining the genre. The first character, *kō* 講, can describe, among other things, a lecture that explains a sutra or set of doctrinal ideas in an easily comprehensible manner. In Japanese, *kō* also has a special usage that can indicate a group gathering for a certain purpose—in the context of a *kōshiki,* it refers to an association of devotees seeking to deepen their understanding and to support each other in their practice. One such association was the Twenty-Five Samādhi Society (*Nijūgo zanmai e* 二十五三昧会), a group of twenty-five monks founded in the late tenth century. This group was instrumental in the invention of *kōshiki,* as the next section of this chapter explains. The second character, *shiki* 式, describes a ceremony or the structure of a ceremony. Accordingly, the term *kōshiki* can be interpreted as the ceremonial structure for meetings of a religious association, or a ceremony with a lecture at its center, or the structure of this type of ceremony.[3] Originally, *kōshiki* texts were written for meetings of associations whose members promised to support each other in their religious practices. Over time, as *kōshiki* began to be used for other purposes, such as expounding doctrine or fundraising, the meaning of the term shifted toward a ceremony with a lecture at its center. This is the meaning often emphasized in modern scholarship, as in Steven Nelson's translation of *kōshiki* as "lecture-sermon" and Lori Meeks's "chanted lecture."[4]

But there is yet another level where the meaning of the term can be seen to oscillate between two poles. *Kōshiki* is a liturgical genre defined by its literary form. Concretely, a work in this genre consists of a pronouncement of intention (*hyōbyaku* 表白) followed by a number of sections (*dan* 段)—usually an odd number—with one or more Chinese verses (*kada* 伽陀, Skt. *gāthā*) after each section. This structure is what defines the genre. Nonetheless, in a ritual centering on this kind of text, other liturgical pieces are usually vocalized as

3. See also Yamada 1995, 13–14; Gülberg 1999, 29; Gülberg 2006, 30; and Gülberg 2018, 53–57 and 67, which emphasizes the importance of religious associations, pointing out that lectures are usually directed to listeners and delivered while facing them, but *kōshiki* are performed while facing the object of worship. In this context, Gülberg mentions the rare example of the *Shunie* 修二会, a repentance ritual performed annually at Tōdaiji in Nara, where the *kōshiki* is read silently.

4. Nelson 2003, 2008a, and 2008b; Meeks 2010. Similar rituals exist in other Buddhist cultures, such as the Sri Lankan *bana,* a two-pulpit preaching ritual. According to Mahinda Deegalle, in *bana* "the Buddhist preacher has assumed the role of an entertainer, a performer, and a religious communicator in addition to being a monk" (2006, 1). What Deegalle ascribes to *bana* could also be said of *kōshiki:* "In order to increase pious wisdom among Buddhist communities, two-pulpit preaching incorporated a variety of popular ritual elements, such as singing, chanting, and dramatic performance, as well as the cultivation of aesthetic pleasure as a means of conveying the lessons of Buddhism" (94).

well. Niels Gülberg thus distinguishes between a narrow definition of the term, referring only to the genre-defining text consisting of a pronouncement of intention, sections, and verses, and a broad definition, which includes all texts vocalized during the ritual. As a consequence of the broad use of *kōshiki,* another term, *shikimon* 式文 (central text of the ceremony), was then used to refer to the genre-defining text. The Buddhist schools still differ in their use of the term *kōshiki.* For example, Shingon clerics employ a narrow definition, whereas Zen monks typically use a broad one. Since scholars usually work with the definition used by the school they study, in the rest of this chapter I shall use the term *kōshiki* as it has been defined by the tradition I am discussing.

That said, a *kōshiki* in the narrow sense (i.e., a *shikimon*) has an internal structure that is demarcated with set phrases at important junctures. The pronouncement of intention explains the meaning of the ritual and addresses the object of veneration and the participants. Customarily, it opens by addressing the object(s) of veneration: "Humbly I speak to [names of the objects of worship] and say..." (*uyamatte* 敬って... *ni mōshite mōsaku* に白して言さく). Then it provides a digest of the virtues of the object of veneration before listing the topics of the following sections, as in a table of contents. Each section that follows introduces a theme, explores it in detail, and closes by asking the assembly to sing a verse and perform prostrations. After singing a Chinese verse—or, in rare instances, a Japanese poem (*waka*)—the assembly intones words of worship (*raihai no kotoba* 礼拝の詞), a short phrase starting with "Homage to..." (*namu* 南無...), and performs one or more prostrations. Most *shikimon* consist of three or five sections, but there are also some with no sections following the pronouncement of intention, and others with as many as nine, ten, or twelve sections. The last section of a *shikimon* is often a transfer of merit.[5]

During the *shikimon,* the officiant recites the pronouncement of intention and the sections in *kundoku* 訓読, a Japanese reading of the Chinese text that involves a complete syntactical reordering according to Japanese grammar.[6] The assembly, by contrast, usually sings the verses of the *shikimon* in Chinese—in other words, the verses retain the Chinese word order but are vocalized with Sino-Japanese pronunciation. This means that when *kōshiki* are described as a ritual genre in the vernacular language, that description is based on the practice of reciting the pronouncement of intention and the sections in *kundoku,* when texts composed in literary Chinese are realized in Japanese. Some texts notated in Japanese using *kana* 仮名 (syllabic Japanese script) have survived, which less literate people (including women) might

5. See Gülberg 1999, 30–31, and 2006, 33 and 36–37.

6. When reading the Chinese text in Japanese, the resulting language is usually close to the original, containing a high percentage of Sino-Japanese terms—a language that Steven Nelson calls "hard Japanese" (2003, 21). Peter Kornicki (2018, 166) calls this rendering of a Chinese text "bound translation," as it keeps closely to the original text. Composing and reading texts aloud in literary Sinitic was an important part of literary culture in premodern Japan; see Steininger 2017 for a detailed study of the practices of literary Sinitic in the mid-Heian period.

have used for reading or recitation, but those works, too, were originally composed and written in Chinese.[7]

The signposting throughout the text of the *shikimon* and its overall structure make it easy for listeners to follow the content. Singing the verses and performing prostrations after each verse further integrate the assembly into the flow of the narrative formed by the pronouncement of intention and the subsequent sections. In this way, expressions of devotion to the object of worship are closely interwoven with the explanation of its virtues during the ritual.

From the standpoint of content, *shikimon* are highly intertextual: they usually quote sutras or other doctrinal texts, and most of the verses are selected from sutras. This means that while a *kōshiki* author did not necessarily need to compose new sentences, he could still give a *kōshiki* his fingerprint through his selection of quotations.

This explanation has covered the primary features of a *shikimon* (or *kōshiki* in the narrow sense). As mentioned earlier, the broad definition of *kōshiki,* meaning the ritual as a whole, includes the vocalization of additional liturgical texts. These other pieces differ according to the school or lineage, the temple, and the occasion, as well as the scale of the ceremony. Manuscripts that contain only a *shikimon* frequently do not specify the variable elements, only giving the instruction "proceed as usual" (*tsune ni gotoshi* 常に如し). Nonetheless, many of the usual elements can be specified: early in the ritual, the assembly sings a communal obeisance (*sōrai* 総礼) in unison, expressing their veneration to the object of worship.[8] Other common elements are the *Hymn of the Four Wisdoms* (*Shichisan* 四智讃)[9] and the *Four Shōmyō Melodies* (*Shika hōyō* 四箇法要).[10] The assembly might also vocalize an invitation (*kanjō* 勧請) addressing the object(s) of worship and asking them to appear at the ceremonial place and accept the offerings, or a text invoking deities (*jinbun* 神分) who protect the ritual space and will help to spread the merit produced through the ritual. Other pieces that might be vocalized are songs of edification (*kyōke* 教化),[11] Japanese hymns (*wasan* 和讃),[12] an offertory declaration

7. See also Yamada 1995, 33; Gülberg 1999, 34; and Gülberg 2006, 36.

8. Certain verses are often used for the communal obeisance, and only a few expressions are changed in them to fit the object(s) of veneration.

9. *Shichisan,* a chant in Sanskrit, is one of the oldest Buddhist chants in the Japanese *shōmyō* repertoire: "It seems likely that this piece derives from seventh-century India, and that it was transmitted to China in the eighth, and to Japan at the beginning of the ninth" (Arai K. 1999, 326).

10. *Shika hōyō,* a ritual sequence that consists of the four chants *Praise of the Thus Come One* (*Nyoraibai* 如来唄), *Gāthā of Falling Flowers* (*Sange no ge* 散華偈), *Gāthā of Sanskrit Sound* (*Bonnon no ge* 梵音偈), and *Gāthā of the Sounding Staff* (*Shakujō no ge* 錫杖偈), is usually performed before the central part of a ceremony. It was performed during the Eye-Opening Ceremony of the Great Buddha of Tōdaiji in Tenpyō 17 (752); see *Tōdaiji yōroku,* 50.

11. *Kyōke* are liturgical texts that explain and praise Buddhist teachings. They constitute one of the oldest *shōmyō* genres in Japanese. The first was supposedly written by Ennin 円仁 (794–864); see Gülberg 1999, 38–40.

12. *Wasan* are hymns in Japanese. The first is said to have been composed by Genshin. See Gülberg 1999, 40–42, for examples of the use of *wasan* in *kōshiki.*

(*saimon* 祭文),[13] and the *Transfer of Merit to Six Offerings* (*rokushu ekō* 六種回向).[14] Of these pieces, around half are vocalized in Chinese (and one in Sanskrit) rather than Japanese, preserving elements of earlier ritual practices. From them it can be seen that the description of *kōshiki* as a liturgy in the vernacular language is based on a narrow understanding of the term.

The Development of *Kōshiki* in Japanese Buddhism

Many aspects of the early development of *kōshiki* remain unclear due to the scarcity of surviving texts. The manuscripts and woodblock prints that were produced were intended to be used in rituals, and unless written by eminent monks and treated as temple treasures, they were subjected to normal wear and tear without great concern for their preservation. Therefore, not all of the *kōshiki* that were composed and performed over the centuries are still extant. In that light, some of the details in the following sketch must be regarded as provisional in that they are based on information in the available sources.

Kōshiki emerged from shorter liturgical forms vocalized in Japanese, such as *hyōbyaku,*[15] as part of a movement to develop a liturgy in Japanese that began sometime in the tenth century. The earliest acknowledged work in this genre is the *Nijūgo zanmai shiki* (Ceremony of the twenty-five samādhi), composed by the Tendai monk Genshin 源信 (942–1017) in Kanna 2 (986) for the Twenty-Five Samādhi Society.[16] The members of this society met each month at the Yokawa temple complex on Mt. Hiei to renew their vows to help each other attain rebirth in Amida Buddha's Pure Land (Gokuraku jōdo 極楽浄土). Once born in the Pure Land, they believed, they would never fall back into the realms of samsaric rebirth and were certain to attain enlightenment.

The *Nijūgo zanmai shiki* had far-reaching influence, inspiring other *kōshiki* compositions. Later it was revised as the *Rokudō kōshiki* 六道講式 (*Kōshiki* on

---

13. *Saimon* invite the object of worship to accept the offerings. These texts are written in Chinese but read in Japanese. Originally they were specifically composed for each ceremony; however, standardized texts were gradually used. The first Japanese *saimon* are recorded in the *Honchō monzui* (*Honchō monzui chūshaku* 2, 747–760). See Friedrich 1982 for a German translation and analysis. It is unclear when *saimon* were first composed for *kōshiki.* According to medieval sources, Myōe wrote one for his *Gojūgo zenchishiki kōshiki* 五十五善知識講式 (*Kōzanji Myōe shōnin gyōjō* (*kana gyōjō*), MSS 1: 56), but this text is not extant; see Gülberg 1999, 42.

14. *Rokushu ekō* transfers the merit produced through the performance of the ritual, and six offerings are made during this chant.

15. *Hyōbyaku,* a pronouncement of intention, have been recited in Buddhist ceremonies since the Heian period (794–1185).

16. Some early *kōshiki* were attributed to Saichō 最澄 (767–822), the founder of the Tendai school, and Kūkai 空海 (774–835), the founder of the Shingon school, but these works were actually composed much later; see Gülberg 1999, 75–78. Sarah Horton doubts Genshin's authorship of the *Nijūgo zanmai shiki,* as there is "little evidence to support this attribution" (2001, 107). However, Gülberg has convincingly shown that this attribution seems highly likely even though Genshin's reputed authorship of ten additional *kōshiki* remains to be confirmed (1999, 44–46). Yamada Shōzen cautiously notes that although it is unclear to what extent the *Nijūgo zanmai shiki* was composed by Genshin, he must have had a close connection to this text (1995, 23).

the six realms) and widely performed.[17] In the next century, the Tendai monk Meiken 明賢 (1026–1098) composed a *Seigan kōshiki* 誓願講式 (*Kōshiki* on [Amida's] vow), and the Sanron monk Yōkan 永観 (or Eikan, 1033–1111) wrote an *Ōjō kōshiki* 往生講式 (*Kōshiki* on rebirth [in Amida's Pure Land], ca. 1079), which became the primary structural model for later *kōshiki.*[18] Yōkan, a former monk of Tōdaiji and a strong advocate of Amida's Pure Land, is said to have had his *Ōjō kōshiki* performed at his deathbed, further highlighting the *kōshiki*'s function to help practitioners attain rebirth in Amida's Pure Land.[19] A century later, it was recorded that Jien 慈円 (1155–1225), head of the Tendai school, instructed his disciples to perform the *Nijūgo zanmai shiki* in order to transfer merit for his well-being after his passing.[20] These cases suggest that the origins of *kōshiki* and its early development lay in rituals related to preparing for rebirth in Amida's Pure Land and the afterlife. Together with the rise of Pure Land devotion—and related deathbed and memorial practices to achieve rebirth in Amida's Pure Land—*kōshiki* were performed at numerous sites in many different local areas as a means of deepening the faith of aspirants who wished to take refuge in Amida Buddha at their final hour.

While most of the early *kōshiki* authors were Pure Land adherents in the Tendai tradition, clerics of other traditions soon adopted this genre. One of them was Kakuban 覚鑁 (1095–1144), the founder of the Shingi branch of the Shingon school, who is credited with the composition of more than ten *kōshiki.*[21] Yamada Shōzen suggests that Kakuban composed many of them not for the propagation of Buddhist doctrine to a wider audience but for his own private practice.[22] Many scholars have acknowledged the role of *kōshiki* for proselytization,[23] but it was also the case, as Kakuban's *kōshiki* show, that some clerics performed *kōshiki* as part of their own devotional and soteriological practice.

As *kōshiki* grew increasingly popular, many new works in this genre appeared—most of them written by highly educated clerics, and some by retired emperors and other literary men.[24] The pinnacle in the creation of works in this genre came in the late twelfth and early thirteenth centuries when the

17. For the *Nijūgo zanmai shiki,* see NKS 4: 246–255. For a detailed analysis, see Gülberg 1999, 101–176.

18. For the *Ōjō kōshiki,* see T 84, no. 2725. Yōkan also composed a *Sanji nenbutsu kanmon shiki* 三時念仏観門式; for a German translation and analysis, see Gülberg 1999, 177–209. On the *Ōjō kōshiki* as a model, see Gülberg 2006, 36–37, and 2018, 60–61.

19. *Shūi Ōjōden* 3: 26, in *Nihon shisō taikei* 7, 384. On the rise of deathbed practices for achieving rebirth in Amida's Pure Land, see Stone 2016, especially chap. 1.

20. Gülberg 2018, 62.

21. Gülberg 1999, 47–49.

22. Yamada 1995, 35.

23. See, for example, Ozaki 1997, 66; Ozaki 1998b, 167; and Stone 2016, 73. Ford also emphasizes that *kōshiki* served "propagational, pedagogical, and even economic" purposes (2005, 45).

24. Gülberg 1999, 43; 2006, 37.

Hossō monk Jōkei 貞慶 (1155–1213) and the Kegon-Shingon monk Myōe 明恵 (1173–1232) became its two most prolific authors. Jōkei is credited with over twenty-nine *kōshiki,* his *Kannon kōshiki* and *Jizō kōshiki* in particular achieving wide popularity.[25] Myōe is credited with twenty-three *kōshiki,* and his *Shiza kōshiki* (*Kōshiki* in four sessions), composed for the Buddha's memorial day, is considered a masterpiece by Japanese clerics and scholars alike.[26]

Because it was taken up by clerics of different traditions, the *kōshiki* genre became part of a ritual repertoire widely shared throughout Japanese Buddhism. In fact, although *kōshiki* originated in the context of Tendai Pure Land devotion, the majority of the extant compositions in the genre are devoted to objects of worship other than Amida. According to James Ford, the increase in number of compositions was also related to socio-political changes in the early medieval period.[27] As power shifted from the nobility and aristocratic families such as the Fujiwara to the Minamoto and the Kamakura shogunate, established temples no longer could rely on state support or aristocratic patrons alone and had to look for new support from a broad range of social strata. In this context, *kōshiki* seem to have been an effective means of securing new patronage as well as devotional allegiance.

Overall, the development of *kōshiki* can be situated amid the broad process of "Japanization" of religious practices and artistic forms introduced from China. This genre emerged at a time when other Japanese liturgical forms, such as *wasan* and *hyōbyaku,* were being developed together with the adaption of Chinese musical styles to suit Japanese tastes. In that sense, these forms of expression became localized practices. The fact that *kōshiki* were vocalized in Japanese and so spoke directly to Japanese audiences was of course a major factor in the popularization of the new genre.

After peaking in the twelfth and thirteenth centuries, the number of *kōshiki* compositions steadily declined, and very few *kōshiki* were written in the Tokugawa period. Most of the late compositions in the genre were by Sōtō monks, and one of these was created in the Meiji era. Then, around twenty years ago, Inoue Gishin, a Sōtō priest from Aichi prefecture, composed two new *kōshiki.* Other than these, I know of no other *kōshiki* composed in the last two centuries. According to Gülberg's chronology, the last *kōshiki* composed in schools other

25. The Kōshiki Kenkyūkai published a compilation of Jōkei's *kōshiki* in 2000; see also Gülberg 1999, 50–58. Jōkei's *Kannon kōshiki* is included in T 84, no. 2728; see Kōshiki Kenkyūkai 1993. For a study of the *Jizō kōshiki,* see Kōshiki Kenkyūkai 1991, 214–222, and 2000, 101–120, 293–299. Jōkei's *Miroku kōshiki* is examined in Ford 2005 and 2006a, 71–100, 207–214, while Quinter 2011 and 2016 study Jōkei's *Monju kōshiki.*

26. Gülberg 1999, 59–64. The *Shiza kōshiki* consists of the *Nehan kōshiki* (*Kōshiki* on the Buddha's passing), *Jūroku rakan kōshiki* (*Kōshiki* on the Sixteen Arhats), *Yuiseki kōshiki* 遺跡講式 (*Kōshiki* on the remaining traces), and *Shari kōshiki* 舎利講式 (*Kōshiki* on relics). Kindaichi 1964 reconstructed the accent of the Japanese language in the Kamakura period using the musical notations included in the manuscripts of the *Shiza kōshiki.* For a study of the performance of the *Shiza kōshiki,* see Arai K. 2008; and Mross 2012c and 2016a. For a translation of the *Nehan kōshiki,* see Mross 2016b. The *Shiza kōshiki* is included in T 84, no. 2731.

27. Ford 2006b, 98–99.

than the Sōtō school were the *Sanbutsu kōshiki* 讃仏講式 (*Kōshiki* on praising [Amida] Buddha), written by the Jōdo-shin monk Jakunyō 寂如 (1651–1725), a Nishihonganji 西本願寺 abbot, and the *Taishi kōshiki* 太子講式 (*Kōshiki* on Shōtoku Taishi) composed in Enkyō 4 (1747) by Hongakubō Hōjun 本覚坊方順 (n.d.), who might have been associated with Hōryūji 法隆寺 in Nara.[28]

At the same time, it should be noted that the composition or invention of a new *kōshiki* is "just" the starting point of a more complex and continuous transmission. After their composition, works were integrated into the liturgical calendar of different Buddhist temples, and the texts were handed down from generation to generation. But over time, many *kōshiki* ceased to be performed and were largely forgotten, their only traces being the ritual handbooks created for them and stored in temple archives. Yet the genre remains alive, and *kōshiki* are still performed in most Japanese Buddhist schools, the most prominent examples being the *Ōjō kōshiki* in the Tendai school and the nightlong performance of Myōe's *Shiza kōshiki* on Mt. Kōya.

Remarkably, eleven different *kōshiki* are performed in the Sōtō school today—more than in any other Buddhist school. One reason might be the centralization of monastic training in the Sōtō school. At each of the two head temples, around 150 novices are in training at any given time, making it possible for monks at these temples to perform rituals that require a large number of performers. Another reason might be that schools with a strong *shōmyō* tradition have other elaborate rituals in their repertoire, whereas *kōshiki,* for Sōtō clerics, constitute the most melodic rituals in their tradition. In any case, *kōshiki* as a genre has continued to thrive over many centuries and are still a vital part of the liturgical repertoire of Japanese Buddhism.

Kōshiki Performance: Actors, Ritual Places, and Music

Performances of *kōshiki* have varied to a high degree. Although *kōshiki* started as rituals performed exclusively by clerics, there were also times when they were performed by mixed groups of lay devotees and clerics, or by groups of laypeople only. Today only monks or nuns perform *kōshiki*—that is, if laypeople are present, they only listen and watch. The exact reason for this reversion to clericalization is unknown, but it might be related to the increasing complexity of both the rituals and the skills required to perform them.[29]

The group of clerics who perform a *kōshiki* (or any other Buddhist ritual) is known as *shikishū* 識衆 / 式衆 or *daishū* 大衆, and the number of participants varies. *Kōshiki* can be performed by small or large assemblies. The ceremony is led by the officiant, called the *dōshi* 道師 or *shikishi* 式師.

Texts of *kōshiki*—unlike many doctrinal texts or literary works meant to

28. Gülberg 1999, 74 and 269; see also his *Kōshiki database.*

29. In the performance of Myōe's *Shiza kōshiki* during his lifetime, for example, lay devotees and clerics sang the name of the Buddha for around two hours between the parts of the ritual. But as more and more *shōmyō* pieces were added over time, it became too difficult for lay devotees to participate. For a detailed study of this development, see Mross 2016a.

be read in private—are vocalized during the ritual.[30] They have become integrated in highly musical ceremonies that feature several styles of Japanese Buddhist chant. A ritual centering on a *kōshiki* often includes all three styles—song (*utau shōmyō* 歌う声明), recitation (*kataru shōmyō* 語る声明), and reading (*yomu shōmyō* 読む声明)—and together they shape its sonic landscape. The art of vocalizing liturgical texts requires extensive training and is transmitted from master to disciple as part of the latter's education. Since each school preserves a distinctive style of vocalization, the characteristics of the musical performance differ depending on the school.

Initially, the vocalization of a *shikimon* may have been improvised using fixed melodic patterns on three different pitch levels. A change in the pitch level highlighted important passages and added variety.[31] Until the Muromachi period (1336–1573), this style of vocalization was probably the common practice, and monks recited *shikimon* in a way they thought could transmit the content most effectively. But as the accent of the Japanese language gradually changed, it became increasingly difficult to improvise the melodies of *shikimon*.[32] As a result, beginning in the early Muromachi period, monks in the Buddhist schools that had a strong *shōmyō* tradition—primarily Shingon and Tendai—added musical notation to the *shikimon* to ensure the transmission of a "traditional" recitation style, albeit without improvisation, through succeeding generations.[33] Clerics in other schools, including Sōtō monks, chose not to add musical notation, and so we no longer know how *shikimon* were recited in the Sōtō school. However, the lack of notation does not mean that a liturgical text was recited without melodic embellishments; even today one can hear some improvised melodic embellishments in the Sōtō school. This kind of improvisation would be unthinkable in the Shingon school, where clerics are taught to follow the traditional musical notation. Nevertheless, although the melodic embellishments in a recitation by Zen monks sometimes resemble those of Shingon or Tendai monks, I have never heard a Sōtō monk reciting a *shikimon* on three different pitch levels.[34]

In the medieval period, some of the *kōshiki* performances were even more elaborate musically. Wealthy temples or patrons occasionally hired professional musicians to play *gagaku* 雅楽 (court music) between the sections of certain *kōshiki*, and so instrumental music, chosen to fit the tonal mode of the

30. One exception is the aforementioned *Shiza kōshiki*, which is read in silence during the *Shunie* repentance ritual at Tōdaiji.

31. Nelson 2001a, 2001b, and 2009.

32. Nelson 2009, 5.

33. For a study of the *kōshiki* recitation method on three pitch levels, see Nelson 2009; Tokita 2015, 34–50; and Mross 2016a, 113–122.

34. For example, Suzuki Eiichi 鈴木永一 always recites the *shikimon* and offertory declaration of a *kōshiki* with melodies, even though no musical notation is included in the liturgical text. In an interview in 2018 at Sōjiji, he said that he learned this style at Sōjiji Soin in Noto as a young monk.

shikimon, was integrated into its performance.[35] Such rituals were called *kangen kō* 管弦講 (lit., assembly of wind and string instruments), and some *kōshiki* were originally composed for this performance style, such as the *Junji ōjō kōshiki* 順次往生講式 (*Kōshiki* on rebirth in the Pure Land), composed in Eikyū 2 (1114) by the Tendai monk Shingen 真源 (d. 1136), and the *Ongaku kōshiki* 音楽講式 (*Kōshiki* on music).[36] The *Junji ōjō kōshiki* featured texts praising Amida and his Pure Land that were set to *gagaku* pieces of Chinese origin (*tōgaku* 唐楽) and *saibara* 催馬楽 (songs in Japanese that might derive from folk melodies).[37] *Kōshiki* that had not been composed as *kangen kō,* such as Yōkan's *Ōjō kōshiki* and Jōkei's *Shari kōshiki* in five sections, were later arranged to be performed with *gagaku.* A description of an elaborate *kangen kō* that featured both instrumental music and *shōmyō* can be found in the medieval war tale *Genpei jōsui ki* (Record of the rise and fall of the Minamoto and Taira). In this tale, the Heike perform the *Ongaku kōshiki* for the deceased Taira no Kiyomori, with sixteen members of the Heike clan playing musical instruments: two play the *shō* 簫 (a flute), two the *fue* 笛 (transverse flute), two the *shō* 笙 (mouth organ), one the *wagon* 和琴 (Japanese zither), one the *kakko* 羯鼓 (an hourglass-shaped drum), one the *shōgo* 鉦鼓 (gong), one the *hōkei* 方磬 (metallophone), one the big drum (*taikō* 太鼓), two the *kin* 琴 (zither), and three the *biwa.*[38]

In many rituals, the object of worship is made present through a visual representation, whether it be a statue or a painting. Likewise, *kōshiki* are performed in front of an image of the central object of veneration. The object of worship is both the buddha, bodhisattva, deity, or text to whom a given ritual is directed and the concrete representation of that sacred entity as a statue or painting enshrined on the altar. Yamada Shōzen interprets the image as the focal point of the ritual because the participants usually face the image.[39] The use of a statue or a painting varied depending on the location of the *kōshiki* performance.

As for the performance site, *kōshiki* were mostly performed in temple halls, as one might expect, but occasional performances also took place in the houses of lay devotees. The elaborateness of the ritual depended on the financial status of the temple or the lay patron. *Kangen kōshiki,* the most elaborate *kōshiki,* could only be performed at wealthy temples like Tōdaiji (Nara),

35. The term *gagaku* describes a wide range of classical music, and the instrumentation varied depending on the style. Today *gagaku* and *shōmyō* are often treated as independent but they shared common settings in premodern Japan. See Nelson 2008a, 2008b.

36. The author of the *Ongaku kōshiki* and the date of its composition are unknown. However, Sugano Fumi (1987) has shown that it must have been written before 1300.

37. For a brief explanation of the *Junji ōjō kōshiki* in English, see Nelson 2003, 13; Gülberg 1993, 71; and Rambelli 2021, 53. Several studies of this *kōshiki* and typographical reprints of a manuscript in the archive of Chi'on'in 知恩院 have been published: see Itō S. 1975, 359–388; Satō T. 1979, 111–158; and Kōshiki Kenkyūkai 1990.

38. *Genpei jōsui ki* 6: 57. See also Gülberg 1999: 91–93. On *kangen kōshiki,* see also Rambelli 2021, 53–54, 62.

39. Yamada 1995, 19–20.

Kōfukuji 興福寺 (Nara), Shōmyōji 称名寺 (Yokohama), and Mt. Kōya, or in the houses of nobility who could afford to engage musicians.[40]

Interestingly, some *kōshiki* were performed outdoors. Myōe is said to have conducted his *Jūmujin'in shari kōshiki* 十無尽院舎利講式 (*Kōshiki* on the relics of Jūmujin'in) outdoors on the Buddha's memorial day. On this occasion, he declared a tree to be the bodhi tree, erected a pile of stones to represent the diamond throne (*kongōza* 金剛座), and built a stupa next to it.[41] In this case, nature replaced the images used in temple halls and represented the sacred sites mentioned in the *kōshiki.*

Even more colorful were *kōshiki* in which participants enacted scenes from sutras or performed dances. Yamada calls the acts performed during these rituals "theater techniques" (*gekiteki sahō* 劇的作法).[42] For example, the *Yokawa kadaiin geikō kiroku* 横川花臺院迎講記録 (Record of the *mukae kō* at Yokawa's Kadaiin) describes performances of Yōkan's *Ōjō kōshiki* in Jōwa 2 and 3 (1346–1347) as a *kangen kō* dramatized as a *mukae kō* 迎講, a ceremony that reenacts the arrival of Amida Buddha with twenty-five bodhisattvas to usher a deceased person to the Pure Land.[43] These rituals were undoubtedly lively events, as the people acting the roles of the bodhisattvas were dressed in costumes and danced or moved to the music. Another example of a *kōshiki* performance in which participants enacted Buddhist scenes is the previously mentioned outdoor performance of Myōe's *Jūmujin'in shari kōshiki.* On that occasion, the lay devotees watered the tree representing the bodhi tree, reenacting a scene from the *Ayuwang jing* 阿育王經 (Sutra of King Aśoka) in which, upon the king's wish, an outcaste maid revived the dying bodhi tree by giving it milk.[44] This shows theater and ritual are closely related in Japanese culture. Early Buddhist rituals could include *bugaku* dances or mask dances known as *gigaku* 伎楽, and the melodies used in the recitation style of Buddhist chant (*kataru shōmyō*) influenced the vocalization style of *nō* theater.

The foregoing examples demonstrate the diversity of *kōshiki* performances in premodern times. Depending on the situation and the resources, *kōshiki* could be made more elaborate by adding instrumental music and more performers, or could be simplified. The colorful performances mentioned in this section by no means represented the typical *kōshiki* performance, just as the financial resources of most temples or ritual sponsors were more modest. Over time *kōshiki* performances became standardized, and certain styles of performance, such as *kangen kō,* were lost. Nonetheless, the performance practices in different Buddhist schools remain diverse, and we still find manifold ways of performing *kōshiki* in contemporary Japan.

40. Gülberg 2006, 35.

41. *Kōzanji Myōe shōnin gyōjō* (*Kana gyōjō*), MSS 1: 47–48; *Kōzanji Myōe shōnin gyōjō* (*Kanbun gyōjō, Jōzanbon*), MSS 1: 130; *Kōzanji Myōe shōnin gyōjō* (*Kanbun gyōjō, Hōoninbon*), MSS 1: 200.

42. Yamada 1995, 12.

43. Suzuki H. 1991. Horton (2008) suggests that the *mukae kō* (welcoming ceremony) originated with Genshin.

44. T 50: 139b10–19.

History of *Kōshiki* in the Sōtō School

Of Japan's two major schools of Zen, only the Sōtō school has developed a rich *kōshiki* tradition.[45] The Sōtō school emerged in the first half of the thirteenth century, and most of its *kōshiki* were composed in later centuries. Thus Sōtō *kōshiki* developed for the most part after the peak of *kōshiki* production in the twelfth and thirteenth centuries, presenting a special case in the development of *kōshiki* as a whole. Nevertheless, although Zen clerics typically downplay the influences of other Japanese Buddhist schools on Japanese Zen, the adoption of *kōshiki* by Sōtō clerics shows how elements of a shared ritual vocabulary entered Zen practice and subsequently were integrated into a distinctive ritual tradition of Sōtō Zen.

Sōtō Definition of *Kōshiki*

Before examining the history of Sōtō *kōshiki* in detail, it is necessary to explain how the term *kōshiki* is used in the Sōtō school. Sōtō clerics in contemporary Japan generally use the term *kōshiki* in a broad sense, applying it to the entire ritual. They refer to the central text, consisting of a pronouncement of intention and thematic sections followed by verses (in other words, *kōshiki* in the narrow sense), as the *shikimon*. In my discussion of Sōtō *kōshiki*, I will follow this usage.[46]

45. *Kōshiki* have also been performed in Rinzai temples. But only the Chinese immigrant monk Lanxi Daolong 蘭渓道隆 (J. Rankei Doryū, 1213–1278) seems to have composed new *kōshiki*. He is credited with the composition of five *kōshiki*, the *Kannon kōshiki* 観音講式, *Nehan kōshiki* 涅槃講式, *Rakan kōshiki* 羅漢講式 (*Kōshiki* on the arhats), *Shari kōshiki* 舎利講式, and *Daruma kōshiki* 達磨講式 (*Kōshiki* on Bodhidharma). These five works were later called *Kenchō go kōshiki* (Five *kōshiki* of Kenchō[ji]). In the Tokugawa period, Lanxi Daolong's *Rakan kōshiki* was performed at Kenchōji 建長寺 (Kamakura), Engakuji 円覚寺 (Kamakura), Shōkokuji 相国寺 (Kyoto), Tenryūji 天龍寺 (Kyoto), and Entsūji 円通寺 (Hakata), and it is still performed annually at Kenchōji and Engakuji. It has been a matter of debate whether his *kōshiki* were recited in Chinese or Japanese (see Gülberg 2006, 36), but because extant Tokugawa-period texts contain *furigana* and *kaeriten*, we can assume that Lanxi's *kōshiki* were recited in Japanese. I was able to see the performance of the *Rakan kōshiki* at Kenchōji and Engakuji several times, and the *shikimon* was always recited in Japanese. For a study of Lanxi's *Rakan kōshiki*, see Mross 2012a. Additionally, the *Rakan kōshiki* credited to Dōgen has been performed in Rinzai temples; monks at Tōfukuji 東福寺 (Kyoto) still conduct it every January, and monks at Myōshinji 妙心寺 (Kyoto) probably used to perform it, as an edition produced by this temple, *Meiji shinkoku Rakan kōshiki*, is extant.

46. However, in earlier times, Sōtō monks also used the term *kōshiki* in its narrow sense. For example, in the *Keizan shingi* edited by the influential Sōtō reformer Manzan Dōhaku 卍山道白 (1636–1715), the *shikimon* of the *Rakan kōshiki* is called *kōshiki*, and the whole ritual is called *Rakan kuyō* 羅漢供養 (T 82: 433b19, 433b21, 435a13). Even within a single work, the usage of the term *kōshiki* is not always consistent. For example, in the *Keizan shingi* copied by the monk Rinkō 麟広 (n.d.) in Meiō 10 (1501), both the *Rakan kōshiki* and the *Nehan kōshiki* are included. The *shikimon* of the *Rakan kōshiki* is called *Rakan kō no shiki* 羅漢講之式, while the *shikimon* of the *Nehan kōshiki* is preceded by the subheading *hyōbyaku* (pronouncement of intention). The latter style is customary in some other schools, and the *Nehan kōshiki* in the Rinkō manuscript follows this convention. Thus the term *kōshiki* was used in a variety of ways, and it has to be understood in its context.

Additionally, Sōtō clerics since the Tokugawa period use the term *kōshiki* in another very particular, even broader sense, applying the term to rituals that are not *kōshiki* in the original sense.[47] These include *Tanbutsue* 歎仏会 (Ceremony of praising the buddhas), *Daifusatsu bosatsu shiki* 大布薩菩薩式 (Grand precepts meeting),[48] and *Kannon senbō* 観音懺法 (Kannon repentance ceremony) despite the fact that these rituals do not contain a *shikimon,* usually the defining criterion for a *kōshiki.* From the perspective of *kōshiki* studies in general, these rituals cannot claim to be *kōshiki.* Yet Sōtō clerics and most scholars of the Sōtō school seem unaware or unconcerned with the discrepancy;[49] they understand *kōshiki* to be grand rituals that include *shōmyō* and therefore belong to the school's *shōmyō* repertoire. In fact, compared to other Sōtō rituals, all the rituals they consider *kōshiki* are relatively similar in terms of their melodic realization. Nevertheless, rather than follow this very broad definition, I use the term *kōshiki* only to refer to rituals that include a *shikimon,* as described above.

Early History of Sōtō *Kōshiki:* Medieval Japan

The history of *kōshiki* in the Sōtō school starts with its founder, Dōgen, who in addition to being an avid practitioner of zazen was also involved in the performance of rituals. During his lifetime, *kōshiki* production was at its peak,

47. The earliest example of this very broad usage of the term *kōshiki* can be found in the manuscript *Shi kōshiki* (Four *kōshiki*), written in Jōkyō 3 (1686) by Kankai 観海 (n.d.) of Hōenji 玉円寺 in Kanazawa, which contains the *Grand Precepts Meeting* in addition to *kōshiki* on the Buddha's passing, Bodhidharma, and the Sixteen Arhats; see Ozaki 2014a, 130–132. Other examples are the two multivolume collections *Tōjō go kōshiki* (Five *kōshiki* of the Sōtō school) and *Sōtō roku kōshiki* (Six *kōshiki* of the Sōtō school), both edited in the middle of the eighteenth century. In addition to *kōshiki* in a traditional sense, the set of five contains *Daifusatsu shiki* and *Tanbutsue shiki,* while the set of six includes *Daifusatsu kōshiki, Tōjō shōrai hō* 洞上唱禮法 (Ceremony of venerating the buddhas in the Sōtō school), *Tanbutsue shiki,* and *Kanromon* 甘露門 ("Ambrosia gate," sung during the ceremony for feeding the hungry ghosts). The second volume of ZSZ includes eleven rituals under the rubric *kōshiki,* but four of them do not contain a *shikimon* and therefore are not *kōshiki* in the original sense: *Tanbutsue hosshiki, Tōjō shōraihō, Kannon senbōhō,* and *Tōjō daifusatsuhō.*

48. Traditionally, *Daifusatsu bosatsu shiki* is a precepts meeting (Skt. *poṣadha*), a central ritual for the *saṃgha* in which monks and nuns recited the rules and confessed their transgressions in front of the assembly. In the Japanese Sōtō school, however, this observance became highly ritualized. Instead of confessing their transgressions, clerics chant *shōmyō* pieces before a lecture about the *Sutra of Brahmā's Net* (*Fanwang jing,* J. *Bonmyō kyō*). For a detailed study on the development of the *Grand Precepts Meeting* in the Sōtō school, see Ozaki 2014a.

49. During my fieldwork at Sōtō temples, I met only one Sōtō monk who was aware of the special usage of the term *kōshiki* in the Sōtō school. Interestingly, Inoue Gishin (2000, 9r–v), a teacher at Eiheiji's satellite temple in Nagoya, provides a categorization of Sōtō *kōshiki* that distinguishes between (*a*) rituals that have an individual character, such as *Senbō, Fusatsu, Tanbutsu,* and *Shōraihō;* (*b*) *kōshiki* with a standard form, such as *Nehan kōshiki, Hokke kōshiki, Daruma kōshiki, Hōon kōshiki,* and *Dentō kōshiki;* and (*c*) rituals that in addition to the standard form have an invitation (*kanjōmon*), such as the *Rakan kōshiki,* as well as rituals that do not include a *Praise of the Four Wisdoms* and the *Four Shōmyō Melodies,* such as the *Daihannya kōshiki.* In this book, only categories *b* and *c* are described as *kōshiki,* because only these rituals contain a *shikimon.*

and *kōshiki* were widely performed in all Buddhist traditions. Although the sources we have give us no information about why or how often he might have been involved himself in *kōshiki* performances, it is reasonable to assume that it was not unnatural for Dōgen to conduct rituals in this genre.

Dōgen is credited with the composition of the *Rakan kōshiki,* a work praising the Sixteen Arhats, a group of Śākyamuni's direct disciples. According to the *Record of the Perpetuity of the Dharma, Narrated by the Great Arhat Nandimitrā* (Skt. *Nandimitrāvadāna,* Ch. *Daaluohan nantimiduoluo suoshuo fazhuji*), Śākyamuni ordered these disciples to remain in this world rather than enter nirvāṇa so that they could protect his teachings and followers after his departure.[50] The attribution to Dōgen is in part based on two fragments of a *Rakan kōshiki* manuscript in his original handwriting, which were designated as national treasures (fig. 1.1).[51] It has been assumed that Dōgen wrote this manuscript around Hōji 3 (1249), when he recorded that heavenly flowers appeared during a ceremony for the arhats—probably the *Rakan kōshiki*—that he conducted at Eiheiji, interpreting the auspicious sign as proof that Eiheiji is a special sacred place, the equal of Mt. Tiantai in China.[52]

There are still many questions concerning the origins of this *kōshiki.* Two theories have been proposed based on premodern sources. The first cites the Zuichō manuscript of the Dōgen biography *Kenzeiki* 建撕記 from Tenshō 17 (1589), which states that according to a colophon of a *Rakan kuyō no shikisahō* 羅漢供養の式作法 (Ritual procedure for the offerings to the arhats), Yōsai 栄西 (or Eisai, 1141–1215), the founder of Japanese Rinzai Zen, composed a *Rakan kōshiki,* and it was transmitted in the Sōtō school.[53] However, neither

50. T 49, no. 2030. For studies of the arhats in Zen, see Lévi and Chavannes 1916, Visser 1923, and Michihata 1983. See also Faure 1991, 266–272, and 1996, 88–96; and Ishida T. 2006. For studies of the *Rakan kōshiki* in the Sōtō school, see Harada 1980; Azuma 1983; Kirino 2002; Mross 2007; Mross 2011. Visser 1923, 182–196, offers a partial English translation of the *Rakan kōshiki* edited by Menzan, and Ichimura 1994 translated the *Keizan shingi* edited by Manzan Dōhaku, which includes a *Rakan kōshiki.* For a complete German translation of the contemporary ritual handbook of the *Rakan kōshiki,* see Mross 2007, 53–91. For a *kundoku* of the *Rakan kōshiki,* see Yamamoto 2010b; for a *kundoku* and a translation into modern Japanese, see Nakano et al. 2002, 167–220.

51. The two fragments are stored in the archive of Daijōji 大乗寺 (Kanazawa) and the archive of Zenkyūin 全久院 (Toyohashi). For a typographical reprint, see DZZ 7: 288–295; DZO 2: 402–404; or ZSZ 1: 23–29. Facsimiles of these manuscripts are included in DZSS, 91–94 and DZSK, 225–237. Manzan Dōhaku confirmed the authenticity of the manuscript stored in the archive of Daijōji (DZSS, 7; ZSZ 1: 29). For a detailed study of these manuscripts, see Kirino 2002.

52. *Jūroku rakan genzui ki;* see DZO 2: 546; DZSK, 950; DZZ 7: 398; and ZSZ 1: v. Dōgen's *Shōbōgenzō* also includes a fascicle on arhats titled *Arakan,* in T 82: 152c–154a; DZZ 1: 403–408. In this fascicle, Dōgen does not discuss the Sixteen Arhats but describes arhats as practitioners who have eliminated all defilements and reached enlightenment.

53. K, 71. Kirino points out that this manuscript uses the term *Rakan kuyō no shikisahō* rather than *kōshiki,* and therefore it is unclear whether the author really meant a *kōshiki* (2002, 71). However, since *kōsahō* and *sahō* can also be used to describe *kōshiki,* it is possible that the text refers to a *kōshiki* here; see Gülberg 1999, 299.

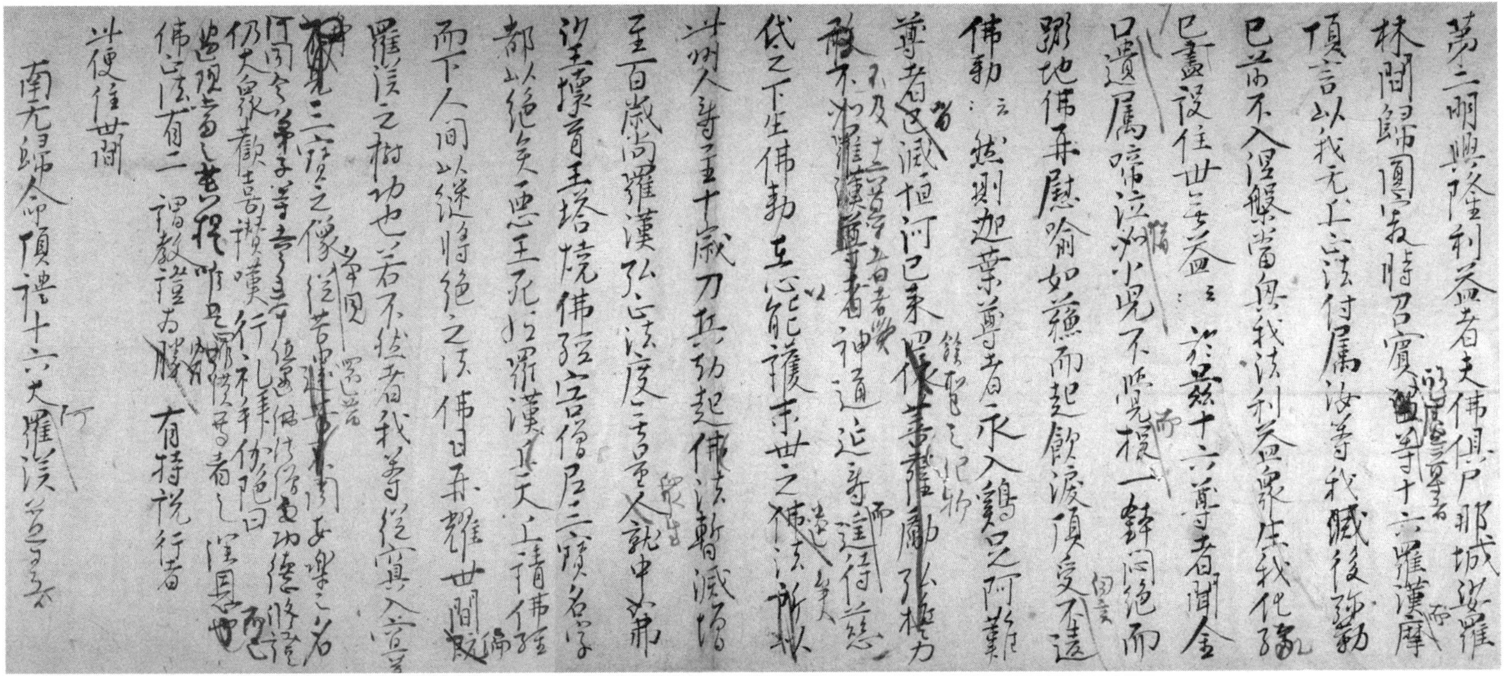

Figure 1.1. *Rakan kuyō shikimon* (1249?) in the hand of Dōgen. Archive of Zenkyūin, Toyohashi. Photo by Toyohashi City Museum of Art and History. Used with permission.

the original postscript nor a *Rakan kōshiki* by Yōsai has been found.[54] It is possible that Yōsai wrote or edited a *Rakan kōshiki* that served as a model for both Myōe's earlier *Jūroku Rakan kōshiki* and Dōgen's *Rakan kōshiki*. This would explain the similarities between these *kōshiki* as well as some passages in the text of the *Rakan kōshiki* of the Sōtō school—for example, the statement that the correct teaching of the Buddha was transmitted to Japan through Saichō and Kūkai, a statement that probably would not have originated with Dōgen.[55]

The second theory is based on the claims of Menzan Zuihō 面山瑞方 (1683–1769), one of the great reformers of Sōtō Zen in the Tokugawa period. He wrote that Dōgen shortened Myōe's *Shiza kōshiki*, which consists of the *Nehan kōshiki* (*Kōshiki* on the Buddha's passing), *Jūroku rakan kōshiki* (*Kōshiki* on the Sixteen Arhats), *Yuiseki kōshiki* (*Kōshiki* on the remaining traces), and *Shari kōshiki* (*Kōshiki* on relics).[56] But only the *Jūroku rakan kōshiki* and *Shari kōshiki* of Myōe's *Shiza kōshiki* are thematically incorporated in the *Rakan kōshiki*. Myōe also composed a *Rakan wasan* (Japanese hymn for the arhats) and a *Rakan kushiki* (Offering ceremony for the arhats).[57] Because Dōgen's *Rakan kōshiki* and Myōe's ritual texts praising the arhats contain many similar sentences and phrases, we can assume that Dōgen was strongly influenced by Myōe's text.[58] Both theories suggest that Sōtō monks neither invented an entirely new ritual for themselves nor simply adopted rituals from the Chinese Chan tradition: rather, they developed their ritual practice from within a Japanese environment and adapted elements from already established Japanese Buddhist schools. This led to the formation of a highly eclectic ritual tradition.

Keizan also performed rituals for the arhats. According to his diary, he performed a *Rakan kuyō* 羅漢供養 (Offering for the arhats) every month since Gennō 1 (1319) at the request of the arhats themselves.[59] We can assume that

54. Nevertheless, according to his *Kōzen gokoku ron* (A treatise on letting Zen flourish to protect the state), Yōsai annually performed an arhat ceremony in the first month; see T 80: 15a12, 15a15. For an English translation of the *Kōzen gokoku ron*, see Tokiwa 2005.

55. Itō Shūken (DZZ 7: 399) and Kawamura Kōdō (DZSK, 950, and ZSZ 1: v) also assume that Myōe and Dōgen have used Yōsai's text as a model. The assumption that Yōsai composed a *Rakan kōshiki* might explain why this *kōshiki* has been performed in Rinzai temples and on Mt. Kōya.

56. *Tōjō sōdō shingi gyōhōshō*, SZ 4: 205.

57. *Rakan wasan*, NKS 4: 46–48. Myōe's close disciple Kikai 喜海 (1178–1250) copied the *Rakan kushiki* in Genkyū 2 (1205). For a facsimile and a typographical reprint, see MSS 5: 327–366.

58. See Kirino 2002. Kirino (2001) also argues that the *Shōbōgenzō* chapter *Menju* 面授 was influenced by Myōe's *Yuiseki kōshiki*.

59. *Tōkokuki*, JDZ, 395; KZ 8: 21. This is also mentioned in the *Keizan shingi*, T 82: 427b19–21. Additionally, an offertory declaration recited during the *Rakan kōshiki* is included in the *Tōkokuki; Rakan ku saimon*, JDZ, 457–458; KZ 9: 35. Yet since it is included only in the widely circulating later version and not in the older manuscript in the archive of Daijōji, we can assume that it was added to the *Tōkokuki* after Keizan's death; see Kawai 2002. Arhats played an important role in Keizan's life and are often mentioned in the *Tōkokuki*. For example, in a dream Keizan saw the eighth arhat, Vajraputra, who told him that the place of his temple is truly superior; see JDZ, 392–393; KZ 8: 5. See Faure 1996, 89, for an English translation of this dream; and Mross 2007, 23–24, for a German translation.

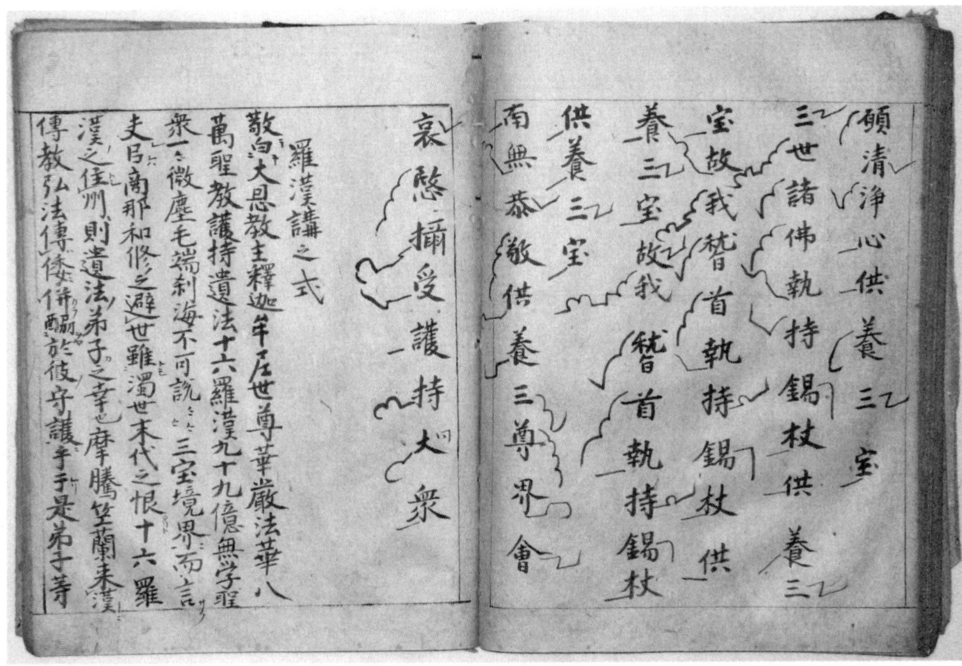

Figure 1.2. *Rakan kōshiki*, in the Rinkō manuscript of the *Keizan shingi* (1501). The right side shows the end of the *Gāthā of the Sounding Staff*, and the left side the beginning of the *shikimon*. The lines next to the Chinese characters in the *Gāthā of the Sounding Staff* indicate the melodic movement. This is the oldest extant musical notation of the Sōtō school. Archive of Yōkōji, Hakui. Photo by the author.

this ritual was a *Rakan kōshiki*. The version in the *Keizan shingi* (Pure rules of Master Keizan), a ritual manual compiled by Keizan, became the standard version of the *Rakan kōshiki* and remained so until the publication of a revised edition of the *kōshiki* in 1966. A *Rakan kōshiki*, however, is included only in the Rinkō manuscript (*Rinkō shoshabon* 麟広書写本) of the *Keizan shingi* written in Meiō 10 (1501) and in the print edition edited by Manzan Dōhaku 卍山道白 (1636–1715) in Tenna 1 (1681).[60] The Rinkō manuscript contains a detailed description of the *Rakan kōshiki* and a *Nehan kōshiki* (fig. 1.2). Unlike Dōgen's manuscript, the two *kōshiki* in the Rinkō manuscript contain musical notation—the oldest extant musical notation of the Sōtō school. This is significant because singing and recitation are probably the most important elements in the performance of a *kōshiki*, and musical notation is one of the very few means to gain insight into the aural world of Buddhist rituals. This manu-

60. The Rinkō manuscript of the *Keizan shingi* is stored in the archive of Yōkōji. It is titled *Nōshū Tōkokusan Yōkōji gyōji shidai* 能州洞谷山永光寺行事次第, but commonly referred to as *Keizan shingi*. The Manzan edition of the *Keizan shingi* is included in T 82, no. 2589.

script shows that the Sōtō school had a *shōmyō* repertoire by the early sixteenth century.

The *Nehan kōshiki,* which narrates the Buddha's passing and explains his last teaching, has been performed during memorial services for the Buddha at Sōtō temples since the Muromachi period. Several different *Nehan kōshiki* have been composed; the one vocalized at Sōtō temples is a variation of the *Nehan kōshiki* attributed to Genshin.[61] It was included in the Rinkō manuscript of the *Keizan shingi,* but it was probably not performed during Keizan's time at Yōkōji, because there is no mention of a *Nehan kōshiki* in the oldest surviving copy of the *Keizan shingi,* the manuscript held at Zenrinji (Zenrinji-bon 禅林寺本, Eiwa 2 [1376]), or in Keizan's temple diary, the *Tōkokuki* (Record of Tōkoku[san]).[62] Yet as it is included in the Rinkō manuscript of the *Keizan shingi* copied in Meiō 10 (1501), we can infer that it was performed at Sōtō temples from at least the beginning of the sixteenth century. Also, a number of Tokugawa-period manuscripts and prints have been discovered, confirming its widespread use during this period.

A third Sōtō *kōshiki* that can be traced back to the medieval period is the *Hokke kōshiki* (*Kōshiki* on the *Lotus* [*Sutra*]) written for Dōgen's memorial service by Giun 義雲 (1253–1333), the fifth abbot of Eiheiji.[63] Although this *kōshiki* was performed in remembrance of Dōgen, the *shikimon* does not give an account of Dōgen's life; rather, it praises the *Lotus Sutra* and explains some of its doctrinal concepts. In its form, the *Hokke kōshiki* belongs to a subgroup of *kōshiki* that Niels Gülberg calls *kōkyō kō* 講経講, *kōshiki* that are similar to sutra lectures and whose sections can be separated into three parts: general overview, explanation of the name of the sutra, and expounding on and classification of the sutra.[64] It is the only *kōshiki* adhering to this form in the Sōtō school.

There may well have been other *kōshiki* performed at medieval Sōtō temples, but from the extant sources we can only confirm the performance of these three *kōshiki.*

---

61. Menzan wrote in his *Tōjō sōdō shingi gyōhōshō* that the *Nehan kōshiki* of the Sōtō school was composed by Myōe; see SZ 4: 206. But Ozaki Shōzen (1997, 1998a, 1998b) has shown that it is actually a variant of the one attributed to Genshin. Genshin's authorship, however, is questionable; see Gülberg 1999, 44. For a *kundoku* of this *kōshiki,* see Shiina 2010a.

62. See also Ozaki 1997, 47, and 1998b, 168–169. Azuma interprets the sources differently: he assumes that Keizan performed a *Nehan kōshiki* because it is included in the Rinkō manuscript of the *Keizan shingi,* which states in the postscript that the *Keizan shingi* is based on Keizan's explanations; see Azuma 2000, 40. He also considers the possibility that Dōgen performed a *Nehan kōshiki,* as the manuscript indicates that it follows the old rules of Eiheiji.

63. Postscript of the *Eiheiji kaisan kigyō Hokke kōshiki* (*Hokke kōshiki* for short) written by Engetsu Kōjaku 円月江寂 (1694–1750) in Enkyō 4 (1747); see ZSZ 2: 819–835. Engetsu Kōjaku was the forty-second abbot of Eiheiji, and according to his postscript, he asked Menzan to edit the *Hokke kōshiki* using an old manuscript in the archive of Hōkyōji 宝慶寺 (Fukui prefecture), which has since been lost. For a *kundoku* and explanation of Menzan's edition, see Sakauchi 2010b. For a *kundoku* and a translation into modern Japanese, see Nakano et al. 2002, 263–321.

64. Gülberg 1999, 36–37.

The Tokugawa Period

The Tokugawa period seems to have been the heyday for the invention of new Sōtō *kōshiki*. During this period, Sōtō monks composed at least nine new *kōshiki* and adopted at least five *kōshiki* from other schools. These new works and the high number of extant manuscripts and woodblock prints from this period suggest that *kōshiki* were widely performed at Sōtō temples. However, it should be noted that no temple conducted all the *kōshiki* discussed here; liturgies were highly localized, and some *kōshiki* were performed only at one or a few temples.

The boom in woodblock printing during the Tokugawa period ensured that large numbers of Buddhist texts were produced. From the seventeenth century on, Japanese monks strove to establish an orthodoxy and orthopraxy in their respective schools, and the print medium played a major role in that trend. Accordingly, ritual manuals were produced as print editions, leading to a standardization of ritual practices. Still, the print medium did not completely replace handwritten texts, which continued to have a place.[65] The numbers of both manuscripts and woodblock print editions of Sōtō *kōshiki* in this period demonstrate the vitality of this genre in the Sōtō school.

The increase in *kōshiki* does not suggest a burgeoning in the number of rituals performed in the Sōtō school, as most of the *kōshiki* discussed in this section did not involve the invention of completely new ritual observances. Rituals for most of the deities venerated in the *kōshiki* were already being performed; however, they consisted of simpler forms, based mostly on sutra chanting, and were in some cases replaced with *kōshiki*—in other words, more elaborate musical rituals. Thus, the increase in *kōshiki* represents an augmentation in the ways of performing a ritual for a certain object of veneration.

New kōshiki *composed in the Tokugawa period.* A high percentage of the new works, five out of the nine currently known *kōshiki,* were written in remembrance of influential Sōtō monks. It had been customary to perform memorial services for school and temple founders, and Sōtō monks accordingly composed *kōshiki* narrating the life and accomplishments of their patriarchs. These works constitute a subgenre of *kōshiki* called *hōon kōshiki* 報恩講式 (*kōshiki* to repay benevolence received).

Current sources suggest that the first *hōon kōshiki* composed for a Sōtō monk was the *Butsuji kōshiki* for Keizan, written before 1679 by an unknown author. This *kōshiki* was performed at both Sōjiji and Yōkōji and is studied in detail in Part II of this book.[66]

---

65. Kornicki (2006) demonstrated that scribal traditions and manuscript culture continued to have an important role in the transmission of knowledge and literary life until the middle of the nineteenth century despite the boom in printing and publishing from the seventeenth century on. Likewise, ritual manuscripts continued to be used at many Sōtō temples, as the extant manuscripts suggest.

66. The earliest document mentioning the *Butsuji kōshiki* is the *Shogakuzan Sōjizenji shogyōji,*

In Hōei 4 (1707), two *hōon kōshiki* for Dōgen were composed independently. One was the *Dōgen zenji kōshiki* 道元禅師講式 (*Kōshiki* on Zen Master Dōgen) by Zuihō Daiki 瑞峰大奇 (d. 1737), the head priest of Hōshōji 法祥寺 (Yamagata prefecture). The other was the *Eihei shoso Dōgen zenji kōshiki* (*Kōshiki* on Zen Master Eihei Dōgen) written by Zenzui Shōzen 禅瑞性泉 (n.d.) of Shinano province (present-day Nagano prefecture).[67] Why Daiki and Shōzen composed *kōshiki* in remembrance of Dōgen is unclear. The 450th anniversary of his death had already been commemorated in Genroku 15 (1702), a few years earlier. As both were in Manzan's lineage—Daiki a direct disciple of Manzan and Shōzen a disciple of Meishū Shushin 明州珠心 (1636–1724), Manzan's successor at Daijōji[68]—they might have been influenced by the reform movement of the Sōtō school (*shūtō fukko undō* 宗統復古運動), in which Manzan was a leading force. This movement lasted from around the middle of the seventeenth century until the middle of the eighteenth century, and its advocates aimed to return to Dōgen's style of Zen and to establish an official orthodoxy. Consequently, Sōtō monks began to intensively study and comment on Dōgen's works, especially the *Shōbōgenzō*.

Around fifty years later, Menzan composed the *Eihei kaisan Hōon kōshiki* (*Kōshiki* to repay benevolence received from the founder of Eihei[ji]), or *Hōon kōshiki* for short, for the five hundredth anniversary of Dōgen's death. According to Menzan, the two *hōon kōshiki* by Daiki and Shōzen contained many mistakes and misspellings, so he composed a new *kōshiki* to correct those mistakes and incorporate new knowledge about Dōgen's life.[69]

During my archival work at Sōjiji Soin, I discovered several manuscripts containing the verses for a *kōshiki* that had been completely forgotten. It was the *Gasan kōshiki,* written for Gasan Jōseki, Sōjiji's second abbot (fig. 1.3). As the first full-time abbot of Sōjiji, Gasan was very important to his temple's success, and monks in his lineage performed an annual memorial service for him that lasted several days. For this annual observance, an unknown author composed the *Gasan kōshiki,* most likely in the eighteenth century.[70]

---

written in Enpō 7 (1679), but it was probably composed earlier; see Muromine 1965, 245. For a translation of this *kōshiki,* see Appendix 2.

67. See Kasai 2003 for a typographical reprint.

68. *Yōhō Renpō keifu,* ZSZ 10: 323.

69. ZSZ 2: 717–734. For a *kundoku,* see Tsunoda H. 2010, and for a *kundoku* and a translation into modern Japanese, see Nakano et al. 2002, 373–429.

70. I discovered seventy-two texts with choral pieces for the *Gasan kōshiki* that had been glued into manuscripts originally copied in Genroku 7 (1694) (*Nehan kō kada narabini Shichisan, Hōyō* 法要). For a study of these choral notations, see Mross 2012b and 2013b. Further, Ozaki Shōzen found the *Ryōson shōki tō sajōchō,* written in Meiji 4 (1871), in the archive of Sōjiji, which includes an illustration of the sitting order for the *Gasan kōshiki.* Additionally, the Sōtōshū Bunkazai Chōsa Iinkai discovered a diary by Minzan Sokō 珉山楚江 (d. 1737), a head priest of Jissōji 実相寺, who served as one of the five abbots at Sōjiji in Kyōhō 6 and 7 (1723–1724). This manuscript, *Hōzan shukujiki,* is listed in Shūhō 2: 116. For a typographical reprint of the *Gasan kōshiki saimon* and *shikimon* included in it, see Mross 2013a. Further details are in Mross 2012b; 2013a; 2013b; and 2014a, 138–140 and 180–183.

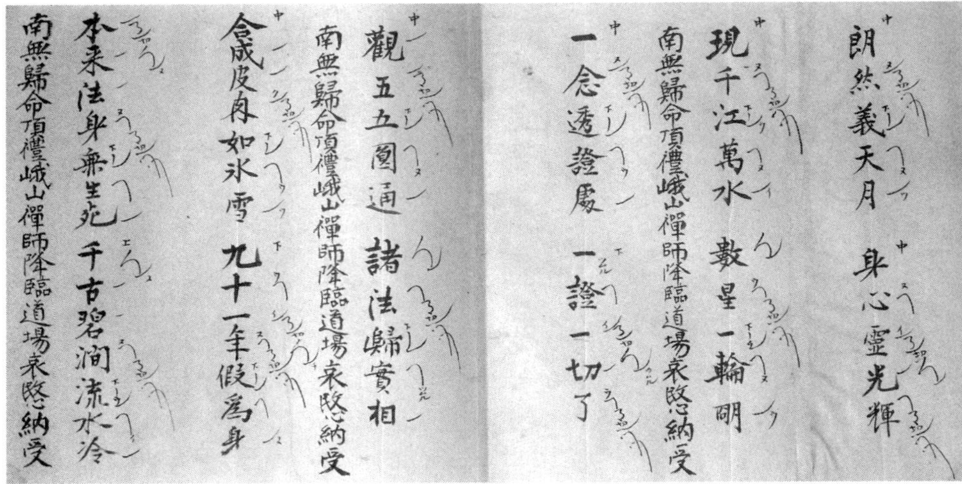

Figure 1.3. Verses of the *Gasan kōshiki*. Tokugawa period. Archive of Sōjiji Soin, Monzen. Photo by the author.

The *hōon kōshiki* for Dōgen, Keizan, and Gasan were not performed in every Sōtō temple. Temples had their own observances and liturgical calendars, and not all chose to conduct rituals for these patriarchs. To a great extent, the liturgy was highly localized. It is therefore likely that the *Gasan kōshiki* was performed only at Sōjiji and the *Butsuji kōshiki* only at Yōkōji and Sōjiji, because Keizan was Yōkōji's and Sōjiji's founding abbot and Gasan was Sōjiji's first full-time Zen abbot. Since neither Gasan nor Keizan had any relation to Dōgen's temple, Eiheiji, these *kōshiki* would not have been performed by the monks there.

At some temples, the presence of particular sacred images led to the performance of rituals dedicated to them. For example, the temple Dairyūji 大隆寺 in Takayama, Gifu prefecture, has a hall in which the bodhisattva Myōken 妙見 (Skt. Sudarśana), an astral deity of the pole star or the Northern Dipper (Ursa Major), is enshrined. This bodhisattva is thought to provide protection from various calamities and to bring rich harvests, ward off disease, and increase longevity. In Japan, he is also believed to cure eye diseases.[71] In the eighteenth century, monks at Dairyūji performed a *Myōken kōshiki* 妙見講式 (*Kōshiki* for Myōken), as recently discovered manuscripts attest, one copied in An'ei 9 (1780) (fig. 1.4).[72] This was most likely a commissioned work written by Daini Sōryū 大而宗龍 (1717–1789), a very active Zen monk

71. For a study of the Myōken cult, see Faure 2016, chap. 2.

72. *Myōken kōshikibon* and *Myōken kōshikibon zen*. This *kōshiki* has five sections. Gülberg's *Kōshiki database* lists three *kōshiki* for Myōken, all titled *Hokuto kōshiki* 北斗講式 or 北斗講私記 (*Kōshiki* on the Northern Dipper), but these works are written in three sections, none of which is titled *Myōken kōshiki*.

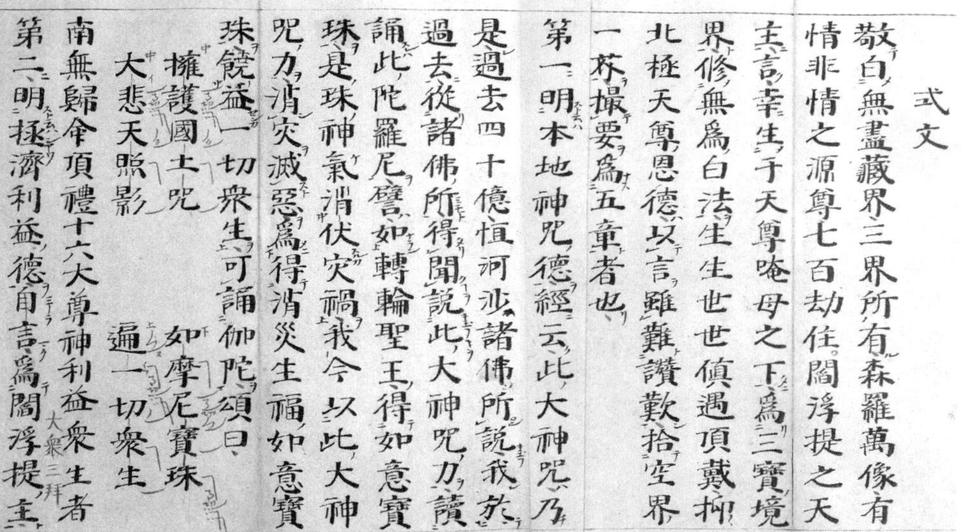

式文
敬白無盡藏界三界所有森羅萬像有
情非情之源尊七百劫住閻浮提之天
主言幸生于天尊唵母之下爲三寶境
界修無爲白法生生世世値遇頂戴抑
北極天尊恩德以言雖難讚歎拾空界
一杯撮要爲五章者也
第一明本地神咒德經云此大神咒乃
是過去四十億恒河沙諸佛所說我於
過去從諸佛所得聞說此大神咒力讀
誦此陀羅尼譬如轉輪聖王得如意寶
珠是珠神氣消伏災禍我今以此大神
咒力消災滅惡爲得消災生福如意寶
珠饒益一切衆生可誦伽陀頌曰
擁護國土咒 如摩尼寶珠
大悲天照影 遍一切衆生
南無歸命頂禮十六大尊神利益衆生者
第二明拯濟利益德用言爲閻浮提主

Figure 1.4. *Myōken kōshiki* (1780). Pronouncement of intention and the first section of the *shikimon.* The officiant read the prose sections, and the assembly sang the verse, following the musical notation to the right of the characters. Archive of Dairyūji, Takayama. Photo by the author.

who traveled throughout Japan to teach and to administer the bodhisattva precepts to laypeople.

Another example of a local *kōshiki* is the *Kasekison nōke kōshiki,* venerating a sacred stone, which was published by the Sōtō temple Tōunji 洞雲寺 in Edo (Tokyo) in Ganji 2 (1864).[73] This *kōshiki* is exceptional in the Sōtō school's *kōshiki* corpus in that it was clearly written for a lay audience who could not read Chinese characters: the text is completely written in Japanese with *furigana* (Japanese reading aids) next to all the Chinese characters (fig. 1.5).

Another *kōshiki* composed in response to a request, this time from the head priest of Chōfukuji 長福寺 (Nara prefecture), was Menzan's *kōshiki* on the *Great Sutra on the Perfection of Wisdom* (*Mahāprajñāpāramitā Sūtra*), the *Daihannya kōshiki,* written in Meiwa 6 (1769). A rolling reading of the *Great Sutra on the Perfection of Wisdom* had been performed in Japan since the early eighth century in the belief that the speed-reading of this long sutra would produce great merit.[74] Japanese Sōtō clerics have performed it since the founding of their school in the thirteenth century. During this ritual, the six hundred volumes of the text are divided among the available clerics, who skim through the text by having the pages of the concertina-folded booklets glide from one

73. On this *kōshiki,* see Gülberg 2016, 155–156.

74. See Visser 1935, 494–519.

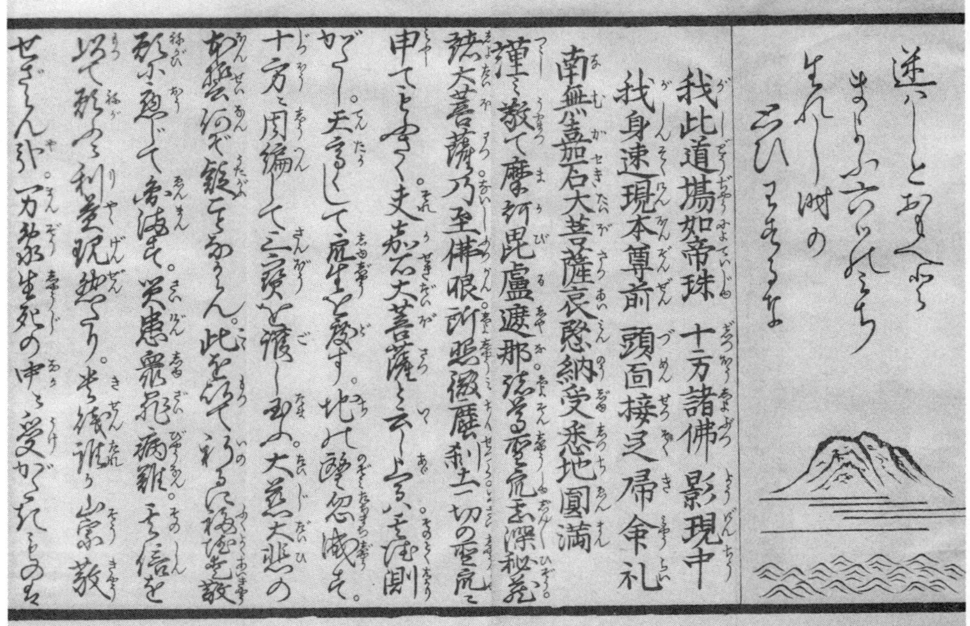

我此道場如帝珠　十方諸佛影現中
我身影現本尊前　頭面接足帰命礼
南無虚空蔵大菩薩哀愍納受悉地圓満

Figure 1.5. *Kasekison nōke kōshiki* (1864). General obeisance and the beginning of the *shikimon*. From the Kadono Konzen Library Collection. Used with permission.

hand to the other, creating a dramatic visual effect of accordion-like pages cascading through the air. Menzan wrote a *shikimon* narrating the benefits of this sutra and integrated it into the ritual of the rolling reading.[75]

Kōshiki *adopted in the Tokugawa period.* In addition to composing new *kōshiki*, Sōtō monks did not shrink from appropriating *kōshiki* performed in other schools, demonstrating their openness to adopting ritual texts from different traditions. When that happened, a cleric would usually take the offertory declaration and *shikimon* of an existing *kōshiki* and insert them into the standard ritual frame used for Sōtō *kōshiki*. The resulting performance would be Sōtō in style, and probably the monks in the assembly would only know where the text had originated if the ritual handbook disclosed it. In this way, liturgical texts imported from other lineages became part of the ritual tradition of the Sōtō school.

The first text to be so adopted in the early Tokugawa period was apparently

75. For a facsimile of this *kōshiki*, see SZ 4: 677–689. A copy of this ritual handbook, printed in An'ei 2 (1773), is stored in the archive of the Research Institute for Japanese Music Historiography, Ueno Gakuen University. For a *kundoku* of the *Daihannya kōshiki*, see Shiina and Sakauchi 2010.

the *Daruma kōshiki* (*Kōshiki* on Bodhidharma), and it was the effort of Bannan Eiju 万安英種 (1591–1654), one of the first monks in this period to advocate a return to Dōgen's Zen. The authorship of this *kōshiki* has been a matter of debate. According to the postscript of one edition, it was composed by Myōe.[76] Menzan, however, asserted that the *Daruma kōshiki* was composed by Kakua 覚阿 (1143–?), who had been credited with the earliest transmission of Zen from China to Japan in the early medieval period.[77] Of course, rituals venerating Bodhidharma are of central importance in the Zen schools, and monks of other Zen traditions independently composed *Daruma kōshiki*. One was written by the Rinzai monk Lanxi Daolong.[78] Another was composed by an unknown monk of the Daruma school, the first independent Zen movement in Japan, founded by Dainichi Nōnin 大日房能忍 (n.d.) at the end of the twelfth century, which was soon marginalized and then disappeared.[79] So far it seems that Sōtō monks did not perform a *Daruma kōshiki* until the early Tokugawa period.

Another *kōshiki* that was adopted is the *Busshōe kōshiki* (*Kōshiki* for the ceremony of the Buddha's birth), which Myōe composed in Karoku 1 (1225).[80] When it was brought into the Sōtō school is unknown. The earliest record of its performance can be found in a ritual manual used at Eiheiji that was written in the first half of the eighteenth century.[81] According to the postscript of a woodblock print from Kan'en 4 (1751), Sugawara Shigehiro 菅原重熈, a local head officer of Kaga, Noto, and Mikawa, requested that the monk Gidō 宜道 of Hōenji 宝円寺 revive the *Busshōe kōshiki* and perform it during the seventh memorial service for his father.[82] This example of a Sōtō *kōshiki*'s performance during a memorial service for a layperson is quite rare.

---

76. ZSZ 2: 851. See also SZ 33: 478. For the *Daruma kōshiki,* see ZSZ 2: 837–851. For a *yomikudashibun* and an explanation of the *Daruma kōshiki* included in the ZSZ, see Shiina 2010b. For a *yomikudashibun* and a translation into modern Japanese, see Nakano et al. 2002, 325–372.

77. *Tōjō sōdō shingi gyōhōshō,* SZ 4: 206.

78. See n. 45 above for other *kōshiki* composed by Lanxi Daolong and their performance history in Rinzai temples. Monks of the Rinzai monastery Myōshinji published a *Daruma kōshiki* in 1877. Because it contains musical notation and guidelines for its performance, we can assume that Rinzai monks had once performed it. Interestingly, this is not Lanxi's *kōshiki* but the one adopted by Sōtō monks.

79. This *kōshiki* survives in a copy from the Kamakura period titled *Jō tōshōgaku ron,* held at Kanazawa Bunkō. It is a major source for the study of the doctrine of the Daruma school; see Ishii 1991, 626–714; and Breugem 2012, chap. 5.

80. For a typographical reprint and study of Myōe's *Busshōe kōshiki,* see Gülberg 1995.

81. *Kichijōzan Eiheiji nenchū teiki* 吉祥山永平寺年中定規. This *shingi* was compiled between Kyōhō 1 (1716) and Kyōhō 14 (1729), during the time of Eiheiji's thirty-ninth abbot, Jōten Sokuchi 承天則地 (1655–1744). For a typographical reprint, see Ozaki 2000.

82. The woodblock print was produced by Hōenji, Tentokuin 天徳院, and Zuiryūji 瑞龍寺 and is currently held in the archive of Shōyōji. It was reprinted in Keiō 1 (1865); see Watarai 1982 for a typographical reprint of this edition. The fact that fifty copies of this print were acquired by Daijōji suggests that this *kōshiki* was also performed there; see Watarai 1982, 107; and Kadono Konzen Library Collection. Two other manuscripts have been discovered at Tentokuin: *Busshōe ryaku kōshiki,* n.d., and *Busshōe ryaku kōshiki,* Keiō 2 (1866). Ritual handbooks containing the choral pieces of the *kōshiki* further confirm the performance of the *Busshōe kōshiki* at other Sōtō temples, including Yōkōji (*Busshō Nehan kōshiki,* Hōreki 3 [1753]).

In the late Tokugawa period, Mugaku Guzen 無学愚禅 (1733–1829), former abbot of Daijōji in Kanazawa, edited Jōkei's *Kannon kōshiki* in Bunka 6 (1809), adding it to the repertoire of Sōtō *kōshiki*.[83] Since the medieval period, the *Kannon senbō* 観音懺法, a repentance ritual directed toward Kannon, had been widely performed in Rinzai and Sōtō temples,[84] but it was replaced by the *Kannon kōshiki* at a few temples toward the end of the Tokugawa period. While the *Kannon senbō* is highly musical, it does not contain a *shikimon*. Thus the adoption of the *Kannon kōshiki* added a ceremony narrating Kannon's virtues in Japanese to the ritual repertoire of the Sōtō school.

Most likely the last *kōshiki* adopted during the Tokugawa period was a gender specific one: the *Anan kōshiki*, venerating Ānanda, which was adopted by Jakushū Kankō 寂宗観光 (1785–1868), a Sōtō nun whose scope of activity in that period was extensive, including participation in the revival of the Rinzai convent Yōrin'an in Kyoto. Śākyamuni was thought to have allowed women to join the Buddhist order through the intercession of Ānanda, so Buddhist nuns traditionally performed rituals for Ānanda to repay their debt to him. Kankō apparently discovered the *kōshiki* for Ānanda in Bunsei 10 (1827) in the archive of Kōzanji, Myōe's temple in the northwest of Kyoto.[85] According to its preface, Myōe was thought to have written the text for a nun, but this attribution is considered questionable,[86] with some scholars suggesting it was probably written by a Tendai monk on the basis of an earlier *Anan keka* 阿難悔過.[87] After copying the text she found, Kankō edited it and asked Kōsen Mujaku 黄泉無著 (1775–1839), the head priest of Manshōji 万松寺 (Owari province) and a well-known Sōtō reformer, to compose an offertory declaration. It was printed in Bunsei 12 (1829) and distributed to Sōtō nuns.

83. See Watarai 1986 for a typographical reprint of an edition from 1892. A copy of this edition is also held at the Komazawa University Library. See also Kōshiki Kenkyūkai 2000, 161–176, for a typographical reprint of a manuscript from Shōō 1 (1288); Tomabechi 1997 for a *kundoku* with extensive annotations; and Kōshiki Kenkyūkai 1993 for a detailed study.

84. The *Kannon senbō* was composed between 998 and 1004 by the monk Zunshi 遵式 (964–1032) in China based on the *Qing guanshiyin pusa xiaofu duhai tuoluoni zhou jing*, T 20, no. 1043, and Zhiyi's 智顗 (538–597) *Fahua sanmei chanyi*, T 46, no. 1941. This ritual was introduced to Japan by the Rinzai monks Yōsai and Ennin Bennen 円爾弁円 (1202–1280) and later adopted by Sōtō monks. For a study of the *Kannon senbō*, see Kawaguchi 1981 and Ikeda 2001. For a description of the present-day performance practice, see Watarai and Sawada 1980, 36–51. The *Kannon senbō* has often been performed for the salvation of the deceased. In this function it was also incorporated into the *nō* play *Tomonaga* 朝長, a play about the death of Minamoto Tomonaga 源朝長 (1143–1160) (Matsuoka 1991).

85. For a description of Kankō's activities, see Sōtōshū Nisōshi Hensankai 1955, 273–283, and Ambros 2016a, 218–222. For a study of the *Anan kōshiki* in the Sōtō school, see P. Arai 2000 and 2008; Ebie 2010; and Ambros 2016a. A complete translation is provided in Ambros 2016b. Lori Meeks examined the *Anan kōshiki* performed at Hokkeji, a convent associated with Eison's vinaya revival movement (2010, 232–237). For studies of the *Anan kōshiki* and its authorship in Japanese, see also Nomura 2002, 371–408; and Katsuura 2008.

86. Gülberg 1999, 61; Ebie 2010, 309–311.

87. Katsuura 2008, 117–118 and 120–121; Nomura 2002, 384–389; and Ambros 2016a, 215–216.

Paula Arai writes that the *Anan kōshiki* is a ritual of gratitude for Sōtō nuns "communally renewing their commitment to life as monastic women," whereas Barbara Ambros maintains "that the ritual has functioned polysemously, affirming nuns' marginalization and their lesser status vis-à-vis the male clergy, while also serving as a means for nuns to celebrate their gender difference."[88]

The widely performed *Jizō kōshiki* composed by Jōkei might also have been adopted during this period.[89] One of the most popular deities in Japanese Buddhism, the bodhisattva Jizō is thought to be a savior of beings dwelling in the hells, and he is often invoked in funeral or memorial services. Jōkei's *kōshiki* explains that until the appearance of the future buddha Miroku 弥勒 (Skt. Maitreya), Jizō saves all sentient beings in the evil time stained with the five defilements (*gojoku akuse* 五濁悪世) together with those suffering in the three lower realms. When Sōtō clerics adopted Jōkei's *kōshiki* is unclear. The oldest edition I was able to locate was printed in 1882 by the abbot of Jigenji 慈眼寺, a Sōtō temple in Kyoto, and while we can confirm that the *Jizō kōshiki* was performed there in the Meiji era, it might have been adopted earlier.[90]

Last but not least, a manuscript of a *Yakushi kōshiki* 薬師講式 venerating the Medicine Buddha was recently discovered at Yōmeiji 永明寺, a Sōtō temple in Shimane prefecture. The origins of this work are unclear, and the manuscript was most likely copied in the Tokugawa period.[91] We cannot say whether it is a new work by a Sōtō monk or a work adopted from another school. Because no other copy of this *kōshiki* has been found, we must assume that it was not widely performed at Sōtō temples and belonged to a local tradition. Nonetheless, its existence underscores the fact that a wide range of *kōshiki* were performed at Sōtō temples.

Except for the *Yakushi kōshiki,* whose author is unknown, all the adopted *kōshiki* I have mentioned were composed by or attributed to well-known authors in other traditions, such as the Tendai monk Genshin, the Hossō monk Jōkei, and the Kegon-Shingon monk Myōe. The adopted *kōshiki* were also directed toward different objects of veneration: Śākyamuni, the Medicine Buddha, Kannon, Jizō, Ānanda, and Bodhidharma. Of these, Bodhidharma was typically an object of devotion only for Zen monks; the others were venerated in all Japanese Buddhist schools. The adoption of these *kōshiki* shows that the ritual tradition of Sōtō Zen incorporated texts from other schools at a time, under the Tokugawa, when the boundaries between schools were as

88. Arai P. 1999, 105; Ambros 2016a, 208.

89. On Jōkei and his *Jizō kōshiki,* see Shimizu 1995 and Kōshiki Kenkyūkai 2000, 101–120, 293–299. In relation to Kasuga, see Glassman 2012, 51–75.

90. *Jizō bosatsu kōshiki,* archive of the Research Institute for Japanese Music Historiography, Ueno Gakuen University. I own a different Meiji-era edition, printed in Nagoya in 1885, with markings made by hand that suggest it was once used in a ritual. Shimizu Kunihiko (2008, 2009) has shown that Jizō played an important role in funerals conducted by Sōtō monks since the fifteenth century. For a study of the Jizō cult in Japan, see Glassman 2012.

91. *Yakushi kōshiki ryakuhon.*

Table 1.1. *Kōshiki* performed at Eiheiji and Sōjiji in the Tokugawa period

Eiheiji	*Sōjiji*
Rakan kōshiki (1 / 8, 5 / 8, 9 / 8)	*Rakan kōshiki* (1 / 15 and 6 / 1)
Nehan kōshiki (2 / 15)	*Nehan kōshiki* (2 / 15)
Busshōe kōshiki (4 / 8)	—
—	*Butsuji kōshiki* (8 / 14)
Hokke kōshiki (8 / 21–28)	—
Daruma kōshiki (10 / 5)	—
—	*Gasan kōshiki* (10 / 19)

clearly defined as they had ever been, a consequence of the head and branch temple system controlled by the bakufu.

Nevertheless, the temple liturgies remained highly localized during that period, and clerics at a particular temple performed only a limited number of *kōshiki*. Monks at the two Sōtō head temples, for example, did not follow the same observances or conduct the same *kōshiki* (table 1.1). The monks of Eiheiji performed the *Rakan kōshiki* three times a year (1 / 8, 5 / 8, and 9 / 8), the *Nehan kōshiki* on the Buddha's memorial day (2 / 15), the *Busshōe kōshiki* on the Buddha's birthday (4 / 8), the *Daruma kōshiki* on Bodhidharma's memorial day (10 / 5), and the *Hokke kōshiki* eight times during Dōgen's memorial service (8 / 21–28).[92] Monks at Sōjiji performed the *Rakan kōshiki* twice a year (1 / 15 and 6 / 1), the *Nehan kōshiki* on the Buddha's memorial day, the *Butsuji kōshiki* during Keizan's memorial service (8 / 14), and the *Gasan kōshiki* during Gasan's memorial service (10 / 19).[93] This comparison shows that the liturgy at Sōtō temples shared common themes such as the *Rakan kōshiki* and the *Nehan kōshiki* while also honoring local traditions through rituals for temple founders and the like.

92. This list is based on the *Kichijōzan Eiheiji nenchū teiki*. For a typographical reprint, see Ozaki 2000. This *shingi* was compiled between Kyōhō 1 (1716) and Kyōhō 14 (1729). At some point, most likely later in the eighteenth century, monks at Eiheiji replaced the *Hokke kōshiki* with Menzan's *Eihei kaisan Hōon kōshiki,* composed in Hōreki 3 (1753), and started to perform the *Daihannya kōshiki,* composed in Meiwa 6 (1769) by Menzan. Eiheiji monks still perform these two *kōshiki.*

93. This list is based on the *Shogakuzan Sōjizenji shogyōji,* which gives an overview of the liturgical year in Enpō 7 (1679). A typographical reprint is included in *Sōjiji shi* (Muromine 1965, 243–246). For a detailed analysis and translation, see Mross 2014a, 112–127. The *Gasan kōshiki* was not mentioned in this text, however, because it seemed to have been composed in the latter half of the Tokugawa period. Earlier, either a *Nehan kōshiki* or a *Rakan kōshiki* was performed during the annual memorial services for Gasan. Moreover, it seems that even after the *Gasan kōshiki*'s composition, a *Rakan kōshiki* was performed in some years. See the *Nōshū shogakuzan nai Myōkōan shingi* (Kansei 10 [1798]), ZSZ 2: 350; the *Shogakuzan rinban nikkan* from Bunsei 11 and 12 (1828–1829) in Itō R. 2003b, 115; and the *Shogakuzan rinbanchū nikki* from Kōka 2 and 3 (1845–1846) in Itō R. 2001b, 44. For a detailed study of the extant manuscripts of the *Gasan kōshiki* and its history at Sōjiji, see Mross 2012b, 2013a, and 2013b.

New Sōtō *Kōshiki* from the Meiji Era to the Present

The Meiji era was marked by dramatic changes in all areas of Japanese society, including Sōtō institutions and doctrine. Nonetheless, Sōtō clerics continued to perform *kōshiki* established in earlier times and produced new print editions for these ceremonies. In addition, they introduced ritual innovations within traditional liturgical genres. In 1893, well after the last creation of *kōshiki* in other schools, Bukkan Bonjō 仏鑑梵成 (d. 1906), a monk affiliated with Sōjiji, composed a new ritual, the *Tōjō dentō kōshiki*, which is a *hōon kōshiki* for Keizan.[94]

Innovations have continued to the present day. Around twenty years ago, Inoue Gishin, then head of training (*tantō* 単頭) at Eiheiji's satellite temple in Nagoya and head priest of Hana'iji 花井寺 in Aichi prefecture, wrote two new *kōshiki*. The first was a *Hakusan kōshiki* composed for Haga Jōmyō's rite of passage in becoming head priest of Tōshōji 東昌寺 in Nagoya, a temple containing a small Hakusan shrine. Hakusan is a sacred mountain range close to Eiheiji and a few other early Sōtō temples such as Hōkyōji 宝慶寺 and Daijōji. Sōtō clerics have venerated the mountain's *kami* as an important protector deity of their school. At Eiheiji, there is a spring said to contain water from Hakusan, and novices make a pilgrimage to the mountain every summer even today. In an interview, Inoue told me that he has a deep connection to the mountain and therefore erected a small Hakusan shrine at Eiheiji's satellite temple in Nagoya, which had no tutelary deity at the time.[95] When the main hall of the temple was rebuilt and opened in October 2017, he and his colleagues performed the *Hakusan kōshiki* to celebrate this occasion.

Inoue's second *kōshiki* was the *Jōyō daishi kōshiki* (*Kōshiki* for Great Master Jōyō), commemorating Dōgen. He composed it for the Shōwakai 正和会, a group of Eiheiji-affiliated monks in Aichi prefecture, of which he has been a leading member. This group had been invited to perform a ritual at Eiheiji to pay respect to Dōgen on the 750th anniversary of his death, and Inoue composed the *Jōyō daishi kōshiki* for the occasion, performing it at Eiheiji on May 20, 2002. Inoue had two aims in this *kōshiki*: to create a shorter ritual and to compose an offertory declaration and *shikimon* that are easily understandable. His *kōshiki* is also unusual in that he added *goeika* 御詠歌 (Buddhist devotional hymns), a style of hymn chanting that differs significantly from *shōmyō*. Sōtō clerics invented this style of chanting in the early 1950s as a religious practice for lay followers,[96] and its integration into a *kōshiki* is remarkable because *goeika* and *shōmyō* are usually regarded as belonging to different spheres, and most *shōmyō* specialists do not sing *goeika*. In my interviews with

94. This *kōshiki* is discussed in detail in Chapter 5. For a translation of its *shikimon*, see Appendix 6. For a *kundoku*, see Sakauchi 2010a and Nakano et al. 2002, 433–490.

95. Interview with Inoue Gishin in June 2017. See also Inoue 2016, 4–5.

96. Sōtō clerics call this school of hymn chanting Baikaryū 梅花流 (lit., style of plum blossoms). The repertoire consists of *goeika* and *wasan* 和讃 (Japanese hymns), which are together referred to as *eisanka* 詠讃歌 (Buddhist hymns).

Sōtō priests who specialize in *shōmyō,* some openly admitted that they dislike the singing of *goeika* in traditional rituals, since, to them, it represents a departure from their tradition. Nevertheless, Inoue created a modern *kōshiki* that could be performed in only ninety minutes—a ritual whose vocal music and gracious movements would, he hoped, offer enjoyment to Sōtō clerics and visitors alike.[97]

At the same time that Inoue was composing his new *kōshiki,* Imamura Genshū, then head of training at Eiheiji's satellite temple in Tokyo, undertook a revision of Menzan's *Eihei kaisan Hōon kōshiki* (also called *Jōyō daishi Hōon kōshiki*) that aimed to create a historically accurate account of Dōgen's life based on medieval sources. Inspired by the Sōtō human rights movement, he also minimized the traditional account of Dōgen's ancestry, barely mentioning his supposed descent from imperial and aristocratic clans, and omitted the honorary posthumous titles given to Dōgen by Japanese emperors.[98] The *kōshiki* was performed at Eiheiji's satellite temple in Tokyo, which issued an audio recording on compact disc to document its contribution to the celebration of Dōgen's anniversary.[99] Today the two new *kōshiki* are performed at Eiheiji's two satellite temples—Inoue's in Nagoya and Imamura's in Tokyo—while monks at Eiheiji still perform Menzan's version. It will be interesting to see whether the monks of Eiheiji adopt one of the new *kōshiki* in the coming years.

The evolution of Sōtō *kōshiki* illustrates the ways in which Sōtō clerics composed new rituals or adopted ritual texts from other traditions, demonstrating the vitality of the genre up to the present. Table 1.2 lists the twenty *kōshiki* performed in Sōtō temples in chronological order according to the first known performance or the date of the oldest extant manuscript or printed edition.[100] In these twenty *kōshiki,* the objects of veneration range

97. Inoue 2002, 47v–48r and 60v–61r.

98. Imamura 2002, 20. The human rights movement in the Sōtō school arose as a reaction to the so-called Machida incident of 1979. At the Third World Conference on Religion and Peace, Machida Muneo 町田宗夫, president of the administrative headquarters of Sōtō Zen, declared that there was no social discrimination in Japan, provoking a scandal. It was reported that Sōtō priests had customarily engaged in a number of discriminatory practices, including giving posthumous names to deceased parishioners identifying them as members of outcast families (*buraku* 部落 or *burakumin* 部落民). Sōtō temples had further allowed access to temple necrologies to private investigators hired by families checking the background of a potential marriage partner and by companies seeking to ensure that executives were not descendants of former outcasts. In response to the uproar, the Sōtō school established a Human Rights Division that sought to eliminate such practices, not least by organizing the eradication of discriminatory names in necrologies stored in temple archives and the replacement of gravestones on which such names had been engraved. Today the monks at Eiheiji and Sōjiji perform an annual ritual to atone for the Sōtō school's previous human rights violations. See Bodiford 1996 for a study of this incident and its consequences.

99. *Dōgen zenji nanahyakugojukkai daionki hōsan: Shinpen Hōon kōshiki.* See also Mross 2015 for a detailed study of Imamura's *kōshiki.*

100. Yokoi wrote that Myōe's *Shiza kōshiki* and *Jūichimen kannon kōshiki* were performed at Sōtō temples (Yokoi 1967, 60). Further, the head priest of Yōshōji 養昌寺 (Tokyo) asserts in a

Table 1.2. Historical outline of *kōshiki* in the Sōtō school

Date	*Title*	*Author*	*Editor*
ca. 1249	*Rakan kōshiki*	Dōgen?	
14th c.	*Hokke kōshiki*	Giun	
1501	*Nehan kōshiki*	Genshin?	
First half 17th c.	*Daruma kōshiki*	Kakua / Myōe?	Bannan Eiju
Before 1694	*Butsuji kōshiki*	?	
First half 18th c.	*Busshōe kōshiki*	Myōe	
1707	*Dōgen zenji kōshiki*	Zuihō Daiki	
1707	*Eihei Dōgen zenji kōshiki*	Zenzui Shōzen	
1753	*Eihei kaisan Hōon kōshiki*	Menzan Zuihō	
1769	*Daihannya kōshiki*	Menzan Zuihō	
1780	*Myōken kōshiki*	Daini Sōryū ?	
18th c. ?	*Gasan kōshiki*	?	
1809	*Kannon kōshiki*	Jōkei	Mugaku Guzen
1829	*Anan kōshiki*	Myōe ?	Jakushū Kankō / Kōsen Mujaku
1865?	*Kasekison nōke kōshiki*		
Tokugawa period?	*Yakushi kōshiki*	?	
1882	*Jizō kōshiki*	Jōkei	
1893	*Tōjō dentō kōshiki*	Bukkan Bonjō	
2001?	*Hakusan kōshiki*	Inoue Gishin	
2003	*Yōjō daishi kōshiki*	Inoue Gishin	

from buddhas and bodhisattvas to disciples of the Buddha, eminent Zen monks, and even *kami* and individual sutras (table 1.3).

Some of the twenty *kōshiki* listed in the tables are no longer performed, for manifold reasons. Earlier *kōshiki* honoring Dōgen and Keizan were replaced by new rituals: the *Tōjō dentō kōshiki* replaced the *Butsuji kōshiki,* and

postscript he wrote for a *Jizō kōshiki* handbook produced in 1982 that a *Shari kōshiki* was also performed at Sōtō temples. However, I could not find any historical source that confirms the performance of these three *kōshiki* at Sōtō temples. A woodblock print edition of the *Benzaiten kōshiki* from Bunsei 10 (1827) has been found at the Sōtō temple Dairyūji, but because it does not use the standard ritual form or musical notation of the Sōtō school, it was most likely bought or presented to the temple.

Table 1.3. Sōtō *kōshiki* categorized according to objects of veneration

Object(s) of veneration	Kōshiki
Buddhas	*Busshōe kōshiki*
	Nehan kōshiki
	Yakushi kōshiki
Bodhisattvas	*Kannon kōshiki*
	Jizō kōshiki
	Myōken kōshiki
Disciples of the Buddha	*Rakan kōshiki*
	Anan kōshiki
Eminent monks	*Daruma kōshiki*
	Dōgen zenji kōshiki
	Eihei Dōgen zenji kōshiki
	Eihei kaisan Hōon kōshiki
	Yōjō daishi kōshiki
	Butsuji kōshiki
	Tōjō dentō kōshiki
	Gasan kōshiki
Kami	*Hakusan kōshiki*
	Kasekison nōke kōshiki
Sutras	*Hokke kōshiki*
	Daihannya kōshiki

Menzan's *kōshiki* for Dōgen replaced the earlier *kōshiki* for Dōgen (*Hokke kōshiki, Dōgen zenji kōshiki,* and *Eihei Dōgen zenji kōshiki*). The *kōshiki* performed for Gasan ceased to be performed because monks at Sōjiji in the Meiji era merged the memorial services for Keizan and Gasan into one service and began performing a *kōshiki* only for their first abbot, who had been officially declared one of the two great patriarchs of Sōtō Zen. In the cases of the *Busshōe kōshiki, Myōken kōshiki, Kasekison nōke kōshiki,* and *Yakushi kōshiki,* we do not know why Sōtō monks stopped performing them, but we can speculate, for the latter three works, that it was due to changes not only in the ritual calendar of Sōtō temples but in their relationship to parishioners in the Meiji era. Today the birthday of the Buddha is still celebrated at Sōtō temples, but the *Busshōe kōshiki,* which requires great expertise in ritual performance and *shōmyō,* has been replaced with a simpler ritual.

Kōshiki Practice in Contemporary Sōtō Zen

Traditional rituals are sometimes described as stagnant or meaningless remnants of earlier times, but throughout my research in Japan, I witnessed *kōshiki* as a living tradition. By no means are *kōshiki* just a relic—some priests still revise *kōshiki* creatively or adopt elements of *kōshiki* for new rituals. Members of the young monks' associations gather to practice *kōshiki* and *shōmyō,* and *shōmyō* specialists of the Sōtō school teach in study clubs of different local areas. In contrast to the Shingon and Tendai schools especially, the Sōtō school has a rather limited repertoire of *shōmyō* pieces. But when one surveys the performance of *kōshiki* in contemporary Japan, one finds that most of the performances are in the Sōtō school. At least eleven *kōshiki* are still performed in Sōtō temples (table 1.4), showing that *kōshiki* are a vibrant part of ritual practice in contemporary Sōtō Zen.

Yet this list is deceptive, for no Sōtō cleric performs all these rituals. Depending on the temple and its area, a cleric might perform one or two, or at most five different *kōshiki.* Most of the *kōshiki* performances take place at the head temples or training temples as part of their annual observances (fig. 1.6). Monks at Eiheiji, for example, annually perform the *Daihannya kōshiki* (1 / 2), *Eihei kaisan Hōon kōshiki* (1 / 26), *Nehan kōshiki* (2 / 15), *Rakan kōshiki* (6 / 15), and *Daruma kōshiki* (10 / 5),[101] whereas monks at Sōjiji perform the

Table 1.4. *Kōshiki* performed in contemporary Sōtō Zen

Object(s) of veneration	Kōshiki
Buddha(s)	*Nehan kōshiki*
Bodhisattvas	*Kannon kōshiki*
	Jizō kōshiki
Disciples of the Buddha	*Rakan kōshiki*
	Anan kōshiki
Eminent monks	*Daruma kōshiki*
	Eihei kaisan Hōon kōshiki
	Yōjō daishi kōshiki
	Tōjō dentō kōshiki
Kami	*Hakusan kōshiki*
Sutras	*Daihannya kōshiki*

101. *Sozan gyōhō shinan.* This ritual manual also lists the three rituals *Tanbutsu kōshiki* (1 / 3), *Kannon senbō* (3 / 24), and *Daifusatsu kōshiki* (7 / 2) as *kōshiki,* but because they do not contain a *shikimon,* I have not counted them as *kōshiki* for the purposes of this book. Audio recordings of *kōshiki* performances at Eiheiji are included in LP sets documenting the music of Sōtō Zen: the

Figure 1.6. *Rakan kōshiki*, performed at Eiheiji on June 15, 2015. Photo by the author.

Rakan kōshiki (11 / 16) and *Tōjō dentō kōshiki* (10 / 14) every year.[102] At these temples, novice monks start practicing the challenging chants a month before each ceremony. Through the practice and performance of these rituals, they acquire the skills to chant in a certain way and to perform ritual functions in a Sōtō style.

Sōtō nuns continue to perform *kōshiki* as well, even though the *kōshiki* are not included in the annual observances of the Aichi Senmon Nisōdō 愛知専門尼僧堂 in Nagoya, the only operating Sōtō nunnery today. The nuns have regular classes in *shōmyō*, and they perform *kōshiki* on special occasions. The classes are currently taught by Maekawa Bokushō, an acclaimed ritual specialist who teaches full-time at Sōjiji. In personal conversations with me, he commented on the nuns' high motivation and how well they progress in their *shōmyō* skills between his classes.

The most important *kōshiki* for the Sōtō nuns is the *Anan kōshiki*. Only performed by nuns, it celebrates the existence of their order and reaffirms their identity. Therefore, they perform it at special occasions such as the one hundredth anniversary of the founding of the Nagoya nunnery in 2003. This performance was captured on video, and a commentary on the *kōshiki* was provided by the abbess Aoyama Shundō 青山俊董.[103] The nuns also perform

Hōon kōshiki is in *Sōtō-Zen: Kōshiki, Tanbutsu, Fusatsu;* the *Rakan kōshiki* is in *Sōtō-Zen: Tange, Kitō, Kuyō;* and the *Daifusatsu shiki* is in *Zen*, vol. 6 of *Shōmyō Taikei.*

102. Sōjiji monks also perform the *Daifusatsu shiki* (5 / 16) and *Tanbutsue* (several times a year). An audio recording of the *Daifusatsu shiki* at Sōjiji is in *Sōtō-Zen: Kōshiki, Tanbutsu, Fusatsu,* and a recording of the *Rakan kōshiki* at Sōjiji is in *Zen,* vol. 6 of *Shōmyō Taikei.*

103. *Anan kōshiki: Aichi Senmon Nisodō sōritsu hyakushūnen kinen;* Aoyama 2003.

the *Rakan kōshiki* and *Jizō kōshiki* on occasion. In March 2018, for example, they performed the *Jizō kōshiki* at the graduation ceremony for nuns who had finished their monastic training. The Sōtō nuns' association had also performed this *kōshiki* at the inauguration ceremony for Sōjiji's Sanshōkaku 三松閣, a building intended to serve as a training center for lay devotees, in 1990. Remarkably, Sōjiji published an audio recording of it as part of the celebration of its relocation to Tsurumi eighty years earlier.[104]

Some *kōshiki* have been performed to celebrate rites of passage. In an interview, Inoue Gishin mentioned that the *Rakan kōshiki* used to be performed at a *shinsanshiki* 晋山式, the occasion when a monk becomes the head priest of a temple, as had happened when he became head priest of his temple. Notably, the *Hakusan kōshiki* he subsequently composed was similarly performed for one of his priest friends. On such occasions, it is the distinctive musical nature of *kōshiki,* so different from regular sutra chanting, that serves to underscore the significance of the rite of passage.

In contemporary Sōtō Zen, *kōshiki* are rarely performed at the request of lay devotees—indeed, laypeople are seldom present when these rituals take place at training temples or the head temples. But in certain areas of Akita prefecture, the *Kannon kōshiki* has been performed during elaborate funeral services for lay devotees.[105] At such a time, the *kōshiki* fulfills the same ritual function as the *Kannon senbō* that is performed at funerals in Niigata prefecture.[106] On the whole, however, *kōshiki* are seldom performed at local temples, primarily because ten or more priests are usually needed and the vocalization of the liturgical texts is challenging for priests who are not used to performing them frequently.[107]

Occasionally, *kōshiki* are performed outside regular temple observances. Terakura Shōyū 寺倉昭雄, for example, who taught *shōmyō* at Sōjiji and is head priest of Sōgenji 曹源寺 in Niigata prefecture, once sang the *Rakan kōshiki* by himself during a tea ceremony. For that occasion, he shortened its length to around thirty minutes. In an interview (October 2015), he also mentioned that he sometimes reads the offertory declaration of the *Nehan kōshiki* during the Buddha's memorial service at his temple, because he feels that it offers a beautiful and instructive account of the Buddha's passing. This has proved especially effective when the lay devotees hear the text while gazing at a pictorial representation of the event.

---

104. *Goitō hachijūnen kinen;* Sōtōzen: Kōshiki no sekai. See Umeda 1990 for a report on this dedication. A video recording of the nuns' performance of a *Jizō kōshiki* at the Aichi Senmon Nisōdō can be found in *Sōtōzen mezame.*

105. Information from the Akita Young Monks Association (October 2010). The *Kannon kōshiki* is also performed as a regular observance at certain temples in Akita prefecture (Watarai 1986, 20).

106. Conversations with monks of Niigata, October 2010.

107. Some Sōtō priests lament that *kōshiki* are rarely performed in local temples; see, for example, Inoue 2000, 31v–32r; Suzuki B. 2010, 13–14; Inoue 2002, 59v; and Kojima in Inoue 2000, foreword.

Finally, some priests do perform concerts on stage or collaborate with musicians representing other musical genres. For these collaborations, Sōtō priests often select liturgical pieces from *kōshiki*—or other ceremonies that feature *shōmyō*—and then integrate these chants into a new performance. These creative projects suggest that at least some Sōtō priests regard the vocalizations of *kōshiki* as an important legacy that can serve to introduce their own religious culture to a wider audience.

From Manuscript to Print

The transmission of *kōshiki* down through the centuries was only possible because the ritual texts were transmitted in written form. Indeed, since *kōshiki* are essentially embedded in manuscript and print culture, one could say that the transmission of *kōshiki* depended on the production of ritual manuals. Originally, *kōshiki* were always handwritten and copied from previous manuscripts by hand. The manuscript medium made local differences and parallel text versions possible, as every new copy offered the possibility of changing the text—a reminder of the fluid nature of ritual texts.[108] One example is the *Nehan kōshiki,* for which there were a number of transmission lineages in the Tokugawa period.[109]

Woodblock prints of *kōshiki* texts began to be produced in the Tokugawa period, around the time of the reform movement when Sōtō monks strove to establish an official orthodoxy and orthopraxy. The change from manuscript to print inevitably led to a standardization of *kōshiki* and a process of canon formation.[110] After their original publication, ritual handbooks were often reprinted or sometimes used as models for new woodblock print editions.

One important change during this period was that many print editions provided all clerics in the assembly access to the offertory declaration and *shikimon* of a *kōshiki.* Previously, the assembly used ritual handbooks that only contained the choral pieces, while the clerics who vocalized liturgical texts solo additionally used manuscripts of these texts. Consequently, only the clerics who vocalized the offertory declaration and *shikimon* could read them. Most print editions, in contrast, include all the texts of the ritual, and so all clerics could now read along with the offertory declaration and *shikimon.* Many editions also contain detailed instructions for how to perform the ritual (fig. 1.7).

But even after the introduction of print editions, some temples contin-

108. Scholars of the new philology movement have discussed the development of parallel versions of texts in European medieval manuscript culture and suggested the concept of a "fluid text"; see Bumke 2010; Cerquiglini 1999; and Nichols 1990 and 1997.

109. For a detailed comparison of the various manuscripts and prints, see Ozaki 1997, 1998a, and 1998b.

110. On the introduction of the print medium to Japan, see Kornicki 1998; see also Chibbett 1977 and Berry 2006 on the history of the printed book in Japan.

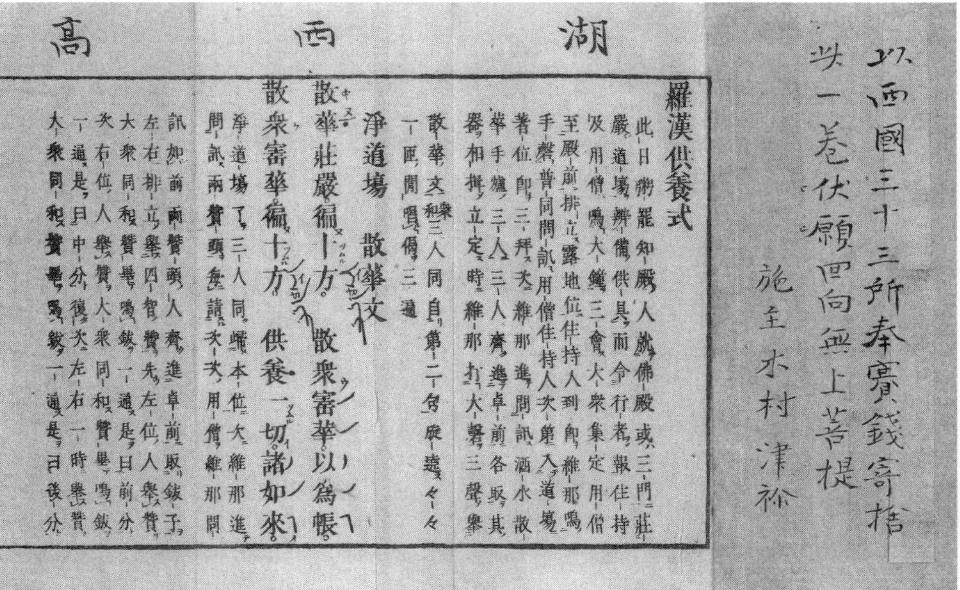
湖西高

羅漢供養式
此日粥罷知殿人就佛殿或三門莊
嚴道場辨備供具而令行者報住持
及用僧鳴大鐘三會大衆集定用僧
至殿前排立露地位住持人到即維那鳴
手磬普同問訊用僧住持人次第入道場
著位即三拜次維那進問訊灑水散
華手爐三人三人齋進卓前各取其
器相揖立定時維那打大磬三聲舉
散華文衆和三人同自第二句旋遶々々
一匝問唱偈三遍
淨道場　散華文
散華莊嚴徧十方　散衆寶華以為帳
散衆寶華徧十方　供養一切諸如來
淨道場了三人同歸本位次維那進
問訊兩贊頭無請次次用僧維那問
訊如前兩贊頭人齋進卓前取鈸子
左右排立舉四智贊先左位人舉贊
大衆同和贊畢鳴鈸一通是曰前分
次右位人舉贊大衆同和贊畢鳴鈸
一通是曰中分復次左右一時舉贊
大衆同和贊畢鳴鈸一通是曰後分

以西國三十三所奉賽銭寄捨
此一巻伏願回向無上菩提
施主　木村津裕

Figure 1.7. *Rakan kuyō shiki*. Late Tokugawa period. This detail shows the first piece, the *Gāthā to Scattering Flowers*, sung to purify the ritual space. The liturgical pieces in this handbook are printed in large script, and the text in smaller script provides instructions for the performers. Collection of the author.

ued to use manuscripts, especially if a particular *kōshiki* was not widely performed or if the temple's version differed from that in the print edition. At Sōjiji, for example, the monks continued to use manuscripts until the middle of the Meiji era, enabling the temple to preserve its own ritual tradition. Remarkably, the monks at Sōjiji produced beautiful and precious manuscripts, written on fine paper, with gold and silver decorations on the covers and gold-inflected paper glued to the inner front cover.[111] The ritual handbooks used at Sōjiji were thus a cut above any woodblock print edition, and their quality reflected the high status of the temple (figs. 1.8 and 1.9).

Even when clerics used printed manuals, they sometimes emended the texts by adding lines with brush and ink or gluing small pieces of paper with a different text over the original. We can also see these practices in manuscripts. Today monks sometimes make changes to print editions by writing the additions on sticky notes and attaching them to the text. Needless to say, this results in a truly fluid text, because once the sticky notes are removed, no traces are left.

111. Manuscripts copied at Sōjiji in Genroku 7 (1694): *Butsuji kō kada narabini Shichisan, Rakan kō kada narabini Shichisan, Nehan kō kada narabini Shichisan, Hōyō*, and *Kada narabini hōyō*. Manuscripts copied in Bunka 10 (1813): *San kōshiki narabini hōyō*.

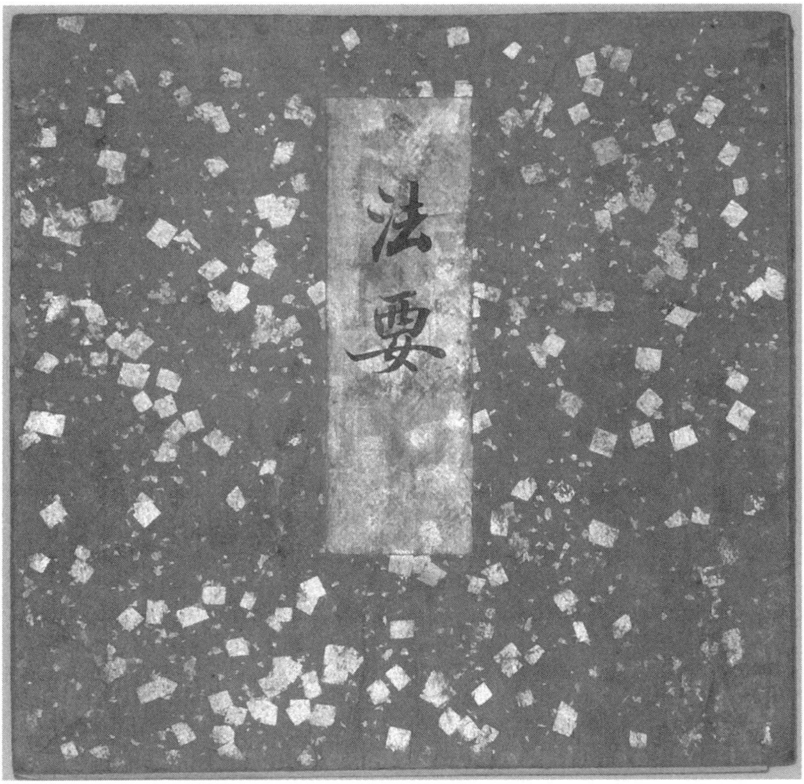

Figure 1.8. Cover of the ritual manuscript *Hōyō* (1694). Archive of Sōjiji Soin. Photo by the author.

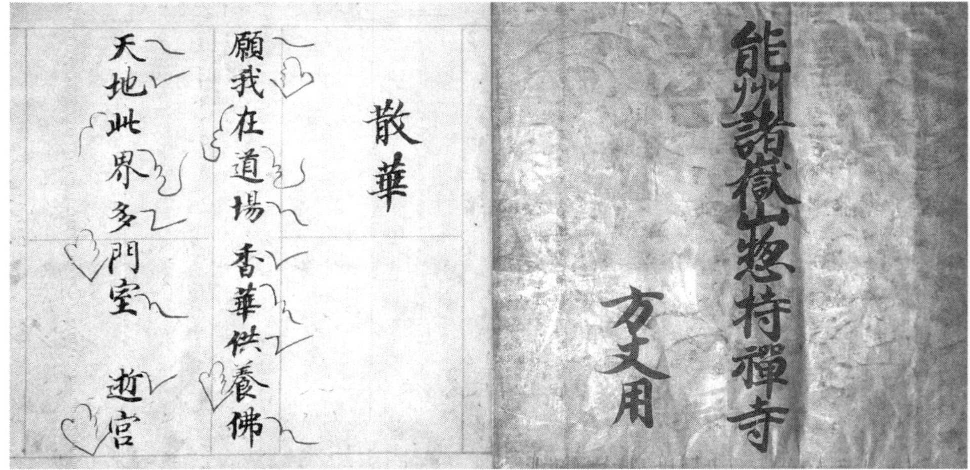

Figure 1.9. *Hōyō* (1694). Beginning of the *Gāthā of Falling Flowers*. Archive of Sōjiji Soin. Photo by the author.

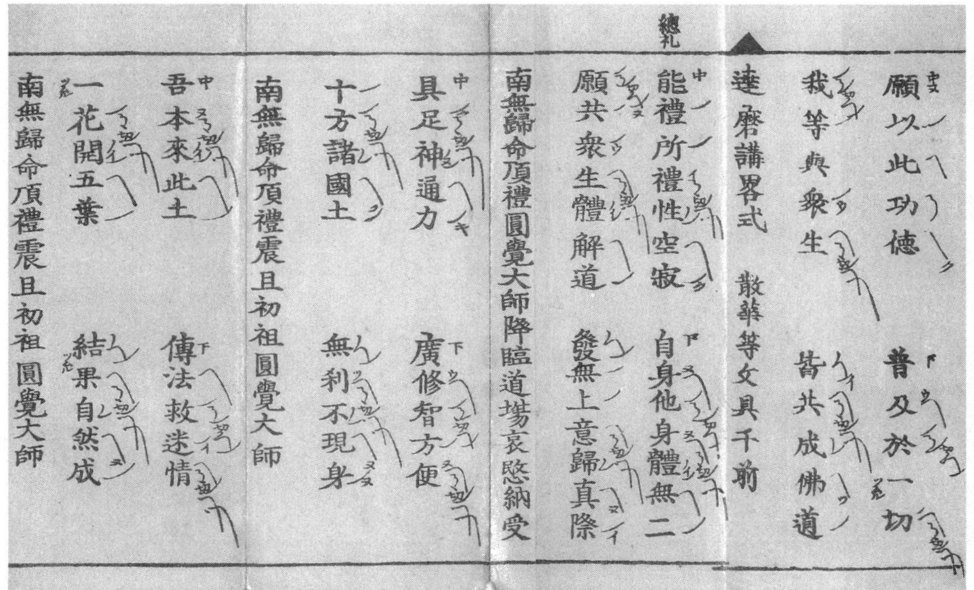
願以此功徳 普及於一切
我等與衆生 皆共成佛道
達磨講畧式 散華等文具于前
能禮所禮性空寂 自身他身體無二
願共衆生體解道 發無上意歸真際
南無歸命頂禮圓覺大師降臨道場哀愍納受
具足神通力 廣修智方便
十方諸國土 無刹不現身
南無歸命頂禮震旦初祖圓覺大師
吾本來此土 傳法救迷情
一花開五葉 結果自然成
南無歸命頂禮震旦初祖圓覺大師

Figure 1.10. *Ryaku kōshiki* (*Daijō shōin*). Late Tokugawa period. The text on the right, the *Universal Transfer of Merit,* is the last verse of the *Rakan kōshiki.* Following it are the choral pieces of the *Daruma kōshiki,* starting with the general obeisance and the verses of the first two sections of the *shikimon.* Collection of the author.

The standardization of *kōshiki* alluded to earlier was especially fueled by the production of multivolume print editions. The first editions of this type were the *Five Kōshiki of the Sōtō School* (*Tōjō go kōshiki*),[112] and the *Six Kōshiki of the Sōtō School* (*Sōtō roku kōshiki*),[113] both published in the middle of the eighteenth century. The volumes of these two editions contain all the texts vocalized during the rituals, as well as instructions for the performance. Also, sometime in or before Hōreki 12 (1762), monks at Daijōji, a major temple in Kanazawa said to have been very influential in the development of Sōtō *shōmyō,* edited a ritual handbook containing the choral pieces for the *Rakan kōshiki, Daruma kōshiki,* and *Nehan kōshiki* (fig. 1.10).[114]

112. This collection consists of the *Rakan kōshiki, Daifusatsu shiki, Tanbutsue shiki, Nehan kōshiki,* and *Daruma kōshiki.*

113. It includes the *Rakan kōshiki, Hōon kōshiki, Daifusatsu kōshiki, Tōjō shōrai hō, Tanbutsue shiki,* and *Kanromon.*

114. *Ryaku kōshiki* (*Daijō shōin*). In addition to the three *kōshiki,* it contains the choral pieces for the *Daifusatsu shiki.* For a typographical reprint, see Watarai 1983. Unfortunately, it is not known who edited this ritual handbook or why. However, an entry in one woodblock print of this edition states that it was used by Unryū 雲龍 of Gakudenji 覺傳寺 in Hōreki 12 (1762), so it must have been printed in that year or earlier (collection of the author). Texts for these four rituals are also included in the manuscript *Shi kōshiki* (*Four Kōshiki*) written by Kankai of Hōenji in Kanazawa in Jōkyō 3 (1686); see Ozaki 2014a, 130–132.

In 1966, a new five-volume edition of elaborate Sōtō rituals was published, titled *Shōwa kaitei Shōmyō kihan* (Regulations for *shōmyō,* revised in the Shōwa era), or *Shōmyō kihan* for short, another milestone in the standardization of *kōshiki.*[115] Today the *Shōmyō kihan* is the standard ritual manual for *shōmyō* in the Sōtō school—one *shōmyō* specialist I talked with called it the "bible of Sōtō *shōmyō.*"[116] In this edition, some of the standardized chants were abbreviated to reduce the length of the ritual, and the *shōmyō* notation was simplified.[117] Changes like these have carried over to new editions of other *kōshiki* and have had a long-lasting influence on the performance practice of Sōtō *shōmyō* and *kōshiki.* A monk who had been in training at Sōjiji when the *Shōmyō kihan* was published told me in an interview that the influential *shōmyō* specialist Maekawa Hakuhō 前川博邦 (1918–2006), who taught *shōmyō* at Sōjiji at that time, introduced both the old and new styles to the novices during the transition period but instructed them mainly in the new style. In other words, the clerics were fully aware of the changes their performance practice was undergoing at the time.

Conclusions

This chapter has traced the development of *kōshiki* since the tenth century and revealed the great diversity within this ritual genre. Although *kōshiki* originated as an expression of Pure Land devotion in the Tendai tradition, it quickly spread throughout the different schools of Japanese Buddhism, and most works in the genre venerate objects of worship other than Amida. Indeed, Sōtō monks did not perform a *kōshiki* for him.

Sōtō clerics have composed, edited, and performed more than twenty different *kōshiki* since Dōgen's lifetime. Some of these were widely performed, such as the *Rakan kōshiki,* but others were performed only at certain temples, because they addressed an object of worship specific to a temple, lineage, or group. Thus liturgies were highly localized. Although the composition of *kōshiki* generally declined after the thirteenth century, Sōtō monks displayed a continuous vitality and creativity in creating new *kōshiki* and adapting older texts. Long after *kōshiki* ceased to be written in other schools, Sōtō monks such as Bukkan Bonjō and Inoue Gishin composed new works in this genre.

The ritual tradition of Sōtō *kōshiki* has been remarkably eclectic. Sōtō clerics adopted several *kōshiki* written by monks of other schools, such as Jōkei's *Kannon kōshiki* and Myōe's *Busshōe kōshiki.* Moreover, the genre itself belongs to a ritual vocabulary that is widely shared in Japanese Buddhism. This shows how Sōtō clerics developed their own ritual tradition within the

115. It consists of separate ritual handbooks for the *Rakan kōshiki,* the *Tanbutsue hosshiki* (Ceremony of praising the buddhas), the *Daifusatsu bosatsu shiki,* and the *Kannon senbō,* together with a volume explaining how to sing the various *shōmyō* pieces and a transcription into Western musical notation.

116. Personal conversation during fieldwork at Tōkōji, November 2010.

117. For a detailed analysis of how the pieces were shortened, see Mross 2007, 70–74.

Japanese religious landscape. By performing *kōshiki,* Sōtō clerics not only express devotion to an object of worship but also connect to clerics of previous generations who performed the same rituals. The performance of the *Rakan kōshiki,* for example, connects the monks to Dōgen, who is said to have composed it. As a senior monk at Sōjiji once said to me, the reason to perform Dōgen's *kōshiki* is to continue the ritual tradition established by the school founder. Thus the performance of *kōshiki* reaffirms the school identity of the clerics. Another example of a *kōshiki* that expresses group identity is the *Anan kōshiki;* performed only by nuns, it celebrates the existence of their order.

Some Sōtō clerics view *kōshiki* as an important cultural asset of their school. This chapter's epigraph eloquently expresses the feelings of Inoue Gishin on this matter.[118] Therefore, Sōtō clerics have been given to composing, editing, and reprinting *kōshiki* at special times, such as the grand death anniversaries of eminent monks commemorated at fifty-year intervals. Special occasions have also been moments when clerics perform *kōshiki,* because what is called for at these times are the most festive and musical rituals the Sōtō school has to offer.

While *kōshiki* has often been described as a genre directed toward lay devotees, many performances in the Sōtō school seem to have been private monastic rituals or to have taken place during important observances of the liturgical year, such as the Buddha's memorial service. Very few sources attest to the involvement of laypeople in Sōtō *kōshiki.* Two rare examples are the *Busshōe kōshiki* and the *Kannon kōshiki,* which were performed as part of death rituals. Another *kōshiki* that probably involved lay devotees was the *Kasekison nōke kōshiki.* Because it was written in Japanese with readings for all Chinese characters, we can assume that lay devotees may have vocalized some of the liturgical texts of the ritual. Some other *kōshiki* that might have been performed for lay devotees are the *Daihannya kōshiki, Myōken kōshiki, Yakushi kōshiki,* and *Jizō kōshiki,* all of which describe the worldly benefits that their respective objects of worship provide. Unfortunately, current sources do not throw any light on the participation of lay devotees in these rituals. Hopefully, new manuscripts will be discovered that will enable us to fill in our understanding of the social side of Sōtō *kōshiki.*

---

118. Inoue 2002, 60r.

2
Ritual Structure of Sōtō Kōshiki

THE PREVIOUS CHAPTER traced the evolution of *kōshiki* by highlighting the invention of new rituals involving the composition or adoption of a *shikimon*, the central text of the ceremony. This chapter examines the structure of *kōshiki* in detail, together with the performance practice that distinguishes the Sōtō school, in order to reveal the dynamics underlying the process of ritual innovation and change.

Like other rituals, most *kōshiki* consist of well-established elements and sequences, with scope for invention limited to only a few components.[1] "New ritual items, even new ritual configurations," noted Victor Turner, "tend more often to be variants of old themes than radical novelties."[2] Authors or editors of rituals borrow elements from preceding rituals that may belong to the same tradition or to others. Burkhard Gladigow refers to this phenomenon as *interrituality*, an extension of the concept of intertextuality that designates the interrelations between the textual and performative dimensions of rituals.[3] The use of previously established elements connects new rituals to an existing ritual tradition. In her study of a new godparent ritual performed in one of the Mi'kmaq First Nations, Anne-Christine Hornborg suggests that "by practicing interrituality—borrowing minor ritual acts or elements including ritual objects from other rituals—it is possible to simultaneously both invent rituals and refer to them as 'tradition.' "[4]

These tendencies are also at play in the invention and performance of Sōtō *kōshiki*. A *kōshiki* author composes a *shikimon* and maybe an offertory declaration, or a cleric selects a *shikimon* written by a monk in another Bud-

---

1. See Rappaport 1999, 32; and Bell 1997, 223–242, on ritual invention.

2. Turner 1973, 1100.

3. Gladigow 2004, 61. See also Stausberg 2014, 238. Similarly, Klaus-Peter Köpping (2004), in his study of Japanese village rituals, Shintō ceremonies, and *nō* theater, describes the borrowing between rituals and theater as *interperformativity*.

It is important to note that there is another definition of interrituality: recently, ritual studies scholars have used the term to describe rituals that are created in the sphere of interreligious dialogue in order to highlight the spaces between different traditions; see, for example, Kreinath 2016 and 2017, Grimes 2017, and Moyaert 2019. In this book, however, I use the term interrituality as an expansion of the concept of intertextuality, acknowledging relations not only between texts but also among the other components or dimensions (acoustic, kinetic, and material) of rituals.

4. Hornborg 2017, 17.

dhist school. In either case, the composer or editor inserts the *shikimon* and offertory declaration into a structure typical for *kōshiki* of his school. I call this structure a ritual frame and demonstrate below that a ritual frame is built from previously established elements that are assembled in accordance with the customs of a particular ritual tradition. Thus while the *kōshiki* genre itself, along with many of the liturgical pieces vocalized during the ritual, belongs to a ritual language shared throughout Japanese Buddhism, the structure and performance practice of a particular ritual signify school or lineage identity.

In this chapter, I analyze the *Rakan kōshiki,* an offertory ritual for the Sixteen Arhats. By examining its structure, including its textual, acoustic, kinetic, and material elements, I demonstrate that the principle of modularity is foundational in *kōshiki* composition and performance. Moreover, the *Rakan kōshiki* is often considered a representative work in that it served as a model for other Sōtō *kōshiki.* But versions of it were also performed in the Rinzai and Shingon schools, and a comparison of their respective ritual frames shows how school identity was vested in, and expressed through, those different frames.

Modules and Frames: Theoretical Considerations

While scholars have proposed a number of models for analyzing the structure of rituals, including ritual grammar and syntax,[5] I prefer the concepts of modules and frames as a more productive way to examine how elements are combined to form the ritual structure of a *kōshiki.* Modules are the individual building blocks of rituals.[6] In his book *Ten Thousand Things: Module and Mass Production in Chinese Art,* Lothar Ledderose argues that the use of modules was vital to the creation and production of ancient bronzes, terracotta figures, porcelain, architecture, and printing. The use of modules, he writes, made it possible to create a large range of variations from a limited repertoire of components.[7] In rituals, modularity is similarly important, making it easy for ritual specialists to learn and perform a variety of rituals

5. Fritz Staal (1979a, 1979b, and 1989) was especially influential in arguing that rituals follow syntactic rules; see also Gane 2014; Payne 1999, 2004, and 2012; Meshel 2014; and Seaquist 2004. Ritual studies scholars, however, have debated whether the idea of ritual grammar is actually useful for a study of rituals; see, for example, Michaels 2016, chap. 2.

6. This term has also been used by other scholars working on rituals. Charles Orzech (1998) describes small units in esoteric Buddhist rituals as modules, and the stringing together of ritual elements as boilerplate, arguing that esoteric rituals consist of a basic template that can be elaborated or abbreviated as needed. Likewise, Daniel Stevenson (2015) calls ritual sequences modules in a recent article on Buddhist rituals in Song China, suggesting that modular assemblages of litany and gesture could be transposed freely from one ritual to another. And Don Handelman (2005) shows that the secular ritual that opens the Holocaust Martyrs and Heroes Remembrance Day in Israel is characterized by a modularity of sequences or performance modules, which together constitute the whole event.

7. Ledderose 1998, 1.

while also providing a foundation for the composition of new rituals in which existing modules are assembled together with new or innovative elements. Michael Oppitz further likens these basic building blocks to prefabricated elements that are mobile and transferrable to other or new rituals by following a construction plan:

> The prefabricated structural elements or units from which rituals are made are the building blocks with which they are composed. They come simultaneously from a number of levels: a material level in the form of certain objects required to conduct the ritual at a set time and at a designated place; a linguistic level of ready formulated utterances such as prayers, magical formulae or recited myths; an acoustic level in a broader sense, with musical and other sonic means of expression; and a kinetic level with special actions, movements and gestures.[8]

All these dimensions come into play in the construction of a *kōshiki,* and I will consider each, together with their interaction, in the structure of the *Rakan kōshiki.*

The concept of ritual frames is another idea central to this study. The concept of framing originated with Gregory Bateson, who wrote: "The first step in defining a psychological frame might be to say that it is (or delimits) a class or set of messages (or meaningful actions)." Bateson then used the analogy of a picture frame to describe what he meant:

> The frame around a picture, if we consider this frame as a message intended to order or organize the perception of the viewer, says, "Attend to what is within and do not attend to what is outside." Figure and ground, as these terms are used by gestalt psychologists, are not symmetrically related as are the set and nonset of set theory. Perception of the ground must be positively inhibited and perception of the figure (in this case the picture) must be positively enhanced.... The picture frame tells the viewer that he is not to use the same sort of thinking in interpreting the picture that he might use in interpreting the wallpaper outside the frame.[9]

For Bateson, frames are psychological concepts for structuring subjective reality. In his monograph *Frame Analysis,* Erving Goffman (1974) developed Bateson's concept further and made it applicable to the analysis of more complex social interactions. In these and other psychological or sociological approaches to the concept, frames are understood to be an abstract form of meta-communication or meta-cognition that influences the experience, emo-

---

8. Oppitz 1999, 73; translation by Michaels 2010, 11. Likewise, Burkhard Gladigow argues that "a special problem of a 'unity' of a complex ritual... lies in the different ways of integrating diverse levels in the sequence of ritual events: the patterns of movement (the motor level), the staging of visual elements (the optical level), the cultic sounds and music (the acoustic level), and the use of language or tituli (the declamatory level)" (2008, 484).

9. Bateson 1987, 192–193.

tions, interpretations, and actions of a subject. In contrast, I use the term "ritual frame" primarily in a structural sense.[10]

In a structural analysis of *kōshiki,* the metaphor of a picture frame is useful in that certain modules can be said to frame a *shikimon.* But in Sōtō *kōshiki,* the ritual frame is large and elaborate—and it is not symmetrical.[11] It bears a psychological dimension, too, because it informs ritual specialists what kind of ritual they are going to perform—or, to use Bateson's expression, it tells the participants that they are not to use the same sort of thinking during the ritual that they might use in interpreting activities and events outside the ritual setting.

Moreover, frames may interlock, and small frames may enclose larger ones. Don Handelman discusses the differences between outward-facing framing (how the frame of a ritual relates to the world around it) and inward-facing framing (frames within a ritual), asking, "How it is that the ritual moves through them, frame after frame, frame within frame, frame entangled with frame?"[12] In my analysis of the ritual structure of the *Rakan kōshiki,* I show how the ritual progresses through multiple framed sequences while at the same time creating a larger ritual frame into which the *shikimon* is set.

A Brief History of the Arhat Cult

As the oldest *kōshiki* in the Sōtō school, the *Rakan kōshiki* has often served as a model for other *kōshiki.*[13] Before delving into its structure and performance, it is helpful to understand its origin in the long-standing veneration of the arhats.[14]

The term *arhat* has multiple definitions. In Mahāyāna Buddhism, arhats are often polemically depicted as the human ideal projected in the so-called Hīnayāna Buddhism (the "Lesser Vehicle"). They are further described as practitioners interested only in their own salvation, in contrast to the bodhisattvas who strive to reach enlightenment for the sake of all beings. However, Mahāyāna Buddhists also venerated the arhats, describing them as embodying the very same qualities as a bodhisattva. Of these, the Sixteen Arhats and

---

10. For a discussion of frames and framing in ritual studies, see Jungaberle and Weinhold 2006 and Stewart and Strathern 2012, a special issue of the *Journal of Ritual Studies* on ritual framing.

11. Don Handelman (2004) criticized Bateson's concept as linear, suggesting the concept of a moebius frame instead. However, Jan Snoek (2006) and Jens Kreinath (2012) have demonstrated that Bateson's concept was not intended to be static or linear. Here it is important to note that I, too, do not regard a ritual frame as static, but as dynamic in the same way that a picture frame can be painted or decorated or even exchanged for another frame around the same picture.

12. Handelman 2012, 74.

13. See chap. 1, n. 50, on studies of the *Rakan kōshiki.*

14. For studies of the arhat cult in China, see Lévi and Chavannes 1916 and Joo 2007 and 2009; for the arhat cult in China and Japan, see Visser 1923 and Michihata 1983; and for the arhat cult in Japan, see Faure 1991, 266–272, and 1996, 88–96; and Ishida 2006. Several art historians have also studied paintings of the arhats in detail; see Fong 1958; Little 1992; and Kent 1995.

Five Hundred Arhats were especially venerated. The locus classicus for the veneration of the Sixteen Arhats is the *Record of the Perpetuity of the Dharma, Narrated by the Great Arhat Nandimitrā* (*Daaluohan nantimiduoluo suoshuo fazhuji*), translated by Xuanzang 玄奘 (600–664). This text, the earliest to name all of the Sixteen Arhats, recounts that Śākyamuni ordered sixteen of his direct disciples not to enter nirvāṇa after his passing but instead to remain in this world to protect his teachings and followers.[15] Beginning a century after Xuanzang's translation, the Sixteen Arhats became a subject for paintings, and arhat veneration slowly grew in popularity.[16] Certain sites became famous, such as the stone bridge on Mt. Tiantai, where the Five Hundred Arhats were thought to live.[17] Among the many pilgrims who made their way to this bridge were a few Japanese monks, notably the Tendai monk Jōjin 成尋 (1011–1081), Chōgen 重源 (1121–1206), who later raised funds for the rebuilding of Tōdaiji, and the Rinzai monk Yōsai.[18]

When returning from China, many Japanese monks brought back paintings of the arhats. The Tōdaiji monk Chōnen 奝然 (938–1016) is said to have brought the first images of the Sixteen Arhats to Japan in Ei'en 1 (987). Members of the Fujiwara family began to perform rituals for the arhats after that date, often to secure the well-being of a deceased family member in the afterlife.[19] With the rise of Zen Buddhism in the Kamakura period, the arhat cult grew in importance, and Dōgen is said to have brought back from China images of the arhats attributed to Li Longmin 李竜眠 (d. 1106), creator of a noted iconographic style for paintings of the Sixteen Arhats.[20]

Although doctrinal Zen texts rarely mention the arhats, ritual texts and extant images do give indications of the significance of the arhat cult; as Bernard Faure observed: "It is impossible to overestimate the role of these figures in Chan and Zen."[21] It should not be surprising, then, that the first and most widely performed *kōshiki* of the Sōtō school was a *kōshiki* for the Sixteen Arhats. Dōgen is credited with the composition of its *shikimon,* and two fragments of a *Rakan kōshiki* written by Dōgen himself survive.[22] That text

15. T 49, no. 2030. For a French translation, see Levi and Chavannes 1916, 6–24. For a detailed study, including an English translation, see Shih 2002. For a study of the three extant versions in Khotanese, Tibetan, and Chinese, as well as a translation of the Khotanese and Tibetan versions, see Chen 2018. Visser (1923, 58–62) translated excerpts of this text.

16. For a study of the relationship between painted depictions of the Sixteen Arhats and the spread of the arhat cult, see Joo 2007, chap. 3.

17. On Mt. Tiantai and how it became a central site of the arhat cult, see Joo 2007, chap. 6.

18. For a study of Jōjin's visit to Mt. Tiantai, see Joo 2007, 218–228. Jōjin also attended a ritual for the arhats at a major temple in Kaifeng; see Joo 2007, 320–325, and 2009, 97–101. On Chōgen and Yōsai, see Shibata 1979, 235, and Michihata 1983, 275–276.

19. Maegawa 2012, 232–233. Arhat rituals performed by members of the Fujiwara family in the eleventh and twelfth centuries are also mentioned in the diaries *Shōyūki* (2: 257) and *Heihanki* (1: 153, 208, 241–242, and 272–273); see also Mross 2013c, 319.

20. Faure 1996, 90–91.

21. Faure 1996, 89.

22. See chap. 1, n. 51.

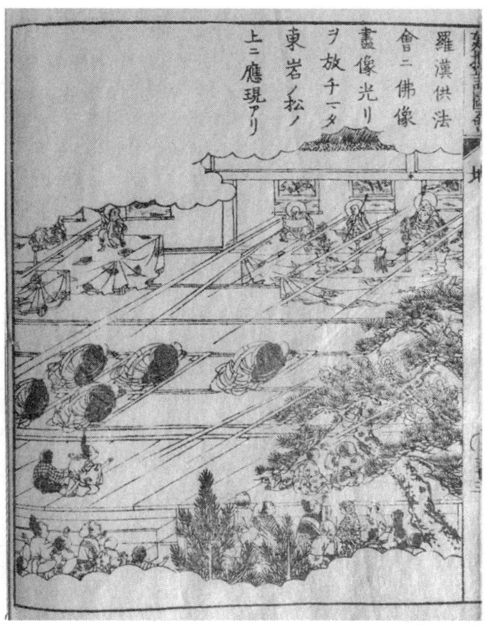

Figure 2.1. Dōgen's performance of a ritual for the arhats. Detail of *Teiho Kenzeiki zue* (1806). Courtesy of East Asia Library, Stanford University. Used with permission.

is thought to date from around Hōji 3 (1249), when heavenly flowers were said to have appeared before the arhat images during a ritual for the arhats. Dōgen recorded this miraculous event and interpreted it as proof that Eiheiji would be a sacred place equaled only by Mt. Tiantai in China.[23] Later hagiographies embroidered the idea, stating that the arhat images emitted light or that the arhats appeared on a pine tree in front of the temple, placing Eiheiji under the protection of the arhats themselves (fig. 2.1).[24] Besides Dōgen, other prominent Sōtō Zen monks such as Keizan and Menzan also had close ties to devotional activities venerating the Sixteen Arhats.[25]

---

23. *Jūroku rakan genzui ki;* see DZO 2: 546, DZSK, 950, DZZ 7: 398, and ZSZ 1: v. For an English translation, see Visser 1923, 149. Dōgen's *Shōbōgenzō* also includes a fascicle on arhats entitled *Arakan;* but here, without discussing the Sixteen Arhats, Dōgen describes arhats as practitioners who have eliminated all defilements and reached enlightenment.

24. See, for example, *Kenzeiki* (K, 71). Also, Menzan's *Rakan ōgenden* mentions that the arhats appeared on a pine in front of the temple (Michihata 1983, 207).

25. Keizan mentioned in his temple diary *Tōkokuki* that he had been a disciple of the fourth arhat, Suvinda, some lifetimes ago. He also indicated that in Shōwa 2 (1313) he had a dream in which the eighth arhat appeared to him (JDZ, 392–393; KZ 8: 5; see also Faure 1996, 89, and Mross 2007, 23–24). A few years later, in Gen'ō 2 (1320), he inaugurated the monthly performance of an offertory ceremony for the Sixteen Arhats at Yōkōji (JDZ, 395; KZ 8: 21).

Menzan wrote two works on the miraculous deeds of the *Arhats: Rakan ōgenden* and *Jūroku rakan fukuden senkōki.* In the former, he describes an occasion when he prayed to the Sixteen Arhats for strong attendance at an upcoming training period. The arhats appeared in his dream and the next day many monks arrived. See Michihata 1983 for a summary of this account. Menzan also edited the *Tōjō Rakan kōshiki.*

Although scholars have often emphasized the popularity of the arhat cult in the Zen schools, veneration of the arhats was not confined to this tradition. The earliest extant *Rakan kōshiki* was written not by a Zen monk but by the Kegon-Shingon monk Myōe.[26] Myōe is also credited with another ritual text for the Sixteen Arhats, the *Rakan kushiki.*[27] Both texts heavily cite the *Record of the Perpetuity of the Dharma* and most likely served as models for the Sōtō school's *Rakan kōshiki.* Later ritual texts written or performed by monks of other schools are also extant, suggesting that the cult of the arhats was widespread.[28]

Many manuscripts and woodblock prints of the *Rakan kōshiki* have been discovered in Sōtō temples, attesting to its popularity. After Dōgen's time, the version included in the *Keizan shingi* seems to have been widely circulated.[29] This version differs to some extent from the manuscript attributed to Dōgen. Based on that manuscript, Menzan edited the *shikimon* and published a woodblock print edition entitled the *Tōjō Rakan kōshiki.* But it seems that Keizan's version was still performed at many Sōtō temples after Menzan's edition was published. In the 1960s, however, the editors of the *Shōwa kaitai Shōmyō kihan,* in which the *Rakan kōshiki* was included, decided to return to Dōgen's version and accordingly revised the *shikimon* based on Dōgen's text.[30] One senior priest at Sōjiji told me that they continue to perform the *Rakan kōshiki* not because they believe in the arhats but to perpetuate the ritual tradition established by Dōgen. This aspiration was a likely motivation for the revision of the *kōshiki* in the 1960s, suggesting that the performance of the *Rakan kōshiki* has become an enactment of collective memory that connects the clerics to their school founder, the author of the ritual.

Today, Sōtō clerics at Zen monasteries perform a number of arhat rituals, not only the elaborate *Rakan kōshiki* for the Sixteen Arhats, but also a sutra reading for the arhats on mornings when the morning service is not abbreviated, and a *Rakan pai* 羅漢拝 on the first and fifteenth days of the month, a relatively simple ritual in the arhat hall on the second story of the main gate.[31]

Many of these arhat rituals, including the *Rakan kōshiki,* also praise the relics of the Buddha. The connection of the Sixteen Arhats to the Buddha's relics is explained in the *Record of the Perpetuity of the Dharma,* which narrates a sermon by the arhat Nandimitrā in response to the questions of his disciples concerning how long the Dharma will continue to exist in this world. Before

26. *Jūroku rakan kōshiki,* part of Myōe's *Shiza kōshiki.*

27. For a study of Myōe and the arhat cult, see Maegawa 2012, 229–238.

28. See, for example, *Rakan ku sahō* (Hōryūji), *Rakan ku* (Ninnaji), and *Rakan kanjō sahō narabini saimon* (Ninnaji).

29. The *Rakan kōshiki* was only included in the Rinkō manuscript, copied in Meiō 10 (1501), and the Manzan edition of the *Keizan shingi,* first printed in Tenna 1 (1681).

30. For a detailed study of the development of the *Rakan kōshiki,* see Mross 2007 and 2011.

31. The *Rakan pai* is similar to the *kanjō* (invitation) sung during the *Rakan kōshiki,* but additionally the monks invoke the ten disciples of the Buddha. Before this text, they chant the *Heart Sutra* and afterwards read a transfer of merit; see *Shogakuzan Sōjiji nikka shokyōyō shū,* 218–228; Inoue 2005, 1: 18 and 74–75; and *Shōwa kaitei Sōtōshū gyōji kihan,* 53–54. For a description of the ritual form at Eiheiji, see *Dōanryō kōmuchō,* 28–29.

foretelling the advent of the future buddha Maitreya, Nandimitrā explains that the Dharma would continue to exist and that the Sixteen Arhats, whom the Buddha had instructed to protect the teaching after this death, would continue to dwell in this world, protecting the teaching, helping practitioners, and bringing great rewards to donors. However, when the life span of humans in Jambudvīpa reaches seventy thousand years, the Dharma would cease to exist. At that time, the Sixteen Arhats and their retinues will gather and build a magnificent stupa in which they will enshrine all the relics of the Buddha. After circumambulating and paying respect to the stupa, the arhats will ascend into the air and enter nirvāṇa, their bodies bursting into flames and leaving nothing behind. The stupa will then sink deep into the earth and disappear.[32] The text suggests that the relics and the arhats will preserve and represent the Buddha's teaching after his passing until the advent of Maitreya.[33] In this way, both the relics and the arhats can establish a connection to the Buddha during the time of his physical absence, and they came to be worshiped together in some rituals, including the *Rakan kōshiki*.[34] In effect, the arhats served as contact relics of Śākyamuni Buddha—objects that had direct contact with the Buddha and can in turn offer practitioners a way to connect with him through their intermediation. Thus, they can reduce the sense of longing for the Buddha long after his passing.[35]

---

32. Some Pali texts maintain that when the Dharma ceases to exist, Śākyamuni's relics will also disappear by burning away with no remainder. In other words, the disappearance of Śākyamuni's relics was apparently a necessary condition for the advent of Maitreya; see Strong 2004, 221–228.

33. Relics have been venerated in all Buddhist cultures. The most revered are relics of the Buddha, but relics of eminent monks or bodhisattvas have also been venerated. The *Record of the Perpetuity of the Dharma* describes the beginning of a relic cult: having expounded his sermon, Nandimitrā dies, ascends into the air, sets his body on fire, and lets the remaining bones drop onto the earth; after which, his disciples collect his relics, build a stupa, and make offerings to it (T 49: 14c08–14c16).

Relics have played an important role in Japanese Zen Buddhism since the beginning. Monks of the Daruma school, for example, transmitted relics of the six patriarchs of Chan and the bodhisattva Fugen Kōmyō 普賢光明 (Skt. Samantabhadra). One of these relics was transmitted to Gikai 義介 (1219–1309), Keizan's master, who in turn gave it to Keizan. Keizan then buried it together with other objects related to his lineage on the Peak of the Five Elders at Yōkōji. Dōgen also brought back from China relics of his teacher Myōzen 明全 (1184–1225), which he interpreted as a sign of authentic transmission (*Shari sōdenki*). In the context of *kōshiki*, it is important to mention that the high number of extant *Shari kōshiki* also suggests the popularity of the relic cult in medieval Japan. On relics in various Asian cultures, see Germano and Trainor 2004. On the veneration of relics in East Asia with a special focus on Zen, see Faure 1991, 132–147, and 1996, 158–173. For a detailed study on the relic cult in medieval Japan, see Ruppert 2000.

34. Early examples of this practice are Myōe's *Shiza kōshiki, Rakan kushiki,* and *Rakan wasan,* in which both the arhats and the relics of Śākyamuni were venerated.

35. Jacob Kinnard (2004) has demonstrated the vagueness of the term "presence" in Buddhist studies. David Eckel notes the power of the Buddha's absence in the ritual formation of Mahāyāna rituals and argues that it is the "subtle combination of presence and absence that gives Buddhist ritual its distinctive power" (1990, 63).

Performance of the *Rakan kōshiki* in Contemporary Japan

The following description is based on my fieldwork at the Sōtō head temple of Sōjiji in 2004 and from 2007 to 2013, together with an analysis of the handbooks used for the ritual. I saw the *Rakan kōshiki* performed several times and observed how the annual performances differed slightly from year to year. This was mostly a result of the unique voices or styles of the individual performers: a lead vocalist might add additional melodic embellishments, or the officiant might improvise subtle melodic variations when vocalizing the *shikimon,* which could also be read with almost no melodic inflections. Based on these observances, I will generalize the performance practice at Sōjiji and not describe any particular performance.

The basic ritual structure is always the same, and the *Rakan kōshiki* is performed in a similar way at other Sōtō temples. Looking back historically, it is not known how Dōgen performed this *kōshiki,* but the earliest extant source containing a description of the *Rakan kōshiki* in the Sōtō school, written in Meiō 10 (1501), lays out the same ritual structure that is used today.[36] This structure is given in subsequent ritual handbooks as well. Nevertheless, it remains likely that the melodic realization of liturgical texts and other details of the performance differed to some degree from today's practice.[37]

Rituals are repetitive. Participants repeat highly formulaic gestures and actions. Performers vocalize certain texts several times. Musical instruments provide the same cues for ritual actions throughout the ritual. Likewise, *kōshiki* are characterized by repetition. As a consequence, the following account is itself repetitive. I hope that it conveys an impression of the various characteristics of the ritual, including its formality and repetition.

Ritual Space and Ritual Actors

At Sōjiji, the *Rakan kōshiki* is performed annually on November 16 as part of the rituals that come midway through the ninety-day training period. More than fifty monks usually participate, and the performance takes place in the Hall of the Great Ancestors (Daisodō 大祖堂), the largest hall at Sōjiji, where most major observances are conducted. At other temples, the *Rakan kōshiki* may be performed in the Dharma hall or the arhat hall located on the second story of the main temple gate. As a rule, lay devotees do not actively participate in the ritual. A few times during my fieldwork at Sōjiji, the members of the temple's women's association attended the ritual but acted more as an audience.[38]

---

36. This is the Rinkō manuscript of the *Keizan shingi* held at Yōkōji. Although the *Rakan kōshiki* in this manuscript does not provide the liturgical text of the *Gāthā to Scattering Flowers,* it does list the three ritual positions that are required for this piece, so I assume that it was also intended to be sung.

37. For example, Sōtō monks changed their musical notation in the Tokugawa period, and a comparison of ritual handbooks suggests that the melodies also changed at that time; see Mross 2014a, 173–174 and 416–418.

38. Rappaport (1999, 39–41) distinguishes between the audience and the congregation

Before the ritual, the novices who are responsible for the hall prepare the ceremonial space (fig. 2.2). Arhat images are not permanently enshrined in the Hall of the Great Ancestors, so the monks first hang scrolls of the Sixteen Arhats above the altar. Then they set up small tables in the central area of the hall for the monks who will perform the main ritual acts (fig. 2.3). On a table in front of the altar, they place ritual implements and the handscrolls that contain the text of the address of invitation (fig. 2.4).[39] They also assist in the preparation of offerings that will be delivered during the ritual. During the ceremony itself, their job is to rearrange the ritual space and bring in implements, texts, or other paraphernalia as needed.

The most important ritual actions take place directly before the altar in the central area of the hall, called *daima* 大間. In this area sit the monks who perform the main ritual functions. Their seating order is strictly prescribed, and no one is able to move around freely. In front of each monk is a small table, on which the ritual handbook is placed. The cantor or chanting leader and the monk who plays the musical instruments sit at the back of the central area.[40] All monks who sit in the central area face the altar. To the left and right of the central area sit the two monks who lead the *Hymn of the Four Wisdoms,* facing each other. They are thus situated in front of the monks in the assembly, who sit on either side of the central area, facing toward the center. The officiant sits on the right side of the altar outside the central area, also facing the altar. Another senior monk, whose role is to lead the delivery of offerings during the address of invitation, sits at the left side of the altar (fig. 2.5). During the ritual, lay devotees are not allowed to enter the central part of the hall or the area where the assembly sits. If members of Sōjiji's congregation are present, they sit behind the assembly on the left or right side. Occasional visitors are not permitted to enter the tatami area and must remain at the very back of the hall, where chairs are set up.

The allocation of roles in the *kōshiki* usually reflects the temple hierarchy. The officiant is a senior priest, most often the *godō* 後堂 (rear hall)[41] or *tantō*

---

when discussing the differences between theater and ritual. However, in traditional Buddhist rituals in Japan, it is sometimes the case that the congregation does not actively participate. While they likely have a different attitude than that of an audience in a theater, they still are observers more than active participants.

39. The setup on the table slightly differs depending on the ritual. For example, fig. 2.4 shows the setup of the *Dentō kōshiki* where the text of the offertory declaration (*saimon*) is placed on the table at the beginning of the ritual because no address of invitation is sung during this ritual.

40. According to the graph in the ritual handbook of the *Shōwa kaitei Rakan kōshiki,* it is the cantor who plays the musical instruments (36v–37r; see fig. 2.2), and it is done this way at Eiheiji. But at Sōjiji the cantor only sings while another monk plays the instruments.

41. *Godō* is a high position in the head temples of the Sōtō school. In principle, it is one position below the superintendent. It is named *godō* because the monk who holds it sits next to the rear door in the monks' hall (*sōdō* 僧堂). It was created in the Meiji era and is one of the most prestigious positions for Sōtō monks. The *godō* is considered the "face" of the monks' hall at a head temple, and is responsible for instructing young monks in zazen and doctrine.

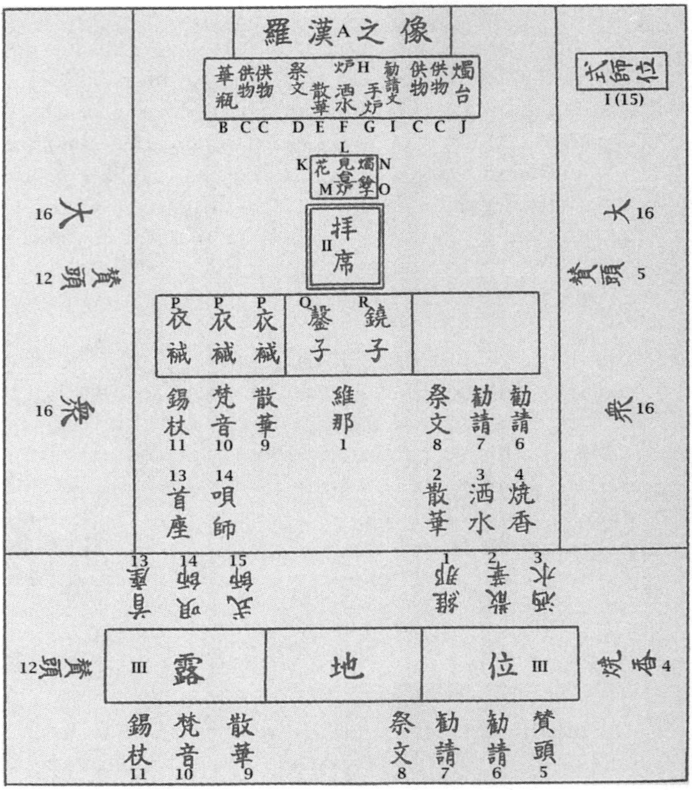

Figure 2.2. Diagram of the setup and positions of the performers. From the *Shōwa kaitei Rakan kōshiki,* 36v–37r. Used with permission.

Implements: **A.** Images of the arhats (*rakan no zō* 羅漢の像); **B.** Flower vase (*kebyō* 華瓶); **C.** Offerings (*kumotsu* 供物); **D.** Text of the offertory declaration (*saimon* 祭文); **E.** Flowers to be scattered (*sange* 散華); **F.** Pure water (*shasui* 洒水); **G.** Portable incense vessel (*shuro* 手炉); **H.** Incense vessel (*ro* 炉); **I.** Text of the address of invitation (*kanjōmon* 勧請文); **J.** Candle holder (*shokudai* 燭台); **K.** Flowers (*hana* 花); **L.** Scripture stand (*kendai* 見台); **M.** Incense vessel (*ro* 炉); **N.** Candle (*shoku* 燭); **O.** Small bell (*reisu* 鈴子); **P.** Golden tray (*ekoku* 衣裓); **Q.** Sounding bowl (*keisu* 磬子); **R.** Gong (*nyōsu* 鐃子).

Performers: **1.** Cantor (*ino* 維那); **2.** Cleric who scatters flowers during the first liturgical piece (*sange* 散華); **3.** Cleric who sprinkles water during the first liturgical piece (*shasui* 洒水); **4.** Cleric who carries the incense vessel during the first liturgical piece (*shōkō* 焼香); **5.** Lead singer of the *Hymn of the Four Wisdoms* (*santō* 賛頭); **6.** Lead singer of the address of invitation (*kanjō* 勧請); **7.** Lead singer of the address of invitation (*kanjō* 勧請); **8.** Cleric who recites the offertory declaration (*saimon* 祭文); **9.** Lead singer of the *Gāthā of Falling Flowers* (*sange* 散華); **10.** Lead singer of the *Gāthā of Sanskrit Sound* (*bonnon* 梵音); **11.** Lead singer of the *Gāthā of the Sounding Staff* (*shakujō* 錫杖); **12.** Singer of the *Hymn of the Four Wisdoms* (*santō* 賛頭); **13.** Cleric who sings the *Praise of the Thus Come One* (*shuso* 首座); **14.** Cleric who sings the *Praise of the Thus Come One* (*baishi* 唄師); **15.** Officiant (*shikishi* 式師); **16.** Assembly (*daishū* 大衆).

Special places: I. Place of the officiant (*shikishii* 式師位); **II.** Place of worship (*haiseki* 拝席); **III.** Place to assemble at the beginning and end of the ritual (*rojii* 露地位).

Figure 2.3. Ceremonial space for the *Rakan kōshiki* in the Hall of the Great Ancestors at Sōjiji. Photo by Sōjiji. Used with permission.

Figure 2.4. Table in front of the altar, showing the setup for the *Dentō kōshiki* at Sōjiji. Photo by the author.

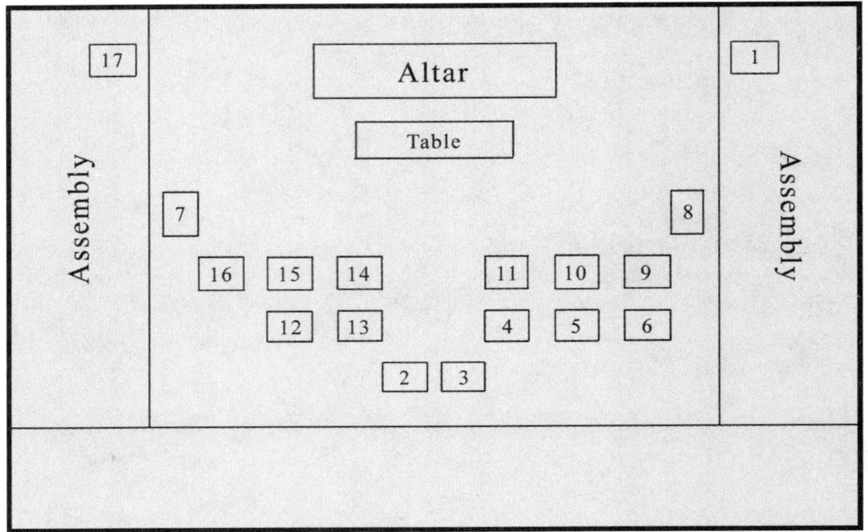

Figure 2.5. Seating diagram for the *Rakan kōshiki* at Sōjiji. The positions here slightly differ from those shown in fig. 2.2 in that a cantor's assistant (3) plays the musical instruments, and a senior monk (17) leads the delivery of offerings during the address of invitation; both positions are absent in the *Shōwa kaitei Rakan kōshiki*. Diagram by Ilona Mross.

1. Officiant; **2.** Cantor; **3.** Monk who plays the main musical instruments; **4.** Monk who scatters flowers; **5.** Monk who carries the incense vessel; **6.** Monk who sprinkles water; **7–8.** Monks who sing the *Hymn of the Four Wisdoms;* **9–10.** Monks who lead the address of invitation; **11.** Monk who recites the offertory declaration; **12–13.** Monks who sing the *Praise of the Thus Come One;* **14.** Lead singer of the *Gāthā of Falling Flowers;* **15.** Lead singer of the *Gāthā of Sanskrit Sound;* **16.** Lead singer of the *Gāthā of the Sounding Staff;* **17.** Monk who leads the delivery of offerings during the address of invitation.

単頭 (head of the meditation platform).[42] The cantor is usually the *ino* 維那, a senior teacher responsible for instructing novices in etiquette, discipline, ritual performance, and *shōmyō*.[43] He usually sings the solo parts in rituals, but at the head temples a novice who has been in training for several years

42. The *tantō* is a senior teacher at a major monastery who instructs novices in Buddhist practice. It is one position below the *godō*.

43. Often translated as rector, the *ino* has a long history as a high monastic official. During the Tang dynasty, the *ino* was mainly responsible for enforcing rules and discipline. In the Song dynasty, and in medieval Japan, he also led sutra-chanting services and recited the verses transferring merit at the end of a ritual. In contemporary Japan, only monasteries have a senior teacher who officially serves as the *ino*. When rituals are performed at local Zen temples, one priest is usually assigned to take on the role of *ino*, and he will lead the sutra chanting and read the transfer of merit. See Foulk 2010b, 168–169, on the historical development of this position. Due to the *ino*'s function in rituals, I translate it as cantor in the context of *kōshiki*.

may be assigned the role of cantor to gain experience in leading a ritual. Advanced novices may also perform other important pieces or ritual actions.[44] The role allocation thus reflects hierarchy, but it also correlates to the length of training and depth of ritual expertise.

Purifying the Ritual Space

While the vibrant peal of the *tenshō* 殿鐘 bell resounds, the clerics slowly enter the Hall of the Great Ancestors. The monks of the assembly, all novices, sit down in neatly arranged rows to the left at the back of the hall, while the monks designated to perform the main ritual actions line up in two rows behind the central area, facing each other (see fig. 2.2, *rojii,* III). The officiant takes a seat in a special area to the very right of the altar, flanked by his two assistants, who face him. A third assistant, responsible for ushering the officiant at the beginning and end of the ritual, takes a seat in front of them, facing the officiant. The monks of the assembly walk through the rows of the monks who had lined up in the back. Passing through the back of the central area, they go to the left or the right of the central area and stand at their assigned places. The officiant, his two assistants, and the usher stand up. The assistants bow three times, while the officiant only lowers his head. Then the officiant and the assistants bow to the left, right, and center. These movements are all coordinated by the clear, high-pitched sound of the handbell (*shukei* 手磬 or *inkin* 引磬), played by the usher, who also bows with the other monks. Then the usher solemnly leads the officiant and his assistants to the two rows in the back of the central area, where all take their places. The monks in the two rows, including the officiant, bow, again to the left, right, and center. One monk after another ceremoniously enters the central area and walks to his assigned place, where he stands. When all the monks have taken their places with the officiant in the center and have spread out sitting cloths (*zagu* 坐具), the cantor's assistant strikes a handbell to coordinate three prostrations. The officiant then moves to his seat at the right side of the altar.

Approaching the three monks who sit in the first row on the left, the cantor invites them to carry out their designated functions during the first chant by performing a full bow in *gasshō* 合唱 (*monjin* 問訊), first spreading his arms wide apart, then bringing his palms together in front of his chest and respectfully bending his head and upper body. (The cantor repeats this formal gesture of invitation whenever he invites other monks to lead chants or perform ritual actions during the ritual.) The three monks respond to this invitation with a bow and stand up. Once the cantor has returned to his place, he and the three monks simultaneously perform one prostration.

Moving to the table in front of the altar, each of the three monks takes

44. The *Shōwa kaitei Rakan kōshiki* (fig. 2.2) further suggests that one of the monks who sing the *Praise of the Thus Come One* is the *shuso* 首座 (lit. head seat), the monk who serves as the head novice during the ninety-day training period. But in reality, the *shuso* does not necessarily sing the *Praise of the Thus Come One.*

up a ritual implement: one an incense holder, one a water vessel and a stick to sprinkle the water, and one a golden tray (*ekoku* 衣裓) with paper flowers on it.[45] The cantor's assistant strikes a large singing bowl (*keisu* 磬子) three times normally, and once muted. The cantor vocalizes the first line of the *Gāthā to Scattering Flowers* (*Sange no ge* 散華偈). Singing slowly in free rhythm, he adds a slight melodic embellishment on the second character, "flower," and then adds longer melismatic embellishments on the last syllable of the line. Another stroke of the singing bowl gives the cue for the assembly to join the chant at the second line, and the cantor's assistant strikes it again at the beginning of each following line. All monks sing the verse in unison, with melodic inflections at the end of each line. They sing:

> Falling flowers decorate all ten directions.
> We scatter many precious flowers forming a curtain (*chō* 帳).[46]
> We scatter many precious flowers in all ten directions
> And offer [these] to all Tathāgatas.[47]

Their singing in free rhythm with slow melodic embellishments, always gliding from one tone to the next, creates a solemn atmosphere.

When the assembly joins the singing of the cantor, the three monks who stand in front of the altar start to circumambulate the hall, one carrying the incense burner, one sprinkling water, and one scattering paper flowers. The water is supposed to cleanse the room; the flowers, to decorate the hall; and the fragrance of incense, to attract buddhas, bodhisattvas, and other deities. After the circumambulation, the three monks put the implements back on the table and return to their places, where they perform one prostration simultaneously with the cantor and sit down.

The cantor goes to the middle of the central area of the hall, on the same level with the two monks who lead the *Hymn of the Four Wisdoms,* and invites them with a formal bow. The two monks rise and walk toward the center, bow toward one another with hands crossed in front of their chests, and kneel down. Two assistants quickly glide in to bring them cymbals. The two monks stand up and start to play the cymbals loudly, in rhythmic patterns of long and short clashes interrupted by a small gong, struck by the cantor's assistant.

45. *Ekoku* (lit. robe), also called *hanazara* 花皿 (flower tray) or *keko* 華籠, is a golden round tray decorated with flowers to which three cords are attached. On it are placed the paper flowers that are scattered during the ritual. Originally, this ritual implement was made out of bamboo or wood.

46. *Chō* is a curtain that hangs on both sides of the altar.

47. *Shōwa kaitei Rakan kōshiki,* 2r. This verse is a variant of a verse in the *Flower Garland Sutra* (*Da fangguang Fo huayan jing*), translated by Buddhabhadra (359–429), T 9: 435a5–6. It is also chanted in the *Grand Precepts Meeting;* see *Keizan shingi,* T 82: 433a14–15. The *Shōwa kaitei Rakan kōshiki,* the ritual handbook used for performances of the *Rakan kōshiki,* is one of the five volumes of the *Shōwa kaitei Shōmyō kihan,* the standard manual for rituals featuring *shōmyō* in the Sōtō school today; see chap. 1. All subsequent references to the text of the *Rakan kōshiki* will be to this edition unless otherwise indicated.

Figure 2.6. *Hymn of the Four Wisdoms.* The photos of the *Rakan kōshiki* in this section were all taken on November 16, 2019, at Sōjiji. Photo by Sōjiji. Used with permission.

Before each long stroke, the monks spread their arms far apart and shift their weight onto the tips of their toes, but when they clash the cymbals in front of their chests, they lower their heels back to the ground. The beautifully choreographed movements add an impressive visual component to the dynamic play of the cymbals (fig. 2.6).[48]

After this instrumental introduction, the two monks sing the *Hymn of the Four Wisdoms,* the only Sanskrit text vocalized during this ritual.[49] The assembly joins in after one stroke of the handbell, sounded by the monk who played the gong and also plays the main musical instruments. This hymn differs markedly from all other pieces: each syllable is sung energetically several times on the same pitch, followed by a very short pause, and when the syllable is sung for the last time, the melody usually drops in glissando fashion. Occasionally, a short melodic pattern is inserted. This piece is thus characterized by an alternation between strongly sung repeated syllables and brief passages with light melodic inflections. Now the two monks who lead the chant clash

48. In 2011, I observed that monks at Sōjiji exchanged this instrumental play for the cymbal and drum play performed in the *Kannon senbō,* which has a different rhythmic pattern. The exchange I witnessed is evidence of the fluidity of rituals, showing that monks do on certain occasions modify the ritual performance.

49. This piece was originally a śloka, a Sanskrit verse consisting of two sixteen-syllable lines. It is one of the oldest pieces in the Japanese *shōmyō* tradition and was probably transmitted from China to Japan at the beginning of the ninth century; see Arai K. 1999, 326.

the cymbals, again intersected by the gong, creating a finale to the chant. Then they hand the cymbals over to the assistants, who take them away. The two monks bow, return to their places, and perform a prostration.

Because the text is a transliteration of the original Sanskrit hymn and not a translation, the monks cannot understand the text when vocalizing it.[50] Although there are explanations written by and for Sōtō monks, the monks who perform the ritual rarely consult them. Reading the transliterated Sanskrit, the monks sing:

> Om. Bazara satanba
> Sōgyaraka bazara
> Ratannō madotanran
> Bazara daramagyayana
> Bazara gerumagya rohaba (3r–v)[51]

A possible translation into English:

> Om. Through receiving the blessing of Vajrasattva,
> We obtain the ultimate Vajraratnaḥ.
> By chanting Vajradharma's name,
> May we attain the Vajrakarma of enlightenment.[52]

The hymn praises the four wisdoms by invoking the names of the four directional bodhisattvas—Vajrasattva (J. Kongōsatta 金剛薩埵, east), Vajraratnaḥ (J. Kongōhō 金剛玉, south), Vajradharma (J. Kongōhō 金剛法, west), and Vajrakarma (J. Kongōgō 金剛業, north)—who are thought to represent the four wisdoms. Vajrasattva represents the wisdom that reflects all phenomena as they are; Vajraratnaḥ, the wisdom of observing the ultimate sameness of everything; Vajradharma, the wisdom of discerning the distinctive features of all phenomena; and Vajrakarma, the wisdom of accomplishing what is to

50. This text is also vocalized in the Shingon and Tendai schools. The pronunciation differs in each school, but the Sōtō pronunciation is closer to the one in the Tendai school; see Watarai and Tsukamoto 1983, 20–21.

51. This chant is based on the mantra: *Oṃ vajra sattva saṃgrahād vajra ratnam anuttaraṃ / vajra dharma gāyanaiḥ vajra karma karo bhava.*

52. For the translation, I used the Chinese translation that has been handed down in the Shingon and Tendai schools; see Sakauchi 1973, 4; Watarai and Tsukamoto 1983, 20; and *Bukkyō ongaku jiten,* 125. In the Shingon tradition this chant is interpreted as a praise of Mahāvairocana, whose wisdom encompasses the four wisdoms; see Arai K. 1999, 327; *Mikkyō daijiten* 2, 969; and Nelson 1998, 477. In contrast to this interpretation, the *Bukkyō ongaku jiten* states that this chant is a praise of Vajrasattva. Accordingly, the following translation would also be possible:

> Through receiving the blessing of Vajrasattva,
> We obtain the ultimate diamond treasure.
> By chanting the diamond words,
> May we fulfill the result of the diamond actions.

be done to benefit sentient beings. Modern commentaries written by Sakauchi Ryūyū and Inoue Gishin explain that this chant is a praise of Mahāvairocana, the cosmic Buddha who is the central object of worship in esoteric Buddhism. They also mention the four directional buddhas who represent the four wisdoms in connection with Mahāvairocana, whose wisdom of understanding the fundamental nature of all phenomena encompasses all four wisdoms.[53] Inoue further writes that in the Sōtō school this chant is vocalized as a praise for all buddhas and bodhisattvas.[54] Because the four directional bodhisattvas represent the four directions, we could say that through the invocation of the four directional bodhisattvas, a sacred space like a mandala is established. However, I have never heard a Sōtō monk explain this chant in this way.

Inviting the Objects of Veneration

Having purified and prepared the ritual space, the monks invite the objects of veneration. Again this part of the ritual starts with a gesture of invitation to the priests who perform ritual actions in the central area. After the cantor has performed a prostration at his place, he approaches the senior monk who is responsible for the delivery of offerings, seated to the left of the altar. They both bow. Then the cantor goes to the two monks who lead the next liturgical piece, the address of invitation (*kanjōmon* 勧請文), and they all bow to each other. These two monks move to the middle, spread their sitting cloths, and perform three prostrations. They walk to the table in front of the altar and offer incense. Each takes an envelope containing a handscroll of the text and moves it over the smoke from the incense burner to purify the texts with the fragrance of incense. After returning to the middle of the hall, the two monks sit down in lotus position on sitting cushions, brought by an assistant. After untying the bands of the handscrolls, they start singing the address of invitation, a long liturgical piece characterized by alternate duo and choral chanting (fig. 2.7).[55]

The two monks first sing, "The great assembly should together venerate the relics of the bodily remains of the Thus Come One, the Sixteen Great Arhats, and the Five Hundred Great Arhats" (5r). Then they invite all Sixteen Arhats individually; the Five Hundred Arhats of the stone bridge on Mt.

53. The four directional buddhas and Mahāvairocana are together called the five wisdom buddhas (*gochi nyorai* 五智如来). They are: Akṣobhya (J. Ashuku 阿閦), representing the east and embodying mirrorlike wisdom; Ratnasaṃbhava (J. Hōshō 宝生), representing the south and embodying equality wisdom; Amitābha (J. Amida), representing the west and embodying observational wisdom; and Amoghasiddhi (J. Fukū 不空) or Śākyamuni, representing the north and embodying the wisdom of perfect practice or accomplishing activities. Mahāvairocana takes the position in the center and embodies the all-encompassing wisdom of understanding all phenomena—in other words, emptiness.

54. Sakauchi 2010a, 260–262; and Inoue 2000, 14r–v.

55. An address of invitation is only chanted in the *Rakan kōshiki, Myōken kōshiki,* and *Daihannya kōshiki.* In the Tendai school, an address of invitation is not sung during *kōshiki.* Therefore, Watarai and Tsukamoto (1983, 23) argued that the performance of an address of invitation in Sōtō *kōshiki* was influenced by the Shingon school.

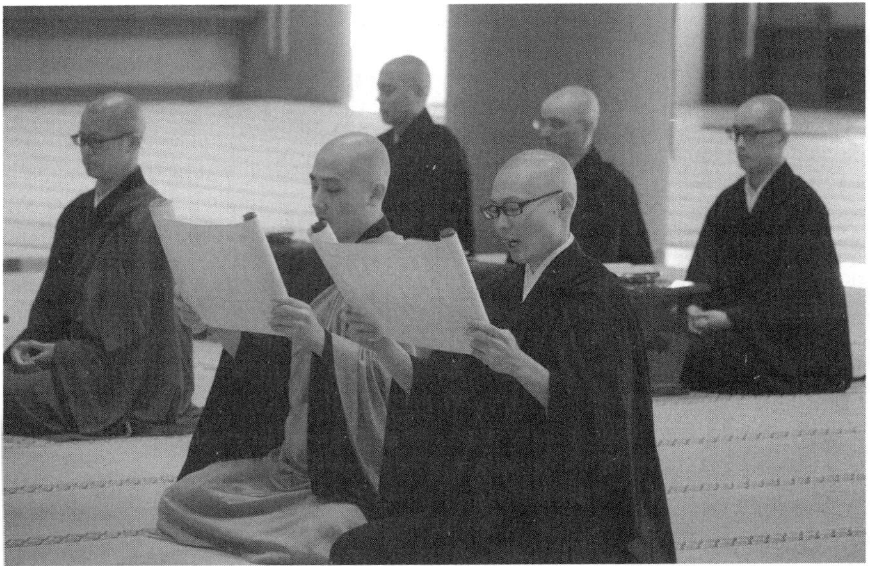

Figure 2.7. Address of invitation. *Rakan kōshiki*. Photo by Sōjiji. Used with permission.

Tientai; Mahākāśyapa, regarded as the first Indian patriarch; Ānanda; Kuṇḍadhāna (J. Kundobakan 君屠鉢漢), one of the four great arhats; and the Buddha's relics. For each, the two monks sing the phrase "Reverently prostrating ourselves, we take refuge in [name] with his entourage of [number of] arhats.[56] May they accept our humble offerings and our veneration with the three activities [of speech, actions, and thought]" (5r–11r). The assembly joins in at the line requesting acceptance of the offerings and veneration. Everyone then performs one prostration except for the two monks leading the piece, who continue singing.[57] In order to invite each object of veneration individually, the monks repeat this phrase twenty-one times.

The address of invitation features a solemn melody that gradually builds up tension. The monks start the beginning of each invocation with light melodic inflections on a middle pitch level, rise to a higher pitch level when they name the object of worship, and then continue with increasing melodic embellishments. However, they sing the short phrase "with his entourage of [number of] arhats" on one tone on the lower pitch level with gusto. Finally, when the assembly joins in, the last part of the phrase is vocalized with light melodic inflections. These melodic variations give each invocation its own dynamic.

56. The phrase "with his entourage of [number of] arhats" is sung only for the Sixteen Arhats.

57. In 2010, monks at Sōjiji performed a bow instead of a prostration after each invocation.

While the monks sing the address of invitation, the senior monk responsible for leading the delivery of the offerings and his assistants provide water, rice, sweets, and tea for all the arhats and objects of veneration. They form a half circle around the altar with the senior monk in the middle. One assistant brings in the offering, which is handed from one monk to the next. When it reaches the senior priest, he lifts it up and censes it over the smoke from the incense burner. The offering is then passed on from one monk to the next and placed on the altar. This is a long ritual sequence as all Sixteen Arhats are thus invited and presented with offerings one by one.

To conclude the invitation, the two monks sing, "Reverently prostrating ourselves, we take refuge in the Sixteen Great Arhats and the Five Hundred Arhats. May they remember their original vow, come, and manifest themselves" (11v). Most of the first sentence is vocalized on one pitch, but starting with its last syllables, the monks sing with slow melodic movements, first descending, then ascending, and finally ending the piece with a tremolo that fades out. They roll up the handscrolls and put them back into the envelopes. Then they walk to the table in front of the altar, bow, and put the texts back on it. They return to the middle of the hall, and everyone performs three prostrations. Finally, the two monks return to their original places.

The cantor now approaches the officiant, and the two bow to one another. The cantor spreads his sitting cloth and performs a quick prostration (*toppai* 頓拝) while the officiant bows once. When the cantor stands with his sitting cloth folded over his arm, he and the officiant bow toward each other again. Then the cantor goes to the monk who will recite the offertory declaration, invites him in the usual manner, and returns to his seat.

Suddenly the sound of the large drum breaks the silence. A novice plays it with strong strokes that become faster and faster, highlighting the significance of the upcoming ritual offering. The officiant, accompanied by his two assistants, walks to the middle, where another assistant has already placed a small tatami mat. On it, one of the assistants spreads out the officiant's sitting cloth. The officiant goes to the table in front of the altar, where he offers incense, and then performs three prostrations in the middle of the central area of the hall. He offers water, rice, sweets, and tea in red lacquerware, aided by his two assistants and other ritual assistants (fig. 2.8). They form a line around the table in front of the altar, with the officiant in the center, and provide offerings in the same formal way as during the address of invitation. Afterward, the officiant returns to his place in the middle, performs three prostrations, and returns to the table, where his assistants are waiting. All of them bow once. Then the officiant returns with his assistants to the place in the middle of the hall and performs three prostrations. Three loud strokes of the large drum resound through the hall. The officiant then reads Dharma words for the incense offering (*nenkō hōgo* 拈香法語), a brief address to the Sixteen Arhats asking them to accept the offerings (fig. 2.9). He walks with his assistants to the table in front of the altar and offers incense. One assistant

Figure 2.8. The officiant offers tea. *Rakan kōshiki*. Photo by Sōjiji. Used with permission.

Figure 2.9. The officiant reads Dharma words to the offering of incense. *Rakan kōshiki*. Photo by Sōjiji. Used with permission.

hands a long incense stick to the other, who takes it up to the altar. The officiant again returns to the place in the middle, bows once, and returns to his original seat.[58]

58. The ritual sequence of the Dharma words is not included in the ritual handbook currently used or in any premodern ritual handbook of the *Rakan kōshiki* that I have seen. The Dharma words are written by the officiant himself and thus vary depending on the priest and

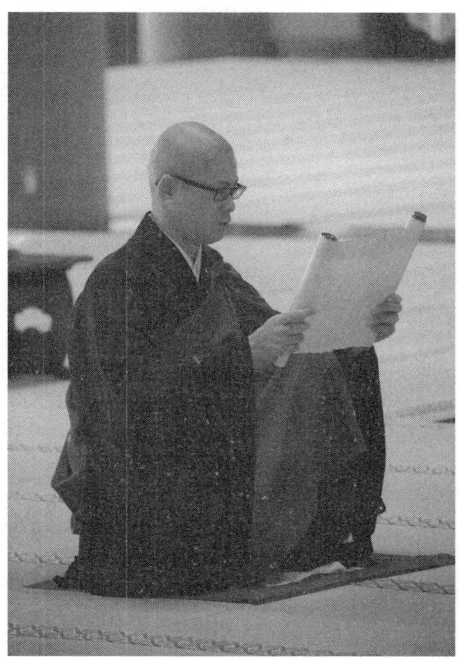

Figure 2.10. Offertory declaration. *Rakan kōshiki*. Photo by Sōjiji. Used with permission.

The monk who will read the offertory declaration performs one prostration at his place and goes to the middle of the hall, where he spreads out his sitting cloth and performs three prostrations. At the table in front of the altar, he offers incense, then takes the envelope with the handscroll containing the offertory declaration, and censes it. Standing in front of his place in the middle, he takes the scroll out of the envelope, kneels down in *chōki* 長跪 (kneeling upright with both knees on the ground while not lowering his buttocks onto his calves),[59] and starts reading the offertory declaration (fig. 2.10):

> Today, on [date], the disciples of the teachings left by Śākyamuni, the Thus Come One, have heard from a distant past that the Sixteen Great Arhats and the Five Hundred Great Arhats have received the direct order of the Buddha. They still dwell in this world and spread the Buddha's teachings. Therefore, in order to repay [their] benevolence (*ontoku* 恩徳), we respectfully offer incense, flowers, tea, sweets, and vegetarian food, though humble, to the Sixteen Great Arhats. (12v)

---

year. At Eiheiji and Eiheiji's satellite temple in Tokyo, the officiant does not read Dharma words. Instead the officiant leads the delivery of offerings during the address of invitation. At Sōjiji, the delivery of offerings during the address of invitation is led by another senior monk.

59. However, in 2010, the monk who read the offertory declaration sat down in *seiza*. In the following year, a different monk recited the text and he sat upright kneeling.

When the date is read, the monk who plays the main instruments sounds the handbell once, and all clerics (except the monk reciting the offertory declaration) bow until they hear the words "have heard." The offertory declaration continues to praise the arhats, stating, for example, that the venerable arhats hoisted the brocade sail of wisdom and crossed the ocean of afflictive desire (*bonnon no yokukai* 煩悩之欲海). The bodies of the arhats are compared to refined gold and their minds to the full moon. Then the text describes their various appearances and dwelling places. They are praised as unicorns (*rin* 麟) and dragons of the Dharma world and for possessing the three wisdoms (*sanmyō* 三明) and the six supernatural abilities (*rokuzū* 六通) (12v–13v). Finally, the monk responsible for the offertory declaration reads:

> If one respectfully prepares incense, flowers, and candles, makes food offerings (*saigu* 斎供), and reverently prays, then for certain [the arhats] will come and answer the request. Even if it is one hundred million *ri* away, [for them] it is like a strong man who closes and opens his arms. They come to the ritual site (*dōjō* 道場) and so accept the offerings. We respectfully wish that the Sixteen Great Arhats lead the whole family of great arhats and come equally to [receive] the offerings (*nōkyō* 納亨) at this place. May they accept them. (13v–14r)

This liturgical piece has a similar function to the address of invitation. Although the monks of the assembly do not vocalize this text, they all hold the ritual handbooks in a prescribed manner and read along.

When the monk has finished reading the offertory declaration, he rolls up the handscroll, stands up, puts it into the envelope, bows, and brings it back to the table in front of the altar. He offers incense and bows again. As he bows, the cantor's assistant strikes the singing bowl once. The monk returns to the place in the middle, and when he bows again, the singing bowl is struck mutely. The cantor starts singing the communal obeisance (*sōrai no ge* 総礼偈) while the monk performs one prostration and then returns to his original place. After the first line of the communal obeisance, the cantor's assistant strikes the singing bowl again, and the assembly sings the verse of the communal obeisance in unison:

> Our place of this rite (*dōjō* 道場) is like the jewels of Indra's palace (*daiju* 帝珠),[60]
> The reflections of all the saints [i.e., the arhats] appearing in each one.
> We face the reflections of the saints
> and place our foreheads at their feet, taking refuge in them. (14r–v)[61]

60. *Daiju* are the jewels reflecting each other endlessly on the vertices of the vast net that hangs over Indra's palace. This metaphor, taken from the *Flower Garland Sutra,* describes mutual interpenetration.

61. This verse is a variation of a verse from the *Fahua sanmei xingshi yunxiang fuzhuyi* (J. *Hokke zanmai gyōji unsō fujo gi*), T 46: 956a2–3, that is widely used for the communal obeisance in *kōshiki.* In the Sōtō school it has also been used in the *Hokke kōshiki* (ZSZ 2: 821) and the *Butsuji*

This verse is sung in a similar style to the opening *Gāthā to Scattering Flowers* and uses the same melodic patterns. At the end of this verse, all perform a prostration, coordinated by the sound of the handbell.[62]

The text suggests that the arhats are thought to have responded to the invitation and arrived at the ceremonial place. This concludes the section of the invitation summoning the objects of worship to the ceremonial space.

A Feast for All Attending

Now the monks perform the *Four Shōmyō Melodies* (*Shika hōyō*). This ritual sequence was performed at the Eye-Opening Ceremony of the Great Buddha of Tōdaiji in Tenpyō 17 (752) and is usually thought to function as a symbolic feast for all attending: the objects of veneration, monks, nuns, and lay believers.[63] It is an integral part of the *shōmyō* repertoire shared throughout Japanese Buddhism.

The sequence starts with the gesture of invitation to the monks who will lead the four chants. Approaching the monk or pair of monks who will sing the *Praise of the Thus Come One* (*Nyoraibai* 如来唄), the cantor extends the formulaic gesture. (This first chant is most often performed by two monks, hence my use of the plural in the following description.) The cantor then does the same with the three monks who will lead the *Gāthā of Falling Flowers* (*Sange no ge* 散華偈),[64] the *Gāthā of Sanskrit Sound* (*Bonnon no ge* 梵音偈), and the *Gāthā of the Sounding Staff* (*Shakujō no ge* 錫杖偈). The three chants are together called the "*San-Bon-Shaku*" 散梵錫.

The two monks who perform the *Praise of the Thus Come One* stand up, and when the cantor has returned to his original place, all three perform one prostration. Then the two monks go to the table in front of the altar, offer incense, go to the middle, spread out their sitting cloths, and perform three prostrations. An assistant places sitting cushions, on which they sit in lotus position. Another assistant brings in a notation stand with elegant movements, each step under total control. Raising his body and standing on the tips of his toes, he lifts the stand high above his head, quickly squats, and places the stand on the tatami, sliding it into position in front of the two monks, who prepare to sing the *Praise of the Thus Come One*. His finely choreographed movement foreshadows the impressive nature of the upcoming chant.

One of the two monks takes up a handbell from the stand in front of him. He strikes it three times and then both monks sing, "Un nyo ra-i" ウン如来

---

kōshiki (Ozaki 1998c, 64). In general, the communal obeisances in most *kōshiki* differ, because the stock verses that are often used are usually modified to fit the specific object of veneration.

62. The *Showa kaitei Rakan kōshiki* (14v), as well as the *Sozan gyōhō shinan* (3: 116) used at Eiheiji, indicates that three prostrations should be performed, but only one is performed at Sōjiji.

63. *Todaiji yōroku*, 50.

64. This *Gāthā of Falling Flowers* has the same title as the *Sange no ge* at the beginning of the ritual, but it is a different chant. To avoid confusion, I translate the earlier *Sange no ge* as *Gāthā to Scattering Flowers* and this *Sange no ge* as *Gāthā of Falling Flowers*.

Figure 2.11. *Praise of the Thus Come One.* This piece is often sung by two monks in unison, but one monk sung it solo during the *Rakan kōshiki* at Sōjiji in 2019. Photo by Sōjiji. Used with permission.

(Om, Thus Come One) in a soft voice (15r). After another strike of the handbell, the two monks raise their voices and begin singing elaborate melismas on the syllable "me"—staccato tones, glissandi, and large vibratos interchange and build a dramatic, magnificent performance of the text: "Hail, Thus Come One, the marvelous!" (15r–16r) (fig. 2.11).[65] Although the text is short, its performance takes around ten minutes, due to the melismatic vocalization. It is the most difficult piece in the Sōtō *shōmyō* repertoire, and the two novices who must sing it practice intensively in the knowledge that every mistake will be immediately audible as they sing together in unison.

At the end of the piece, one of the two monks strikes the handbell twice and returns it to the stand. The other monk, who had placed his ritual handbook on the stand, puts it back into his robe and both stand up. The assistant

65. Originally, the text was "The wondrous body of the Thus Come One, [unequaled] in the world," but the editors of the *Shōwa kaitei Shōmyō kihan* shortened it in the 1960s. The text is the beginning of a verse from the Śrīmālā *Sūtra* (Ch. *Shengman shizi hou yisheng da fangbian fangguang jing*). The whole verse is known under the title *Verse of the Praise of the Thus Come One* (*Nyoraibaimon* 如来唄文), which is sometimes sung instead of the *Praise of the Thus Come One.* The complete verse is: "The body of the Tathāgata, excellent in form, Is unequaled in the world, Being incomparable and inconceivable. Therefore, we now honor you. The Tathāgata's form is inexhaustible And likewise his wisdom. All things eternally abide [in him]. Therefore, we take refuge in you." (Paul 2004, 10; for the original, see T 12: 217a24–27.) However, we rarely find the *Verse of the Praise of the Thus Come One* in premodern Sōtō manuscripts, and substituting this piece for the *Praise of the Thus Come One* seems to be a relatively new development. Nonetheless, the *Shōwa kaitei Shōmyō kihan* provides it as an alternative.

who brought in the stand returns and takes it to the back of the altar area, again with precise, elegant movements. The two monks stand up, and another assistant comes to take away the sitting cushions. Then the two monks perform one prostration, bow, and return to their places. At the sign of their bow, the three monks who will sing the next three liturgical pieces stand up, and when the previous pair have returned to their places, all five simultaneously perform one prostration at their places.

The three monks who will sing the *San-Bon-Shaku* now take up the flower trays from their small tables. One of them additionally picks up a sounding staff (*shakujō* 錫杖), which had been prepared at his place. This staff has six metal rings attached to its upper end that make a metallic rattling sound when it is shaken or beat on the ground. The monk holding it now strikes the tatami with the bottom of the staff and shakes it three times in a fixed, short rhythm. Then the three monks walk in a prescribed way to the table in front of the altar: they first turn to the right, then to the front, then to the left, then to the front again, and finally to the right, going up to the table in front of the altar. Every time they turn at 90 degrees, the monk with the sounding staff strikes it on the tatami and shakes it.

When they arrive at the table, the monk with the sounding staff strikes it on the tatami again and shakes it three times. All three bow, and then proceed to lead the three successive chants (18v–21v) (fig. 2.12). The *Gāthā of Falling Flowers* praises Śākyamuni and explains that the ritual participants offer incense and flowers to him. The *Gāthā of Sanskrit Sound* declares that the participants offer flowers to Śākyamuni and all bodhisattvas. The *Gāthā of the Sounding Staff* describes how clerics dedicate themselves to Buddhist practice holding a sounding staff in their hands. The monk leading each piece sings the first line, and then is joined by the whole assembly on the next line, each piece

Figure 2.12. Three monks lead the *San-Bon-Shaku*. *Rakan kōshiki*. Photo by Sōjiji. Used with permission.

alternating between solo and communal singing. In contrast to what has gone before, these three pieces are sung with a fixed rhythm, and all three have a cheerful melody. The monk who leads the *Gāthā of Falling Flowers* scatters paper flowers during the first and third chants, and the monk who leads the third chant beats the tatami with the sounding staff in a lively rhythm three times at the end of each communally sung section of the *Gāthā of the Sounding Staff.* When the three monks have completed this ritual sequence, they bow and return to their places in the same way that they had come forward, again with the monk holding the sounding staff playing it with the same lively rhythm several times during their progression. When they arrive at their places, the monk with the sounding staff strikes it three times on the tatami again. All bow, put down their implements, perform one prostration, and sit.

The Central Ritual Sequence: *Shikimon*

Now the *shikimon,* a vocalization of the longest text of the ritual, begins. Including the verses, its full performance would most likely take at least thirty minutes or longer, depending on how quickly the officiant reads the text. Sōtō clerics often abbreviate it, however, choosing to recite three of the five sections to shorten the time required to perform the ritual. For example, in 2010 when Morita Shōkō 盛田正孝, then *godō* at Sōjiji, served as officiant, he read the pronouncement of intention and the first, third, and fifth sections.[66] In the following description, I provide summaries of all five sections while indicating where cuts in the performance of the *shikimon* were made.[67]

Again, a gesture of invitation signals the start of the *shikimon.* The cantor invites the officiant to begin his recitation with the same movements used for the Dharma words earlier. When the cantor has returned to his place, the officiant moves into the middle of the hall, helped by two attendants who carry his incense vessel and sitting cloth. Two ritual assistants take the small ceremonial table and the tatami mat on which the officiant sat and carry these to the middle. The officiant bows, goes to the table in front of the altar, and offers incense while the assistants finish their task. Returning to the middle, he performs three prostrations and sits. Then he rings a small bell (*rei* 鈴) three times and recites the words of worship: "Homage to the Sixteen Great Arhats who protect the transmitted teachings. May we meet them lifetime after lifetime" (22r). At the end of this phrase, he rings the bell again and bows once. He repeats this phrase two more times and then reads the beginning of the pronouncement of intention (fig. 2.13):

66. The following year, Suzuki Eiichi, then *godō* at Sōjiji, only vocalized the pronouncement of intention and the first and fifth sections of the *shikimon.* In June 2015, I attended the *Rakan kōshiki* at Eiheiji. During the ritual, the officiant read the pronouncement of intention and the first, third, and fifth sections of the *shikimon.* He did not read the complete first section, but omitted the list of names and dwelling places of the Sixteen Arhats at the beginning of the section. During my fieldwork at Sōjiji, Eiheiji, and Eiheiji's satellite temple in Tokyo, I never heard a recitation of a complete *shikimon.* But even with abbreviations, the performance of a *kōshiki* still takes around two hours.

67. For a detailed analysis of the sources used in the *Rakan kōshiki,* see Mross 2007, 74–89.

Figure 2.13. The officiant reads the *shikimon*. *Rakan kōshiki*. Photo by Sōjiji. Used with permission.

> Reverently, I address the great compassionate teacher, Śākyamuni, the World-Honored One; the eighty thousand sacred teachings such as the *Kegon* and *Lotus Sutras;* the Sixteen Arhats, who protect the teachings left by the Buddha; the nine billion nine hundred millions of saints who have exhausted all practices (*mugaku* 無学); the realms of the Three Treasures [Buddha, Dharma, and Saṃgha] that are as small as single particles of dust or the tip of a hair and as vast as the universe (*sekkai* 刹海), so inexpressible; and say: (22v)

When he reads the first word, the cantor's assistant strikes the handbell once and all lower their heads until the next sound of the handbell, which is struck when the officiant voices the words "Sixteen Arhats." When Morita performed in 2010, he read the *shikimon* at a moderate speed, lengthening the last syllable of each sentence or adding a pause between sentences. Consequently, his vocalization was easy to follow. His intent was to clearly convey the content of the text, and so he read it as recitative, although without adding melodic inflections.[68]

The pronouncement of intention briefly explains the transmission of the Dharma from India to China and Japan, proclaiming that the Dharma was

68. I have seen many *kōshiki* performances at a number of Sōtō temples. Sometimes the *shikimon* is read very quickly without pauses, making it difficult to understand the text. When the reading occurs at such a fast tempo, the verses that are sung during the *shikimon*, which are slowly vocalized in free rhythm, contrast sharply with the officiant's reading and sound even more solemn.

transmitted by Saichō and Kūkai to Japan, and praising the arhats for having protected the teaching. Then the text states that the assembly has prepared incense and flowers to offer to the Buddha's relics, as well as tea and sweets for the arhats (22v–23v). Thereafter, it elucidates the reason for the ritual:

> Respectfully, we ask the Three Treasures to illuminate the thoughts of the disciples. Today's lecture has a particular reason: we only bathe in a single drop of the ocean of virtue (*tokudai* 徳海) and hope to be saved from the towering waves of the ocean of suffering (*kukai* 苦海). The Sixteen Venerable Arhats internally conceal the practice of bodhisattvas while externally appearing in the form of śrāvakas.[69] Step by step, they transform the Dharma world; moment for moment, they respond to the good deeds of donors. They understand the profound meaning of the scriptures of the twelve divisions of the Buddhist canon and the treatises on the five ancient sciences (*gomyō* 五明)[70] and four vedas (*shii* 四韋).[71] Their eloquence is never obstructed. The praise of their virtues cannot be exhausted. (23v–24r)

The pronouncement of intention ends with a statement of the topics of the ensuing five sections (24r). Although Morita only delivered the first, third, and fifth sections, he still read the whole list. These sections explore aspects of the Sixteen Arhats in detail.

The first section introduces the names of the Sixteen Arhats and where they reside. Their teaching activities and practices for which they are known are also described: Some of them meditate, some preach the Dharma, others hold precept meetings, and still others explain the commentaries on the precepts. The section ends with the stipulation that to invite the arhats, one should face in the direction of their abode, burn incense, offer flowers, and perform prostrations. If one invites the arhats once, they will come once; if one invites them three times, they will appear three times. It is the same for one hundred or one thousand times. Just as the moon's reflection appears on the water, the arhats certainly come (24r–26r). Then the officiant proclaims the line: "Therefore, assembly, we should rely on their promise [to follow the Buddha's order], intone a verse, and perform a prostration. We sing a verse" (26r–26v). When Morita served as officiant, he held the last word and added a subtle melodic inflection, providing a cue for the entrance of the cantor.

The cantor's assistant strikes the singing bowl once, muted, and the

69. The term śrāvaka (*shōmon* 声聞, or voice-hearer) originally described direct disciples of the Buddha. In later Mahāyāna texts, śrāvakas were depicted as disciplined renunciants who strive for arhatship for their own sake, following the so-called Hīnayāna (Lesser Vehicle). This path was seen as inferior to that of bodhisattvas, the Mahāyāna ideal, who strive for buddhahood for the sake of all beings.

70. *Gomyō* 五明 are the five sciences in ancient India. These were grammar and linguistics (*śabda vidyā*, J. *shōmyō* 声明), logic (*hetu vidyā*, J. *inmyō* 因明), psychology (*adhyātma vidyā*, J. *naimyō* 内明), medicine (*cikitsā vidyā*, J. *ihōmyō* 医方明), and craft (*śilpakarma sthāna vidyā*, J. *kugyōmyō* 工巧明).

71. The four vedas are the Rig Veda, Sama Veda, Yajur Veda, and Atharva Veda.

cantor sings the first line of the verse by himself. The assembly enters on the second line, and the cantor's assistant sounds the singing bowl at the beginning of each line. The verse following the first section says:

> We bow our heads down to the great arhats.
> The Dharma nature is pure and clear as the moon.
> When the mind of sentient beings is like still water,
> The reflections of the arhats will appear in it.[72]
>
> Humbly prostrating ourselves, we take refuge (*namu kimyō chōrai* 南無帰命頂礼) in the Sixteen Great Arhats. May we meet them lifetime after lifetime. (26v–27r)

The monks sing this verse with melodic patterns that are similar to those in the opening *Gāthā to Scattering Flowers*. The *shikimon* thus offers two contrasting styles of vocalization: the officiant's reading of the *shikimon* is performed with very few if any melodies, while the singing of the verses by the assembly is replete with solemn melodies. Both convey devotion to the arhats, but in different modes. When the verse is concluded, all the monks perform a prostration to the sound of the handbell.

The second section explains how the Buddha on his deathbed instructed his disciples not to enter nirvāṇa but to remain in this world after his passing to help all sentient beings and protect the Dharma until the coming of the next buddha, Maitreya. The section describes the lament of the Sixteen Arhats when they heard the Buddha say that he was about to enter nirvāṇa: they all cried like small children, fell on the ground, and lost their senses. But when the Buddha consoled them, they regained consciousness, drank their tears, and agreed to follow the Buddha's order. Since then, they have used their supernatural powers to extend their lives and protect the Dharma. The text poetically describes how the practitioners are able to encounter the Buddhist teaching due to the accomplishment of the arhats and expresses joy about this (27r–29r) before ending by addressing the assembly: "Therefore, assembly, you should rejoice, praise [the arhats], and perform a prostration. We sing a verse" (29r).

When this section is performed, the assembly sings the following verse:

> The Buddha's true Dharma has two [sides]:
> Namely, doctrine (*kyō*) and enlightenment (*shō*) as its essence.[73]

72. This verse is a variation of the following *gāthā:* 菩薩清涼月 遊於畢竟空 衆生心水淨 菩提影現中, which is included in the *Nianfo sanmei baowang lun* (J. *Nenbutsu zanmai hōō ron*), T 47: 137a29–b1, and *Qixinlun shubi xiaoji* (J. *Kishinron shohissakki*), T. 44: 393c25–26. The first two lines are taken from the *Flower Garland Sutra* (T 9: 670c21).

73. According to the explanation following this verse in the *Jushelun* (J. *Kusharon*), *kyō* 教 are sutras (*kaikyō* 契經, i.e., sermons), regulations (*jōbuku* 調伏, a translation of the term Vinaya), and *abhidharma* (*taihō* 對法, i.e., philosophical treatises) (T 29: 152b03–04). *Shō* 証 are the factors of enlightenment (*bodai bunpō* 菩提分法) of the three vehicles, i.e., the vehicles of śrāvaka 声聞, pratyekabuddha 縁覚, and bodhisattva 菩薩 (T 29: 152b04).

If people live who embrace, explain, and practice [the teaching accordingly],
[The true Dharma] abides in this world.[74]

Humbly prostrating ourselves we take refuge in the Sixteen Great Arhats. May we meet them lifetime after lifetime. (29r–v)

Morita skipped over this second section when he performed the ceremony in 2010. After the concluding verse of the first section, he rang the small bell and then read the third section, which expounds the benefits of providing offerings to the arhats. Those who venerate arhat images, the text states, will always be free from enduring poverty, and the friends who invoke the names of the arhats will quickly receive protection. Whether reward or punishment, the results of one's actions will be right in front of one's eyes. The text then summarizes a passage from the *Record of the Perpetuity of the Dharma* that explains how the arhats appear incognito in multiple forms when devotees prepare a vegetarian feast and offer it to the clergy. Secretly receiving the offerings, they let the donors receive superior rewards in turn. Further examples of the benefits to be gained in this world from arhat veneration are recounted in four miracle tales describing the appearance of a gushing spring in an arid land, the transformation of a poor woman into a queen, the acquisition of riches after making offerings to the arhats, and the light emitted by arhat sculptures on fasting days. The section closes by praising the benefits of arhat veneration and admonishing listeners to take delight in the arhats' unlimited response to prayers. The officiant invites the assembly to perform a prostration in front of the Sixteen Arhats, pray for the benefits of the field of merit, and sing a verse (29v–31v). The assembly responds by vocalizing this verse:

The Sixteen Great Arhats
Are the greatest superior field of merit.
Those who venerate them and give offerings,
Will naturally obtain great benefit.

Humbly prostrating ourselves we take refuge in the Sixteen Great Arhats. May we meet them lifetime after lifetime. (31v–32r)

The fourth section, which Morita skipped over, describes at length how the arhats help to prevent or eliminate misfortunes. Following a string of stories and quotations, the text offers this summary: "Thus we know that it is solely the supernatural abilities of the arhats that can eliminate the misfortunes of humans and gods" (33r). The section then lauds the disciples who gave rise to the thought of attaining enlightenment and traveled throughout China and Japan seeking the pure teaching of Śākyamuni. Without fail they

74. This is a verse from the *Jushelun,* T 29: 152b1–2.

held bimonthly precepts meetings and provided offerings every single day, setting an example of zealous practice for all people who believe in the Dharma. This is due to the protective power of the arhats, which also manifests in the capacity of the Dharma to abide forever in this world (33r–33v). The officiant finally addresses the assembly: "Therefore, assembly, in order to eliminate misfortune, bestow happiness, and enable the Dharma to abide forever, we should perform a prostration. We sing a verse" (33v). The assembly sings the following verse (when this section is vocalized):

> The Sixteen Great Arhats
> Are like jewels protecting the country.
> One invocation and one prostration
> Can eliminate all calamities.
>
> Humbly prostrating ourselves we take refuge in the Sixteen Great Arhats. May we meet them lifetime after lifetime. (34r)

The fifth section, which Morita read and is the shortest, explains the significance of making offerings to the Buddha's relics. The text first establishes that the arhats continue to dwell in this world and protect humans, because the Buddha out of pity had ordered them to do so. And to further benefit deluded beings, the Buddha has left physical relics (34v). The text closes by saying:

> At dusk under the Sāla trees, the Buddha shed tears of pity and great compassion and entrusted us to the bodhisattvas and śrāvakas. In the morning of the five evils, he left solid bodily relics (*kengo kosshari* 堅固骨舎利) and thus carried out buddha acts that provide miraculous benefits. The pity (*awaremi* 哀) [expressed] during his lifetime and after his entry into nirvāṇa, and the compassion (*megumi* 恵) [expressed through] his physical body (*shōshin* 生身) and dispersed body (*saishin* 砕身) are beyond expression. Therefore, in order to venerate this inexhaustible benefit, we should sing a verse and perform a prostration. We sing a verse. (34v–35r)

All the monks sing the last verse of the *shikimon* and then perform a prostration, concluding this ritual sequence:

> Unborn, he showed his birth in Kapilavastu.
> Undying, he showed his death in Kuśinagara.
> Eternally abiding on the Vulture Peak, he saves all sentient beings.
> Therefore we bow before the venerable Śākyamuni.
>
> Humbly prostrating ourselves we take refuge in the relics of the remaining body. May we meet them lifetime after lifetime. (35r–v)

Closure: Transfer of Merit

The ritual ends with a transfer of merit. Because *kōshiki* in the Sōtō school are usually not sponsored by lay devotees, the merit is not dedicated to a specific individual. Instead the monks transfer the merit to all beings. The cantor's assistant strikes the singing bowl once, muted, and then the cantor sings the first line of the *Universal Transfer of Merit* (*Fuekō* 普回向). The assembly comes in on the second line, and the cantor's assistant strikes the singing bowl at the beginning of each line. The monks sing:

> We wish that this merit
> Extends universally to all.
> May we and all sentient beings
> Together realize the Buddha way. (36r)[75]

They sing this chant with melodic patterns similar to those in the opening *Gāthā to Scattering Flowers*. After the verse, the cantor alone vocalizes the final phrase: "Homage to the Dharma realm of self and others. May we equally benefit." He ends the line with a tremolo that becomes softer and softer and so concludes the ritual.

The monks of the assembly turn to face the altar and perform three prostrations synchronized by strikes of the handbell. The monks sitting in the middle area of the hall—except the officiant—return to their starting positions at the back of the hall, and when they arrive at their place they bow to the left, right, and center. The officiant resumes his starting place among the other monks, and all bow again in the same manner. As the monks of the assembly disperse, the usher leads the officiant and his two assistants back to his seat to the right of the altar. Once there, he and his assistants bow three times, and then all bow to the left, right, and center, thus departing from the ceremony.

At Sōjiji, a group photo of the monks who performed the central ritual functions, most of them advanced novices, is usually taken before the ritual assistants start the hall cleanup. The photo not only documents the occasion in the ritual tradition of Sōjiji, but also serves as a memento of the monks' training when they have left the head temple.

Although the foregoing description has detailed the movements that occur during the ritual, the performance of the *Rakan kōshiki* actually requires very little movement on the whole, and most monks stay at their place the whole time, only performing prostrations when required. For the monks in the assembly, who do not have an opportunity to move throughout the ritual, the experience of kneeling for over two hours can be an ordeal. Yet the well-

---

75. This verse, taken from the *Lotus Sutra* (T 9: 24c21–22), is sung in many *kōshiki* and other rituals. Notably, it was sung in the earliest *kōshiki* on record, Genshin's *Nijūgo zanmai shiki;* see NKS 4: 254.

rehearsed and finely choreographed movements of the monks with central roles and their assistants add immensely to the aesthetic character of the ritual; and anyone filming or photographing strives to capture the subtlety of their elegant and refined gestures. Early in my fieldwork, a young instructor who sometimes accompanied me during filming took delight in directing my attention to special movements. It seemed that the monks who performed these movements enjoyed them as well. One of the teachers at Sōjiji said that when he was a novice at Sōjiji over twenty years ago, they tried to refine the movements as much as they could and would showcase them to a higher degree than today's novices would. This bespeaks the physicality of ritual practice as well as the embodied nature of Zen practice.

Ritual Frames and the Structure of the *Rakan kōshiki*

Having described the performance of the *Rakan kōshiki* in detail, I now turn to examining its ritual structure. I show how the *shikimon* was set into a ritual frame and how smaller frames encompass sequences that form the larger frame, creating a flow in which the ritual unfolds. Other than naming the liturgical texts incorporated in the ritual, Sōtō monks do not propose a structural analysis of their *kōshiki*. Yet, as the preceding sections of this chapter have outlined, the order and content of the chants suggest a structural division into five parts (table 2.1). The first consists of the purification of the ritual space, and it incorporates the *Gāthā to Scattering Flowers* and the *Hymn of the Four Wisdoms.* The second part invokes the objects of veneration and invites them to come to the place. It comprises the address of invitation, the Dharma words during the offering of incense, the offertory declaration, and the communal obeisance—at the end of which, the objects of veneration are thought to be present at the ritual site. The third part, the *Four Shōmyō Melodies,* functions as a symbolic feast. All the liturgical pieces performed so far, from the opening *Gāthā to Scattering Flowers* to the *Gāthā of the Sounding Staff,* the last of the *Four Shōmyō Melodies,* constitute the preparatory sequences leading into the central sequence of the *kōshiki:* the *shikimon,* which I interpret as the heart of the ceremony. The function of the *shikimon* is twofold: it addresses the invisible audience, consisting of the objects of veneration—in this case, the arhats as well as the Buddha relics—and praises them. Vocally and semantically, this is done through the pronouncement of intention and thematic sections recited by the officiant and the verses and words of worship sung by the assembly. In addition, the performers express their devotion bodily by performing full prostrations after each verse. The recitation of the officiant can further be interpreted as a lecture about the virtues of the objects of veneration for the clerics and lay devotees attending the ritual. The fifth and last part is the transfer of merit and closing of the ceremony. Because the *shikimon* is the central sequence of the ritual, I view the preceding and concluding sequences as forming a ritual frame, in which the *shikimon* is set. This frame is not symmetrical, as the preparatory sequences are much longer than

Table 2.1. Standard ritual form of *kōshiki* in the Sōtō school

Ritual sequence	*Function*
Gāthā to Scattering Flowers (*Sange no ge* 散華偈) *Hymn of the Four Wisdoms* (*Shichisan* 四智讃)	Purification of the ritual space
Address of invitation (*kanjōmon* 勧請文) Offertory declaration (*saimon* 祭文) Communal obeisance (*sōrai no ge* 総礼偈)	Invitation to the objects of veneration
Four Shōmyō Melodies (*Shika hōyō* 四箇法要): – *Praise of the Thus Come One* (*Nyoraibai* 如来唄) – *Gāthā of Falling Flowers* (*Sange no ge* 散華偈) – *Gāthā of Sanskrit Sound* (*Bonnon no ge* 梵音偈) – *Gāthā of the Sounding Staff* (*Shakujō no ge* 錫杖偈)	Feast
Shikimon 式文	Lecture / praise / worship
Universal Transfer of Merit (*Fuekō* 普回向)	Transfer of merit

The pieces highlighted in gray constitute the ritual frame. (Because the Dharma words that accompany the incense offering [*nenkō hōgo*] are not included in the ritual handbooks, I do not list them among the ritual sequences for the invitation to the objects of veneration.)

the concluding transfer of merit. But like a picture frame enclosing a picture, the ritual frame of the *kōshiki* encloses the *shikimon*.

During the ritual, texts that were written for a particular *kōshiki* are vocalized along with standard liturgical pieces used in other rituals. The opening and closing parts—the purification of ritual space and transfer of merit—along with the third part of the symbolic feast, tend to be standard liturgical pieces. The second and fourth parts—the invitation and *shikimon*—address the objects of worship directly and therefore incorporate texts that were composed or adapted for the needs of a particular *kōshiki*. Consequently, we find an alternation between standard liturgical pieces, which belong to a shared ritual vocabulary of Japanese Buddhism, and newly composed texts or pieces that have been adapted for the *kōshiki*.

The beginning and the end of the ritual are mirrored: the monks assemble in a prescribed fashion at the back of the hall close to the doors, while the officiant waits in a back area to the right of the altar, from which he is the last to enter the central space. The ritual ends in the same way, but in the reverse order. So the frame enclosing the *shikimon* is set into a larger frame consisting of entering and exiting the hall.

Within the *kōshiki,* we also find smaller frames. Each ritual sequence is framed by a set of related actions: when the opening action is the cantor's gesture of invitation to the monks who will lead a certain liturgical piece and their movement into the middle of the hall, the closing action is the return of the monks to their original places. The first three pieces—*Gāthā to Scattering Flowers,* the *Hymn of the Four Wisdoms,* and the address of invitation—are all framed in this way. The closing action of a ritual sequence usually overlaps with the opening action of the next sequence, because the cantor times his movement to initiate the next invitation to coincide with the final prostration of the monks who have completed the last sequence. Hence ritual sequences are framed by corresponding actions, and these frames are coordinated with one another and set within the overall frame of the *kōshiki.*

Some sequences are tied together by the fact that they are initiated at the same time. For example, the cantor invites the officiant who reads the Dharma words and the monk who vocalizes the offertory declaration one after the other, and these sequences thus share the same starting point. Then, when the monk who read the offertory declaration performs a final prostration, the cantor begins to sing the communal obeisance, creating a transition to the next piece and tying the three pieces into a unit. Similarly, the performers of the *Four Shōmyō Melodies* are invited by the cantor at the same time, and the interlocking structure knits the four individual pieces and the sequences together.

The larger ritual structure, moreover, follows a guest-host paradigm. That is, the ritual is seen as a banquet or entertainment to which the deities (the guests) are invited by the performing clerics (the hosts). During the *Rakan kōshiki,* for example, the clerics chant the *Gāthā to Scattering Flowers* and the *Hymn of the Four Wisdoms* to prepare the ritual space. Then they vocalize the address of invitation and the offertory declaration to invite and welcome the objects of worship, and they sing a communal obeisance paying respect to the deities who are thought to have just arrived at the ceremonial site. The *Four Shōmyō Melodies* subsequently serve as a banquet of praise for the objects of worship. During the *shikimon* the clerics continue praising the objects of worship, expressing devotion while detailing their virtues. And at the close of the ritual, we can assume that the *Universal Transfer of Merit* serves to send off the objects of worship, although it does not state this aim.[76]

While the guest-host model is well known as an analytical framework for interpreting Shingon rituals, many other Buddhist rituals are also based on

76. Maekawa Bokushō ([2000–2001], 48) suggests that the transfer of merit functions to send off the objects of worship.

it.[77] For example, during the memorial services for Chan patriarchs and former abbots in Song China, the spirit of a patriarch or former abbot was invited to attend as the honored guest, and offerings of hot water, tea, and food were provided for him.[78] Another example is the sutra-chanting services performed at Sōtō temples. While the objects of worship might not be explicitly invited through a particular invocation, offerings for them are still provided and the merit is transferred to them at the end of the ritual.

Surprisingly, while the *shikimon*, the genre-defining text, was originally the main ritual sequence in a *kōshiki*, contemporary Sōtō monks do not always see that text as the center of the ritual. Officiants today rarely vocalize the entire text and usually choose to abbreviate it. What the clerics seem more interested in is the performance of the *shōmyō* pieces, which they sing with melodies, in contrast to the recitations that occur with few if any melodic inflections. The liturgical piece that often receives the most attention—and consequently feels like the musical climax of the ritual—is the *Praise of the Thus Come One*. When I took part in the creation of a new ritual that incorporated elements of a *kōshiki* while stopping short of being one, the Sōtō monks I worked with regarded the *Praise of the Thus Come One* as the high point, insisting that it had to be placed in a position to form the climax of the ritual. Likewise, when I mentioned that I was studying *kōshiki* to classmates at Komazawa University, who were all young Sōtō clerics, some immediately started half humming, half singing to vocalize the *Praise of the Thus Come One* in a halting way, as if to indicate that, to them, this piece was the most memorable part of the ritual. Thus, even though it was not intended to be the center of the ritual, it draws attention to itself due to its dramatic musical quality. That contemporary Sōtō clerics seem to value the *shōmyō* pieces more highly than the *shikimon* may also be reflected in their definition of *kōshiki* as any ritual featuring a high percentage of *shōmyō*. The results of my fieldwork suggest that the frame—the *shōmyō* pieces—do in fact receive more attention than the picture—the *shikimon*. We could even say that among contemporary Sōtō clerics there has been a reversal of figure and ground with the music of the ritual eclipsing its original logic.

Variations of the Basic Ritual Form

The structure of the *Rakan kōshiki* served as a model—or template—for other *kōshiki*.[79] Clerics composing a new *kōshiki* drew from a repertoire of ritual

77. For an analysis of the guest-host model in esoteric rituals, see Payne 1991, 88–89, and Sharf 2003. For an analysis of Myōe's *Shiza kōshiki* through the lens of the guest-host paradigm, see Mross 2016a, 110–111.

78. See Foulk and Sharf 1993, 193–194; and Foulk 1993, 173–174. Stevenson (2015) analyzes the structure of Buddhist rituals in Song China (mostly repentance rituals) and finds that they also began with invocations and offerings of incense and flowers, followed by veneration of the assembled deities, confession, transfer of merit, and profession of vows (318–390 and 443–448). Such rituals can be interpreted as instances of the guest-host paradigm as well.

79. For example, the afterword of the *Dōgen zenji kōshiki* states that the sitting order and

elements—or modules—derived from earlier *kōshiki*, and they usually inserted an offertory declaration and a newly composed or adapted *shikimon* into a standard ritual frame. This meant that the process of innovation was deeply rooted in a preexisting ritual tradition, yet that grounding did not preclude the possibility of introducing variations in the standard ritual frame as well. Such changes were evidence of a dynamic vitality in an otherwise static-seeming ritual form.

Of the nineteen Sōtō *kōshiki* that I studied, eleven follow a basic ritual structure derived from the *Rakan kōshiki* with some variations.[80] Most do not contain an address of invitation or Dharma words during the incense offering—perhaps unsurprising in that the latter goes unmentioned in the ritual handbooks for the *Rakan kōshiki* and seems to be a special addition by Sōjiji's monks.[81] According to the extant ritual handbooks, even when a *kōshiki* follows the standard ritual form, there can be variations depending on the particular needs of the temple or occasion. If necessary, the form can be simplified, or it can be elaborated by the addition of other ritual elements. A typical elaboration might be to add a sutra recitation to the *kōshiki*. For example, according to some ritual handbooks, the *Nehan kōshiki* at Sōjiji and Menzan's *Hōon kōshiki* ended with sutra recitations.[82] Adding a closing hymn might be another possibility, as the monks at Sōjiji may have done in the Tokugawa period by singing the *Final Praise* (*Gobai* 後唄)[83] at the end of their *kōshiki*.[84] In other circumstances, *kōshiki* could also be abbreviated, as in the

role allocation of the *kōshiki* follows the *Rakan kōshiki*. Inoue Gishin also used the same standard structure (with the exception of the invitation) in the two new *kōshiki* he recently composed (*Hakusan kōshiki* and *Jōyō daishi kōshiki*). He considers the structure without the address of invitation to be the representative form of *kōshiki* (Inoue 2000, 9r, 12v–13r).

80. The eleven *kōshiki* are the *Nehan kōshiki, Daruma kōshiki, Dōgen zenji kōshiki,* Menzan's *Hōon kōshiki,* Inoue's *Jōyō daishi kōshiki, Butsuji kōshiki, Dentō kōshiki, Jizō kōshiki, Hakusan kōshiki, Hokke kōshiki,* and *Anan kōshiki.*

81. Only two other Sōtō *kōshiki,* the *Daihannya kōshiki* and the *Myōken kōshiki,* contain an invitation. Interestingly, these *kōshiki* diverge from the standard form.

82. According to the *San kōshiki narabini hōyō,* written in Bunka 10 (1813) at Sōjiji, the monks read the *Sutra of the Teachings Left by the Buddha* (*Yiyao jing*) and the chapter *Lifespan of the Buddha* (*Juryōbon* 寿量品) of the *Lotus Sutra* before the *Universal Transfer of Merit* during the *Nehan kōshiki.* As for Menzan's *Hōon kōshiki,* the clerics had the option to recite the chapter *Peace and Contentment* (*Anrakugyōbon* 安楽行品) of the *Lotus Sutra* at the end of the ritual; see, for example, *Jōyō daishi Hōon kōshiki* in ZSZ 2: 732.

83. The *Final Praise,* usually vocalized at the end of a ritual, praises the buddha(s) for abiding undefiled in this world. In the Sōtō school, it is also called *Sho sekai* (*no*) *bon* 処世界梵 (Hymn of abiding in this world), as the hymn begins with these words. Sōtō monks have vocalized it during the *Grand Precepts Meeting* and after the morning meal since Dōgen's time; see the *Shōbōgenzō* fascicle *Jukai* 受戒 (Receiving the precepts), DZO 1: 621; DZZ 2: 299; and T 82: 307c26; and *Fushuku hanpō* 赴粥飯法 (Procedures for taking food), DZO 2: 356; DZZ 6: 70; and T 82: 329a23–24. Today, Sōtō clerics do not sing this piece during *kōshiki* anymore, and it seems to have been a rare case in premodern times. For a translation of this verse, see Ichimura 1994, 10.

84. No extant handbook indicates the ritual structure of *kōshiki* performed at Sōjiji in the Tokugawa period. But the ritual handbooks used for *kōshiki* at Sōjiji include the *Final Praise,* and therefore I suspect that monks at Sōjiji sang this liturgical piece; see *Kada narabini hōyō* and *San kōshiki narabini hōyō.*

performance of the *Nehan kōshiki* and *Daruma kōshiki* at Yōmeiji 永明寺 in Shimane prefecture where monks omitted the *Hymn of the Four Wisdoms, Praise of the Thus Come One,* and possibly the *San-Bon-Shaku.* By omitting these five chants, the form of the ritual became relatively simple, consisting of the *Gāthā to Scattering Flowers,* the offertory declaration, the communal obeisance, the *shikimon* (including the respective verses), and the *Universal Transfer of Merit.*[85]

A more complex kind of variation occurred when *kōshiki* deviated in more substantial ways from the standard ritual structure. In these cases, important liturgical texts, taken from well-established rituals related to the object of worship, were incorporated to align the *kōshiki* more closely with its actual object of worship. The modularity that allowed these texts to be integrated into a *kōshiki* proved vital for the design of new rituals.

Six of the *kōshiki* I studied do not adhere to the standard ritual structure of Sōtō *kōshiki.* In Menzan's *Daihannya kōshiki,* for example, the monks sing the piece *Gāthā of Praising Incense* (*Kōsan no ge* 香讃偈) before the invitation and omit the *Praise of the Thus Come One* and *San-Bon-Shaku.* After the *shikimon,* the monks recite the *Heart Sutra* and perform a rolling reading of the *Great Sutra on the Perfection of Wisdom* before ending with a *dhāraṇī* and a special transfer of merit. In other words, for a *kōshiki* on the *Great Sutra on the Perfection of Wisdom,* Menzan fused elements of a *kōshiki* with a rolling reading of that sutra, a ritual that was widely performed in Japanese Buddhism.[86] Similarly, the author of the *Myōken kōshiki* omitted the *Praise of the Thus Come One* and *San-Bon-Shaku* while adding an invocation, sutra readings, and *dhāraṇī* before the *shikimon.* He also added a votive text and the *Final Praise* at the end of the ritual.

A contrasting example is the *Kannon kōshiki,* edited by Mugaku Guzen, which was simplified. Mugaku decided to omit the *Hymn of the Four Wisdoms,* offertory declaration, and *San-Bon-Shaku,* using the *Ten Great Vows* [*of Kannon*] (*Jū daiganmon* 十大願文) instead. He also replaced the *Praise of the Thus Come One* with the *Verse of the Praise of the Thus Come One.* Then, after the *Universal Transfer of Merit,* he added a recitation of the *Kannon Sutra* with an optional circumambulation of the hall and a final *Transfer of Merit for the Offerings to the Great Kannon* (*Kannon daishi jōgu ekō* 観音大士上供回向).[87]

Table 2.2 shows at a glance the structural innovations of the six *kōshiki* that deviate from the standard ritual structure of the *Rakan kōshiki.* It reveals that underlying the many variations is a common substrate consisting of a communal obeisance, *shikimon,* and transfer of merit. The communal obeisance, a verse that expresses veneration for the object(s) of worship, is selected for each *kōshiki* and can differ accordingly, but there are a few verses that are

85. *Kakuōzan Yōmeizenji nai shingi* (Hōei 7, 1710).

86. The oldest extant edition of the *Daihannya kōshiki* was edited in Meiwa 6 (1769) and printed in Anei 2 (1773). For a *kundoku,* see Shiina and Sakauchi 2010.

87. A woodblock print edition of the *Kannon kōshiki* from Meiji 4 (1871) is in the Komazawa University Library. For a typographical reprint, see Watarai 1986.

Table 2.2. Comparison of the *Rakan kōshiki* and *kōshiki* that deviate from its ritual form

Rakan kōshiki	*Daihannya kōshiki*	*Myōken kōshiki*	*Eihei shoso Dōgen zenji kōshiki*	*Kannon kōshiki*	*Busshōe kōshiki*	*Kasekison nōke kōshiki*
Gāthā to Scattering Flowers	*Gāthā to Scattering Flowers*	*Gāthā to Scattering Flowers*	Communal obeisance	*Gāthā to Scattering Flowers*		
	Gāthā of Praising Incense	Invocation (*keibyaku* 啓白)	*Gāthā to Scattering Flowers*	*Ten Great Vows [of Kannon]*		
Hymn of the Four Wisdoms		*Hymn of the Four Wisdoms*	*Hymn of the Four Wisdoms*			
Invitation	Invitation	Invitation				
Offertory declaration	Offertory declaration	Offertory declaration	Offertory declaration			
Communal obeisance	Communal obeisance	Communal obeisance		Communal obeisance	Communal obeisance	Communal obeisance
		Heart Sutra, Marvelously Beneficial Disaster Preventing Dhāraṇī, Dhāraṇī of Myōken, other *dhāraṇī, Shingon of Universal Offerings*				

(*continued*)

Table 2.2. Comparison of the *Rakan kōshiki* and *kōshiki* that deviate from its ritual form (*continued*)

Rakan kōshiki	*Daihannya kōshiki*	*Myōken kōshiki*	*Eihei shoso Dōgen zenji kōshiki*	*Kannon kōshiki*	*Busshōe kōshiki*	*Kasekison nōke kōshiki*
Praise of the Thus Come One			*Praise of the Thus Come One*	*Praise of the Thus Come One*	*Praise of the Thus Come One*	
San-Bon-Shaku			*San-Bon-Shaku*		*Gāthā to Scattering Flowers*	
Shikimon	*Shikimon*	*Shikimon*	*Shikimon*	*Shikimon*	*Shikimon*	*Shikimon*
	Heart Sutra		"Ease in Practice" chapter of the *Lotus Sutra*			*Dhāraṇī*, words of worship
	Rolling reading of the *Great Sutra on the Perfection of Wisdom*					
	Disaster Preventing Dhāraṇī					
Universal Transfer of Merit	Transfer of merit	*Universal Transfer of Merit*	*Universal Transfer of Merit*	*Universal Transfer of Merit*	*Universal Transfer of Merit*	*Universal Transfer of Merit*

	Votive text (*ganmon* 願文)		Verses of the *Kannon Sutra*	Section for protector deities (*jinbun* 神分)	Text for arousing the aspiration for enlightenment (*bodaishin* 菩提心)
	Final praise (*Gobai* 後貝)		*Transfer of merit for offerings to the Great Kannon*	Transfer of merit	

I used the following texts for comparison:

- *Tōjō Rakan kōshiki* (1756); *Rakan kuyōshiki* (ZSZ 2: 787–803); *Shōwa kaitei Rakan kōshiki* (1966).
- *Daihannya kōshiki* (1773).
- *Myōken kōshikibon* (1780); *Myōken kōshikibon zen* (n.d.).
- *Eihei shoso Dōgen zenji kōshiki* (1707).
- *Kannon kōshiki* (1871), Komazawa University.
- *Busshōe kōshiki* (1751; 1865); *Busshōe ryaku kōshiki* (1886; n.d.). (However, there is one edition in the archive of the Research Institute for Japanese Music Historiography at Ueno Gakuen University produced in 1894 that does follow the standard ritual form.)
- *Kasekison nōke kōshiki* (1864).

Although the *Yakushi kōshiki* in the archive of Yōmeiji probably differed from the standard form, it is not included in this table because the ritual handbook does not clearly outline its ritual form.

often used for this purpose. A *shikimon,* as the genre-defining text, is required in all *kōshiki.* Since it is customary for all Buddhist rituals to transfer the merit produced through the performance of the ritual, all *kōshiki* end with a transfer of merit. In other words, the communal obeisance, *shikimon,* and transfer of merit are the basic elements shared by all *kōshiki,* and the variations in structure shown in the table illustrate the modularity, fluidity, and interrituality of this ritual genre.

Modules in the *Rakan kōshiki*

The preceding sections have shown that the ability of clerics to create a ritual frame or structure for *kōshiki* out of selected liturgical pieces depended on a modularity that was vital in the invention of rituals. In the actual performance of *kōshiki,* we find the deployment not only of textual modules but of sonic, kinetic, and material ones as well. This section introduces the multiple dimensions in which the complex modularity of Sōtō *kōshiki* plays out in performance.

Many of the elements introduced below appear in other rituals besides *kōshiki* and thus are part of the embodied knowledge that clerics acquire during their training. The interrituality of these building blocks, both within the Sōtō repertoire of rituals and across the Japanese Buddhist traditions, enables Sōtō clerics to perform a wide range of rituals without extensive rehearsals.

Textual Modules

While *kōshiki* authors have a high degree of freedom in the composition of a *shikimon* and the selection of complementary liturgical pieces, the performers do not. They cannot utter any words spontaneously, and all texts are fixed. An officiant might choose to abbreviate the *shikimon,* but he does not change its words. Rituals, as Roy Rappaport suggested, are "performances of more or less invariant sequences of formal acts and utterances, not entirely encoded by the performers."[88] Such utterances function as textual modules. Some are relatively short, whereas others are more extensive and may consist of entire liturgical pieces.

When a monk creates a new *kōshiki,* he composes a new *shikimon* and maybe an offertory declaration. Texts in these liturgical genres use certain phrases at particular junctures—for example, the offertory declaration usually ends with a phrase asking the objects of worship to accept the offerings. Or in the thematic sections of a *shikimon,* phrases like "first / second / third, I explain . . ." and "let us all perform a prostration and sing a verse" appear at the beginning and end of each section. Moreover, if an author chooses to include a passage from a sutra, he also adds connecting sentences. All of these formulaic phrases are textual modules that a *kōshiki* author has at his command.

Additionally, the ritual frame into which a *kōshiki* author sets his *shikimon* and offertory declaration consists of standard liturgical pieces and further

88. Rappaport 1999, 24.

employs shorter common phrases such as the patterns used in the address of invitation or the words of worship sung after certain verses, many of which are learned by the clerics in other rituals or *kōshiki.* All of these textual passages can be regarded as building blocks or modules that an author selects for a new ritual, which consequently is highly intertextual.

Acoustic Modules

Sounds and music, while often overlooked in ritual studies, play a central role in many Buddhist ceremonies. In *kōshiki,* the texts may be foundational in the invention of a new ritual, but they are only realized in the vocalization that takes place during the performance. That is, ritual languages "even when written, remain tacitly sonic."[89] Sōtō monks usually speak of "*kōshiki shōmyō*" when they talk about these rituals, acknowledging music as a vital component of *kōshiki.*

Acoustic modules fall into two categories. The first is vocal music: most pieces are performed with melodies, and the clerics vocalize the texts using melodic inflections or patterns. Each melodic pattern has a name, clearly demarcating it from other patterns, and when combined they form the melody of a piece.

The second category comprises the sounds of the musical instruments. These specific sounds signal the beginning of a piece or a line of verse and coordinate physical movements. They also frame liturgical pieces or sequences. Most of the patterned sounds—for example, the strikes of the handbell to coordinate prostrations—are similarly used in other rituals and thus are very familiar to the clerics, accentuating the interrituality of *kōshiki.* Moreover, the sounds of the instruments not only structure the ritual but give it a rhythm: "By demarcating a beginning, ending, transition, or high point, sounds can lay out a narrative track even when they don't contain narratives."[90] The musical soundscape of *kōshiki* will be studied in detail in the next chapter.

Kinetic Modules

Conduct in a Sōtō monastery is regulated by precisely executed postures, gestures, and movements. This concentration on etiquette is a core doctrine of Sōtō Zen, often expressed in the proverb: "Proper conduct is the Buddha Dharma; etiquette is the principle of our school" (*igi soku buppō, sahō kore shūshi* 威儀即仏法、作法是宗旨).[91] Novices learn the proper forms of bodily

89. Grimes 2014, 275.

90. Grimes 2014, 274.

91. The origins of this proverb are unknown, but it was likely created in the late Meiji era to describe the detailed etiquette that Dōgen promotes in his writings. Dōgen himself does not use this phrase. The second part is said to be based on a passage in the *Shōbōgenzō* fascicle *Senjō* 洗浄 (Washing and purifying), in which Dōgen states: "Etiquette is the principle of our school, attaining the way is etiquette" (*sahō kore shūshi nari, tokudō kore sahō nari* 作法これ宗旨なり、得道これ作法なり); see DZO 1: 466; DZZ 2: 81; and T 82: 30a19–20. Ishihara Jōmyō (2020, 179), who studied the origins of this proverb, found the earliest recorded instance in a report of a Sōtō leadership meeting, published in 1915 in the *Sōtōshūhō* 曹洞宗報.

conduct during their training, and the exact execution of these forms is drilled over and over again. As a result, the performance of these postures, gestures, and movements is integral to the deeply internalized embodied knowledge that Sōtō clerics acquire.[92] This same knowledge informs *kōshiki* as the kinetic modules employed in the ritual. Some convey important messages, functioning "as a second language articulated simultaneously alongside of words."[93] Others frame ritual sequences and can be interpreted as punctuation marks (periods, colons, or commas) that create a pulse on which the ritual unfolds.

Sitting and hand postures follow the common etiquette of ritualized actions in the Sōtō school. In the basic sitting posture, the monks kneel while resting the buttocks on their heels (*seiza* 正坐). All other sitting postures indicate the special character of a certain liturgical piece or sequence. For example, the monks leading the address of invitation and the *Praise of the Thus Come One* sit in lotus position, the posture of seated meditation, whereas the monk who recites the offertory declaration takes an upright kneeling posture. In his explanations of *kōshiki,* Inoue Gishin suggests that sitting in lotus position during the *Praise of the Thus Come One* underscores the high skill that is necessary to perform this piece well. The offertory declaration is an expression of yearning for the arrival of the objects of veneration at the ceremonial place, so upright kneeling declares one's veneration. He points out, too, that the *Praise of the Thus Come One* and the offertory declaration are traditionally vocalized by senior monks, and the *San-Bon-Shaku* is usually led by young monks while standing. Thus the sitting (or standing) postures and the role allocation reflect the temple hierarchy. He further remarks that the changes in sitting posture, which usually does not happen in other rituals, add color to the ritual.[94] The hand postures of the monks are also prescribed. Either they join their palms together in front of their chests (*gasshō* 合唱), or they place the left hand on top of the right hand, palms up on their lap with the tips of their thumbs lightly touching (*hokkaijō in* 法界定印), or they hold the ritual handbook in front of their eyes in a specified way.

The numerous prostrations performed by the monks during the ritual express deep respect and devotion to the object of worship and give additional weight to the statements vocalized. When the monks invite the arhats one by one to appear at the ceremonial site, they perform a prostration after each invocation. They also perform at least one prostration whenever they sing words of worship. Thus they convey the meaning of their words not only vocally but also physically.[95]

Other ritual actions are also minutely prescribed, such as how to enter

---

92. The *Shōwa kaitei Sōtōshū gyōji kihan,* the current ritual manual of the Sōtō school, includes a section on bodily etiquette, bows, prostrations, and sitting positions (391–395). For an English translation, see Foulk 2010a, 497–503.

93. Grimes 2010, 77.

94. Inoue 2000, 21r, 30v–31r.

95. Tambiah (1979, 130–142) argued that the transmission of the same message on differ-

the central area of the hall, how to walk to reach an assigned place, how to bow in greeting, how to circumambulate the hall, and how to deliver offerings. Kinetic modules, as noted above, enclose the ritual as a whole, as well as all ritual sequences. Framing the entire ritual is a distinctive style of entering and exiting the hall, and ritual sequences are framed by the cantor's gesture of invitation to perform a particular ritual function and by the monks' return to their places at the end of the sequence. Using the metaphor of punctuation marks, one could interpret these actions as semicolons or periods marking the end of a message that is conveyed, and the beginning of another.

Material Modules

Another type of module is formed by the objects and materials used in the ritual. Some traditions do not sacralize their ritual objects and instead try to minimize costs. The iconoclastic discourse found in some records of Chan encounters might suggest that Zen monks would devalue icons and ritual objects. However, during my fieldwork, I witnessed how clerics at Sōjiji are accustomed to using highly refined materials that display their temple's status to visitors and guests, and how other wealthy temples openly show off their new acquisitions.[96] During the *kōshiki,* material modules fulfill various functions, some vital to the particular ritual, others needed to bring off the performance, and still others part of clerical attire in general.

The most important consideration is that the object of worship must be made present through an image. If there is none present in the hall, images are prepared. In the case of the *Rakan kōshiki,* sixteen hanging scrolls depicting the arhats are usually suspended in the center of the hall beside or behind the altar area. In the *Nehan kōshiki,* which is concerned with the Buddha's entry into nirvāṇa and is sometimes performed during his annual memorial service, a scroll depicting the scene of the Buddha's last night is hung as the central image in the hall, and the participants in the ritual gaze at it while listening to the recitation of the officiant.

Texts are both heard and handled during the ritual. They are present not only as a vocalized text, but also as material objects in the form of printed books and manuscripts. All monks use a ritual handbook; even when they do not vocalize a particular text themselves, they hold the ritual handbook in front of their eyes and read along.[97] The handbooks they use are concertina-fold booklets, the standard format for sutra books used in Buddhist rituals. The address of invitation and the offertory declaration are produced as handscrolls, however, and are put on the table in front of the altar in a special envelope. Both the format of these texts and their placement in ceremonial envelopes underscore the special character of these liturgical pieces.

---

ent channels can be seen in various rituals and that this redundancy helps to support ritual efficacy.

96. On Zen and material culture, see Winfield and Heine 2017.

97. The only exception is the two monks who vocalize the *Hymn of the Four Wisdoms* by heart.

There are other materials that fulfill essential functions during the ritual. To invite the objects of veneration to the ritual space, implements such as the water vessel and stick for sprinkling water, the paper flowers that are scattered, and the incense holder are used at the beginning of the ritual to purify and prepare the ritual space. Offerings to welcome the objects of worship, such as incense, tea, sweets, and rice, are provided in special vessels. The particular offerings made and their manner of delivery will be familiar to the monks who place them on the altar, since offerings similar to those in the *Rakan kōshiki* are provided in other Sōtō rituals as well. Also, the room is decorated. Flowers and candles are set up on the altar, and an open vessel for offering incense sticks is put on the table in front of the altar. Some of the other decorations, however, are permanent fixtures in the hall that do not need to be set up beforehand.

In addition to regular articles of attire, such as clerical robes, sitting clothes, and other accessories, the monks also carry a sitting cloth on which they sit in rituals. The officiant holds a scepter staff (*nyoi* 如意) to signify his status (see fig. 2.9),[98] and he wears red shoes at the beginning and end of the ritual when he walks to the back of the central area where the monks wait and then back to the right side of the hall. His ceremonial place is also specially set up: he sits in front of a small table on which a candle and flowers have been prepared. In the middle of the table is a special bookstand, which is sometimes covered with fine fabric, and a small bell is placed to its right, which he plays at the beginning of all sections during the *shikimon* (see fig. 2.13). Moreover, while the other monks spread their sitting cloths directly on the floor, the officiant has a mat under his sitting cloth as a further sign of his status.

Ritual paraphernalia include small tables set up for the monks sitting in the central area of the hall, on which round golden trays with five-colored cords are sometimes placed. These trays are only brought out on special occasions, such as when the abbot of Sōjiji serves as the officiant in an important ritual. Common implements that aid a successful performance of the ritual include a sutra stand for the cantor and the singers of the *Praise of the Thus Come One,* microphones, and sitting cushions for the monks who perform the *Praise of the Thus Come One* and the address of invitation.

Ritual sequences and the larger structures of the ritual fuse the textual, acoustic, kinetic, and material modules, forming new wholes that exceed the sum of their parts. Additionally, some central ritual objects are complex in themselves, occupying two or more dimensions: Liturgical texts, for example, are simultaneously present as linguistic entities, sound (linguistic patterns vocalized with or without melodies), and material objects (the books and handscrolls present in the ritual). Moreover, since the ritual handbook contains procedural directions as well as liturgical texts, which are then embodied or put to action in the ritual, we can say that the text is also realized kineti-

98. At Sōjiji, usually the officiant holds a scepter staff (*nyoi*), but at a few other temples, such as Eiheiji and Eiheiji's satellite temple in Tokyo, the officiant holds a fly-whisk (*hossu* 払子). For a discussion of Zen staffs, see Heine 2017.

cally. Musical instruments are another example. They are objects in themselves, but it is their sound in the acoustic dimension that is essential, and they are played by monks moving their bodies in prescribed ways. Probably the most vivid example is the cymbal playing, which the monks perform with carefully choreographed movements. And of course the music notation in the texts makes the musical instruments present in the form of text.

The *Rakan kōshiki* on the Move

The *Rakan kōshiki,* credited to Dōgen and performed by Keizan, was adopted and performed by monks in the Rinzai and Shingon schools, providing a strong basis for comparison of the ritual frames used in different traditions. Apart from minor variants, the *shikimon* and the offertory declaration are the same in the three schools, reflecting a pan-sectarian understanding of arhat veneration. However, the ritual structure in which the common elements are held differs according to the school, for each developed its own unique way of performing *kōshiki.* The following comparison, it should be noted, is based on ritual manuals from different time periods, but that latitude does not vitiate the observation that the separate identities of the schools are reflected in the different ritual frames they developed.

The *Rakan kōshiki* in the Rinzai School

The origins of this *kōshiki* in the Rinzai school are unclear, but we know that Yōsai (or Eisai, 1141–1215), the so-called founder of Rinzai Zen in Japan, annually performed an arhat ceremony in the first month of the year.[99] At Tōfukuji 東福寺, the influential Rinzai temple in Kyoto founded in Katei 2 (1236), monks have performed arhat rituals since the late thirteenth century, but we do not know when a *Rakan kōshiki* was first performed at a Rinzai temple or who might have introduced it.[100] The only two ritual handbooks that I was able to study were produced by the print shop Baiyōshoin 貝葉書院 in Kyoto for Myōshinji 妙心寺 (Kyoto), another major Rinzai monastery (fig. 2.14), and Tōfukuji.[101] At the latter temple, the *Rakan kōshiki* is still performed

99. *Kōzen gokoku ron,* T 80: 15a12, 15a15.

100. The earliest record of an arhat ceremony at Tōfukuji is included in *Kuge Kantō ōdanna kitō tō chūshin bun* 公家関東大檀那御祈祷等注進文, written by Enni Ben'en 円爾弁円 (1202–1280) in Kōan 3 (1280). This text states that the monks at Tōfukuji performed an arhat ceremony on the first day of every month (Shiraishi 1930, 139). According to the *Enichi Tōfukuzenji gyōrei kihō* 慧日山東福禅寺行令規法, a monastic code of Tōfukuji written in Bunpō 2 (1318), the monks at Tōfukuji performed an arhat ceremony in the first seven days of the new year as a prayer (*kitō* 祈祷) for the year and on the first day of the other months (Ozaki 1999b, 58–60). Although these sources provide evidence of the early performance of arhat rituals at Tōfukuji, we do not know whether the monks performed a *kōshiki* or not. Interestingly, a manuscript in the archive of Zōfukuin on Mt. Kōya states that the author of this *Rakan kōshiki* would be Enni (*Shōketsu sho* 聲决書, n.d., Zōfukuin). However, I have not come across any other attribution of this *kōshiki* to Enni.

101. *Meiji shinkoku Rakan kōshiki* (Myōshinji-ban), originally edited in Ansei 6 (1823), recarved in the Meiji era; and *Kaisei Rakan kōshiki* (Tōfukuji-ban), n.d.

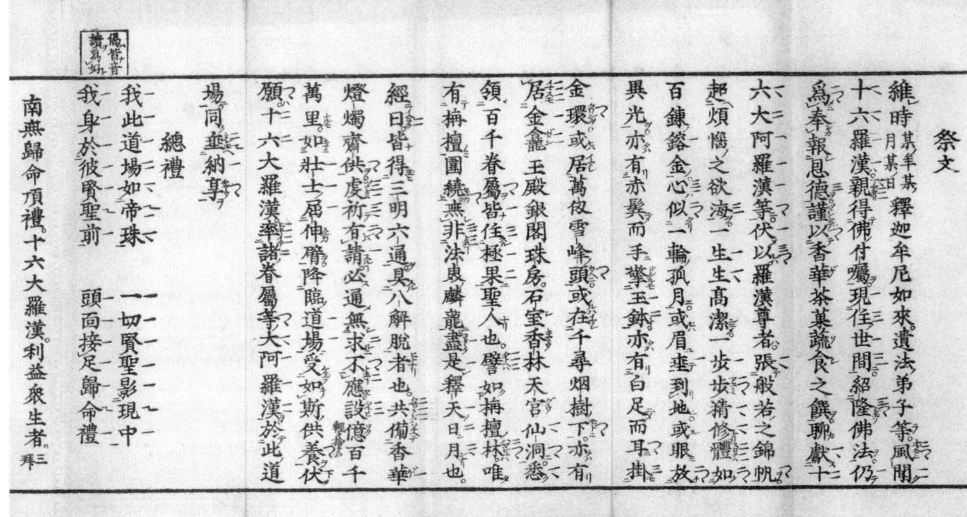

祭文

維時某年某月某日釋迦牟尼如來遺法弟子等風聞
十六羅漢親得佛付囑現住世間紹隆佛法仍
為奉報恩德謹以香華茶菓蔬食之饌聊獻十
六大阿羅漢等伏以羅漢尊者張般若之錦帆
超煩惱之欲海一生一生高潔一步一步精修體如
百錬鎔金心似一輪孤月或眉垂到地或眼放
異光亦有赤髮而手擎玉鉢亦有白足而耳掛
金環或居萬仞雪峰頭或在千尋烟樹下亦有
居金龕玉殿銀閣珠房石室香林天宮仙洞悉
領百千眷屬皆住極果聖人也譬如栴檀林唯
有栴檀圍繞無非法鳳麟龍盡是釋天日月也
經日皆得三明六通具八解脫者也共備香華
燈燭齋供虔祈有請必通無求不應設億百千
萬里如壯士屈伸臂降臨道場受如斯供養伏
願十六大羅漢率諸眷屬等大阿羅漢於此道
場同垂納享

總禮

偈皆音讀爲好

我此道場如帝珠　一切賢聖影現中
我身於彼賢聖前　頭面接足歸命禮

南無歸命頂禮十六大羅漢利益衆生者　拜三

Figure 2.14. *Meiji shinkoku Rakan kōshiki,* Myōshinji. Edited in 1823; woodblock recarved in the Meiji era. This excerpt shows the offertory declaration and communal obeisance. The markings to the right of the Chinese characters indicate the melodic inflections. Collection of the author.

annually during the first three days of the year. The Myōshinji version was originally edited in Ansei 6 (1823), but the corresponding date for the Tōfukuji version is not known. Nevertheless, according to both ritual handbooks, the ritual form of the *kōshiki* was as follows:

Invitation
Offertory declaration
Communal obeisance
Shikimon[102]
Universal Transfer of Merit

At first sight, it is already clear that this structure is much simpler than its counterpart in the Sōtō school: the Rinzai *Rakan kōshiki* contains fewer liturgical pieces. The same structure is outlined in both handbooks, but the texts of the invitation differ, with the Myōshinji version being similar to the Sōtō text.[103] The offertory declaration, the communal obeisance, and the *shikimon*

102. The *shikimon* is not called *shikimon* in the Rinzai school. According to the Tōfukuji ritual handbook, it was called *kōshiki,* and in the Myōshinji handbook it was entitled "*hyōbyaku.*" However, for ease of comparison, I have adopted the Sōtō terminology here.

103. The Tōfukuji version uses a different pattern for the invitation, starting each invocation with *isshin bujō namu* 一心奉請南無 (Single-mindedly, we respectfully pay homage to…)

are more or less identical. The Rinzai *kōshiki* also ends with the *Universal Transfer of Merit* in the same way as the *kōshiki* of the Shingon and Sōtō schools.[104] During the *Rakan kōshiki* performed at Tōfukuji that I attended in 2010, the monks additionally performed a rolling reading of the *Great Sutra on the Perfection of Wisdom* after the *kōshiki*.

The *Rakan kōshiki* in the Rinzai school also differs from its counterparts in the Sōtō and Shingon schools in its musical performance. In general, Rinzai monks do not sing elaborate melodies or pieces with many melodic inflections. Nonetheless, as the musical notation in the ritual handbooks indicates, they vocalize the offertory declaration with a few melodic inflections. In addition, the communal obeisance and the verses of the *shikimon* contain a musical notation that consists mainly of straight lines, which most likely indicate a sustained tone. Therefore, I assume that the verses were sung mostly on one pitch with very limited melodic variation. In sum, the limited melodic realizations of the texts reflect the fact that the Rinzai school does not have an extensive *shōmyō* repertoire.

The *Rakan kōshiki* in the Shingon School

Monks on Mt. Kōya, the center of the Nanzan Shin school 南山進流 of Shingon *shōmyō*, also performed the *Rakan kōshiki*.[105] They called it *Sakujitsu Rakan kōshiki* 朔日羅漢講式 (*Kōshiki* for the arhats on the first day of the year), as they usually performed it on that day. Extant manuscripts and woodblock prints suggest that they performed it from the Muromachi until the Tokugawa period.[106] Unfortunately, we do not know when it was first performed at Mt.

instead of *kimyō chōrai*..., as in the Myōshinji and Sōtō versions. The Myōshinji and Sōtō texts also state the place where the respective arhat dwells and how many arhats are in his entourage, details that the Tōfukuji version omits. Furthermore, the objects of worship and their order differ slightly in the different versions. The Tōfukuji version first addresses the bodhisattvas Mañjuśrī (J. Monjū) and Samantabhadra (J. Fugen), who are often depicted as Śākyamuni's attendants, and thereafter addresses the ten great disciples of the Buddha, who are not invoked in the other versions, and then the Sixteen Arhats. These different forms of the invitation indicate a ritual change that cannot yet be accounted for but also show that similar liturgical texts can fulfill the same function. These differences further suggest that lineage identity can be expressed by slight variations in the texts of shared rituals.

104. The *shikimon* of the Myōshinji version and the Tōfukuji version differ to a certain extent. Interestingly, the Myōshinji version is closer to Menzan's edition of the *Rakan kōshiki*, which the editor of the Myōshinji version in his afterword mentions having consulted.

105. For a detailed study and comparison of the Shingon school's *shikimon* with the Sōtō school version, see Mross 2013c.

106. The *Kōyasan kōshikishū* contains the following manuscripts of the *shikimon* of the *Sakujitsu Rakan kōshiki* (in chronological order): 四1 (Muromachi period); 四2 (Tenbun 6, 1537); 四53 (Muromachi period); 四3 (Genroku 14, 1701); 四4 (Tokugawa period); 四6 (Kanpō 3, 1743); 四49 (Kansei 1, 1789); and 四5 (Tokugawa period). Other ritual manuscripts from the Tokugawa period provide information for the assembly in how to perform this ritual: *Rakan kō hossoku* (around 1811); *Shokō sahō shū* (Manji 4 [1661], printed on Mt. Kōya); *Shōketsu sho* (n.d.); *Jūnigatsu shōmyō kō yakusha hossoku* (n.d.); and *Kōgon shūyō shū* (Tenpō 5, 1834).

Kōya or who introduced the ritual text to this branch of the Shingon school. Today, Shingon monks no longer perform this *kōshiki.*

One of the ritual manuals for the *Rakan kōshiki* printed on Mt. Kōya in the Tokugawa period was the *Rakan kō hossoku,* edited in or before Bunka 8 (1811) (fig. 2.15). Because it is the only ritual handbook that I was able to find that contains all the texts vocalized by the assembly, I use it here to analyze the ritual form. According to this handbook, the form of the *Rakan kōshiki* on Mt. Kōya was as follows:

Invitation[107]
Hymns for the Delivery of Offerings:[108]
  Sanskrit Hymn of the Four Wisdoms (*Shichi no bongo* 四智梵語)[109]
  Sanskrit Hymn of Mahāvairocana (*Shinryaku no bongo* 心略梵語)[110]
  Hymn of Vajrakarma (*Kongōgō* 金剛業)[111]
Offertory Declaration
Communal Obeisance
Four Shōmyō Melodies:
  Praise of the Thus Come One
  Gāthā of Falling Flowers
  Gāthā of Sanskrit Sound
  Gāthā of the Sounding Staff

---

107. The address of invitation in the Shingon school is very similar to the one in the Sōtō school, but the order of the words is slightly different. Furthermore, the Sōtō version also addresses Ānanda, whereas the Shingon version invokes Kūkai, the founder of Japanese Shingon Buddhism. Consequently, the Shingon's address of invitation became more representative of the school.

108. The following three *shōmyō* pieces are sung during the delivery of offerings to the objects of veneration. Therefore, this ritual sequence is called "delivery of offerings" (*tengu* 伝供, also read as *dengu*).

109. This piece, also called *Shichi no bongo san* 四智梵語讃, is the same as the *Hymn of the Four Wisdoms* in the Sōtō school. In the Shingon school, two versions of the *Hymn of the Four Wisdoms* exist: one is a transliteration called *Shichi no bongo,* which is sung here, and the other is a Chinese translation called *Shichi no kango* 四智漢語 (Chinese hymn of the four wisdoms).

110. This chant praises Mahāvairocana (J. Dainichi 大日) of the womb realm and is therefore also known under the title *Dainichi san* 大日讃. Like *Shichisan,* this chant was originally a śloka and was composed in seventh-century India. Again, two versions exist: a transliteration (*Shinryaku no bongo*) and a translation into Chinese (*Shinryaku no kango* 心略漢語). As Nelson explains, "The term *shinryaku* may be translated as 'abbreviation of the heart,' and refers to the fact that the text of this *san* is an abbreviation of a longer text which is 32 verses in length" (1998, 488). For a translation, see Nelson 1998, 489.

111. The full title of this *shōmyō* piece is *Kongōgō bosatsu san* 金剛業菩薩讃 (Hymn of the bodhisattva Vajrakarma). It is a praise of the bodhisattva Vajrakarma, who dwells in the north. Therefore, this chant is also called *Hymn of the North* (*Hoppō no san* 北方讃). It is a Sanskrit piece and was originally a śloka, composed in seventh-century India. The *Hymn of Vajrakarma* is also used as a praise of the Buddha; see Arai K. 2008, 27, and *Shōmyō jiten,* 245.

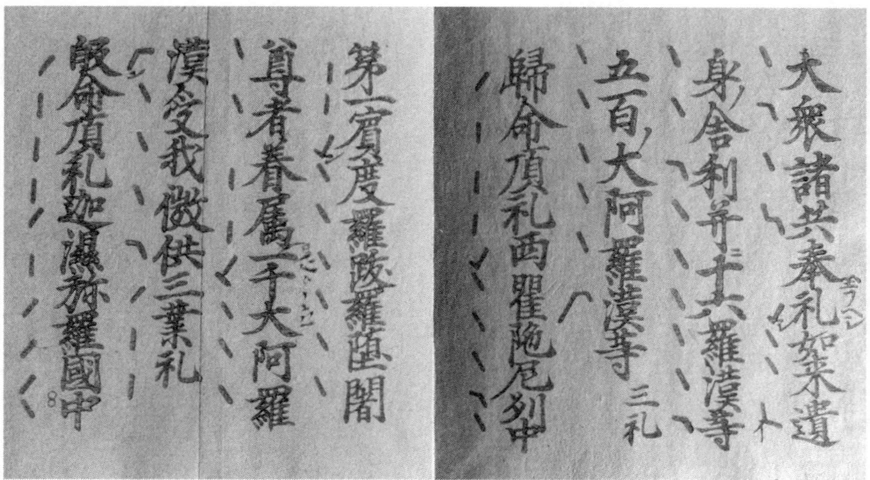

大衆諸共奉礼如来遺
身舎利并十六羅漢等
五百大阿羅漢等 三礼
帰命頂礼西瞿陀尼洲中
第一賓度羅跋羅堕闍
尊者眷属一千大阿羅
漢受我微供三業礼
帰命頂礼迦湿弥羅国中

Figure 2.15. *Rakan kō hossoku,* printed at Mt. Kōya (1811?). This excerpt shows the invitation (*kanjō*) at the beginning of the ritual. The lines to the left of the Chinese characters indicate the melodies of the chant. Courtesy of East Asia Library, Stanford University. Used with permission.

Shikimon[112]
Universal Transfer of Merit[113]
Praise of Relics (*Shari rai* 舎利礼)[114]

This structure is more complex than the ritual form in the other two schools. However, this brief overview also shows that the Shingon version shares more similarities with the Sōtō than with the Rinzai version. Impor-

112. Shingon clerics usually call the *shikimon kōshiki.* However, for ease of comparison, I adopt the Sōtō terminology here.

113. Shingon clerics call this piece *ekō kada* or *ekō no kada* 回向伽陀 (*gāthā* for transferring merit). However, for ease of comparison, I adopt the Sōtō terminology here.

114. The *Praise of the Relics* is a Chinese text praising the Buddha's relics. It is performed in many Buddhist schools, often during funerals. Several ritual manuals that contain descriptions of various rituals contain also an entry on the *Rakan kōshiki.* The form in these ritual handbooks differs slightly from the form in the *Rakan kō hossoku.* First, the other ritual handbooks offer two or three variations for the pieces chanted during the *tengu.* The printed ritual handbooks (*Shokō sahōshū* and *Kōgon shūyō shū*) state that the clerics chant the *Sanskrit Hymn of the Four Wisdoms,* the *Sanskrit Hymn of Mahāvairocana,* and either the [*Sanskrit*] *Hymn of Fudō* (*Fudō no san* 不動讃) or the *Auspicious Chinese Hymn* (*Kikkyō no kango* 吉慶漢語). The manuscripts in the archive of Zōfukuji (*Shōketsu shō* and *Jūnigatsu shōmyō kō yakusha hossoku*) additionally provide the option of singing the *Sanskrit Hymn of the Four Wisdoms, the Sanskrit Hymn of Mahāvairocana,* and *the Hymn of Vajrakarma;* this is the only option indicated in the *Rakan kō hossoku.* Second, some ritual handbooks postulate that the clerics only sing the *Praise of the Thus Come One* and the *Gāthā of Falling Flowers,* in other words, the sequence *Two Shōmyō Melodies* (*Nika hōyō* 二箇法要) instead of the *Four Shōmyō Melodies* (*Shokō sahōshū, Kōgon shūyō shū, Shōketsu shō,* and *Jūnigatsu shōmyō kō yakusha hossoku*).

tantly, the order of liturgical pieces at the beginning is different. In the Sōtō school, the ritual starts with the *Gāthā to Scattering Flowers,* which is not included in the Shingon version. On Mt. Kōya, the *Rakan kōshiki* started with an address of invitation, which in the Sōtō school follows the *Hymn of the Four Wisdoms.* Moreover, instead of only one Sanskrit piece—the *Hymn of the Four Wisdoms*—Shingon clerics vocalized three Sanskrit hymns during the delivery of offerings. And at the end of the ritual, they sang the *Praise of the Relics,* which is absent from the Sōtō version. The fifth section of the *shikimon* praises the Buddha's relics, and by including the *Praise of the Relics,* Shingon monks added another piece that expresses veneration for the Buddha's relics. Yet, despite these differences, the ritual structures in both schools share many similarities.

Finally, I would like to note that the Shingon school is one of the mainstream traditions of *kōshiki.* Many *kōshiki* originated within this school, and Shingon monks have performed rituals in this genre over the centuries. Additionally, this school has a rich *shōmyō* repertoire, and *shōmyō* has always been a central element of the school's monastic curriculum. Therefore, Shingon clerics spent considerable time and effort mastering and refining their vocal skills, developed detailed musical notation systems, and wrote treatises on *shōmyō.* As expected, the *Rakan kōshiki* performed at Mt. Kōya had more musical features than the corresponding ritual in the Sōtō or Rinzai schools: The manuscripts of the *shikimon* and the offertory declaration include musical notation indicating melodic inflections on every syllable.[115] According to that notation, the *shikimon* was recited with melodic patterns on three different pitch levels. The officiant started on the first pitch level, occasionally went up to the second pitch level, and in the fourth and fifth sections recited certain passages on the highest pitch level. These alterations in pitch emphasized changes of topic, the words of the Buddha or the arhats, and other important passages. In this way, the narrative part of the *shikimon* became an expressive musical piece that required training and practice to perform well.[116] All the other pieces were also sung with distinct melodies, spanning a wide range of *shōmyō* styles, creating a rich sonic landscape.

Ritual Form and School Identity

This brief overview of the ritual structures used in the respective schools has highlighted the differences between them. Yet there were also significant similarities. All three schools use the invitation, offertory declaration, communal obeisance, *shikimon,* and *Universal Transfer of Merit.* These elements

115. The following manuscripts contain the offertory declaration: *Sakujitsu Rakan kō saimon* 朔日羅漢講祭文, in *Shosaimon* (printed in Kan'ei era, 1624–1645), and *Sakujitsu Rakan kō saimon* 朔日羅漢講祭文, in *Shosaimon* (printed in Enbō era, 1673–1681).

116. For a detailed description of the style of vocalization, see Nelson 2008b, 2009; Tokita 2015, 34–50; or Mross 2016a, 113–122. In the Tendai school, the *shikimon* is also vocalized on three different pitch levels. For a study of how Tendai *kōshiki* are vocalized, see Amano 2000, 74–95.

Table 2.3. Comparison of the *Rakan kōshiki*'s structure in the Sōtō, Rinzai, and Shingon schools

Sōtō school	*Rinzai school*	*Shingon school*
Gāthā to Scattering Flowers		
		Invitation
Hymn of the Four Wisdoms		*Sanskrit Hymn of the Four Wisdoms* *Sanskrit Hymn of Mahāvairocana* *Hymn of Vajrakarma*
Invitation	Invitation	
Offertory declaration	Offertory declaration	Offertory declaration
Communal obeisance	Communal obeisance	Communal obeisance
Praise of the Thus Come One *Gāthā of Falling Flowers* *Gāthā of Sanskrit Sound* *Gāthā of the Sounding Staff*		*Praise of the Thus Come One* *Gāthā of Falling Flowers* *Gāthā of Sanskrit Sound* *Gāthā of the Sounding Staff*
Shikimon	*Shikimon*	*Shikimon*
Universal Transfer of Merit	*Universal Transfer of Merit*	*Universal Transfer of Merit* *Praise of Relics*

constitute the basic form used in the Rinzai school. In contrast to the five-part structure outlined above, the Rinzai version omits the first part devoted to purifying the ritual space and the third part featuring the *Four Shōmyō Melodies.* Therefore, the ritual frame in the Rinzai school consists only of the invitation of the objects of worship and the transfer of merit. In the Sōtō and Shingon schools, the form is more complex. Sōtō monks sing a *Gāthā to Scattering Flowers, Hymn of the Four Wisdoms,* and the *Four Shōmyō Melodies,* while the Shingon monks vocalized three Sanskrit hymns, the *Four Shōmyō Melodies,* and at the end the *Praise of the Relics.* The Sōtō and Shingon versions are similar in many ways. Interestingly, the Shingon monks sang the *invitation* at the beginning of the ritual before the *Hymn of the Four Wisdoms*—in effect, reversing their order. In the Sōtō version, I have interpreted the *Gathā to Scattering Flowers* and the *Hymn of the Four Wisdoms* as a preparation and purification of the ritual space, and the invitation, offertory declaration, and communal obeisance as a welcoming of the objects of worship. In the Shingon version, the ritual starts with the invitation, and the monks vocalize the three Sanskrit hymns during the delivery of offerings before the offertory declaration. Consequently, the first part consists of a relatively long invitation to the objects of worship, and basically includes the preparation of the ritual space.[117]

These contrasting frames and performance practices seem to reflect the different ways the three schools valorize the performance of rituals in general and *shōmyō* in particular. The Rinzai school, with the simplest ritual form, places less importance on refined performance—for example, exact positioning of the body is not demanded as it is in the Sōtō school—and focuses instead on *kōan* study. Furthermore, the Rinzai school has a very limited *shōmyō* repertoire. Shingon clerics, on the other hand, place high value on ritual practice, especially the vocalization of sacred texts, and novices intensively practice the singing of liturgical pieces. Daily services in the Shingon school, moreover, integrate fundamental *shōmyō* chants, giving the clerics ample practice in vocalizing texts with melodic embellishments. The Sōtō school lies somewhere in the middle; it has a *shōmyō* repertoire, but most Sōtō clerics (with some regional exceptions) do not sing *shōmyō* on a regular basis as part of their duties. Also, the *shōmyō* repertoire in the Sōtō school is more limited than that in the Shingon school. Nevertheless, most Sōtō clerics do not question the value of their *shōmyō* tradition and see it as an essential part of their religious culture. Furthermore, they especially emphasize in their training the acquisition and execution of precise bodily postures, not only in zazen and *kinhin* 経行 (walking meditation) but also in the performance of *kōshiki* and other Sōtō rituals. The highly choreographed precision of their movements in these rituals is a distinguishing trait of the tradition they treasure, going back to Dōgen's own emphasis on correct body position.

Although these schools use many of the same chants and draw on a shared ritual vocabulary, they have each developed their own ways of structuring and performing *kōshiki* such that priests or devoted laypeople can readily tell when a performance represents a different tradition than the one they are familiar with. Additionally, such differences—observable in any or all of the concrete dimensions of *kōshiki* (textual, acoustic, kinetic, and material)—can signify allegiances that extend beyond school identity down to specific lineages. At Eiheiji and Sōjiji, for example, the etiquette slightly differs. Monks at these two temples not only tie their robes differently, they even have different ways of holding a handbell. Thus, minute details can indicate lineage identity.

Conclusions

This chapter has explored the interrituality of Sōtō *kōshiki* to show that many of the liturgical elements they incorporate are part of a ritual repertoire widely shared in Japanese Buddhism. The modularity at the core of these rituals

117. It seems that there is some freedom for variation in the order of liturgical pieces in the Shingon school. For example, the memorial service for the Buddha's passing, which features Myōe's *Shiza kōshiki,* starts with the invitation, communal obeisance, the three hymns for delivery of offerings, and the offertory declaration; see Mross 2016a, 105.

allows clerics easily to add new rituals to their repertoire, since the basic modules—various kinds of prostrations or hand gestures, for example—are part of the embodied knowledge they acquire during their training. By the same token, the use of already familiar elements allows a *kōshiki* composer to create a new ritual by writing a new *shikimon* and offertory declaration and setting them into the standard ritual frame of Sōtō *kōshiki.*

I also showed that a *kōshiki* consists of ritual frames: smaller frames that enclose all ritual sequences, a larger frame into which the *shikimon* is set, and a still larger frame regulating entry to and exit from the ceremonial place. Thus we find frames within frames. I further argued that the ritual structure or frame into which a *shikimon* is set signifies the school's identity. Although the *Rakan kōshiki* has been performed in the Sōtō, Rinzai, and Shingon schools and all schools use the same *shikimon,* each encloses the *shikimon* in a ritual frame that follows its own tradition.

Finally, this chapter has demonstrated that a *kōshiki* performance is complex and consists of many more elements than just the written texts that have been the main focus in most scholarship so far. In fact, *kōshiki* are multidimensional ritual performances that incorporate carefully choreographed movements as well as elaborate vocalizations, often with refined melodies. Since Sōtō clerics themselves emphasize the sonic dimension of *kōshiki,* the next chapter explores their understanding of musical performance as a Zen practice.

3
Kōshiki *as Music Practice*

All of life is music. In my case, it is *shōmyō;* I only sing *shōmyō,* nothing else.
Shōmyō is the voice of the realization of buddhahood.
—Maekawa Bokushō

MUSIC AND SOUNDS have long been vital components in religious rituals. Distinctive soundscapes help to separate ritual time and space from daily life, to transport participants into a different world, and to evoke particular emotions. Special sounds and music also serve as vehicles for communication with the sacred. Sounds can also carry cosmological and soteriological significance and help to make the sacred present. Rituals can have manifold soundscapes, consisting of the sounds of instruments such as drums and bells and the vocalization of sacred texts, as well as silence or ambient sounds.

The sonic dimension also plays a vital role in Buddhist rituals, including *kōshiki.* Buddhist clerics sing or recite texts, but only the monks who vocalize the liturgical pieces read them; lay devotees usually just listen. In some cases, liturgical texts are vocalized in a language unintelligible to listeners, and the sound of the vocalization eclipses the meaning of the text.[1] Scholars working on Buddhist rituals, however, have tended to focus on ritual texts and their content without acknowledging that most of these texts were meant to be vocalized, and only through their vocalization do they fulfill their function.

Ritual procedures (*hosshiki* 法式) also play an important role in the performance of Sōtō rituals. "*Kōshiki* offer something for the eyes and the ears," Inoue Gishin writes, emphasizing that *kōshiki* are impressive not only because of their music but as an aesthetic whole, a *Gesamtkunstwerk* (total work of art), so to speak.[2] Thus, carefully choreographed movements are a vital part of the performance, as the previous chapter has shown. Contemporary Sōtō monks

1. On ritual music, see also Michaels 2005, 33. Other researchers have also emphasized the role of the voice in the reading of Buddhist texts. See, for example, Rambelli 2007, 94 and 114, and Eubanks 2011, 6, 17, and 140.

2. Inoue 2002, 48.

use the term *hosshiki shōmyō* 法式声明 (ritual procedures and Buddhist chant) or *hosshiki kōshiki* 法式講式 (ritual procedures and *kōshiki*) to describe the fusion of music and ritual procedures in the performance of *kōshiki*. This terminology underscores the fact that Sōtō priests do not regard the music as independent from the movements and ritual procedures; rather they understand rituals holistically.

However, many of the movements and gestures performed in *kōshiki* are also part of other rituals; what actually distinguishes *kōshiki* from other ceremonies is the style of vocalization. Accordingly, this chapter focuses on the sonic aspect of *kōshiki,* mainly in contemporary Sōtō Zen, in order to demonstrate the significance of chanting as a Zen practice. First I introduce the vocalization styles and musical instruments to illustrate the diverse sounds and *shōmyō* styles that characterize Sōtō *kōshiki*. Next I briefly discuss the musical notation, touching on the long history of *shōmyō* in the Sōtō school. Based on my fieldwork in Japan, I then detail how Sōtō monks learn to sing *shōmyō* and show how the art of vocalizing liturgical texts is still transmitted orally despite the recent use of audio and video recordings to aid the acquisition of ritual expertise. Finally, I elucidate how contemporary Sōtō priests interpret *shōmyō* and *kōshiki,* demonstrating that for many of them the musical realization of *kōshiki* is inseparable from the soteriological goals of Zen practice.

The Music of *Kōshiki*

Kōshiki as Vocal Music

The musical styles of liturgical pieces vary widely: a few are sung with many melismas in free rhythm, three are sung with a clear melody and a fixed rhythm, and others are vocalized with only minor melodic inflections. Broadly speaking, all the pieces belong to the *shōmyō* categories of song (*utau shōmyō*) and reading (*yomu shōmyō*).[3] The different styles create a manifold soundscape that leads the participants sonically through the ritual. Moreover, the different vocalization styles have a strong influence on the listeners' comprehension of the content; some pieces are sung in a way that makes it impossible to understand the text, whereas others are read or recited so as to remain intelligible.

Pieces categorized as reading are usually performed by a solo voice and without melodies apart from a few minor melodic inflections at the end of the text or section. This style of vocalization was originally chosen for liturgical texts that should be easily understandable to the audience—so naturally all the texts belonging to this category of *shōmyō* are vocalized in Japanese. In a Sōtō *kōshiki,* the category of reading is represented by the offertory declaration and the *shikimon*'s pronouncement of intention and thematic

3. A third category in *shōmyō* is recitation (*kataru shōmyō*), but this usually does not occur in Sōtō *kōshiki*.

sections.[4] Because these texts were composed in Chinese but are vocalized in Japanese, a reading of these two texts includes frequent Sino-Japanese terms and the use of a rather formal language, described by Steven Nelson as a "hard Japanese."[5] Although the *shikimon* is considered the central ritual sequence in a *kōshiki,* its performance is usually shortened in contemporary Japan because Sōtō priests strive for rituals that last around one hour, and a *kōshiki* with a reading of even an abbreviated *shikimon* lasts more than two hours. Therefore, some officiants additionally read the *shikimon* at lightning speed, making it difficult for listeners to actually understand the text. Inoue Gishin complains about this state of affairs and encourages clerics to read the *shikimon* more slowly and with more attention to its content.[6]

Pieces classed as song are written in different languages and are vocalized with melodies in a wide range of styles. Most of these are choral pieces sung by the assembly. In general, they are vocalized slowly in free rhythm, and the melodies glide from one tone into the next, creating a smooth flow that fits the free rhythm well. Considering the different styles and languages, I group these pieces into four subcategories: (1) Chinese verses sung with Sino-Japanese pronunciation; (2) highly melismatic chants on a few syllables; (3) Sanskrit hymns; and (4) prose pieces. Most of the liturgical pieces vocalized in a Sōtō *kōshiki* belong to the first subcategory, Chinese verses. This group includes the *Gāthā to Scattering Flowers,* the communal obeisance, the *Verse of the Praise of the Thus Come One,*[7] the three pieces of *San-Bon-Shaku,* the verses sung during the *shikimon,* and the *Universal Transfer of Merit.* All feature choral singing in unison, although the voices sometimes break off in spontaneous tone clusters. *San-Bon-Shaku* has a special status in this subcategory: it is sung with a clear rhythm and a songlike melody, so that one could leave the ceremony humming it,[8] whereas every other piece in this subcategory is sung in free rhythm, as is typical for *shōmyō.* Moreover, while all other pieces are led

4. In the Tendai and Shingon schools, the *shikimon* is recited with melodic patterns on three different pitch levels (low, medium, and high). This style of vocalization constitutes the *shōmyō* style of recitation. The change of the pitch level adds emphasis to selected passages, as well as an emotional layer to the text. For a detailed study of the musical realization of *shikimon,* see Amano 2000, 74–95; Nelson 2008b and 2009; Tokita 2015, 34–50; and Mross 2016a, 113–122. During my fieldwork at Sōjiji, I sometimes heard Suzuki Eiichi using similar melodic structures when he vocalized an offertory declaration or a *shikimon.* His vocalization style qualifies for the category of recitation, but he is an exception.

5. Nelson 2003, 21.

6. Inoue 2000, 12r. In recommending a slow and dedicated reading so that lay devotees can actually understand the text, Inoue seems to suggest that he sees lay devotees as part of the intended audience. However, at most *kōshiki* I attended, very few lay devotees, if any, were present. I have not attended a *kōshiki* at Eiheiji's satellite temple in Nagoya, where Inoue teaches, and cannot judge whether lay devotees attend the *kōshiki* (either the *Jōyō daishi kōshiki* or *Hakusan kōshiki*) performed there in October.

7. *Verse of the Praise of the Thus Come One* is an alternative to the piece *Praise of the Thus Come One.* During my fieldwork at Sōjiji, I heard this piece only once.

8. This style of vocalization is specific to the Sōtō school. In other schools, the three pieces of *San-Bon-Shaku* are sung in free rhythm; see also Watarai and Tsukamoto 1983, 27.

by the cantor, who sings the first line solo and then is joined by the assembly, *San-Bon-Shaku* is led by three other monks and consists of alternations between soloists and choir.

The second subcategory—highly melismatic chants—has just one representative in a Sōtō *kōshiki*: *Praise of the Thus Come One.* Its short text is sung with long and elaborate melismas on the syllabi *me.* Consequently, it is the most impressive piece in a *kōshiki* and forms a musical climax in the ritual. It is also the most difficult piece in a Sōtō *kōshiki.* Usually it is sung by two monks in unison, which makes it even more challenging, as a mistake by one of the two is immediately audible to everyone. Needless to say, the countless melismas make it impossible to understand the text that is sung.[9]

Only one piece, the *Hymn of the Four Wisdoms,* belongs to the subcategory of Sanskrit hymns. The vocalization style is to hold each syllable on one pitch and then repeat the syllable on the same pitch a few times, inserting only a few melodic embellishments at the end of certain lines. This chant is led by the two monks who play the cymbals, using long and short clashes intersected by a strike on a small gong, before and after the chant.

The fourth subcategory is represented by the address of invitation, a prose text in Chinese that invites the objects of worship to the ritual site by invoking each object of worship individually. This text is sung with melodic patterns similar to those used in the Chinese verses, but it has a larger pitch range. The invocation formula for each object of worship is initiated by two monks, and the assembly joins in for the close of each formula. With the separate invocations for the objects of worship—the Sixteen Arhats in the *Rakan kōshiki,* for example—there is a constant alternation between the duo chanting of the two monks and the choral singing of the assembly.

Since most of the pieces categorized as song are vocalized in Chinese or Sanskrit, large parts of the *kōshiki* are difficult for listeners to understand. As George Tanabe notes:

> Chanting produces liturgical rhythms valued for their audible or musical effects rather than their textual messages. Since chants consist of words, they have linguistic meaning, but chanting often produces sounds that cannot be recognized as a regular spoken language. The *Heart Sūtra* (*Prajñāpāramitāhṛdaya-sūtra*), for example, is popular in East Asia as a Chinese text about emptiness, a fundamental Mahāyāna teaching, but when it is chanted in Japan, each Chinese character is given a Japanese pronunciation without any change in the Chinese grammatical

9. This piece used to be much longer than it is today; the editors of the *Shōwa kaitei Rakan kōshiki* shortened it to one-quarter of its original length (15r–17r). This new ritual handbook also contains the *Verse of the Praise of the Thus Come One* as an alternative to the *Praise of the Thus Come One* (17v–18r). The former is easier to sing and therefore chosen in circumstances where no cleric is present who can sing the *Praise of the Thus Come One* or when an easier piece is required. This new addition and the abbreviation of the *Praise of the Thus Come One* suggest that the editors wanted to make the performance of *kōshiki* easier.

> word order of the text. The audible result is neither Japanese nor Chinese, but a ritual language unto itself.[10]

This kind of sonic ritual language can also be found in Sōtō *kōshiki.* Apart from the recitation in Japanese of the *shikimon* and the offertory declaration, listeners (lay devotees or visiting clerics) are not able to understand the words being sung unless they can see the text. The participating monks see all texts and can thus understand the Chinese verses, but they too cannot understand the content of the *Hymn of the Four Wisdoms,* as that text is a transliteration of the Sanskrit sounds and no translation is given in the ritual handbooks. In these cases, the sound eclipses the content.

Instrumentation

Although *kōshiki* are known for their vocal music, percussion instruments play an essential role during the ritual.[11] These instruments are called *narashimono* 鳴物, literally "sounding things." The use of instruments is not limited to rituals like *kōshiki;* instead the sounds of these instruments guide the monks through their daily life at the head or training temples with a cumulative effect that has been described as a grand percussion concert.[12] Starting with the wake-up bell in the early morning, instruments signal the beginning and end of activities, but the sounds they make, as Watarai Sōjun and Sawada Atsuko suggest, are not just signals but the rhythm of *shingi* 清規 (rules of purity), which transmits unlimited reverberations.[13] Thus, one can interpret these sounds as a pillar of monastic discipline and etiquette.

Ritual manuals explain when and how to play the instruments, and a few monastic codes contain sections on them.[14] For example, Dongyang Dehui's 東陽徳輝 *Chixiu Baizhang qinggui* (Imperial revision of Baizhang's rules of purity), compiled from 1335 to 1338, includes a section on Dharma instruments (*hōgi* 法器), which states that the Buddha introduced various sound signals to assemble his followers, and that Chinese monks inherited this custom from their Indian predecessors:

> Following the practice of the sound instruments used in Indian monastic temples, the Zen institution has continued to use various sound instruments after their fashion even today for the purpose of warning against confusion and idleness,

10. Tanabe 2004, 137.

11. In Taiwanese Buddhism, similar instruments are used; see Wei-Yu Lu's (2012) dissertation on the performance practice of sound instruments and Li-Hua Ho's (2006) survey.

12. Giesen 1990, 1204.

13. Watarai and Sawada 1980, 52.

14. The *Shōwa kaitei Sōtōshū gyōji kihan,* the official monastic code of the contemporary Sōtō school, also includes a detailed section on how to play the instruments (397–411 and 415–424); see Foulk 2010a, 506–527 and 534–571, for an English translation. The text provides information on how to play the instruments without commenting on their deeper meaning.

> encouraging compliance with the teachings and regulations, giving guidance for those who abide in dark subhuman states, and pleasing gods and humans.
>
> If great concentration (*dading* 大定) is always maintained and if transcendent function (*dayong* 大用) always remains quiescent, while hearing one does not hear, and while being aware one has no awareness. Thinking thus, one strikes a sound object and the mysterious wind [of religion] should suddenly arise (i.e., spontaneous transformation). There is neither thinking (*wusi* 無思), nor is there any orientation toward achieving a goal (*wuwei* 無思無爲), the Buddha's spontaneous conversion in itself shines forth forever, and the world of his benevolent longevity opens limitlessly. Is this not the veritable capital city of purity and peace?[15]

In this way, the *Chixiu Baizhang qinggui* stresses the importance of the musical instruments in Buddhist practice and their soteriological function to guide practitioners on their path.

Instruments are to be found in all Sōtō temples, but the larger temples have more instruments as well as better sounding ones. Priests value well-sounding instruments, and the head temples are known for the high quality of their large singing bowls and *mokugyo* (lit. "wooden fish," a round hollow wooden drum). One senior priest who occasionally helps out at Sōjiji explained to me what kind of reverberation a good singing bowl makes and proclaimed that Sōjiji's large singing bowl would have exactly that kind of sound. The quality of the instruments, which is immediately apparent to the trained ear, reflects the status and relative wealth of a temple.

In the rest of this section, I introduce the instruments that are sounded in a *kōshiki*. The clerics play them in a prescribed way; nothing is improvised. I consider the sounds produced as acoustic modules, as explained in the previous chapter. Most of them give monks cues to perform movements or to start singing. Some also frame a ritual sequence or the ritual as a whole, and others are thought to serve as a vehicle for communication with the objects of worship. Over time, some of the instruments or the way they are played have inevitably changed. Rather than describe these changes in detail here, I will give just a few examples in order to demonstrate the fluidity in the performance of *kōshiki* through their history.

Tenshō *and* kanshō *bells.* In a Sōtō *kōshiki* performed in contemporary Japan, the beginning of the ritual is signaled by the *tenshō* 殿鐘, the bell of the hall (fig. 3.1). The *tenshō* hangs from the ceiling and is struck from the outside with a wooden stick or beam, depending on the size of the bell. At Sōjiji, the *tenshō* is in a small gallery along with several other musical instruments. To announce the beginning of the ritual, there are four strikes of the bell. When the monks hear its sound, they know it is time to assemble in the hall. After

15. Translation adapted from Ichimura 2006, 410; for the original, see T 48: 1155b17–21.

Figure 3.1. *Tenshō* in the Hall of the Great Ancestors at Sōjiji. In other halls, the *tenshō* is not as large and usually hangs from the ceiling on a thick cord. Photo by Sōjiji. Used with permission.

the four strikes, the *kanshō* 喚鐘, a small bell that hangs in a small rack and is played with a wooden stick, is sounded twice. Then a monk plays the *tenshō* in three long sequences according to a predetermined pattern (*san'e* 三会). After the second sequence, the handbell (see below) is played twice, guiding the monks of the assembly.

Kōshiki handbooks before the publication of the *Shōwa kaitei Shōmyō kihan* in the 1960s indicate that a monk was to strike the large temple bell to signal the beginning of the ritual.[16] The sound of the large temple bell, which is housed in a wooden frame outside the hall in the temple complex, was thought to have the capacity to reach into the lower realms of existence to save the living beings there.[17] While the change to the *tenshō* is only a detail, it nonetheless indicates that *kōshiki* performances have continued to change over time.

16. See, for example, *Nehan kōshiki* (Genroku 9 [1696] and Kyōhō 10 [1725]) and *Tōjō go kōshiki*.

17. The origin of this interpretation is explained in the *Chanyuan qinggui* (Pure rules of the Zen garden), which states that the king of Zha was reborn as a thousand-headed fish whose heads were continually being severed by a wheel of swords. But each time a bell was sounded, the wheel of swords stopped and the king was relieved of his pain; see X 63: 534a7–9; and Yifa 2002, 169, for an English translation. However, as Yifa remarks, the *Chanyuan quiggui* mistakenly refers to the king of Zha instead of the king of Kaniska (291).

Handbell. The instrument played most often in a *kōshiki* is the *shukei* 手磬, which I translate as handbell. It is a small singing bowl mounted on a handle so that it can be played while walking or standing (fig. 3.2). It is struck with a metal or wooden rod from the outside and has a clear, bright sound. This instrument is also called *inkin* 引磬. The first character, *in,* indicates that the handbell guides the monks throughout the day. During a *kōshiki,* it is played in clearly defined patterns to coordinate movements, such as prostrations and bows. For example, every time all the monks in the assembly perform three prostrations, the cantor or his assistant first plays the handbell with slowly accelerating strikes. He then indicates the start of the first and second prostrations with a single strike and then sounds the handbell twice, with a brief pause between the strikes, for the third. If all are sitting and must perform one prostration, he strikes the handbell twice to give the signal for all to stand, then once more for the onset of the prostration, followed by another strike to indicate that no subsequent prostration follows. To give the signal for all to sit again, he sounds the handbell twice. During the *Hymn of the Four Wisdoms* and *San-Bon-Shaku*—in other words, during choral pieces that are not led by the cantor—the handbell has an additional function to give cues for the assembly to join the singing.

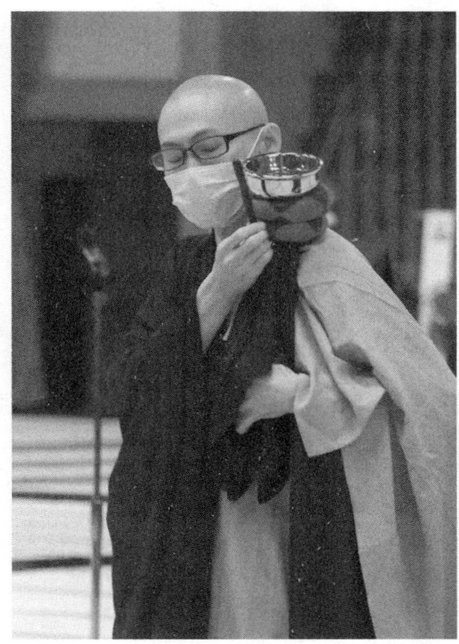

Figure 3.2. Handbell. This photo was taken during the *Dentō kōshiki* performed at Sōjiji on October 14, 2020, when all monks wore face masks due to the Covid-19 pandemic. Photo by Sōjiji. Used with permission.

Large singing bowl. The large singing bowl (*daikei* 大磬) rests on a brocade cushion and is played with a thick wooden striker with a fabric-covered top (fig. 3.3). At Sōjiji the *daikei* has a diameter of around 70 cm.[18] Its mellow, deep sound reverberates with rich overtones. There are two ways to play it: One is to strike it and let it reverberate until its sound fades out. The other way is to mute its reverberation after it is struck, either with the striker or the sleeve of the monk's robe.

In the *Rakan kōshiki,* the cantor or his assistant sounds the singing bowl

18. Sōjiji has an even larger singing bowl, which is set up on the right side of the altar and played during the morning service, but it is not played during a *kōshiki.*

to give cues for entrances during the *Gāthā to Scattering Flowers,* address of invitation, communal obeisance, verses of the *shikimon,* and *Universal Transfer of Merit.* He strikes it at the beginning of a piece and then at the start of each line except for the address of invitation, during which he only strikes it once, when the assembly joins the singing. At the beginning of the *Gāthā to Scattering Flowers,* the first piece in the ritual, he strikes it three times in synchrony with the movements of the three monks who circumambulate the hall during this piece. At the first strike, the monks leave their place to go to the table in front of the altar. The cantor or his assistant strikes it a second time when the three monks arrive at their position, and a third time when they bow. Then he strikes it once muted and the cantor starts singing the piece. The reverberations of the singing bowl mark the beginning of the central ritual acts, as it is only then that this instrument is played four times. At the beginning of other verses, it is struck once with letting it reverberate and then once muted, or only once muted. Nonetheless, in all instances, the sound of the singing bowl provides cues for the performers to begin singing.

Figure 3.3. Large singing bowl. Photo by Sōjiji. Used with permission.

Cymbals and gong. In contrast to the other instruments, the cymbals (*hatsu* or *hachi* 鈸) and small gong (*nyō* 鐃) do not give cues for entrances but frame the *Hymn of the Four Wisdoms* (figs. 3.4 and 3.5). This is the only instrumental play during a *kōshiki.* The monk who plays the large singing bowl and the main handbell (either the cantor or his assistant) is responsible for striking the gong, while the two monks who lead the *Hymn of the Four Wisdoms* play the cymbals with carefully choreographed movements. Preparing to clash the cymbals, they lift the cymbals up to shoulder level and stand on their

Figure 3.4. Cymbals. Photo by Arai Ikkō. Used with permission.

toes. When they clash the cymbals, they move their hands together in front of their chests and come down onto their feet. In this way, as Inoue said, the performance offers something for the eyes and ears.[19]

Figure 3.5. Small gong. Photo by Sōjiji. Used with permission.

The cymbals are played in fixed patterns of slow long and short clashes, producing a powerful sound. After most patterns, the gong is sounded, reverberating softly. The instrumental play develops through introductory, middle, and final parts. Today the first two parts are performed before the hymn, and the last part after, framing the hymn. However, earlier handbooks provide different instructions: The *Hymn of the Four Wisdoms* was to be sung three times and the cymbals and the gong were played after each time through the piece.[20] First the monk who stood on the left led the chant, the assembly joined in, and then the monk leading the chant played the cymbals' introductory part, accompanied by the gong. Thereafter the monk on the right started singing the piece, all joined in, and the monk leading this repetition played the cymbals' middle part. Finally the piece was sung a third time, with both monks leading the piece. When the assembly finished singing, both monks played the cymbals' final part together. One can imagine that this structure led to an interesting sonic experience: first, the sound came from one side, then from the other, and finally, the volume increased when both monks sung together and played the cymbals at the same time, creating a finale to the chant. Assuming the tempo did not change, this ritual sequence must have lasted over twice as long as it does today.

Sounding staff. The sounding staff (*shakujō* 錫杖) is a wooden staff on whose upper end a round metal ring is affixed, from which six smaller metal rings are attached (figs. 3.6 and 3.7).[21] The six rings are supposed to symbolize the six practices of a bodhisattva: charity, morality, forbearance, effort, meditation, and wisdom.[22] If one moves the sounding staff or hits it on the ground, the rings make a metallic sound upon contact with each other.

The sounding staff, called *khakkhara* in Sanskrit, originated in India and

19. Inoue 2002, 48.

20. See *Tōjō go kōshiki,* for example.

21. See the *Dedao ticheng xizhang jing* for a detailed description of the symbolic meaning of the sounding staff; see also Heine 2017 on staffs in Zen Buddhism.

22. ZGD, 469.

Figure 3.6. Sounding staff (*shakujō*). The monk carrying the staff walks to the place where he will lead the *Gāthā of the Sounding Staff.* Photo by Sōjiji. Used with permission.

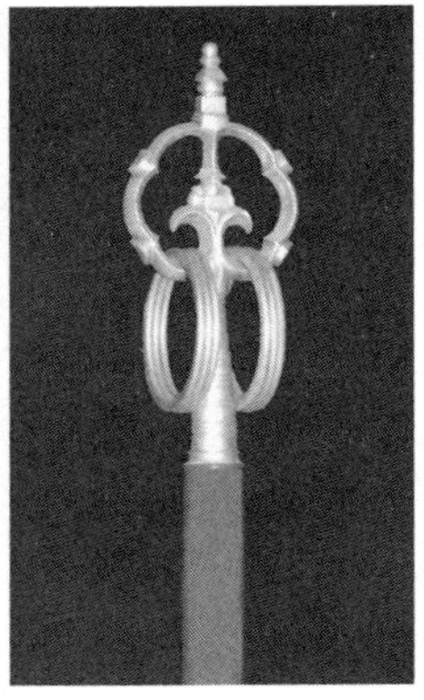

Figure 3.7. Top of the sounding staff. Photo by Sōjiji. Used with permission.

is one of the eighteen essential belongings of monks. According to the *Mūlasarvāstivāda Vinaya,* the Buddha is said to have told his disciples "to affix a ring as big as the mouth of a cup to the end of their sticks and to attach small rings to the big ring" and to shake the stick in order to signal their approach to donors.[23] In contemporary Sōtō Zen, clerics still use the sounding staff in the same way during their begging rounds. In the *Four Part Vinaya,* it is further said that the monks should use this staff to scare away insects.[24] The *Chixiu Baizhang qinggui* explains the meaning of the sounding staff (here translated as pewter staff):

> According to the *Pewter Staff Sutra* 錫杖經 (*Dedaotichengxizhangjing*), the Buddha is said to have told his disciples that they should keep a staff topped by pewter because all the buddhas of the past, present, and future have kept and will keep [such a staff]. The staff in question is also called a "wisdom staff" or "staff of virtue," because it symbolizes the source of insight and practice and their merit. Mahākāśyapa asked the Buddha, "Why does the cane have pewter rings on top?" The Buddha replied, "*Xi* 錫 ('pewter-top') symbolizes lightness. Relying on this staff, its holder can remove his defilements and escape from this triple world. *Xi* symbolizes insight. Because it helps its holder to realize wisdom and insight, *xi* symbolizes awakening. Because it awakens its holder to the ultimate nature of the

23. Yifa 2002, 249–259.
24. Yifa 2002, 249.

triple world as suffering and empty, *xi* symbolizes separation. That is to say, its holder is to be freed from the five kinds of desires."[25]

In the Sōtō school, the sounding staff has a long shaft that is pounded on the ground, but other schools also use a version with a short shaft, which is shaken in the air. In a *kōshiki,* the monk who leads the *Gāthā of the Sounding Staff* plays the sounding staff as he and the other two monks who lead the *San-Bon-Shaku* go to the front and later return to their places, marking the beginning and end of the *San-Bon-Shaku.* The monk who leads the *Gāthā of the Sounding Staff* also shakes it three times at the end of each choral section during this chant. At some temples, clerics just strike the sounding staff on the floor a couple of times without a discernible rhythm, but monks at Sōjiji often shake it in a jazz-like rhythm, which gives the piece a lively character.

Small bell. During a *kōshiki,* the officiant plays a small handheld bell (*rei* 鈴) with a clapper inside that makes a piercing high-pitched sound when it is rung (fig. 3.8). The officiant rings it three times at the beginning of the *shikimon,* at the conclusion of each section of the *shikimon* just before the assembly sings the verse, and at the beginning of a new section. Its sound thus frames the *shikimon* and its sections. It is said that the sound of this small bell attracts the attention of buddhas, bodhisattvas, and other deities and invites them to the ceremonial place.[26]

Figure 3.8. Small bell (*rei*). Photo by Arai Ikkō. Used with permission.

Large drum. The only membranophone played during a *kōshiki* at Sōjiji is the large drum (fig. 3.9).[27] Played with a thick wooden stick, it is the loudest instrument in a *kōshiki,* and its deep sound reverberates in one's body. At Sōjiji, this drum is placed in the small gallery of the hall, like the *tenshō.* The sound of the drum announces the delivery of offerings by the officiant and the reading of his Dharma words, a statement addressing the arhats. When the officiant goes to the front to present the offerings delivered to the altar, a novice plays the drum with strong strikes in accelerando. When the officiant has finished the delivery of offerings and has performed his prostrations, the novice strikes the drum three times with great force. Then the officiant reads a statement asking the Sixteen Arhats to accept the offerings. The two pieces that are vocalized before and after this ritual sequence invite the objects of worship to the ceremonial place. One

25. Translation adapted from Ichimura 2006, 253; for the original, see T 48: 1139b18–b24.

26. Watarai and Sawada 1980, 89.

27. The ritual handbooks do not mention this drum. The ensuing sequence consisting of Dharma words read by the officiant, which might be unique to Sōjiji as I only heard it there during my fieldwork, is not included in the ritual manuals.

can imagine that the loud strikes of the large drum support this aim by capturing the attention of the objects of worship.

Figure 3.9. Large drum. Photo by Sōjiji. Used with permission.

These are the instruments that are played during a *kōshiki* in the Sōtō school. The *mokugyo,* often heard in other Sōtō rituals, is not played in *kōshiki* unless the *kōshiki* ends with a sutra reading (fig. 3.10).[28] The reason is that sutras are recited in a steady rhythm and the *mokugyo* is used to indicate the tempo, whereas most *shōmyō* pieces of the Sōtō school, with the exception of *San-Bon-Shaku,* are sung or recited in free rhythm. *Kōshiki* offer a very different soundscape from that of other Sōtō rituals, due to the melodic character of the liturgical pieces and the musical instruments played—or not played.[29]

It is also important to mention that there are many silent moments during the ritual. These occur when monks prepare to move to the designated place for leading a chant or fulfilling a ritual function. These silent spaces stand in contrast to the manifold sounds of the ritual, creating pauses of anticipation.

Music and Ritual Form

Among Sōtō rituals, *kōshiki* are characterized by the abundance of musical variation. Its five parts (with one exception, the fifth, which consists of only one piece) each contain at least two different vocalization styles and feature an instrument whose sound is unique to that part. As a result, the music creates a rich multicolored arc through which the ritual unfolds.

The ritual starts with the clear sound of the *tenshō* played in a sequence of strikes with pauses in between, creating a slow-paced atmosphere. The first part of the ritual, the purification of the room, starts with the *Gāthā to Scatter-*

28. Today the term *mokugyo* 木魚 (wooden fish) is used to describe the round wooden drum. However, the term was originally used to describe the wooden fish that hangs from the ceiling in front of the monks' hall and is played before meals. Sōtō monks are said to have adopted today's *mokugyo* in the Tokugawa period after Yinyuan Longqi 隠元隆琦 (J. Ingen Ryūki, 1592–1673), founder of the Ōbaku school 黄檗宗, introduced it to Japan (ZGD, 1225). In his *Tōjō sōdō shingi kōtei betsuroku,* Menzan reflects on the new instrument and suggests that it was developed in Ming dynasty China (1368–1644). After the introduction of the new instrument, the "older" wooden fish was renamed *hō* 梆 (SZ 4: 273–275). The influential Rinzai scholar-monk Mujaku Dōchū 無着道忠 (1653–1744) provided a similar explanation of the two different *mokugyo* and their correct names (*Zenrin shōkisen,* 749).

29. One regular ritual that incorporates *shōmyō* is the ceremony for feeding the hungry ghosts (*sejikie*), in which the *Ambrosia Gate* (*Kanromon*) is vocalized. *Ambrosia Gate* is a set sequence of invocations and *dhāraṇī* that ends with a special transfer of merit sung with melodies. Another example of *shōmyō* is the singing of the piece *Gāthā to Scattering Flowers* at the beginning of the rolling reading of the *Great Sutra on the Perfection of Wisdom,* adding musical color to the ritual.

Figure 3.10. Large *mokugyo* in the Hall of the Great Ancestors at Sōjiji. Other *mokugyo* are not as large and usually played while sitting. Photo by Sōjiji. Used with permission.

ing Flowers, a solemn Chinese verse. The cantor leads this chant, which is sung in free rhythm with the melodic patterns often used for Chinese verses. Upon its conclusion, the soundscape dramatically changes when two monks energetically play the cymbals, interspersed by the soft sound of a gong. This instrumental play frames the Sanskrit piece *Hymn of the Four Wisdoms,* which is sung in a more dynamic and forceful way than the opening *gāthā.*

The second part, which invites the objects of worship to the ceremonial place, starts with the address of invitation, a solemn piece that uses patterns from the *gāthā* and similar verses but with a larger pitch range. The repetitions of the invocations for each object of worship—sixteen times for the Sixteen Arhats—intensify a sense of gravity. This is punctuated by the loud drum strikes announcing the offerings and Dharma words delivered by the officiant. Then a monk reads the offertory declaration in Japanese, praising and supplicating the objects of worship. This part of the ritual ends with the communal obeisance, a Chinese verse vocalized in a style similar to that of the opening *gāthā,* returning to the musical style of Chinese verses.

The next part, which I interpret as a feast, is musically distinct from all the others. The vocalization of the first piece, *Praise of the Thus Come One,* offers dramatic melismas and represents the musical climax of the ritual, while the following three pieces, composing the *San-Bon-Shaku,* are sung with clear rhythm and a cheerful melody. Unique to this part is the sounding staff, whose bright metallic ring adorns the *San-Bon-Shaku.*

The fourth part is the *shikimon,* the center of a *kōshiki,* and it alternates between the officiant's recitation of the prose in Japanese with little or no melodic inflections and the assembly's choral singing of verses in Chinese with melodic patterns reminiscent of the opening *gāthā*. At the beginning of each section of the *shikimon,* the officiant rings a small, high-pitched bell, which resonates in a high sound to attract the attention of the objects of worship.

In the fifth part, the only piece that is sung is the *Universal Transfer of Merit,* a Chinese verse vocalized with melodic patterns similar to those in the first piece. The *kōshiki* ends with the sound of the handbell coordinating the final prostrations. So the ritual concludes as it began—with the sounds of bells and the singing of Chinese verses.

In this musical arc, only the second and fourth parts contain liturgical texts that are intelligible to the listeners, and these pieces are framed by chants sung in Chinese or Sanskrit—ritual sequences in which the sound eclipses the meaning of the text. The sounds of the instruments, moreover, provide cues to the performers throughout the ritual, the deep reverberations of the singing bowl signaling entry into solo or choral singing, and the clear ring of the handbell prompting the prostrations performed at the end of liturgical pieces. The overall effect is inescapable: participating in the ritual is a multisensory experience in which the textual component is one part of a larger whole, and perhaps a smaller part than most text-oriented scholars have acknowledged. The manifold soundscape of *kōshiki*—including the interplay of instrumentation and vocalization styles that characterizes each part of the ritual—is summarized in table 3.1.

Musical Notation in the Realm of Oral Transmission

Because it is inherently fluid, music cannot be grasped after its moment of production as a picture or a sculpture can. However, the extant ritual handbooks containing musical notation (*hakase* 博士) gesture toward sounds that ceased long ago.[30] Musical notation has a long tradition in Japanese Buddhism with the earliest extant examples dating from the eleventh century.[31] Many different styles of musical notation were developed, which vary according to the school and time period. Attesting to the importance of music in Japanese Buddhism, the oldest printed musical notation in the world is a *shōmyō* notation printed at Mt. Kōya in Bunmei 4 (1472).[32] The earliest extant musical notation of Sōtō *shōmyō* was written around three decades later and is included in the Rinkō manuscript of the *Keizan shingi,* copied in Meiō 1 (1501) (fig. 3.11).

This manuscript proves that Sōtō monks have vocalized texts with melodies since at least the sixteenth century. Since then, many *kōshiki* handbooks

30. See Arai K. 1986, 1995, and 1996 for detailed studies on the development of *shōmyō* notation.

31. Arai K. 1995, 2, and 1996, viii.

32. *Shōmyōshū*. See Fukushima 1995 and Fukushima, Arai, and Nelson 2018 for a facsimile and detailed study.

Table 3.1. Musical performance of *kōshiki*

Part	*Title*	*Style of vocal performance*	*Performers*	*Instruments*
Purification of the ritual space	*Gāthā to Scattering Flowers*	Song (Chinese verse)	Cantor (1), assembly	Singing bowl, handbell
	Hymn of the Four Wisdoms	Song (Sanskrit hymn)	Two monks (5,12), assembly	**Cymbals**, **gong**, handbell
Invitation to the objects of veneration	Address of invitation	Song (prose)	Two monks (6,7), assembly	Singing bowl, handbell
	Dharma words to incense offering		Officiant (15)	**Large drum**
	Offertory declaration	Reading	One monk (8)	—
	Communal obeisance	Song (Chinese verse)	Cantor (1), assembly	Singing bowl, handbell
Feast	*Praise of the Thus Come One*	Song (highly melismatic piece)	One or two monks (14)	Handbell
	Gāthā of Falling Flowers	Song (Chinese verse)	One monk (9), assembly	Handbell
	Gāthā of Sanskrit Sound	Song (Chinese verse)	One monk (10), assembly	Handbell
	Gāthā of the Sounding Staff	Song (Chinese verse)	One monk (11), assembly	**Sounding staff**, handbell
Lecture / praise / worship	*Shikimon*	Reading	Officiant (15)	**Small bell**
		Song (Chinese verse)	Cantor (1), assembly	Singing bowl, handbell
Transfer of merit	*Universal Transfer of Merit*	Song (Chinese verse)	Cantor (1), assembly	Singing bowl, handbell

Instruments that are unique to a ritual sequence are indicated in bold. The numbers identifying the performers indicate their seating position as shown in fig. 2.2

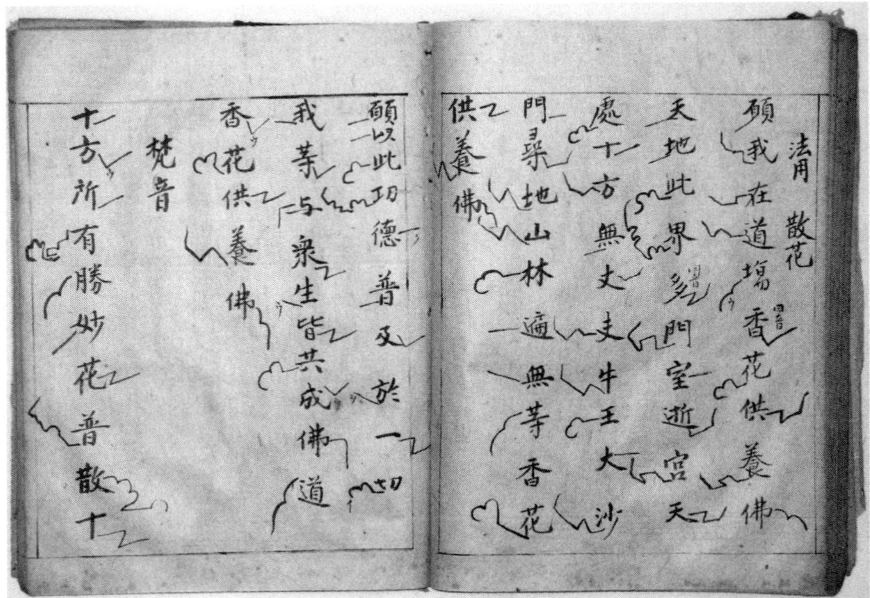

Figure 3.11. The *Gāthā of Falling Flowers,* followed by the first line of the *Gāthā of Sanskrit Sound. Rakan kōshiki* in the Rinkō manuscript of the *Keizan shingi* (1501). The lines next to the Chinese characters indicate melodic movements. Archive of Yōkōji, Hakui. Photo by the author.

with musical notation were produced, and Sōtō clerics continue to use a traditional musical notation today. In learning to read this notation, a novice needs a teacher. As many priests emphasized in interviews, *shōmyō* is part of the realm of oral transmission. The musical notation serves as an aid to memory, a function it similarly had in Christian chanting practices in the early ninth century, as Susan Rankin has shown:

> That memory and recall continued to play a central part in musical practice is abundantly evident in the notations created in the ninth century. These notations remind the reader of sounds that he has heard, but do not provide primary instructions as to how to make those sounds.... [I]f oral practice was the primary basis of transmission, the purpose of notation was to lead the reader back into remembrance of it.[33]

Notation was therefore a way of "music writing in a context of highly trained musical memory."[34] Likewise, the purpose of *ṣhōmyō* notation is to prompt one's memory to recall the melodies and subtleties of the performance learned from one's teacher.

33. Rankin 2011, 111.
34. Rankin 2011, 171.

The use of musical notation shows that the vocalization and the playing of the instruments are not done randomly but are performed in a structured and precisely controlled manner. Sōtō monks have taken great efforts to notate the melodies and instruments in the ritual handbooks in order to support clerics in their performance and preserve the traditional performance practice. One of them, for example, was the monk Shinryū 真龍 (n.d.), who copied several manuscripts at Sōjiji in Bunka 10 (1813). In a colophon, he remarked that the oral transmission of *shōmyō* was starting to disappear: monks sang however they liked and had difficulty in singing the melodies skillfully. Therefore, he encouraged his fellow monks to practice *shōmyō* and copied earlier manuscripts that had started to show signs of wear and tear.[35]

Over the centuries, Sōtō clerics employed two different notation systems. In the early stages, they adopted a system that visually represents the contours of the melodic movement by the direction of lines. This system derived from the early musical notation used in other schools, especially Tendai, and is called *tada bakase* 只博士 (lit. *hakase*—), that "which lacks any standard criterion for indicating pitch."[36] We find this kind of musical notation in the Rinkō manuscript of the *Keizan shingi* and in *kōshiki* manuscripts written at Sōjiji in Genroku 7 (1694) and Bunka 10 (1813) (figs. 3.11–3.14).[37] Unfortunately, it is not possible to reconstruct the melodies in the old notations because no explanation of how to read them has been found. Additionally, Sōtō monks cannot sight-read this notation system anymore, as it was gradually superseded by a new system developed by Sōtō clerics in the Tokugawa period that formed the basis for today's musical notation (figs. 3.15 and 3.16).[38] We do not know exactly when the change occurred, who made the

35. *San kōshiki narabini hōyō*. See Ozaki 1998c, 67, for a typographical reprint; and Mross 2014a, 166, for an English translation. Fear of the degeneration of the *shōmyō* tradition and the worry that everybody sings as he likes seem to have been a common concern in *shōmyō* transmission. For example, Fujiwara no Takamichi 藤原孝道 (1166–1237) lamented about this in his treatise *Shiki hossoku yōi jōjō* 式法則用意条々; see Nelson 2001a for a typographical reprint.

36. Arai K. 1995, 2. *Tada bakase* notation is sometimes called *meyasu hakase* or *meyasu bakase* 目安博士, literally "easily readable notation." However, Arai Kōjun distinguishes between *tada bakase* and *meya hakase* where the latter has additional markings for melodic embellishments (1996, viii–ix). But Tendai monks use both terms for the same notation. In some schools, notation systems that indicate concrete pitch levels using graphs (*zu hakase* 図博士 and *goin bakase* 五音博士) were developed, making it possible to reconstruct the melodies. See Arai K. 1995 and 1996 for a detailed explanation of the graph notation systems. Sōtō monks, however, did not adopt any of these systems and continued to use the earlier system that indicated melodic movements by the direction of lines.

37. Sōjiji manuscripts copied in Genroku 7 (1694): *Butsuji kō kada narabini Shichisan, Rakan kō kada narabini Shichisan, Nehan kō kada narabini Shichisan, Hōyō,* and *Kada narabini hōyō*. Manuscripts copied in Bunka 10 (1813): *San kōshiki narabini hōyō*.

38. Another possibility is that depending on the local area monks used different notation systems, one of which became the standard notation. The oldest notations we currently have are from Sōjiji and Yōkōji, and they represent the older style. The two temples are located in close proximity and belong to Keizan's lineage—factors that might have contributed to their using the same system. In any case, I think it is more likely that Sōtō monks first adopted a notation used in other schools and then developed it further to fit their needs.

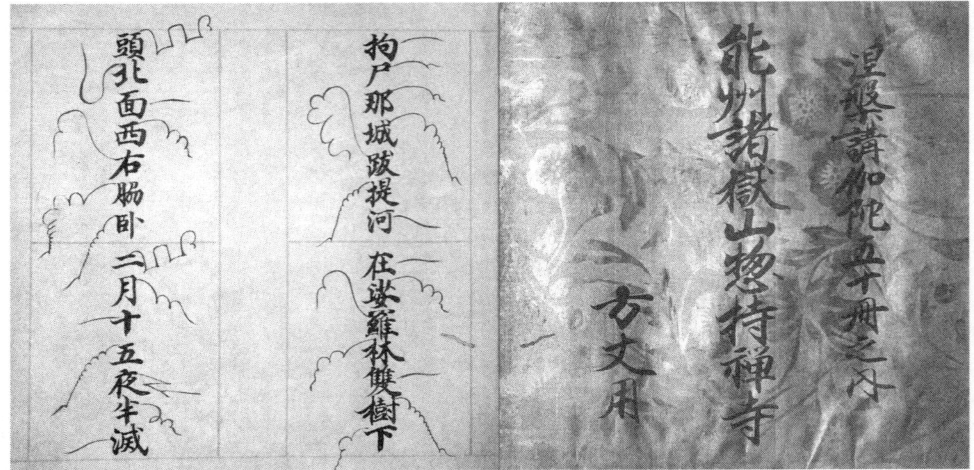

Figure 3.12. First page of the *Nehan kō kada narabini Shichisan,* a manuscript containing the verses of the *Nehan kōshiki* (1694). The verse shown here is the general obeisance. The musical notation next to the Chinese characters is written in red ink. Archive of Sōjiji Soin, Monzen. Photo by the author.

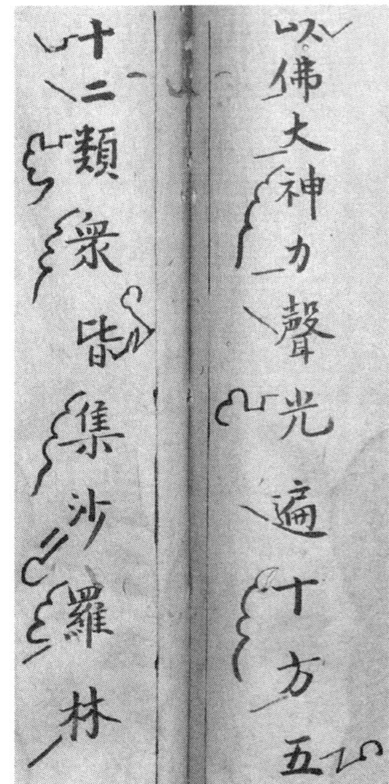

Figure 3.13. Old style of Sōtō *shōmyō* notation. Verse of the first section of the *Nehan kōshiki,* in the Rinkō manuscript of the *Keizan shingi* (1501). Archive of Yōkōji, Hakui. Photo by the author.

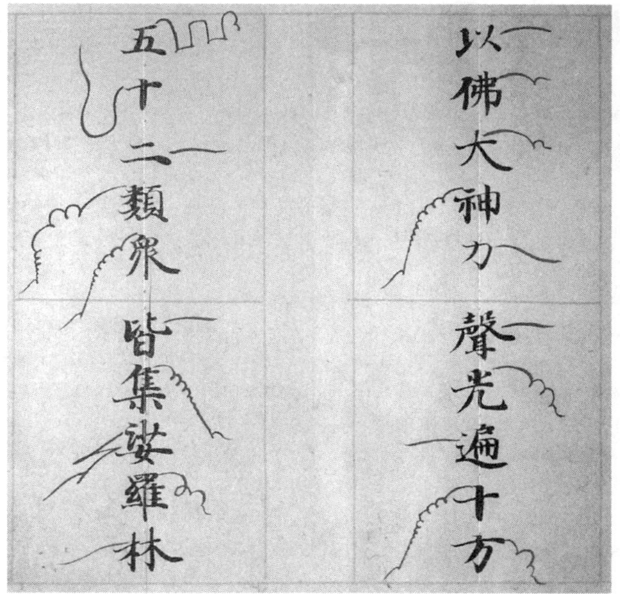

Figure 3.14. Old style of Sōtō *shōmyō* notation. Verse of the first section of the *Nehan kōshiki,* in *Nehan kō kada narabini Shichisan* (1694). Archive of Sōjiji Soin, Monzen. Photo by the author.

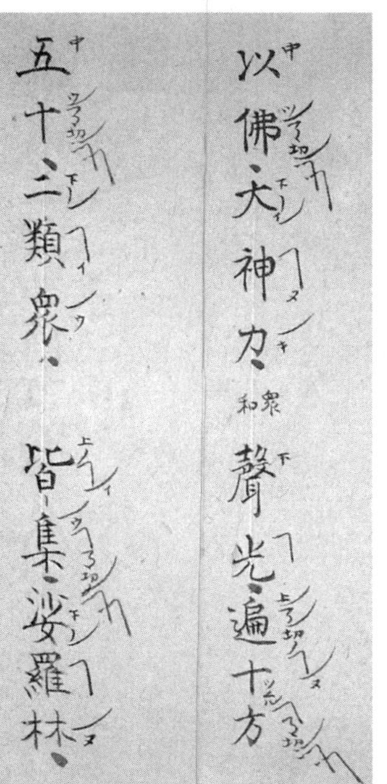

Figure 3.15. New style of Sōtō *shōmyō* notation. Verse of the first section of the *Nehan kōshiki,* in a text added to the *Nehan kō kada narabini Shichisan* around the end of the Tokugawa period or the early Meiji era. Archive of Sōjiji Soin, Monzen. Photo by the author.

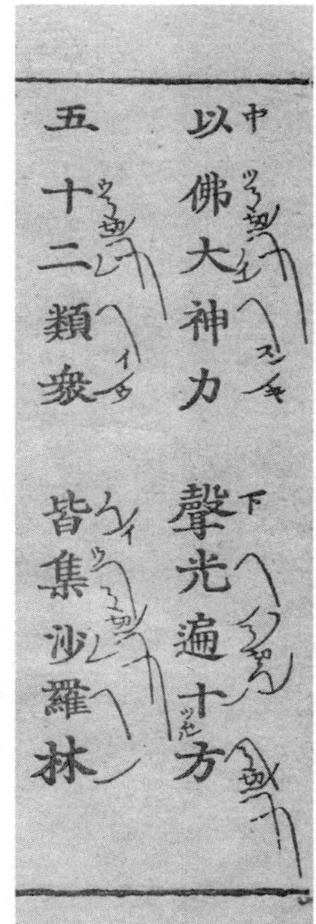

Figure 3.16. New style of Sōtō *shōmyō* notation. Verse of the first section of the *Nehan kōshiki,* in the *Ryaku kōshiki* (*Daijō shoin*), a widely used ritual handbook printed during the late Tokugawa period. From the Kadono Konzen Library Collection. Used with permission.

decision to invent a different system of notation, or how the new system became the standard notation used in the Sōtō school. While the older notation represents the contours of the melodies by the direction of lines, the new notation employs a fixed set of standardized symbols (or symbolic lines) that indicate melodic patterns. These patterns, as well as the symbols themselves, are called *fushi* 節.

The new notation system was in use as early as the seventeenth century. However, it did not immediately replace the older system; instead both systems were in use for a long period of time, and there seem to have been local differences as to when a given temple adopted the new system. Monks at Sōjiji, for example, most likely continued to use the older system into the nineteenth century, because it was still employed in the ritual handbooks that Shinryū copied in Bunka 10 (1813).[39] The first indication that Sōjiji monks were using the new notation system does not appear until the late Tokugawa period or early Meiji era, when they inscribed texts using the new system in older *kōshiki* manuscripts in their possession.[40] That cache of manuscripts had been copied using the old style of notation in Genroku 7 (1694); at around the same time, clerics at other temples were writing ritual manuals using the new system, including Kankai 観海 (n.d.) of Hōenji 玉円寺 (Kanazawa), who copied the *Four Kōshiki* in Jōkyō 3 (1686),[41] and monks at both Shōbōji 正法寺 (Iwate prefecture) and Saifukuji 西福寺 (Nagano prefecture), who copied the *Nehan kōshiki* in Genroku 5 (1692) and Genroku 9 (1696), respectively (fig. 3.17). Over time, the new system became the standard. A major factor was that woodblock print editions of *kōshiki,* which began to appear in the eighteenth century, used the new notation system, and these print editions became a driving force in standardizing ritual practice across Japan.

It seems likely that the new style of musical notation proved attractive to many clerics because it provided more information about the performance than did the earlier notations (figs. 3.15, 3.16, and 3.17). Next to the *fushi* we find indications about the pitch level: low (*ge* 下), middle (*chū* 中), and high (*jō* 上). Long melodic lines include notations as to where the monks should take a breath (切). Some texts give additional information, such as the pronunciations for a few characters or when the assembly should join the chanting. Over the course of its development, the musical notation of *shōmyō* in general has become increasingly detailed over time, motivated by the aim to better preserve *shōmyō* as much as to provide clerics with more details regard-

39. *San kōshiki narabini hōyō.*

40. Sōjiji monks added texts using the new notation system on the back side of manuscripts originally written in Genroku 7 (1694): *Butsuji kō kada narabini Shichisan, Rakan kō kada narabini Shichisan, Nehan kō kada narabini Shichisan,* and *Hōyō* (archive of Sōjiji Soin). Because one of these texts (a notation of the *San-Bon-Shaku*) is dated 1890, I surmise that the new texts were added sometime between Bunka 10 (1813) and 1890. For a detailed study of these manuscripts, see Mross 2014a, chap. 5.

41. *Shi kōshiki.* See Ozaki 2014a, 130–132.

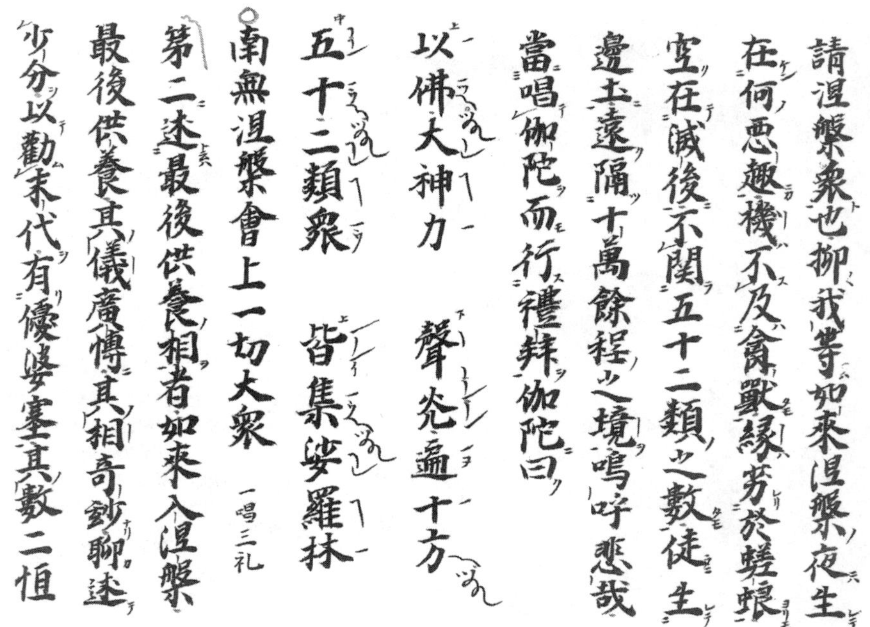
請涅槃衆也抑我等如來涅槃夜生
在何悪趣機不及貪獸縁劣於蛣蜋
空在滅後不聞五十二類之數徒生
邊土遠隔十萬餘程之境嗚呼悲哉
當唱伽陀而行禮拜伽陀曰
以佛大神力　聲光遍十方
五十二類衆　皆集娑羅林
南無涅槃會上一切大衆　一唱三礼
第二述最後供養相者如來入涅槃
最後供養其儀廣傳其相奇鈔聊述
少分以勸末代有優婆塞其數二恒

Figure 3.17. *Shikimon* of the *Nehan kōshiki* (1692), showing the end of the first section, verse with musical notation, and beginning of the second section. This manuscript contains an early form of the new style of *shōmyō* notation; in later texts, the squiggly lines used here are replaced by other symbols (cf. 3.16). Archive of Shōbōji, Iwate prefecture. Facsimile produced by Sōtōshū Bunkazai Chōsa Iinkai. Used with permission.

ing the performance. The same development can be found in the Sōtō notations.

In some cases, the change in musical notation coincided with a change of melodies. For example, a close comparison of the *fushi* for the verses of the *Butsuji kōshiki* written at Sōjiji in Genroku 7 (1694) and on the back of the same manuscripts sometime in the nineteenth century hints at melodic change: The curvy line next to the first character (一) in the third line in the Genroku 7 manuscript (fig. 3.18) indicates several melodic inflections, whereas no *fushi* appear in the notation from the nineteenth century (fig. 3.19), suggesting that the character was now sung on one pitch without any melodic inflection. The notation from Genroku 7 further shows different melodies for the last characters in the first and third lines (食 and 結), but those characters were later sung with the same melodic patterns according to the new notation.

Both notation systems reveal the same concept of melodic organization. When comparing the notation for the verses sung during the *shikimon,* we see that the same melodic patterns were used for the verses, similar to

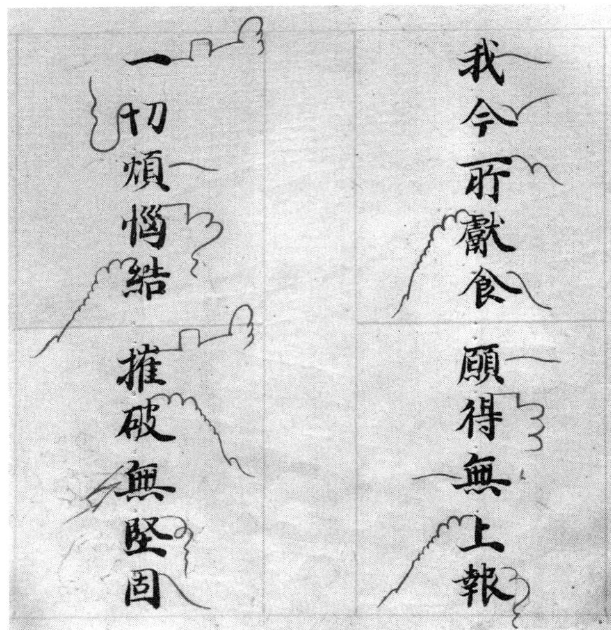

Figure 3.18. Verse of the second section of the *Butsuji kōshiki,* in *Butsuji kō kada narabini Shichisan* (1694). From the Kadono Konzen Library Collection. Used with permission.

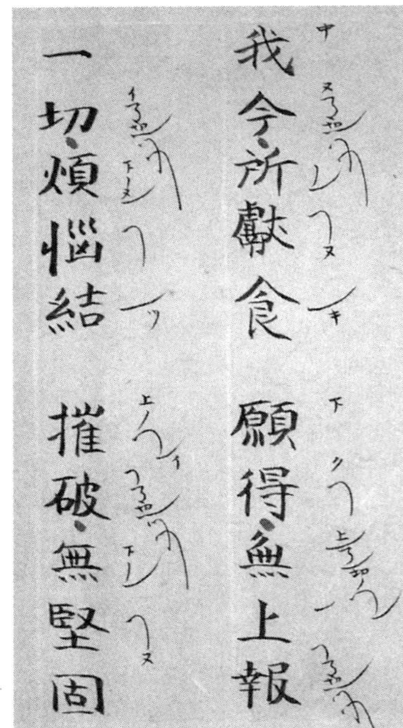

Figure 3.19. Verse of the second section of the *Butsuji kōshiki,* in a text added to the *Nehan kō kada narabini Shichisan* (1694) around the end of the Tokugawa period or early Meiji era. Archive of Sōjiji Soin, Monzen. Photo by the author.

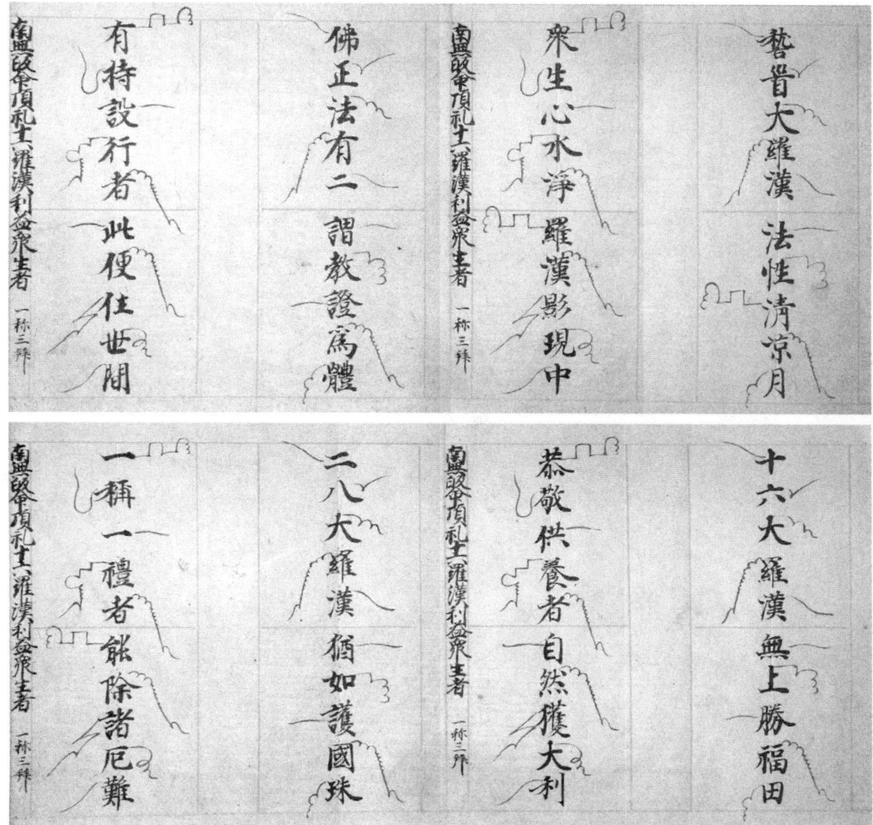

Figure 3.20. Verses of sections one through four of the *Rakan kōshiki,* in *Rakan kō kada narabini Shichisan* (1694). This notation shows that verses were sung with standard melodic patterns, as the melodic movement appears to be almost the same for all verses. Archive of Sōjiji Soin, Monzen. Photo by the author.

songs where the melody stays the same while the text changes with each verse, making it easier for the monks to learn the melody and sing the verses (fig. 3.20).[42]

It is important to note that the individual *fushi* have names. When learning to sing the different pieces, monks in contemporary Japan first learn how to sing the individual *fushi.* The *Shōwa kaitei Shōmyō kihan* (80v–81r) lists thirteen basic *fushi,* some of which have additional variations (fig. 3.21). I interpret these *fushi* or patterns as melodic modules, which are assembled to form melodies. One example of a *fushi* is *marubushi* 円節, which is

42. Two choral notations in the archive of Kanazawa Bunko illustrate this concept very well. The manuscripts provide the melodic framework for verses by substituting squares for the Chinese characters; see Kanazawa Bunko 2006, 15.

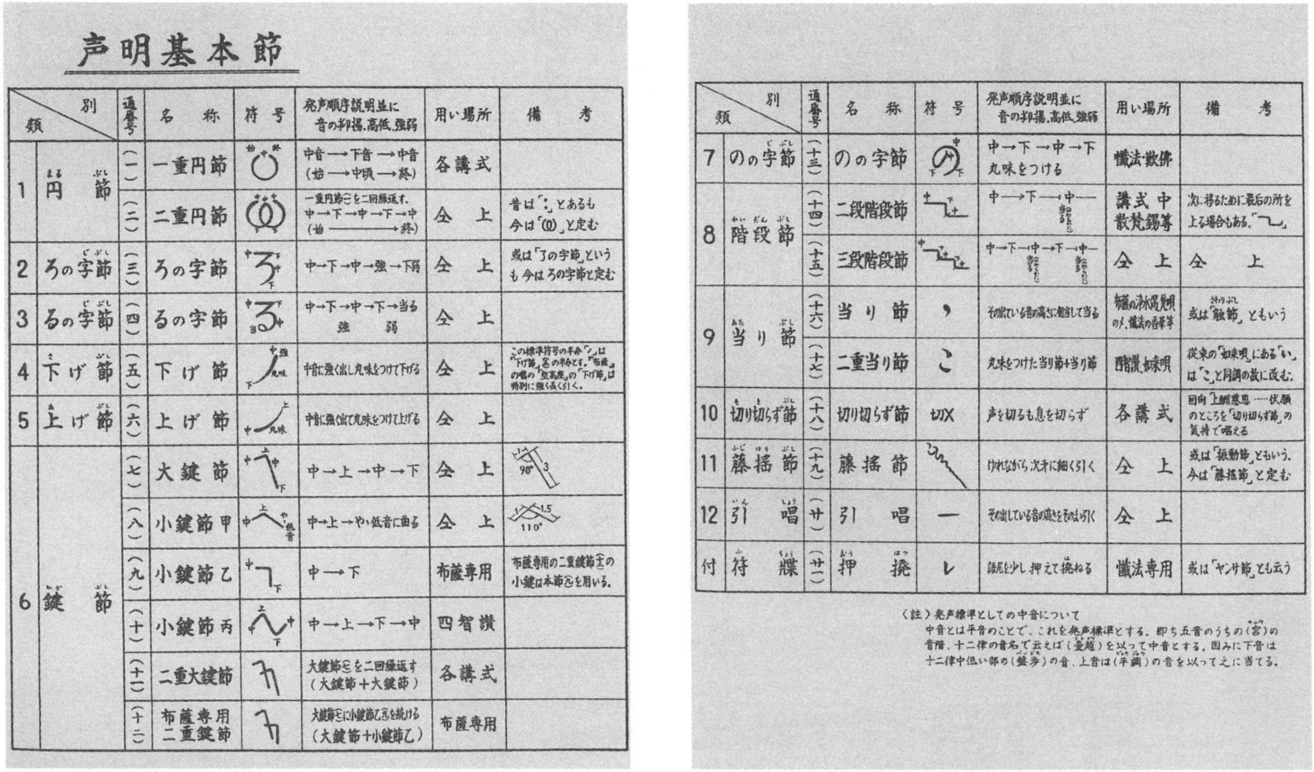

声明基本節

類 \ 別	通番号	名称	符号	発声順序説明並に音の抑揚、高低、強弱	用い場所	備考
1 円節	(一)	一重円節		中音 → 下音 → 中音（始 → 中頃 → 終）	各講式	
	(二)	二重円節		一重円節(一)を二回繰返す．中 → 下 → 中 → 下 → 中（始 → 終）	仝上	昔は「:」とあるも今は「(0)」と定む
2 ろの字節	(三)	ろの字節		中 → 下 → 中 → 強 → 下弱	仝上	或は「了の字節」というも今はろの字節と定む
3 るの字節	(四)	るの字節		中 → 下 → 中 → 下 → 当る 強 弱	仝上	
4 下げ節	(五)	下げ節		中音に強く出し丸味をつけて下げる	仝上	この標準符号の半分「ノ」は「下げ節」(五)の半分とす。「布薩」の唱の「独高座」の「下げ節」は特別に強く長く引く。
5 上げ節	(六)	上げ節		中音に強く出て丸味をつけて上げる	仝上	
6 鍵節	(七)	大鍵節		中 → 上 → 中 → 下	仝上	1 90° 3
	(八)	小鍵節甲		中 → 上 → やゝ低音に曲る	仝上	1 1.5 110°
	(九)	小鍵節乙		中 → 下	布薩専用	布薩専用の二重鍵節(十二)の小鍵は本節(九)を用いる。
	(十)	小鍵節丙		中 → 上 → 下 → 中	四智讃	
	(十一)	二重大鍵節		大鍵節(七)を二回繰返す（大鍵節＋大鍵節）	各講式	
	(十二)	布薩専用二重鍵節		大鍵節(七)に小鍵節乙(九)を続ける（大鍵節＋小鍵節乙）	布薩専用	

類 \ 別	通番号	名称	符号	発声順序説明並に音の抑揚、高低、強弱	用い場所	備考
7 のの字節	(十三)	のの字節		中 → 下 → 中 → 下 丸味をつける	懺法・歎佛	
8 階段節	(十四)	二段階段節		中 → 下 → 中 — （当る）	講式中 散梵錫等	次に移るために最后の所を上る場合もある。
	(十五)	三段階段節		中 → 下 → 中 → 下 → 中 — （当る）	仝上	仝上
9 当り節	(十六)	当り節	❜	その出ている音の高さに相当して当る	布薩の浄水偈、覚明のメ、懺法の香華等	或は「触節」ともいう
	(十七)	二重当り節	こ	丸味をつけた当り節＋当り節	四智讃、如来唄	従来の「如来唄」にある「い」は「こ」と同調の故に改む。
10 切り切らず節	(十八)	切り切らず節	切X	声を切るも息を切らず	各講式	回向「上酬慈恩……伏願」のところを「切り切らず節」の気持で唱える
11 藤揺節	(十九)	藤揺節		ゆれながら次才に細く引く	仝上	或は「振動節」ともいう。今は「藤揺節」と定む
12 引唱	(廿)	引唱	—	その出している音の高さをそのまゝ引く	仝上	
付 符牒	(廿一)	押撥	レ	語尾を少し押えて撥ねる	懺法専用	或は「ヤンサ節」とも云う

（註）発声標準としての中音について
中音とは平音のことで、これを発声標準とする。即ち五音のうちの（宮）の音階、十二律の音名で云えば（壹越）を以って中音とする。因みに下音は十二律中低い部の（盤渉）の音、上音は（平調）の音を以ってこれに当てる。

Figure 3.21. Explanation of the standard melodic patterns (*fushi*) used in Sōtō *shōmyō*. From *Shōwa kaitei Shōmyō kihan* (1966), 79v–81r. Used with permission.

represented as a circle with an opening at the top. The melody starts on the middle pitch, goes to the lower pitch, and then returns to the middle pitch, which usually means going from one pitch a fourth lower and then back. This simple version is called one *marubushi* (*ichijū marubushi* 一重円節). A close variation is two *marubushi* (*nijū marubushi* 二重円節), which is the same melodic pattern repeated; this is represented by two circles with openings on the top that merge with each other. *Marubushi* is one of the most basic *fushi*, and its graphic representation resembles the melody. However, there are also *fushi* where the graphic representation does not resemble the melodic movement.

As noted earlier, the *Praise of the Thus Come One* holds a special status within the ritual and forms a musical climax with its many magnificent melismas. The special character of this piece is reflected in its musical notation, which additionally hints at the eclectic nature of Sōtō rituals. Today the notation looks very similar to the notation used in the Tendai school, called *meyasu hakase*, which is based on the simple *hakase* notation (*tada bakase*) with additional information about embellishments. This kind of notation can be seen in several manuscripts and in the extant Sōtō print editions from the Tokugawa period (figs. 3.22 and 3.23).[43] Remarkably, however, the notation produced at Sōjiji in the Tokugawa period looks similar to the musical notation for the *Praise of the Thus Come One* used in the Shingon schools (figs. 3.24 and 3.25). This notation provides detailed explanations of how the chant is sung—for example, textual notes written next to the lines indicate how many vibratos to sing on a certain note or where to take a breath.[44] The oldest extant musical notation for the *Praise of the Thus Come One* in the Sōtō school looks again different: in the Rinkō manuscript of the *Keizan shingi*, this piece is notated with the same simple *hakase* used in old Tendai manuscripts (fig. 3.26).[45] This form of notation is actually similar to the earlier notation system used for verses. Thus Sōtō clerics have employed three different notation systems for the *Praise of the Thus Come One* throughout the centuries. This is worth noting because other researchers have argued that the *shōmyō* of the Sōtō school was highly influenced by the Tendai school.[46] However, the different notations of the *Praise of the Thus Come One* suggest that the music of the Sōtō school was highly eclectic because Sōtō monks borrowed from other traditions.

Moreover, in contemporary Japan the traditional style of musical notation does not stand alone. First, the appendix of the *Shōmyō kihan* includes a

43. Although the Tendai example in fig. 3.23 is from the Taishō era, Tendai monks used this style of notation in earlier times. See, for example, the *Gyosan rokkan jō* compiled by Shūen 宗淵 (1786–1859) and printed in Bunsei 1 (1818) in *Zoku Tendaishū zensho Hōgi* 1: 113–114.

44. *Kada narabini hōyō, San kōshiki narabini hōyō.*

45. For an example of the early Tendai notation of the *Praise of the Thus Come One*, see Tōyō Ongaku Gakkai 1972, 277–278, or Arai K. 1986, 16, where it is reprinted.

46. See, for example, Watarai and Sawada 1982, 89–91.

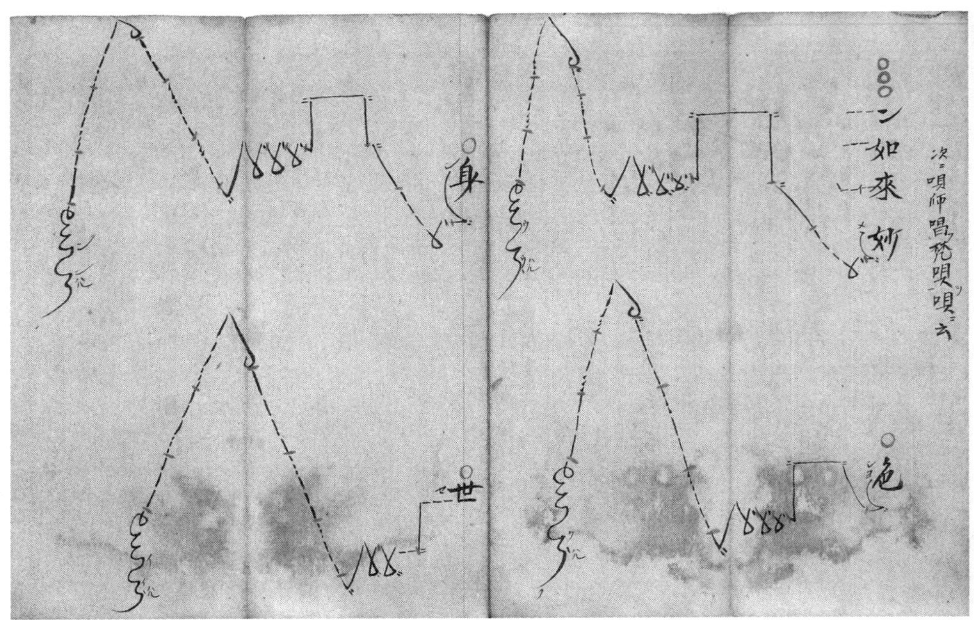

Figure 3.22. Musical notation of the *Praise of the Thus Come One* in "Tendai" style, in *Rakan kōshiki,* a Sōtō school manuscript from 1779. Collection of the author.

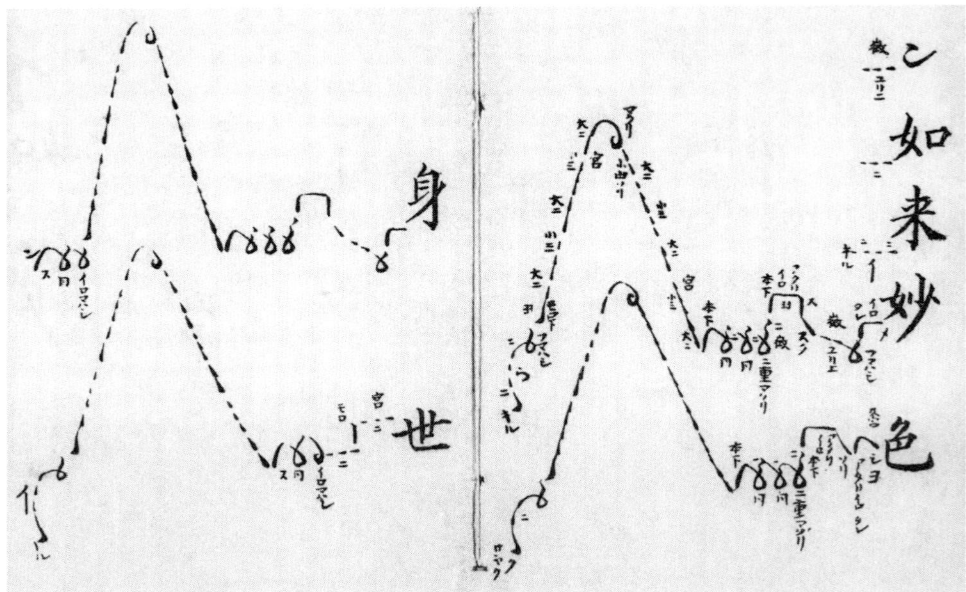

Figure 3.23. *Praise of the Thus Come One,* in *Shōmyō zenshū* 声明全集 (1924), a ritual manual edited by the Tendai monk Taki Dōnin 多紀道忍 (1890–1949). From the National Diet Library Digital Collections.

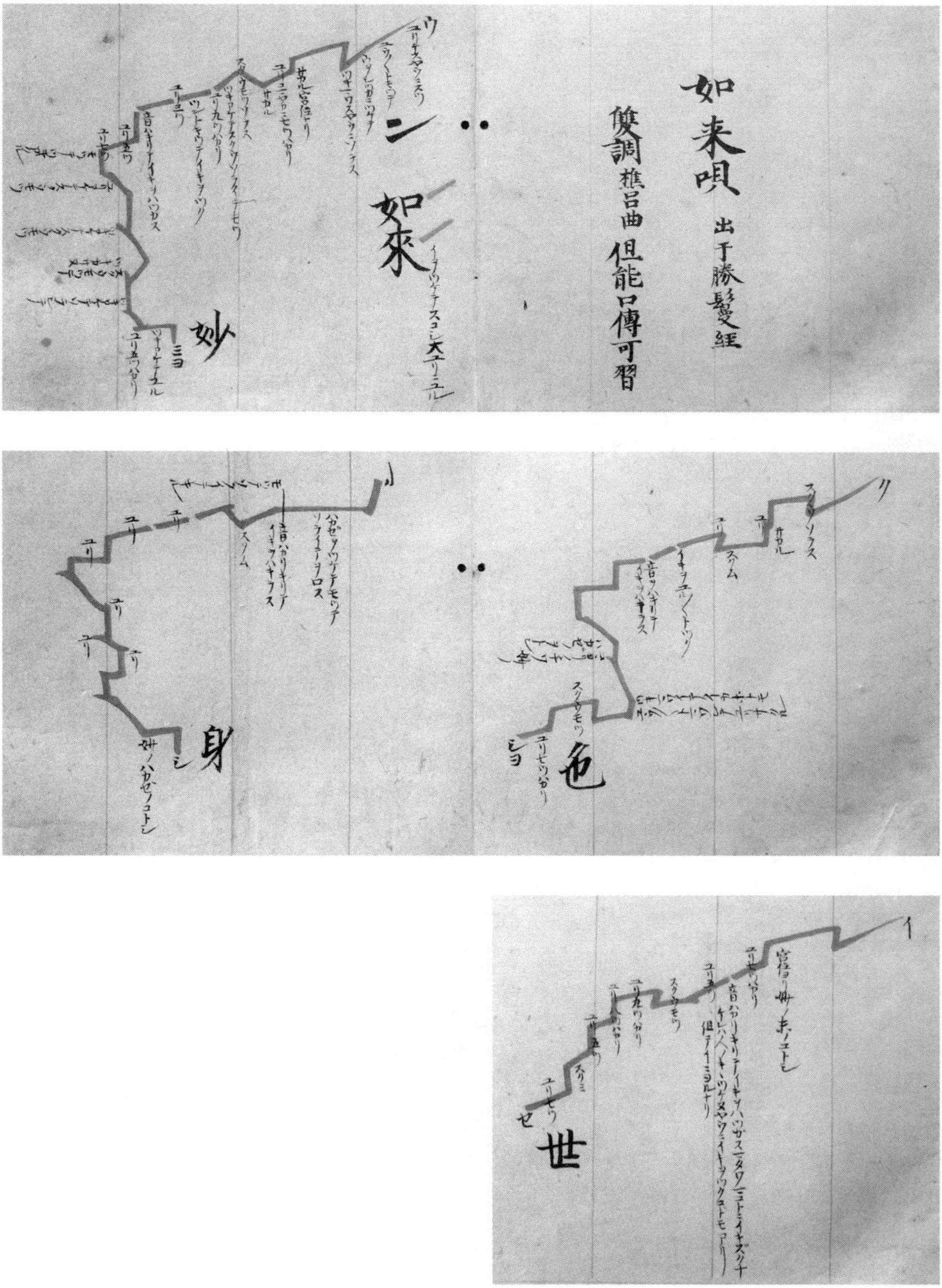

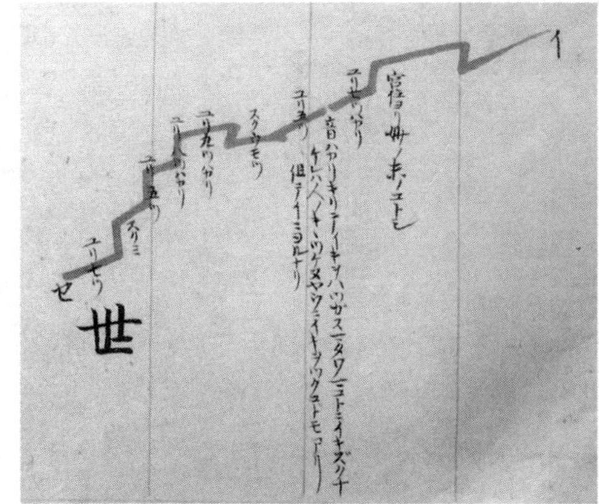

Figure 3.24. Musical notation of the *Praise of the Thus Come One* in "Shingon" style, in *Kada narabini hōyō* (1694), a compilation of all the *shōmyō* pieces sung during *kōshiki* at Sōjiji. The bold lines in red ink indicate the melismas. The *katakana* script in black next to the red lines provides detailed instructions. Archive of Sōjiji Soin, Monzen. Photo by the author.

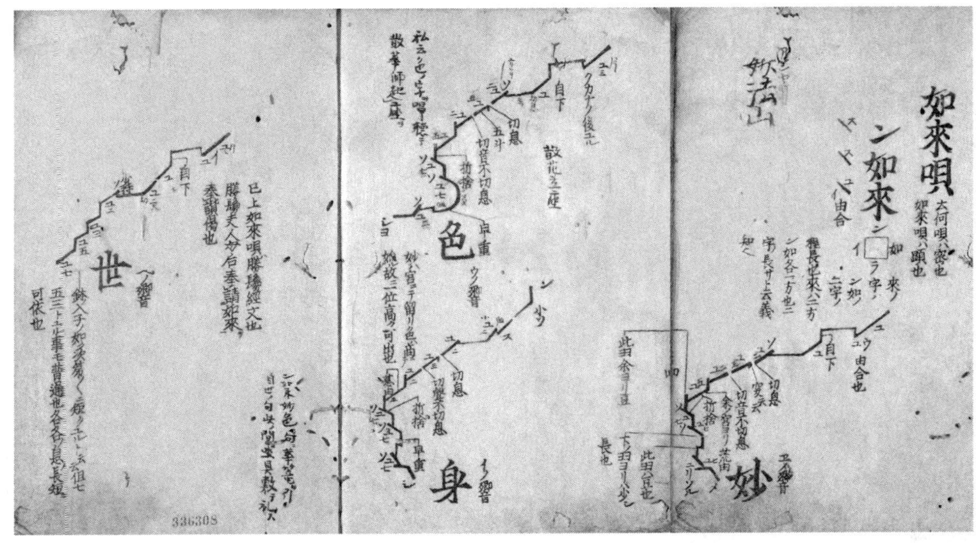

Figure 3.25. *Praise of the Thus Come One,* in *Gyosan shishō* 魚山私鈔 (1646), a *shōmyō* manual compiled by the Shingon monk Chōe 長恵 (1458–1524). From the National Diet Library Digital Collections.

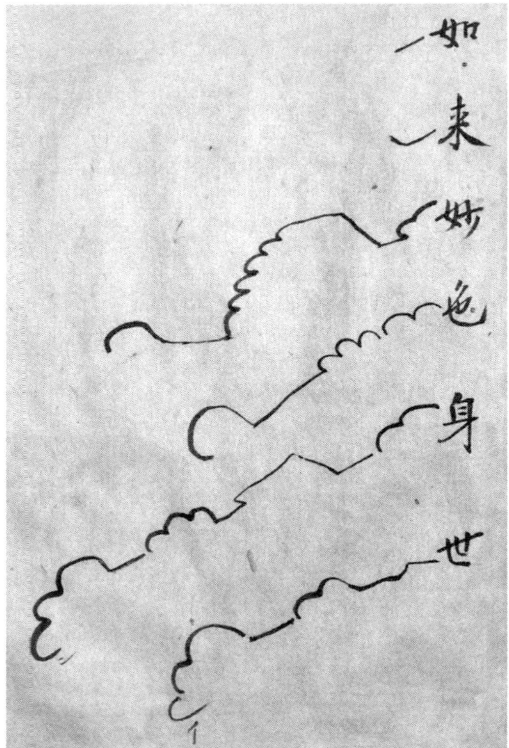

Figure 3.26. *Praise of the Thus Come One.* Detail of the *Rakan kōshiki*, in the Rinkō manuscript of the *Keizan shingi* (1501). Archive of Yōkōji, Hakui. Photo by the author.

Western notation for all pieces.[47] Yet I have never seen a monk using the Western notation, most likely because it does not well represent the characteristics of the *shōmyō* melodies that glide from one tone to the next and are sung very slowly in a free rhythm. Second, some *shōmyō* specialists have invented their own notation system to use as an aid in teaching. Maekawa Bokushō, for example, uses a staff with five lines, in which each line indicates a tone in the pentatonic scale (fig. 3.27).[48] Suzuki Bunmei, a former *shōmyō* teacher at the training temple Kasuisai, uses a more complex system with eight lines in which the spaces between the lines (alternating in gray and white) indicate the notes (fig. 3.28).[49] These intricate systems visually capture melodic movements (as well as some melodic embellishments) and make it easier for the beginner to learn the melodies of *shōmyō* pieces.[50] However, as the instructional devices of two individual teachers, they are not widely used. Instead the traditional musical notation remains the notation used in Sōtō rituals as it is a visual representation that well reflects the musical characteristics of Sōtō *shōmyō*.

Notation for Musical Instruments

The ritual handbooks also contain a notation for the musical instruments to be played during the liturgical pieces. This notation is relatively basic and uses different symbols or terms to describe the sounds of the instruments. The earlier ritual handbooks do not contain detailed instrumental notation, but over time the amount increased. The oldest extant example is a graph notation for cymbals and gong of the *Praise of the Four Wisdoms,* found in the Rinkō manuscript of the *Keizan shingi*. Short and long lines indicate short or long clashes of the cymbals, and a Chinese character—in later manuscripts, a circle—indicates one strike of the gong (fig. 3.29). The playing of the cymbals and gong is the only instrumental music in a *kōshiki,* which might have led the copyist of the Rinkō manuscript to include it. In contrast, notations for the instruments that are used to signal the beginning of pieces or lines are not included in the earliest extant ritual handbooks.

One instrument that is often played during the performance of a *kōshiki* is the singing bowl. In the notation, strikes of the singing bowl are indicated by circles, and if the sound is muted, a triangle is used (fig. 3.30). These marks are often highlighted in red, both in manuscripts and in woodblock prints, to give performers additional visual cues. Among the other instruments, the handbell

---

47. *Shōmyō kihan furoku,* 17v–r. The extensive liner notes to the LP records on Sōtō *shōmyō* (Watarai and Sawada 1980, 60–72; Watarai and Sawada 1982, 64–74; Watarai and Tsukamoto 1983, 91–98) and the explanations of the *Precepts Meeting* and the *Rakan kōshiki* in the *Shinpen Sōtōshū jissen sōsho* also contain Western notation; see Yamamoto 2010a and 2010b.

48. See, for example, Maekawa [2000–2001], 155–170.

49. Suzuki B. 2010, 38–42. He writes that his system is based on a Tendai notation he learned when studying with the Tendai priest Amano Denchū 天納傳中, a well-known *shōmyō* specialist and scholar.

50. This is a conclusion based on my own fieldwork. See also Suzuki B. 2010, 23–24.

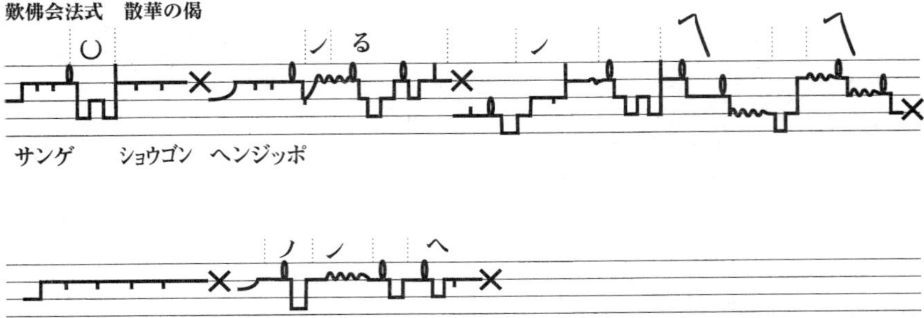

Figure 3.27. Maekawa Bokushō's *shōmyō* notation of the *Gāthā to Scattering Flowers.* The upper staff notation indicates the first line of the verse, and the lower staff the second line of the verse. Each line of the staff indicates a tone in the pentatonic scale. Maekawa [2000–2001], 162. Used with permission. (For the traditional notation of this piece, see fig. 3.30.)

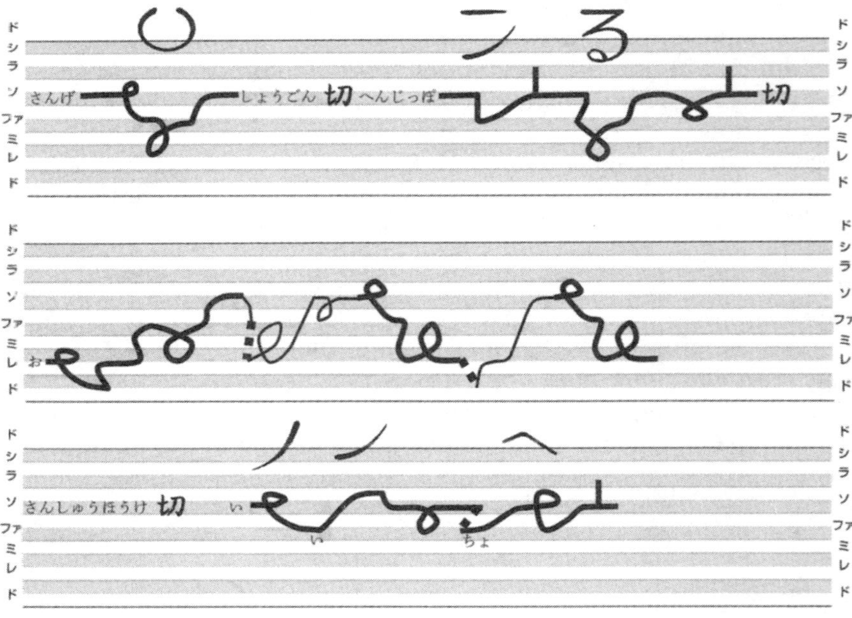

Figure 3.28. Suzuki Bunmei's *shōmyō* notation of the first two lines of the piece *Gāthā to Scattering Flowers.* The upper two sections indicate the melodic movement of the first line of the verse, and the lower section gives the melody of the second line of the verse. The spaces between the lines of the staff represent the notes of a major scale, as the solfège on the left and right shows. The notation visually shows how a performer glides from one tone to the next. Suzuki 2010, 39. Used with permission.

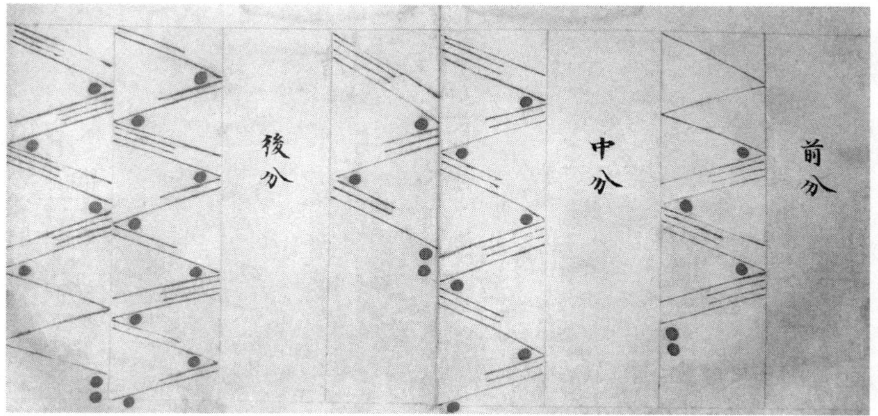

Figure 3.29. Musical notation for cymbals and gong in *Kada narabini hōyō* (1694). Archive of Sōjiji Soin, Monzen. Photo by the author.

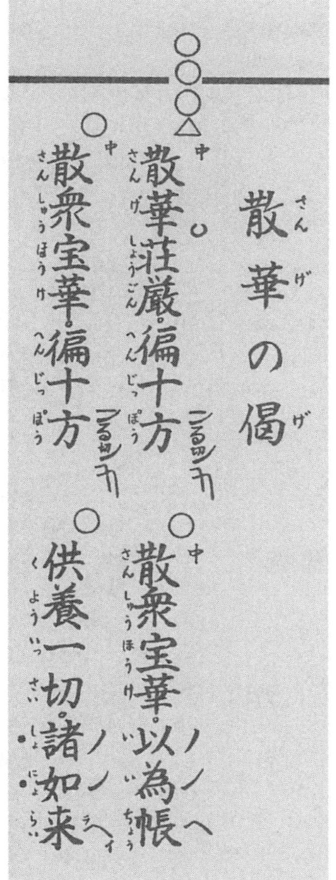

Figure 3.30. *Gāthā to Scattering Flowers,* in the *Shōwa kaitei Rakan kōshiki* (1966), 2r. This is the musical notation in the ritual manual used by Sōtō clerics today. A larger circle indicates a regular strike of the singing bowl, and a triangle a muted strike. The small black circles at the end of the piece indicate strikes of the handbell. Used with permission.

is usually notated with small circles, and the sounding staff is indicated not with symbols but by statements like "shake once" or "shake three times."

The Study and Transmission of *Shōmyō*

Skillful performance of the musical aspects of the ritual is the result of intensive training. A novice needs dedication and, most importantly, a teacher, since the vocalization of liturgical texts has long been a skill passed on from master to disciple. Mastering the skills required is a process that is similar to learning other musical styles, secular as well as religious, because novices and teachers employ similar methods to support learning.

Study at Training Temples

Young monks usually begin the study of *shōmyō* during their monastic training at one of the two head temples or a training temple. Participating in sutra-chanting services every day, they quickly gain expertise in sutra recitation and have many opportunities to recite sacred texts that do not require singing elaborated melodies. *Shōmyō,* however, requires far more training than sutra chanting and is only performed on special occasions. Consequently, the novices need to practice intensively before these observances.

The *ino* at a monastery is responsible for instructing the novices in *shōmyō* and other aspects of ritual expertise. At the head and major training temples, the senior priests who serve as *ino* are usually well-respected *shōmyō* specialists who have spent many years polishing their vocal skills. For them, teaching novices provides an opportunity to transmit their skills to the next generation.

How much *shōmyō* instruction a novice receives depends on a number of factors, including where he trained and how long he stayed there. The head temples generally offer more opportunities to learn *shōmyō* because the monks there perform more rituals that feature elaborate melodies than are performed in smaller temples. Novices assigned solo parts in a *kōshiki* or another *shōmyō* ritual receive individual instruction. At the head temples, not all novices are given the chance to sing a solo part in a *kōshiki.* Nowadays, most novices stay for just one year and are therefore too junior to perform a main part in a *kōshiki* or any other major ritual. Only novices in their second or third year or even later are assigned such important roles. Nevertheless, most novices do get a chance to sing the choral parts in a *kōshiki* and thus learn the choral pieces. The novices who serve in the *dōanryō* 堂行寮 (office of *ino* assistants) at the head temples usually receive regular instruction in the vocalization of texts and the playing of the musical instruments, since they lead the chants and play the instruments during rituals.

In local training temples, the situation is very different. If *kōshiki* are performed, all novices are usually assigned important roles, as there may be only around ten to fifteen novices at the temple (versus around 150 novices at a head temple). Suzuki Bunmei recalls that when he was a novice at Nittaiji

Senmon Sōdō, most novices would stay longer than one year.[51] Back then, the positions for the next year's *kōshiki* were assigned right after they had finished that year's performance. In this way, the novices had a year to polish their *shōmyō* skills. Today, in some of the smaller training temples, *kōshiki* are not performed at all, either because too few monks are available to perform these rituals or because ritual practice is deemphasized at a particular temple.

At temples where *kōshiki* are performed, *shōmyō* instruction and study take place during the preparation for the performance of a *kōshiki* or another ritual that features *shōmyō*. What surprised me at first during my fieldwork at Sōjiji was that the monks did a "dress rehearsal" the night before the actual performance. After running through the ritual in its entirety, the *ino,* together with other senior teachers and possibly a few advanced novices, would give detailed feedback to the younger monks. This was the last step in a long process of group instruction, individual lessons, and rehearsals that often had begun approximately one month before the day of the ritual. In the individual lessons, the novices performing the solo parts would meet with the *ino* one-on-one: The teacher would sing a line and the novice would repeat it. This went back and forth, usually until they had worked through the entire piece. The same method was used in group practice sessions for the assembly: the *ino* would sing and the novices repeated what he sang. At Sōjiji, individuals were not asked to sing alone during group sessions, although that can happen at smaller training temples. When Haruki Shōshū, who had been *ino* at Eiheiji for six years and is currently *ino* at Kasuisai, explained to me how he teaches at Kasuisai, he said that he sings first and then the novices sing one after another so that he can give feedback to each novice. If all sing together, he cannot judge the performance of each one.[52]

In an interview, Maekawa Bokushō expounded on the importance of imitation in the learning process apart from lessons or lectures. He said that a young novice needs a good role model in order to develop an understanding of the aesthetics, melodies, dynamics, and other musical aspects of the ritual. A *shōmyō* teacher provides this model when performing himself in rituals, demonstrating an ideal performance practice to the novices, who then can imitate him.

Although *shōmyō* is learned via oral transmission, the novices do employ new technologies such as voice recorders to support their learning. After recording a lesson, they will listen to the teacher over and over in private. Kōya Kennin 高屋継仁, the current *ino* at Sōjiji and the youngest *shōmyō* specialist I interviewed, mentioned that he records the pieces for the novices himself and then gives them the recordings for practice. As one might expect, Kōya, as well as other younger *shōmyō* specialists, had used recording devices to learn *shōmyō*. As Munakata Gihō 宗像義法, a former *ino* at Eiheiji, remarked, if you

51. Suzuki B. 2010, 14.

52. See also Suzuki B. 2010, 36, for his own reflections on how he teaches in relation to how he learned *shōmyō*.

hear it just once, it is difficult to remember.[53] Thus, recordings can supplement the memory.[54]

Some of the *shōmyō* teachers whom I interviewed shared their reflections on their own learning experience and how they have adjusted their teaching methods in order to transmit *shōmyō* more effectively. Kōya, for example, said that what his teacher taught was "perfect *shōmyō*." Rather than laying out the steps to get there, his teacher jumped right into the performance. Kōya thinks that a more step-by-step approach might be easier for the novices. Although he demonstrates all the variations there are at the very beginning, he teaches the very basics of the liturgical pieces first and adds embellishments and other details as he goes along. Similarly, Haruki said that he first teaches the basic melodic patterns and then starts to teach *Tanbutsue* or other rituals.[55]

The commitment to improve the skills of the novices is also shown in the detailed feedback that senior priests give to young monks after rehearsals and ritual performances. Remarkably, I occasionally saw the teachers at Sōjiji giving points for the level of performance with 100 points for the highest, sometimes for individual pieces sung by novices and sometimes for the ritual performance as a whole. They judged the performances on several levels, including melodic correctness, vocal production, dynamics, breaks, and timing. When I asked Maekawa Bokushō about the custom of grading, he said that it is an important aspect of the training that young monks receive, because by getting detailed feedback, they are able to further polish their skills.

Kōya remarked that he used to give points to the novices who led the chanting, but recently, instead of giving points, he tries to explain in greater detail why the performance fell short of perfection. He thinks that a novice needs to understand what should be improved and that points alone do not provide this information. Kōya further mentioned that he records the performance of a novice who is leading a ritual for the first time and then gives the sound recording to the novice along with detailed feedback.

As mentioned earlier, a number of formulaic movements are executed by the monks during a *kōshiki*. Unlike *shōmyō* that is only sung in special rituals like *kōshiki*, the movements and gestures used in *kōshiki* are largely the same as those that the clerics perform in daily or regular rituals. Therefore, novices learn these movements early in their training, and the conduct quickly becomes part of the embodied knowledge they acquire. Watching their carefully choreographed movements, *kōshiki*, as well as most other Sōtō rituals, feel almost like a dance. The movements seem effortless—but it is an effortlessness born of intensive training. Novices who are newly assigned to bring

53. Interview, June 15, 2015.

54. Another use of recording devices was mentioned by Haruki, who recommends to his novices that they record and listen to their own performances. By checking whether they actually sang in the way they thought, they can hear for themselves what needs to be improved. This method is also used by music students—for example, my fellow students and I recorded ourselves on a regular basis when we studied jazz performance at the Berklee College of Music.

55. The widely performed *Tanbutsue* is probably the most basic *shōmyō* ritual of the Sōtō school, and therefore *shōmyō* teachers often start instruction with this ritual.

ritual implements into the central area of the hall or help with the delivery of offerings to the objects of worship enshrined on the altar practice their movements daily under the watchful instruction of one or two senior novices, until they can perform them skillfully and simultaneously at the same speed.

Study after Leaving a Training Temple

Once the novices leave a training temple, they might have fewer opportunities to participate in *kōshiki*.[56] But those who are interested can continue studying *shōmyō*. Joining *shōmyō* practices organized by their local young monks' association is one option. There also are several *shōmyō* study groups in different parts of Japan that allow priests to study under the guidance of a *shōmyō* specialist. Between meetings, the members of these groups make use of sound recordings of the group sessions to practice at home. They might also use CD or DVD recordings by a *shōmyō* specialist to enhance their study and listen to the performance over and over or sing along with it.[57] These recordings do not typically contain lectures on the vocal technique or other technical aspects of *shōmyō;* instead they consist of performances of *shōmyō* pieces or complete rituals. One exception is worth mentioning here: the second disc in a three-DVD set featuring Maekawa Hakuhō, probably the most renowned *shōmyō* specialist of his generation, provides more information than most other recordings and seems to be a good introduction to *shōmyō*. The video shows the musical notation on the screen and visually indicates where in the notation Maekawa is at each point. This is a great help in learning how to read the musical notation. Additionally, at the beginning of each piece, a narrator states what is special about the piece and what aspect should be given particular attention.[58] However, as many *shōmyō* specialists remarked in interviews, recordings alone cannot teach *shōmyō*. One needs a teacher who corrects one's use of the voice and imparts the subtleties of tone production and melodic movement.[59] Nonetheless, the recordings can supplement direct instruction by a teacher and also preserve the current chanting style for future generations.[60]

---

56. Priests in some areas perform rituals featuring *shōmyō* at elaborate funeral services and thus continue to be engaged in singing *shōmyō*. In Niigata prefecture, one of the strongholds of Japanese Sōtō *shōmyō,* priests perform either a *Kannon senbō* or a *Tanbutsue*. In some areas of Akita prefecture, the priests perform a *Kannon kōshiki*. In Aichi prefecture, there used to be a similar custom of performing a *Tanbutsue* or a *Kannon senbō*. But these cases are exceptions and most Sōtō priests do not need *shōmyō* skills to fulfill their regular duties.

57. See, for example, the DVD sets *Shōmyō no tebiki* and *Sōtōshū hosshiki shinan: Ino dōan kōshū*.

58. *Kobutsu no manebi: Hosshiki shōmyō*.

59. Haruki mentioned an additional caveat of the recordings as practice tools: some masters featured might use a lot of additional embellishments, which is confusing for young monks who do not yet know the basics (interview, July 7, 2017).

60. In her study of contemporary shamans in Korea, Laurel Kendall discusses how young shamans use audiotapes to learn complicated chants. Recordings, she writes, are useful because they provide the rhythms and intonations that are missing in a written text. Nevertheless, she hints at the limits of sound recordings, as they cannot help an apprentice to master the use of the voice, body posture, or facial expression. She also describes a case in which a master told an apprentice who had tried to learn a piece from a commercial recording that the rhythm is off. The master then offered to make a recording of herself for the disciple. See Kendall 2009, 109–110.

Dedicated young novices have always sought out *shōmyō* specialists for private instruction, and this guidance proved vital for their becoming well-known *shōmyō* singers in their own right. One example is Baba Gijitsu 馬場義実, a priest in Yokohama, who is locally known for his *shōmyō* skills and often performs as cantor in the Yokohama area. He intensively studied *shōmyō* for around six months with Imai Gen'yū 今井玄雄, who had been *ino* at Eiheiji and *tantō* at Hōkyōji 宝慶寺, while living with Imai at his temple in Niigata. Imai instructed Baba privately on a daily basis, starting with the basic melodic patterns before learning whole pieces. Similarly, Munakata Gihō visited his *shōmyō* teacher every evening for three months to study with him, until the teacher was satisfied with Gihō's performance. Maekawa Bokushō, as the son of Hakuhō, studied solely with his father over decades and continued to receive instruction even when he had become a teacher at Nittaiji Senmon Sōdō himself. Terakura Shōyū, who had been *ino* at Sōjiji and now is head priest at a temple in Niigata prefecture, is another very different case, as he studied *shōmyō* with several teachers. His training started when he entered the training temple Hōonji 報恩寺 in Morioka, Iwate prefecture, at the age of fifteen. He recalled that he first learned the pieces that he needed to recite during funerals. The master taught *shōmyō* by instructing Terakura in various *fushi*. Later, he went to Sōjiji to study with Maekawa Hakuhō. After leaving Sōjiji, Terakura sought instruction from other *shōmyō* specialists, most of them active in Niigata prefecture. Thus, Terakura studied with several specialists over many years. Most of the *shōmyō* specialists said that during their intensive study of *shōmyō*, they had many opportunities to participate in rituals that featured *shōmyō*. Baba further remarked that although he does not perform these kinds of rituals regularly anymore, he remembers the melodies very well and can still sing them, because he had studied them so intensively.

These four cases demonstrate the need for intensive study under a master in order to become skilled at *shōmyō* oneself. Learning *shōmyō* and *kōshiki* resembles the way traditional art forms in Japan are transmitted. It is basically a matter of learning by imitating a master, and for that reason Japanese priests insist that *shōmyō* belongs to the realm of oral transmission. Maekawa Bokushō and Terakura emphasized in interviews the concept of *denjū* 伝授, transmission from master to disciple. This is the most important aspect of all traditional Japanese arts. A master instructs his disciple, and after years of intensive study the disciple becomes a master himself. *Denjū* is, of course, also central in the transmission of Zen from mind to mind. But in some cases, a disciple might have only a brief meeting with a master before receiving a verification of understanding, or the relationship might be more of a formal nature. However, in *shōmyō* and ritual expertise, as well as in traditional arts, the transmission of knowledge over an extended time period is a necessity in order to master a skill.

Vocal Training: From *Kangyō* to Karaoke

Like singers of secular music, *shōmyō* specialists also use strategies to train their voices. A few priests, for example, told me about *kangyō* 寒行, or practicing in the cold—in this case, reciting in the cold.[61] Depending on the area and teacher, the monks who do this either recite a sutra or just sing a long "*hō*" in a very loud voice. For example, Haruki recalled how as a young monk at Eiheiji in the cold winter mountains he recited for two to three hours a day to make his voice stronger. He just sang "*hō*" for as long as he could, holding the tone. Nowadays, he does it in a car when he drives as nobody can hear him. Maekawa Bokushō also mentioned that he recited sutras in the cold wind when he was young. Baba further said that he also had done *kangyō* when he went on begging rounds with his father as a teenager. When he lived with Imai he did not do it anymore, but when he was driving home from Imai's temple, a three-hour drive, he sang while listening to the tape. Also, sometimes he sang outside where nobody could hear him, since one has to recite with a loud voice—otherwise the body does not remember.

But another priest told me that he would not do *kangyō* as there is a chance it will hurt one's voice; in fact, Baba said he did actually hurt his voice during begging rounds. Notably, Haruki and Maekawa seem to not instruct their novices to do this practice. Maekawa's son, for example, does not do it, but during the morning recitation at his temple, the hall is very cold, and he thought that this would be a good substitute. The best would be to read sutras beside the graveyards outside, Maekawa said, because there are no roofs or walls and the sound does not reflect back. This would be a good way to improve the volume of one's voice.

When I spoke with Kōya, he mentioned another interesting way he improved his voice: he used to sing a lot of karaoke as a university student, and that was a very good preparation for him to study *shōmyō*, as he had intensively studied vocal techniques before he learned to sing *shōmyō*. In the same way as Maekawa, he emphasizes that one learns by actually participating in regular observances; certain texts requiring a long breath are vocalized daily at Sōjiji and in this way, train the voice. Thus, the novices practice by the daily vocalizations and not through some special exercises. It is a learning by doing.

The learning process of *shōmyō* showcases how similar it is to the study of other musical styles. A novice needs to undergo a long training before he can master the subtleties of *shōmyō* and become a skilled performer who might one day teach *shōmyō* at one of the head or training temples. Becoming a *shōmyō* specialist is like becoming a professional singer.

Kōshiki Shōmyō as Zen Practice

The last section of this chapter analyzes how contemporary Sōtō priests interpret their *shōmyō* practice and addresses the question: What role does the

61. The term *kangyō* describes ascetic practices that are traditionally done in the midst of the winter, often for thirty days. Practices varied and could include zazen, sutra recitation, the recitation of the name of a buddha, and going on begging rounds. An early examplar of such practices was the Nichiren monk Kuonjōin Nisshin 久遠成院日親 (1407–1488), who recited verses from the *Lotus Sutra* for four hours every night for one hundred days from autumn through winter at the graveyard of his temple Hokekyōji 法華経寺 (Stone 1999, 389).

vocalization of liturgical texts play in Sōtō Zen? Unfortunately, there are no historical sources that explain how monks in the Tokugawa period or earlier understood the role of *shōmyō*. However, a few contemporary *shōmyō* specialists have written essays or liner notes to recordings that detail how they interpret *shōmyō*. I also interviewed Sōtō priests but soon realized— as other ritual studies scholars have done—that ritual specialists and practitioners are mainly concerned about their own performance practice and often seem unable to answer theoretical questions. The priests talked more about the technical details of their performance, the history of *shōmyō* and *kōshiki* in their school, and how they learned to perform *shōmyō*. But most of them did not provide answers to my philosophical or theoretical questions, so the following analysis is primarily based on the writings of contemporary Sōtō priests, supplemented by information from my interviews and fieldwork.

The headquarters of the Sōtō school does not promote an official interpretation of *shōmyō*, and thus there seems to be room for a wide range of individual views regarding the role of *shōmyō* and *kōshiki* in Sōtō Zen. Most priests interpret *shōmyō* in accordance with their understanding of general Buddhist concepts and the core ideas of the Sōtō school. The views I outline below are not necessarily shared by all Sōtō clerics. Nevertheless, the monks I cite are well-respected and influential ritual specialists; most have taught at one of the two head temples or major training temples. It is impossible to judge how their opinions differ from understandings hundreds of years ago, due to the lack of sources, but the views described here reflect how some of today's leading *shōmyō* specialists interpret singing as a Zen practice.

An important caveat is that unlike the preceding chapters, here I follow the Soto priests' loose definition of *kōshiki* as referring to any Sōtō ritual that features *shōmyō*. This is in fact how Sōtō priests talk about these rituals: since the vocalization styles of *kōshiki* (rituals centering around a *shikimon*) and other rituals featuring *shōmyō* are similar, Sōtō clerics do not distinguish between these kinds of rituals, which stand in sharp contrast to the regular sutra-chanting services of their school. I start with Maekawa Bokushō and Suzuki Bunmei's views on *shōmyō* and then introduce the ideas of other *shōmyō* specialists, mainly those affiliated with the head temple Sōjiji.

Maekawa Bokushō

One of the leading *shōmyō* specialists of the Sōtō school, Maekawa served twice as the *ino*, then as the *tantō*, and currently is the *godō* at Sōjiji. It is rare for a *shōmyō* specialist to become the *godō* at a head temple, since the *ino*, responsible for instructing monks in etiquette and rituals, and the *godō*, responsible for instructing monks in zazen and doctrine, usually represent different fields of specialization. Maekawa also gives lectures to *shōmyō* study groups in several different areas of Japan and teaches Sōtō nuns at the convent in Nagoya, Aichi Senmon Nisodō. As the son of Maekawa Hakuhō, the most acclaimed *shōmyō* specialist of the postwar generation, he developed an intimate relation to *shōmyō* while listening to his father's vocalization from an early age.

Maekawa is an untypical *shōmyō* specialist because he has deeply reflected on ritual practice and developed a philosophical view of it. Other *shōmyō* specialists I talked to were mainly concerned with the technical details of their performance practice and did not readily discuss the meaning or interpretation of *shōmyō*. Maekawa, however, has long been engaged in zazen practice and studied under the guidance of several masters who were all disciples of the prominent Zen teacher Sawaki Kōdō 澤木興道 (1880–1965). These include Kishigami Kōjun 岸上興詢, Sawaki's last disciple; Sakai Tokugen 酒井得元 (1912–1996) and Suzuki Kakuzen 鈴木格禅 (1926–1999), two Komazawa University professors; Kawase Genkō 川瀬玄光 (1908–1988), the only nun to receive Dharma transmission from Sawaki Kōdō; and Okamura Kōbun 岡村光文, a nun who widely taught the sewing of the robe. Maekawa's practice and understanding of Sōtō Zen have been doubly influenced by Sawaki's emphasis on zazen and his father's expertise in Sōtō rituals and *shōmyō*. He has admitted that when he was young he did not think that *shōmyō* was actually important. But Suzuki Kakuzen, who respected his father's *shōmyō* skills, corrected that view and told him that *shōmyō,* too, is part of practice. From then on, Maekawa practiced *shōmyō* with enthusiasm. He has also been interested in doctrinal texts, including the *Shōbōgenzō,* and has read extensively in religion, Japanese traditional music, and literature. This wide reading might have inspired him to reflect more deeply on his own ritual practice.

Among his writings is a twenty-page essay entitled "Zen Master Dōgen and Religious Rituals" (Kōso Dōgen zenji to shūkyō girei), in which he elaborates his views on *shōmyō* and sutra recitation as Zen practices.[62] In this essay, Maekawa begins a paragraph on ritual procedures and *shōmyō* (*hosshiki shōmyō*) with the following statement:

> As for zazen, its practice is the realization of buddhahood. The robe is the fabric of the realization of buddhahood. Thus, *shōmyō* is the voice of the realization of buddhahood, and ritual procedures (*hosshiki* 法式) are the actions of the realization of buddhahood. The point to keep in mind when practicing these is to strictly cut yourself off from the ordinary mental state. Zazen should not be [done sitting in] *seiza,* it must be [done sitting in] full lotus or half lotus position. The robe cannot even be changed a little from the Buddha's rules. The words before the altar are verses (*shiika* 詩歌), and when read, should be sung (*shō* 唱) or recited (*ju* 誦); it should not be [like] regular conversation that is spoken from the

62. This unpublished article was distributed to Maekawa's colleagues, disciples, and students, and I cite it here because it is the most comprehensive essay he has written about ritual practices. He had previously expressed these ideas in more condensed form: in the liner notes to a set of VHS cassettes showing *shōmyō* performances by his father, and in an essay in *Sōtōzen mezame,* a book accompanying a set of audio and video recordings of Sōtō rituals; see Maekawa [1989] and Maekawa [2000–2001]. In the following citations from "Zen Master Dōgen and Religious Rituals," I include references to corresponding passages in the latter essay.

> ordinary mental state. Also, the actions are not the actions of the ordinary mental state, and therefore they are ritual procedures.[63]

In this paragraph, Maekawa mentions four aspects of Sōtō Zen—zazen, the robe, *shōmyō,* and ritual procedures—and describes them as expressions of the realization of buddhahood. His interpretation reflects one of the core principles of Sōtō Zen: the unity of practice and realization (*shushō ittō* 修証一等), a concept based on Dōgen's writings.

One of Dōgen's earliest works, *Bendōwa* 辦道話 (Talk on pursuing the way), is considered the locus classicus for this idea. To a fictive question on what someone who has understood the true Dharma should expect from zazen practice, Dōgen answered:

> To think practice and realization are not one is a non-Buddhist view. In the Buddha Dharma, practice and realization are one and the same. As your present practice is practice within realization, your initial negotiation of the Way is in itself the whole of original realization. That is why from the time you are instructed in the way of practice, you are told not to anticipate realization apart from practice. It is because practice points directly to original realization.[64]

Thus, rather than seeing practice as a gradual process that leads to some future enlightenment, Dōgen asserts that practice and realization are one. Throughout his *Bendōwa,* Dōgen advances the superiority of zazen. In particular, he states that from the start of a consultation with a teacher, there is no need for incense offerings, making prostrations, reciting the name of a buddha, repentance, and sutra recitation; one should just sit and cast off body and mind.[65] This passage is often cited to show that Dōgen advocated an exclusive practice of zazen, and it laid a foundation for some interpretations of Sōtō Zen as focused solely on seated meditation. In other writings, however, Dōgen promoted various practices, including those disparaged in the foregoing passage from the *Bendōwa.*[66] In his famous essay *Tenzō kyōkun* 典座教訓 (Instructions for the cook), for example, he explains how the work of a cook is by no means inferior to zazen.[67] Today, the practice of novices at the head temples of the Sōtō school is not limited to seated meditation; rather, they

---

63. Maekawa n.d., 9; Maekawa [2000–2001], 48.

64. Translation by Waddell and Abe 2002, 19; for the original, see DZO 1: 737; DZZ 2: 470. On Dōgen and his interpretation of the unity of practice and realization, see Cook 1983 and Leighton 2008.

65. DZO 1: 731; DZZ 2: 462.

66. Foulk (2012) has shown that Dōgen enthusiastically promoted in other works the practices he dismissed in *Bendōwa.* On this point, see also Kubovčáková 2018 for an interpretation of how zazen and devotional practices are closely connected in Dōgen's thought. On the role of monastic discipline in Dōgen's *Shōbōgenzō,* see Heine 2020, chap. 8.

67. See DZO 2: 295–303, DZZ 6: 2–25, or T 82: 320a02–323a15. For an English translation, see Foulk 2001.

engage in a wide range of monastic observances, including the performance of rituals, all of which are intended to be done with the same mindset as zazen and are viewed as an expression of realization.

Likewise, Maekawa relates the principle of realizing buddhahood not only to zazen but also to other practices such as the wearing of the robe, the singing of liturgical texts, and other ritual procedures. For Maekawa the performance of rituals and the singing of *shōmyō* are not opposed or subordinated to zazen; rather, they share the very same quality.[68] In this way, the voice of *shōmyō* and the singing of sacred texts are also an expression of the realization of buddhahood. He does not distinguish between ritual observances and zazen as Zen practices—for him, both are based on the same principle, the idea that practice and realization are one. Throughout my fieldwork at Sōjiji, I saw him performing in numerous ritual functions. His bearing and posture always seemed as focused as it was during zazen, and he appeared to be performing the rituals with the same concentration. One of the novices was moved to remark on this, saying that Maekawa is a *mihon* 見本, a model, for how to practice.

The next section of Maekawa's essay is devoted to *shōmyō*. He first explains the ritual form of *kōshiki:* the preparatory pieces before the *shikimon* function to decorate the room; the *shikimon* praises the virtues of the buddhas, bodhisattvas, and patriarchs while the monks pay respect to the objects of worship and express prayers; the transfer of merit serves as a musical send-off to the objects of worship.[69] He goes on to say that *shōmyō hosshiki* and musical instruments have other functions as well:

> When the music created to invite the buddhas is performed, then just by hearing this music we know what [ritual] is performed, and finally the music confirms their presence. As for the decoration (*shōgon* 荘厳), both the ritual procedures and the music are performed in time and space; the ritual that cuts off the ordinary mental state is at the same time the realization of buddhahood. The person

68. It is important to mention that some Sōtō teachers promote zazen as superior to other practices and that there are a few small training temples in Japan that focus primarily on zazen. Additionally, there are a few temples that offer monastic training but are not official training temples. One famous example is Antaiji 安泰寺, founded by Sawaki Kōdō. Uchiyama Kōchō 内山興正, who succeeded Sawaki after his death, focused on "zazen practice with minimal ceremony, ritual, and formality" (Okumura 2012, xi) and started *sesshin* (meditation periods) "without toys": no Dharma talks, no *kyōsaku* 警策 (wake-up stick), no cleaning, no work, no chanting, and no bathing (http://antaiji.org/archives/eng/adult26.shtml). Another example of a temple with minimal focus on rituals is Bukkokuji 仏国寺 in Obama City (Fukui prefecture). But the practice at these temples is very different from the practice at the head temples of the Sōtō school. Moreover, according to Maekawa Bokushō, Sawaki Kōdō was entirely capable of vocalizing *shōmyō*, and when he was *godō* at Sōjiji he is said to have devotedly recited *shikimon*. At Myōgenji 妙元寺 in Nagoya, the temple of his nun disciple, clerics often performed the abbreviated repentance ceremony and nuns who had studied directly under Sawaki would have annually performed the *Jizō kōshiki* and *Rakan kōshiki* (email exchange with Maekawa).

69. Maekawa n.d., 11; Maekawa [2000–2001], 48.

seeing a buddha is nobody else but a buddha. Therefore, the people providing offerings in front of one's eyes are the family of the buddha(s).

Since the olden times, we have strictly avoided departing from the rules of the ceremonies, because when people perform Buddhist rituals, solemnity is necessary. It can be said that this strictness is the separation between the buddhas and the ordinary mental state. . . .

It can be said that only through *shōmyō,* the instruments, zazen, and rituals do we symbolically express the state of the Buddha without mediation. In other words, all myriad things collectively, all sentient beings, both ordinary and enlightened, and everything in existence preserve the reverberation of the universe from the time of the Buddha. This is called pure sound (*bonnon* 梵音).[70] I conclude that we cannot deny that *shōmyō* and the instruments are the expression of this reverberation.[71]

Maekawa stresses the importance of rituals and again explains that ritual practice offers the opportunity to realize buddhahood. Music and ritual procedures differ from the ordinary mental state and symbolically express buddhahood. Remarkably, he describes *shōmyō* and the sound of the musical instruments as a kind of Ur-sound that has reverberated through the universe since the time of the Buddha. Thus he implies that through sound one can connect with the Buddha in the time of his physical absence while expressing the state of a buddha oneself.

He then discusses the necessity of training and practice:

Further, *shōmyō* needs special training. One might say that zazen does not need it, but when conducting *sesshin* 攝心 it becomes clear by itself that this needs steadfast physical and mental stamina. Both ritual procedures and *shōmyō* are the honing of [one's] life. Through Buddhist rituals we extinguish the ordinary mental state; however, in that respect, *shōmyō* has an especially complicated side. Nowadays, everybody performs Buddhist rituals. But considered from the point of the practitioners, we do not say that one should conduct *hosshiki shōmyō* and *kōshiki,* but instead one practices and cultivates [them], and as a human expression, one must reach excellence [in them]. Because it is an action directed at something that transcends humans, it is called expression (*hyōgen* 表現), it is

70. The term *bonnon* has several meanings; it can describe the voice of Brahma, the teaching of the Buddha, a particular liturgical piece, or ceremonial music. It is also used to describe a pure voice, and in this sense, it is often used as a metaphor for the beautiful voice of the Buddha. Based on a conversation with Maekawa Bokushō, I have translated *bonnon* here as pure sound. Maekawa explained that all sounds could be *bonnon*—however, not all sounds are *bonnon.* Ordinary sounds and speech would not be *bonnon.* He also clearly stated that he did not mean Sanskrit sounds or Sanskrit as a language here. On the other hand, he said that all sounds in a ritual are *bonnon.* Therefore, a translation as "ceremonial music" might be possible. However, as he also maintained that sound outside the ritual context could be *bonnon,* I translated the term here as "pure sound" (interview, July 17, 2017). Interestingly, in Hinduism *nāda brahma,* which is usually translated as *bonnon,* is regarded as a kind of Ur-sound of the cosmos.

71. Maekawa n.d., 11–12; Maekawa [2000–2001], 48–49.

> called craft (*gigei* 技芸), it is called art (*geijutsu* 芸術). It is not a means for humans to interact with one another.
>
> There is nothing more difficult than to actually perform Buddhist rituals while intoning [texts]. But as for old basic guidebooks, there are close to none; further, of those [that remain] there are aspects that cannot be learned [from them]. In recent years, it has become possible to produce sound recordings and the study has changed completely; nevertheless, there are aspects that cannot be transmitted [this way]. [Trying to learn from recordings] does not match the actual [experience of] hearing how a practitioner intones [a text], as it disappears in an instant. Truly, there is no substitute for learning step by step, in person, under the guidance of a master.[72]

Here Maekawa shifts from a soteriological perspective to the aesthetic side, emphasizing that one must reach excellence in *shōmyō* in terms of practice as well as aesthetics. On the one hand, *shōmyō* is an expression of the realization of buddhahood, and on the other, it is an art form that requires cultivation in order to achieve excellence. So, it becomes clear that *shōmyō* has a soteriological as well as an aesthetic and artistic side. Maekawa further emphasizes that one needs to learn directly from a teacher. In an interview, he further noted that a beginner would not know what to improve and has to learn by listening to specialists. A teacher can instruct a student and tell him what needs to be amended to cultivate his skills.

In the remainder of the essay, Maekawa discusses mostly technical aspects of *hosshiki shōmyō* such as naturalness, tonal structure, tone production, tone color, musical notation, speed, and breathing method. In the following, I translate only the paragraphs that illuminate his understanding of rituals as a Buddhist practice. The first explains the conduct of a buddha (*butsugyō* 仏行):

> It is practicing as personal practice and not to intone for other people. It is to reverently and sincerely practice. As for the conduct of a buddha, fundamentally it is not skilled or unskilled. But the emotion of the practitioner must be strong. In the [*Sōtōshū*] *Gyōji kihan* 行持規範 (Standard observances [of the Sōtō school]) and other texts, there are instructions on vocalization. It is the voice of delight and sublime beauty; it should not be like sinking into darkness. On a high tone, it has grace and strictness. There are many terms, such as singing (唱), reciting (誦), and reading (曰), but every time [you intone a text] in front of the Buddha altar you want to keep the tension. To avoid mistakes, you should practice beforehand, further make all the preparations, and during reciting you must refrain from coughing and the like.[73]

Thus, ritual practice requires sincerity, and this devoted concentration lays the foundation for a graceful vocal performance. Maekawa's ensuing

72. Maekawa n.d., 12–13; Maekawa [2000–2001], 49–50.
73. Maekawa n.d., 13; Maekawa [2000–2001], 50.

elucidation of naturalness in vocalization concludes with the statement that "in order to truly reach naturalness, training and technique are necessary."[74] Although he stated earlier that a dualistic view of skilled and unskilled cannot be applied to the conduct of a buddha, this statement points to the reality that expertise in *shōmyō* cannot be reached without devoted training and practice. In the end, Maekawa, along with other *shōmyō* specialists, distinguishes between levels of performance and shows an appreciation of a skilled vocalization.

Next, Maekawa begins a discussion about tone production (*hassei* 発声) with an interesting statement on the relation between *shōmyō* and zazen:

> For [us] who practice zazen, voice production is clearly influenced by the breathing method of zazen. It is difficult to explain this fully in writing, but it involves the stillness that we experience in *shōmyō,* the long sensation of the breath, and the calmness. When the patched-robed monks practice *shōmyō,* they pay attention to following the posture of zazen. *Shōmyō* has a unique voice production method; although it is very similar to Japanese traditional music, by no means can you just borrow it [from other genres]. It can be said that what makes *shōmyō shōmyō* solely depends on this voice production method. Awareness of the posture of zazen is automatically awareness of the posture of the voice production for *shōmyō.*[75]

In suggesting that *shōmyō* and zazen share a similar breathing method and an awareness of posture, Maekawa again describes both practices as equal. We could say that practitioners bring the breathing method and concentration of zazen from the meditation hall to the Buddha or Dharma hall, where they perform rituals.

Then Maekawa explains some details about the special voice production of *shōmyō*. First, there are two different timbres: dark (*jigoe* 地声 or *yō* 陰) and bright (*kasei* 仮声 or *on* 陽). Second, he comments on the dynamics: in traditional Japanese music, there is no crescendo; a note is either loud or soft. There are more subtle aspects of voice production, such as the sustaining of notes and accentuation, that are difficult to express in musical notation, he writes, again emphasizing the necessity of training in order to be able to control one's voice to the extent required.[76] Maekawa continues expounding on the limitations of the musical notation included in the *Shōwa kaitei Shōmyō kihan* and the aesthetics of *shōmyō:*

> In Shōwa 40 (1965), the committee members of the *Shōmyō kihan* compared and examined the old *kōshiki* books, and then they selected and standardized the musical notation (*hakase*). But [their] simplification of that musical notation also has inconsistencies. Traditional melodies come first; notation marks (*fugō* 符号)

74. Maekawa n.d., 13; Maekawa [2000–2001], 50.
75. Maekawa n.d., 15; Maekawa [2000–2001], 51.
76. Maekawa n.d., 15; Maekawa [2000–2001], 51.

> do not. The reason is that between the musical notation that is not included in the *kihan* and the musical notation [that is], there are *fushi*. Further, it could be thought that the only reason these *fushi* cannot be written down is because they are subtle and extremely difficult to notate; yet combined with the voice production of the dark tone [the *fushi*] are very beautiful. This, we can say, is the key to *shōmyō*. To rigidly intone [according to] the musical notation cannot be called *shōmyō*. Further, there are also people who display [stylistic] differences depending on [their] master and [their affiliation with one of] the two head temples; but that is not the point here. The music of our school is something that has a position that has been studied and fixed in relation to Japanese traditional music. It preserves the characteristics of medieval music well.
>
> To study and perceive the beautiful as beautiful is to train in the sensibility of our predecessors who have perfected [*shōmyō*] over hundreds of years. It truly is profound.[77]

Since the musical notation is incomplete, oral instruction is necessary to provide the information that is missing from the ritual handbooks. But the meaning of *shōmyō* study goes further. For Maekawa, *shōmyō* training enables the practitioner to connect through his vocalization with the Buddha himself and the Sōtō lineage.

Throughout the essay, Maekawa acknowledges the two sides of *shōmyō*. On the one hand, it is a religious practice with soteriological significance that expresses the realization of buddhahood in the same way that zazen does. On the other hand, it is an artistic expression that has its own aesthetic principles and requires dedicated training. Yet the two sides are intimately connected: in the practice of *shōmyō*, it is necessary to polish one's artistic and technical skills, and at the same time, practicing *shōmyō* is the honing of oneself.

Suzuki Bunmei

Suzuki Bunmei is a priest who trained under Maekawa Bokushō and his father Hakuhō and formerly taught *shōmyō* at the training temple Kasuisai. Interestingly, his view differs strongly from Maekawa Bokushō's. Suzuki is very active in the promotion of *shōmyō* and helped to edit the new edition of a book on *shōmyō* for Sōtō clerics.[78] In the introduction, he recalls that when he was a novice at the training temple Nittaiji Senmon Sōdō in Nagoya, he wondered why they, as zazen practitioners, would need to practice and perform *shōmyō*. Therefore, he asked Maekawa Hakuhō, then the *godō* at Nittaiji Senmon Sōdō, "Why do we need *shōmyō* in our school?" Hakuhō answered, "We must pay respect and provide offerings to the buddhas and patriarchs." Suzuki writes that he later asked other masters the same question, but Hakuhō's answer left a deep and long-lasting impression on him.[79] Suzuki continues:

77. Maekawa n.d., 16; Maekawa [2000–2001], 51–52.
78. Suzuki B. 2010.
79. Suzuki B. 2010, 3.

> We use *shōmyō* in order to pay respect to the buddhas and patriarchs and to provide offerings to them. In itself, the meaning of these words is simple, but somehow it is a magnificent theme. Who are the buddhas and patriarchs? And what do "paying respect" (*raihai* 礼拝), "providing offerings" (*kuyō* 供養), and "ceremonies" (*hōyō* 法要) mean? I remember that since that time my interest in *shōmyō* shifted from solely focusing on the technique of *shōmyō* to the meaning of *shōmyō* performed during ceremonies.[80]

Like many practitioners, Suzuki's foremost concern as a young monk was with the technical and aesthetic aspects of *shōmyō,* but when he reached a certain level, he began to inquire into the religious meaning of the ritual. Several other priests hinted at the same development when I spoke with them about *shōmyō.* Baba, for example, mentioned that he intellectually understood the meaning of the pieces when he was young, but not with his heart. His only concern at the beginning was the correct performance practice of *shōmyō,* and it was not until much later that he developed a deep understanding of its religious meaning. He added that it is probably always like that when first learning: one is just concerned about building one's skills.

Other priests gave a variety of answers when I asked them Suzuki's question. Some expounded on the history of *shōmyō* and *kōshiki* in the Sōtō school; others talked about rituals and their connection to lay devotees. Maekawa Bokushō's answer was intriguing, especially as he is the son of Hakuhō. He said that he does not agree with his father on this point and then stated, "If one does not perform *shōmyō,* then there is no Buddha." When I asked him about *kōshiki,* mentioning the *kōshiki* for the Sixteen Arhats, he confirmed: "Only when one performs a *kōshiki* do the Sixteen Arhats exist." Thus he further emphasized that without *shōmyō* and rituals the objects of worship—whether it be buddhas, bodhisattvas, or other deities—would not exist. Only at the time of the ritual is their existence affirmed, and only then do they exist. The same applies to zazen practice: When one practices zazen, then there is a buddha. When one does not, then buddha does not exist.[81]

Interestingly, when I asked Maekawa on another occasion why *shōmyō* is necessary, he said that the priests are artists, and they need to do art. Dōgen and Keizan were artists who understood music, literature, and daily life. Today it is the same. He said he only understood that idea when he was close to fifty, after having studied *shōmyō* for thirty years. "All of life is music," he said. "In my case, it is *shōmyō,* I only sing *shōmyō,* nothing else."[82]

Thus we have two very different perspectives on the meaning of ritual: while Suzuki and Maekawa Hakuhō emphasize Buddhist devotion in their interpretation, Maekawa Bokushō bases his view on the core concept of Sōtō

80. Suzuki B. 2010, 3.
81. Interview on July 14, 2017.
82. Conversation, October 20, 2015.

Zen that practice and realization are one. In his essay, Suzuki further expounds the definition of Buddhist ceremonies:

> If one looks up *hōyō* 法要 in [the dictionary] *Daijirin,* it says a "Buddhist ceremony; especially funerals and rituals to transfer merit to one's deceased family members." In other words, it has the meaning of a ceremony セレモニー. Additionally, it says, "the central part of the Buddhist teachings." Of course, it is the latter that we emphasize when it comes to *hōyō*. The ultimate goal of performing *hōyō* is to use rituals (*gishiki*) to accomplish the realization of the correct way taught by many patriarchs, starting with the Buddha and the two patriarchs [Dōgen and Keizan]. During Śākyamuni's lifetime, all those who laid out decorations, such as flowers and lights, intimately received this teaching below the space that was decorated solemnly and neatly. Also today, after Śākyamuni's passing, when we cannot look up to his [physical] appearance [anymore], we welcome the buddhas and patriarchs through images or we welcome the spirits [of the deceased] through memorial tablets. Below the decorated space, just as in the time of the Buddha, we intimately meet the Buddha and receive correct guidance. Although the buddha sculptures do not speak or preach in the same way as Śākyamuni, by giving life and voice to the teachings through sutra recitations and by the actual sermons and Dharma talks of the officiant, we can become intimate with the teachings of the Buddha. In the ceremonial space, one can meet the Buddha through rituals that regulate the space that is decorated, and thus it is a precious space in which one becomes intimate with the Buddha.[83]

Hence Suzuki views rituals as special spaces where one can meet the Buddha and receive his guidance. The ritual space is special because it is completely regulated and no ordinary affairs infiltrate the ritual realm. In distinguishing it from daily affairs, Suzuki invests the ritual space with the power to make possible an intimate encounter with the Buddha and his teachings. He elaborates on this further:

> Regarding the sutra readings and the texts of the transfer of merit, when one performs a ceremony (*hōyō*), one has to intone the specified texts. It is the same for the instruments: one has to play a specific instrument with specific timing and volume; everything is regulated. Due to the regulated sound, the atmosphere of the ceremonial place is maintained and the attention of everybody who is involved in the ceremony is directed toward the Buddha. On the contrary, when something occurs that differs from the rules, attention is drawn away from the Buddha. This is common sense. We protect the place of the Buddha that is regulated during the ceremony and perform the sounds in order to maintain [it]. We must also cultivate the [proper] voice production; it is the same for the instruments.[84]

83. Suzuki B. 2010, 3–4.
84. Suzuki B. 2010, 4.

Here Suzuki suggests that the strict regulation of conduct helps to create a space where the Buddha and his teachings can manifest. Thus he offers an explanation of ritual that is similar to the definitions proposed by many ritual studies scholars who maintain that formality and stereotypy are vital for the efficacy of a ritual.

After expounding on some technical aspects of *shōmyō,* such as breathing, tone production, and pronunciation, Suzuki closes his essay with a statement that expands the meaning of *hōyō* (ceremony) beyond the ritual context:

> If ceremony is not limited to ritual, then all the more does one animate the experience of the ceremony in all of daily [life]. *This* daily [life] is the Buddha Dharma. All actions are the Buddha Dharma, and they are the actions of a buddha. [In any case,] with regard to ceremony as ritual, its meaning shows itself directly to us. It is an important guidance.... It is not a ceremony to showcase; shouldn't we aim to realize ceremony as practice?[85]

Thus Suzuki touches on the soteriological dimension of *shōmyō* within and beyond the ritual setting. Yet his focus throughout remains on the devotional aspect of rituals, in contrast to Maekawa's understanding of *shōmyō* as a practice, like zazen, that in itself is an expression of the realization of buddhahood. For Suzuki, rituals are the place where practitioners can hear the teaching of a buddha and receive his guidance, which they can subsequently put into practice.

Views of Other *Shōmyō* Specialists

Other priests explained further aspects important for the practice of *shōmyō.* One of them is Terakura Shōyū, who studied under several masters, including Maekawa Hakuhō. He began an interview with the following remark:

> The most important aspect is that one has to vocalize *shōmyō* [pieces] that praise the Buddha with the feeling of praising him. In the *kōshiki* for Zen master Keizan, one has to have the feeling of praising the virtue of Zen master Keizan. If at the outset one misses this point, then however skillful one is in *shōmyō,* there will be no substance [in one's chanting]. Vocalizing *shōmyō* also has a musical element, and it is important. But everyone has his own *fushi* [or personal style], because all have their own individuality.... I personally think that it is good like that. It is like the flow of water: in the end all [rivers] run into the same sea.[86]

Then Terakura explained that at Sōjiji there are more than one hundred novices. Consequently, the teachers instruct the novices not to display their personality, as they have to sing together like a choir. Later a novice has to find his own way and make recitation practice his own.

85. Suzuki B. 2010, 25.
86. Interview on October 15, 2015.

The ideas that Terakura had stated at the beginning run through the interview like a red thread. Throughout the interview, as well as in other conversations, he emphasized that one must have a clear understanding of the meaning of the text before one can vocalize it. This requires that one study the texts before vocalizing them, and doing so helps one to decide where to take a breath or put an accent. In this way, the listeners will be able to actually understand the text. He was mainly referring to dedications (*sho* 疏) and transfer of merit texts written specially for a particular ritual when he said this. But we can assume he would say the same about offertory declarations and *shikimon,* since understanding a text is in fact the basis for being able to recite it with the requisite praise.

Terakura returned to the musical aspect of *shōmyō* several times. He said, for example, that "*shōmyō*... has a musical element. Of course, it is music (*ongaku* 音楽). But it is not simply reciting, one has to have the object [of worship] in mind. When reciting a *Rakan kōshiki,* if one does not think about the form of the arhats while reading it, then it is nothing but empty *nenbutsu* (*kara nenbutsu* 空念仏)." He also said, "When one vocalizes but nothing is conveyed, then it has no value. It is not about whether 'this is beautiful' or 'one has a nice voice.'... If the listeners are not moved by the heart of this person, then it is useless."

Like Terakura, other current or previous *ino* of Sōjiji, such as Kōya and Nozaki Taiyū 野崎泰雄, emphasize that it is important to understand the meaning of the text and to recite it in a way that listeners can follow. Nozaki even remarked that it is like karaoke: "There are many people who are good, but they do not move peoples' hearts. One needs *tamashii* (soul) in one's chanting."[87] Nozaki went on to say that zazen is the basis for *shōmyō,* and every time I met him during a ritual at Sōjiji, he would reiterate his view that to understand *shōmyō,* one has to study zazen; it cannot be done without it.

Terakura likened chanting to the central practice of Sōtō Zen, *shikan taza* 只管打坐 (just sitting).[88] Contemporary Sōtō clerics describe *shikan taza* in slightly different ways, but it is generally understood as zazen practice that straightforwardly engages in sitting; it is not a means to reach enlightenment. There is no need for a gradual progress to reach enlightenment; zazen itself is already the fulfillment of the realization of buddhahood, as Dōgen said in his *Bendōwa.* Even when one sits for the first time, all realization is already attained.[89] The official Sōtō school webpage further explains that the posture one takes when doing zazen is the posture of the Buddha and therefore the posture of enlightenment. In this posture realization is attained.[90] In applying

87. Interview on October 15, 2015.

88. Although Dōgen used the phrase *shikan taza* only a few times in his *Shōbōgenzō,* it became the stock phrase for describing the core practice of Sōtō Zen. See Foulk 2012 and 2015, and Kubovčáková 2018, for detailed studies of Dōgen and *shikan taza.*

89. DZO 1: 737; DZZ 2: 470.

90. Sōtō Zen Net, "Sōtōshū no zazen" 曹洞宗の坐禅, https://www.sotozen-net.or.jp/propagation/zazentop.

this concept to other activities, Terakura said that *shikan* 只管, single-mindedness, is what is important, not just in the act of sitting but also in cleaning, reciting, and the like. Suzuki Eiichi, former *tantō* at Sōjiji and current abbot of Sōjiji Soin, echoed this point when he spoke of "single-minded *shōmyō*" (*isshin no shōmyō* 一心の声明) and stated that both zazen and *shōmyō* share the same foundation of "just doing" (*tada yaru*). Thus *shōmyō* practice can be understood as "just singing," as it shares the same foundation as *shikan taza.* In other words, this interpretation views singing *shōmyō* not as goal oriented or as a devotional practice but as an expression of the realization of buddhahood based on the principle that practice and realization are one, as Maekawa also suggested in his essay.

Tsuruoka Hakuhō 鶴岡白鳳, another priest who wrote an essay on *shōmyō,* also relates *shōmyō* and other observances to a Sōtō interpretation of Zen practice:

> "Through our observances, we actualize the observances of the buddhas and thus penetrate the great way of the buddhas" (*Shōbōgenzō, Gyōji* 正法眼藏行持). The characteristic of these observances, which can be called our school's profound meaning, is also directly expressed by the aspects of the melodies that are transmitted through *shōmyō.* The melodies do not reach controlled grandeur; the rhythm is also simple; the mode, the pauses, the sustaining of notes, and the like are also plain and basic.
>
> However, the rhythm, mode, pauses, and the like aforementioned bring the deportment of a practicing buddha (*gyōbutsu igi* 行佛威儀) to life when *kōshiki* and other rituals are performed following the pure rules. [The deportment of a buddha means that] "through *shikan taza,* we obtain liberation at this time and place." We should therefore correct what is heard and seen [i.e., the vocalization and movements].[91]

Tsuruoka interprets *shōmyō* as a fundamental Sōtō practice and relates it to zazen by quoting Dōgen's *Shōbōgenzō.* Both zazen and rituals, he affirms, are to be conducted as the practice of a buddha and as such are an expression of realization.

Kojima Shōin 小島璋允, a former *kannin* 監院 (superintendent) of Eiheiji's satellite temple in Nagoya and *godō* at Eiheiji, surprisingly connects ritual practice, which he describes as the embodiment of the Dharma, to the expectations of lay devotees. He wrote the following statement while serving in Nagoya:

> ...when all dress in correct robes and follow the proper conduct (*igi* 威儀) according to the rules (*nyohō* 如法), their sutra reading and voices completely resemble the sutra reading of a single person. Then their movements, their circumambulation of the hall, and their music are all performed with the officiant in

91. Tsuruoka 2010, 44–45.

> the center, and both walking and sitting are performed synchronously, solemnly and correctly. Thus the aspects that satisfy the religious desire of lay devotees flourish. This is the special character of our school's ritual tradition, which is expressed by the proverb "Proper conduct is the Buddha Dharma, and etiquette is the principle of our school" (*igi soku buppō, sahō kore shūshi* 威儀即仏法、作法是宗旨).[92]

Kojima seems to be tacitly admitting that Sōtō monks perform rituals for the laity, but the proverb he cites at the end encapsulates the Sōtō school's principle that the correct performance of rituals is the embodiment of the Dharma. In other words, by affirming that proper conduct is an expression of the realization of buddhahood in the same way that zazen is, he suggests that rituals work on multiple logics: they not only are an expression of buddhahood but serve the needs of lay devotees as well.

In the same publication, Inoue Gishin, now *kannin* of Eiheiji's satellite temple in Nagoya, gives a detailed explanation of the history of *shōmyō* and *kōshiki* and writes the following about the meaning of *kōshiki:*

> Now in *kōshiki* we also vocalize the verses following the traditional rhythm and praise the virtues of the buddhas. At the requisite time, the buddhas, bodhisattvas, heavenly beings, and benevolent deities appear. Therefore, before their eyes, we praise and provide offerings [to them], and as the merit from vocalizing [their] names and paying respect accumulates, we receive the protection and mercy [of the buddhas and bodhisattvas] (*kabi onchō* 加被恩寵). May we continue to practice the way and further answer the pure faith of the devotees and their prayers and offerings to the ancestors.[93]

Like Kojima, Inoue relates ritual practices to the wishes of lay devotees, but he additionally hints at the this-worldly benefits that rituals are thought to provide. Interestingly, Maekawa and Suzuki, as well as the Sōjiji-affiliated priests I spoke with, never mentioned lay devotees in relation to *shōmyō* or *kōshiki* in their writings or our conversations. For them, *shōmyō* was a practice as delineated by the practice-realization paradigm central to Sōtō Zen doctrine, or an expression of devotion, or—for Maekawa—an art. But Kojima and Inoue, both active at Eiheiji's satellite temple in Nagoya, emphasize the role of rituals for lay propagation. The reason might be that Kojima's and Inoue's statements appeared in a publication alongside three rituals, two of which, the *Kannon senbō* and *Tanbutsue,* are sometimes performed during elaborate services for lay devotees. But like Suzuki, Inoue also stresses the devotional aspect of rituals.

Last but not least, several of the priests I talked with mentioned that they find singing and chanting enjoyable. This was certainly a reason for focusing

92. Inoue 2000, foreword.
93. Inoue 2000, 1v.

on *shōmyō* and seeking to improve their chanting skills. Baba, for example, said that it feels good to recite or perform *shōmyō,* and if you become more skilled in singing *shōmyō,* it feels even better.[94] Munakata Gihō similarly remarked, "It's fun to sing *shōmyō*. It is like karaoke."[95] He said that he had enjoyed learning *shōmyō,* and so he tries to teach *shōmyō* in an enjoyable manner to the novices at Eiheiji. Several *shōmyō* specialists also mentioned that they play musical instruments, such as electric guitar or electric bass, and had been enthusiastic about playing music before learning *shōmyō*. Their musical background might have played a major role in their decision to devote considerable time and energy to the music of Sōtō Zen. Finally, there is an additional, often vital factor: several priests mentioned that when they were young, they heard a senior priest sing *shōmyō* beautifully and were deeply touched by the performance. Such a moment seems to have sparked a deep interest in learning *shōmyō* in not a few Sōtō clerics.

Conclusions

This chapter has demonstrated that the performance of *kōshiki* is intimately related to music practice. Clerics vocalize liturgical pieces in a number of styles, ranging from a reading with very little to no melodic embellishment to highly melismatic singing. Instruments are played throughout the ritual to provide cues for singing and to coordinate ritual actions. These musical styles and sounds blend to form an arc through which the ritual unfolds.

Young monks need dedicated training to develop the ability to sing the liturgical pieces. Most importantly, they need a teacher who can give them direct instruction in the correct performance of the melodies and the subtleties of vocal production in *shōmyō*. This training starts when a novice enters a training temple, and upon his departure it can continue in *shōmyō* study groups, local young monks' associations, and other informal ways. Monks who are seriously interested in *shōmyō* usually seek out a master to continue polishing their skills through individual lessons. Passed down from one generation to the next, *shōmyō* is part of the oral transmission of ritual expertise in Sōtō Zen. Over the centuries, this transmission has been supported by musical notation—an aide-memoire for melodies—and audio and video recordings more recently, but as all *shōmyō* specialists aver, there is no substitute for in-person instruction.

The *shōmyō* specialists who teach in the head and training temples interpret their practice in different ways. Many view it through the lens of Sōtō Zen doctrine and regard *shōmyō* as an integral part of their Zen practice. Maekawa Bokushō understands *shōmyō* based on the core principle of the unity of practice and realization and suggests that through both zazen and the vocalization of liturgical texts "we symbolically express the state of the

94. Interview on July 17, 2017.
95. Interview on June 15, 2015.

Buddha without mediation." Other priests mention the core idea that "proper conduct is the Buddha Dharma, and etiquette is the principle of our school," and of course they do include *shōmyō* and rituals in this paradigm. Others, however, such as Suzuki Bunmei, approach *shōmyō* from a more general Buddhist perspective and interpret it as a devotional practice, one that expresses devotion to buddhas, bodhisattvas, and patriarchs. For Suzuki, rituals also offer a space for receiving guidance from the Buddha's teachings. Two priests who have worked in a smaller training temple, Kojima and Inoue, add another dimension to the understanding of rituals when they acknowledge their importance in fulfilling the expectations of lay devotees. These contrasting views illustrate the multivocality of interpretations of ritual practice within the Sōtō school.

Most *shōmyō* specialists evaluate *shōmyō* and *kōshiki* from an artistic standpoint and teach methods that will lead to a skilled performance. Maekawa, in particular, details several aspects of *shōmyō,* including the two different timbres, tone production, dynamics, and breathing, whose subtleties cannot be captured by musical notation. For him, *shōmyō* cannot be considered *shōmyō* if all a performer does is rigidly intone a melody by reading the musical notation; one has to sing following the subtle aesthetic ideal of Sōtō *shōmyō.* These different ways of approaching *shōmyō* are not mutually exclusive. For Maekawa, the aesthetic and soteriological perspectives form a unity. Singing *shōmyō* is the honing of one's life: by practicing and performing *shōmyō,* a practitioner polishes his artistic skills, and this very practice is at the same time an expression of the realization of buddhahood. Terakura emphasizes the devotional nature of rituals by expounding on the need to understand the texts before one can recite in a way that communicates the content. But he also relates *shōmyō* to *shikan taza* when he comments that one needs to perform all activities single-mindedly. All these different perspectives highlight that *shōmyō* specialists view the art of chanting as a musical skill completely intertwined with religious practice.

PART TWO

Kōshiki *and Collective Memory: The Case of Keizan*

4

Early Modern Lineage Divergences

Suzuki Bunmei: "Why do we need *shōmyō* in our school?"
Maekawa Hakuhō: "We must pay respect and provide offerings to the buddhas and patriarchs."

AT THE END of the seventh month in Bunsei 11 (1828), Donge Zenzui 曇華禅瑞 (d. 1856), the twenty-first head priest of Keijūji 渓寿寺 in today's Eihime prefecture, arrived with three attendants at the head temple Sōjiji in the remote village of Monzen on the Noto peninsula, to serve as one of the abbots there for a year. In the next few days, he met the resident monks at Sōjiji, the current abbots, and the other soon-to-be abbots. He was also introduced to Sōjiji's etiquette and participated in a number of small-scale rituals. The first major observance Zenzui attended was the memorial service for Keizan, Sōjiji's first abbot, conducted every year from the thirteenth to the fifteenth day in the eighth month.[1] Many monks from temples affiliated with Sōjiji in the nearby provinces of Kaga, Etchū, and Noto came to Sōjiji to attend this service and pay their respects to Keizan. Among the rituals performed was a *kōshiki* for Keizan, the *Butsuji kōshiki* (*Kōshiki* on Zen Master Butsuji).[2] This *kōshiki* was the only ritual during the memorial service that detailed Keizan's life, adding a concrete commemoration of his accomplishments to the memorial service.

The *kōshiki* performed for Keizan at Sōjiji echoed a performance of an earlier version of the same *kōshiki* during the memorial service at Yōkōji, another temple founded by Keizan on the Noto peninsula. The *kōshiki* were important rituals for each temple: they not only served to repay the benevolence of the temple founder, but also functioned to help consolidate a

1. *Shogakuzan rinban nikkan*, written by Shunkō 俊光, Zenzui's assistant. See Itō R. 2003b for a typographical reprint.

2. The *Butsuji kōshiki* uses Keizan's posthumous name Zen Master Butsuji (Butsuji Zenji 仏慈禅師), which Emperor Gomurakami 後村上天皇 (1328–1368) is supposed to have bestowed on him in Shōhei 8 (1353). It is unclear whether Sōjiji monks actually accepted this title, because, according to extant letters, the temple's first full-time abbot, Gasan, declined it. Nevertheless, by the Tokugawa period Zen Master Butsuji had become a commonly used name for Keizan; see Takeuchi K. 1998 and Satō Shūkō 1999, 21–24, on this issue.

collective memory on which the future success of the temple and its community was based.[3] Part II of this book studies the historical development of these alternate versions of the *kōshiki* for Keizan, tracing the modifications that appeared in each *shikimon* over time and highlighting the dynamics of ritual innovation and change.

Both versions of the *kōshiki* for Keizan express gratitude to him as the founder of the largest lineage of Sōtō Zen. They commemorate his life and narrate the early history of his lineage. Consequently, a performance of the ritual is a recounting of history in which the community engages by hearing the *shikimon* read aloud. The performance is thus an enactment of a community of memory—a community of fellow practitioners who remember their past in the same way and who retell the same foundational stories about their lineage or school.[4]

In other religions, similar communities form around ritual remembrances of saints or decisive events. Derek Krueger calls these rituals a "liturgy of memory" and proposes that Byzantine Christian rituals and hagiographies created a liturgical "we," a community of religious individuals demarcated by a shared communal memory. This liturgical "we" is formed not only by sharing a set of stories and ideas but also by experiencing the bodily and vocal expressions of these beliefs in communal rituals.[5] Similarly, Gavin Flood, in exploring the formation of subjectivity, relates ritualized practices to the performance of a tradition's memory.[6] He mainly focuses on ascetic practices, but his ideas can be applied to commemorative rituals as well: rituals remembering a saint or an influential religious figure often retell key narratives that incorporate the central ritual practices of the tradition.

Preserving the memory of its own history has been vital to the collective memory of Zen lineages. Biographies of eminent Zen monks and other forms of Zen literature, including the *kōan* collections narrating old cases, exemplify the central ideas and practices of the tradition through individual stories and legends. The biographies are thus part of the constant retelling of the collective memory—or *imaginaire*—of Zen Buddhism.

---

3. Memory has been an important research focus in several humanities disciplines. One of the founding fathers of this field is the sociologist Marice Halbwachs, who coined the phrase "collective memory." For an overview of memory studies, see Olick, Vinitzky-Seroussi, and Levy 2011, 3–62, or Kattago 2015, 1–19. Aleida Assmann and Jan Assmann proposed the concept of cultural memory to describe the knowledge handed down within one culture; see J. Assmann 1992 and 2000.

4. Several scholars have used the concept of communities of memory. Robert Bellah and his collaborators, for example, employ the concept to analyze contemporary American society (Bellah et al. 1985, 152–163), and Mario Poceski uses it to describe the Chan school (2015, 24–28). For studies on memory in East Asian Buddhism, see also Poceski 2018.

5. Krueger 2000 and 2014, chap. 3. In his work on hagiographies and writing, Krueger suggests that the hagiographies are an act of remembering and "sought to make present in narrative a holy essence that might otherwise be irretrievably absent" (2000, 484). See also Krueger 2004, chap. 6.

6. Flood 2004.

Before unraveling the *kōshiki* for Keizan, a few words are in order on *kōshiki* performed in remembrance of eminent monks. Memorial services for school founders and influential patriarchs have been important observances throughout East Asian Buddhism. However, the ritual form of these memorial services has varied over time. In Japanese Buddhism, sutras were read and sometimes offertory declarations were recited. If the memorial service was conducted for a school or lineage founder at a major temple, the clerics would perform multiday ceremonies during which they conducted a variety of rituals. The development of the ritual genre of *kōshiki* added another option to the repertoire of Buddhist liturgy, and *kōshiki* offered the possibility of narrating the biography of an eminent monk while expressing gratitude for the benevolence received. Therefore, *kōshiki* for school founders were composed in various schools. For example, Ryūkan 隆寛 (1148–1227) composed a *kōshiki* for Hōnen (1133–1212), the founder of the Jōdo school, entitled *Chion kōshiki,* and Kakunyo 覚如 (1270–1351) composed a *kōshiki* for Shinran 親鸞 (1173–1263), the founder of the Jōdo-shin school, entitled *Hōon kōshiki.*[7] Interestingly, most of the *kōshiki* in the Sōtō school were actually composed in remembrance of eminent monks, as seen in the outline of the development of Sōtō *kōshiki* in chapter 1. These works constitute a subgenre of *kōshiki* called *hōon kōshiki* (*kōshiki* to repay kindness), which express gratitude to eminent monks and at the same time shape the collective memory of a lineage—through both the retelling of the biography and the communal performance of the ritual.[8]

This chapter explores the first *kōshiki* composed in remembrance of Keizan, the *Butsuji kōshiki.* I show that the temples Yōkōji and Sōjiji developed alternate versions of the *kōshiki* that reflected the rivalry between them during the medieval period. First, I introduce each temple's background and then explain the context of the ritual's performance during Keizan's memorial service. Turning to the *kōshiki* itself, I examine its origins and ritual structure before analyzing the *shikimon* and the differences they reveal between the two communities of memory.

Keizan's Temples: Yōkōji and Sōjiji

The history of Yōkōji begins in Shōwa 1 (1312) when patrons donated land to Keizan to found a new temple in Hakui in Noto province. Five years later, in Bunpō 1 (1317), Keizan moved to Yōkōji upon completion of the abbot's

7. The *Chion kōshiki* is included in *Shinshū seikyō zensho* 5, 715–719; see Kushida 1976 for a typographical reprint. Kushida (1965) studies the *Chion kōshiki* as an important source for the life of Hōnen. The *Hōon kōshiki* is included in T 83, no. 2665; see Callahan 2011 and 2016 for detailed studies.

8. In this book, I use the term "biography" to describes works narrating the lives of Buddhist monks and nuns. These biographies do not present objective accounts of the clerics' lives and often serve a devotional or didactic purpose. They could also be regarded as hagiographies. However, the two literary categories are in many cases interchangeable, and the subjects of secular biographies are often idealized as well. On this point, see Poceski 2015, 42–43.

quarters.[9] In Genkō 1 (1321), Jōken 定賢 (n.d.), a master of esoteric Buddhism who was the resident priest of a small Kannon chapel in the northern part of the Noto peninsula, placed his chapel under the guardianship of Keizan.[10] Keizan renamed it Sōjiji. The details of this transfer remain unclear, and the nature of the relationship between Keizan and Jōken is unknown. In the fifth month of Shōchū 1 (1324), Keizan traveled to Sōjiji to open its monks' hall, and he installed Gasan as Sōjiji's first full-time Zen abbot two months later. Keizan then returned to Yōkōji.[11]

In Shōchū 2 (1325), just a month before his death, Keizan gave six of his disciples instructions concerning the succession of Yōkōji's abbotship and ordered that the monks of his lineage serve as abbot in the order of their seniority.[12] After his death, four of these disciples—Meihō Sotetsu 明峰素哲 (1277–1350), Mugai Chikō 無涯智洪 (d. 1351), Gasan Jōseki, and Koan Shikan 壺菴至簡 (d. 1341)—served successively as abbot of Yōkōji, and the temple flourished. After completing their own terms, the four cooperated in appointing their own disciples to Yōkōji's abbotship, and Yōkōji was jointly managed by the heirs of these four monks, ensuring its prosperity. Yet by 1379, the system had failed, and the next ten abbots all belonged to Meihō's lineage.[13]

At the same time, Gasan's disciples established an abbot rotation system at Sōjiji that did secure stability and institutional success.[14] An intense rivalry between Yōkōji and Sōjiji developed. Both temples had few parishioners, and since they were not pilgrimage sites, they depended on wealthy patrons and the support of monks in their lineage. By 1430, Sōjiji, which had been one of Yōkōji's branch temples during Keizan's lifetime, had become independent and was able to challenge Yōkōji for preeminence.[15] In Genna 1 (1615), Sōjiji was declared one of the two head temples of the Sōtō school, alongside Eiheiji, and by the end of the seventeenth century, it was able to claim more than 90 percent of all Sōtō temples as its branch temples.[16] Sōjiji had eclipsed Yōkōji, and Yōkōji, struggling economically, would even become a branch temple of Sōjiji later in the Tokugawa period.[17]

At the same time, a severe rivalry between Eiheiji and Sōjiji, the two head

9. Azuma 2002, 8.

10. *Morookadera Kannondō jiryōshikichi kishinjō.*

11. *Tōkokuki,* JDZ, 430–431; KZ 8: 270–271. For a history of Sōjiji in English, see Mross 2014a, chap. 3, and Bodiford 1993, 81–84, and chap. 9. See Bodiford 1993, 85–88, on Yōkōji.

12. JDZ, 430–431. These six disciples were Meihō Sotetsu, Mugai Chikō, Gasan Jōseki, Koan Shikan, Kohō Kakumyō 孤峰覚明 (1271–1361), and Genshō Shinzan 源照珍山 (n.d.).

13. Bodiford 1993, 101.

14. After Gasan's death, his disciples installed an abbot rotation system on the model of Yōkōji's system and continued to develop it over the years. For a detailed account, see Itō R. 1998a, 1998b, 2001a, 2001b, 2002a, 2002b, 2003a, 2005a, and 2005b, and Mross 2014a, chap. 3.

15. Itō R. 1999; 2005a, 59.

16. Tamamuro 2008, 13, 71–74.

17. Bunkazai 7: 631.

temples, had also developed, fueling disputes over a range of issues.[18] The matters that caused the greatest conflict involved the regulations governing the changing of the robe (*tenne* 転衣), a rite of passage that allowed a cleric to change from a black robe to a different colored robe and so ascend the ecclesiastical ranks. Since the fees paid by the monks were an important source of income for the two head temples, the monks of both temples tried to influence the Bureau of Temples and Shrines (Jisha Bugyō 寺社奉行) to issue regulations that favored their temple. Aware of its favorable location, Eiheiji argued that it should be possible to conduct the ceremony of changing the robe at both head temples, whereas Sōjiji averred that branch temples should undergo the changing of the robe at their own head temple, knowing that more than 90 percent of all Sōtō temples belonged to their faction. It seems that the bureau might have favored Eiheiji, because nearly 51 percent of all monks who underwent the changing of the robe between 1641 and 1790 visited Eiheiji for the rite of passage, while 49 percent did so at Sōjiji.[19]

In the 1890s, the rivalry between Sōjiji and Eiheiji worsened, fueling an independence movement at Sōjiji. But after two years of intense conflict, the two head temples agreed to reconcile. Sōtō leaders now proclaimed the doctrine of "two head temples, one essence" (*ryōzan ittai funi* 両山一体不二). Officially, any veneration of Sōjiji or Eiheiji was a veneration of both, and doctrinal differences between the writings of Dōgen and Keizan were to be considered alternative expressions of the same essence.[20] In this environment, Sōjiji monks wrote a new *kōshiki* for Keizan, which will be studied in the next chapter.

In 1898, Sōjiji was almost completely destroyed by a fire. The leadership decided to move Sōjiji to Yokohama but rebuild the original temple on a smaller scale at its former site. That temple was renamed Sōjiji Soin, while Sōjiji itself relocated to Tsurumi ward in Yokohama, where it continues to meet the needs of numerous parishioners while serving as a flagship training temple for young monks.

Yōkōji, by contrast, was impoverished by the early Meiji era. Kohō Hakugan 孤峰白巌 (1845–1909), Yōkōji's abbot from 1882 to 1909, worked diligently toward its rebuilding, and a *kōshiki* played a role in his revival movement. Today Yōkōji is a relatively small temple that is dependent on the donations of other Sōjiji-affiliated temples that endeavor to preserve it as an important historical site for their school.

---

18. This rivalry had already begun in the middle of the sixteenth century when Eiheiji monks claimed precedence for Eiheiji on the basis of its historical position as the temple founded by Dōgen. When Eiheiji was acknowledged by the court as a training place whose abbot was entitled to receive the imperial robe (*shusse dōjō* 出世道場), Sōjiji protested, and in Tenbun 9 (1540) the title of *shusse dōjō* was suspended; see Takeuchi M. 1981, 71 and 73–74.

19. See Tamamuro 2008, 71, 73–76, and 166–198, on these controversies.

20. Takeuchi M. 1981, 126; Bodiford 1993, 84.

Memorial Service for Keizan at Sōjiji

In the Tokugawa period, the *Butsuji kōshiki* was performed during the memorial services for Keizan at both Yōkōji and Sōjiji. These services were multiday ceremonies modeled on the memorial service for the Buddha. At Sōjiji the service was much more elaborate than at Yōkōji, reflecting the status of the two temples at the time. A directive issued by the Tokugawa bakufu in Genna 1 (1615) further ordered all monks of Sōjiji's branch temples in the three provinces of Kaga, Noto, and Etchū to attend the service at Sōjiji.[21] However, according to sources from Genroku (1688–1704) onward, the monks from these provinces rotated their attendance so that monks from four to five temples per province usually traveled to Sōjiji for each service.[22] Nevertheless, with more than one hundred monks living permanently at Sōjiji, all of whom most likely attended, the memorial service remained a grand ritual.[23] At Yōkōji, on the contrary, Keizan's memorial service drew far fewer monks. The different scales are also indicated by the number and kinds of manuscripts produced for the *Butsuji kōshiki* at the two temples: whereas Sōjiji monks produced fifty manuscripts written on expensive paper with decorated covers and in a large format, Yōkōji monks produced fifteen without any decorations and in a standard size.

At both temples, the memorial service lasted three days, from the thirteenth to the fifteenth day of the eighth month. Unfortunately, we do not have sources that detail all the activities during the commemoration at Yōkōji. But one extant source gives us a brief overview. Rituals of different types, many of them featuring sutra chanting, were performed by Yōkōji's resident monks and monks visiting from its branch temples. On the morning of the last day, the service culminated with the performance of the *Butsuji kōshiki* and formal offerings.[24]

About the memorial service at Sōjiji, we have detailed information from several sources. One of them is a record written by Shunkō, one of Zenzui's attendants, who listed the activities and rituals performed in Bunsei 11 (1828):[25]

21. *Various Regulations for Sōjiji* (*Sōjiji shohatto*), issued by Tokugawa Ieyasu 徳川家康 (1542–1616) in Genna 1 (1615); see Mross 2014a, 96–97, for an English translation. The monks were also required to attend the memorial services for Gasan at Sōjiji. Early Sōjiji monks had used the memorial services for Keizan, as well as those for Gasan, to decide organizational matters that ensured Sōjiji's institutional success, ordering that all monks affiliated with Sōjiji had to attend the memorial services for Keizan and Gasan if they did not want to be excluded from their lineage; see Directive from Kōraku 2 (1380), *Sōjiji monto keiyakujō.*

22. See the *Nōshū shojiin kaisanki nidaiki shūrai chō* 能州諸寺院開山忌二代忌集来帳, written in Genroku 9 (1696), in Muromine 1965, 258. See also Tamamuro 2008, 151.

23. Tamamuro 2008, 151–152; Muromine 1965, 257–259.

24. *Nikkan,* written in Hōryaku 13 (1763). This manuscript states that a separate text provides a detailed list of the rituals performed during the memorial service, but I was not able to locate it.

25. *Shogakuzan rinban nikkan,* in Itō R. 2003b, 146–147. The oldest extant source that gives

8/12

- The visiting monks from Kaga, Etchū, and Noto greet the abbots of Sōjiji
- In the evening, rehearsals for the rituals

8/13

- Morning recitation in the Buddha hall
- Sutra chanting for coming together (*shūrai fugin* 集来諷経) in the guests' hall
- Rolling reading of the *Great Sutra on the Perfection of Wisdom*
- Breakfast
- Verses and "Sanskrit sound" (*kada bonnon* 伽陀梵音)[26]
- Reading of the *Sutra of the Teachings Left by the Buddha* (*Yiyao jing*) and the *Lotus Sutra*, offering of rice, and circumambulation of the hall
- Lunch
- Sutra chanting for the cleaning of Keizan's grave and circumambulation of the hall during the recitation of the *Heroic March Dhāraṇī* (*Lengyan zhou* 楞嚴呪)[27]

---

information about the ritual structure of the memorial service for Keizan is the *Shogakuzan Sōjizenji shogyōji*, written in Enpō 7 (1679), in Muromine 1965, 243–246. However, it only offers a basic outline of the ritual structure; see Mross 2014a, 112–127, for a translation and study.

26. The exact meaning of *kada bonnon* is unclear. *Kada* are verses, but this term can also describe the monk who is singing solo the first lines of chants. *Bonnon* has several meanings. It can be the abbreviated title of the *shōmyō* piece *Bonnon no ge* (Gāthā of Sanskrit sound), which is the second piece of *San-Bon-Shaku*. It can also describe Buddhist chant in general, chants in Sanskrit, or the beautiful voice of a buddha. Although we do not know what texts were meant here, we can assume that this rite featured *shōmyō*.

27. The full title of the *Heroic March Dhāraṇī* (J. *Ryōgon ju*) is *Great Buddha's Uṣṇīṣa Heroic March Dhāraṇī of the Ten Thousand Practices* (*Dafoding wanxing shoulengyan tuoluoni* 大佛頂萬行首楞嚴陀羅尼, J. *Daibutchō mangyō shuryōgon darani*). It is included in the seventh fascicle of the *Heroic March Sutra* (*Dafoding rulai miyin xiuzheng liaoyi zhupusa wanxing shoulengyan jing*, J. *Daibutchō nyorai mitsuin shushō ryōgi shobosatsu mangyō shuryōgon kyō*), or *Lengyan jing* (J. *Ryōgon kyō*) for short, an apocryphal sutra composed in the Tang dynasty. The *Heroic March Dhāraṇī* explains that through the virtue of this *dhāraṇī* practitioners can overcome all obstacles and practice successfully, developing the wisdom of a buddha and escaping from the world of birth and death. It is frequently recited during training periods in a ceremony called the *Heroic March Assembly* (Ch. *Lengyanhui* 楞厳会, J. *Ryōgon'e*). The *dhāraṇī* is also recited during the three central Buddhist celebrations, the memorial service for Bodhidharma, and funerals for clerics. According to one theory, the Chinese monk Zhanglu Qingliao 長蘆清了 (J. Chōro Seiryō, 1088–1151) invented the *Heroic March Assembly* during his abbacy at a monastery on Butuoshan 補陀山 in Mingzhou. When an epidemic had spread among the monks, he was advised by Avalokiteśvara (J. Kannon) in a dream to circumambulate the hall while chanting the *Heroic March Dhāraṇī*. After performing this ritual, the epidemic ended, and the ritual became popular as a means of protecting monastic retreats from unfortunate occurrences. Another theory suggests that the recitation of the *Heroic March Dhāraṇī* for the success of the training period originated with Shenxiu 神秀 (J. Jinshū, 606?–706), considered to be the sixth patriarch in the Northern school of Chan. See Ozaki 2010, 165–166, and Foulk 2010b, 128. For a study of the *Heroic March Dhāraṇī* in Chinese Buddhism, see Ho C. 2010.

– Recitation of the *Three Dhāraṇī* (*san darani* 三陀羅尼),[28] offering of incense, and nine prostrations
– Dinner
– Formal meeting in the main kitchen

8 / 14

– Morning recitation
– Offering of rice gruel
– Breakfast
– *Butsuji kōshiki*
– Dharma words to the offering of incense
– Recitation of the *Heroic March Dhāraṇī* and circumambulation of the hall
– Midday chanting
– Lunch
– Night preceding the memorial day (*tsūya* 逮夜) at *hōji* 晡時 [i.e., 2–4 p.m.]:
Grand offering of incense
Prostrations
Communal offering of incense
Heroic March Dhāraṇī in "grand true" reading style (*daishindoku* 大真読)[29]
Sutra chanting in the afternoon before the memorial day
Recitation of the *Three Dhāraṇī*
– Dinner
– The resigning abbots visit the various departments and announce their resignation

28. The *Three Dhāraṇī* were probably the *Dhāraṇī of the Mind of Great Compassion* (*Dabeixin tuoluoni* 大悲心陀羅尼, J. *Daihishin darani*), the *Dhāraṇī of the Jubilant Corona* (*Foding zunsheng tuoluoni* 仏頂尊勝陀羅尼, J. *Butchō sonshō darani*), and the *Marvelously Beneficial Disaster-Preventing Dhāraṇī* (*Xiaozai miao jixiang tuoluoni* 消災妙吉祥陀羅尼, J. *Shōsai myōkichijō darani*).

The *Dhāraṇī of the Mind of Great Compassion* is very popular in the Zen schools. This *dhāraṇī* is included in the *Qianshou qianyan guanshiyin pusa guangda yuanman wuai dabeixin tuoluoni jing* (J. *Senju sengen kanzeon bosatsu kōdai enman mugi daihishin darani kyō*). Its recitation is supposed to cure all illnesses and cast away bad spirits, and those who recite it will obtain the mind of a bodhisattva and be able to benefit all beings. Zen monks call it the *Dhāraṇī of the Mind of Great Compassion* because of its unlimited virtue.

The *Dhāraṇī of the Jubilant Corona* is supposed to prolong one's life and keep illnesses away. It is included in the *Foding zunsheng tuoluoni jing* (J. *Butchō sonshō darani kyō*) and was often recited in prayer rituals for the elimination of calamities and long life. See Copp 2005 for a study of this *dhāraṇī* in Chinese Buddhism.

The *Marvelously Beneficial Disaster-Preventing Dhāraṇī* is supposed to eliminate calamities and bring good fortune. It is based on the *Foshuo chichengguang daweide xiaozai jixiang tuoluoni jing* (J. *Bussetsu shijōkō daiitoku shōsai kichijō darani kyō*). Menzan Zuihō wrote a small book entitled *Shōsai kichijō kyō jikisetsu* about the merit of the recitation of this *dhāraṇī* in Meiwa 6 (1769).

29. *Daishindoku* is a special reading of sutras in which the text is recited very slowly with melodies. The *Heroic March Dhāraṇī* also used to be chanted to the playing of drums in prayer rituals at Sōjiji; see Yamaguchi 2012, 144. However, these two styles of reciting the *Heroic March Dhāraṇī* have been lost.

8 / 15

- Circumambulation of the hall at dawn
- Sutra chanting to the offering of rice gruel
- Breakfast
- Sutra chanting for the longevity of the emperor in the Buddha hall
- Ceremonies in the halls as usual
- Three Buddhist rites:
  - Offering of hot water
  - Dharma words to the offering of tea
  - Offering of incense
- Rite of wearing the purple robe for the last time:[30]
  - Grand offering of incense
  - Communal offering of incense
- Recitation of the *Heroic March Dhāraṇī* in the "grand true" reading style during the circumambulation of the hall
- Lunch
- Greetings of the resigning and new abbots
- Ascending the hall (*jōdō* 上堂) sermon in the Buddha hall
- The resigning five abbots leave the temple
- The five new abbots take up residence and greet the abbots of the subsidiary temples (*tatchū* 塔頭) of Sōjiji

The rituals performed during the three-day memorial service started on the thirteenth with a morning recitation and a sutra-chanting service to mark the monks' coming together. This was followed by a rolling reading of the six hundred volumes of the *Great Sutra on the Perfection of Wisdom*. On the second day, the *Butsuji kōshiki* was performed after breakfast. The service ended on Keizan's memorial day, the fifteenth, with more offerings, recitations, and an ascending the hall sermon.

Most of the texts vocalized were not specific to Keizan's memorial service

30. In Buddhism, the purple robe was an indicator of clerical status loaded with symbolic meaning. The custom of conferring a purple robe started in Tang dynasty China with the imperial gift of a purple robe to monks of special merit. In the eleventh century, the government started to sell purple robes, turning them into a commodity. According to the scholar-monk Mujaku Dōchū, Yōsai and Dōgen were the first monks to receive purple robes in Japan (ZGD, 415). However, the emperor had conferred purple robes on monks before the thirteenth century—the Tendai monk Gyōgen 行玄 (1097–1155), for example, is said to have received a purple robe after curing the emperor of a severe illness in Eiji 1 (1141) (*Kachō yōryaku*, in *Dainihon bukkyō zenshō* 128, 5). Later, the conferral of the purple robe became an institutional matter, and abbots of temples that were acknowledged as imperial prayer temples could wear one. In the Tokugawa period, the wearing of the purple robe was strictly regulated by the bakufu. In the Sōtō school, only the abbots of Eiheiji and Sōjiji were allowed to wear one; see *Sōjiji shohatto*, and Mross 20014a, 96–97, for an English translation. See also Kieschnick 2003, 87–107, for a discussion of the robe and its symbolism. On the robe in Japanese Buddhism, see Diane Riggs 2010; and on the robe in Sōtō Zen in particular, see Faure 1995, Diane Riggs 2004 and 2017, and Williams 2009.

and could be performed on other occasions as well. The *Sutra of the Teachings Left by the Buddha* performed on the thirteenth, for example, explains the last teaching of the Buddha and is traditionally read during the days prior to the Buddha's memorial day. Similarly, the monks chanted the *Sutra of the Teachings Left by the Buddha* two days before Keizan's memorial day. Generally speaking, the memorial service for Keizan was modeled on the Buddha's memorial service, suggesting not only that the monks perceived the two services as parallel, but that Zen masters, who were thought to have received the uninterrupted transmission of the true essence of Śākyamuni's enlightenment, were seen as equal to the Buddha. And indeed the *Butsuji kōshiki* presents Keizan as a substitute for the Buddha.

Some of the vocalized texts were specific to Keizan's memorial service. These were the *Butsuji kōshiki,* the Dharma words accompanying the incense offering, and most likely the transfers of merit vocalized at the end of each ritual.[31] Of these texts, the *shikimon* of the *Butsuji kōshiki* was by far the longest, and it narrated Keizan's life and accomplishments in detail. It also added a narration of Sōjiji's origins to the service. Musically, the *Butsuji kōshiki* contrasted with the sutra chanting and *dhāraṇī* recitations, which were vocalized without melodic embellishment. Significant exceptions were the *Heroic March Dhāraṇī,* which was vocalized in "true grand" style—probably resembling the slow, melodic chanting of the *Dhāraṇī of the Mind of Great Compassion* (*Dabeixin tuoluoni* 大悲心陀羅尼) every morning at Sōjiji today—and the *kada bonnon,* which probably featured *shōmyō.* Nevertheless, as a long ritual featuring a range of *shōmyō* styles, the *Butsuji kōshiki* must have stood apart.

Scholars have often emphasized the role of *kōshiki* in propagating Buddhist teachings to laypeople.[32] This observation may apply to some cases, but not to the *Butsuji kōshiki.* Like Yōkōji, Sōjiji had only a few parishioners and was located in a very remote area. A few laypeople may have attended some of the rituals during Keizan's memorial service, but the monks would no doubt have far outnumbered them. The memorial service for Keizan was a service for and by the monks of the Sōjiji branch, not a celebration for the laity. In fact, lay devotees are not mentioned at all in Shunkō's record. The *Butsuji kōshiki,* and Keizan's memorial service as a whole, was not performed to proselytize; they served instead as a means for the monks to remember Keizan, pay their respects to him, and celebrate their heritage in a grand manner.

At the same time, Keizan's memorial service played an important role in Sōjiji's administration. Sōjiji had an abbot rotation system, and the memorial service was the time when the current abbots turned over their responsibilities to their successors. This rotation was central to the administrative system that Sōjiji employed from the second half of the sixteenth century until Meiji

31. Unfortunately, I have not found any manuscript containing the Dharma words and the transfers of merit vocalized during Keizan's memorial service. But the Dharma words during the offering of incense and the special transfers of merit usually follow standard patterns, so we can assume they did not detail Keizan's life.

32. See Ford 2005, 45; Ozaki 1998b, 167; and Callahan 2011.

3 (1870). Every year, five monks from Sōjiji's branch temples came to Sōjiji to serve alternating terms as abbot of Sōjiji for seventy-five days.[33] The five prospective abbots came before the memorial service, attended it, and when on the fifteenth day of the eighth month the standing five abbots resigned, they assumed their positions as abbots of Sōjiji's five subtemples, with one of them also becoming the new standing abbot of Sōjiji itself. The memorial service for Keizan was completely interwoven with this turnover, as the meetings in the evenings of the thirteenth and the fourteenth and in the early afternoon of the fifteenth show.

During the memorial service, the five resigning abbots served as officiants in the important rituals, and one of them recited the *shikimon* of the *Butsuji kōshiki.*[34] This meant that every year a different monk, who usually did not reside permanently at Sōjiji, recited this text. Some of these high-ranking monks may have taken a copy of the *shikimon* to their home temple after finishing their tenure at Sōjiji, and so the texts were disseminated to other temples, albeit in a limited way.[35]

For its participants, the memorial service was like a family gathering. During the three days, they could meet their distant Dharma relatives, talk with them, perform rituals together, and experience the fellowship of their Dharma lineage in a concrete way. As the most elaborate musical ritual during the memorial service, the *Butsuji kōshiki* provided a narration of their founder's life and a retelling of the origin of their lineage—a key narrative around which a distinct community of Sōjiji-affiliated monks formed.

Butsuji kōshiki

Combining biography and founder worship, the *Butsuji kōshiki* embedded a narration of Keizan's life and the collective memory of his lineage within the ritual frame of a *kōshiki.* Yōkōji and Sōjiji had their own versions of the *kōshiki,* which mainly differed in how each temple accounted for its founding while also diminishing the role of the other temple.[36] The rivalry between the two

---

33. Each branch temple was affiliated with one of Sōjiji's five subtemples: Fuzōin 普蔵院, Myōkōan 妙高庵, Tōsen'an 洞川庵, Denpōan 伝法庵, and Nyoian 如意庵. These subtemples, built around 1400, represented the lineages of Gasan's five disciples: Taigen Sōshin 太源宗真 (d. 1370), Tsūgen Jakurei 通幻寂霊 (1322–1391), Mutan Sokan 無端祖環 (d. 1380), Daitetsu Sōrei 大徹宗令 (1333–1408), and Jippō Ryōshū 実峰良秀 (1318–1405). See Takeuchi M. 1981, 72–73; Itō R. 2005a, 60; Tamamuro 2008, 88–89; and Nodomi 2011, 60–62.

34. For lists of the important rituals in which the abbots served as officiants, see *Myōkōan shingi* (Kansei 10, 1798) and *Kaisan kokushi Butsuji kōshiki* (list written in Tenpō 2, 1831); see also Mross 2014a, 128–130.

35. The two extant manuscripts of the *shikimon* of Sōjiji's *Butsuji kōshiki* have been found not in the archive of Sōjiji or Sōjiji Soin but in archives of branch temples whose head priests had served as abbots at Sōjiji and had recited the *shikimon* during their time there: *Kaisan kokushi Butsuji kōshiki* (Bunka 3, 1806) and *Shogaku kokushi zenji kōshikibon* (Kaei 2, 1849).

36. See Ozaki 1998c and 1999a, and Mross 2010 and 2012d, on the two transmission lineages. Appendix 1 lists the manuscripts of the *Butsuji kōshiki* that have been found in temple archives.

temples was thus condensed into competing narratives that sought to shape how Sōtō monks construed their own history, tradition, and collective identity.

Origins and Ritual Structure

Like all *kōshiki,* the *Butsuji kōshiki* began with the composition of a *shikimon.* However, its author and the date of its composition are unknown, and we have no sources that can illuminate its origin.[37] The oldest extant manuscripts were produced at Sōjiji in Genroku 7 (1694), but it is mentioned in an earlier document, written in Enpō 7 (1679), that lists the regular observances performed at Sōjiji.[38] For this reason, we can assume that the *Butsuji kōshiki* was composed before 1679.

It is reasonable to suppose that a Yōkōji monk originally composed the *Butsuji kōshiki* and that Sōjiji monks adopted it later, because a comparison of the *shikimon* with extant biographies of Keizan shows that it is largely based on the biographical account included in the *Tōkoku goso gyōjitsu,* a work containing biographies of the first five abbots of Yōkōji, namely, Keizan, Meihō, Mugai, Gasan, and Koan.[39] The date of this work's composition is also unknown, but most likely an abbot of Yōkōji or a closely affiliated monk compiled it in the middle of the Muromachi period.[40] Consequently, the *kōshiki* reflects the biographic image of Keizan developed before the Tokugawa period.

The author(s) of the *Butsuji kōshiki* relied on the modular structure of *kōshiki* described in chapter 2. After composing the *shikimon* and an offertory declaration, they inserted these texts into a ritual frame that was similar to the structure of the *Rakan kōshiki,* one difference being the lack of an address of invitation in the *Butsuji kōshiki.* The monks at Yōkōji used a simpler form and did not sing the *Four Shōmyō Melodies.* In other words, when they performed the *Butsuji kōshiki,* the pieces they vocalized were the *Gāthā to Scattering Flowers, Hymn of the Four Wisdoms,* offertory declaration, communal obeisance, *shikimon,* and *Universal Transfer of Merit.*[41] At Sōjiji, however, the monks did sing the *Four Shōmyō Melodies* before the *shikimon,*[42] perhaps because of the greater resources

37. Other titles were also used for this *kōshiki,* e.g., *Shogaku kokushi zenji kōshiki, Kaiso kokushi kōshiki, Kaiso kōshiki,* and *Taiso Butsuji kōshiki* (1892). In the archive of Sōjiji Soin, I also discovered manuscripts with the titles *Taiso kokushi hōon kōshiki* 太祖國師報恩講式 and *Dentō kōshiki* 傳燈講式. Because Keizan came to be called Taiso 太祖 (Great Ancestor) in 1877, these manuscripts must have been written in or after 1877. I have not seen any other reference to the *Butsuji kōshiki* under the title *Dentō kōshiki,* which is actually the title of a new *kōshiki* commemorating Keizan composed by Bukkan Bonjō in 1891.

38. *Shogakuzan Sōjizenji shogyōji,* in Muromine 1965, 243–246.

39. SZ 16: 595–599. Ozaki Shōzen (1999a, 119) was the first to propose the thesis that monks of Yōkōji originally composed the *kōshiki.* However, the oldest extant manuscripts were produced at Sōjiji in Genroku 7 (1694), whereas the earliest extant Yōkōji manuscript is dated Shōtoku 5 (1715).

40. SZ 33: 366; Azuma 1974a, 17–18.

41. This ritual form is laid out in the *Kaiso kōshiki* (Shōtoku 5, 1715).

42. No handbook has yet been discovered that clearly lays out the ritual structure of *kōshiki*

available: as many of monks lived there, it must have been easier for Sōjiji to identify the solo singers that a more elaborate *kōshiki* required.

Shikimon of the *Butsuji kōshiki*

Praising the Three Treasures, the Zen lineage, and Keizan. Here I introduce the *shikimon* of the Yōkōji version of the *Butsuji kōshiki* before discussing the differences between the Yōkōji and Sōjiji texts.[43] The first part of the *shikimon,* the pronouncement of intention, does not focus on Keizan; instead it gives the reason for performing the ritual and recounts the transmission of the Dharma from India to China to Japan. In other words, by recalling the Zen lineage to which Keizan belongs, it affirms the authority whereby Keizan is presented as an equal of the Buddha.

The pronouncement of intention is relatively short and opens by addressing the Three Treasures—the Buddha, the Dharma, and the Saṃgha:

> Reverently, I address the great compassionate saviors of the world [i.e., buddhas and bodhisattvas] in the lands [as many as] various dust motes, all pure teachings of the oceanic storehouse, and the ordinary and holy monks of the ten directions, and say:[44]

Keizan is not explicitly mentioned in the first sentence of the pronouncement of intention. However, he is indirectly included in the address to the Buddha, Dharma, and Saṃgha. Then the pronouncement of intention declares the reason for performing the ritual:

> Respectfully, we gather every year on the memorial day of the founder of this mountain, Zen Master Butsuji, great venerable Keizan. We prepare this lecture and perform this Buddhist service. In general, we praise the excellent virtue of

---

performed at Sōjiji in the Tokugawa period. The assumption that the monks at Sōjiji performed the *Butsuji kōshiki* using the standard ritual form is based on liturgical texts included in the ritual handbooks used at Sōjiji (*Butsuji kō kada narabini Shichisan, Kada narabini hōyō,* and *San kōshiki narabini hōyō*). However, some of the ritual handbooks include the piece *Final Praise,* indicating that this liturgical piece may have been sung during *kōshiki* at Sōjiji in the Tokugawa period (*Kada narabini hōyō* and *San kōshiki narabini hōyō*).

43. Unless otherwise noted, excerpts from the Yōkōji version of the *kōshiki* have been translated from an untitled manuscript stored at Yōkōji that is usually referred to as *Butsuji kōshiki* (ca. 1725). Here I call it the Yōkōji manuscript. Since a complete translation with detailed annotation is provided in Appendix 2, the annotation in this chapter has been kept to a minimum. Appendix 7 provides a facsimile of this manuscript made available by Sōtōshū Bunkazai Chōsa Iinkai. For a typographical reprint, see Ozaki 1998c. Page citations for my translations in this chapter are to Ozaki's publication.

44. Since the first part of the Yōkōji manuscript that includes the beginning of the pronouncement of intention have been lost, I translate here the opening passage from the Sōjiji version, *Kaisan kokushi Butsuji kōshiki* (Bunka 3, 1806), stored at Taineiji and henceforth referred to as the Taineiji manuscript.

> the Three Treasures and so develop the great heart to spread the Dharma and to benefit all beings. In particular, we praise the original vow of the venerable great master to propagate the teachings in place of the Buddha, and so we repay one drop of the milky ocean. (Ozaki 1998c, 59)

The text indicates that it was written to be recited during Keizan's memorial service in order to repay the benevolence received from the master who appeared "in place of the Buddha." Keizan's authority to propagate the Dharma is based on the idea that he stands in the lineage of the direct, mind-to-mind transmission of the Dharma that started with the Buddha. To Zen clerics, the understanding of each patriarch in this lineage is the same as the Buddha's. Hence the pronouncement of intention lays out the Zen genealogy:

> First, [Śākyamuni] left the palace of Tuṣita Heaven. For a time, he sat on the throne of the king; finally, he went to [Bodh]gayā and was completely rewarded for [his] way to enlightenment (*kakudō* 覺道) [i.e., his practice] on the snow peaks [i.e., Himalayas]. He displayed the beauty of the marvelous attributes [of a Buddha] and manifested eternal life.
>
> As various flowers sent out fragrance, from the tips of the tongues of many forests gushed the ocean of the boundless essence of the Dharma body [i.e., the Buddha preached enthusiastically]. As the crane trees returned to [their] roots, the full moon of the Buddha nature assembled in the lapis lazuli vase [i.e., the Buddha left relics when he entered nirvāṇa]. Therefore, [the Buddha] gathered all sentient beings of the five natures and explained the one Buddha vehicle. Once on the top of Vulture Peak, he picked up a flower and made Mahākāśyapa smile. In front of the Stupa of Many Sons, he transmitted the mind seal [to him] and let [him] cultivate the wisdom-life of the marvelous Dharma body.
>
> Kāśyapa hid at Kukkuṭapāda, and Ānanda died at the Ganges. But they transmitted the robe and belief, which were successively transmitted face-to-face for twenty-eight generations until they reached the honorable Bodhidharma. The honorable one first received the prophecy from Prajñātāra. He went far away to China and swept away the questions of Emperor Liang [i.e., Emperor Wu]. Then he obtained the respect and enlightenment of Shenguang [i.e., Huike]. From then on, Caoxi [i.e., Huineng] spread out a net, and the house of Dong [i.e., Dongshan Liangjie] mended the robe.
>
> [The teaching of the Caodong (J. Sōtō) school] was transmitted over thirteen generations and then reached our nation's Great Master Eihei [i.e., Dōgen]. First, he left the peak of [Ten]dai (Tairei 台嶺) [i.e., Mt. Hiei] and entered the room of Kennin[ji]. Finally, he crossed the southern sea and climbed the Great White Peak [i.e., Tiantongshan]. He let go of body and mind in a foreign country and explained the original face on his home mountain. He revived the Buddha's sun and popularized the style of the ancestors. (59)

This central passage describes the transmission of the Dharma, originating with Śākyamuni, from India to China to Japan. The pronouncement of intention does not resemble the daily transfer of merit during the morning service, in which all the names of the patriarchs of a lineage and previous abbots of a respective temple are recited. Instead the *Butsuji kōshiki* mentions only the best-known patriarchs—Kāśyapa, Ānanda, Bodhidharma, Huike, Caoxi, Dongshan, and Dōgen—and gives brief accounts of their lives, thereby enlivening the Dharma lineage with concrete examples. The description envisions Keizan in this lineage without explicitly mentioning him, giving him a place in the *imaginaire* of Zen transmission that is both linear in the sense that Keizan is one in a sequence of patriarchs, and circular in the way that the enlightenment of the Buddha and of each patriarch is thought to be the same.[45] As a result, Keizan and his temple are equally legitimized by the unbroken lineage starting with the Buddha. Through this pronouncement of intention, as well as the daily transfer of merit during morning services when monks recite the names of the patriarchs, Sōtō monks remember their lineage and heritage.

In reality, such a simple lineage does not exist, because monks studied with multiple masters, as a reading of the biographies of Zen monks immediately reveals and as the next section of the *kōshiki* suggests.[46] But in the family tree of Zen, these complex relationships are reduced to a single line. Nevertheless, these abstract lineages played a fundamental role in the collective memory of the Zen tradition, as the pronouncement of intention reminds us.

After the description of the transmission of the Dharma, the *Butsuji kōshiki* praises Zen by stating that "Zen transmits the mind of the Buddha" whereas "the scriptures transmit the words of the Buddha." It then states that Zen and the teaching schools share the same principle and complement each other, but that foolish people get stuck in doctrinal debates whereas wise men understand the truth and widely propagate the true teaching.

Finally, the purpose of the ceremony—praising the Three Treasures in general and Keizan in particular—is restated, and the topics of the following three sections are introduced, providing listeners with a map of the narration that follows.

Keizan's past lives, auspicious birth, and accomplishments. The first and longest section of the *shikimon* details Keizan's life, starting with his auspicious birth and previous lifetimes and ending with his passing. The text also narrates the early history of Sōtō Zen in Japan and the founding of Keizan's lineage. In

45. Here I follow Bernard Faure's interpretation of the term *imaginaire,* based on Jacques Le Goff's definition (Faure 1996, 10–12). Ritual practices do not represent an eternal reality but are products of imagination. Faure suggests that "a 'purely' Zen form of imagination, a reservoir of images and *exempla* specific to Chan" exists, in which the images and stories "are *topoi,* mnemonic devices (like the mantras and *dhāraṇī* of esoteric Buddhism) helping in the memorization of essential points of Chan doctrine" (1996, 11). Similarly, it could be said that the ritual language and practices of the *Butsuji kōshiki* express the *imaginaire* of the monks of both Sōjiji and Yōkōji.

46. See Bodiford 1993 on the complex network of horizontal relationships in the early Sōtō community.

their respective versions of the *kōshiki,* both Yōkōji and Sōjiji present themselves as Keizan's main temple. Here I focus on Yōkōji's version and show how it describes Yōkōji as a special sacred site, thereby expressing its communal memory.

The section opens by stating Keizan's name and place of birth, followed by Keizan's description of his previous lives:

> First, I explain the accomplishments of the Zen master. The Zen master's real name (*imina* 諱) was Jōkin, called Keizan. He was born in the village Tane in Echizen. He did not explain his family descent at all. Once he said during a Dharma talk: "In a previous life I was the deity of a Kubara tree. In the old days during the time of the Buddha Vipasyin, I realized the state of an arhat. Later I followed the fourth honorable [arhat] Sohinda and lived with him together on the snow mountains [i.e., the Himalayas] in [the northern continent] Uttarakuru. Because of these causes, I have now been reborn at the foot of Mt. Haku 白山 in the northern region [of Japan]." (60)

Keizan's account of his previous lives reminds us of the Jātaka stories, tales of the former lives of Śākyamuni Buddha. Keizan's practice over these earlier lifetimes is depicted as the reason he became a great master. Through the description of his former existences, another linearity is added to that of the Dharma transmission described in the pronouncement of intention—namely, the linearity of Keizan's previous lives and his rebirth as a result of his practice during his previous lifetimes.

The section then recounts the auspicious birth of Keizan. His mother dreamed that she drank sunlight and became pregnant. She then performed 1,333 prostrations, recited the *Kannon Sutra* (a chapter of the *Lotus Sutra* explaining the virtues of Kannon) thirty-three times daily, and prayed to Kannon to give birth to a holy boy. The symbolism of a special birth is rooted in the biography of the Buddha, whose mother, Māyā, dreamed that an elephant entered her womb, and she became pregnant. The *Butsuji kōshiki* and other biographies of Keizan maintain the topos of a very devoted mother and include descriptions of her dreams or prayers. Likewise, many biographies of eminent monks mention the dreams their mothers had before becoming pregnant; the biographies of Gasan and the *Gasan kōshiki* are other examples.[47] Menzan's *Hōon kōshiki* for Dōgen and the influential Dōgen biography *Kenzeiki* 建撕記 do not mention dreams but include wondrous events that accompanied Dōgen's birth.[48] In this way, the *hōon kōshiki* of the Sōtō school follow the standard pattern of Buddhist biographies.

---

47. After praying either to Monju 文殊 (Skt. Mañjuśrī) or to Kannon that she might have a holy son, Gasan's mother dreamed that she swallowed a sword and then became pregnant. See *Sōji nidai oshō shōtō, Sōji dainise Gasan oshō gyōjō, Tōkoku goso gyōjitsu,* and *Nichiiki tōjō shosoden;* see also Mross 2013a, 125, on the *Gasan kōshiki.*

48. *Hōon kōshiki,* ZSZ 2: 724; K, 3.

The *Butsuji kōshiki* describes Keizan as an extremely intelligent child. It then explains Keizan's entry into the clergy and his study under early Sōtō masters, situating him in a network of masters who had all practiced under Dōgen:

> At the age of thirteen, he secretly developed a wish to leave the household. Then he entered the room of Master Koun [Ejō] 孤雲[懷奘] (1198–1280) of Eihei[ji] and shaved his head [i.e., became a monk].
>
> Then, under Jakuen 寂圓 (1207–1299), the master of the stupa (*tassu* 塔主), he aroused the thought (*hosshin* 發心) [of attaining enlightenment] and received the [bodhisattva] precepts from Zen master Gien 義演 (d. 1314). Suddenly, when he heard the phrase from a sutra, "With the eyes given by their parents, they all see the three thousand worlds,"[49] he awakened. He immediately instructed (*teishō* 提唱): "If you change the self, you make all things, and if you change all things, you make the self."
>
> Again [Keizan's] eyes were opened through Master [Tettsū Gi]kai [徹通義]介 (1219–1309) of Daijō[ji] [when] he practiced alone "The ordinary [mind] is the way" and rode the black jewel in the darkness.[50] He was appointed the second abbot of Daijō[ji]. (60–61)

In the pronouncement of intention, a single lineage of transmission from India to China to Dōgen was sketched out, and Keizan was imagined in it without being explicitly mentioned. The first section of the *Butsuji kōshiki* now situates Keizan in a complex network of connections to Dōgen by describing how he studied under Dōgen's principal disciple Ejō and the Chinese monk Jakuen, who had come to Japan to study with Dōgen, as well as with Gien and Gikai, both of whom had studied under Dōgen. After Dōgen's death, Jakuen, Gien, and Gikai became disciples of Ejō, from whom they received Dharma transmission. Keizan is therefore connected to four important monks of the early Sōtō community and is legitimatized through a horizontal network connecting him not only to Dōgen but also to Chinese Chan, via Jakuen and Gikai, who had studied there.

Another point of interest is the description of Keizan's enlightenment experience upon hearing the phrase "With the eyes given by their parents, they all see the three thousand worlds" from the *Lotus Sutra*. This account is based on the *Tōkoku goso gyōjitsu:*

> When he was twenty-two years old, he incidentally read the phrase from a sutra, "With the eyes given by their parents, they all see the three thousand worlds," and

---

49. This is a sentence from the nineteenth chapter of the *Lotus Sutra,* T 9: 47c17.

50. This account is based on an exchange between Gikai and Keizan. Gikai tested Keizan's understanding of the famous *kōan* "The ordinary mind is the way," and Keizan answered that the night before he had ridden on a black jewel in the darkness. See *Tōkoku goso gyōjitsu,* SZ 16: 595; see also Azuma 1974a, 93–95.

> reached enlightenment and said: "If you change the self, you make all things, and if you change all things, you make the self. The cool breeze and the bright moon are originally right in front of your eyes." (SZ 16: 595)

But where that text uses the verb "said" to introduce Keizan's statement upon reaching enlightenment, the author of the *Butsuji kōshiki* substitutes "immediately instructed." According to the *Tōkoku goso gyōjitsu,* Keizan was twenty-two years old when he had this experience. But the *Butsuji kōshiki* describes him already as a master.

Subsequently, the section describes Keizan as a religious leader, attesting to his role as the great popularizer of Sōtō Zen: as his fame spread, many monks and lay believers visited him. Then the section states that he composed the *Denkōroku* 傳光錄 (Record of the transmission of the light), one of the central texts of the Sōtō school today.[51] This is followed by a brief quotation from the *Genkō shakusho* 元亨釈書, Japan's first comprehensive Buddhist history, compiled by the Rinzai monk Kokan Shiren 虎関師錬 (1278–1346). The author of the *Butsuji kōshiki* remarked "Was it not at that time that Shiren said, 'The teaching of [Dō]gen spreads in the northern region'?,"[52] implying that the spread of Dōgen's teaching was due to Keizan's activities.

The section now describes the founding of Yōkōji in detail, presenting it as a special sacred site:

> One day the master had the idea to resign [from Daijōji]. At that time, there were, among others, the daughter of the local regent Sakawa Hachirō Heishi Yorichika 酒勾八郎頼親 of the Taira family of the province of Nō [i.e., Noto], with the Dharma name Sonin 祖忍, as well as her husband Unno Sanrō Shigeno Nobunao 海野三郎滋野信直 of the province of Shin [i.e., Shinano]. They invited [Keizan] to come to this province. Together they exhausted their reverence. Moreover, they searched for the tranquility of this mountain and told [Keizan] about it. It accorded well with the master's plan to retire [from the abbotship of Daijōji]. Then they informed the administration in Kamakura, donated land, and built a temple. With the help [of the *kami*] of the Keta 氣多 [shrine], they allowed the Dharma to be protected and the assembly to be at ease.
>
> [Keizan] called this mountain Tōkoku 洞谷 and so revered the old style of Dongshan 洞山. He called this temple Yōkō 永光 and venerated the remaining accomplishments of Dayang [Jingxuan] 大陽[警玄] (943–1027).
>
> [Pilgrims] hung torn straw sandals on the branches of the *enoki* tree [in front of the temple gate], and [Keizan] established a very special place under the pine trees where he arrived. Myōshōgon'in 妙荘嚴院 [i.e., the abbot's quarters] was

51. The *Denkōroku* was first printed in Ansei 4 (1857) in an edition by Busshū Sen'ei 仏洲仙英 (1794–1864). Before this edition, it was handed down in manuscript form, and only a limited number of monks had access to it. Besides the *Tōkoku goso gyōjitsu,* no other premodern biography of Keizan mentions this work; see Azuma 1974a, 113–118. See also Bodiford 2015 and 2017 on the *Denkōroku;* and Cleary 1990, Cook 2003, and Foulk 2017 for English translations.

52. Fujita 2011, 128.

> opened at a special place, and a land filled with fragrance (*kōshaku kokudo* 香積國土) manifested itself at this site. Furthermore, Tomosada 朝定 built Saishōden 最勝殿 [i.e., the Buddha hall] and solemnly opened the place of practice for prayers for the imperial court. [Fujiwara] Iemasa [藤原]家方 built the Fukōdo 普光堂 [i.e., the Dharma hall], and there [Keizan] explained his Dharma lineage for the first time. The officer [Fujiwara] Yukifusa [藤原]行房 (d. 1337) wrote name plaques and made these protectors of the temple. The nun Sonin worshiped Kannon and lived in Enzū[in] 圓通[院]; Jōken had a dream, and the southern emperor [i.e., Emperor Godaigo] sent questions.
>
> [Keizan] responded nine times to the requests of people and served as abbot at eight places of practice. On this mountain in particular, the five elders and the four wise men protect this one peak; and the three sages and the two heavenly kings push the two wheels [of food and doctrine]. (61)

This passage praises Yōkōji as a sacred place protected by the *kami* of the Keta shrine. Located in Hakui, the Keta shrine was the main shrine in Noto, at which the deity Ichinomiya 一宮 was worshiped. According to the *Tōkokuki,* Ichinomiya appeared to Keizan in a dream to request offerings, and asked Keizan to enshrine a Bishamon 毘沙門 statue as the main object of worship for the storehouse at Yōkōji. Keizan interpreted this dream as a sign that Ichinomiya would protect Yōkōji.[53]

The naming of temples, halls, and mountains has long been an important means to create imaginative connections to eminent monks or sacred places, with the affiliations thus established providing historical and geographical precedents for the sacredness of temple sites. This practice was followed in the naming of Tōkokusan Yōkōji 洞谷山永光寺, as is evident when the author of the *shikimon* explains that the mountain name Tōkoku was chosen in remembrance of Dongshan Liangjie, the co-founder of the Caodong school, and the temple name Yōkō was selected in remembrance of Dayang Jingxuan, an important reviver of the Caodong tradition. In his *Tōkokuki,* Keizan explained:

> As the sixteenth-generation heir to the founding patriarch Tōzan 洞山 [Ch. Dongshan], I revere his house style (*kafū* 家風). Therefore, I named this mountain Tōkoku 洞谷, simply replacing [the character] mountain (*san / zan* 山) with [that of] valley (*koku* 谷), just as Sōzan 曹山 [Ch. Caoshan, i.e., Caoshan Benji] was derived from a change in Sōkei 曹渓 [Ch. Caoxi, i.e., Huineng]. As I am the eleventh-generation heir to the founding patriarch Dayang [Jingxuan] 大陽

53. JDZ, 393, or KZ 8: 7–12; see Faure 1996, 84, for an English translation. Dreams played an important role in the lives of monks. For a detailed study of dreams in Buddhist biographies, see Quenzer 2000, 185–242. Keizan's *Tōkokuki* suggests that he found legitimation and guidance through dreams; see Faure 1996, chap. 5. Myōe is especially famed for the dreams and visions that he recorded in his dream diary and that guided his practice. For detailed studies of Myōe, see Girard 1990 and Tanabe 1992.

> [警玄], I revere the clear vision (*meimoku* 盈目) of Dayang (Great Sun) and named this monastery Yōkōji 永光寺 (Monastery of Eternal Light).[54]

Although Keizan established a clear imaginative connection to Dongshan and Dayang in the naming of his temple, the name Dayang was later crossed out in the Yōkōji manuscript and next to it "Eihei" 永平, i.e., Dōgen, was written. In this way, the monks of Yōkōji sought to affiliate themselves with Dōgen and Eiheiji, shifting their connections from Dongshan and Dayang to Dongshan and Dōgen. We do not know anything about the background of this change, but the new affiliation with Dōgen and Eiheiji reflected a changing *imaginaire* and possibly an attempt to elevate Yōkōji's status.

In the passage of the Yōkōji manuscript translated above, we find several other changes that reflected alterations in the collective memory. For example, in the sentence stating that Yukifusa wrote the name plaques for the temple, the term "seven halls" was added later. This addition emphasized Yōkōji's high status by suggesting that it was built according to the Southern Song model of a seven-hall temple compound (*shichidō garan* 七堂伽藍), consisting of a mountain or main gate and a Buddha hall, Dharma hall, monks' hall, kitchen, latrine, and bathhouse. Keizan mentions in his *Tōkokuki* that temples usually received only one or two name plaques, but that he fortunately received seven at Yōkōji.[55]

The Yōkōji version of the *Butsuji kōshiki* identifies Yōkōji as Keizan's main temple and the source of his lineage. In the passage translated above, only two statements hint at the existence of Sōjiji. First, it mentions Jōken, who entrusted his temple, the future Sōjiji, to Keizan after having an auspicious dream. Then it states that Keizan founded eight temples and served as abbot at nine.[56] But only Daijōji and Yōkōji are mentioned in the passage, leaving Sōjiji, which had long surpassed Yōkōji in status when the *Butsuji kōshiki* was written, among the unnamed. We might suspect that in looking past Sōjiji, the Yōkōji monks were deliberately downplaying the position of its powerful rival.

Also mentioned in this passage is a vital source that was central to Yōkōji's claim to status and authority: the questions of Emperor Godaigo. The *kōshiki* refers here to the ten questions that Emperor Godaigo is said to have sent to Yōkōji in Gen'ō 2 (1320); after receiving Keizan's answers, he supposedly declared Yōkōji to be an imperial prayer temple, the first Sōtō temple to receive

54. Translation adapted from Faure 1996, 53; for the original, see JDZ, 395 or KZ 8: 21–22.

55. JDZ, 431.

56. According to the *Sansō yuiseki teradera okibumiki,* Keizan instructed his disciples that the eight temples of Yōkōji, Enzūin, Hōōji, Kōkōji, Hōshōji, Jōjūji, Daijōji, and Sōjiji should be upheld by monks of his lineages; see JDZ, 416–418, or KZ 8: 171–179; and *Yōkōji no meihō,* 34, for a photo of this document. Except for Daijōji, all these temples were founded by Keizan; not mentioned in this source is Jōmanji. Adding this temple to the list, Keizan founded eight temples and served as abbot of nine.

this recognition.[57] Sōjiji, however, also possesses documents claiming the same question-and-answer exchange and recognition, written in Genkō 2 (1322).[58] Although both sets of documents are later forgeries, they nevertheless played an important role in the intense rivalry between the two temples, with each claiming for itself the cherished imperial recognition.

Another statement that hints at Yōkōji's role as Keizan's main temple is that Yōkōji is protected by the five elders (Rujing, Dōgen, Ejō, Gikai, and Keizan) and four disciples (Meihō, Mugai, Gasan, and Koan). The text refers here to the Peak of the Five Elders (Gorōhō 五老峰), where Keizan is said to have buried the recorded sayings of Dōgen's master Rujing, a fragment of one of Dōgen's bones, a sutra Ejō had copied using his own blood, pieces of Gikai's bones, Gikai's Dharma transmission certificate, relics that had been handed down in the Daruma school, Chinese relic beads, and sutras Keizan had copied himself.[59] These relics endowed the site with the spiritual authority of the five Zen masters, and Yōkōji with unimpeachable standing as the center of Keizan's ancestral lineage. This statement in the *shikimon* is therefore an assertion of Yōkōji's authority both in Keizan's lineage and in the Sōtō school.

The *shikimon* continues by praising Keizan's teaching activities. It explains that Keizan died in Shōchū 2 (1325) at the age of fifty-eight and that a stupa named Dentōin 傳燈院 was built for him.[60] This first section of the *shikimon* closes by stating that Keizan became a great master due to accumulated practice during his five hundred lifetimes before the present manifestation. To repay the kindness received from Keizan, the assembly is invited by the officiant to sing a verse and perform a prostration:

---

57. *Jūshu gitai; Godaigo tennō shusse dōjō gorinji.*

58. *Jūshu chokumon; Godaigo tennō rinji sha.*

59. *Tōkokuki,* JDZ, 411–416; KZ 8: 129–168. However, according to the *Tōkokusan jinmiraisai okibumi,* which was signed by Keizan and Sonin in Gen'ō 1 (1319), Keizan did not bury sutras copied by him but rather his transmission certificate; see Azuma 2002, 20–21; *Yōkōji no meihō,* 30 and 76–77; and *Tōkokuki,* JDZ, 419–420; KZ 8: 182–194. Although Keizan mainly buried items related to his Sōtō lineage, he notes in his *Tōkokuki* that he also buried relics handed down in the Daruma school. Many monks of the early Sōtō community were monks of the Daruma school, which had been founded by Dainichi Nonin 大日能忍 (n.d.). Keizan's teacher Gikai was also a former Daruma monk, and through him Keizan inherited the lineage of the Daruma school. Faure (1987, 26) argues in his study on the Daruma school: "We may well wonder to what extent Dōgen was influenced by, rather than influenced, his new disciples. In other words, who converted whom is perhaps not so clear as the tradition would have us believe."

60. The *Butsuji kōshiki* is a Tokugawa-period source, so it states that Keizan died when he was fifty-eight years old. However, Matsuda Bun'yū (1974) and Yamahata Shōdō (1974) have convincingly shown that Keizan lived from 1264 until 1325, dying when he was sixty-two. By stating that Keizan died when he was fifty-eight and had been a monk for forty-seven years, the *kōshiki* implies that Keizan was ordained when he was twelve. The *Tōkokuki* and *Tōkoku goso gyōjitsu,* however, state that he was ordained when he was thirteen and died after being a monk for forty-six years; see JDZ, 435; KS 8: 209–301; SZ 16: 595–596. It is unclear whether the statement in the *Butsuji kōshiki* is a copying mistake or was already a mistake in the source that its author used.

We bow our heads to the honorable Butsuji.
The Dharma nature is pure and clear as the moon.
When the mind of sentient beings is like still water,
The reflection of feeling and response (*kannō* 感應) will appear in it.[61]

Humbly prostrating ourselves, we take refuge in Zen Master Butsuji, who benefits all sentient beings. (62)

Except for the name of the object of worship in the first line and *kannō* in the last one, this verse is the same as the one used at the end of the first section in the *Rakan kōshiki*.[62] The Sōjiji version of the *Butsuji kōshiki* uses a different verse, but it too is taken from the *Rakan kōshiki*, which served as a model for many of the new *kōshiki* in the Sōtō school.

Keizan and his disciples. The second section of the *Butsuji kōshiki*, which is considerably shorter than the first, remembers Keizan as an influential teacher whose lineage was responsible for the spread of Sōtō Zen all across Japan. It starts by mentioning those whom Keizan taught and ordained:

Second, I explain the manifestation in response during his lifetime. When the Zen master was first at Jōman[ji] in Unbe, he widely sent out the bright light of the one precept and ordained around seventy people, such as [Gen]ka Tekkyō 眼可鐵鏡 (d. 1321). Furthermore, even Butsurin 佛林 [i.e., Kyōō Unryō 恭翁運良, 1267–1341] and Sankō 三光 [i.e., Kohō Kakumyō (1271–1361)] of different schools bathed in the light of the precepts and received a prophecy. The donors Sakawa 酒勾 [Sonin] and Unno 海野 [Sanrō Shigeno Nobunao] thoroughly consumed the taste of the Dharma and took the tonsure.

The four great disciples [Meihō] Sotetsu, Mugai [Chikō], [Gasan] Jōseki, and [Koan] Shikan were formerly dragons of the doctrine and tigers of the rules. But finally they entered the melting pot [of Keizan] and all became great vessels. Thereafter, the far descendants of the four wise men filled Japan and built around twenty thousand Zen temples. (62)

This section presents Keizan as an active teacher who widely administered the precepts and taught many capable disciples. Among them were Keizan's four main disciples, who had been proponents of other traditions before converting to Zen and becoming pillars of Keizan's lineage. Thanks to their effort, Sōtō Zen spread all across Japan. The monks of this lineage were well aware that it is their branch that was responsible for the success of the Sōtō

61. This verse is a variation of a *gāthā* from the *Flower Garland Sutra,* T 9: 670c21. It is also included in the *Nianfo sanmei baowang lun,* T 47: 137a29–b1, and *Qixinlun shubi xiaoji,* T 44: 393c25–26.

62. In the Manzan edition of the *Keizan shingi,* which includes the *Rakan kōshiki,* this verse can be found in T 82: 435b25–26.

school in Japan, and thus they remembered their history during Keizan's memorial service.

The text then highlights the contributions of both Dōgen and Keizan: Dōgen transmitted Zen, whereas Keizan established the monastic rules. By presenting these two masters as a pair, the *shikimon* presents them as the two central figures of Sōtō Zen and Keizan as equally important as the school founder, Dōgen.

The text goes on to describe the sacred protection of Yōkōji: "At the black stone, the mountain spirit stays for a long time in the jewel belt. In the deep pine tree grove, Isurugi shows sweet pears for eternity."[63] The allusions here to one or more temple legends have remained obscure, as no source has yet come to light to explain them. But in suggesting that mountain spirits and *kami* protect Zen temples, the statement reflects the importance of temple legends and demonstrates the eclecticism in the makeup of the pantheon of Japanese Zen.[64]

Finally, this section praises Keizan for his continuous practice and earnest teaching and invites the monks to sing a verse, summarizing the content of the *shikimon:*

> The monk who realized enlightenment five hundred existences ago
> Completed the practice to reach enlightenment and has an immeasurable body.
> We only wish that he may widely save the world of sentient beings,
> May he not abandon the wheel of the correct vow for eternity. (62–63)

Most verses in *kōshiki* are quotations from sutras, but this verse seems to have been specially composed to praise Keizan, most likely for the *Butsuji kōshiki.* It describes Keizan's enlightenment and expresses the wish that he will save all sentient beings.

Keizan's influence and repaying his kindness. The third and final section of the *shikimon* expresses the monks' gratitude to Keizan, who is described as eternally abiding at Yōkōji. The first paragraph once more declares the intention of the ritual:

> Third, I explain the salvation of all beings after his death. Now we have been born four hundred years later and gather here every year on the day of [his] passing. Although there is no one [among us] whose three modes of activity [of body, speech, and mind] are pure, we are fortunate to have joined the numbers of the disciples of [Keizan's] transmitted teaching. We revere his wondrous remains and hold this memorial service. There are no offerings from patrons, but we offer as many mountain flowers and vegetables as we can. [We] are but a few distant

---

63. Ozaki 1998c, 62.

64. See Hirose 1988 for a study on the role of legends in the founding of Zen temples.

> descendants from various provinces; we have walked through rain and frost, protected by bamboo hats and shoes, and have gathered [here]. (63)

The monks repay Keizan's benevolence with humble offerings suited to their station. In noting explicitly that there are no offerings from patrons, the *kōshiki* declares that it is a ritual by and for the monks of Keizan's lineage.

The sacred nature of Yōkōji is then praised once more, and Keizan is described as eternally abiding and teaching there:

> If we think respectfully, the bright moon stays long in front of the Peak of the Five Elders and shows intimately the eternal form of the Dharma body. The running stream (*seisui* 逝水) flows for eternity in the valley of Tōkoku and captures the pure voice and the sound of the rolling tide. All day long we can hear the talk of the great master; why always use the guidance of other people? (63)

The text intimates that Keizan's voice can be heard at Yōkōji, still offering guidance to his distant disciples. The section closes by explaining that the way to repay kindness is to practice for the sake of all beings:

> One step forward, one step backward, and we still do not depart from the mountain of wholesome roots. One veneration, one prostration, and together we enter the forest of virtue.
>
> We have a profound mind [deeply seeking enlightenment] and offer [it] to the worlds as numerous as dust motes. This is called the offering to repay kindness. We have this aspiration for enlightenment and extend it to the world. This is called the salvation of all beings after his death. (63)

The ritual ends with the assembly singing the *Universal Transfer of Merit,* dedicating the merit accumulated through the performance of the *kōshiki* to all sentient beings.

Differences between the Two Transmission Lineages

While similar in most passages, the *shikimon* in the Yōkōji and Sōjiji versions differ at important junctures. Both present their own temple as Keizan's main temple and neglect describing the other in any depth. But by the Tokugawa period, the rivalry between Sōjiji and Yōkōji had lost much of its salience for Sōjiji, which had risen to the status of one of the two head temples of the Sōtō school. For Sōjiji, the true rival was Eiheiji. Nevertheless, the rivalry between Sōjiji and Yōkōji had shaped the collective memory of both temple communities and is reflected in the two versions of the *Butsuji kōshiki.*

The greatest differences between the two transmission lineages appear in the first section of the *shikimon* in connection with the founding of Keizan's temple. While the Yōkōji version gives an extensive explanation of how Keizan founded Yōkōji after he had left Daijōji, the Sōjiji version, after lightly passing over the founding of Yōkōji, focuses on how Keizan opened Sōjiji:

In Ōchō 1 (1311), [Keizan] stepped down from the temple affairs [of Daijōji] and surprised [the monks] with the drum [announcing the ascending the hall sermon] for [his] resignation.[65] The local regents and the common people yearned from afar and venerated [him] deeply. Some people built temples, invited the master, and let him live there. These were Jōman[ji] 城満[寺], Jōjū[ji] 浄住寺, and Kōkō[ji] 光孝[寺].

Then Shigeno no Nobunao 滋野信直 of Nō province and his wife of the Taira family respected his virtue, donated one mountain in the district of Sakai, built a temple compound, invited [Keizan], and made him the founding abbot. Together they exhausted their reverence. Therefore, [Keizan] came, and when he arrived at this temple [i.e., Yōkōji], the peaks were lined up and enclosed a flat area that was like a grindstone. He truly felt completely pleased.

[Jōken][66] had a wondrous dream of Kannon and [entrusted his] temple to the master. [Keizan] followed Jōken's deep request and changed [the temple] from a teaching to a Zen [temple]. He named the mountain Shōgaku 諸嶽 and saved the old name [given by] Gyōki 行基 (668–749). He wrote Sōji on the temple and responded to the wondrous talisman (*reifu* 靈符) of the bodhisattva.[67]

The water of the blue valley river was pure, and [Keizan] put a twining vine stick on the ground. The moss of the white cliff was smooth, and [Keizan] mended torn clothes [there]. The gate of the three pine trees (*sanshō* 三松) [widely] opened like the character eight 八. The sweet spring of the one lineage fills one hundred rivers.

Furthermore, the emperor sent ten questions, promoted [Sōjiji], and made it a prayer temple of the imperial household. Kakumyō drank bitterness for three years [i.e., he practiced for three years under Keizan] and then he received the transmission (*kechimyaku* 血脈) of the bodhisattva precepts. The officer [Fujiwara] Yukifusa wrote the name plaque and made it a protector of the temple. The elder Gasan protected the Dharma robe and supported the sagely guidance.

[Keizan] opened the place of practice for prayers for the fortune of the imperial court and vigorously set up a Dharma seat for imperially appointed abbots (*shusse no hōseki* 出世法席). [Keizan] responded nine times to the requests of the people and served as abbot at eight places of practice. On this mountain especially, the five shrines and the four *kami* protect the Three Treasures; the three sages and the two heavenly kings push the two wheels [of food and doctrine]. (61)

This passage recounts the founding of Sōjiji in detail, presenting it as a special sacred site. But first the text alludes to the temple that Keizan founded before Sōjiji, saying that Shigeno Nobunano and his wife invited Keizan to Noto and that Keizan was pleased with the location, yet never mentioning Yōkōji's name.

65. Before resignation, an abbot gives an ascending the hall sermon, which is usually announced with the sound of a drum.

66. Jōken's name is not given in the two extant Sōjiji manuscripts. We can assume that an earlier scribe forgot to copy "Jōken" and later it was not corrected.

67. "The bodhisattva" most likely refers to Kannon here because Morookadera was a temple in which Kannon was worshiped and Jōken is said to have had a dream of Kannon requesting him to entrust the temple to Keizan; see *Sōjiji kaibyaku no engi*.

Similarly, the Yōkōji version is silent about Sōjiji, confining itself to a brief mention of Jōken's dream.

The Sōjiji version then turns to Sōjiji itself. First, it retells the story of Jōken's auspicious dream, which led to his entrusting of the temple to Keizan. As in the text of the Yōkōji version, the mountain name and the temple name are explained. Shōgaku 諸嶽 is an alternative reading of Sōjiji's former temple name Morooka, a name supposedly given by the famous monk Gyōki 行基 (668–749), who is said to have traveled around the country and preached to a wide range of people; and Sōji refers to the protection of the bodhisattva Kannon. Through the connection to Gyōki, Sōjiji claimed legitimacy as a sacred place with a long history.

The text supports Sōjiji's claims to power by mentioning the ten questions that Emperor Godaigo is said to have sent to Keizan at Sōjiji, and by stating that Sōjiji was recognized as an imperial prayer temple. Afterward, Kakumyō is mentioned, who is supposed to have mediated between Emperor Godaigo and Keizan.[68]

The passage closes with a description of the sacred protection that Sōjiji enjoys, stating that "the five shrines and the four *kami* protect the Three Treasures," and "the three sages and the two heavenly kings push the two wheels [of food and doctrine]." The latter statement also appears in the Yōkōji manuscript, but instead of the former statement, the Yōkōji version says, "the five elders and the four wise men protect this one peak," referring to the Peak of the Five Elders and Keizan's four main disciples. Despite my efforts, I was not able to find another document that mentions the presence of five shrines and four *kami* at Sōjiji; hence it seems likely that the *kōshiki* originated at Yōkōji and the monk(s) of Sōjiji who adopted it changed this sentence in the *shikimon.*

In a similar way, many of the other differences in the *shikimon* seem to be the result of emendations of the original text, assuming it was written at Yōkōji. In the first section, the Yōkōji version states that Keizan instructed his four main disciples, Meihō, Mugai, Gasan, and Koan, and "encouraged the practice of the 'four friends,'" whereas the Sōjiji version only mentions Gasan by name, followed by the same clause about the "four friends."[69] This slight difference may reflect the different histories of the two temples: Meihō, Mugai, and Koan played no role at Sōjiji and were therefore omitted, in contrast to Gasan, who inherited Sōjiji and whose five disciples upheld Sōjiji after his death. Yet the Sōjiji version still mentions the "four friends"—another conspicuous indication that this text was first composed at Yōkōji and then edited, however carefully, at Sōjiji.

The second and third sections of the two versions are almost identical, apart from a few expressions and passages that describe the unique sacred nature of each temple. One of the few differences in the second section can be found in the passage where the Yōkōji version states: "At the black stone, the mountain spirit stays for a long time in the jewel belt. In the deep pine

68. *Jūshu gitai,* JDZ, 376–380; KZ 9: 227–261.

69. Ozaki 1998c, 61.

tree grove, Isurugi shows sweet pears for eternity." In its place, the Sōjiji text reads: "At the deep green pine trees, [the dragon king] Sāgara holds high a light of the night for a long time. At the thickly growing oak tree, the mountain *kami* shows sweet pears for eternity."[70]

In the third section, the intent of the Sōjiji editors' emendations appear obvious in the following passage:

> If we think respectfully, the bright moon stays long in front of the Peak of the Five Elders [Sōjiji version: "on top of Shogaku"] and shows intimately the eternal form of the Dharma body. The running stream flows for eternity in the valley of Tōkoku [Sōjiji version: "in front of the gate of Sōji(ji)"] and captures the pure voice and the sound of the rolling tide. All day long we can hear the talk of the great master; why always use the guidance of other people? (63)

The two versions of the *Butsuji kōshiki* differ in the events that are included and the explanations of those events. In general, the competing understandings of history they offer follow the existing biographies of Keizan, which can also be broadly categorized into Yōkōji- or Sōjiji-branch works.[71]

Additionally, the concluding verses of the first two sections differ in the two transmission lineages: while they do not draw on different collective memories, they do suggest that each temple aimed to create its own *kōshiki* distinct from that of its rival. At the end of the first section, where the Yōkōji version adopted the verse from the same section of the *Rakan kōshiki,* the editors at Sōjiji took a verse from the second section of that work:[72]

> Buddha's true Dharma has two [sides]:
> Namely, doctrine and enlightenment as its essence.
> If people live who embrace, explain, and practice [the teaching accordingly],
> [The true Dharma] abides in this world.[73]

At the end of the second section, where the Yōkōji version has a verse summarizing the content of the section, the Sōjiji version adopted a verse from the *Nehan kōshiki,* another widely performed *kōshiki:*

> We now offer food
> And wish that we may obtain the greatest rewards;
> The attachments to all afflictions,
> May we overcome [them] and may [they] not be strong.[74]

---

70. Ozaki 1998c, 62.

71. See Azuma 1974a, 14–20, for a discussion of the two transmission lineages of the biographies of Keizan.

72. In the Manzan edition of the *Keizan shingi,* this verse can be found in T 82: 435c19–20.

73. Ozaki 1998c, 62. This verse was originally taken from the *Jushelun,* T 29: 152b1–2.

74. Ozaki 1998c, 63. This *Nehan kōshiki* is based on the one attributed to Genshin, which also includes this verse; see *Dainihon bukkyō zensho* 33, 184. A very similar verse can also be found in the *Nirvāṇa Sutra,* T 12: 612b19–20.

If we assume that the Sōjiji version of the *Butsuji kōshiki* was based on the *kōshiki* performed at Yōkōji, we can surmise that monks at Sōjiji felt compelled to substitute two verses from other well-known Sōtō *kōshiki,* both performed annually at Sōjiji, again highlighting the intertextual character of *kōshiki.*

Conclusions

The *Butsuji kōshiki* was a combination of biography and founder worship—a "liturgy of memory," to borrow Krueger's terminology. For the Yōkōji and Sōjiji communities, it was a unique and important ritual that annually helped renew, through its retelling, the collective memory of their founder and their temple. The text offered a narration of Keizan's life during his memorial service, and at the same time it praised him. Additionally, the chanting by the assembly and the prostrations performed during the ritual physically expressed the monks' veneration of Keizan, who, having descended to the place of the ritual, was thought to be present.

The singing of verses by the monks and the prostrations after each verse provided a ritual structure into which the narrative of Keizan's biography was set. The entire *shikimon* was itself placed within a larger frame: the typical ritual frame of Sōtō *kōshiki,* consisting of liturgical pieces that build a highly musical soundscape clearly distinct from that of other Sōtō rituals. Thus, during the three-day memorial service at both Yōkōji and Sōjiji, the *Butsuji kōshiki* offered a musical and narrative expression of religious devotion.

The *Butsuji kōshiki* and the memorial services for Keizan played a role in constructing tradition, group identity, and collective memory. The two transmission lineages of the *kōshiki* narrate different versions of the early history of Keizan's lineage, with distinct accounts of temple history and religious authority. When differences in collective memory induce modifications of liturgical texts, the changes highlight the fact that rituals and ritual texts are fluid. In the Meiji era, the two versions of the *kōshiki* for Keizan responded to new developments within the school, a subject to be explored in the next chapter.

5

Innovations in the Meiji Era

Monks at both Yōkōji and Sōjiji continued to perform *kōshiki* in remembrance of Keizan in the Meiji era, but the two transmission lineages saw dramatic changes. In the middle of this era, Yōkōji's abbot, Kohō Hakugan, revised the *Butsuji kōshiki,* and a Sōjiji-affiliated monk, Bukkan Bonjō, wrote an entirely new one. Like the earlier *kōshiki,* the new ritual texts expressed the communal memories of the opposing lineages and sought to shape each temple's future in an attempt to establish its version of history, in which it held the more sacred position, in the collective memory of the Sōtō school.

Sōjiji aimed to consolidate itself as the equal of Eiheiji, the other head temple of the Sōtō school. The memory of Keizan was vital to this goal because he had been recognized in the early Meiji era as one of the two great patriarchs of Sōtō Zen, the master who stood next to Dōgen, the founder of Eiheiji. Yōkōji, in contrast, was in disrepair and in need of financial support to survive. Its monks used the memory of Keizan and Yōkōji's early role in the Sōtō school to encourage clerics to donate funds for its upkeep and rebuilding. These intentions formed the backdrop against which Hakugan and Bonjō compiled their new *kōshiki.*

This chapter studies these two new *kōshiki.* First, I outline the new developments in the Meiji era. I then examine the new edition of the *Butsuji kōshiki* produced by Hakugan at Yōkōji, which developed in continuity with the earlier tradition, before turning to the new *kōshiki* composed by Bonjō for Sōjiji. I explore the backgrounds of both works, analyzing for what purposes they were created, their historical and institutional contexts, and how they differed from the earlier *Butsuji kōshiki* of the Tokugawa period. In this way, the present chapter illuminates how the *kōshiki* of remembrance of Keizan continued to play a vital role in the construction of communal memory in the Meiji era.

The Sōtō School in the Meiji Era

The Meiji era was a time of tremendous change in all aspects of Japan's society. A new government had been established by a group of samurai whose wish to reestablish imperial rule led them to overthrow the Tokugawa bakufu. This development strongly affected Buddhist temples. The abolition of the parishioner system, which had been central to the structure of Buddhist institutions in the Tokugawa period, meant the sudden loss of the financial security that Buddhist temples had enjoyed since the seventeenth century. In the process of forging a national identity, the new leaders established Shintō as *the* Japanese religion and promoted the divinity of the emperor, who was seen as the highest representative of Shintō. Buddhism and Shintō were intimately intertwined and had been influencing each other for centuries. But to establish Shintō as an independent religion, the new Meiji government ordered the separation of *kami* and buddhas (*shinbutsu bunri rei* 神仏分離令) and the removal of Buddhist images, implements, and texts from Shintō shrines. This demotion devolved into a general persecution of Buddhism. Statues, texts, and implements were destroyed, temples were merged or dissolved, and temple lands were confiscated. Sōjiji, to take one example, lost 400 *koku* 石 of land.[1] After the persecution ended, the Buddhist schools had to redefine their doctrines based on new ideologies and find alternative methods of institutional organization.

In the first half of the Meiji era, the Sōtō school also faced internal struggles, marked by continuous rivalry and conflict between its two head temples, Eiheiji and Sōjiji. In Meiji 1 (1868), the abbot of Eiheiji seized the moment and proposed to the new government that Eiheiji should be recognized as the single head temple of the Sōtō school. A year later, in light of Sōjiji's objection, the Meiji government acknowledged both Eiheiji and Sōjiji as head temples but granted Eiheiji higher status at the same time.[2] Then the government ordered Eiheiji and Sōjiji to resolve their differences. After hundreds of years of intense rivalry, the two head temples agreed to a formal truce, signed by the abbots of Eiheiji and Sōjiji in Meiji 5 (1872). The agreement stated that Eiheiji and Sōjiji are the two head temples of a united Sōtō school, but that because Eiheiji was founded by Dōgen, it stands above Sōjiji. The truce also stipulated that all past differences will be resolved and the two head temples will work together to prevent future disputes.[3]

In the following years, the leaders of the Sōtō school modernized their institution. In 1877, representatives of the two head temples issued a directive that declared Dōgen and Keizan to be the two patriarchs of the Japanese Sōtō school and announced titles for both: Kōso 高祖 (Eminent Ancestor) for Dōgen and Taiso 太祖 (Great Ancestor) for Keizan.[4] They published biographies of Dōgen and Keizan in Japanese that could be easily understood by a wide audience. In this context, a new biographic image of Keizan was developed, which monks at Sōjiji soon integrated into a new *kōshiki*.

Despite the truce, new controversies developed, and the conflict between Eiheiji and Sōjiji reignited. The election of officers to serve at Eiheiji from the ranks of Sōjiji-affiliated temples attracted especially severe criticism. At the beginning of 1891, a group of Sōjiji-affiliated monks who had begun to advo-

1. Nodomi 2007, 13–14. See Ketelaar 1993 on the persecution of Buddhism in the Meiji era.
2. SZ *Nenpyō* 年表: 582–583; Takeuchi M. 1981, 92–94; and Nodomi 2007, 14.
3. Takeuchi M. 1981, 95–97; Nodomi 2007, 15.
4. *Sōtōshū ryōhonzan futatsu zensho*, Meiji 5 (1872)–Meiji 11 (1878): 109v–110r.

cate for Sōjiji's autonomy submitted a request to that effect to Azegami Baisen 畔上楳仙 (1825–1901), Sōjiji's abbot.[5] Acknowledging the momentum, Azegami declared Sōjiji's independence in March 1892.[6] To justify the bold action, supporters published a series of tracts in which they made three claims: first, that it was Keizan, not Dōgen, who was responsible for the spread of Sōtō Zen in Japan; second, that Keizan was the true founder of the Japanese Sōtō school, because it was he—rather than Dōgen—who had established its institutional base and fundamental religious practices; and third, that the name of the school, Sōtō, had originated at Sōjiji when Emperor Godaigo issued to Keizan his edict recognizing Sōjiji as an imperial prayer temple.[7] Of course, Eiheiji opposed these claims, and its supporters published their own studies of early Japanese Sōtō Zen in order to refute Sōjiji's arguments. Nevertheless, Sōjiji was close to realizing its plan when, in November 1893, the minister of internal affairs intervened to rule against Sōjiji's independence, based on the truce of Meiji 5 (1872), and ordered the two factions to reconcile.[8]

To accomplish a reconciliation, Sōtō leaders proclaimed the compromise doctrine of "two head temples, one essence" (*ryōzan ittai funi*) whereby any separate veneration of Sōjiji or Eiheiji is a veneration of both, and any differences between the doctrines in the writings of Dōgen and Keizan are to be considered alternative expressions of the same essence.[9] This idea has since shaped the ideology of the modern Sōtō school.

Yōkōji had no perceptible influence on the reformation of the Sōtō school during this period. Instead it struggled for survival, and in the early Meiji era its abbot even had to sell temple lands and buildings.[10] When Kohō Hakugan took over the abbotship in 1882, Yōkōji was dilapidated and had incurred high debt. He depended on the support of other Sōtō temples, including Sōjiji, and of lay patrons to rebuild his temple. Amid this turbulence, Hakugan and Bonjō produced their new *kōshiki* for Keizan. The rituals continued to express the communal memories of Sōjiji and Yōkōji while reflecting the temples' altered self-identities in the new times.

Hakugan's Revision of the *Butsuji kōshiki*

Hakugan revised the *Butsuji kōshiki* for the 550th memorial service of Emperor Godaigo and performed it with his fellow monks at Yōkōji in October 1892.[11]

5. Yokozeki 1970, 217–218; Bodiford 1993, 83.

6. Takeuchi M. 1981, 120–121.

7. Yoshioka 1982, 1374; Bodiford 1993, 83.

8. Takeuchi M. 1981, 122–124; Yoshioka 1982, 1374–1375; see also Ozaki 2014b and 2020, and Mross 2014b on Sōjiji's movement for independence.

9. Takeuchi M. 1981, 126; Bodiford 1993, 84.

10. Yokoyama 1974, 19.

11. A headnote in the *Butsuji kōshiki* informs us that the 550th memorial year of Emperor Godaigo was actually in 1888, but because the repair of temple buildings was not completed, its commemoration was delayed.

We can interpret his revision and its performance as an attempt to reestablish Yōkōji as Keizan's original main temple in the collective memory of the Sōtō school in order to help secure its survival.[12]

Hakugan was a well-known Zen teacher who ordained around fifty monks.[13] One of them was Kohō Chisan 孤峰智璨 (1879–1967), who would later become Sōjiji's abbot.[14] From 1882 until his death in 1909, Hakugan served as abbot of Yōkōji. The temple had become impoverished by the end of the Tokugawa period, and its buildings were so dilapidated that Hakugan devoted all his energy to their restoration. To solicit funds for it, he used the remembrance of Keizan as the basis of his appeal to clerics to assist in the repair of Yōkōji so that it could be maintained as an important historical site of the Sōtō school.

During his time at Yōkōji, Hakugan was offered the prestigious position of *godō* at Eiheiji, but he declined and instead continued to teach at Yōkōji and Zuiryūji 瑞龍寺 (Toyama prefecture). In 1891, Hakugan was nominated for the abbotship of Eiheiji.[15] Even though he lost the election, this nomination reflected his high reputation and status, which we can assume helped him to secure financial support for rebuilding Yōkōji.

Hakugan's Intentions in Revising the *Butsuji kōshiki*

How Hakugan got the idea to edit the *Butsuji kōshiki* is unknown, but the preface he wrote and other notes in his edition suggest that the *kōshiki* fulfilled several functions for him.[16] First, it was a means to express gratitude to Keizan and to pay him respect. In the preface, Hakugan praises Keizan for having taught many disciples and helping them attain enlightenment. Hakugan further expressed his appreciation that it was due to Keizan's activities that Sōtō Zen had spread all across Japan. He also highlights the *kōshiki*'s pedagogical functions:

> I let the monks of the whole mountain regularly perform it, and wish that the narrow minded among the present-day patch-robed monks of the Sōtō school [may] bathe in the wind of the ancestors and open the eye that penetrates all things through the informal sermon on the venerable Great Master. (Abe 2019, 86)

12. Published under the title *Taiso Butsuji kōshiki*. A copy of Hakugan's edition is in the possession of the Kanazawa Shiritsu Tamagawa Toshokan Kinsei Shiryōkan. This edition was reprinted in 1924. The *Kōshiki database* offers a facsimile of this edition (no. 361). For a typographical reprint, see Abe 2019.

13. The description of Hakugan's life is based on the *Yōkō Hakugan zenji gyōjō, Tōkokusan Yōkōji shi*, 52–58, and Bunkazai 7: 587.

14. Chisan published the *Yōkō Hakugan zenji iroku*, a compilation of Dharma words of his master.

15. Kawaguchi 2002, 708–709.

16. See Appendix 3 for a translation of the preface. In the following extracts, references to the typographical reprint of the *Butsuji kōshiki* edition from 1924, in Abe 2019, are provided.

In this way, he expressed his hope that Sōtō clerics would learn from the *shikimon* of the *Butsuji kōshiki,* since the narration of Keizan's life could offer a model for practice.

Beyond those functions, Hakugan aimed to demonstrate the high status formerly enjoyed by Yōkōji and its original role as Keizan's main temple, a fact that had almost been forgotten by the Meiji era. By reminding Sōtō clerics of Yōkōji's place in history, he hoped to enlist support. Accordingly, his revised edition of the *Butsuji kōshiki* was printed and distributed to sponsors, increasing the audience and helping build awareness of Yōkōji's illustrious past.

By revising and introducing the *Butsuji kōshiki* on the occasion of Emperor Godaigo's 550th memorial service, and not at a memorial service for Keizan, Hakugan subtly reminded his contemporaries of the imperial recognition that Yōkōji had received in earlier times. In the preface, he writes:

> The Great Master [Keizan] answered the ten questions of Emperor Godaigo. [His] logic and righteousness, as well as [his] profound explanations, deeply satisfied the mind of the emperor, who bestowed an imperial edict [recognizing Yōkōji as] the first training place of the Sōtō school whose abbot wears the purple robe. It is truly a rare honor. (86)

This passage refers to the ten questions that Emperor Godaigo is said to have sent to Keizan at Yōkōji. Because the emperor was satisfied with Keizan's answers, he recognized Yōkōji as the first Sōtō training center and declared it to be an imperial prayer temple. Hakugan refers to documents purportedly bestowed upon Yōkōji that granted it the highest rank among all Sōtō temples. As mentioned in chapter 4, Sōjiji also possesses documents claiming that Emperor Godaigo sent questions to Keizan at Sōjiji and then bestowed an edict upon Sōjiji. Both sets of documents are later forgeries, but they nonetheless played an important role in the rivalry between the two temples, each of which argued that Emperor Godaigo had declared it to be the highest Sōtō temple in Japan.

Hakugan further added brief comments in his edition that attest to Yōkōji's former position. In the explanatory notes, for example, he and his assistants wrote, "Needless to say, this mountain was the main residence of the Great Master" (86). They also pointed to the many original imperial edicts and important manuscripts that are stored at Yōkōji. And at the end of the ritual handbook, a stamp with the inscription "The first training place opened by Zen Master Butsuji" asserts Yōkōji's original position.[17] These comments suggest that Hakugan wanted to gain recognition of Yōkōji's former status from Sōtō clerics, especially from his supporters.

In explanatory notes, Hakugan and his disciples expressed their wish that

---

17. Jōmanji, however, was the first temple Keizan opened. But Yōkōji became Keizan's main temple during his lifetime, and Keizan does not seem to have had any connection to Jōmanji in his later years.

the publication of the newly revised *kōshiki* would help increase general recognition of Keizan's accomplishments and lead to the official bestowal of a Great Master title (*daishigō* 大師号) on Keizan. Conferring such honorary titles was the prerogative of the emperor, and honoring a monk for his accomplishments gave imperial recognition to both the monk and his lineage. Thus the editors of the *Butsuji kōshiki* wrote:

> Earlier in the Hōryaku era (1751–1764), the elder Menzan wrote the *Hōon kōshiki* for the Eminent Ancestor. He venerated the Eminent Ancestor and called [him] Great Master (*daishi* 大師). Finally, in the prospering time of Meiji, [the emperor] bestowed on Dōgen the posthumous title Great Master Jōyō 承陽大師. Here the words of the elder [Menzan] truly had an effect. Now we do not yet know [a *kōshiki*] praising Great Master Butsuji. Will it have an effect in later days or not? (86)

Hakugan and his disciples suggest here that because Menzan honored Dōgen by calling him Great Master in his *Hōon kōshiki,* Dōgen subsequently received an official Great Master title from the Meiji emperor. Following this precedent, Hakugan refers to Keizan as "Great Master Butsuji" in the preface and throughout the *kōshiki* instead of using the correct Zen Master title (*zenjigō* 禅師号) with Keizan's posthumous name Butsuji. Sōjiji monks had already called for the bestowal of a Great Master title on Keizan when Dōgen was awarded the title Great Master Jōyō in 1879.[18] Hakugan and his disciples seem to have hoped that *kōshiki* could be vehicles with which to contest authority, and that using the Great Master title themselves might pave the way to the actual bestowal of this title by the emperor.

Content and Ritual Structure

In contrast to earlier ritual handbooks, Hakugan's new edition of the *Butsuji kōshiki* was a comprehensive one that contained all the pieces to be vocalized. Woodblock printing made this possible. When manuscripts had to be copied by hand, it would have taken an unreasonable amount of time to copy an entire *shikimon* multiple times when only one monk needed to recite it; but with woodblock printing, it was relatively easy to reproduce a text many times.

Printing the *Butsuji kōshiki* consequently made its *shikimon* accessible to a much wider audience. Previously only clerics who vocalized the *shikimon* had the opportunity to read it—most participants only listened, so for them it was an oral text. Through woodblock printing, the *shikimon* gained an additional function as a written text that could also be read outside the specific ritual setting.

Earlier printed *kōshiki* served as a model for Hakugan's edition. In the Tokugawa period, the monks at Yōkōji used separate manuscripts for the choral and solo parts of the *Butsuji kōshiki.* The assembly used ritual manuals that only contained the choral pieces, while the officiant read a manuscript

18. Kawaguchi 2002, 365.

that contained only the *shikimon,* and the monk who recited the offertory declaration similarly used a manuscript containing only that text.[19] Most printed editions of *kōshiki* in the Sōtō school, by contrast, contain all the texts chanted, together with instructions for the performance and a diagram showing the sitting order. Following their example, Hakugan fused the two kinds of ritual handbooks—choral pieces and solo texts—and added detailed instructions on how to perform the ritual, as well as diagrams for the sitting order and for the announcement of the role allocation. He also included his own preface, explanatory notes by the editors, and a postscript by Hasegawa Ten'ei 長谷川天潁 (d. 1923), the abbot of Jōjūji. Remarkably, the volume also contains explanatory headnotes about the content, a very rare feature in *kōshiki* editions.

Hakugan used the manuscripts of the *Butsuji kōshiki* stored at Yōkōji as his model and followed the earlier ritual structure.[20] However, this time he included the *Four Shōmyō Melodies,* and the resulting form is therefore the standard ritual structure of Sōtō *kōshiki* except for the omission of the address of invitation: *Gāthā to Scattering Flowers, Hymn of the Four Wisdoms,* offertory declaration, communal obeisance, *Four Shōmyō Melodies, shikimon,* and *Universal Transfer of Merit.*

Hakugan's Revision of the *Shikimon*

Although Hakugan only lightly revised the offertory declaration by changing a few terms and phrases, he heavily revised the *shikimon.* In particular, he added many quotations from historical documents, which served to contest the status of his temple and remind listeners and readers of its important role in the early history of Japanese Sōtō Zen. He also adopted passages from other *kōshiki.* All these revisions highlight the intertextual character of the *shikimon.*

In the pronouncement of intention and the first section of the *shikimon,* he made only minor modifications. For example, he changed the beginning of the pronouncement of intention, adding these words of worship at the outset: "Homage to the Great Master Butsuji, venerable master Keizan, who protects the Dharma; may we meet him lifetime after lifetime."[21] No other *kōshiki* praising Keizan starts with words of worship. But the *Rakan kōshiki* begins with a similar phrase, so I assume that Hakugan adopted it from the *Rakan kōshiki,* the *kōshiki* that served as the model for most Sōtō *kōshiki.*[22]

After these words of worship, the address that follows differs from that in the original *Butsuji kōshiki:*

---

19. The extant manuscripts of the *Butsuji kōshiki* are listed in Appendix 1. One extant text at Yōkōji, however, contains both the *shikimon* and the offertory declaration.

20. Most likely he consulted the following manuscripts: *Kaiso kōshiki* (Shōtoku 5, 1715), *Butsuji kōshiki* (ca. 1725; see Appendix 7), and *Butsuji kōshiki saimon* (Bunsei 10, 1827).

21. The typographical reprint in Abe 2019 does not include this phrase.

22. The *Rakan kōshiki* begins with "Homage to the Sixteen Great Arhats who protect the teaching left behind by the Buddha; may we meet them lifetime after lifetime" (T 82: 435a14–15).

> Reverently, I address the Three Treasures existing eternally in the three times [of past, present, and future] and the ten directions, the inconceivable and inexpressible realm of enlightenment, especially the successive generations of ancestors who transmitted the light from rightful successor to rightful successor in the three countries [India, China, and Japan], and especially the holy spirit of the Great Master Butsuji, the Great Ancestor of the Japanese Sōtō school, who received the correct transmission in the fifty-fourth generation of Śākyamuni, the World-Honored One; and say:[23]

A comparison with Menzan's *Hōon kōshiki* commemorating Dōgen,[24] the only *hōon kōshiki* for a Japanese Zen patriarch printed in the Tokugawa period, shows that Hakugan's beginning is very similar. Therefore, we can assume that he adopted it from Menzan's *kōshiki,* slightly abbreviated it, and substituted Keizan for Dōgen in the list of objects of veneration. With the exception of this passage, Hakugan's pronouncement of intention is almost the same as the one in the earlier *Butsuji kōshiki* of the Yōkōji transmission lineage.

In the first section, which details Keizan's life, we find only two brief insertions. Hakugan added Keizan's remark that the place of Yōkōji is truly pure and that there would be no hindrances for spreading the Dharma at this sacred location. He also included the death verse of Keizan.[25]

Most importantly, Hakugan greatly expanded the second and third sections, which were originally much shorter than the first. The second section is now almost twice as long as before, and the third section almost three times longer. To the second section Hakugan added several quotations from historical documents certifying Yōkōji's once-held position and included explanations about these sources: First, he inserted a statement that Emperor Godaigo sent ten questions to Keizan, and because the emperor was deeply satisfied with Keizan's answers, Keizan received an imperial edict in Genkō 1 (1321). Hakugan then quoted this order in full, which declares Yōkōji to be the first imperial prayer temple of the Sōtō school.[26] Next, Hakugan explained that Emperor Gomurakami bestowed the posthumous title of Zen Master Butsuji on Keizan.[27] He then stated that Yōkōji received an imperial edict from Emperor Gotsuchimikado 後土御門天皇 (1442–1500) in Bunmei 11 (1479), which confirmed Yōkōji's status as an imperial prayer temple, and provides parts of this document.[28] Subsequently, he recounted that Emperor Kōmyō 光明天皇 (1331–1380) gave one grain of Buddha relics to Yōkōji for enshrinement and inserted a quote from the *Ashikaga Tadayoshi kishin jōan* (Donation proposal by Ashikaga Tadayoshi).[29] This text refers to the estab-

23. Abe 2019, 87.

24. ZSZ 2: 723.

25. Abe 2019, 88.

26. *Godaigo tennō shusse dōjō gorinji.*

27. *Gomurakami tennō kuzenan* (Shōhei 8, 1353).

28. *Gotsuchimikado tennō rinji.*

29. The bestowal of Buddha relics for a stupa is also mentioned in other sources, e.g., the *Kōgen jōkōin sen, Ashikaga Tadayoshi migyōsho,* and *Yoshimi Yoritaka hōnō jō.*

lishment of a Buddha reliquary to benefit sentient beings (*rishō tō* 利生塔) at Yōkōji as part of Ashikaga Takauji 足利尊氏 (1305–1358) and Ashikaga Tadayoshi's 足利直義 (1306–1352) project to build such a stupa in each of the sixty-six provinces and two islands of Japan.[30] Finally, Hakugan quoted the *Moriyoshi shinnō reisen'an* 護良親王令宣案 (Order by Prince Moriyoshi), written in Genkō 3 (1333), in which Moriyoshi (1308–1335) requested the monks of Yōkōji to perform prayers for the imperial family.[31] The sources Hakugan added—some of which are of highly questionable historicity—all suggest that Yōkōji had been an imperial prayer temple that was highly valued by the court in medieval Japan.

In the third section, Hakugan inserted almost the full text of the *Tōkokusan jinmiraisai okibumi* (Will on the future of Tōkokusan), written by Keizan in Gen'ō 1 (1319),[32] in which Keizan identified the relics he enshrined at the Peak of the Five Elders and ordered the monks in his lineage to protect the site. This explanation conveys the idea that Keizan designed Yōkōji to stand at the center of his lineage. In the same text, Keizan also emphasized that the practice of the monks is possible only because of the support of patrons, and the monks should therefore respect them.[33]

After this long quotation, Hakugan included three excerpts from the *Sansō yuiseki teradera okibumiki* (Will on the temples I leave behind), in which Keizan declared his wishes concerning the succession of his eight temples in Genkō 3 (1323). Of these, Hakugan chose to quote Keizan's instructions for Daijōji, Jōjūji, and Sōjiji.[34] In the case of Sōjiji, Keizan wrote that it is the third temple in the province of Nō and that although the patron still lacked proper faith, Jōken wished that it should be upheld by the monks of Keizan's lineage, who should work toward its prospering. With this quotation, Hakugan put Sōjiji explicitly in its historical place: it once was a branch temple of Yōkōji, and not Keizan's main temple. This was most likely one of the most vital arguments in Hakugan's revival movement.

Shōun Setsugan's Reprint of Hakugan's *Butsuji kōshiki*

For the six hundredth memorial service of Keizan in 1924, Shōun Setsugan 松雲雪巖 (d. 1943), Hakugan's successor at Yōkōji, reprinted Hakugan's *Taiso Butsuji kōshiki*.[35] This is an example of how grand memorial services every fifty

30. Azuma 2002, 43–45; *Yōkōji no meihō,* 38–39 and 88–89; and *Tōkokusan Yōkōji shi,* 23–27. See Collcutt 1981, 106–109, and Ruppert 2000, 254–258, on the Buddha reliquaries that benefit sentient beings.

31. Abe 2019, 88–89.

32. Abe 2019, 89.

33. For a photo of the original *Tōkokusan jinmiraisai okibumi,* see Azuma 2002, 20–21, and *Yōkōji no meihō,* 30, 76–77. The text is also included in the *Tōkokuki* (JDZ, 419–420; KZ 8: 182–194)

34. Abe 2019, 89–90.

35. A typographical reprint of this edition is included in Abe 2019. For the commemoration of Keizan's six hundredth memorial service, a history of Yōkōji, the *Tōkokusan Yōkōji shi,* was also published. As a temple history, the *Tōkokusan Yōkōji shi* promoted Yōkōji's original status and was an attempt to regain recognition of what Yōkōji once was—namely, Keizan's main temple. Like the *hōon kōshiki* for Keizan, temple histories were vehicles for asserting authority.

years provided clerics with a chance to publish and distribute liturgical texts. The content of the ritual handbook is exactly the same as in Hakugan's original edition. Setsugan only added one headnote, explaining the purpose of the *kōshiki* and his own intentions:

> This *Butsuji kōshiki* is said to be a composition to repay kindness and express gratitude for Zen Master Keizan's four hundredth memorial service. The previous master Hakugan printed it for the five hundred fiftieth memorial service of Emperor Godaigo and distributed it to the clerics and laypeople of the Sōtō school. In the fall of Taishō 13 (1924), we commemorate the correct six hundredth memorial day of Great Master Jōsai and further reprint five hundred volumes and make these commemorations of repaying kindness.[36]

Thus for Setsugan, too, the *kōshiki* fulfilled the function of repaying kindness and expressing gratitude. Since Hakugan's edition, the Meiji emperor had bestowed the title of Great Master Jōsai (Jōsai Daishi 常済大師) on Keizan in 1909, so Setsugan used that title in his note.

The distribution of five hundred volumes of the *Butsuji kōshiki* suggests that Yōkōji tried to use it as a means to regain recognition as Keizan's main temple. Both the Tokugawa-period *Butsuji kōshiki* of Sōjiji (discussed in chapter 4) and the new *kōshiki* produced at Sōjiji in the Meiji era talked past this part of history and presented Sōjiji as though it had been Keizan's main temple. In aiming to revive Yōkōji, Hakugan tried to re-establish its status as the original temple of one of the two patriarchs of Japanese Sōtō Zen in order to argue that it deserved recognition and financial support. Setsugan continued the trajectory of Hakugan's project, and we can assume that he used the reprint of Hakugan's *Butsuji kōshiki* for the same ends that Hakugan worked to achieve.

Today monks no longer perform the *Butsuji kōshiki* at Yōkōji, which is maintained as an important historical temple visited by priests and lay devotees who wish to remember the origins of the Sōtō school. Because it is a small temple where only one or two priests live, it is difficult for them to perform a *kōshiki*. They might, however, consider doing so for Keizan's seven hundredth memorial service in 2024.

Tōjō dentō kōshiki: A New *Hōon kōshiki* for Keizan

At the same time that Hakugan edited the *Butsuji kōshiki,* Bukkan Bonjō, a Sōjiji-affiliated monk, composed a new *kōshiki* for Keizan entitled *Tōjō dentō kōshiki* (*Kōshiki* on the transmission of the light in the Sōtō school), or *Dentō kōshiki* for short, to replace the *Butsuji kōshiki* at Sōjiji. As another example of the intertextuality of works in this genre, this *kōshiki* reveals how an author employs textual elements from other rituals or texts when composing a new

36. Abe (2019) does not include this headnote in his typographical reprint of the *kōshiki.*

kōshiki. Bonjō, in particular, was strongly influenced by new biographies of Keizan that had been written in the early Meiji era and that presented a new biographic image of this master. Therefore, I will first describe these new biographies before introducing Bonjō and examining the *kōshiki* itself.

Biographies of Keizan Written in the Early Meiji Era

The impetus for the composition of new biographies of Keizan came from a meeting in 1875 at which representatives of the Sōtō school decided that biographies of Dōgen and Keizan "should be written in Japanese so that even women and children can easily read and understand them."[37] The first to be published was the Dōgen biography *Eihei kōso gyōjō tekiyō* (Outline of the life of Eminent Ancestor Eihei), written in 1878 by Kimura Bunmei 木村文明 (1852–1921). One year later, the first Keizan biography was published: the *Sōji kaisan Taiso ryakuden* (Brief biography of the Great Ancestor, founder of Sōji[ji]), or *Taiso ryakuden* for short, by Takiya Takushū 瀧谷琢宗 (1836–1897). Takiya played an important role in the re-formation of the Sōtō school and held many important positions over the course of his life. When he wrote the *Taiso ryakuden*, he was the representative of Sōjiji in Tokyo. Remarkably, a few years later, from 1885 to 1891, Takiya served as the abbot of Eiheiji, Sōjiji's rival, thus becoming one of the most influential Sōtō monks of his time.[38]

Takiya's *Taiso ryakuden* laid the foundation for a new biographic image of Keizan. His main source was the Keizan biography included in the *Nihon tōjō rentōroku* (Transmission of the lamp in the Japanese Sōtō school), or *Rentōroku* for short, a compilation of biographies of Japanese Sōtō monks written in the early eighteenth century.[39] But in his introductory notes, Takiya mentions that he also consulted other biographies and claims to have used manuscripts that were secretly stored at Sōjiji, Daijōji, and Yōkōji. Biographies of Keizan written before the Meiji era can generally be categorized as Yōkōji- or Sōjiji-lineage works. Takiya's biography evidently stands in the Sōjiji lineage, but it includes many details and episodes that are not mentioned in any extant biography previous to his. For most of these accounts, it has proved impossible so far to confirm a historical source. First of all, Takiya's biography contains new details about Keizan's childhood. For example, Takiya writes that Keizan put his hands together in prayer and chanted "*Namu, namu*" (Homage, homage) when he was three and took great joy in performing Buddhist rituals with his mother. But Keizan's prior lives, which are described by Keizan himself in his *Tōkokuki* and recounted in the *Butsuji kōshiki*, are not mentioned in Takiya's biography. Takiya also omits other wondrous elements but keeps the dream Keizan's mother had before his birth. He quotes many historical

37. Kawaguchi 2002, 321. Previous biographies of the two patriarchs had been written in Chinese.

38. Kawaguchi has intensively studied Takiya's role in the early Meiji era; see Kawaguchi 2002, 679–749.

39. The *Nihon tōjō rentōroku* was compiled by the monk Reinan Shūjo 嶺南秀恕 (1675–1752), who finished this extensive work in Kyōho 12 (1727).

documents, including the complete text of the ten questions that Emperor Godaigo is said to have sent to Keizan at Sōjiji, making it clear that the *Taiso ryakuden* had a clear agenda: to propagate awareness of Keizan's historical role in the formation of the Sōtō school, and to consolidate Sōjiji's authority in that school. Thus Azuma Ryūshin characterized Takiya's work as a "biography of Great Ancestor veneration" (*Taiso sankō no denki* 太祖讃仰の伝記).[40]

Later biographies of Keizan, mostly written by Sōjiji-affiliated monks, followed in Takiya's footsteps.[41] One of these was written by Ōuchi Seiran 大内青巒 (1845–1918), a very influential Buddhist scholar and thinker who played a major role in the modernization of the Sōtō school and was instrumental in the creation of the *Shushōgi* 修証義 (The meaning of practice-realization), a core text of modern Sōtō Zen.[42] Ōuchi compiled biographies of Dōgen and Keizan in a book entitled *Sōtōshū ryōso denryaku* (Short biographies of the two patriarchs of the Sōtō school), published around 1884.

Bukkan Bonjō: Author of the *Tōjō dentō kōshiki*

The new biographic image of Keizan was soon incorporated in the *Tōjō dentō kōshiki* (hereafter *Dentō kōshiki*), composed by Bukkan Bonjō. Bonjō played an active role in the formation of modern Sōtō Zen. From 1871 until 1885, he was the abbot of Myōkōji 明光寺 in Hakata, a major temple in Fukuoka.[43] From 1886 to 1887, Bonjō served at Sōjiji as the principal instructor, or *godō,* a prestigious position in the Sōtō school.[44] Thereafter, he returned to Myōkōji. Only a few years later, in 1891, Bonjō, together with Hakugan, was selected as a candidate for the abbotship of Eiheiji, to serve as successor to Takiya.[45] Although neither was elected, their inclusion in the list of candidates reflects their high standing in the Sōtō school of the Meiji era.

Throughout his career, Bonjō had studied Buddhist doctrine intensively and authored many books. Among them are a compilation of sayings by Zen

---

40. Azuma 1974b, 1115.

41. Azuma argued that all biographies of Keizan were influenced by sectarian agendas. His seminal work *Keizan Zenji no kenkyū* (1974a) was the first critical study of the historical Keizan in light of the available biographical sources. For an overview of Keizan biographies, see Azuma 1974c, 1137–1146.

42. In the late 1880s, Ōuchi compiled the *Tōjō zaike shushōgi* 洞上在家修証義 (The meaning of practice-realization for lay members of the Sōtō school), a short text consisting of phrases from Dōgen's *Shōbōgenzō* originally created for lay devotees. After several revisions by other monks, among them the abbots of Eiheiji and Sōjiji, this text was published under the title *Sōtō kyōkai shushōgi* 曹洞教会修証義 (The meaning of practice-realization in the Sōtō fellowship), or *Shushōgi* for short, by the headquarters of the Sōtō school in 1890. For detailed studies, see Heine 2003 and LoBreglio 2009.

43. *Myōkōji rekishi nenpyō;* SZ *Kaidai sakuin* 解題・索引: 479; Sakurai 1981, 265–266; and Sakauchi 2010a, 280. Myōkōji is an official training center for young monks of the Sōtō school today.

44. SZ *Nenpyō:* 611, 613; *Meikyō shinshi,* no. 2068, 3, and no. 2294, 2; *Sōtōshū ryōhonzan futatsu zensho,* Meiji 19 (1886)–Meiji 22 (1889), 16v, 46r.

45. Kawaguchi 2002, 708–709.

patriarchs[46] and commentaries on important doctrinal works, such as Zongmi's 宗密 (780–841) *Yuanren lun* (Inquiry into the origin of humanity)[47] and the *Shaoshi liumen ji,* six treatises attributed to Bodhidharma.[48] Bonjō included the *shikimon* of the *Daruma kōshiki* in an appendix to his commentary on Bodhidharma's treatises, evidently thinking that it would be beneficial to the study of Zen doctrine and giving it, perhaps for the first time, a function outside its ritual setting.

Bonjō was also influential in the Sōtō school's outreach movement, compiling materials for propagation to laypeople such as the fourteen-volume *Sekkyō rakusōdan* (Discourse on preaching while "falling into the grass")[49] and the two-volume *Sekkyō hitsukei: Shurin tekiyō shitoku shō* ("Calf-licking" notes: Essentials from the *Forest of Pearls,* a handbook for preaching).[50] Bonjō also compiled biographies of Dōgen and Keizan with pictures.[51] These biographies were published in 1893, the same year as Bonjō's *Dentō kōshiki.*

Composition of the *Dentō kōshiki*

Bonjō did not decide on his own to compose a new *kōshiki.* The abbot of Sōjiji, Azegami Baisen, had asked him to do so, making the *kōshiki,* in essence, a commissioned work.[52] In a preface to the ritual handbook, Azegami wrote that he had thought about it for years before asking Bonjō to write a new *kōshiki.*[53] What set off the final spark is unknown.

The *Dentō kōshiki* was written in 1891, but it was not printed until almost two years later, in August 1893, probably due to Sōjiji's movement for independence.[54] Hakugan's *Butsuji kōshiki* had already been printed in October 1892. It is unlikely that Hakugan saw Bonjō's manuscript or that Bonjō saw Hakugan's draft before its publication. However, since Sōjiji and Yōkōji were only around 50 kilometers apart, it is possible that Azegami and Hakugan exchanged news about important matters, such as changes in liturgy, and thus became aware of each other's projects.

Azegami's preface and a postscript written by Bonjō suggest that it was

46. *Zenkai danju yōketsushū* (1902).

47. *Gennin ron keimōshō* (1888). See Gregory 1995 for an English translation of the *Yuanren lun,* and Gregory 1991 for a study of Zongmi and his thought.

48. *Kōsei sanchū Shōshitsu rokumon shū* (1890).

49. The *Sekkyō rakusōdan,* originally published as a woodblock print in 1881–1886, was republished as a typographical reprint in Sōtōshū Sensho Hankōkai 1981a and 1981b.

50. *Shitoku* 舐犢 describes a cow licking her calf—metaphorically, indicating maternal love. In this case, it suggests that the handbook, published in 1885, was compiled for novices.

51. *Kōso Jōyō daishi gyōjitsu zue* and *Taiso Kōtoku enmyō kokushi gyōjitsu zue.*

52. Azegami made his request in a letter to Bonjō that appears to be preserved in the archive of Myōkōji; see Sakauchi 2010a, 280. Unfortunately, I was not able to see the document, so I do not know when Azegami wrote it or what he said.

53. See Appendix 4 for a translation of the preface to the *Dentō kōshiki,* and Appendix 9 for a photographic reproduction. The preface is not included in the edition that is reproduced in the *Zoku Sōtōshu zensho* (ZSZ 2).

54. See Ozaki 2014b, 2020, and Mross 2014b on Sōjiji's movement for independence.

Azegami who chose the title *Tōjō dentō kōshiki* (*Kōshiki* on the transmission of the light in the Sōtō school).[55] The transmission of the Dharma has often been metaphorically described as the transmission of light or of a lamp, where the light or lamp represents enlightenment. Records of the transmission of the light (*dentōroku* 伝灯録)—or lamp records—form an important genre of Zen literature, providing biographies of Zen clerics organized by genealogy. Keizan also gave lectures on the lives of monks in his lineage, starting with the Buddha and ending with his teacher Gikai, and these were compiled by his acolyte(s) in the *Denkōroku*.[56] In their paratexts, both Azegami and Bonjō repeatedly use the image of light to represent the transmission of the Dharma, including this poem in Bonjō's postscript:

> In the past, the Great Ancestor transmitted one light.
> The one light was divided into one hundred thousand lights.
> The lights continue to burn and the radiance has no end.
> Eternally [the lights] break the darkness. This is his [i.e., Keizan's] light.
> (ZSZ 2: 868)

Azegami's preface includes a very similar passage:

> Our Great Ancestor, the National Master, lifted up one light at the precious temple Sōji[ji], and so he brightened the interior of the nine levels [of the heavens] above, and illuminated the outer limits of the eight directions below. ...His many children and grandchildren divided [his] one light and made ten million lights. Now, around five hundred eighty years have passed and around fifteen thousand temples have been founded. Everywhere [his teaching] breaks and brightens the darkness for certain.

Both passages explain the transmission or division of light and celebrate the idea that Keizan's teaching is breaking the darkness of ignorance and leading practitioners to the realm of enlightenment.

Bonjō and Azegami revere Keizan as the Zen master whose lineage is responsible for the spread of Sōtō Zen all across Japan. Knowing that the *kōshiki* was written just before the onset of Sōjiji's movement for independence, we could interpret the title as a premonition of the argument Sōjiji would soon make that Keizan, and not Dōgen, was the true founder of the Japanese Sōtō school.[57] Azegami also states in his preface that the names of the Sōtō school and the temple Sōjiji originated with an imperial order, alluding to Emperor Godaigo's ten questions and his designation of Sōjiji as an imperial prayer temple and the highest temple of the Sōtō school. Another possibility is that

55. See Appendix 5 for a translation of Bonjō's postscript to the *Dentō kōshiki*, and Appendix 9 for a photographic reproduction.

56. See chap. 4, n. 51.

57. See Yoshioka 1982, 1374; Bodiford 1993, 83; and Mross 2014a, 106–108, and 2014b.

the title is based on the name of Keizan's mausoleum, Dentōin, and has nothing to do with Sōjiji's argumentation during its independence movement. However, because the *kōshiki* and the comments by Azegami and Bonjō emphasize Keizan's role as the popularizer of Sōtō Zen, I assume that Azegami chose the title to highlight Keizan's role as the founder of the largest branch of Japanese Sōtō Zen.

Ritual Structure and Content

Like other rituals, the *Dentō kōshiki* was not a complete novelty, and Bonjō relied on established forms in writing it. He first composed an offertory declaration and a *shikimon*. Then he inserted these new texts into the typical ritual frame of Sōtō *kōshiki*. In other words, the resulting ritual form was the *Gāthā to Scattering Flowers, Hymn of the Four Wisdoms,* offertory declaration, communal obeisance, *Four Shōmyō Melodies, shikimon,* and *Universal Transfer of Merit*—basically the same structure employed in both the Tokugawa-period *Butsuji kōshiki* performed at Sōjiji and Hakugan's revised edition. After the *Universal Transfer of Merit,* however, Bonjō added a reading of the *Dhāraṇī of the Mind of Great Compassion* and a final transfer of merit. For the communal obeisance, he decided to adopt a verse that had been used in the *Gasan kōshiki* and Menzan's *Hōon kōshiki* commemorating Dōgen.[58]

Like Hakugan, Bonjō produced a comprehensive ritual manual that included all the texts to be vocalized. He also added information for the monks about how to perform the ritual, a diagram of the sitting order, and another for announcing the role allocation, as was customary for printed *kōshiki* handbooks of the Sōtō school. The handbook therefore appears similar to a playscript, containing all the vocalized parts with other information required for a performance.[59] Both Hakugan's and Bonjō's *kōshiki* were printed, enabling the texts to reach a wider audience than the earlier *Butsuji kōshiki* texts, which were only available in the form of handwritten manuscripts.

---

58. Bonjō chose the following verse for the communal obeisance:

The nature of we who venerate and those who are venerated is empty.
The essence of self and others is not different.
We wish that we together with all sentient beings may realize the way,
Give rise to the aspiration for supreme [enlightenment], and return to the ultimate truth. (ZSZ 2: 855)

This is a widely used verse, commonly known as *Raihai no ge* 礼拝偈, which is said to have originated in Ennin's *Jōgyō zanmaidō gyōhō* 常行三昧堂行法. Genshin quotes this verse in his *Ōjō yōshū* (T 84: 48a06–08), and it was sung in other *kōshiki* of the Sōtō school—for example, the *Dōgen zenji kōshiki, Eihei Dōgen zenji kōshiki,* Menzan's *Hōon kōshiki* (ZSZ 2: 721), and the *Gasan kōshiki* (Mross 2013b, 177). But it was not used in the *Butsuji kōshiki.*

59. In later years, the *Dentō kōshiki* was reprinted several times. For Keizan's grand memorial service in 1974, five thousand volumes were produced and presented as memorial gifts to the attending priests (Sakauchi 2010a, 280), ensuring that the text would be widely disseminated.

Shikimon

In composing his *shikimon,* the longest part of the *kōshiki,* Bonjō quoted from the new Keizan biographies described earlier and incorporated elements from other ritual texts, including the earlier *Butsuji kōshiki.* He also selected verses from influential Mahāyāna sutras. It seems, however, that his primary model for the new *shikimon* he envisioned for Keizan was the *shikimon* in Menzan's *Hōon kōshiki* commemorating Dōgen. Because Dōgen and Keizan were officially recognized as the two patriarchs of the Sōtō school in the Meiji era, and both were seen as representing the essence of Sōtō Zen, the composition of the *Dentō kōshiki* seems to have been an attempt to create a parallel *kōshiki* that would equally venerate the second of the two patriarchs.

First, Bonjō constructed his new *shikimon* in the same way Menzan did, distributing the biography of Keizan over five sections. In both *shikimon,* the first section covers the future master's birth and leaving the household; the second recounts his visits to Zen masters and receiving Dharma transmission; the third expounds his teaching activities; the fourth records imperial recognition; and the last section describes his death and heritage. Bonjō even refers to the five sections as "gates" (*mon* 門), as Menzan did. The *Butsuji kōshiki,* in contrast, consists of only three sections, and the content is distributed very differently. Moreover, the term "gate" is never used in the *Butsuji kōshiki* to describe the sections of the *shikimon.* Finally, as mentioned earlier, Bonjō used the same verse for the communal obeisance that Menzan used in the *Hōon kōshiki.* Considering the intertextual relationship between the *Dentō kōshiki* and the *Hōon kōshiki,* it's highly likely that Bonjō simply borrowed it from Menzan's work.

Praising the Zen lineage and Keizan. As in the *Butsuji kōshiki,* the pronouncement of intention of the *Dentō kōshiki* states the purpose of the ritual and narrates the transmission of Zen.[60] It first addresses the Three Treasures, all the patriarchs of the Zen lineage, and Keizan:

> Reverently, I address all the Three Treasures abiding eternally throughout the entirety of the Dharma realms of the three times [past, present, and future] and the ten directions; the successive generations of ancestor bodhisattvas of the transmission of the light of the three countries [India, China, and Japan]; and especially the venerable spirit of the Great Ancestor, National Master Kōtoku Enmyō [i.e., Keizan] of the Japanese Sōtō school, who received the correct transmission in the fifty-fourth generation of Śākyamuni, the World-Honored One; and say: (ZSZ 2: 858)

The text explicitly addresses Keizan as a patriarch who received the correct transmission of the Dharma in the Zen lineage. It is based not on the

60. See Appendix 6 for a thoroughly annotated translation. Appendix 9 provides a photographic reproduction of the *shikimon* from the original woodblock print. In this chapter, I provide references to the photographic reproduction included in the *Zoku Sōtōshū zensho* (ZSZ).

earlier *Butsuji kōshiki,* which addresses only the Three Treasures, but on Menzan's *Hōon kōshiki* (ZSZ 2: 723). Hakugan also adapted Menzan's address, but he abbreviated it differently. The text then narrates the transmission of the Dharma from the Buddha to Bodhidharma to Dōgen, more or less following the *Butsuji kōshiki.*[61] However, Bonjō shortens the description: he abbreviates the explanation of Śākyamuni's life, and instead of providing an account of Dōgen's life, he praises him:

> Later [the Dharma] was transmitted thirteen times, and then it reached the Eminent Ancestor, Great Master Jōyō [i.e., Dōgen], and the Buddha's sun shone for the first time in our Japan. Truly this [happens only] once in a thousand years. Therefore, it is said that [this] is good fortune for the country and good luck for the people. Earlier [Dōgen was given] the posthumous name Busshō Dentō [Kokushi][62] 佛性傳東[國師] (National Master of the Transmission of the Buddha Nature to the East). Yes, it is truly like this! (ZSZ 2: 858–859)

Here Bonjō presents Dōgen as the first monk to transmit the correct Buddhist teaching to Japan, whereas the *Butsuji kōshiki* describes him only as a master who revived the true Dharma. Considering the intensifying crisis between Eiheiji and Sōjiji when Bonjō was writing the *shikimon,* his praise of Dōgen is interesting and seemingly at variance from the discourse of Sōjiji at the time, whose representatives were arguing that Keizan, not Dōgen, was the true founder of the Japanese Sōtō school.[63]

After the description of the transmission of the Dharma, Bonjō's *shikimon* continues with a passage based on the *Butsuji kōshiki* that praises Zen and goes on to state that Zen and the written teachings share the same essence. However, people of lower and middle capacity get stuck in the net of doctrine, while superior disciples understand the truth and widely promulgate the teaching of the Zen school.

In the pronouncement of intention in the *Butsuji kōshiki,* Keizan is only mentioned three times. Yet in the *Dentō kōshiki,* Bonjō praises Keizan extensively, describing him as the great popularizer of Sōtō Zen:

> Moreover, our Great Ancestor, the national master, had from early on a strong will, full of energy, which exceeded that of ordinary people. Finally, he understood the essence (*yōki* 要機) of transcending the basic tenets of a particular school and going beyond the norms (*chōshū okkaku* 超宗越格). He stayed high on the jeweled seat of Sōji[ji]. The thunder of the Dharma roared far and wide between heaven and earth, and he widely disseminated the correct transmission

---

61. See Mross 2014a, 247–249, for a comparison of the beginning of the pronouncement of intention of the *Butsuji kōshiki* and that of the *Dentō kōshiki.*

62. National Master Busshō Dentō is a posthumous title of Dōgen. It was bestowed in Kaei 7 (1854) by Emperor Kōmei 孝明天皇 (1831–1866).

63. I have not seen Bonjō's name in the documents concerning Sōjiji's movement for independence. Whether Bonjō was involved in this movement is a question for further research.

> of Eihei [Dōgen]. The rain of compassion moistened the whole land everywhere, and now the backward-flowing waters of [Mt.] Dong (Ch. *Dong shui* 洞水, J. *Tō sui*)[64] expand and spread in the world. This is only his remaining grace.
>
> We are grateful that fortunately we draw from this stream and fully bathe in the wave of compassion. Surely we should dedicate a sincere heart and so repay one drop of the milky ocean. Therefore, we respectfully welcome now the time of the memorial day / monthly memorial day,[65] lead the pure monks of the whole mountain, and respectfully offer humble food of village herbs. In this connection we explain and praise the teaching of [Keizan's] complete lifetime. So it is a response to the unlimited virtue [of Keizan]. We humbly wish that [Keizan] may be truly compassionate and show pity; may he accept [our appeal]. (ZSZ 2: 859)

The second half of this passage states the purpose of the ritual: to show gratitude to Keizan for having spread the teaching of the Sōtō school and for showing compassion. By repaying the benevolence received from Keizan, the monks hope that Keizan will show pity for them and accept their appeal. The statement "lead the pure monks of the whole mountain" suggests that Bonjō thought about the *Dentō kōshiki* as a monastic ritual in the same way the *Butsuji kōshiki* had been one, and that it functioned for the clerics in Keizan's lineage as a means to express their gratitude to the founder of their school.

Keizan's birth, childhood, and entry into the clergy. The first section of the *shikimon* explains Keizan's birth and childhood, much of it new information when compared to the *Butsuji kōshiki*. Bonjō's account starts with Keizan's family descent, birthplace, and date of birth, based on Takiya's and Ōuchi's biographies. The *Butsuji kōshiki,* in contrast, says that Keizan did not reveal his family descent and instead presents a statement by Keizan about his previous lives. Besides omitting any mention of previous lives, Bonjō does not describe Keizan as a supernatural bodhisattva-like being, depicting him instead as an extraordinary human.

Both the *Dentō kōshiki* and the *Butsuji kōshiki* mention the dream that came to Keizan's mother and her prayers after she became pregnant. Keizan is described as an extremely gifted child. Then the *Dentō kōshiki* explains:

> His play was also different from [that of] ordinary children. When he was five, he followed his mother, and they recited the *Universal Gate* [of Kannon] (Ch. *Pumen pin* 普門品, J. *Fumon bon*) [i.e., the *Kannon Sutra*] and always performed Buddhist services together. He took great delight in this.
>
> In Bun'ei 10 (1273), when he was just six, he looked up at a holy statue of Kannon and asked his mother: "What virtue does this bodhisattva have that [so]

64. On *Dong shui,* see Appendix 6, n. 20.

65. The temporal expressions "memorial day / monthly memorial day" are printed beside each other in a small font, giving the officiating priest the option to choose the appropriate phrase.

many people venerate [it] and make offerings? Furthermore, is this bodhisattva, too, a human being?" [His] mother heard [this] and was very amazed.

Then suddenly he developed the ambition to leave the household and seek the Dharma. In Kenji 1 (1275), he finally begged [his] father and mother, repeatedly seeking to leave the household. [So] even [his] father and mother could not refuse. Then he entered Eihei[ji] under Master Tettsū [Gi]kai and had his head shaved. At that time, he was eight. (ZSZ 2: 859–860)

The biographies of Keizan prior to the Meiji era had not provided any details about his childhood. This gap was filled by Takiya's biography, and the new information made its way into the *Dentō kōshiki.*[66] The *Butsuji kōshiki* says that Keizan entered Eiheiji under Ejō when he was thirteen, whereas the *Dentō kōshiki* states that he entered Eiheiji at the age of eight under Gikai and received the precepts from Ejō when he was thirteen. This is one of the novel aspects of Keizan's new biographic image that is reflected in Bonjō's *kōshiki.*

The description of Keizan's entry into monastic life ends with Ejō's prophecy that Keizan will become a great master:

Then in spring, in the second month, when he was thirteen, he followed Master Kōun [E]jō and received the great precepts. The master observed his ambition; then he praised [him] and said: "This child has the capacity to [become] a great man. One day he will surely become a teacher for humans and heavenly beings." [This] prophecy was not an empty one. (ZSZ 2: 860)

The first section concludes with the officiant expressing gratitude to Keizan and the assembly singing a verse praising the Buddha and his dedicated practice:

We now answer the good causes of the wholesome roots planted in previous lifetimes. Gratefully we receive the mercy of the Dharma milk. Therefore, we should intone a verse and perform prostrations. We sing a verse:

Long ago the Buddha left the household
Of the Śākya clan and approached Gayā.
He thoroughly studied the bodhisattva path
And was not defiled by worldly affairs.[67]

Humbly prostrating ourselves, we take refuge in the Great Ancestor, National Master Kōtoku Enmyō. (ZSZ 2: 860)

By intoning the concluding words of worship, the monks of the assembly express their taking refuge in Keizen. The verse itself, however, praises the

66. *Taiso ryakuden,* 8v–11r (1897 ed., 9–11). See also Azuma 1974a, 34–41.
67. This verse was adopted from the fifteenth chapter of the *Lotus Sutra,* T 9: 42a01, 42a05.

Buddha. In context, it suggests that Keizan, who left the life of a householder and wholeheartedly practiced the bodhisattva way just as the Buddha did, is an equal of the Buddha.

For each section of the *shikimon,* Bonjō selected a verse from an influential Mahāyāna sutra—this one from the *Lotus Sutra.* All the verses illustrate or echo the central theme of their section, but they also portray Keizan as a buddha or an equal of the historical Buddha by virtue of his having received the direct transmission of the Dharma. This is a trope embedded in the praise of Keizan that pulls away from the biographical account presented in the *shikimon,* which seems intent on depicting Keizan more as a human being.

Training and enlightenment. The second section of the *shikimon* covers Keizan's early years as a monk, describing his practice and realization. It starts by explaining how Ejō, just before his death, told Keizan to follow Gikai. Ten years later, Keizan left Gikai and visited Jakuen; then the Rinzai masters Tōzan Tanshō 東湛照 (1231–1291) and Hakuun Ekyō 白雲慧暁 (1223–1298); Mt. Hiei, the center of the Tendai school; and finally Shinchi Kakushin 心地覚心 (1207–1298), founder of the Hōtō branch 法燈派 of Rinzai Zen. This passage is largely based on the *Rentōroku,* though Bonjō adds the account of Keizan's visit to Mt. Hiei from Takiya's *Taiso ryakuden.*[68] Other extant pre-Meiji-era sources do not mention that Keizan visited Tōzan Tanshō, Hakuun Ekyō, or Shinchi Kakushin. Likewise, Keizan's visits to masters of other schools are not mentioned in the *Butsuji kōshiki,* which only states that Keizan studied with important monks of the early Sōtō community, who had all studied under Dōgen. The *Rentōroku,* Takiya's *Taiso ryakuden,* and the *Dentō kōshiki* give a very different picture of Keizan's early career, suggesting that he had been influenced by teachers of other traditions as well.

The *Dentō kōshiki* then describes how Keizan moved with Gikai to Daijōji and practiced intensely. Like the *Butsuji kōshiki,* the *Dentō kōshiki* says that Keizan had an enlightenment experience when he encountered the phrase "With the eyes given by their parents, they all see the three thousand worlds," from the nineteenth chapter of the *Lotus Sutra* (T 9: 47c17). The *Dentō kōshiki* describes how Keizan explained his understanding to Gikai, and adds that, because Gikai was not satisfied with Keizan's answer, Keizan continued to practice intensively for six more years. The *Butsuji kōshiki,* in contrast, explains Keizan's understanding but does not mention anything about Gikai. The *Dentō kōshiki* goes on to describe how Keizan awakened when he heard a Dharma talk on Zhaozhou's 趙州 (J. Jōshū, 778–897) *kōan* "The ordinary mind is the way," and recounts the following exchange with Gikai:[69]

---

68. *Rentōroku,* SZ 16: 244; *Taiso ryakuden,* 12v (1897 ed., 14–15). Since Takiya's biography was published, Keizan's visit to Mt. Hiei has become part of the collective memory of the Sōtō school. But no medieval source supports this account, and Keizan himself does not mention it in his own writings. On this point, see Azuma 1974a, 74–76.

69. This famous *kōan* is included in the *kōan* collection *Wumenguan* (J. *Mumonkan*), case 19, T 48: 295b13–b24.

> Master [Gi]kai said: "What have you understood?" The national master said: "The deep black jewel runs in the middle of the night." Master [Gi]kai said: "Not enough, say more!" The national master said: "When I have tea, I drink tea. When I have rice, I eat rice." Master [Gi]kai smiled and said: "In the future you will surely spread the teaching of the Sōtō school." (ZSZ 2: 861)

Here the *Dentō kōshiki* presents an exemplary Zen encounter whereas the *Butsuji kōshiki* only states that Keizan "rode the black jewel in the darkness," and the conversation between Gikai and Keizan is not mentioned.

The *Dentō kōshiki* continues with a description of how Gikai transmitted the Dharma to Keizan and gave him Dōgen's robe, signifying that Keizan was now an heir and patriarch of the Sōtō lineage. The *kōshiki* then praises the results of Keizan's teachings, and the assembly is invited again to sing a verse:

> From then on, the wind of truth blew strongly [i.e., the Buddhist teaching prospered], and the correct rules of the successive generations of patriarchal ancestors continued for a long time. The sun of wisdom always shines and opens wide the wisdom eyes of latter-day students. What a fortune for us! Gratefully, we have been able to become descendants in [this] lineage. We should make the great vow and pay our respects generation after generation. Therefore, we should intone a verse and perform prostrations. We sing a verse:
>
> When [Keizan] deeply entered the various samādhis
> And lived peacefully in the truth of nondiscrimination,
> All things were completely pure
> And he realized the perfect enlightenment.[70]
>
> Humbly prostrating ourselves, we take refuge in the Great Ancestor, National Master Kōtoku Enmyō. (ZSZ 2: 861)

Here Bonjō selected a verse from the *Wenshu suoshuo zuisheng mingyi jing* (Sutra spoken by Mañjuśrī on the supreme meaning), attributing to Keizan the accomplishment of the original subject of the verse. Because of the narration that preceded, the verse now describes Keizan's complete realization and so summarizes the section.

Transmitting the Dharma. The third section of the *shikimon* details how Keizan propagated Sōtō Zen. It starts by explaining how Keizan was invited to the province of Awa and served as abbot of Jōmanji. Bonjō underscores that Keizan attracted many people by stating, "When the national master performed the consecration ceremony, clerics and laypeople gathered and it was impossible to count them" (ZSZ 2: 862).

---

70. This verse is from the *Wenshu suoshuo zuisheng mingyi jing* (J. *Monju shosetsu saijō myōgi kyō*), T 20: 817b28–29.

According to the *Dentō kōshiki,* Keizan returned to Daijōji, where he taught in place of Gikai and gave the sermons that were recorded in the *Denkōroku.* Then he succeeded Gikai and became the second abbot of Daijōji. The text states that all kinds of people came and took refuge in Keizan as their teacher, including Gasan Jōseki, Meihō Sotetsu, and Mugai Chikō, who are identified as Keizan's superior disciples. Bonjō quotes long excerpts from the biographies of Gasan and Meihō in the *Rentōroku.*[71] In contrast, the *Butsuji kōshiki* does not provide any details about Gasan's or Meihō's lives.

The *kōshiki* continues with an explanation of how Keizan became abbot of Jōjūji, Yōkōji, and Kōkōji. The description of Yōkōji is a little longer than those for Jōjūji and Kōkōji, but Bonjō does not state that Yōkōji was originally Keizan's main temple and the one Keizan designed to be the center of his lineage. Instead, the account of Yōkōji is embedded between those concerning Jōjūji and Kōkōji. Thus Bonjō elides Yōkōji's former importance and Keizan's original intentions for it. The sources that Bonjō used—Takiya's *Taiso ryakuden* and the *Rentōroku*—give more details about Keizan and Yōkōji than Bonjō does, but Takiya also obscures Yōkōji's original status. He discusses Yōkōji but gives it far less attention than he gives to Sōjiji, whose image he burnishes with extensive quotations from historical documents. Through this strategy, Takiya manages to create the impression that Sōjiji was Keizan's main temple.

Indeed, as Sōjiji gained power and status in the Sōtō school, most Sōtō monks came to perceive Sōjiji as Keizan's main temple. Bonjō naturally follows this perspective. Yōkōji was hardly a factor: it had lost its power and had even become a branch temple of Sōjiji during the Tokugawa period,[72] so by the time Bonjō composed the *Dentō kōshiki,* Yōkōji's original status had been forgotten.

Bonjō explains the founding of Sōjiji in detail, highlighting the special nature of the site:

> Morookadera 諸嶽寺 in Kushihi-shō of the Fugeshi district in Nō [i.e., Noto] was originally a Vinaya temple. The abbot, Vinaya master Jōken, had a wondrous dream of the Light-Emitting Bodhisattvas (Hōkō bosatsu 放光菩薩) [Kannon and Jizō]. He respectfully followed the virtuous words of the national master and changed the Vinaya temple into a Zen temple. He sincerely invited the national master and made [him] the founding abbot. [Keizan] called the mountain Shogaku 諸嶽 and so kept the old temple name. He named the temple Sōji and so took the Dharma words that had been advocated in a dream. Then, in Genkō 1 (1321), on the eighth day of the sixth month, he gave the consecration sermon. (ZSZ 2: 863)

At the end of the section Keizan is praised for his propagation of the Dharma, and the officiant invites the assembly to intone a verse:

71. SZ 16: 249–251.
72. Bunkazai 7: 631.

> From the earlier founding of Jōman[ji] until the opening of Sōji[ji] here, as for the transmission of the Dharma at many places, the wind of the way bends the grass; and as for the saving of sentient beings of the five realms, the light of virtue bends the hollyhock.
>
> To praise the great benefit of the propagation [of the Dharma], we should now intone a verse and perform prostrations. We sing a verse:
>
> [Keizan] has expounded the essence of all things
> And revealed the teaching of the one vehicle.
> He has extensively led all sentient beings,
> Causing them to quickly attain enlightenment.[73]
>
> Humbly prostrating ourselves, we take refuge in the Great Ancestor, National Master Kōtoku Enmyō. (ZSZ 2: 863)

This verse praises Keizan's teaching activities, which are linked to the spread of Sōtō Zen all across Japan. As in the first section, Bonjō chose a verse from the *Lotus Sutra,* and here too, while not the original subject of the verse, Keizan is identified with the subject through the narrative content of the section.

Imperial recognition. The fourth section of Bonjō's *shikimon* describes the imperial recognition of Keizan and Sōjiji in detail. This section can be interpreted as a discourse demonstrating Sōjiji's high status, as Bonjō, following Takiya's example in his Keizan biography, uses historical documents to bolster Sōjiji's claim to authority and precedence over Eiheiji. The *shikimon* explains that Emperor Godaigo sent ten questions to Keizan and quotes the first and tenth questions. It cites the *Godaigo tennō rinji sha* (Edict by Emperor Godaigo), supposedly written by Godaigo in Genkō 2 (1322), which declared Sōjiji to be an imperial prayer temple, and the *Gomurakami tennō rinji sha* (Edict by Emperor Gomurakami), attributed to Gomurakami and dated Shōhei 9 (1354), which confirmed Sōjiji's status as an imperial prayer temple.[74]

These documents had originally played a role in the rivalry between Yōkōji and Sōjiji, with each temple claiming to have received imperial protection earlier than the other. But since Sōjiji had eclipsed Yōkōji by the end of the sixteenth century, these documents had lost that role until they gained salience in the rivalry between Eiheiji and Sōjiji in the Tokugawa period. Then in the Meiji era, when Eiheiji tried to outplay Sōjiji, the latter used the same documents to authenticate its high position and status in the history of the Sōtō school. By including quotations from these documents in his *shikimon,* Bonjō emphasized Sōjiji's importance as well. Nonetheless, it should be noted

---

73. This verse was taken from the twelfth chapter of the *Lotus Sutra,* T 9: 35b10–11.

74. The historicity of both documents is problematic, but in the Meiji era Sōtō monks were more interested in demonstrating the superiority of the Sōtō school than in examining the veracity of the documents they used to support their claims.

that he was using the same rhetorical strategy that Hakugan employed—the quotation of "official" documents—to assert the primacy of Yōkōji's status.

Bonjō then states that Keizan's writings all express the essence of the buddhas and patriarchs, underscoring that clerics can still learn from Keizan. Among the writings he mentions are the *Zazen yōjin ki* 坐禪用心記 (Instructions on the practice of zazen), *Sankon zazen setsu* 三根坐禪説 (Explanation of the three kinds of Zen practitioners), and *Shinjin mei nentei* 信心銘拈提, a commentary on the *Shinjin mei* (Ch. *Xinxin ming*) said to be written by the third Chan patriarch, Sengcan 僧璨 (d. 606). The section closes by praising Keizan for his compassion and teachings and requesting the monks to sing a verse and perform prostrations:

> Now, in order to repay a drop of the ocean of mercy, we should intone a verse and perform prostrations. We sing a verse:
>
> Indra and Brahma both pay homage.
> Bowing their heads, they wish to inquire
> How the Buddha has liberated the beings of this world
> And [his] blessing circulates everywhere.[75]
>
> Humbly prostrating ourselves, we take refuge in the Great Ancestor, National Master Kōtoku Enmyō. (ZSZ 2: 864)

The devas Indra and Brahma pay homage to the Buddha in the same way that Emperor Godaigo venerated Keizan, illustrating the imperial protection that Keizan and Sōjiji enjoyed. Bonjō selected this verse from the *Changshouwang jing* (Sutra of the long-life king), and like the previous verses, it originally had nothing to do with Keizan, but the new context puts Keizan at its center.

Keizan's heritage. The fifth and final section of the *shikimon* in the *Dentō kōshiki* relates how Keizan entrusted his temples to his disciples before his death and the subsequent formation of his lineage, which became the largest branch of the Sōtō school. Keizan handed Sōjiji over to Gasan and established ten rules for the monks there; then he gave a sermon in order to resign from the abbotship of Sōjiji and returned to Yōkōji, which he entrusted to Meihō. Jōjūji went to Mugai, and Kōkōji to Koan. The *Dentō kōshiki* goes on to explain how Keizan passed away. Here it quotes the *Butsuji kōshiki,* stating that Keizan's mausoleum was called Dentō and that Keizan had lived fifty-eight years and was a monk for forty-seven summers. The name Dentō could be interpreted as a nod to the title of the *kōshiki,* but it is only mentioned casually, with no emphasis. No other biography states that Keizan was a monk for forty-seven years; earlier in this text, Bonjō himself wrote that Keizan entered Eiheiji when he was eight and received the precepts at the age of thirteen, so the

75. This is a verse from the *Changshouwang jing* (J. *Chōjūō kyō*), T 3: 388a8–9.

shikimon contradicts itself, a contradiction that likely resulted from the fusion of the new Meiji-era sources with the earlier *Butsuji kōshiki*.

Bonjō presents both Dōgen and Keizan as expressing the same truth but in different forms: whereas Dōgen refused the imperial purple robe, Keizan accepted it. Bonjō explains that these two different approaches are expressions of the same underlying principle, chosen based on the capacity of the audience. The thrust of this passage shows that the new biographic image of Keizan was constructed in opposition to that of Dōgen, and consequently that the *Dentō kōshiki* was similarly constructed in relation to Dōgen and Menzan's *Hōon kōshiki*. The passage is also noteworthy in being an early example of the new concept that the different expressions of Buddhist doctrine by Dōgen and Keizan are expressions of the same essence, an idea that was developed in the Meiji era as a means to reconcile the head temples.[76]

Next, the *kōshiki* details Keizan's heritage by naming Keizan's disciples and the disciples of Gasan and Meihō. From there the narration continues: "From then on, the Dharma water has pervaded everywhere in the four oceans and the true wind blows widely throughout the whole world" (ZSZ 2: 866), underscoring again the fact that Sōtō Zen's dissemination throughout Japan was due to the activities of monks in Keizan's lineage.

Bonjō acknowledges that Keizan's accomplishments were honored with the posthumous names Zen Master Butsuji and National Master Kōtoku Enmyō bestowed by the emperor at the time. In the print edition, we find an additional entry by brush, stating Keizan's new posthumous name: "Further, the Emperor Meiji ordered and bestowed the posthumous name Great Master Jōsai." This entry must have been made in or after 1909, the year the Meiji emperor bestowed this title. This demonstrates again the fluidity of ritual texts, and also that even printed texts can be changed.

Finally, Keizan is praised in a poetic style, and the text invites the assembly to sing a verse:

> Surely you should be deeply delighted and show utmost respect. Lifetime after lifetime you should continually cultivate the seed of buddhahood and everywhere raise Dharma banners [to teach].
>
> Reverently, we wish that the moon of brilliant truth may shine without ever quietly ruffling the original source (*hongen* 本源). May the marvelous mind of the Buddha's compassion feel [with us], finally understand us, and secretly offer wondrous responses.[77] The Dharma world has no borders and all sentient beings are included. May we equally reach marvelous enlightenment and all realize the origin of truth.

---

76. This idea was also the basis of the new central image of worship of the Sōtō school, placing Śākyamuni at the center with Dōgen and Keizan to either side. This icon was understood to symbolize the unification of the two head temples.

77. This sentence contains a wordplay with Keizan's title "Zen Master Butsuji." It may be read as "May the marvelous mind (*myōshin* 妙心) of Buddha's compassion (*butsuji* 佛慈) feel..." or "May the marvelous mind of [Zen Master] Butsuji feel...."

Therefore, because we honor the unlimited manifestation in response, we should intone a verse and perform prostrations. We sing a verse:

The great teacher of devas and humans
Feels compassion for the world.
The sentient beings of the ten directions
All universally receive benefits.[78]

Humbly prostrating ourselves, we take refuge in the Great Ancestor, National Master Kōtoku Enmyō. (ZSZ 2: 866)

This final verse, taken from the *Lotus Sutra,* praises Keizan as a great teacher of all beings. The *kōshiki* remembers him as the great popularizer of Sōtō Zen, and the last section accordingly highlights his compassion and guidance of many people.

Intertextuality of the *Dentō kōshiki*

Comparing the *shikimon* of the *Butsuji kōshiki* and the *Dentō kōshiki,* we can say that the *shikimon* of the *Dentō kōshiki* describes Keizan's life chronologically and is therefore easier to follow. Because of this, it may seem at first glance that Bonjō composed the *Dentō kōshiki* with a lay audience in mind, especially considering that he actively propagated Buddhism to lay devotees and compiled multivolume materials for sermons. But a closer look reveals that his main sources, Takiya's *Taiso ryakuden* and Ōuchi's *Sōtōshū ryōso denryaku,* had been written for laypeople. Therefore, the fact that the *Dentō kōshiki* is easy to understand may be more a reflection of the intended audience of Bonjō's main sources than an indication of his own intended audience. Indeed, the statement "and lead the pure monks of the whole mountain" in the pronouncement of intention suggests that the *Dentō kōshiki* was intended to be a monastic ritual like the *Butsuji kōshiki.* And in fact, the *Dentō kōshiki* has remained a monastic ritual since its composition and first performance.

Bonjō modeled his new *kōshiki* on Menzan's *Hōon kōshiki,* which commemorates Dōgen. As a ritual for Keizan, the *kōshiki* he composed may have been undertaken in an attempt to establish two parallel rituals paying respect to Dōgen and Keizan, in the same way that Bonjō wrote a biography of each of the two patriarchs of the Sōtō school. These works also reflect the formation of a new collective memory in the Meiji era in which the two patriarchs have become the central figures of the school.

Additionally, *kōshiki* authors heavily quote from other sources. In the case of the *Dentō kōshiki,* Bonjō borrowed statements from Keizan biographies such as the *Rentōroku,* Takiya's *Taiso ryakuden,* and Ōuchi's *Sōtōshū ryōso denryaku.* He also included passages from the *Butsuji kōshiki,* Menzan's *Hōon kōshiki,*

78. This is a verse from the eighth chapter of the *Lotus Sutra,* T 9: 23b11–12.

Godaigo tennō rinji sha, and *Gomurakami tennō rinji sha,* all of which were written in Chinese. Because *shikimon* were written in Chinese, it was easy to add Chinese extracts to them. But Takiya's and Ōuchi's Keizan biographies were written in Japanese, so Bonjō had to translate the passages he used from them into Chinese. During the ritual itself, the officiant would then transform the *shikimon* into a Japanese rendering of the Sinitic text. In this way, some passages of the *Dentō kōshiki* underwent two transformations: from Japanese into Chinese and then back into Japanese.

While the *shikimon* of the *Dentō kōshiki* quotes biographies as well as historical documents and was influenced by other *kōshiki,* its verses were all taken from Mahāyāna sutras. This is a common feature of *kōshiki,* and verses are often adopted from sutras or other doctrinal texts. Bonjō carefully selected verses that foreground the main theme of each section, relating Keizan to the Buddha and thereby presenting him as an equivalent of the Buddha.

The intertextuality of *kōshiki* highlights the central role of texts in Buddhist rituals. Through the composition of new texts, *kōshiki* are invented. But these ritual texts are not completely new; they quote other ritual texts as well as doctrinal or biographical works. Although other performative aspects, such as the vocalization, are important in the performance of *kōshiki*—and might even seem to be more relevant to the efficacy of the ritual—without texts, *kōshiki* would not come into existence.

After Bonjō composed his new *kōshiki,* the new ritual was firmly integrated into Sōjiji's liturgical calendar, replacing the earlier *Butsuji kōshiki.* Today the *Dentō kōshiki* is still performed at Sōjiji on October 14 during the annual memorial service for Keizan and Gasan, who are now commemorated together (figs. 5.1 and 5.2). The *Dentō kōshiki* remains a monastic ritual and is not intended to be performed for a lay audience. It is performed in the evening, a time of day when the doors of the main hall are closed and no laypeople can enter. During many years of fieldwork at Sōjiji, I have never seen a Japanese lay devotee attending this ritual. Instead, the only people watching were priests visiting Sōjiji to help during the memorial service or to perform as an officiant in one of the other rituals during this service. The *Dentō kōshiki* has retained its character as a monastic ritual, performed to repay the benevolence received from Keizan.

Conclusions

For the monks at Yōkōji and Sōjiji, both the *Butsuji kōshiki* and the *Dentō kōshiki* were first and foremost rituals to express their gratitude to Keizan. The narration of Keizan's life by the officiant during the *kōshiki* explained why Keizan deserved veneration, and after listening to the recitation of the officiant, the monks expressed their veneration for Keizan by singing verses and performing prostrations. Therefore, we can interpret the *kōshiki* as a vocalized and enacted remembrance of Keizan, a liturgy of memory.

Moreover, by participating in the memorial service and the *kōshiki,* the

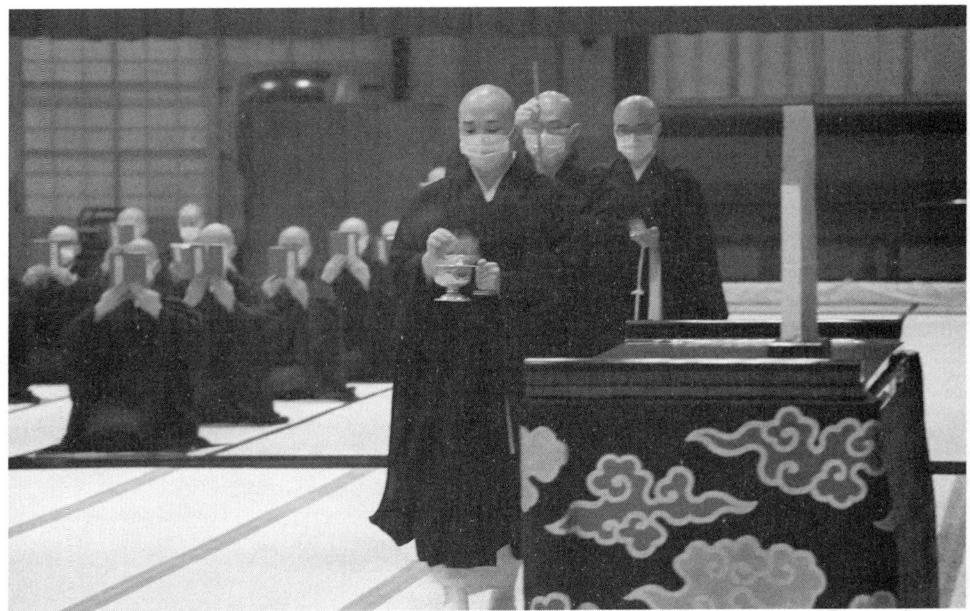

Figure 5.1. Three monks circumambulate the hall during the *Gāthā to Scattering Flowers*. *Dentō kōshiki,* performed at Sōjiji on October 14, 2020, when all monks wore face masks due to the COVID-19 pandemic. Photo by Sōjiji. Used with permission.

Figure 5.2. Singing a verse during the *shikimon*. *Dentō kōshiki,* performed at Sōjiji on October 14, 2020. Photo by Sōjiji. Used with permission.

monks were able to remember and affirm their own lineage and identity. As a result, Keizan's memorial service helped to deepen the lineage consciousness of the monks and build a community. The *kōshiki* itself further strengthened these bonds through its narration of Keizan's biography together with the communal performance of the ritual. In a way, the *kōshiki* was a performance and enactment of the collective memory of a specific community.

In addition, the biographical narrative in the *shikimon* provided a model to Sōtō monks for how to practice, as Hakugan suggests in his foreword when he writes that he wishes Sōtō monks would "open the eye that penetrates all things through the informal sermon on the venerable Great Master."[79] Likewise, Robert Buswell emphasizes this function of biographies in his article about the Korean monk Wonhyo 元曉 (617–686):

> East Asian hagiography was principally intended to preserve for posterity the achievements of an eminent individual who personified a particular spiritual ideal, cultural symbol, or religious accomplishment. Hagiography also functioned as a didactic tool, offering a spiritual exemplar for religious adherents, a model of conduct, morality, and understanding that could be imitated by the entire community. East Asians tended consciously to emulate the lives of past moral paragons, which meant that religious virtuosi tended to follow strikingly similar patterns in their vocations.[80]

Keizan modeled his own life on established ideals for the life of a Buddhist monk, and the biographies about him, as well as the *Butsuji kōshiki* and the *Dentō kōshiki,* became models for future generations.

The two transmission lineages of the *Butsuji kōshiki,* together with Hakugan's *Butsuji kōshiki* and Bonjō's *Dentō kōshiki,* express different collective memories and reflect the rivalry between Yōkōji and Sōjiji. Parallel histories and texts coexisted next to each other and formed the collective memories of opposing lineages. These *kōshiki* were intended to shape the future of Sōjiji or Yōkōji, each temple trying to gain acceptance of the version of history in which it held the more powerful and revered position. Both Hakugan and Bonjō used quotations from historical documents to support their claims. In her study of the founding legends of the temple Tsubosakasan Minami Hokkeji 壺阪山南法華寺, Katja Triplett discovered a similar process in which different legends were transmitted side by side and were used by different factions to promote their interests.[81] Triplett called this process a politics of memory (*Erinnerungspolitik*). In the case of the *hōon kōshiki* for Keizan, we do not have different interest groups at one temple but two interest groups at rival temples. Borrowing Jan Assmann's terminology, we could call these *kōshiki* rituals of collective remembrance—in

79. Abe 2019, 86.
80. Buswell 1995, 553.
81. Triplett 2010.

German, "*kollektives Gedächtnisritual.*"[82] Hence the *kōshiki* and the memorial services for Keizan played a role in constructing tradition, group identity, and history.

Hakugan's *Butsuji kōshiki* stood in opposition to Sōjiji, while Bonjō's *Dentō kōshiki* reflected a new biographic image of Keizan that contrasted Keizan and Sōjiji primarily with Dōgen and Eiheiji. This opposition is also reflected in Bonjō's selection of Menzan's *Hōon kōshiki* as a model for his work, leading him to create a *shikimon* for Keizan that uses the same structure as the *kōshiki* commemorating Dōgen. In effect, this led to the establishment of two parallel *kōshiki* for Dōgen and Keizan. The *Dentō kōshiki* presents Keizan as the counterpart to Dōgen, which Keizan officially became in 1877, when Sōtō leaders designated Dōgen and Keizan as the two patriarchs of the Japanese Sōtō school and settled on the titles Eminent Ancestor and Great Ancestor for them. About the remembrance of Dōgen, Bodiford writes:

> Dōgen's memory has helped keep Eiheiji financially secure, in good repair, and filled with monks and lay pilgrims who look to Dōgen for religious inspiration. Eiheiji has become Dōgen's place, the temple where Dōgen is remembered, where Dōgen's Zen is practiced, where Dōgen's *Shōbōgenzō* is published, where Dōgen's *Shōbōgenzō* is read, and where one goes to learn Dōgen's Buddhism. As we remember Dōgen, we should also remember that remembrance is not value neutral. It cannot be a product of pure, objective scholarship. We should perhaps remind ourselves that the Dōgen we remember is a constructed image, an image constructed in large measure to serve the sectarian agendas of Eiheiji in its rivalry with Sōjiji.[83]

The same can be said for Keizan and Sōjiji. Sōjiji has become the place where Keizan is remembered, where Keizan's writings are published, where Keizan's Zen is taught and practiced; and this remembrance keeps Sōjiji financially stable and attracts a large number of novice monks and lay devotees alike.

The remembrance of Keizan is also vital for Yōkōji's survival: it inspires clerics to support Yōkōji financially, because of its history as Keizan's main temple, and also attracts clerics and lay devotees to visit Yōkōji, albeit in significantly fewer numbers than Sōjiji or Eiheiji. Although Yōkōji stands in the large shadow of Sōjiji, it too depends on Keizan's legacy. In this way, tensions between the three temples shimmer in the depths of the *kōshiki* commemorating Keizan

The new biographies of Keizan were not the result of historical scholarship, as this study of the *Butsuji kōshiki* and the *Dentō kōshiki* has shown. Instead they present a "constructed image," as Bodiford terms it, and this biographic image was constructed in the course of the rivalry between Sōjiji and Yōkōji, and / or Eiheiji. *Kōshiki* were not texts that presented new biographic images

82. Assman 2000, 20.
83. Bodiford 2012, 222.

ab ovo; they were reflections of already existing or evolving images. Takiya's biography was the first text to present a new biographical account of Keizan in the early Meiji era. The transformation in Keizan's biographic image in the Meiji era, first proclaimed by Takiya, was so pronounced for the monks of Sōjiji that it entailed the composition of a new *hōon kōshiki* for Keizan, not a mere revision of the *Butsuji kōshiki.* The new biographic image constructed by Takiya was adopted by other authors and then promoted through subsequent biographies and other works, among them the *Dentō kōshiki,* all of which helped propagate this new understanding and established it as *the* biographic image of Keizan. The parallel transmission lineages of the *Butsuji kōshiki* and the *Dentō kōshiki* show that biographic images remain fluid and change according to the socio-historical environment. This case further suggests that ritual texts that narrate "history" stand in close relation to their historical and institutional contexts and are actually influenced by them. When these contexts change, ritual texts can also change.

We cannot judge whether it was the *Dentō kōshiki* or Hakugan's *Butsuji kōshiki* that was created first, or know whether Bonjō and Hakugan were aware of each other's project when engaged in their own effort. For this reason, it is impossible to say whether Hakugan's *Butsuji kōshiki* was a response to Bonjō's new *kōshiki* or vice versa. Nevertheless, the two ritual texts demonstrate that *kōshiki* still played an important role in the liturgy of Sōjiji and Yōkōji in the Meiji era. These texts also suggest that Sōtō monks in the Meiji era still thought that *kōshiki* were an effective means to express gratitude to their temple founder and to form a collective memory that placed their own temple in a position of power vis-à-vis rival temples.

Epilogue

THIS BOOK has explored the evolution of *kōshiki* in Japanese Sōtō Zen and illuminated the diversity of ritual practices within this tradition. The history of *kōshiki* in the Sōtō school starts with the school founder, Dōgen, who is credited with the composition of a *kōshiki* for the Sixteen Arhats. The heyday of *kōshiki* in the Sōtō school seems to have been during the Tokugawa period, a time when the production of *kōshiki* in other schools had long been in decline. During that time, Sōtō clerics regularly performed around twenty different works in this genre. However, no individual cleric performed twenty different *kōshiki;* rather, liturgies were highly localized and many *kōshiki* were performed exclusively at certain temples. From the Tokugawa period onward, the widespread adoption of print culture for ritual manuals led to a higher degree of standardization; nonetheless, ritual practices remained local. For example, only clerics at Sōjiji—and occasionally those at a few affiliated major temples—perform the *Dentō kōshiki,* commemorating Keizan; only temples in Akita prefecture perform a *kōshiki* for the bodhisattva Kannon during elaborate funeral services; and only nuns at the convent in Nagoya perform a *kōshiki* for Ānanda.

Kōshiki are not relics of earlier times but rituals that continue to evolve. The production of new *kōshiki* did not end in the Tokugawa period: Bukkan Bonjō composed a new *kōshiki* for Keizan in the late nineteenth century, and around twenty years ago, Inoue Gishin compiled two *kōshiki,* one for Hakusan and one for Dōgen. Inoue tried to create *kōshiki* that satisfy contemporary interests by limiting the performance time to around ninety minutes and integrating *goeika* (Buddhist hymns) into the rituals. Additionally, other *kōshiki* continued to be edited or revised. For instance, around 2001 Imamura Genshū edited the *Hōon kōshiki,* composed by Menzan in the mid-eighteenth century in remembrance of Dōgen. Imamura revised the *shikimon* based both on medieval manuscripts about Dōgen's life and on new concerns raised by the human rights movement in the Sōtō school. These cases reflect the fact that *kōshiki* are still part of a living tradition.

The ritual tradition of Sōtō Zen is highly eclectic. Sōtō monks adopted several *kōshiki* composed by authors of other schools, such as Jōkei's *Kannon kōshiki* and Myōe's *Busshōe kōshiki.* Nevertheless, although Sōtō clerics freely borrowed liturgical texts from other schools, they adapted them to their own tradition by inserting them into a ritual structure typical for Sōtō *kōshiki*—and by performing them in a Sōtō style.

Such adaption and performance in the style of a particular school were made possible by the modularity of *kōshiki*. A *kōshiki* author composes a *shikimon* and perhaps an offertory declaration, or a cleric selects a *shikimon* written by a monk of another Buddhist school. In either case, the composer or editor then inserts the *shikimon* and offertory declaration into the structure of *kōshiki* typical for his school. I have described the structure into which the *shikimon* is set as a ritual frame because several liturgical pieces enclose the *shikimon* in the same way that a picture frame encloses a picture. Most Sōtō *kōshiki* share a similar form, one that can be regarded as a standard ritual frame. In chapter 2, I compared the ritual structures of the *Rakan kōshiki* as performed in the Sōtō, Rinzai, and Shingon schools and outlined the different form it takes in each school. While most of the liturgical pieces vocalized in the *kōshiki* come from a shared ritual repertoire, the distinctive structures—or ritual frames—in which the liturgical pieces are placed reflect the school's identity.

In a particular *kōshiki*, Sōtō clerics also use elements from other *kōshiki* or rituals of their tradition. The borrowing of ritual elements—or modules—of various dimensions (textual, kinetic, sonic, and material) showcases the intertextual or interritual quality of rituals. Like texts, rituals draw from a repertoire of modules. Thus, clerics employed elements of an established tradition in the invention of new *kōshiki*, and a new ritual would naturally become part of the tradition. Consequently, the newly composed rituals were easy for the clerics to perform since they were familiar with their basic building blocks.

Many scholars working on Buddhist rituals have privileged written texts and their content. However, as this book has shown, *kōshiki* are multidimensional performances that feature formulaic movements and gestures, melodic patterns, and various materials. An exclusive focus on texts limits our understanding of the power of rituals. The elements of *kōshiki* described in this book—ritual frames and modules related to the material, linguistic, acoustic, and kinetic dimensions—all come together in a *kōshiki* performance to form a ritual that is more than its parts. All these elements contribute to the aesthetic quality of the ritual.

A large percentage of Sōtō *kōshiki* have been composed and performed in remembrance of eminent monks. Like the *kōshiki* commemorating Keizan, the *shikimon* of these rituals narrate the life of an influential Zen patriarch. We can consider the texts as expressions of a collective memory, a memory shared by members of the school or by a certain faction of the school. These texts are then set into the ritual frame of Sōtō *kōshiki*, and their performance enacts this collective memory through the vocalization of the liturgical texts and the bodily expression of veneration.

This book has recognized that life in Zen temples or monasteries offers a rich soundscape. Within the diverse repertoire of Zen rituals, *kōshiki* form the most musical genre that Sōtō Zen has to offer. The vocalization of texts in these rituals is not random—nor as simple as a reading of a sutra on one pitch. Rather, most texts of a *kōshiki* are vocalized with prescribed melodies—indicated with a traditional musical notation in the ritual handbooks—and sung with a highly controlled use of the voice. The *shōmyō* specialists introduced in chapter 3 approach the study of *shōmyō* as a musical practice and constantly aim to refine their skills while keeping in mind the religious function of their activity. That they value *kōshiki* and *shōmyō* as a cultural property of their school is demonstrated by their willingness to produce audio and video recordings to preserve their tradition. Monks of Eiheiji's satellite temple in Tokyo, for example, produced a compact disc containing their newly revised *kōshiki* for Dōgen and submitted it to a performing arts competition organized by the Ministry of Cultural Affairs. Although they did not win a prize, the very fact of their submission is testament to the value they attach to their music.

Many Sōtō clerics view *shōmyō* as the most important element in the performance of a *kōshiki*. This has led them to emphasize the liturgical pieces that are sung to melodies more than the *shikimon* that is read without or with very few melodic inflections, even though the *shikimon* was the original center of the ritual. In contemporary Japan, a cleric reading the *shikimon* usually abbreviates the text. Most clerics also read it relatively quickly, making it difficult for the listeners to understand its content. The center of attention has therefore shifted from the *shikimon* to the pieces that frame it, with the sonic character of the *shōmyō* pieces eclipsing the semantics of the *shikimon*.

Other elements, such as physical movements, further contribute to the aesthetic quality of a *kōshiki*. Although most clerics do not move much during the ritual, the movements of the assistants are carefully choreographed and performed with great precision. Additionally, offerings are carefully prepared, and often refined ritual implements are used. As Inoue wrote, *kōshiki* offer something for the eyes and ears. They must be understood holistically, as they are constructed of texts, movements, melodies, and the deployment of various materials.

The performance of *kōshiki* also has a vital soteriological function. Although publications on Zen often emphasize zazen as the core practice of Zen, Sōtō clerics consider a wide range of activities—including cleaning, cooking, and sutra chanting—to be part of their practice. This idea forms the basis of the proverb, "Proper conduct is the Buddha Dharma, and etiquette is the principle of our school," often cited by contemporary Sōtō clerics. Likewise, Maekawa Bokushō suggested that the performance of rituals and the singing of liturgical texts are an expression of the realization of buddhahood, an interpretation based on the idea that practice and realization are one (*shushō ittō*). This core doctrine was promoted at the outset in Dōgen's writings, and Maekawa has interpreted the performance of Buddhist rituals through this lens. Other *shōmyō* specialists I interviewed also stressed that *shōmyō* and zazen share the same quality and that zazen provides the basis for singing liturgical texts.

The headquarters of the Sōtō school does not promote any specific interpretation of *shōmyō*. Consequently, individual priests have developed their interpretations based on their own understanding and practice. A few have chosen to interpret rituals from a more general Buddhist perspective and not through the lens of Sōtō Zen doctrine. One of them is Suzuki Bunmei, introduced in chapter 3, who emphasizes the devotional function of *kōshiki* and *shōmyō*. These contrasting views illustrate the multivocality within the Sōtō school.

This book has outlined the wide range of contexts in which works belonging to the *kōshiki* genre are performed. *Kōshiki* have often been described as rituals directed toward lay devotees or performed for purposes of outreach. While there are *kōshiki* that did serve such aims, there are also instances of *kōshiki* being performed strictly as monastic rituals. The first work in this genre, the *Nijūgo zanmai shiki* (Ceremony of the twenty-five samādhis), was originally performed by a group of twenty-five clerics who had vowed to help each other achieve rebirth in Amida's Pure Land. Another example can be found in Kakuban, who seems to have composed *kōshiki* for his own private practice. As this book has demonstrated, most Sōtō *kōshiki* seem to have been monastic rituals that were not directed to lay devotees. The *kōshiki* commemorating Dōgen and Keizan were an integral part of the memorial services performed by clerics to pay respect to them. Before the twentieth century, these memorial services at Eiheiji and Sōjiji were held by and for the monastic community, and few parishioners could have been expected to visit the remote head temples. Today, lay devotees do attend these annual memorial services, but at Sōjiji the *kōshiki* for Keizan remains off-limits to lay devotees as it is performed at night behind closed doors. At Eiheiji's satellite temple in Tokyo, in contrast, the *kōshiki* commemorating Dōgen is conducted in the afternoon, and a few lay devotees attended the *kōshiki* when I visited. Still, there are some *kōshiki* that Sōtō clerics do perform for lay devotees, the most prominent being the *Kannon kōshiki* that is performed during elaborate funeral services in Akita prefecture. Also, when *kōshiki* are performed during the day, the doors to the halls are usually open, and at Eiheiji, for example, tourists or parishioners who happen to come by can stay to observe the ritual. The crucial point is that *kōshiki* as a genre is defined by its form and not by the time or occasion when the ritual is performed. Because of this, *kōshiki* has been able to accommodate a wide range of religious functions and performance practices over the course of its history.

Considering that more than four hundred *kōshiki* have been written and performed through the centuries, scholarship has only scratched the surface of this important genre. So far, *kōshiki* written by well-known figures such as Myōe and Jōkei have received considerable scholarly attention while those written by unknown or less-recognized monks have been passed over. *Kōshiki* of the so-called New Kamakura schools, in particular, have not yet been studied thoroughly.

In this book, I have only mentioned the elaborate *kangen kōshiki* in which *gagaku* pieces were performed between the sections of the *shikimon.* A study of the development of these rituals and their performance practice can provide new insight into elite Buddhist practices in medieval Japan, as well as the relations between *gagaku* and *shōmyō* and the role of performative arts in Buddhist rituals. Many premodern sources on Japanese Buddhist music and ritual practices are available to shed light on different aspects of Buddhist chant, including chanting as a Buddhist practice, doctrinal interpretations of sounds, performance practice, and ritual change.

Although this book has explored the development of Sōtō *kōshiki* in detail, many questions still remain, such as those pertaining to how Sōtō clerics first came to adopt this ritual form and the performance practices that characterized it in medieval Japan. In addition, very few sources have been found that can elucidate the social side of Sōtō *kōshiki.* As more premodern manuscripts and woodblock prints stored in temple archives become available for research, we may anticipate discovering new aspects of the evolution of *shōmyō* and *kōshiki* that will deepen our understanding of these ritual practices not only in Zen Buddhism in particular but in Japanese Buddhism as a whole.

APPENDICES

Kōshiki *Commemorating Keizan*

Appendix 1

Extant Manuscripts of the *Butsuji kōshiki*

Several manuscripts of the *Butsuji kōshiki* commemorating Keizan have been found in temple archives. The extant Tokugawa-period manuscripts can be divided into two groups: first, ritual handbooks that contain a *shikimon* and, in one case, the offertory declaration as well, and second, manuscripts containing the verses sung by the assembly (all with musical notation). These manuscripts can be further categorized as texts belonging to the Yōkōji or Sōjiji transmission lineage.

Manuscripts containing the offertory declaration and *shikimon* of the Yōkōji transmission lineage

1. Untitled, but commonly referred to as *Butsuji kōshiki* 仏慈講式, probably written around 1725. I refer to it as the Yōkōji manuscript. Concertina-fold book (*orihon* 折本). Copyist unknown. It contains the *shikimon,* whose verses are written with musical notation, and the offertory declaration. Archive of Yōkōji. Typographical reprint in Ozaki 1998c, 59–64. Facsimile available at the Sōtōshū Bunkazai Chōsa Iinkai; listed in Bunkazai 7: 614. Reproduced in Appendix 7.
2. Untitled, but I refer to it as *Butsuji kōshiki saimon* 仏慈講式祭文, written in Bunsei 10 (1827). Handscroll. Copyist unknown. It contains only the offertory declaration. Archive of Yōkōji. Facsimile available at the Sōtōshū Bunkazai Chōsa Iinkai; listed in Bunkazai 7: 614.[1]

Manuscripts containing the *shikimon* of the Sōjiji transmission lineage

1. *Kaisan kokushi Butsuji kōshiki* 開山國師佛慈講式, inner title: *Kaiso kokushi kōshiki* 開祖國師講式, written in Bunka 3 (1806). I refer to it as the Taineiji 太寧寺 manuscript. "Bound-pocket" book (*fukurotoji* 袋とじ). It contains only the *shikimon,* and the verses are written without any musical notation. It was copied by the monk Gihō 義鳳 (n.d.) of Taiseiin 太清院, a subtemple (*tatchū* 塔頭) in the precincts of Sōjiji. Twenty-five years after

1. The catalogue of the Sōtōshū Bunkazai Chōsa Iinkai refers to it by the provisional title *Keizan Zenji jijaku daiki saimon* 瑩山禅師示寂大忌祭文.

Gihō had copied it, Taikō Ryūdō 大興隆道 (n.d.), the twenty-fourth head priest of Taineiji (Hyōgo prefecture), used it to recite the *shikimon* when he served as rotating abbot at Sōjiji from Tenpō 1 (1830) to Tenpō 2 (1831).[2] After finishing his tenure, Ryūdō took this manuscript home to Taineiji, where it is still stored today. Typographical reprint in Ozaki 1998c, 59–64. Facsimile available at the Sōtōshū Bunkazai Chōsa Iinkai; listed in Bunkazai 5: 359. Reproduced in Appendix 8.

2. *Shogaku kokushi zenji kōshikibon* 諸嶽國師禅師講式本, inner title: *Kaiso kokushi kōshiki* 開祖國師講式, written in Kaei 2 (1849). "Bound pocket" book. It was copied by So'myō 祖明 (n.d.), an attendant at Fuzōin 普藏院, a subtemple in the precincts of Sōjiji. This manuscript was used by Tōkai Hyakugawa 東海百川 (n.d.), rotating abbot at Sōjiji from Kaei 1 (1848) to Kaei 2 (1849).[3] He was the forty-first head priest of Untōan 雲洞庵 (Niigata prefecture) and took the manuscript home after finishing his tenure at Sōjiji. Archive of Untōan. Facsimile available at the Sōtōshū Bunkazai Chōsa Iinkai; listed in Bunkazai 7: 808.

Manuscripts containing the choral pieces of the Yōkōji transmission lineage

1. *Kaiso kōshiki* 開祖講式, written in Shōtoku 5 (1715). Concertina-fold book. Copied by Ankyō 安教 (n.d.), who might have been a disciple of Yōkōji's 485th abbot, Unkei Antaku 雲渓安宅 (d. 1716). It includes the pieces *Gāthā to Scattering Flowers, Hymn of the Four Wisdoms,* communal obeisance, verses of the *shikimon,* and *Universal Transfer of Merit* (as the last verse of the *shikimon*). This manuscript is one of fifteen produced and used at Yōkōji, where it is still stored today. Typographical reprint in Ozaki 1998c, 64–66. Facsimile available at the Sōtōshū Bunkazai Chōsa Iinkai; listed in Bunkazai 7: 614.

Manuscripts containing the choral pieces of the Sōjiji transmission lineage

1. *Butsuji kō kada narabini Shichisan* 佛慈講伽陀並四智讃, written in Genroku 7 (1694). Concertina-fold book. Copied by Chimon 智門 (n.d.), a monk of Unkokuji 雲谷寺, a subtemple in the precincts of Sōjiji. It includes the communal obeisance, verses of the *shikimon, Universal Transfer of Merit,* and *Hymn of the Four Wisdoms* (including musical notation for cymbals and gong). Fifty copies of this manuscript were produced. Today forty-two copies are stored at Sōjiji Soin, and one each at Shōyōji (Yamagata prefecture) and the Kadono Konzen Library Collection. Typographical reprint in Ozaki 1998c, 64–65. Facsimiles of copies in possession of Sōjiji

2. Satō Shinyū 1973, 97; SZ 32: 1047.
3. Satō Shinyū 1973, 57; SZ 32: 1041.

Sōin and Shōyōji are available at the Sōtōshū Bunkazai Chōsa Iinkai; listed in Bunkazai 2: 276 and Bunkazai 7: 429.

2. *Kada narabini hōyō* 伽陀並法要, written in Genroku 7 (1694). Concertina-fold book. Also copied by Chimon. It contains all the *shōmyō* pieces vocalized during *kōshiki* performed at Sōjiji in the late seventeenth century (*Butsuji kōshiki, Rakan kōshiki,* and *Nehan kōshiki*). Five copies of this text were produced. Today three copies are stored in the archive of Sōjiji Soin, and one in the Kadono Konzen Library Collection. Partial typographical reprint in Ozaki 1998c, 65–66. A facsimile of a copy stored at Sōjiji Sōin is available at the Sōtōshū Bunkazai Chōsa Iinkai; listed in Bunkazai 7: 429.
3. *San kōshiki narabini hōyō* 三講式并法要, written in Bunka 10 (1813). Concertina-fold book. Copied by Shinryū 真龍 (n.d.) of Taiseiin 太清院, a subtemple in the precincts of Sōjiji. It is based on the *Kada narabini hōyō* and contains the *shōmyō* pieces for the *Butsuji kōshiki, Rakan kōshiki,* and *Nehan kōshiki.* Five copies were produced at Sōjiji. At least one copy is still stored in the archive of Sōjiji Soin and one in the Kadono Konzen Library Collection. Partial typographical reprint in Ozaki 1998c, 66–67. A facsimile of the copy stored at Sōjiji Sōin is available at the Sōtōshū Bunkazai Chōsa Iinkai; listed in Bunkazai 7: 420.
4. *Butsuji kōshiki kada* 佛慈講式伽陀, probably written at the end of the Tokugawa period. Copyist unknown. Written on separate paper glued to the back side of the following manuscripts originally produced at Sōjiji in Genroku 7 (1694): *Nehan kō kada narabini Shichisan* 涅槃講伽陀並四智讃 (fifty copies) and *Hōyō* 法要 (thirteen copies). Archive of Sōjiji Soin.
5. *Dentō kōshiki ino yō* 傳燈講式 維那用, written between 1877 and 1892. Copyist unknown. Written on the back of one copy of the *Butsuji kō kada narabini Shichisan,* originally produced at Sōjiji in Genroku 7 (1694). It includes the pieces *Gāthā to Scattering Flowers, Hymn of the Four Wisdoms,* communal obeisance, verses of the *shikimon,* and the *Universal Transfer of Merit,* as well as detailed instructions for the performance of the ritual. Archive of Sōjiji Soin.
6. *Dentō kōshiki shikishi yō* 傳燈講式 式師用, written between 1877 and 1892. Copyist unknown. Written on the back of one copy of the *Butsuji kō kada narabini Shichisan,* originally produced at Sōjiji in Genroku 7 (1694). It includes the pieces *Gāthā to Scattering Flowers, Hymn of the Four Wisdoms,* communal obeisance, verses of the *shikimon,* and *Universal Transfer of Merit,* as well as detailed instructions for the performance of the ritual. Archive of Sōjiji Soin.[4]

---

4. See Mross 2014, chap. 5, for a detailed study of these six different ritual manuals produced at Sōjiji.

Later editions

In the Meiji era, Kokō Hakugan, Yōkōji's abbot, produced a complete woodblock print edition containing all the liturgical pieces vocalized in the *Butsuji kōshiki,* including his revised *shikimon,* together with detailed instructions for performance.

1. *Taiso Butsuji kōshiki* 太祖佛慈講式, printed in 1892. Concertina-fold book. A copy is in the possession of the Kanazawa Shiritsu Tamagawa Toshokan Kinsei Shiryōkan.
2. *Taiso Butsuji kōshiki* 太祖佛慈講式, printed in 1924, reprint of the 1892 edition. Concertina-fold book. Copies are in the possession of Yōkōji, the Kanazawa Shiritsu Tamagawa Toshokan Kinsei Shiryōkan, and the Kadono Konzen Library Collection. For a typographical reprint of this edition, see Abe 2019. The *Kōshiki database* includes a facsimile of this edition (no. 361)

Appendix 2

Shikimon of the *Butsuji kōshiki* (Translation)

Three Tokugawa-period manuscripts containing the *shikimon* of the *Butsuji kōshiki* are extant, as listed in Appendix 1. This translation is based on the Yōkōji manuscript, the oldest of the three, on the assumption that the *Butsuji kōshiki* originated at this temple. Textual variants found in the Taineiji manuscript, the oldest extant manuscript containing Sōjiji's version of the *shikimon,* are indicated in the notes. I also translate, at the end of the *shikimon,* a passage from the Taineiji manuscript dealing with the founding of the two temples that differs substantially from the Yōkōji text.

Kohō Hakugan's revised *shikimon* from 1892 includes explanatory headnotes and many new passages from historical documents stored at Yōkōji. A complete indication of Hakugan's insertions is beyond the scope of this translation, which focuses on the Tokugawa-period *Butsuji kōshiki.*

Butsuji kōshiki (*Kōshiki* on [Zen Master] Butsuji)

[Pronouncement of intention]
Reverently, I address the great compassionate saviors of the world (*daihi kuse sha* 大悲救世者) [i.e., buddhas and bodhisattvas] in the lands (*sekkai* 刹界) [as many as] various dust motes, all pure teachings (*bonpō* 梵法) of the oceanic storehouse (*kaizō* 海蔵), and the ordinary and holy monks of the ten directions, and say:[1]

Respectfully, we gather every year on the memorial day of the founder of this mountain, Zen Master Butsuji, great venerable Keizan. We prepare this lecture and perform this Buddhist service. In general, we praise the excellent virtue of the Three Treasures and so develop the great heart to spread the Dharma and to benefit all beings. In particular, we praise the original vow of the venerable great master (*daiso oshō* 大祖和尚)[2] to propagate the teachings

1. This opening statement (before "Respectfully, we gather") is missing from the Yōkōji manuscript, so I have supplied it from the Taineiji manuscript, which goes on to address Keizan not as "Zen Master Butsuji, great venerable Keizan" but as "National Master Kōtoku Enmyō, great venerable Keizan."

2. The Taineiji manuscript has here "the founder of this temple, the National Master" (*kaisan kokoshi* 開山國師).

in place of the Buddha, and so we repay one drop of the milky ocean (*nyūkai* 乳海).[3]

If we think about it, the attributes of delusion and enlightenment (*meigo* 迷悟) did not exist before the Buddha Bhīṣmagarjitasvararāja,[4] but since Śākyamuni the concepts of ordinary and sage (*bonshō* 凡聖) completely exist. First, [Śākyamuni] left the palace of Tuṣita Heaven (*soddagu* 率陀宮).[5] For a time, he sat on the throne of the king; finally, he went to [Bodh]gayā and was completely rewarded for [his] way to enlightenment (*kakudō* 覺道) [i.e., his practice] on the snow peaks (*setsurei* 雪嶺) [i.e., Himalayas].[6] He displayed the beauty of the marvelous attributes [of a Buddha] and manifested eternal life (*kuon juryō* 久遠壽量). As various flowers sent out fragrance, from the tips of the tongues of many forests gushed the ocean of the boundless essence of the Dharma body (*biru shōkai* 毘盧性海)[7] [i.e., the Buddha preached enthusiastically]. As the crane trees (*gakuju* 鶴樹)[8] returned to [their] roots, the full moon of the Buddha nature assembled in the lapis lazuli vase (*ruri hōbyō* 瑠璃寶瓶) [i.e., the Buddha left relics when he entered nirvāṇa]. Therefore, [the Buddha] gathered all sentient beings (*gunki* 群機) of the five natures (*goshō* 五性)[9] and explained the one Buddha vehicle (*ichijitsu butsujō* 一實佛乘). Once on the top of Vulture Peak, he picked up a flower and made

---

3. *Nyūkai* stands here for Dharma milk (*hō'nyū* 法乳), a metaphor that compares the teachings of a Buddhist master to milk. In the same way that milk aids in the growth of a baby, the guidance of a great master promotes the student's development. The term "Dharma milk" describes the compassion of a Buddha or Buddhist master that is as vast as the ocean. According to Sakauchi Tatsuo, it is impossible to completely repay the kindness received. Therefore, the monks wish to repay just one drop of the milky ocean (2010a, 271).

4. According to the twentieth chapter of the *Lotus Sutra,* Bhīṣmagarjitasvararāja (J. Ionō 威音王) is the name of countless buddhas who successively appeared a long time before the Buddha Śākyamuni; see T 9: 50b23–51c07; and for an English translation, see Kubo and Yuyama 2007, 265–270. According to the Zen tradition, Bhīṣmagarjitasvararāja is the first Buddha who reached enlightenment in a *kalpa* without any Buddha before him.

5. *Soddagu* describes the palace of Tuṣita Heaven (J. *Tosotten* 兜率天). Tuṣita Heaven is the fourth of the six heavens of the desire realm. In its inner palace, future buddhas are supposed to practice and teach. Śākyamuni resided there before his birth into this world, and now the next Buddha, Maitreya, is said to await his birth into this world there.

6. In one of his former existences, Śākyamuni is thought to have been an ascetic in the Himālayas who practiced the bodhisattva way (*sessen dōji* 雪山童子); see the *Nirvāṇa Sutra,* T 12: 449b08–b19.

7. *Biru shōkai* is a metaphor that compares the limitlessness of the essence of the Dharma body with the ocean.

8. *Gakuju* are the Śāla trees in the grove at Kuśinagara where Śākyamuni passed away. The leaves of these trees turned white like crane feathers when Śākyamuni died; hence they are called crane trees (*gakuju* 鶴樹).

9. According to Hossō doctrine, beings are divided into five groups depending on their capacity for enlightenment. The five groups are (1) śrāvakas (voice-hearers), referring to Hinayana followers, (2) pratyekabuddhas (self-enlightened buddhas), (3) bodhisattvas, (4) those of indeterminate natures, and (5) those lacking the capacity for enlightenment. However, this idea was later criticized, especially by proponents of the one-vehicle teaching of the *Lotus Sutra,* which proposes that the distinction between the three vehicles of the śrāvakas, pratyekabuddhas, and bodhisattvas is only provisional.

Mahākāśyapa (Daikishi 大龜氏)[10] smile. In front of the Stupa of Many Sons (Tashitō 多子塔),[11] he transmitted the mind seal [to him] and let [him] cultivate the wisdom-life (*emyō* 慧命)[12] of the marvelous Dharma body (*myōhōshin* 妙法身).

Kāśyapa (Kashō 迦葉) hid at Kukkuṭapāda,[13] and Ānanda (Keiki 慶喜)[14] died at the Ganges. But they transmitted the robe and belief, which were successively transmitted face-to-face for twenty-eight generations until they reached the honorable Bodhidharma. The honorable one first received the prophecy from Prajñātāra (J. Hannyatara 般若多羅, n.d.).[15] He went far away to China and swept away the questions of Emperor Liang [i.e., Emperor Wu]. Then he obtained the respect and enlightenment (*haigo* 拝悟) of Shenguang 神光 [i.e., Huike].[16] From then on, Caoxi 曹溪 (638–713) [i.e., Huineng] spread out a net, and the house of Dong (*dongjia* 洞家)[17] [i.e., Dongshan Liangjie 洞山良价, 807–869] mended the robe.[18]

[The teaching of the Caodong / Sōtō school] was transmitted over thirteen generations and then reached our nation's (*honchō* 本朝)[19] Great Master Eihei 永平大師 [i.e., Dōgen 道元] (1200–1253). First, he left the peak of [Ten-]dai (Tairei 台嶺) [i.e., Mt. Hiei 比叡山] and entered the room of

---

10. Daikishi is another name for Mahākāśyapa (Kāśyapa), one of Śākyamuni's closest disciples. He was famous for his ascetic discipline. In the Chan / Zen tradition, he is regarded as the first of the twenty-eight Indian patriarchs.

11. The Stupa of Many Sons was a famous stupa located northwest of the ancient Indian kingdom of Vaiśālī. In Chan literature, we find two theories about the place where the Buddha transmitted the Dharma to Mahākāśyapa: one held that it was at Vulture Peak, and the other that it was at the Stupa of Many Sons. Like the *Butsuji kōshiki,* some texts combine both ideas and suggest that the Buddha transmitted the Dharma secretly at the Stupa of Many Sons and publicly on Vulture Peak. Dōgen held that the Buddha transmitted the Dharma to Mahākāśyapa at Vulture Peak, whereas Keizan followed the explanation that the Buddha transmitted the Dharma to Mahākāśyapa at the Stupa of Many Sons. See Kurebayashi 1960, Tsunoda T. 1997, Ikeda 2010, and Foulk 2017, 2: 229–236.

12. *Emyō* is a metaphor based on the idea that just as the physical body is nourished by food, the Dharma body is nourished by wisdom.

13. Kukkuṭapāda is a place in central India, where Mahākāśyapa is said to be still living.

14. Keiki is a translation of the name Ānanda (J. Anan 阿難). He was a cousin of Śākyamuni and became one of his main disciples. He is said to have had a perfect memory and thus was able to retell all of the Buddha's sermons.

15. According to Chan / Zen tradition, Prajñātāra was the twenty-seventh Indian patriarch and the teacher of Bodhidarma.

16. Shenguang is the birth name of Huike (J. Eka 慧可), regarded as the second patriarch of Chinese Chan.

17. I assume that house of Dong refers to Dongshan Liangjie (J. Tōzan Ryōkai), one of the founders of the Caodong / Sōtō school, because the following sentence states that after thirteen generations Dōgen inherited the Dharma.

18. There are two explanations concerning the origin of the name Caodong / Sōtō 曹洞. One is that the Caodong / Sōtō school was named after the sixth ancestor Huineng 慧能, also called Great Master Caoxi 曹溪大師, and Dongshan Liangjie 洞山良价). This explanation was developed in Japan and is followed in this *kōshiki.*

19. The Taineiji manuscript has *wa* 我 (our) instead of *honchō* 本朝.

Kennin[ji] 建仁[寺].[20] Finally, he crossed the southern sea and climbed the Great White Peak (Dabaifeng 大白峯)[21] [i.e., Tiantongshan 天童山]. He let go of body and mind in a foreign country and explained the original face on his home mountain (*kozan* 故山). He revived the Buddha's sun (*butsunichi* 佛日)[22] and popularized the style of the ancestors (*sofū* 祖風).

It is said that Zen transmits the mind of the Buddha and the scriptures (*kyō* 教) transmit the words of the Buddha. The buddhas and patriarchs (*busso* 佛祖) line up their faces (*kutsubami* 鑣)[23] and mutually show [their] reflections in the mirror. Zen and the scriptures share the same principle (*ki* 揆) and equally show their fists and palms. Foolish people are momentarily stuck in the net of doctrine (*gimō* 義網), but wise men certainly open the gate (*yūkan* 幽關). Here the wind of truth (*shinpō* 眞風) extends afar and unwavering light (*jōkō* 定光) at once appears. In other words, this is the spreading of the one vehicle school (*ichijō shū* 一乘宗) of southern India (*nanten* 南天) [i.e., Bodhidharma's teaching].[24]

And so I generally praised the excellent virtue of the Three Treasures. [In the following,] I will praise in particular the prosperous activities (*kōke* 興化) of the first master of this mountain, Zen Master [Butsuji],[25] and abbreviate in three sections: First, I explain the accomplishments of the Zen master.[26] Second, I explain the manifestation in response (ōke 應化) during his lifetime. Third, I explain the salvation of all beings (*fudo* 普度) after [his] death.

[First section]

First, I explain the accomplishments of the Zen master. The Zen master's real name (*imina* 諱) was Jōkin 紹瑾, called Keizan 瑩山. He was born in the village Tane 多禰 in Echizen 越前.[27] He did not explain his family descent at all.[28] Once he said during a Dharma talk:

---

20. Kenninji was founded by Yōsai 栄西 (or Eisai, 1141–1215), and Dōgen went to this temple to study Rinzai Zen. There he met Myōzen 明全 (1184–1225), Yōsai's disciple, with whom he went to China.

21. Dabaifeng (J. Daihakuhō) is another name for Tiantongshan 天童山 (J. Tendōzan), where Dōgen's master Rujing 如浄 (J. Nyojō, 1163–1228) served as abbot.

22. The Buddha's light or the Buddha's sun is a metaphor for the virtue of a Buddha that drives away the darkness of ignorance like the sun eliminates darkness.

23. *Kutsubami* is a Japanese term for the bit of a horse. I have translated it freely as "faces."

24. *Nanten ichijōshū* 南天一乘宗 (one vehicle school of southern India) is a term for the school founded by Bodhidarma, who was originally from southern India.

25. The Taineiji manuscript has "the founder of this mountain, the National Master" instead of "the first master of this mountain, Zen Master."

26. Throughout the Taineiji manuscript, Keizan is addressed as National Master instead of Zen Master. Keizan received the posthumous title National Master Kōtoku Enmyō in An'ei 1 (1772) before both extant Sōjiji-lineage manuscripts were copied. Because this is a constant variant, I do not indicate every occurrence below.

27. The Yōkōji manuscript states 前越, which I assume is a copying mistake. Two theories exist about the location of Tane in today's Fukui prefecture: one holds that it was in Takefushi Hoyamachō, the other that it was in Sakaigun Maruokachō Yamasakisanga; see Azuma 1974a, 21–24.

28. The account of Keizan's youth and upbringing in this first section is based on the *Tōkoku goso gyōjitsu*, SZ 16: 595.

> In a previous life I was the deity of a Kubara tree (*kubaraju* 倶婆羅樹). In the old days during the time of the Buddha Vipasyin (J. Bibashi 毘婆尸),[29] I realized the state of an arhat. Later I followed the fourth honorable [arhat] Sohinda (J. Sobinda 蘇譜陀) and lived with him together on the snow mountains (*sessen* 雪山) [i.e., the Himalayas] in [the northern continent] Uttara-kuru (J. Hokukurushū 北倶盧洲). Because of these causes, I have now been reborn at the foot of Mt. Haku 白山 in the northern region [of Japan].[30]

One day his honorable mother dreamed that she drank sunlight and then she was pregnant. Immediately she prayed to Kannon Bodhisattva, whom she had carried in her topknot her whole life, to give birth to a holy boy. Every day she performed 1,333 prostrations[31] and recited the "Universal Gate [of Kannon]"[32] thirty-three times. As a result, the delivery was not difficult.[33]

When he was young, he was very intelligent and bright; his mood surpassed [that] of ordinary people.[34] [His] face looked angry, but his nature was calm.[35]

At the age of thirteen, he secretly developed a wish to leave the household. Then he entered the room of Master Koun [Ejō] 孤雲[懐奘] (1198–1280)[36] of Eihei[ji] 永平[寺] and shaved his head [i.e., became a monk].[37]

---

29. Vipasyin (in Pāli, Vipassin) is the first of the seven Buddhas of the past. He is said to have taught Śākyamuni and Maitreya in a former incarnation.

30. This is a variation of the description of Keizan's previous existences in the *Tōkoku goso gyōjitsu* (SZ 16: 595). A more detailed explanation is in Keizan's *Tōkokuki*; see JDZ, 395; KZ 8: 26–33; Kawai 2002, 206–207; and Faure 1996, 30, for an English translation. Interestingly, the *Tōkoku goso gyōjitsu* mistakes Sohinda for the eighth arhat, and in the Yōkōji manuscript the number eight was first written and later corrected to four.

31. Keizan mentions his mother's dream and her devotion to Kannon in his *Tōkokuki*, but the two extant manuscripts of the *Tōkokuki* give different numbers of prostrations: the older manuscript in the archive of Daijōji mentions 3,333, whereas the widely circulating edition (*rufubon* 流布本) states that she performed 1,333; see Kawai 1999, 197; JDZ, 405; and Faure 1996, 35, for an English translation. The *Tōkoku goso gyōjitsu* follows the latter version, SZ 16: 595, and the *Shogaku kaisan Keizan Butsuji zenji gyōjitsu*, SZ 16: 21, gives 333 prostrations.

32. The *Pumen pin* 普門品, or in full the *Guanshiyin pusa pumen pin* 觀世音菩薩普門品 (J. *Kanzeon bosatsu fumon bon*), is the twenty-fifth chapter of the *Lotus Sutra*, T 9: 56c02–58b07. Popularly known as the *Kannon Sutra*, it explains how Kannon helps all sentient beings. See Kubo and Yuyama 2007, 295–302, for an English translation.

33. This passage is again based on the *Tōkoku goso gyōjitsu*, SZ 16: 595. A fuller account of Keizan's mother's prayer and his birth is given in the *Tōkokuki*; see JDZ, 405; Kawai 2002, 222; and Faure 1996, 35, for an English translation.

34. This sentence is a quotation from the *Tōkoku goso gyōjitsu*, SZ 16: 595.

35. A passage in the *Tōkoku goso gyōjitsu* states that Keizan's mother prayed to Kannon to calm her son's temper, and then Keizan became calmer (SZ 16: 595). Keizan himself talks about it in detail in his *Tōkokuki*; see JDZ, 406, and Faure 1996, 35–36, for an English translation.

36. Koun Ejō, Dōgen's closest disciple, became the second abbot of Eiheiji. Originally a monk of the Daruma school, he joined Dōgen's community in Bunryaku 1 (1234). He recorded Dōgen's colloquial instructions in the *Zuimonki* 随聞記 and copied most of the fascicles of Dōgen's *Shōbōgenzō* 正法眼蔵.

37. I assume this passage too is based on the Tōkoku goso *gyōjitsu*, SZ 16: 595.

Then, under Jakuen 寂圓 (1207–1299),[38] the master of the stupa (*tassu* 塔主), he aroused the thought (*hosshin* 發心) [of attaining enlightenment] and received the [bodhisattva] precepts from Zen master Gien 義演 (d. 1314).[39] Suddenly, when he heard the phrase from a sutra, "With the eyes given by their parents, they all see the three thousand worlds,"[40] he awakened (*seigo* 省悟). He immediately instructed (*teishō* 提唱): "If you change the self, you make all things, and if you change all things, you make the self."[41]

Again [Keizan's] eyes were opened (*tenpa* 點破) through Master [Tettsū Gi]kai [徹通義]介 (1219–1309)[42] of Daijō[ji] 大乘[寺] [when] he practiced alone "The ordinary [mind] is the way" (*byōjō ze dō* 平常是道) and rode the black jewel in the darkness.[43] He was appointed the second abbot of Daijō[ji] and cut the *Baojing sanmei* 寶鏡三昧 with the branch [of a tree] [i.e., he received the *Baojing sanmei*].[44]

Learned men (*gakushi* 學士) of other lineages (*takō* 佗泓) were gushing

38. Jakuen (Ch. Jiyuan) was a Chinese monk, who had also been a disciple of Dōgen's teacher Rujing. Some sources suggest that he first met Dōgen in China. When Rujing died, Jakuen came to Japan to join Dōgen's community. After Dōgen's death, he became a disciple of Ejō and later founded Hōkyōji 宝慶寺. His lineage would dominate Eiheiji until the Tokugawa period.

39. Gien was also originally a disciple of Dōgen and became Ejō's disciple after his former master's death. Later, he served as the fourth abbot of Eiheiji. This account is based on the *Tōkoku goso gyōjitsu*, SZ 16: 595, but that text states that Keizan developed the wish to visit other Sōtō masters when he was eighteen and first visiting Jakuen. Gien is not mentioned until after the insight Keizan attained upon hearing the phrase, "With the eyes given by their parents, they all see the three thousand worlds."

40. This sentence is from the nineteenth chapter of the *Lotus Sutra*, T 9: 47c17.

41. The two sentences describing Keizan's awakening are based on the account in the *Tōkoku goso gyōjitsu*, SZ 16: 595. However, just before Keizan's remark, the *kōshiki* author inserted the statement, "He immediately instructed" (*teishō* 提唱), whereas the *Tōkoku goso gyōjitsu* only says that he "reached enlightenment and said." The latter also explains that Keizan was twenty-two when he had this experience.

42. Originally a monk of the Daruma school, Tettsū Gikai entered Dōgen's community in Ninji 2 (1241) together with other monks from the Daruma school. After Dōgen's death, he became a disciple of Ejō, inherited his Dharma, and became the third abbot of Eiheiji. Later, he left Eiheiji and founded Daijōji, where Keizan received his Dharma transmission. Gikai's departure from Eiheiji is often interpreted as a stage of the schism that is supposed to have occurred between different factions in the early Japanese Sōtō community (*sandai sōron* 三代相論).

43. This account is based on Keizan's exchange with Gikai as recounted in the *Tōkoku goso gyōjitsu*, SZ 16: 595. Gikai tested Keizan's understanding of the *kōan* "The ordinary mind is the way," a famous *kōan* included in the *kōan* collection *Wumenguan* 無門關 (J. *Mumonkan*, case 19, T 48: 295b13–b24). Keizan answered that he had ridden on a black jewel in the darkness the previous night. Other biographies of Keizan narrate this encounter in slightly different ways; see Azuma 1974a, 93–95.

44. The *Baojing sanmei* (J. *Hōkyō sanmai*), a Chan text explaining the doctrine of the five ranks and the interfusion of the eternal and the transitory, was written by Dongshan Liangjie. According to the *Tōkoku goso gyōjitsu*, Gikai was satisfied with Keizan's understanding. He therefore foretold that Keizan would popularize Dōgen's teaching and transmitted secret initiation texts of the Sōtō school such as the *Baojing sanmei* to him (SZ 16: 595). The phrase "cut with a branch" presumably means that Keizan received and understood these secret texts.

forth like a spring; the protecting patrons reverberated as a valley. Further, [Keizan] answered the requests for instruction of the assembly. He composed five volumes of the *Denkō*[*roku*] 傳光[録] (Record of the transmission of the light) and [so] expounded the encounters (*kien* 機縁) of the buddhas and patriarchs before (*jūjō* 従上)[45] [him].[46] Was it not at that time that Shiren 師練 (1278–1346)[47] said: "The teaching of [Dō]gen spreads in the northern region"?[48]

One day the master had the idea to resign [from Daijōji].[49] At that time, there were, among others, the daughter of the local regent Sakawa Hachirō Yorichika 酒勾八郎頼親 of the Taira family (Heishi 平氏) of the province of Nō 能州 [i.e., Noto], with the Dharma name Sonin 祖忍, as well as her husband Unno Sanrō Shigeno Nobunao 海野三郎滋野信直 of the province of Shin 信州 [i.e., Shinano]. They invited [Keizan] to come to this province. Together they exhausted their reverence. Moreover, they searched for the tranquility (*yūsui* 幽邃) of this mountain and told [Keizan] about it. It accorded well with the master's plan to retire [from the abbotship of Daijōji]. Then they informed the administration in Kamakura, donated land, and built a temple.[50] With the help [of the *kami*] of the Keta 氣多 [shrine],[51] they allowed the Dharma to be protected and the assembly to be at ease.

[Keizan] called this mountain Tōkoku 洞谷 and so revered the old style of Dongshan 洞山. He called this temple Yōkō 永光 and venerated the

---

45. The term *jūjō* has been crossed out in the Yōkōji manuscript. Both Sōjiji manuscripts contain this expression.

46. The passage on the *Denkōroku* is based on the *Tōkoku goso gyōjitsu,* SZ 16: 595. The *Denkōroku* was first printed in Ansei 4 (1857) in an edition by Busshū Sen'ei 仏洲仙英 (1794–1864). Before this edition, it was handed down in manuscript form, and only a limited number of monks had access to it. Besides the *Tōkoku goso gyōjitsu,* no other premodern biography of Keizan mentions this work; see Azuma 1974a, 113–118. See also Bodiford 2015 and 2017; and Cleary 1990, Cook 2003, and Foulk 2017 for English translations.

47. The scribe of the Yōkōji manuscript mixed up the order of the characters of Shiren and wrote 練師 instead of 師練.

48. This citation from the Dōgen biography included in the *Genkō shakusho* 元亨釈書 compiled by Kokan Shiren 虎関師錬 implies that the spread of Dōgen's teaching was due to the activities of Keizan; see Fujita 2011, 128.

"At that time" (*kono toki* 此時) was later crossed out in the Yōkōji manuscript. The Sōjiji texts follow the original version.

49. From here until "Jōken had a dream and the southern emperor sent questions," the texts of the Yōkōji and Sōjiji transmission lineages completely differ. A translation of the Sōjiji version is given at the end of this appendix.

50. This passage about Keizan's resignation of his abbotship at Daijōji and the invitation to become the founding abbot of a new temple in Noto is based on the *Tōkoku goso gyōjitsu,* SZ 16: 595.

51. Located in Hakui, Keta was the main shrine in Noto and dedicated to the deity Ichinomiya 一宮. According to the *Tōkokuki,* Ichinomiya appeared to Keizan in a dream, requested offerings, and asked Keizan to enshrine a Bishamon 毘沙門 statue as the main object of worship in the storehouse of Yōkōji. Keizan interpreted this dream as a sign that Ichinomiya would protect Yōkōji. See JDZ, 393; KZ 8: 7–12; and Faure 1996, 84, for an English translation.

remaining accomplishments (*yuiretsu* 遺烈) of Dayang [Jingxuan] 大陽[警玄] (943–1027).[52]

[Pilgrims] hung torn straw sandals on the branches of the *enoki* 榎 tree [in front of the temple gate], and [Keizan] established a very special place (*kongoken* 金剛圏) under the pine trees where he arrived.[53] Myōshōgon'in 妙莊嚴院 [i.e., the abbot's quarters] was opened at a special place, and a land filled with fragrance (*kōshaku kokudo* 香積國土) manifested itself at this site. Furthermore, Tomosada 朝定 built Saishōden 最勝殿 [i.e., the Buddha hall] and solemnly opened the place of practice for prayers for the imperial court.[54] [Fujiwara] Iemasa [藤原]家方 built the Fukōdo 普光堂 [i.e., the Dharma hall], and there [Keizan] explained his Dharma lineage for the first time. The officer (*kō* 公)[55] [Fujiwara] Yukifusa [藤原]行房 (d. 1337) wrote name plaques and made these protectors of the temple.[56] The nun (*ni* 尼)[57] Sonin worshiped Kannon and lived in Enzū[in] 圓通[院]; Jōken had a dream[58] and the southern emperor [i.e., Emperor Godaigo 後醍醐天皇 (1288–1339)] sent questions.[59]

---

52. Dayang Jingxuan (J. Daiyō Kyōgen) was a Chinese Chan master who revived the Caodong / Sōtō tradition. Keizan rendered the name Daiyō 大陽 (Great Sun) as Yōkō 永光 (Eternal Light). The *Tōkoku goso gyōjitsu* does not elucidate the naming of Tōkokuzan Yōkōji, but Keizan provides a detailed explanation in his *Tōkokuki* and also identifies Daiyō as the source of the name Yōkō; see JDZ, 395; KZ 8: 21–22; and Faure 1996, 53, for an English translation. Later, however, a monk crossed out Dayang in the Yōkōji manuscript and wrote "Eihei" 永平 [i.e., Dōgen] next to it, seeking in this way to affiliate Yōkōji with Eiheiji and Dōgen, the founder of the Sōtō school. Interestingly, even Hakugan kept "Eihei" in his revised edition of the *Butsuji kōshiki* (Abe 2019, 88). In his headnote, Hakugan cites the first half of Keizan's explanation of the name in the *Tōkokuki,* and so he must have been aware that the *kōshiki* text deviates from the original account, but he did not change this passage or add any explanation to it.

53. This sentence is based on a dream that Keizan recorded in his *Tōkokuki:* after he had seen the future site of Yōkōji for the first time, he dreamed that many monks would come and hang their straw sandals on the *enoki* tree close to the gate, an omen that his temple would prosper; see JDZ, 392 and 397; KZ 8: 2 and 36–37; and Faure 1996, 114–115, for an English translation. This dream is also mentioned in the *Tōkoku goso gyōjitsu,* SZ 16: 595.

54. The first part of the sentence is a slightly changed quotation from the *Tōkoku goso gyōjitsu,* SZ 16: 596. "Furthermore" (*shikanominarazu* 加旃) at the beginning of the sentence was crossed out later.

55. The term *kō* was also crossed out later.

56. Later, "seven halls" (*shichidō* 七堂) was added in front of "name plaques." Keizan had mentioned in his *Tōkokuki* that Yōkōji was extremely fortunate to have received seven imperial name plagues, because temples would usually receive only one or two; see JDZ, 431, and KZ 8: 274.

57. The term *ni* was crossed out later.

58. Jōken, the head priest of Morookadera, was said to have entrusted this temple to Keizan. This was the origin of Sōjiji.

59. Godaigo was the first emperor of the southern court. Both Yōkōji and Sōjiji possess documents claiming that Emperor Godaigo, after sending ten questions to Keizan and feeling deeply satisfied with Keizan's answers, declared the temple to be an imperial prayer temple. However, both documents are later forgeries. For Yōkōji's version, see *Jūshu gitai* 十種疑滞, dated Gen'ō 2 (1320), JDZ, 376–380, or KZ 9: 227–261. For Sōjiji's version, see *Jūshu chokumon* 十種勅問, dated Genkō 2 (1322), JDZ, 381–386, or KZ 9: 263–325.

[Keizan] responded nine times to the requests of people and served as abbot at eight places of practice.[60] On this mountain especially, the five elders (*gorō* 五老)[61] and the four wise men (*shitetsu* 四哲)[62] protect this one peak (*ichihō* 一峯);[63] and the three sages (*sanshō* 三聖)[64] and the two heavenly kings (*niten* 二天)[65] push the two wheels [of food and doctrine] (*nirin* 二輪). The so-called mountain of wholesome roots is a forest of virtue.

The Zen master continuously taught with lion's speech (*shiku* 獅口)[66] and did not get tired, but physical weakness (*horyū no genshitsu* 蒲柳幻質) made him gasp for breath and exhausted him. Here he kindly let Meihō 明峯 (1277–1350), Mugai 無涯 (d. 1351), Gasan 峩山 (1276–1366), and Koan 壺菴 (d. 1341) venerate the high remains of the five elders and further encouraged

60. According to the *Sansō yuiseki teradera okibumiki,* Keizan instructed his disciples that the eight temples Yōkōji, Enzūin, Hōōji, Kōkōji, Hōshōji, Jōjūji, Daijōji, and Sōjiji should be upheld by monks of his lineage; see *Yōkōji no meihō,* 34, for a photograph of this document. Apart from Daijōji, where Keizan had received his Dharma transmission, the other temples were all founded by Keizan. Jōmanji, however, is not mentioned in this source. Adding Jōmanji to the list would confirm the claim that Keizan opened eight temples and served as abbot at nine.

61. The five elders refers to the five masters—Rujing, Dōgen, Ejō, Gikai, and Keizan—whose relics Keizan enshrined on the Peak of the Five Elders (Gorōhō 五老峰) at Yōkōji; see *Tōkokuki,* JDZ, 411–416; Azuma 2002, 20–21; and *Yōkōji no meihō,* 30 and 76–77.

62. The four wise men (or disciples) are Meihō Sotetsu 明峰素哲 (1277–1350), Mugai Chikō 無涯智洪 (d. 1351), Gasan Jōseki 峨山韶碩 (1276–1366), and Koan Shikan 壺菴至簡 (d. 1341).

63. The Taineiji manuscript has this variant: "On this mountain especially, the five shrines and the four *kami* protect the Three Treasures." If we assume that monks at Yōkōji first composed the *kōshiki,* the editor(s) of the Sōjiji version replaced the characters 老 and 哲 with 社 and 神. They further changed "one peak" to "Three Treasures." Of course, *kami* have been worshiped at Sōjiji, but I could not find any source that explicitly mentions five shrines and four *kami* at Sōjiji.

64. In the case of Yōkōji, the three sages are Śākyamuni Buddha, Kannon, and Kokūzō 虚空蔵, who are enshrined as a triad in the Buddha hall called Saishōden. Keizan adapted the name Saishō from the title of the sutra *Zuishengwang jing* 最勝王経 (J. *Saishōō kyō*), in which Kannon and Kokūzō sit next to Śākyamuni; see *Tōkoku goso gyōjitsu,* SZ 16: 596; *Tōkokuki,* JDZ, 395; and KZ 8: 22. Who the three sages are in the case of Sōjiji is not easy to determine. According to Keizan's *Sōjiji chūkō engi,* the two light-emitting bodhisattvas Kannon and Jizō were supposed to be enshrined on the second floor of the main gate. Keizan wrote that the empresses in China and Japan prayed to these bodhisattvas for a safe birth for their children and the women who pray at Sōjiji would receive the same benefits; see Monzenshi 2, 11–12. But these are only two bodhisattvas. The editor(s) of the Sōjiji version might have simply copied this phrase from the Yōkōji version without changing it.

65. According to the *Tōkoku goso gyōjitsu* and the *Tōkokuki,* the two heavenly kings are Bishamon or Tamonten 多聞天 and Karaten 迦羅天; see SZ 16: 596 and JDZ, 394 and 398; KZ 8: 12 and 37. Of course, the *Tōkoku goso gyōjitsu* describes the life of Keizan at Yōkōji. Whether the Sōjiji version refers to the same deities is unclear; other pairings would also be possible.

66. Lion (*shishi* 獅子, sometimes written as 師子) is an epithet for Śākyamuni Buddha, who is the king among humans in the same way that the lion is the king of all animals. Other eminent monks, who preach to large audiences, are also called lions. The "words of a lion" is a metaphor for the teaching of the Buddha or an eminent monk.

the practice of the four friends (*shihai* 四輩).[67] His last wish was very important. Then in Shōchū 2 (1325) on the fifteenth day of the eighth month, Keizan wrote a verse and passed away. [His disciples] cremated [him] and received relics. He was fifty-eight years old and had sat for forty-seven summers.[68] His assistant Daichi 大智 (1290–1366)[69] entered Dentōin 傳燈院 and built a stupa.[70] The southern court ordered that he be given the title Zen Master Butsuji 佛慈禅師.[71]

Thinking about it, if [Keizan] had not fostered the Dharma and benefited all sentient beings (*kōbō rishō* 興法利生) five hundred lifetimes before his present manifestation,[72] then how could he have become a great master for humans and heavenly beings in this world of defilements and evil (*jakuaku se* 濁惡世)? Therefore, in order to repay the kindness received, we should intone a verse and perform a prostration. We sing a verse:

---

67. In the Taineiji manuscript, the first part of the sentence reads: "Here he let Master Jō [i.e., Gasan Jōseki] follow in his footsteps and respect the Ten Rules (*jūjō kikyō* 十條亀鏡)." The editor(s) of this text probably refer here to the *Tōji jūgejō no kikyō* 当寺十箇条之亀鏡, a document laying out the rules for the monks of Sōjiji. It is dated Shūchō 1 (1324) and signed by Keizan. It had been assumed that this document was handwritten by him, but recent research has shown that it is a later composition. Comparing the two versions, the Yōkōji version reads more smoothly and its content is more logical, particularly since the Taineiji manuscript does not mention Keizan's four disciples before concluding the sentence with Keizan's encouragement of the four friends. This conspicuous omission supports the thesis that the *Butsuji kōshiki* was originally composed at Yōkōji.

68. The statement here that Keizan was a monk for forty-seven summers implies that he was ordained when he was twelve. Other sources, such as the *Tōkoku goso gyōjitsu,* SZ 16: 596, state that he sat for forty-six years. To my knowledge, no other biographical source claims that Keizan sat for forty-seven summers or was ordained when he was twelve. Even this *kōshiki* states that Keizan left the household at the age of thirteen. Interestingly, Kohō Hakugan did not correct this statement in his revised edition of the *Butsuji kōshiki;* see Abe 2019, 88. And even Bonjō, author of the *Tōjō dentō kōshiki,* cited this passage without correcting it; see ZSZ 2: 865.

69. Daichi had studied under Keizan in his youth. Later he visited many other masters and also traveled to China. Following his return to Japan, he joined Keizan's community again, and after Keizan's death, he received Dharma transmission from Keizan's disciple Meihō.

70. This sentence is a quotation from the *Tōkoku goso gyōjitsu,* SZ 16: 596. The Taineiji manuscript does not include this sentence. Instead, after the sentence that the disciples obtained relics, we find the sentence: "The stupa is called Dentō[in]."

71. Emperor Gomurakami 後村上天皇 (1328–1368) is supposed to have bestowed the name Zen Master Butsuji to Keizan in Shōhei 8 (1353). But the bestowal of the posthumous title Zen Master Butsuji is still a matter of debate, because Gasan is said to have declined it. For a discussion of this issue, see Takeuchi K. 1998 and Satō Shūkō 1999, 21–24.

In the Taineiji manuscript, we find an additional sentence here: "Around four hundred winters later, the present emperor (*kōjō* 皇上) especially ordered and bestowed the title National Master Kōtoku Enmyō 弘德圓明國師." Kōjō is a term for the present emperor. Therefore, we can assume that this sentence was first added when Emperor Gomomozono 後桃園天皇 (1758–1779) bestowed this title.

72. The statement about five hundred lifetimes is a quotation from the *Tōkoku goso gyōjitsu,* SZ 16: 595. Keizan does mention in his *Tōkokuki* that he was reincarnated five hundred times in order to spread the Dharma and bring profit to all beings after he attained arhatship; see JDZ, 395, and KZ 8: 26–33.

We bow our heads to the honorable Butsuji.
The Dharma nature is pure and clear as the moon.
When the mind of sentient beings is like still water,
The reflection of feeling and response (*kannō* 感應)[73] will appear in it.[74]

Humbly prostrating ourselves, we take refuge in Zen Master Butsuji, who benefits all sentient beings.[75] (When finished [chanting] three prostrations.)

[Second section]
Second, I explain the manifestation in response during his lifetime. When the Zen master was first at Jōman[ji] 城万[寺] in Unbe 海部, he widely sent out the bright light of the one precept (*ichikai kōmyō* 一戒光明) and ordained around seventy people, such as [Gen]ka Tekkyō [眼]可鐵鏡 (d. 1321).[76] Furthermore, even Butsurin 佛林[77] [i.e., Kyōō Unryō 恭翁運良, 1267–1341] and Sankō 三光[78] [i.e., Kohō Kakumyō 孤峰覚明, 1271–1361] of different schools

73. *Kannō* describes the communication between a practitioner and buddhas or bodhisattvas. A practitioner's feeling evokes a response in a buddha or bodhisattva, or vice versa. The verse here refers to the response of Keizan.

74. This verse is a variant of the verse sung at the end of the first section of the *Rakan kōshiki;* only the name of the object of worship in the first line and "*rakan*" in the last one have been changed. See chap. 2, n. 72. In the Taineiji manuscript, we find another verse:

Buddha's true Dharma has two [sides]:
Namely, doctrine (*kyō* 教) and enlightenment (*shō* 證) as its essence.
If people live who embrace, explain, and practice [the teaching accordingly],
[The true Dharma] abides in this world.

This verse is from the *Jushelun* 倶舎論 (J. *Kusharon*), T 29: 152b1–2, and it is also used as the verse for the second section of the *Rakan kōshiki.* According to the explanation following this verse in the *Jushelun, kyō* are sutras (*kaikyō* 契經, i.e., sermons), regulations (*jōbuku* 調伏, a translation of the term *vinaya*), and *abhidharma* (*taihō* 對法, philosophical treatise collections) (152b03–04). These three stand for the three categories of Buddhist doctrine (*sanzō* 三藏). And *shō* are the factors of enlightenment (*bodai bunpō* 菩提分法) of the three vehicles, i.e., the vehicles of śrāvaka (*shōmon* 声聞), pratyekabuddha (*engaku* 縁覚), and bodhisattva (*bosatsu* 菩薩) (152b04).

75. The Taineiji manuscript does not contain words of worship after the verses of the sections.

76. Genka Tekkyō was one of Keizan's first disciples at Jōmanji in Einin 4 (1296). He served as the head monk at Jōmanji and also at Daijōji and Yōkōji later; see Azuma 1974a, 85 and 138.

77. Kyōō Unryō was a monk of the Hōtō branch 法灯派 of the Rinzai school who received Dharma transmission from Muhon Kakushin 無本覚心 (1207–1298). He was a Dharma brother of Kohō Kakumyō. Unryō received the titles Zen Master Butsue 仏慧禅師 and Zen Master Butsurin Enichi 仏林慧日禅師. He also studied under Keizan and became the third abbot at Daijōji.

78. Kohō Kakumyō was a monk of the Hōtō branch of the Rinzai school who also studied under Keizan. He instructed Emperor Godaigo and received the title National Master Kokuzai 国済国師 from him. Later, Emperor Gomurakami 後村上天皇 (1328–1368) gave him the title National Master Sankō 三光国師, and it was through Kakumyō's intermediation that Emperor Gomurakami is said to have bestowed the posthumous title Zen Master Butsuji on Keizan.

(*isei* 異姓) bathed in the light of the precepts (*kaikō* 戒光)[79] and received a prophecy. The donors Sakawa [i.e., Sonin] and Unno[80] [i.e., Shigeno Nobunao] thoroughly consumed the taste of the Dharma and took the tonsure (*teido* 剃度).

The four great disciples [Meihō] Sotetsu, [Mugai] Chikō, [Gasan] Jōseki, and [Koan] Shikan were formerly dragons of the doctrine and tigers of the rules (*giryū ritsuko* 義龍律虎).[81] But finally they entered the melting pot [of Keizan] and all became great vessels. Thereafter, the far descendants of the four wise men filled Japan (Tōkai 東海) and built around twenty thousand Zen temples. The bright mirror of the five elders[82] brightens high the northern heaven; [since then] around five hundred years have passed.

When [Dōgen] fully showed (*zentei* 全提) the seal of the ancestors (*soin* 祖印), the exoteric house and the esoteric gate (*kenka mitsumon* 顯家密門) recommended his teaching (*shū* 宗), which is called the rules (*shūgi* 宗儀) of Eihei [i.e., Dōgen]. When [Keizan] popularized the etiquette (*menzetsu* 綿蕝), the offering of incense in the morning and chanting in the evening (*shinkō yūju* 晨香夕誦) follow his regulations (*nori* 則), which are called the *Keizan shingi* 瑩山清規 (Pure rules of Keizan).[83]

At the black stone, the mountain spirit stays for a long time in the jewel belt. In the deep pine tree grove, Isurugi 石動 shows sweet pears for eternity.[84]

---

79. *Kaikō* usually describes the virtue that is obtained by observing the precepts. But here it is an abbreviation of the previously mentioned *ichikai kōmyō* 一戒光明.

80. Many members of the Sakawa family supported Keizan and the early Yōkōji community. Sakawa here presumably indicates Sonin, the daughter of Sakawa Hachirō Yorichika. She was the founding patron of Yōkōji together with her husband Unno Sanrō Shigeno Nobunao. After the death of her husband, she became a nun and lived in Enzūin. Her Dharma name was Sonin. Unno's Dharma name was Myōjō 妙浄; see Azuma 1974a, 217.

81. In the Taineiji manuscript the four monks are named Tetsu 哲, Kō 洪, Seki 碩, and Kan 簡. See n. 62 above.

82. In the Taineiji manuscript "two treasure moons" was written instead of "bright mirror of the five elders." Two moons refers to a well-known exchange between Keizan and Gasan in which Gasan was asked whether he knows that there are two moons. When Gasan said no, Keizan replied that someone who does not understand this cannot become a Zen master. See *Sōji dainise Gasan oshō gyōjō*, SZ 17: 263.

83. The Taineiji manuscript states "pure rules of the national master" (*kokushi no shingi* 國師清規) instead of *Keizan shingi*.

84. Isurugi refers to Sekidōsan 石動山, a sacred mountain to the northeast of Yōkōji that is also called Isurugiyama. Here the *kōshiki* hints at the protection Yōkōji is thought to have received from the *kami* of Sekidōsan. In the Taineiji manuscript, we find: "At the deep green pine trees, [the dragon king] Sāgara (Shakatsu 娑竭) holds high a light of the night for a long time. At the thickly growing oak tree, the mountain *kami* shows sweet pears for eternity." This must allude to a legend associated with Sōjiji, but I have not been able to find a source for any such legend. However, in Sōtō *kirigami* 切紙, the deity of Hakusan, who is thought to have protected Sōtō Zen and was a vital factor in the expansion of Sōtō Zen, is usually associated with the dragon king (*ryūten* 竜天); see Ishikawa 2001, 1: 352–371. Young monks today still receive from their master a roll entitled *Ryūtenjiku* 竜天軸 inscribed with the text: "The dragon king, protector of the Dharma, great good deity. Hakusan, wondrous principle, *daigongen* 大権現"; see Sekiguchi

In the days when the Zen master lived in this world, he sat on a broken cushion, and for forty years he did not sleep on the nights of both the seventh and ninth days [of the twelfth month] (*shichiku no ryōya* 七九両夜).[85] When he faced the assembly and played with a broken wooden dipper, he did not spill one drop of the Sōtō spring (*tōgen* 洞源) for thirty years. [He] taught in alleys and discoursed in the lanes (*kōsetsu kaidan* 巷説街談) and earnestly explained practice and realization (*gyōshō* 行證). Even a brush as big as a mountain and ink as wide as an ocean cannot exhaust the traces of [his] teaching (*keseki* 化迹). Therefore, we intone a verse and praise his manifestation in response. We sing a verse:

The monk who realized enlightenment five hundred existences ago
Completed the practice to reach enlightenment and has an immeasurable body.
We only wish that he may widely save the world of sentient beings,
May he not abandon the wheel of the correct vow for eternity.[86]

Humbly prostrating ourselves, we take refuge in Zen Master Butsuji, who benefits all sentient beings.

[Third section]
Third, I explain the salvation of all beings after his death. Now we have been born four hundred years later[87] and gather here every year on the day of [his]

1995: 34–35, and Azuma 1996, 40–41, and 2002: 67. Azuma (1996, 41) assumes that this custom originated with a text written by Keizan himself, so the mountain spirit showing sweet pears in the *kōshiki* could be an allusion to Hakusan.

85. The Buddha is thought to have reached enlightenment on the eighth day of the twelfth month, and Huike is remembered on the tenth day of the twelfth month for having cut off his arm and offered it to Bodhidharma to show his sincerity. The zazen begun the night before these two observances commemorate the Buddha and Huike. Keizan mentioned his forty years of nightlong zazen practice on the seventh and ninth days of the twelfth month in a sermon delivered on the tenth day of the twelfth month of Genkō 3 (1323); see *Tōkokuki,* JDZ, 420; KZ 8: 195 and 198; and Kawai 2002, 247. The *Keizan shingi* also cites Keizan's practice and suggests that it should be a regular observance; see T 82: 449b12–b14.

86. The Yōkōji manuscript contains a note next to the last line indicating that the ritual handbook for the cantor reads "wheel of the true Dharma" (*shōbōrin* 正法輪), making the last line: "May he not abandon the wheel of the true Dharma for eternity." The Taineiji manuscript has this verse instead:

We now offer food
And wish that we may obtain the greatest rewards;
The attachments to all afflictions,
May we overcome [them] and may [they] not be strong.

This verse is from the *Nirvāṇa Sutra,* T 12: 612b19–20. It is also used as the verse of the second section in the *Nehan kōshiki* of the Sōtō school, as well as in the *Nehan kōshiki* attributed to Genshin; see ZSZ 2: 746, and *Dainihon bukkyō zensho* 33: 184.

87. The Taineiji manuscript has instead "five hundred years."

passing. Although there is no one [among us] whose three modes of activity (*sangō* 三業)[88] are pure, we are fortunate to have joined the numbers of the disciples of [Keizan's] transmitted teaching. We revere his wondrous remains and hold this memorial service (*saie* 齋會). There are no offerings from patrons, but we offer as many mountain flowers and vegetables as we can. [We] are but a few distant descendants (*unson* 雲孫)[89] from various provinces; we have walked through rain and frost, protected by bamboo hats and shoes, and have gathered [here].

If we think respectfully, the bright moon stays long in front of the Peak of the Five Elders (Gorōhō 五老峯)[90] and shows intimately the eternal form of the Dharma body. The running stream (*seisui* 逝水) flows for eternity in the valley of Tōkoku 洞谷,[91] and captures (*tozasu* 鎖す)[92] the pure voice (*bonnon* 梵音)[93] and the sound of the rolling tide (*kaichō* 海潮).[94] All day long we can hear the talk (*keigai* 謦欬) of the great ancestor (*taiso* 大祖); why always use the guidance of other people? Stubborn ears (*ganji* 頑耳) turn away from listening from beginning to end, whereas wisdom eyes (*egen* 慧眼) end the arising and going of limited opinions.[95]

One step forward, one step backward, and we still do not depart (*hanarezu* 離れず)[96] from the mountain of wholesome roots. One veneration, one prostration, and together we enter the forest of virtue.

We have a profound mind [deeply seeking enlightenment] (*jinshin* 深心) and offer [it] to the worlds as numerous as dust motes. This is called the offering to repay kindness (*hōji kuyō* 報慈供養). We have this aspiration for enlightenment (*dōshin* 道心) and extend it to the world. This is called the salvation of all beings after his death.

---

88. The three modes of activity are body, speech, and mind.

89. The Taineiji manuscript has *unjō* 雲仍 instead of *unson* 雲孫.

90. The Taineiji manuscript has "on the top of Shogaku" 諸嶽 instead of "in front of the Peak of the Five Elders."

91. The Taineiji manuscript has "in front of the gate of Sōji[ji]" instead of "in the valley of Tōkoku."

92. In the Taineiji manuscript, we find *gensu* 現す (manifest) instead of *tozasu*.

93. *Bonnon* describes a beautiful voice and is used as a metaphor for a buddha's voice. It is one of the thirty-two marks of a buddha. The term also describes the voice of Brahma. Here I assume that *bonnon* represents the voice of Keizan.

94. *Kaichō* is the preaching of a buddha. *Kaichōon* 海潮音 describes a buddha's voice, which is as loud as the ocean and therefore can be heard widely. The phrase *bonnon kaichōon* 梵音海潮音 is a quotation from the *Kannon Sutra*, i.e., the twenty-fifth chapter of the *Lotus Sutra*, T 9: 58a26, where it represents the virtue of Kannon. Here the expression is used to describe the voice of Keizan, which is thought to still be present at his temple.

95. I have translated this sentence freely, because the original seems to be corrupt. The Yōkōji manuscript has 頑耳反聞入流了慧眼絶見發見去, and the Taineiji manuscript states 頑耳反聞亡流了慧眼絶見發見. The original sentence might have been 頑耳反聞入聞了慧眼絶見發見去.

96. In the Yōkōji manuscript, 離 was crossed out and 出 (leave) written next to it. The Taineiji manuscript follows the earlier version of the Yōkōji text.

We should intone a verse and transfer the merit universally. We sing a verse:[97]

We wish that this merit
Extends universally to all.
May we and all sentient beings
Together realize the Buddha way.[98]

Humbly prostrating ourselves, we take refuge in the luminous mirror (*heikan* 炳鑑) of the Three Treasures and the wisdom (*shōchi* 照知)[99] of the five elders.[100]

Textual Variant from the First Section of the Taineiji Manuscript[101]

In Ōchō 1 (1311), [Keizan] stepped down from the temple affairs [of Daijōji] and surprised [the monks] with the drum [announcing the ascending the hall sermon] for [his] resignation (*taiku* 退鼓).[102] The local regents and the common people yearned from afar (*fū o hoshite* 風を望て) and venerated [him] deeply. Some people built temples, invited the master, and let him live there. These were Jōman[ji] 城満[寺], Jōjū[ji] 浄住[寺], and Kōkō[ji] 光孝[寺].[103]

Then Shigeno no Nobunao 滋野信直 of Nō province [i.e., Noto] and his wife of the Taira family respected his virtue, donated one mountain in the district of Sakai 酒井, built a temple compound, invited [Keizan], and made him the founding abbot. Together they exhausted their reverence. Therefore, [Keizan] came, and when he arrived at this temple [i.e., Yōkōji], the peaks were lined up and enclosed a flat area that was like a grindstone. He truly felt completely pleased.

[Jōken] had a wondrous dream of Kannon and [entrusted his] temple to the master. [Keizan] followed Jōken's deep request and changed [the temple] from a teaching (*kyō* 教) to a Zen [temple]. He named the mountain

97. In the Yōkōji manuscript, there are a few later entries by hand around the verse, which I have not translated here (see Appendix 7).

98. This *gāthā*, usually called *Fuekō* 普回向 (Universal transfer for merit), is a verse from the *Lotus Sutra*, T 9: 24c21–22. It is known to have been chanted in Genshin's *Nijūgo zanmai shiki;* see NSS 4: 254. It is sung in *kōshiki* and other rituals to transfer the merit that has been accumulated through the performance of the ritual. All *kōshiki* of the Sōtō school use this verse either at the end of the last section or as the transfer of merit following the verse of the final section.

99. In the Yōkōji manuscript, 昭知 is written instead of 照知. I assume that this is a scribal mistake. Therefore, I provided 照知 above. Hakugan also used 照知 in his new edition.

100. This last sentence is not included in the Taineiji manuscript.

101. See n. 49 above.

102. Before his resignation, an abbot usually ascends the Dharma hall to deliver a sermon (*jōdō* 上堂), which is announced by the sound of the large drum.

103. In both Sōjiji manuscripts, the order of the characters for Kōkōji has been reversed (孝光 instead of 光孝). I have rendered the temple name correctly above.

Shōgaku 諸嶽[104] and saved the old name [given by] Gyōki 行基 (668–749).[105] He wrote Sōji on the temple and responded to the wondrous talisman (*reifu* 靈符) of the bodhisattva.[106]

The water of the blue valley river was pure, and [Keizan] put a twinning vine stick on the ground. The moss of the white cliff was smooth, and [Keizan] mended torn clothes [there]. The Gate of the Three Pine Trees (*sanshō* 三松) [widely] opened like the character eight 八.[107] The sweet spring of the one lineage fills one hundred rivers.

Furthermore, the emperor sent ten questions, promoted [Sōjiji], and made it a prayer temple (*kudokuji* 功徳寺) of the imperial household. [Kohō] Kakumyō drank bitterness for three years [i.e., he practiced for three years under Keizan] and then he received the transmission of the bodhisattva precepts. The officer [Fujiwara] Yukifusa wrote the name plaque and made it a protector of the temple (*jichin* 寺鎮).[108] The elder Gasan protected the Dharma robe and supported the sagely guidance (*shōke* or *seika* 聖化). [Keizan] opened the place of practice for prayers for the fortune of the imperial court (*shukuri* 祝釐) and vigorously set up a Dharma seat for imperially appointed abbots (*shusse no hōseki* 出世法席).

104. Sōjiji's original name was Morookadera 諸嶽寺. Keizan used these characters for the mountain name of Sōjiji and changed the reading to Shogakuzan 諸嶽山.

105. According to the *Sōjiji chūkō engi,* the Morooka Kannon hall (i.e., Morookadera) was originally built by the famous monk Gyōki.

106. Because Morookadera was a temple for Kannon worship and Jōken is said in the *Sōjiji kaibyaku no engi* to have dreamt that Kannon requested him to entrust the temple to Keizan, we can assume that "bodhisattva" refers to Kannon here. *Sōji* is also a translation of the term *dhāraṇī,* so the explanation given about the temple name can also be interpreted as a reference to *dhāraṇī.*

107. Three pine trees were planted next to the first gate of Sōjiji; hence it is called Sanshōkan 三松関 (Gate of the Three Pine Trees); see Satō M. 2011, 8. Before Keizan took over at Sōjiji, he is supposed to have had wondrous dreams. In one he saw the main gate of Sōjiji opening like the character 八; see *Sōjiji chūkō engi.*

108. This is also mentioned in the *Sōjiji chūkō engi.* However, the historicity that Yukifusa wrote a name plaque for Sōjiji is highly questionable; see Azuma 1974a, 246.

Appendix 3

Kohō Hakugan's Preface to the *Taiso Butsuji kōshiki* (Translation)

Preface to the *Butsuji kōshiki*

All Buddhas appear in this world for just one great purpose alone (*ichidaiiji inen* 一大事因縁).[1] For us, it is so again with Great Master Butsuji. Originally from the first turning of the wheel of Dharma until the evening of the complete nirvāṇa at Tōkokusan 洞谷山, the Great Master widely saved humans and heavenly beings. He surrounded himself with dragons and elephants (*ryūzō* 龍象)[2] and wanted to let them unfold the Buddha's wisdom and obtain purity. He explained the profound and expounded the marvelous. One blow with a stick and one shout (*ichibō ikkatsu* 一棒一喝) and the matter is resolved. Thus the Buddhist teaching of Jōyō 承陽 [i.e., Dōgen] spreads in the worlds as numerous as the sands of the Ganges. Truly, you have to hear this!

The Great Master answered the ten questions of Emperor Godaigo. [His] logic and righteousness, as well as [his] profound explanations, deeply satisfied the mind of the emperor, who bestowed the imperial edict [recognizing Yōkōji as] the first training place of the Sōtō school whose abbot wears the purple robe. It is truly a rare honor. Now, in the fall of the year of the water dragon, we respectfully perform the five hundred and fiftieth memorial service for the emperor.

In this context, I publish the *Butsuji kōshiki* and offer [it] to the Peak of the Five Elders. I let the monks of the whole mountain regularly perform it, and wish that the narrow-minded among the present-day patch-robed monks of the Sōtō school [may] bathe in the wind of the ancestors and open the eye that penetrates all things (*katsugan* 活眼) through the informal sermon on the venerable Great Master. Truly, a ceremonial book [for this *kōshiki*] has

Hakugan's revised edition of the *Butsuji kōshiki* was published in 1892 and reprinted in 1924. The *Kōshiki database* contains a facsimile of the 1924 edition (no. 361); for a typographical reprint, see Abe 2019.

1. This is a quotation from the "Skillful Means" (*Hōben bon* 方便品) chapter of the *Lotus Sutra,* T 9: 7a21–22.

2. Originally, the term *ryūzō* (lit. dragons and elephants or dragon elephant) referred to a great elephant (Skt. *hastināga*), but it is often used as a metaphor for superior practitioners.

existed secretly in the treasure house of Tōkokusan for almost two hundred years.

Recently, with two or three disciples I revised it, gave it to a woodblock carver, and [now] distribute it in the world to like-minded men. Further, I wish that it may allow all sentient beings to enter the way of the Buddha's wisdom.

Meiji 25 (1892), October 1
Tōkokusan, the Peak of the Five Elders, the keeper of the stupa, five hundred and tenth abbot, the monk Kohō Hakugan humbly wrote this.

Appendix 4

Azegami Baisen's Preface to the *Tōjō dentō kōshiki* (Translation)

Preface to the *Dentō kōshiki*

This *kōshiki* praises his [i.e., Keizan's] virtue. Generally, when there is virtue, then certainly there will be praise. Thinking about this, you should study the teachings in prose and verse of the various sutras. Our Great Ancestor (Taiso 太祖), the National Master, lifted up one light high at the precious temple Sōji[ji], and so he brightened the interior of the nine levels [of the heavens] above, and illuminated the outer limits of the eight directions below. The term Sōtō and the name of this mountain were both inaugurated by imperial order. His many children and grandchildren divided [his] one light and made ten million lights. Now, around five hundred eighty years have passed and around fifteen thousand temples have been founded. Everywhere [his teaching] breaks and brightens the darkness for certain. His great virtue was exactly like this.

Why should we not produce a *kōshiki?* Since the old times of the rotating abbots, this ceremony has been performed year after year, but a complete ceremonial book for it did not yet exist. [I], the mountain monk, have secretly lamented [about it] for years. Therefore, I asked the former *godō* 後堂 of this mountain, Master Bonjō of Myōkō[ji] in Tsukushi [i.e., Kyūshū], to supplement and revise it. Then I proofread, published, and entitled [it] *Dentō kōshiki.*

Moreover, [the *Dentō kōshiki*] should spread in the world. I wish that without interruption [his] grandchildren value the blessing of the Great Ancestor and gather at the source of [his] lineage [at Sōjiji].

Meiji 24 (1891), on a day of the summer training retreat[1]
The present abbot of Sōji[ji], Dharma grandchild Baisen, respectfully wrote [this].

Azegami's preface to the original woodblock print edition of the *Tōjō dentō kōshiki,* published in 1893, is not included in the photographic reproduction of the *kōshiki* found in ZSZ 2: 853–869. See Appendix 9 for a photographic reproduction of the preface, *shikimon,* and postscript in the original print edition.

1. At Sōjiji, the summer training retreat was conducted from April 15 to July 15.

Appendix 5

Bukkan Bonjō's Postscript to the *Tōjō dentō kōshiki* (Translation)

Postscript to the *Dentō kōshiki*

The abbot of Nōzan[1] 能山 [i.e., Sōjiji], Zen master Hōun Fugai 法雲普蓋 [Azegami Baisen], asked me from far away to compile a *Taiso kokushi dentō kōshiki* 太祖國師傳燈講式 (*Kōshiki* on the transmission of the light by the Great Ancestor and National Master). Because his order was sincere, I could not refuse. Now, I do not look back on awkward sentences; I chose this and that and finally produced a one-volume ceremonial book. I only worry that it may be difficult to escape the criticism of the wise. I deeply wish that the superior disciples of the National Master do not criticize the clumsiness of the sentences. [May they] only perform this ceremony with sincerity and thus repay the inexhaustible mercy of the National Master. If we are not yet able to do this, we are not descendants of the transmission of the light. We would only be slaves of Han Yu 韓愈 (J. Kan Yu) and Ouyang Xiu 歐陽脩 (J. Ōyō Shū) in vain.[2] Wholeheartedly, I ask that the Three Treasures verify and the buddhas and patriarchs clearly witness [this composition]. In this context, I have composed two verses in lieu of a postscript.

In the past, the Great Ancestor transmitted one light.
The one light was divided into one hundred thousand lights.
The lights continue to burn and the radiance has no end.
Eternally [the lights] break the darkness. This is his [i.e., Keizan's] light.

Bonjō's postscript is included in ZSZ 2: 868–869. See Appendix 9 for a photographic reproduction of the postscript as it appeared in the original woodblock print edition of 1893.

1. Nōzan is another name for Sōjiji because it is the head temple located in the province of Nō 能州, i.e., Noto.

2. In the Japanese original, Bonjō uses only the first characters 韓歐 (Han Ou) to refer to the two poets Han Yu (768–824) and Ouyang Xiu (1007–1072).

Now the *Dentō kōshiki* is completed.
For its performance only sincerity is needed.
Stop saying, "The patriarch has no words."
The running water and the wind in the pine trees are the voice of the preaching of the Dharma.

In Meiji 25 (1892), on an auspicious day in January
Bonjō, an unworthy distant descendant of the provinces of Chiku [i.e., Chikuzen and Chikugo], respectfully wrote [this].

Appendix 6

Shikimon of the *Tōjō dentō kōshiki* (Translation)

Shikimon

[Pronouncement of intention]
Reverently, I address all the Three Treasures [Buddha, Dharma, and Saṃgha] abiding eternally throughout the entirety of the Dharma realms (*gūjin hokkai* 窮盡法界) of the three times [past, present, and future] and the ten directions; the successive generations of ancestor bodhisattvas (*dentō rekidai soshi bosatsu* 傳燈歷代祖師菩薩) of the transmission of the light of the three countries [India, China, and Japan]; and especially the venerable spirit (*sonrei* 尊靈) of the Great Ancestor (Taiso 太祖), National Master Kōtoku Enmyō 弘德圓明國師 [i.e., Keizan] of the Japanese Sōtō school, who received the correct transmission in the fifty-fourth generation of Śākyamuni, the World-Honored One; and say:[1]

If we think about it, before Bhīṣmagarjitasvararāja[2] (J. Ionō 威音王) the concepts (*na* 名) of sentient beings and buddhas (*shōbutsu* 生佛) did not exist, but since Śākyamuni the marks (*ato* 迹) of delusion and enlightenment (*meigo* 迷悟) have manifested completely.[3]

This is a complete translation of the *shikimon* of the *Tōjō dentō kōshiki* 洞上傳燈講式, first published in a woodblock print edition in 1893. A photographic reproduction of portions of this edition can be found in Appendix 9.

1. The first sentence of the *shikimon* is similar to the first sentence of the *shikimon* in the *Butsuji kōshiki* edited by Kohō Hakugan in 1892. Both also resemble the first sentence of the *Hōon kōshiki*'s *shikimon*, written by Menzan, ZSZ 2: 723. We can assume that Bonjō and Hakugan used Menzan's text as a model, and did so independently, because they abbreviated the text of the *Hōon kōshiki* differently.

2. According to the twentieth chapter of the *Lotus Sutra,* T 9: 50b23–51c07, Bhīṣmagarjitasvararāja is the name of countless buddhas who successively appeared a long time before the Buddha Śākyamuni; see Kubo and Yuyama 2007, 265–270, for an English translation. In the Zen schools, however, it is thought that Bhīṣmagarjitasvararāja was the first Buddha to reach enlightenment in a *kalpa* without any Buddhas before him.

3. This sentence is a variation of a sentence in the *Butsuji kōshiki* (Ozaki 1998c, 59; if not otherwise noted, the passages that Bonjō quotes are included in both transmission lineages of the *kōshiki*). Bonjō changed *meigo no sō* 迷悟相 to *shōbutsu no na* 生佛名 and in the next part of the sentence *bonshō no na ari* 有凡聖名 to *meigo no ato o genzu* 現迷悟迹. The two new expressions *shōbutsu* 生佛 and *meigo* 迷悟 can be found in Menzan's *Hōon kōshiki,* ZSZ 2: 723, and we can assume that Bonjō adopted these words from it.

[Śākyamuni] picked up a flower on Vulture Peak and made the attendant (*bōnin* 傍人)[4] [Mahākāśyapa] smile. In front of the Stupa of Many Sons (Tashitō 多子塔),[5] he transmitted the mind seal (*shin'in* 心印) [to Mahākāśyapa] and thus showed the succession (*shijō* 嗣承) of the gate of transformation (*kemon* 化門).[6] Afterwards [the Dharma] was successively transmitted from face to face for twenty-eight generations, and then it reached the honorable Bodhidharma, the Great Master Engaku (Engaku daishi 圓覺大師). The Great Master first received the prophecy from Prajñātāra.[7] He went far to China. Finally, he obtained Shenguang (J. Jinkō 神光)[8] [as his disciple] and intimately transmitted the robe and the Dharma (*ehō* 衣法).[9] Thereafter, Caoxi 曹溪 (J. Sōkei)[10] [i.e., Huineng] (638–713) soon had two supreme disciples [i.e., Qingyuan Xingsi 青原行思 and Nanyue Huairang 南嶽懷讓].[11] Then [the Dharma] reached Dongshan [Liangjie] 洞山良价 (807–869) and the style of the school (*monpū* 門風) became increasingly prosperous.[12] Later

4. Śākyamuni's attendant was Mahākāśyapa, who was famous for his ascetic discipline. In the Chan / Zen tradition, he is considered the first of the twenty-eight Indian patriarchs.

5. The Stupa of Many Sons was a famous stupa located northwest of the ancient Indian kingdom of Vaiśālī. In Chan literature, we find two theories about the place where Buddha transmitted the Dharma to Mahākāśyapa: one says that it was on Vulture Peak and the other that it was at the Stupa of Many Sons. Some texts combine both ideas and suggest that the Buddha transmitted the Dharma secretly at the Stupa of Many Sons and publicly at the assembly on Vulture Peak. Dōgen held that the Buddha transmitted the Dharma to Mahākāśyapa on Vulture Peak, whereas Keizan maintained that it was at the Stupa of Many Sons. See Kurebayashi 1960, Tsunoda T. 1997, Ikeda 2010, and Foulk 2017, 2: 229–236.

6. The passage until "he transmitted the mind seal" is similar to a sentence in the *Butsuji kōshiki* (Ozaki 1998c, 59). Only four characters and the beginning of the conjunction are different.

7. According to the Chan / Zen tradition, Prajñātāra (J. Hannyatara 般若多羅, n.d.) was the twenty-seventh Indian patriarch and the teacher of Bodhidarma.

8. Shenguang is the birth name of Huike, who is regarded as the second patriarch of Chinese Chan.

9. This part is very similar to the *Butsuji kōshiki*. Bonjō added "Great Master Engaku" and instead of "*sonsha*" 尊者 he used "*daishi*" 大師 (Ozaki 1998c, 59). Bonjō omitted the account of Emperor Wudi. Instead he added that Bodhidharma transmitted the robe and the Dharma, which is not mentioned in the *Butsuji kōshiki*. Nakano and Sakauchi provide "the robe and the bowl" (*ehatsu* 衣鉢) instead of "the robe and the Dharma" (Nakano et al. 2002, 442; Sakauchi 1973, 11).

10. Caoxi is a stream southeast of Shaozhou, near the temple Caoxi Baolinsi 曹溪宝林寺. The sixth patriarch Huineng (J. Enō) was active at this temple, and therefore Huineng is also called the old Buddha of Caoxi.

11. Qingyuan Xingsi (J. Seigen Gyōshi, also written as 清源行思, d. 740) and Nanyue Huairang (J. Nangaku Ejō, 677–744) are said to be two important disciples of Huineng. Qingyuan Xingsi is considered to be the founder of the Qingyuan branch of the Southern school of Chinese Chan. From this branch, the Yunmen 雲門 (J. Unmon), Caodong 曹洞 (J. Sōtō), and Fayan 法眼 (J. Hōgen) schools emerged. Nanyue Huairang became a monk at the age of fifteen and is said to have studied under the sixth patriarch Huineng. Later he moved to the Banyao temple in Nanyue, where he taught for around thirty years. From his branch, the Hongzhou 洪州 (J. Kōshû) and Linji 臨済 (J. Rinzai) schools emerged. One of his major disciples was the influential Chan monk Mazu Daoyi 馬祖道一 (709–788).

12. There are two explanations of the origin of the name Caodong (J. Sōtō). One, devel-

[the Dharma] was transmitted thirteen times, and then it reached the Eminent Ancestor (Kōso 高祖), Great Master Jōyō 承陽[13] [i.e., Dōgen] (1200–1253) and the Buddha's sun shone for the first time in our Japan (*fusō* 扶桑).[14] Truly this [happens only] once in a thousand years. Therefore, it is said that [this] is good fortune for the country and good luck for the people. Earlier [Dōgen was given] the posthumous name (*shigō* 謚號) Busshō Dentō [Kokushi] 佛性傳東[國師] (National Master of the Transmission of the Buddha Nature to the East).[15] Yes, it is truly like this!

It is said that Zen transmits the mind of the Buddha and the scriptures (*kyō* 教) transmit the words of the Buddha. The buddhas and patriarchs line up their faces (*kutsubami* 鑣)[16] and mutually show [their] reflections in the mirror. Zen and the scriptures share the same principle and equally show their fists and palms.[17] When people of lower and middle capacity encounter a problem, they are stuck in the net of doctrine. The superior disciples certainly open the profound gate (*yūkan* 幽關).[18] Thus the way of the ancestors has gradually blossomed and the teachings of the [Zen] school (*shūjō* 宗乘) have circulated widely.[19]

Moreover, our Great Ancestor, the National Master, had from early on a strong will, full of energy, which exceeded that of ordinary people. Finally, he understood the essence (*yōki* 要機) of transcending the basic tenets of a particular school and going beyond the norms (*chōshū okkaku* 超宗越格). He stayed high on the jeweled seat of Sōji[ji]. The thunder of the Dharma (*hōrai* 法雷) roared far and wide between heaven and earth, and he widely disseminated the correct transmission of Eihei [Dōgen]. The rain of compassion moistened the whole land everywhere, and now the backward-flowing waters

oped in Japan, is that the Sōtō school was named after the sixth patriarch Huineng, also called the great master of Caoxi, and Dongshan Liangjie. This is the explanation followed in this *kōshiki*. The *Butsuji kōshiki* also mentions Huineng and Dongshan and their contributions to the spread of Zen (Ozaki 1998c, 59).

13. Sōtō monks settled on the titles Eminent Ancestor (Kōso 高祖) for Dōgen and Great Ancestor (Taiso 太祖) for Keizan in 1877. In 1879, Dōgen was given the posthumous title Great Master Jōyō by the Meiji emperor.

14. This passage is based on the *Butsuji kōshiki* (Ozaki 1998c, 59). However, the short biography of Dōgen in it calls him "Great Master Eihei" instead of "Eminent Ancestor, Great Master Jōyō," because the *Butsuji kōshiki* had been written before the title Great Master Jōyō was bestowed on Dōgen. Additionally, the *Butsuji kōshiki* explains that Dōgen revived the Buddha's sun and not that the Buddha's sun shone for the first time in Japan.

15. National Master Busshō Dentō is a posthumous title given to Dōgen by Emperor Kōmei 孝明天皇 (1831–1866) in Kaei 7 (1854).

16. *Kutsubami* is the bit of a horse. I have translated it freely as "faces."

17. This passage is a direct quote from the *Butsuji kōshiki;* see Ozaki 1998c, 59–60.

18. Here Bonjō changed the *Butsuji kōshiki*'s "foolish people" and "the wise" to "people of lower and middle capacity" and "superior disciples"; see Ozaki 1998c, 59–60.

19. This passage is a free adaptation of the text in the *Butsuji kōshiki,* which also states that the correct tradition still prevails; see Ozaki 1998c, 59–60.

of [Mt.] Dong (Ch. *Dong shui* 洞水, J. *Tō sui*)[20] expand and spread in the world. This is only his remaining grace.

We are grateful that fortunately we draw from this stream and fully bathe in the wave of compassion. Surely we should dedicate a sincere heart and so repay one drop of the milky ocean (*nyūkai* 乳海).[21] Therefore, we respectfully welcome now the time of the memorial day / monthly memorial day,[22] lead the pure monks of the whole mountain, and respectfully offer humble food of village herbs. In this connection we explain and praise the teaching of [Keizan's] complete lifetime (*ikke no honmatsu* 一化之本末). So it is a response to the unlimited virtue [of Keizan]. We humbly wish that [Keizan] may be truly compassionate and show pity; may he accept [our appeal].[23]

Today's lecture abbreviates and explains the five gates:[24] first, the gate of [his] birth and [his] leaving the household; second, the gate of visiting [various] masters and [his] enlightenment; third, the gate of Dharma transmission and the saving of sentient beings; fourth, the gate of the emperor's sentiment (*kōkan* 皇感) and the appointment of the abbot by the imperial court; and fifth, the gate of the spreading of the aromatic flame (*hōen* 芳談) [i.e., Keizan's teaching].

[First section]
First, I explain the gate of [Keizan's] birth and [his] leaving the household. The national master was a child of the powerful Fujiwara family of the Tane 多禰 district in Echizen.[25] He was born during the reign of the eighty-ninth emperor, Emperor Kameyama 龜山天皇 (1249–1305), in Bun'ei 5 (1268),

---

20. I translate *Dong shui* here as "waters of Mt. Dong," but it actually refers to a creek or stream in the vicinity of Mt. Dong. The passage is an allusion to a *kōan* describing an exchange between Dongshan and his student Longya 龍牙 (835–923): when Longya asked Dongshan why Bodhidharma came from the West, Dongshan's reply that he would tell him when the Dong stream flows backward prompted Longya's awakening; see *Ruizhou Dongshan Liangjie chanshi yulu,* T 47: 522c19–20. In the *kōshiki,* the statement that the waters of Dong flow backward and spread in the world presumably means that Keizan openly teaches and his teaching is available to all who inquire.

21. *Nyūkai* stands here for Dharma milk (*hō'nyū* 法乳), a metaphor that compares the teachings of a Buddhist master with milk. In the same way that milk aids in the growth of a baby, the guidance of a great master promotes the student's development. The term describes the compassion of a Buddha or Buddhist master that is as vast as the ocean. According to Sakauchi Tatsuo (2010, 271), it is impossible to completely repay such kindness, so the monks can only endeavor to repay one drop of the milky ocean. The last part of this sentence is a quote from the *Butsuji kōshiki* (Ozaki 1998c, 59). The expression "sincere" (*suntan* 寸丹) earlier in the sentence also appears in the *Hōon kōshiki,* ZSZ 2: 724.

22. The two expressions "memorial day / monthly memorial day" are printed beside each other in a small font, giving the officiant the option to choose the appropriate phrase.

23. The entire passage starting with "Therefore, we respectfully welcome . . ." is based on Menzan's *Hōon kōshiki,* ZSZ 2: 724.

24. In this *kōshiki,* the sections of the *shikimon* are called gates (*mon* 門) as in the *Hōon kōshiki.*

25. This explanation is based on Takiya Takushū's *Sōji kaisan Taiso ryakuden,* or *Taiso ryakuden* for short, written in 1879; see *Taiso ryakuden,* 1r (1897 ed., 1). There are two theories about the location of Tane, one claiming that it was in Takefushi Hoyamachō, Fukui prefecture,

the year of the wooden dragon, on the eighth day of the tenth month.[26] Earlier the holy mother had dreamt that she drank the morning sun and then she was pregnant. From then on, she paid homage to the bodhisattva Kannon of the district, performed prostrations, chanted, and prayed that she would be certain to give birth to a holy child.[27] Soon she gave birth.

[His] endowment was excellent as expected. His magnanimity surpassed [that of] ordinary children by far. His play was also different from [that of] ordinary children.[28] When he was five, he followed his mother, and they recited the *Universal Gate* [of Kannon][29] and always performed Buddhist services together. He took great delight in this.[30]

In Bun'ei 10 (1273), when he was just six, he looked up at a holy statue of Kannon and asked his mother: "What virtue does this bodhisattva have that [so] many people venerate [it] and make offerings? Furthermore, is this bodhisattva, too, a human being?" [His] mother heard [this] and was very amazed.[31]

Then suddenly he developed the ambition to leave the household and seek the Dharma.[32] In Kenji 1 (1275), he finally begged [his] father and mother, repeatedly seeking to leave the household. [So] even [his] father and mother could not refuse. Then he entered Eihei[ji] under Master Tettsū [Gi]Kai 徹通[義]介 (1219–1309) and had his head shaved. At that time, he

---

and the other that it was in Sakaigun Maruokachō Yamasakisanga, Fukui prefecture; see Azuma 1974a, 21–24.

26. This is a slightly altered quote from Ōuchi Seiran's *Taiso kokushi goden* (15), included in his *Sōtōshū ryōso denryaku,* written in 1884–1885. Interestingly, Bonjō does not use Ōuchi's term *tanjō* 誕生 but substitutes *gōtan* 降誕, a term usually used for buddhas and bodhisattvas who come down into this world to teach sentient beings. In the biographies of Keizan written prior to the Meiji era, Keizan's birth date is only mentioned in the *Sōjiji kyūki* 総持寺旧記, written between 1661 and 1673. In all other sources Keizan's birth date is not mentioned; see Azuma 1974a, 21.

27. This account of Keizan's mother's dream and prayer is based on the *Nihon tōjō rentōroku,* or *Rentōroku* for short, SZ 16: 244. But Bonjō changed "mother" (*haha* 母) to "holy mother" (*kenbō* 賢母), following the *Butsuji kōshiki,* and he added *daishi* 大士 to Kannon, using *Kannon daishi* as Takiya did in his *Taiso ryakuden,* 8r (1897 ed., 8).

28. The source for these three sentences has not been identified. The *Butsuji kōshiki* states that Keizan excelled above ordinary children (Ozaki 1998c, 60), whereas the *Taiso ryakuden* and *Rentōroku* state that Keizan was different from ordinary children (*Taiso ryakuden,* 8v [1897 ed., 9]; *Rentōroku,* SZ 16: 244).

29. The *Pumen pin* 普門品, short for the *Guanshiyin pusa pumen pin* 観世音菩薩普門品 (J. *Kanzeon bosatsu fumon bon*), is the twenty-fifth chapter of the *Lotus Sutra,* T 9: 56c02–58b07, popularly called the *Kannon Sutra* (Ch. *Guanyin jing* 観音経, J. *Kannon gyō*). See Kubo and Yuyama 1993, 295–302, for an English translation.

30. This account is based on Takiya's *Taiso ryakuden,* 9r (1897 ed., 9), and Ōuchi's *Taiso kokushi goden,* 15. Ōuchi, however, does not state that Keizan took delight in it.

31. This passage is again based on *Taiso ryakuden,* 10r–v (1897 ed., 10), and *Taiso kokushi goden,* 15–16. Ōuchi, however, abbreviated the *Taiso ryakuden*'s account; he does not mention that this was a conversation between Keizan and his mother and shortens Keizan's questions. Bonjō abbreviates Keizan's questions in the same way.

32. This sentence is based on *Taiso ryakuden,* 11r (1897 ed., 11), and *Taiso kokushi goden,* 16.

was eight.[33] He received the Dharma name Jōkin 紹瑾 and the name Keizan 瑩山. Do these express the character of a beautiful jewel reflecting and absorbing light?[34]

Then in spring, in the second month, when he was thirteen, he followed Master Kōun [E]jō 孤雲[懐]奘 (1198–1289) and received the great precepts. The master observed his ambition; then he praised [him] and said: "This child has the capacity to [become] a great man. One day he will surely become a teacher for humans and heavenly beings." [This] prophecy was not an empty one.[35] Sure enough, it has come about that the waters of the valley of Tō (Tōkoku 洞谷)[36] overflow and equally moisten the withering three grasses and two trees (*sansō niboku* 三草二木);[37] the clouds cover the gate of the pine trees (*shōkan* 松關)[38] and everywhere in the four directions [the shadow of these clouds] covers the sentient beings of the whole world.

We now answer the good causes of the wholesome roots planted in previous lifetimes. Gratefully, we receive the mercy of the Dharma milk (*hō'nyū* 法乳). Therefore, we should intone a verse and perform prostrations. We sing a verse:

> Long ago the Buddha left the household
> Of the Śākya clan and approached Gayā.
> He thoroughly studied the bodhisattva path
> And was not defiled by worldly affairs.[39]

> Humbly prostrating ourselves, we take refuge in the Great Ancestor, National Master Kōtoku Enmyō. (Recite once, three prostrations.)

[Second section]
Second, I explain the gate of [Keizan's] visit to other masters and [his] enlightenment. In the fall of Kōan 3 (1280), in the eighth month, when Master

33. This passage about Keizan becoming a monk is based on *Taiso ryakuden,* 11v (1897 ed., 11–12).

34. The source for these two sentences is unclear. Azuma attributes the choice of the name Jōkin to Gikai but does not state his source. He also assumes that Keizan gave himself the name Keizan; see Azuma 1974a, 46.

35. This passage is based on the *Rentōroku,* SZ 16: 244, and *Taiso ryakuden,* 13r (1897 ed., 13). Ejō's comment is a direct quotation from the *Rentōroku.* Bonjō only changed the character 成 to 為.

36. Tōkoku is the mountain name of Yōkōji.

37. The term "three grasses and two trees" is based on a parable in the fifth chapter of the *Lotus Sutra,* T 9: 19a18–20b24. Tall plants represent bodhisattvas, medium-sized plants śrāvakas and pratyekabuddhas, and small plants ordinary men and devas. Tall trees represent bodhisattvas of the distinct teaching of the one vehicle, and small trees bodhisattvas of the shared teaching. As the rain moistens all plants equally, the teaching of a buddha enlightens all beings equally.

38. The gate of the pine trees is a reference to the outer gate of Sōjiji, called the Gate of the Three Pine Trees (Sanshōkan 三松関).

39. This verse was adopted from the fifteenth chapter of the *Lotus Sutra,* T 9: 42a01 and 42a05.

[E]jō was about to pass away, [Ejō] ordered the national master to follow Master [Gi]kai. The national master obediently followed and never forgot [Ejō's order]. He lifted his robe (*kotsui* 摳衣)[40] and followed Master [Gi]kai.[41] This was for around ten years.[42]

In the spring of Kōan 8 (1285), the year of the wooden rooster, he left Master [Gi]kai and wandered from master to master. First, he passed Hōkyō[ji] 寶慶[寺] in Etsu and met the eminent Jakuen 寂圓 (1207–1299). Next, he went to the capital [i.e., Kyōto] in the south and visited many venerable masters like Hōkaku 寶覺 [i.e., Tōzan Tanshō 東山湛照, 1231–1291][43] of Manju[ji] 萬壽[寺] and Hakuun Ekyō 白雲慧暁 (1223–1298).[44] Then he ascended Mt. Hiei 比叡山 and studied Tendai doctrines. Further, he went to Kōkoku[ji] 興國寺 in Nanki and met National Master Hōtō 法燈國師 [i.e., Shinchi Kakushin 心地覚心, 1207–1298].[45] [Already], at first sight he was greatly praised. In the following year, he returned and visited the eminent Jakuen again. Finally, he went home to Eihei[ji] and returned to Master [Gi]kai.[46]

In Shōō 2 (1289), the year of the earth ox, he followed Master [Gi]kai and went to Dajō[ji] 大乘[寺] in Ka [i.e., Kaga]. At that time, he was

---

40. Lifting one's robe used to be a way of greeting a higher-ranked person; see *Dai kanwa jiten* 5: 370.

41. This passage is a slightly altered quotation from the *Rentōroku*, SZ 16: 244. To this Bonjō added the year Kōan 3 from the more detailed account in the *Taiso ryakuden*, 13r–v (1897 ed., 13–14).

42. The *Taiso kokushi goden* states that Keizan became a monk when he was eight and practiced for ten years under Gikai before he left to study with other masters (16). Therefore, I assume that Bonjō took this sentence from Ōuchi's biography. But Ōuchi does not mention that Keizan received the bodhisattva precepts from Ejō when he was thirteen.

43. Tōzan Tanshō was a Rinzai monk who was given the posthumous name Zen Master Hōkaku. He first studied Pure Land Buddhism but then became a Zen monk, receiving Dharma transmission from Enni 円爾 (1202–1280). Later he served as abbot of Manjūji, and after Enni's death, he became the second abbot of Tōfukuji 東福寺.

44. Hakuun Ekyō was a Rinzai monk who first studied at Mt. Hiei. At the age of twenty-five, he entered Sennyūji 泉涌寺 and became a Risshū monk. When he was thirty-nine, he went to China. Upon his return to Japan, he received Dharma transmission from Enni and became the fourth abbot of Tōfukuji in Shōō 5 (1292).

45. Shinchi Kakushin (aka Muhon Kakushin 無本覚心) was a very influential Rinzai monk and the founder of the Hōtō branch of Rinzai Zen. He was ordained at Tōdaiji 東大寺 and later studied esoteric Buddhism and Zen at Mt. Kōya 高野山. When visiting many Zen masters in Kyoto, he is said to have received the bodhisattva precepts from Dōgen. Later he went to China and received Dharma transmission from the Rinzai master Wumen Huikai 無門慧開 (1183–1260). After his return, he went to Mt. Kōya and became abbot of Kongō Zanmaiin 金剛三昧院. Then he was invited by the shogun to found Saihōji 西方寺 (later renamed to Kōkokuji 興国寺). He received the posthumous title National Master Hōtō Enmyō 法燈円明国師.

46. This entire passage is largely based on the *Rentōroku*, SZ 16: 244. Bonjō added to it a new beginning and the account of Keizan's visit to Mt. Hiei, probably drawn from the *Taiso ryakuden*, 14r–15v (1897 ed., 14–15). The *Rentōroku*, however, states that Gikai was residing at Daijōji when Keizan returned to him, whereas Takiya writes that Gikai was at Eiheiji at that time. Bonjō follows the latter. Interestingly, of the extant pre–Meiji era sources, only the *Rentōroku* mentions that Keizan visited masters of other schools. In his own writings, Keizan does not mention this and no medieval source supports this account; see also Azuma 1974a, 74–76.

twenty-two.[47] Day and night, he practiced intensively and was not idle for a moment.[48] By happenstance, he was reading the *Lotus Sutra* and reached [the line], "With the eyes given by their parents, they all see the three thousand worlds,"[49] and he suddenly had an insight. Therefore, he went to the abbot's quarters and explained his understanding. Master [Gi]kai said: "If you want to study this matter, you cannot take your realization as complete. Go deeper and exert yourself diligently." The national master bowed and left. From then on, he controlled his mind and did not rest.[50] It was exactly like being in the same place with an enemy. Six years passed in this manner.[51] Whenever he read the one great Buddhist canon, he completely understood and penetrated [its] meaning.

In the winter of Einin 2 (1294), in the tenth month, he awakened (*katsunen* 豁然) and understood the truth when he heard Master [Gi]kai raising the story of Zhaozhou's 趙州 (J. Jōshū, 778–897) "The ordinary mind is the way" in an ascending the hall sermon. Then he said, "I have understood." Master [Gi]kai said, "What have you understood?" The national master said, "The deep black jewel runs in the middle of the night." Master [Gi]kai said, "Not enough, say more!" The national master said, "When I have tea, I drink tea. When I have rice, I eat rice." Master [Gi]kai smiled and said, "In the future you will surely spread the teaching (*shūgū* 宗風) of the Sōtō school."[52]

Next spring, in the first month, Master [Gi]kai let the national master enter his room and transmitted the Dharma. Further, [Gikai] entrusted to him the Dharma robe that had been transmitted from the Eminent Ancestor [i.e., Dōgen] and [ordered him]: "Do not cut off [the transmission of the correct teaching]."[53]

From then on, the wind of truth (*shinpū* 眞風) blew strongly [i.e., the Buddhist teaching prospered], and the correct rules of the successive generations of patriarchal ancestors continued for a long time. The sun of wisdom (*enichi* 慧日) always shines and opens wide the wisdom eyes (*egen* 慧眼) of

47. The first sentence of this passage is based on the *Taiso ryakuden,* 16r (1897 ed., 16). The second sentence might be a direct quote from the *Rentōroku,* SZ 16: 244, but the brief statement of Keizan's age at that time could be based on the Meiji-era sources.

48. I assume that this sentence is based on the *Taiso ryakuden,* 16r–v (1897 ed., 16). But in that text this description follows the account of Gikai's instruction to Keizan to endeavor further, which comes next in the *Dentō kōshiki.*

49. This is a sentence from the nineteenth chapter of the *Lotus Sutra,* T 9: 47c17.

50. The *kōshiki* gives two readings of the character 寢, one meaning sleep (*inuru*), the other meaning rest (*yasumu*).

51. The passage starting with "By happenstance, he was reading the *Lotus Sutra*..." is based on the *Rentōroku,* SZ 16: 244. But in the last sentence the *Rentōroku* has seven years instead of six. Possibly Bonjō was counting the years until Keizan's next major enlightenment experience, which occurred when he was twenty-seven, according to the *Taiso ryakuden,* 17r (1897 ed., 17).

52. This paragraph is based on the *Rentōroku,* SZ 16: 244, but Bonjō altered a few expressions based on the account in the *Taiso Ryakuden,* 17r–v (1897 ed., 17–18). I also assume that Bonjō added the date from the *Taiso ryakuden,* as the *Rentōroku* does not provide a date.

53. This paragraph is largely based on the *Rentōroku,* SZ 16: 245, but Bonjō added to it "transmitted the Dharma."

latter-day students. What a fortune for us! Gratefully, we have been able to become descendants in [this] lineage. We should make the great vow and pay our respects generation after generation. Therefore, we should intone a verse and perform prostrations. We sing a verse:

When [Keizan] deeply entered the various samādhis
And lived peacefully in the truth of nondiscrimination
All things were completely pure
And he realized the perfect enlightenment.[54]

Humbly prostrating ourselves, we take refuge in the Great Ancestor, National Master Kōtoku Enmyō. (Recite once, three prostrations.)

[Third section]

Third, I explain the gate of Dharma transmission and the saving of sentient beings. In Einin 4 (1296), the year of the fire monkey, a local officer of the Kaifu district in Awa province, whose name is unknown and who was related to Hosokawa 細川, the senior assistant of the minister of justice, honored the wish of the way (*dōbō* 道望) [i.e., aspiration] of the national master. He built the temple Jōman[ji] 城満[寺], invited the national master, made [him] the founding master, and venerated him deeply. When the national master performed the consecration ceremony, clerics and lay people gathered and it was impossible to count them.[55]

Then in Shōan 1 (1299), the year of the earth boar, following Master [Gi-]kai's order, [Keizan] returned home to Daijō[ji]. He expounded the Dharma in place of [his] master. The instructions of the *Denkō*[*roku*] 傳光[録][56] took place exactly at that time.[57] Soon he succeeded to the Dharma seat of Master [Gi]kai and the propagation of the tradition (*kefū* 化風) increasingly flourished.[58]

---

54. This verse is a quotation from the *Wenshu suoshuo zuisheng mingyi jing*, T 20: 817b28–29. While Keizan was not the original subject of this verse, the context of the *kōshiki* establishes Keizan as its new focus.

55. This account is based on the *Taiso ryakuden*, 17v–18r (1897 ed., 18). The phrase "venerated him deeply" can also be found in the *Rentōroku*, SZ 16: 245, which gives only a brief explanation about the founding of Jōmanji. See Azuma 1974a, 80–85, on Keizan's abbotship at Jōmanji.

56. One of the main texts of the Sōtō school, the *Denkōroku* is today considered Keizan's main work. It was first printed in Ansei 4 (1857) in an edition by Busshū Sen'ei 仏洲仙英 (1794–1864). Before this publication, it was handed down in manuscript form, and only a limited number of monks had access to the text. Besides the *Tōkoku goso gyōjitsu*, no other premodern biography of Keizan mentions this work; see Azuma 1974a, 113–118. See also Bodiford 2015 and 2017 for studies of the *Denkōroku;* and Cleary 1990, Cook 2003, and Foulk 2017 for English translations.

57. This account is based on the *Taiso ryakuden*, 19v–20r (1897 ed., 20). The *Rentōroku* does not mention the *Denkōroku*.

58. The expressions differ, but the content here follows the *Taiso ryakuden*, 21v–22r (1897 ed., 21).

Then the dragons and elephants (*ryūzō* 龍象)[59] of the various schools of the four directions (*gōko* 江湖),[60] feudal lords, officers, and common people all took refuge [in him] and flocked together. Men of superior capacity like Gasan Jōseki 峩山紹碩 (1276–1366), Meihō Sotetsu 明峯素哲 (1277–1350), and Mugai Chikō 無涯智洪 (d. 1351) all changed their robes and became disciples [of Keizan].[61]

Of these the eminent Gasan [Jō]seki had once been at Mt. Hiei (Eigaku 叡嶽) and had studied the main points of calming and contemplation (*shikan* 止觀). He revered the style of the way (*dōfū* 道風) of the national master and came to meet [Keizan]. Then he asked, "The liberated mind (*dattai kijō* 脱體機情) does not acquire delusions (*mōjō* 妄情). Further, it does not acquire Dharma nature (*hosshō* 法性). In nature (*shō* 性), Dharma nature does not exist. This is the secret content of the Tendai school. Why is the essence of the teaching outside the [Tendai] doctrine different?" The national master smiled and said, "Different, different!" [Jō]seki said, "What is different?" Immediately, the national master entered the sleeping quarters. From then on, [Jō]seki was very strongly determined and quickly three years passed. One night he sat in the lotus position facing the moon. The national master snapped [his] fingers once at [Gasan's] ear. [Jō]seki awakened and was completely enlightened. Finally, he received the seal of approval (*inka* 印可).[62]

Also the eminent Meihō [So]tetsu left the household [and became a monk] at Mt. Hiei. He thoroughly studied the exoteric and esoteric doctrines and penetrated [their] essence. Unexpectedly, he came to visit the national master at Daijō[ji]. The national master appointed him as an acolyte. He always would call [him] and say, "Attendant [So]tetsu!" And [So]tetsu would answer. The national master would say, "What is this?" [And So]tetsu had no answer. It went on like this for eight years. Finally, he became one with the profound principle.[63]

Later there were Koan Shikan 壺庵至簡 (d. 1341) and Chinzan Genshō 珍山源照 (n.d.). Together they revered [Keizan's] style and followed [his] teaching.[64] They stood straight on the field of original existence (*hon'u/ honnu denchi* 本有田地) and did not drop the many affairs of past and present.

---

59. The term *ryūzō* (lit. dragons and elephants or dragon elephant) originally referred to a great elephant (Skt. *hastināga*), but it is often used as a metaphor to describe superior practitioners.

60. Jianghu 江湖 refers to the provinces of Jiangxi and Hunan. It can also be a contraction of the expression "three rivers and five [great] lakes" (*sankō goko* 三江五湖). The term came to be used as a metaphor for "the four directions" or "all places under heaven."

61. This account is based on the *Taiso ryakuden,* 21r (1897 ed., 21). Bonjō added "feudal lords (*shokō* 諸侯), officers (*daiyūshi* 大夫士), and common people (*shonin* 庶人)" to this passage.

62. This paragraph is based on the Gasan biography included in the *Rentōroku,* SZ 16: 250–251.

63. This paragraph is based on the Meihō biography included in the *Rentōroku,* SZ 16: 249.

64. Koan Shikan first studied *yuishiki* 唯識 (consciousness-only doctrine), Tendai, and other teachings. Later he joined Keizan's community and received Dharma transmission from Keizan. He became the second abbot of Kōkōji and later the fifth abbot of Yōkōji. Chinzan Genshō first studied under Genka Tekkyō 眼可鐵鏡 (d. 1321). After Tekkyō's death, he became Keizan's dis-

Then in Ōchō 1 (1311), the year of the golden boar, because of the request of the retired abbot (*seidō* 西堂) [Gen]ka Tekkyō[65] [眼]加鐵鏡 (d. 1321), [Keizan] became the founding master of Jōjū[ji] 浄住[寺] in Ka [i.e., Kaga].[66] In the following year, the year of the water rat, he accepted the appeal of Shigeno Nobunao 滋野信直 of the province of Nō [i.e., Noto]. He entered the district of Sakai, built a temple and named it Tōkokusan Yōkōzenji 洞谷山永光禪寺.[67] Also, a local official of Hakui named Tokuda 得田 built Kōkōji 光孝寺, invited the national master [there], and made him the founding master.[68]

Morookadera 諸嶽寺 in Kushihi-shō of the Fugeshi district in Nō [Noto] was originally a Vinaya temple. The abbot, Vinaya master Jōken 定賢律師, had a wondrous dream of the Light-Emitting Bodhisattvas (Hōkō bosatsu 放光菩薩) [Kannon and Jizō].[69] He respectfully followed the virtuous words of the national master and changed the Vinaya temple into a Zen temple. He sincerely invited the national master and made [him] the founding abbot. [Keizan] called the mountain Shogaku 諸嶽 and so kept the old temple name. He named the temple Sōji 總持 and so took the Dharma words that had been advocated in a dream. Then, in Genkō 1 (1321), on the eighth day of the sixth month, he gave the consecration sermon.[70]

From the earlier founding of Jōman[ji] until the opening of Sōji[ji] here, as for the transmission of the Dharma at many places, the wind of the way bends the grass; and as for the saving of sentient beings of the five realms (*gosetsu* 五刹), the light of virtue bends the hollyhock.

To praise the great benefit of the propagation [of the Dharma], we should now intone a verse and perform a prostration. We sing a verse:

[Keizan] has expounded the essence of all things
And revealed the teaching of the one vehicle.
He has extensively led all sentient beings,
Causing them to quickly attain enlightenment.[71]

Humbly prostrating ourselves, we take refuge in the Great Ancestor, National Master Kōtoku Enmyō. (Recite once, three prostrations.)

---

ciple. Koan Shikan and Chinzan Genshō are both mentioned in the *Taiso ryakuden,* which states that they "changed their robes and took refuge in Keizan" (24v [1897 ed., 25]).

65. Genka Tekkyō was one of Keizan's first disciples at Jōmanji, where he served as head monk (*shuso* 首座). Later he was head monk at Daijōji and Yōkōji; see Azuma 1974a, 85 and 138.

66. This account is based on the *Taiso ryakuden,* 22v–23r (1897 ed., 23–24).

67. Here Bonjō might have greatly abbreviated the account of Yōkōji's founding in the *Rentōroku,* SZ 16: 245, and the *Taiso ryakuden,* 23r–24v (1897 ed., 24–25).

68. This passage is based on the *Taiso ryakuden,* 24v (1897 ed., 25). The *Rentōroku* also states that Keizan was invited as the founding abbot of Kōkōji, and Bonjō might have adapted the last part of the sentence from the *Rentōroku,* SZ 16: 245.

69. According to the *Sōjiji chūkō engi,* the two Light-Emitting Bodhisattvas Kannon and Jizō were enshrined on the second floor of the main gate; see Monzenshi 2: 11–12.

70. Takiya gives a detailed account of Sōjiji's founding in the *Taiso ryakuden,* 28r–30v (1897 ed., 29–31). Here Bonjō could be summarizing Takiya's description.

71. This verse is from the twelfth chapter of the *Lotus Sutra,* T 9: 35b10–11.

[Fourth section]
Fourth, I explain the gate of the emperor's sentiment and the appointment of the abbot by the imperial court. Emperor Godaigo 後醍醐天皇 (1288–1339) thoroughly revered the style of the way of the national master.[72] Then in the year when Sōji[ji] opened, he sent ten questions through the imperial messenger Kohō Kakumyō 狐峯覺明 (1271–1361).[73] The first [question] was: "Are the intent of the Zen patriarchs (*soi* 祖意) and the intent of the scriptures (*kyōi* 教意) the same or are they different?" And the tenth was: "I have contemplated Zhaozhou's *kōan* "Mu" 無 for many years.[74] That I have not yet penetrated [it] makes me sorrowful. How can I endeavor to strive forward?"[75] The national master broke [his] doubts at once. It was just like the spring wind that melts the ice, leaving not a trace behind in the water. The answers fit the mind of the emperor and the emperor's admiration was deep. Therefore, he promoted Sōjiji especially and made it an imperial temple.[76] Soon he designated it as the first training place of the Japanese Sōtō school whose abbot receives the imperial purple robe (*Nihon Sōtō shusse daiichi shishi no dōjō* 日本曹洞出世第一賜紫道場).[77] Then [Sōjiji] received the emperor's edict stating: "Shogakuzan Sōjizenji in the province of Nō directly inherited the correct transmission of Caoxi [i.e., Huineng] and exclusively propagates the profound style of the Sōtō school. In particular, it is an unparalleled Zen garden of Japan. Therefore, I designate [it] as a training place of the Sōtō school whose abbot receives the imperial robe (*Sōtō shusse dōjō* 曹洞出世道場). It should be ranked equally with Nanzen[ji] 南禪[寺], the first of the highest ranked temples. [Its abbot] should wear the purple Dharma robe and pray for the long reign of the emperor. Thus, the wish of the emperor is like this and so the imperial order is as stated above."[78]

Further, [Sōjiji] received Emperor Gomurakami's 後村上天皇 (1328–1368) edict stating: "The abbot of Sōjiji in the province of Nō still transmits

72. The *Rentōroku* includes a similar statement; see SZ 16: 245.

73. Kohō Kakumyō (1271–1361) was a monk of the Hōtō branch of the Rinzai school, but he also studied under Keizan. He instructed Emperor Godaigo and received the title National Master Kokuzai 国済国師 from him. Later he received the title National Master Sankō 三光国師 from Emperor Gomurakami. Through his intermediation, Emperor Gomurakami is said to have bestowed the posthumous title Zen Master Butsuji 仏慈禅師 on Keizan.

74. A monk ask Zhaozhou, "Does a dog have Buddha nature?" Zhaozhou answered, "*Mu*" 無 (no). This famous exchange appears in many *kōan* collections, including *Wumen guan,* where it is the first case (T 48: 292c20–21). See Heine 2014 for a detailed study of this *kōan.*

75. The two questions are a quotation from the *Jūshu chokumon.* Whether Bonjō consulted the original is unclear, since Takiya and Ōuchi also quote this source; see *Taiso ryakuden,* 31v and 37v (1897 ed., 32 and 38–39), and *Taiso kokushi goden,* 21–22. Takiya cites the questions and answers in full, whereas Ōuchi cites only the ten questions. The original was written in Chinese, but Takiya and Ōuchi provide a Japanese rendering of the original.

76. This sentence is a quotation from the *Taiso ryakuden,* 39r (1897 ed., 40).

77. The *Taiso ryakuden* contains a similar sentence at 39v (1897 ed., 41), but Bonjō could be drawing from the *Godaigo tennō rinji sha,* which he quotes in full in the following.

78. Here Bonjō quotes *Godaigo tennō rinji sha,* the document supposedly written by Emperor Godaigo. The manuscript is dated Genkō 2 (1322).

the correct transmission from Vulture Peak and corrects directly the excellent precedent of Caoxi. [Its] rank is the same as Zuiryū[zan]'s 瑞龍[山] [Nanzenji] and the doctrinal essence of the school (*shūkō* 宗綱) flourishes in the world. [Sōjiji] has popularized the way of the ancestors and has propagated the Buddha Dharma, [and the monks of Sōjiji] pray forever that the plan of the emperor may last ten thousand springs and one thousand autumns long. Increasingly, they let the wonderful scent of Shaolin 少林[79] flourish like one flower with five petals (*ikke goyō* 一華五葉).[80] Thus, the wish of the emperor is like this and so the imperial order is stated as above."[81]

From then on, the beautiful color of Shogaku rose more and more and the teaching (*hōmon* 法門) of Sōji[ji] increasingly prospered. Moreover, the fundamental principles (*kōshū* 綱宗) that [Keizan] preached, such as the *Zazen yōjin ki* 坐禪用心記 (Instructions on the practice of zazen), *Sankon zazen setsu* 三根坐禪説 (Explanation on the three kinds of Zen practitioners), and *Shinjin mei nentei* 信心銘拈提 (Commentary on the *Xinxin ming* 信心銘 written by the third Chan patriarch Sengcan 僧璨), are all the essence (*yōki* 要機) of the buddhas and patriarchs. It is like one bright pearl that fills all the worlds in the ten directions (*jin jippō sekai ikka no myōju* 盡十方世界一顆明珠)[82] and the perfect and boundless space that has no boundaries.

If we think about it, if he had not developed the great vow of compassion and wisdom five hundred lifetimes ago, how could he have become a great teacher of humans and heavenly beings in [this] degenerate age (*jokuakuse* 濁悪世)?[83] We should venerate the benefit [he extended] during his lifetime. The rain, bamboo, wind, and pine tree explain fully the practice and realization (*gyōshō* 行證). Even a brush as big as a mountain and ink as wide as the ocean do not exhaust the traces of [his] teaching (*keseki* 化跡).[84]

---

79. Shaolinsi 少林寺 is the monastery where Bodhidharma is said to have spent nine years.

80. The five petals can be interpreted as an allusion to the five generations of patriarchs that followed Bodhidharma: Huike 慧可, Sengcan 僧粲, Daoxin 道信, Hongren 弘忍, and Huineng 慧能. The term has also been interpreted as an allusion to the so-called five houses, the five main branches of the Chan lineage: Guiyang 潙仰 (J. Igyō), Linji 臨濟 (J. Rinzai), Caodong 曹洞 (J. Sōtō), Yunmen 雲門 (J. Unmon), and Fayan 法眼 (J. Hōgen).

81. Here Bonjō quotes the entire document supposedly bestowed by Emperor Gomurakami in Shōhei 9 (1354), the *Gomurakami tennō rinji sha,* with one difference: for Sōtō 曹洞 in the original, Bonjō substitutes Sōkei 曹渓.

82. "All the worlds in the ten directions are one bright pearl" (盡十方世界是一顆明珠) is a saying attributed to Xuansha Shibei 玄沙師備 (J. Gensha Shibi; 835–908), who is said to have used it to instruct people. The locus classicus is an exchange in his biography in the *Jingde chuandeng lu:* A monk asked Xuansha how a student is supposed to understand this saying. Xuansha replied by asking what use would there be in understanding. The next day, Xuansha asked the monk the same question, and the monk repeated Xuansha's answer from the day before. Xuansha then said, "Now I know that you make your living in the cave of demons under the mountains." See T 51: 346c16–21; and Foulk 2017, 2: 118, for an English translation. Dōgen devoted one fascicle of his *Shōbōgenzō, Ikka Myōju* 一顆明珠, to this *kōan;* see DZZ 1: 76–81.

83. There is a similar sentence at the end of the first section of the *Butsuji kōshiki;* see Ozaki 1998c, 61–62.

84. This sentence is a quotation from the *Butsuji kōshiki;* see Ozaki 1998c, 62.

Now, in order to repay a drop of the ocean of mercy (*onkai* 恩海), we should intone a verse and perform prostrations. We sing a verse:

Indra and Brahma both pay homage
Bowing their heads, they wish to inquire,
How the Buddha has liberated the beings of this world (*dose* 度世)
And [his] blessing (*fukuse* 福施) circulates everywhere.[85]

Humbly prostrating ourselves, we take refuge in the Great Ancestor, National Master Kōtoku Enmyō. (Recite once, three prostrations.)

[Fifth Section]
Fifth, I explain the gate of the spreading of the aromatic flame. In Shōchū 1 (1324), the year of the wooden rat, the national master entrusted the Dharma seat of Sōji[ji] to the eminent Gasan [Jō]seki. He stipulated ten rules and so admonished the practice of the disciples.[86] His last wish was very important. He ascended the hall and said, "I stand in front of students and alone cross over to the realm beyond all things (*bubbyō* 物表). [Like] the steep green mountain and the moving mountain clouds, father and child do not part from each other for many years. The king and subjects unite, and there is no [distinction between] inner and outer." Then he descended from the seat and returned to Tōkoku [i.e., Yōkōji].[87]

In the next year, the year of the wooden ox, in autumn, in the eighth month, [Keizan] became ill. Therefore, he selected the eminent Meihō [So-]tetsu and entrusted him with the temple affairs of Tōkoku.[88] He called the eminent Mugai [Chi]kō and let him manage Jōjū[ji] 浄住[寺]. He ordered the eminent Koan [Shi]kan and let him protect Kōkō[ji].[89]

In the night of the fifteenth day, he called his attendant, took a bath, and shaved his hair. He uttered a verse and passed away. The verse was: "This peaceful field that I have cultivated by myself, how often I have gone to sell or buy [its fruits], it is still like a virgin land. At the place where infinite seeds are growing thick, ascending the Dharma hall, I see people holding a hoe."[90] Then a cremation was done and relics collected. The stupa was called Dentō 傳燈. [Keizan] had lived for fifty-eight years and had sat for forty-seven summers.[91]

---

85. This verse is from the *Sutra of the Long-Life King* (*Changshouwang jing*, J. *Chōjūō kyō*), T 3: 388a8–9.

86. Takiya cites all ten rules and states that Keizan entrusted Sōjiji to Gasan; see *Taiso ryakuden*, 40r–41v (1897 ed., 41–43). Ōuchi and the *Rentōroku* do not mention the ten rules.

87. This passage is a quotation from the *Rentōroku*, SZ 16: 246, but there the Dharma talk continues after the excerpt quoted in the *Dentō kōshiki*.

88. This is a slightly expanded quote from the *Rentōroku*, SZ 16: 246.

89. Here the *shikimon* gives the characters of the temple Kōkōji in the wrong order (孝光 instead of 光孝). This was most likely due to a scribal error, because the correct characters were given in the third section of the *shikimon*.

90. This is a slightly altered quote from the *Rentōroku*, SZ 16: 246.

91. This sentence is based on the Sōjiji version of the *Butsuji kōshiki*; see Ozaki 1998c, 61.

During his lifetime the Eminent Ancestor, Great Master [Dōgen], refused the imperial purple robe, followed the rules, and practiced virtue; and so he felt compassion with the descendants.[92] The national master specially received the imperial edict designating [Sōjiji] as the training place whose abbot wears the imperial purple robe (*shishi shusse dōjō* 賜紫出世道場), and he received the imperial edict that the monks of one school [i.e., the Sōtō school] could change their robe and make their debut [as imperial appointees] (*ten'e zuise* 轉衣瑞世) [at his temple]. Now, the one great benefit of the gate of transformation through the changing of the robe is fully due to the great mercy of the national master. Further, the different expressions of our school (*shūmon* 宗門) are the activities of the two ancestors in accordance with the capacity of the audience.

The men who succeeded the wheel of the true Dharma were the five superior disciples Gasan, Meihō, Chikō, Shikan, and Genshō.[93] Gasan had twenty-five superior disciples, among them Taigen [Sōshin] 太源[宗真] (d. 1371), Tsūgen [Jakurei] 通幻[寂霊] (1322–1391), Mutan [Sokan] 無端[祖環] (d. 1387), Daitetsu [Sōrei] 大徹[宗令] (1333–1408), and Jippō [Ryōshū] 実峯[良秀] (1318–1405).[94] Meihō had eight superior disciples, among them Gida Daichi 祇陀大智 (1290–1366) and Shugan Dōchin 珠巖道珍 (n.d.). From then on, the Dharma water (*hōsui* 法水)[95] has pervaded everywhere in the four oceans (*shikai* 四海)[96] and the wind of truth blows widely throughout the whole world. Therefore, in Shōhei 9 (1354), on the second day of the third month, Emperor Gomurakami ordered and bestowed the posthumous name Zen Master Butsuji.[97] Further, in An'ei 1 (1772), on the twenty-ninth day of the eleventh month, Emperor Gomomozono 後桃園天皇 (1758–1779) ordered and bestowed the posthumous name National Master Kōtoku Enmyō.[98]

Fortunately, because of the [good] causes from previous lifetimes, we are grateful to be distant descendants. [Keizan's] mind moistens the water of wisdom (*esui* 慧水) and flows into the ocean of the six ways in which monks

---

92. This sentence is a variation of a passage in the *Hōon kōshiki,* SZ 2: 731.

93. Traditionally, Gasan and not Keizan is said to have had five superior disciples. Keizan is said to have had six great disciples: Meihō, Chikō, Gasan, Shikan, Kohō Kakumyō, and Gensho. Kakumyō is not mentioned in this passage.

94. The exact source has not been identified, but there is a similar statement in the *Hōon kōshiki,* ZSZ 2: 731. Because Gasan's disciples were famous and very influential in the history of Sōjiji, it is difficult to judge whether Bonjō wrote this sentence based on the *Hōon kōshiki.*

95. Dharma water is a metaphor for the benefits of the Dharma: as water washes away stains, the Dharma erases delusions.

96. *Shikai* are the oceans in the four cardinal directions around Mt. Sumeru.

97. This sentence is based on the *Rentōroku,* SZ 16: 246, and the *Taiso ryakuden,* 44r (1897 ed., 45).

98. This sentence is probably based on the *Taiso ryakuden,* 44r–v (1897 ed., 45–46), where Takiya quotes Emperor Gomomozono's edict in full. In the ritual handbook of this *kōshiki* in the Kadono Konzen Library Collection, a monk added by hand the sentence "Further, Emperor Meiji ordered and bestowed the posthumous name Great Master Jōsai," most likely around the time the title was bestowed in 1909.

should live in harmony (*rokuwakyō* 六和敬).[99] [His] body bends in the wind of compassion, settling peacefully behind the clouds of the four offerings (*shikuyō* 四供養).[100] This is the remaining kindness (*ion* 遺蔭) of the great compassionate vow of the national master. [Mt.] Sumeru is lower than his mercy and the ocean is shallower than his virtue. Surely you should be deeply delighted and show utmost respect. Lifetime after lifetime, you should continually cultivate the seed of buddhahood (*busshu* 佛種) and everywhere raise Dharma banners (*hōdō* 法幢) [to teach].[101]

Reverently, we wish that the moon of brilliant truth may shine without ever quietly ruffling the original source (*hongen* 本源). May the marvelous mind (*myōshin* 妙心) of the Buddha's compassion (*butsuji* 佛慈)[102] feel [with us], finally understand us, and secretly offer wondrous responses. The Dharma world has no borders and all sentient beings are included. May we equally reach marvelous enlightenment (*myōkaku* 妙覺) and all realize the origin of truth (*shingen* 眞源).

Therefore, in order to honor the unlimited manifestation in response, we should intone a verse and perform prostrations. We sing a verse:

The great teacher of devas and humans
Feels compassion for the world.
The sentient beings of the ten directions
All universally receive benefits.[103]

Humbly prostrating ourselves, we take refuge in the Great Ancestor, National Master Kōtoku Enmyō. (Recite once, three prostrations.)

---

99. The six ways by which monks harmonize with each other are body, speech, thought, precepts, view, and practice.

100. The four kinds of offerings are clothing, food and drink, bedding, and medicine.

101. In India, monks raised a banner at the gate during a sermon. Likewise, banners are raised in Zen temples during the biannual training periods and for special ceremonies.

102. Because Butsuji is also a posthumous name for Keizan, this passage can also be translated as "May the marvelous mind of Butsuji [Keizan]..."

103. This verse is from the eighth chapter of the *Lotus Sutra*, T 9: 23b11–12.

Appendix 7

Butsuji kōshiki (ca. 1725): Yōkōji Manuscript (Facsimile)

Facsimile by Sōtōshū Bunkazai Chōsa Iinkai. Used with permission.

佛慈禪師瑩山大和尚恒歳
示宗正諱設此講會舉此
佛事總歎三寶殊勝功德
以發弘法利生大心別顯大
祖和尚代佛揚化本誓以報
乳海一滴者也夫惟威音王
已前誰無迷悟相釋迦文已
還既有凡聖名始降率陀
宮假居金輪寶位終逾伽耶
城普報雪嶺覺道現妙相
端嚴顯久遠壽量也雜華
飛香則諸林香端湧沸毘
盧性海鶴樹歸根則佛性
圓月收拾瑠璃寶瓶是以攝
五性群機演一寶佛乘或時
靈鷲山頭拈一華弄引大

龜氏微笑多子塔前傳心印
培養妙法身慧命雖有迦葉
遁雞足慶喜沒恒河猶傳
衣信展轉而授二十八傳至
菩提達磨尊者尊者始受
般若多羅讖記逞來震旦徹
梁皇宸聽亦獲神光拜悟從
此曹溪張綱洞家補袞一十
三傳乃至本朝永平大師始出
台嶺投建仁室終截海南登
大白峯脫身心於異鄉具眼目
於故山挽回佛日勃興祖風所
謂禪傳佛心教傳佛語佛祖
並鑣互現鏡裏影像禪教
同揆等視手中拳掌者有
[illegible]絆義網哲人必啓幽關於

蔵真風遊布定光忽顕即是
南天一乗宗之流播也謂之総
歎三寳殊勝功悳也別讃當
山始祖禅師興化者畧有三段
第一明禅師行實第二明在世
應化第三明滅後普度　一明
禅師行實者禅師諱紹瑾號
瑩山前越多禰邑産也不曽
說氏族或時垂示云予前生者
倶婆羅樹神也毘波尸佛時曽
成阿羅漢果後随第四尊者
蘇賓陀倶住北倶盧洲雪山
依有斯宿因故今降生於北陸
白山下云々賢母一日夢飲日
光後托胎便祈一生髻中
頂戴観世音菩薩聖児

每日行一千三百三十三禮誦
普門品二十三遍然兮元無
雖幼時穎異聰敏氣歷庸
類而雖有忿怒相性元存温
柔十三歳竊發脫白志終
入永平孤雲和尚室雖髮亦
發心於寂圓塔主受戒於義
演禪師依聞父母所眼未見
三千界教文皆悟且有變有
己成万物變万物成自己之提
唱再被大乘灸公秘爲點破
獨步平常是道騎駕暗裏
毘崙蒲廓於大乘二世代
柯於寶鏡三昧佗泓學子士
衆湧外護檀盟谷響亦
應衆請益著述傳光五篇

拈提從上佛祖機縁而練師。
所謂光化播北地者此時乎。一
日師動隠退懷時有能州府主
酒勾八郎平氏頼親女法名祖忍同
夫信州海野三郎滋野信直等
請到本州倶盡供敬且探當山
幽邃告之師愜隠棲思詔于鐮
倉官衙施地建寺籍氣多幽
谷護法安衆號山於洞谷慕
洞山古風帝寺於永光仰大陽
遺烈樓樹枝頭掛破艸鞋下
馬松下設金剛圏梦莊嚴院
特地開香積國土當處現加
彌朝定建最勝殿嚴啓祝
釐道場家方造普光堂始演
師業所據行房書額字爲

寺鎮。祖忍[illegible]奉観音住圓通。
定賢感夢。
南帝北闕九應衆請八坐道
場就中當山者。五老四皓護
一峯三聖二天推二輪所謂。
善根山功德林也。禪師雖獅
口譲々不倦蒲柳幻質奄々將。
盡於茲。敎明峯無涯哉山臺

菴宗豊五老之高蹤且警策
罪業之行持其遺嘱甚切也時
正中二年八月十五書偈唱滅闍
維歛舎利羅世壽五十有八坐夏
四十七移龕大智侍者入傳燈院
起塔
南帝勅諡佛慈禪師想夫非
五百生前興法利生現身奚得
濁悪世中為人天大師耶同爲
報恩可唱伽陀行禮拜伽陀曰
稽首佛慈悲　法住清涼月
衆生心水淨　感應影現中
南無歸命頂禮佛慈禪師利益
衆生者
第二明在世應化者禪師始在海
部城時普放一戒光明度

可識鏡等七十餘人且佛林三光
果娃猶添戒光東識記灒句
海野檀越飽嘗法味遍利度
四大弟子哲洪碩簡者住日鍾
遅義龍律虎之勢終授爐
燼命成大器從此四哲流裔
充溢東海建二万有餘禅刹
五老明鑑懸北天歷五百餘歳
星霜全提祖印則顯家露門
推其宗謂之水平宗儀張皇
綿蕝則晨香夕誦衆其則謂
之瑩山清規山寺鳥石者山
神永留王帯森々松林者
石動遠示其崇也禅師在世
日坐破蒲團則四十年未不寐
七九兩夜臨衆時弄破木杦則

三十歳中不泄洞源一滴巷說。
街談徧暢行證十乘。海硯盡。
盤化迹同唱伽陀可歎無窮之。

應化頌曰

五百生前證是人　覺行圓滿無邊身
惟願普度群生界　永劫不捨願輪

南無歸命頂禮佛慈禪師利益

衆生者

第三明滅後普度者我等今
生四百歳後茲遇毎歳示寂日
雖非三業清淨者頼列遺法弟
子數慕茲靈蹟嘗茲齋會雖
無禮越供給山華野蔬隨分供
養繞列國雲孫雨笠霜鞋
運歩來聚共惟五老山峯前
永遺明月親示法身常在相。

入の

洞谷溪畔久注迴水鎖林花音
海潮音終日得聞大祖之聲言
欬唾常豈假別人提撕複耳
交聞亦流了甚志眼絶見發見
去一進一退未離善根山一瞻
一禮俱入功德林將此深心奉
塵剎謂之報慈供養將此道
心施世間謂之滅後普度宜
唱伽陀普願同向伽陀曰（祖師自贊之可辭法乳恩頌云）
願以此功德　普及於一切
我等與衆生　皆俱成佛道
南無歸命頂禮　三寶炳鑑（不用）
五老昭知

Appendix 8

Kaisan kokushi Butsuji kōshiki (1806): Taineiji Manuscript (Facsimile)

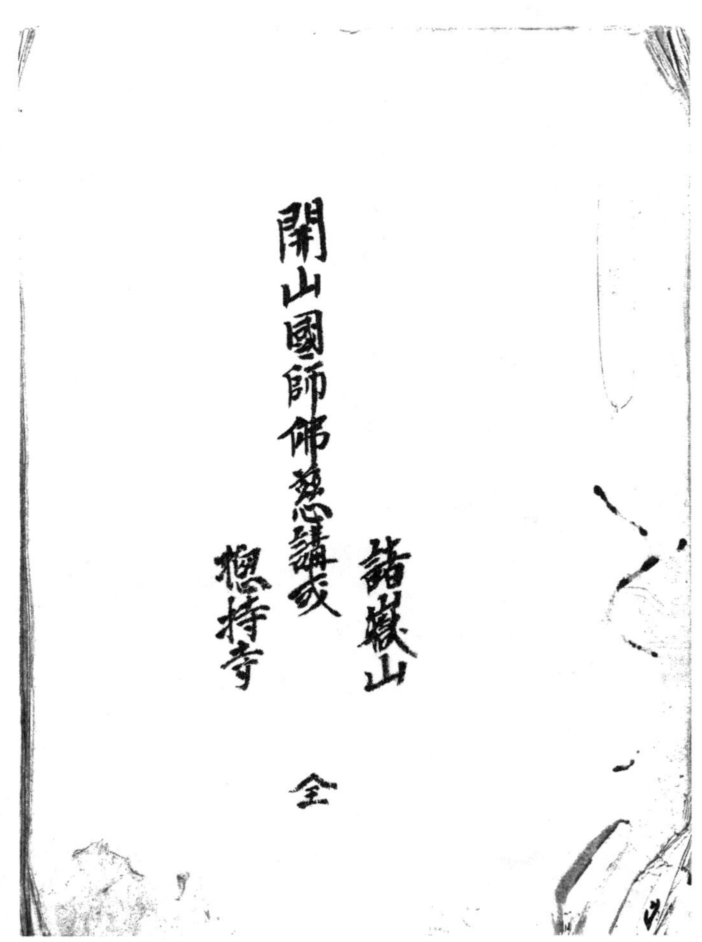

開山國師佛慈講式

諸嶽山

摠持寺

全

The Taineiji manuscript contains additional entries about the annual rituals at Sōjiji and other information about the head temple, written by Taikō Ryūdō (n.d.), who served as rotating abbot at Sōjiji in 1830–1831, which are not reproduced here. Facsimile by Sōtōshū Bunkazai Chōsa Iinkai. Used with permission.

越前刕彌足産也吊前生者倶婆羅樹神也

攝持開山弘德圓明國師佛慈大禪師

諱ハ 紹瑾瑩山大和尚

開山忌

每年八月十三日ゟ十四日十五日迄 二代忌 十月十八日ゟ十九日廿日ニ

加越能三ヶ國寺院集來也

開祖國師講式

謹啓諸塵刹界大悲救世者海藏所有梵法十方凡
聖僧等ニ而言恭遍當山開闢
弘德圓明國師瑩山大和尚恒歳ニ示寂ノ辛諱ニ設此講會ヲ擧ニ
此佛事ヲ總數ニ寶殊勝功德ヲ以發弘法利生ノ大心ヲ別ハ
讃ス開山國師代佛揚化ノ本誓ヲ以報報恩海ノ一滴ヲ者也
夫惟レハ威音王已前ニ雖無迷悟相ノ釋迦文已還ハ既ニ有
凡聖ノ名始降率陀宮ヨリ毀君金輪尊位ヲ終ニ遁伽耶
城ヲ普報雪嶺覺道ヲ現妙相ノ端嚴ヲ顯久遠ノ壽量ヲ
也雜華飛香則諸林ノ吉端濃ニ沸昆靈世海ヲ

萬樹歸根則佛性圓月收拾精魂牢瓶
是以攝五性群機演一實佛乘或時
靈鷲山頭拈一華弄百非龜毛微笑多子塔前
傳心印培養妙法身繼慧命雖有迦葉阿難遞代遞慶
喜沒中恒河上猶傳衣信展轉面授二十八傳至菩
提達磨尊者始受般若多羅讖記遙來
震旦徹梁皇聽亦獲神光拜悟從此曹溪張
綱洞家補袞十三傳乃至我永平大師始出
台嶺投建化室終截南海登大白峯脱身心於輿
鄉具面目於故山拈出佛日勃興祖風所謂禪傳
佛心教傳佛語佛祖並鑣互現鏡裏影像
禪教同揆等覩手中拳掌味薰猶鮮義絲細
人必啓幽關於茲真風退而定光忽顯即是
南天一來宗之流播也謂之總數千至殊勝
功德也別讚當山開祖國師興化爲最有
三段第一明國師行實第二明在世應
化第三明滅後普度第一明國師行

實者國師諱紹瑾號瑩山越前州彌色産也
不審說此時或時舉示云前生者倶挐
羅樹神也毘婆尸佛時曾成阿羅漢果後
隨第四尊者蘇賓陀倶住北倶盧洲雪
山依有斯宿因故今降生於北陸白山下云
云賢母一日夢飲日光後花胎便祈一生
影響中頂戴觀世音菩薩聖像且毎日行一
千三百三十三禮誦普門品三十三返然分免
無難幼時穎異聽敏氣稟肅然雖有忿怒
相性元存過棄十三歲禱髮脫白志級
入永平孤雲和尚雖髮亦發心於寂圓塔主
受戒於義演禪師條聞父母所生眼悉見三
千界之教文省悟且有變自己成萬物
變萬物成自己之提唱耳被大衆介
公和尚點破獨步平常是道騎驢暗裡

崐崘神帝於大乘之世伐柯於空鏡三
昧俺泓學士泉瀏外護擅盟合如響
亦應衆請叅著述傳光平等拓提從上
佛祖機緣也鍊師所謂木化播北地者此
時乎應長段元謝院事動退数几諸候
庶民無不望風瞻敬或建寺迎師居之蓋城濫
㵎住奔走箒郷州滋野信重及吉人平武欽
其德於酒井忠施一山創伽藍請為開山之
祖一俱盡恭敬同事繆相到當山則竒峯
繙從中間平地礙貴惜懷感觀青瑞夢將
院付師籍更賢懇請革教為禪宗山諸嶽
認行基古跡扁寺放總持應蓮靈符碧巖
木清阜葛藤子白嶽苔滑神破爛衫三枝
機關八字開一脈甘泉百川張加諭皇帝
垂十種問陞為天泉功德寺覺明禅
三年之傳受菩薩戒血脈衍方八書額字

為寺鎮蔵光護法衣羽翼聖化啓祝璧道場
興此世法席九應衆請八坐道場就中當山
者五祖四神護三宝三聖三大推一輪所謂善根
山功德林也國師雖御口諄々不倦蒲柳幻質
奄々將盡許茲教領師擣臨崇重十條之龜
鏡且發許衆四輩之行持其八遺囑甚切也于時
正中二年八月十五日書偈唱滅闍維斂舎利羅
号塔曰傳燈世壽五十八坐夏四十七南帝勅
諡佛慈禪師四面飾之後白上温綸特陞
諡弘德圓明國師想丈非五百生前興法利生
現身至得濁悪世中為人天大師耶因為
報恩可唱伽陀行禮拜伽陀曰、

佛正法有二　謂教證為躰
有持說行者　此使住世間

第二明在世應化者國師始在海部城方時香放飛光明度可鐵鑊等七十餘人旦佛林三光毘嵐猶沐戒光稟誡記酒句海鄙檀越飽嘗法味遇剃度四大弟子撒碩箇香性昭鎔逞義龍律亂之擬終投爐燼僉成大器漫此四哲流衣缽元遙東海二十餘禪刹雨箇宝月高懸北夫歷五百餘歲星霜

全提祖印則顯家寶門推其宗謂之永平宗儀張皇綿蕝則晨香夕誦兼其則謂之國師清規葱葱青松香鶴永捧夜光一燈栢樹為山神鎮於甘棠也國師在世日坐破蒲團則四十年來不涅七九兩夜臨與下時弄破木杓則三十歲中不洩涓源一滴吞説街談偏歸衍證山峯海硯盛鬱化迹因唱伽陀可歎無窮之雁花頌曰

我今所獻食　願得無上報
一切煩惱結　摧破無堅固

第二明滅後普度者我等今生五百歳後茲遇毎歳示寂日雖非三業清淨者願列遺法弟子數莫茲靈蹟營茲廠開會雖無權機供給山華野蔬隨分供養總有列國西天作雨笠霜鞋運歩來聚恭惟諸嶽峯頭永遺明月法身常在相總持門前久注逝水現梵音海潮音終日潺聞大祖之聲教常豈餒別人提誨願耳及聞比流了慧眼絶見發見一進一退未離善根山一膳一禮俱入一切德林持此深心奉塵刹謂之報恩供養得此道心說世間謂之滅後普度宜唱伽陀普願回向伽陀曰

願以此功德　普及於一切
我等與衆生　皆共成佛道

文化第三丙寅年八月十日

太清院
義鳳謹寫

天保二卯八月十四日畢
本山輪住兼傳法菴弘老
太寧廿四世隆道誦之

御両尊遠忌
開山大和尚五百年忌
二世大和尚四百五十年忌

Appendix 9

Tōjō dentō kōshiki (1893) (Facsimile)

This ritual handbook contains all texts vocalized as well as detailed instructions for the performance. But here only Azegami Baisen's preface, the *shikimon,* the *Universal Transfer of Merit,* and Bukkan Bonjō's postscript are reproduced. From the Kadono Konzen Library Collection. Used with permission.

鉢大本

傳燈講式序

夫講式者頌其德也凡有德必有頌矣蓋諸經中散華賛華之法可以觀焉吾　太祖國師高挑一燈於總持之寶刹上照　九重之中下耀八紘之外曹洞之稱本山之號皆自　勅定出焉而兒孫詵詵一燈分作千萬之燈今也閱世五百八十餘載創寺一萬五千餘所到處無不照破冥暗其洪德旣如此豈可無講式之設哉自中古輪住之時雖年年行其式而未有其完備之式本山僧窃憂之有年于茲因今本山前後堂筑之明光梵成和尚補充改定之乃考𨯢上梓名曰傳燈講式以公于世欲俾繩繩仍孫奉重　太祖之恩德朝宗流泒之淵源也

時明治二十四年夏安居日

現住總持法孫楳仙敬撰

治廿六年

次維那至式師前頭拜請之式師進眞前燒香三拜胡跪具上唱式文也第一門畢維那擧伽陀自第二句大衆和之次次皆同之

式文

敬白三世十方窮盡法界一切常住三寶三國傳燈歷代祖師菩薩特釋迦牟尼世尊第五十四世正傳日本洞上太祖弘德圓明國師常濟大師太和尚尊靈言

夫惟威音王已前雖無生佛之名釋迦文以還旣現迷悟之迹是以靈鷲山頭拈一華惹起傍人微笑多子塔前傳心印表示化門嗣承從是展轉面授二十八傳至菩提達磨圓覺大師大師始受般若多羅讖記遙來震旦遂獲神光親傳衣法爾來曹溪旣出二神足後至洞山門風益振復一十三傳乃至高祖承陽大師佛日初耀於我扶桑實是千載一時也所以道國之運也人之幸也向有佛性傳東之諡號也亦宜矣哉所謂禪傳佛心教傳佛語佛祖並鑣互現鏡裏影象禪教同揆等視手中拳掌中下

動滯義綱上士必啓幽關於是祖道漸
興宗乘流播也姝吾太祖國師早懷蓋
世抜群志操遂得超宗越格要機高據
總持寶座法雷遐震於普天大弘永平
正傳慈雨偏霑於率土如今逆流洞水
汪洋彌綸海內是偏其遺澤也我等幸
辱酌其流飽浴恩波須傾誠實之寸丹
以酬乳海之一滴仍之茲恭迎示寂月忌之
辰率闔山清衆虔獻谿毛之微饌因講
讃一化之本末以奉報答罔極恩德者
也伏冀眞慈垂哀愍納受

今此講讃畧明五門一者降誕出家門
二者遍參見性門三者轉法度生門四
者皇感瑞世門五者芳蹤流通門

第一明降誕出家門者國師越前多禰
莊豪族藤原氏今子乃人皇八十九代
龜山天皇文永五年戊辰十月八日降
誕先是賢母夢呑朝暾而有娠焉爾來
日詣郡之觀音大士禮拜唱誦祈其必
生聖子既及分娩資性果穎敏氣宇迥

超常兒遊戲亦異庸俗。五歲之頃從母共諷普門品等。常以作佛事自爲其樂。文永十年甫六歲。仰瞻觀音聖像問母。此大士有何功德。諸人恭敬供養。且大士亦爲人乎。母聞大歎異焉。於是忽發出家求法之志。至建治元年。遂乞父母頻求出家。父母亦不奪其志。乃投徹通介祖於永平。祝髮時年八歲也。法諱紹瑾。號曰瑩山。表其有美玉璨爛含光之氣稟者歟。尋十三歲春二月。從孤雲弉祖禀受大戒。祖察其志。輙歎曰。此子有大人作。他日爲人天師必矣。讖記不空。果至洞谷水派等。潤三草二木之枯槁。松關雲鎖普蓋四維八荒之群類。我等今答宿殖善根良因。蒙法乳之恩。

仍可唱伽陀行禮拜。伽陀曰

佛昔從釋種。　出家近伽耶。
善學菩薩道。　不染世間法。

南無歸命頂禮太祖弘德圓明國師　常済大師　一唱三拜

第二明遍參見性門者。弘安三年秋八

月荓祖將謝世。囑國師依介祖。國師佩服不敢忘。攝衣隨介祖。凡十年矣。弘安八年乙酉春。辭介祖遊方。首過越之寶慶。謁寂圓公。次南趨中原。參萬壽寶覺。白雲慧曉等諸老。又登叡山。扣天台法門。更造南紀之興國。見法燈國師。一見大賞歎焉。明年復歸參寂圓公。尋還永平。省于介祖。正應二年巳丑。隨從介祖赴加之大乘。時年廿二矣。日夜實參精修。須臾不怠。會看妙經云。父母所生眼。悉見三千界。忽有省。仍詣方丈陳所解。介祖曰。欲究此事。不得於此子覺觸取。則汝更去做工夫。國師拜退。自爾攝心無寢。恰如仇同處。如是六經星霜間。閱一大藏經。無不意解釋然矣。永仁二年冬十月。聞介祖上堂舉趙州平常心是道話。豁然徹證。乃曰。我會也。介祖曰。汝作麼生會。國師曰。黑漆崑崙夜裏奔。介祖曰。未在更道。國師曰。逢茶喫茶。逢飯喫飯。介祖微笑曰。子向後當起洞上宗風翌春正月介祖使國師入室嗣法且以高祖所傳法衣付之勿令斷絶矣從是眞風大扇永繩列祖之眞規慧日常輝廣開後學之慧眼我等何幸忝得系聯於末裔也宜發大誓願世世奉重焉

仍可唱伽陀行禮拜伽陀曰

深入諸三昧　安住平等理
諸法悉清淨　成正等正覺

南無歸命頂禮太祖弘德圓明國師 一唱三拜

第三明轉法度生門者永仁四年丙申細川刑部大輔屬將阿波國海部郡司某仰國師道望剏立城滿精舍屈請國師爲開山祖大加禮敬國師開堂緇素輻湊不能筭數焉至正安元年巳亥依介祖命歸省大乘代祖演法垂誡傳光録之宗誨蓋在此時也尋董介祖法席化風愈起於是江湖諸宗龍象及諸侯大夫士庶人悉歸依駢闐峩山紹碩明峯素哲無涯智洪等秀群之士皆更衣師事焉就中峩山碩公嘗在叡嶽曉止

觀等大旨慕國師道風來謁乃問曰脫體機情不得妄情又不得法性性不存法性是台宗容旨也豈與教外之旨異國師微笑曰別別碩曰別處作麽生國師便入寢堂碩自是激勵甚切既逾三歳一夜對月趺坐國師於其耳畔彈指一聲碩豁然大悟遂蒙印可又明峯哲公初出家于叡嶽精究顯密貫通旨趣忽來參國師於大衆國師令居侍司常喚曰哲侍者哲應諾國師曰是什麽哲無對如是者凡八年遂契玄旨矣後有壺庵至簡珍山源照共慕風從化驀直蹈著本有田地不落古今事物之數既而應長元年辛亥由可鐵鏡西堂之請爲開祖于加之淨住翌年壬子應能州滋野信直之懇請入酒井保建立梵刹號洞谷山永光禪寺又羽喰郡司得田某建光孝寺迎國師爲開山之祖爰能之鳳至郡櫛比莊諸嶽寺舊爲律院院主定賢律師感放光菩薩之靈夢欽服

國師德音革律院爲禪林懇請國師爲
開山始祖山嶼諸嶽以存舊寺號寺名
總持而取于夢中所唱之法語也乃以
元亨元年六月八日開堂演法嚮自城
滿創建此至總持開闢數處轉法道風
偃草五利度生德光傾葵我等今爲讃
廣大化益乃可唱伽陀行禮拜伽陀曰

演暢實相義。開闡一乘法——
廣導諸群生。今速成菩提。

南無歸命頂禮太祖弘德圓明國師 一唱三拜

第四明皇感瑞世門者後醍醐天皇曾
欽慕國師道風乃以總持開闢之年勅
使孤峯覺明垂十種疑問其第一曰祖
意教意是同是別耶乃至第十曰朕以
趙州無字公案提撕年尚矣以未透徹爲
恨如何工夫用心耶如是疑團國師一
鎚擊碎了也恰如春風消氷水不留痕
奏對稱聖旨叡感有餘矣於是特陞總
持寺爲官寺尋補日本曹洞出世第一
賜紫道場乃賜綸旨曰能州諸嶽山總

持禪寺者直續曹溪之正脈專振洞上
之玄風特依爲日域無雙之禪苑補任
曹洞出世之道場宜相並南禪第一之
上利著紫衣法服奉祈寶祚延長者天
氣如此仍執達如件又後村上天皇賜
綸旨曰能州總持寺住持職位之事紹
傳鷲嶺之正脈直匡曹溪之勝躅祖位
齊瑞龍宗綱振天下恢弘祖道舉揚佛
法鎭奉祈皇圖長久於萬萅千秋益令
榮少林芬芳於一華五葉者天氣如此
仍執達如件從爾諸嶽之秀色彌聳總
持之法門益昌加之其所舉示之綱宗
坐禪用心記三根坐禪說信心銘拈提
等皆是佛祖要機究如盡十方界一顆
明珠圓滿無際空無稜角顧夫自非五
百生前發悲智弘誓願奚得濁惡世中
爲人天大導師耶在世利益可以此仰
知也雨竹風松偏暢行證山筆海硯難
罄化跡今爲酬恩海涓滴可唱伽陀行
禮拜伽陀曰

釋梵齊敬意。　稽首欲受問——
所以佛度世。　福施以周匝。
南無歸命頂禮太祖弘德圓明國師　一唱三拜
第五明芳澄流通門者正中元年甲子。
大國師將付總持之法席於峩山碩公撰
定十條龜鑑。以警策末亂之行持。其遺
囑甚切也。上堂曰。卓立機前獨超物表。
峩峩青山。蒸蒸山雲。父子長年不相離。
君臣道合無內外云云。便下座歸于洞
谷。其翌年乙丑秋八月示疾。因舉明峯
哲公囑洞谷院事。召無涯洪公董淨住。
命壼庵簡公守孝光。至十五夜半喚侍
者沐浴淨髮。說偈示寂。偈曰。自耕自種
閑田地。幾度賣來買去新。無限靈苗繁
茂處。法堂上見插鍬人。乃荼毘斂舍利。
號塔曰傳燈。世壽五十八。坐夏四十七。
其在世也。雖高祖大師辭皇帝之紫服。
行儉修德以隣愍子孫。大國師者持受皇
帝之賜紫。出世道場之綸旨。蒙可令一
宗僧侶轉衣瑞世之勅宣。今以轉衣爲

化門一大利益者悉由國師之洪恩而
宗門之抑揚共是兩祖隨機之活作用
也有紹續正法輪者峩山明峯智洪至
簡源照之五哲峩山下出太源通幻無
端大徹實峯等二十五哲明峯下出祇
陀大智珠巖道珍等八哲爾來法水大
漲于四海眞風遐扇于一天因之正平
九年三月二日後村上天皇勅謚佛慈
禪師更至安永元年十一月二十九日
後桃園天皇勅謚弘德圓明國師（更ニ明治天皇ニ勅シテ常済大師ト謚シ玉フ）某等
幸賴夙因忝爲苗裔心霑慧水逍遙於
六和敬海中身偃慈風安住於四供養
雲裏是併國師大悲願之遺蔭也其恩
須彌尚低其德滄海亦淺須是深心歡
喜恭敬頂戴生生紹隆佛種處處建立
法幢仰願圓明眞月照而常寂不動本
源佛慈妙心感而遂通潛施靈應法界
無邊群生無盡同歸妙覺咸悟眞源仍
爲仰無窮應化可唱伽陀行禮拜伽陀
曰

天人之大師　哀愍於世間

十方諸衆生　普皆蒙饒益

南無歸命頂禮太祖弘德圓明國師　一唱三拜

普回向

願以此功德　普及於一切

我等與衆生　皆共成佛道

南無自他法界平等利益　維那一人唱之唱了鳴手

磬三　普同一拜立

次誦大悲呪回向云

上來講讚諷經功德奉爲大祖弘德圓

題傳燈講式後

能山貫主法雲普蓋禪師遙託余令編輯　太祖國師傳燈講式也其命懇篤余不克固辭於是乎不顧不文彼此折衷遂製一部式本只恐難免識者譏誚敢冀　國師傑雲英仍不咎文之陋拙而惟運至誠心行此法式以酬　國師無窮恩德儻或未能然者不是傳燈兒孫也徒爲韓歐奴隸已矣伏請三寶證明佛祖炳鑒因賦一偈用代跋語

太祖當初傳一燈一燈分作百千燈燈燈續焰光無盡長破闇冥是此燈
令也傳燈講式成行之只要竭丹誠休言乃祖無消息流水松風說法聲

時明治廿五年一月穀旦

筑州遠孫不肖梵成謹撰

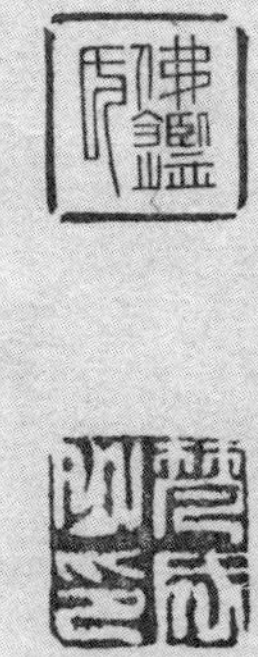

諸嶽山藏版

Bibliography

Primary Source Collections and Reference Works

Bukkyō ongaku jiten 仏教音楽辞典. Edited by Amano Denchū 天納傳中 et al. Kyoto: Hōzōkan, 1995.

Bukkyōgo jiten 仏教語辞典. Edited by Nakamura Hajime 中村元. 3 vols. Tokyo: Tōkyō Shoseki, 1975.

Bussho kaisetsu daijiten 仏書解説大辞典. Edited by Ono Genmyō 小野玄妙. 15 vols. Tokyo: Daitō Shuppan, 1936.

Dai kanwa jiten 大漢和辞典. Edited by Morohashi Tetsuji 諸橋轍次. 13 vols. Tokyo: Taishūkan, 1955–1960.

Daizōkyō zenkaisetsu daijiten 大蔵経全解説大辞典. Edited by Kamata Shigeo 鎌田茂雄 et al. Tokyo: Yūzankaku Shuppan, 1998.

Digital Dictionary of Buddhism (DDB). Edited by Charles Muller. http://buddhism-dict.net/ddb.

Dōgen zenji shinpitsu shūsei 道元禅師眞筆全集 (DZSS). Edited by Ōkubo Dōshū 大久保道舟. Tokyo: Chikuma Shobō, 1970.

Dōgen zenji shinseki kankei shiryōshū 道元禪師眞蹟關係資料集 (DZSK). Edited by Daihonzan Eiheijinai Eihei Shōbōgenzō Shūsho Taisei Kankōkai 大本山永平寺内永平正法眼藏蒐書大成刊行會. Tokyo: Taishūkan shoten, 1980.

Dōgen zenji zenshū 道元禅師全集 (DZO). Edited by Ōkubo Dōshū 大久保道舟. 2 vols. Tokyo: Chikuma Shobō, 1969–1970.

Dōgen zenji zenshū 道元禅師全集 (DZZ). Edited by Kawamura Kōdō 河村孝道 et al. 7 vols. Tokyo: Shunjūsha, 1988–1993.

Encyclopedia of Buddhism. Edited by Robert E. Buswell, Jr. New York: Macmillan Reference, 2004.

Iwanami Bukkyō jiten 岩波仏教辞典. Edited by Nakamura Hajime 中村元 et al. 2nd ed. Tokyo: Iwanami Shoten, 2002.

The Japanese-English Zen Buddhist Dictionary. By Yūhō Yokoi. Tokyo: Sankibō Busshorin, 1991.

Jōsai daishi zenshū 常濟大師全集 (JDZ). Edited by Kohō Chisan 孤峰智璨. Yokohama: Daihonzan Sōjiji, 1967. First published 1937.

Kanazawa Bunko shiryō zensho 金沢文庫資料全書. 10 vols. Yokohama: Kanagawa Kenritsu Kanazawa Bunko, 1974–1991.

Keizan Zen 瑩山禅 (KZ). Edited by Kōchi Eigaku 光地英学 et al. 12 vols. Tokyo: Sankibō, 1985–1994.

Kōshiki dētabēsu 講式データベース [*Kōshiki database*]. Compiled by Niels Gülberg. Online from 2000 to 2019; available for download at DOI: 10.13140/RG.2.2.30498.99527.

Kōyasan kōshikishū 高野山講式集. Edited by Kōyasan Daigaku Fuzoku Kōyasan Toshokan 高野山大学附属高野山図書館. Osaka: Kobayashi Shashin Kōgyō, 2001, 2 CD-ROMs.

Mikkyō daijiten 密教大辭典. Edited by Mikkyō Daijiten Hensankai 密教大辞典編纂會. Rev. ed. 6 vols. Kyoto: Hōzōkan, 1969–1970.

Mikkyō jiten 密教辞典. Edited by Sawa Ryūken 佐和隆研. Kyoto: Hōzōkan, 1975.

Mochizuki Bukkyō daijiten 望月仏教大辞典. Edited by Mochizuki Shinkō 望月信亨 et al. Expanded and revised by Tsukamoto Zenryū and Sekai Seiten Kankō Kyōkai. 10 vols. Tokyo: Sekai Seiten Kankōkyōkai, 1954–1974.

Myōe shōnin shiryō 明恵上人資料 (MSS). Edited by Kōzanji Tenseki Monjo Sōgō Chōsadan 高山寺典籍文書綜合調查団. 5 vols. Tokyo: Tōkyō Daigaku Shuppankai, 1971–2000.

Nihon kayō shūsei 日本歌謡集成 (NKS). Edited by Takano Tatsuyuki 高野辰之. Rev. ed. 12 vols. Tokyo: Tōkyōdō Shuppan, 1960.

Nihon kokugo daijiten 日本国語大辞典. Edited by Nihon Kokugo Daijiten Dainihan Henshū Iinkai 日本国語大辞典第二版編集委員会. 2nd ed. Daijiten Henshūbu. Tokyo: Shogakukan, 2001–2003.

Reibun Bukkyōgo daijiten 例文仏教語大辞典. Edited by Ishida Mizumaro 石田瑞麿. Tokyo: Shōgakkan, 1997.

Shinsan Dai Nihon zoku zōkyō 新纂大日本續藏經 (X). Edited by Kawamura Kōshō 河村孝照, Nishi Yoshio 西義雄, and Tamaki Kōshirō 玉城康四郎. 90 vols. Tokyo: Kokusho Kankōkai, 1975–1989.

Shinshū Monzenchō shi, Shiryōhen 2: Sōjiji 新修門前町史　資料編2 総持寺 (Monzenshi 2). Edited by Monzenchō Shihensan Senmon Iinkai 門前町史編さん専門委員会. Monzenchō: Ishikawaken Monzenchō, 2004.

Shohon taikō Eihei kaizan Dōgen zenji gyōjō Kenzeiki 諸本對校永平開山道元禅師行状建撕記 (K). Edited by Kawamura Kōdō 河村孝道. Tokyo: Taishūkan Shoten, 1975.

Shōmyō jiten: Shōmyō taikei tokubetsu furoku 声明辞典：声明大系特別付録. 2nd ed. Kyoto: Hōzōkan, 2012.

Sōgō Bukkyō daijiten 総合仏教大辞典. Edited by Sōgō Bukkyō Daijiten Henshū Iinkai 総合佛教大辞典編集委員会. 3 vols. Kyoto: Hōzōkan, 1987.

Sōtōshū bunkazai chōsa mokuroku kaidaishū 曹洞宗文化財調査目録解題集 (Bunkazai). Edited by Sōtōshū Bunkazai Chōsa Iinkai 曹洞宗文化財調査委員会. Vols. 3–7. Tokyo: Sōtōshū Shūmuchō, 1996–2006.

Sōtōshū komonjo 曹洞宗古文書 (Komonjo). Edited by Ōkubo Dōshū 大久保道舟. 3 vols. Tokyo: Chikuma Shobō, 1972.

Sōtōshū shūhō chōsa mokuroku kaidaishū 曹洞宗宗宝調査目録解題集 (Shūhō). Edited by Sōtōshū Shūhō Chōsa Iinkai 曹洞宗宗宝調査委員会. 2 vols. Tokyo: Sōtōshū Shūmuchō, 1991–1994. For vols. 3–7, see *Sōtōshū bunkazai chōsa mokuroku kaidaishū*.

Sōtōshū zensho 曹洞宗全書 (SZ). Edited by Sōtōshū Zensho Kankōkai 曹洞宗全書刊

行會. 20 vols. Tokyo: Sōtōshū Shūmuchō, 1970–1973. Vols. 1–19 are a reprint of 1929–1938 ed.

Taishō shinshū daizōkyō 大正新脩大蔵経 (T). Edited by Takakusu Junjirō 高楠順次郎 and Watanabe Kaigyoku 渡辺海旭 et al. 85 vols. Tokyo: Taishō Issaikyō Kankōkai, 1924–1934.

Zengaku daijiten (shinpan) 禪學大辭典 (新版) (ZGD). Edited by Zengaku Daijiten Hensanjo 禪學大辭典編纂所. Tokyo: Taishūkan, 1985.

Zenyaku Kanjikai 全訳漢辞海. Edited by Satō Susumu 佐藤進 and Hamaguchi Fujio 濱口富士雄. Tokyo: Sanseido, 2006.

Zōfukuin bunko zenpon shūsei 増福院文庫善本集成. Edited by Kōyasan Daigaku Fuzoku Toshokan 高野山大学附属図書館. Osaka: Kobayashi Shashin Kōgyō Kabushiki Kaisha, 2006, 12 DVDs.

Zoku Sōtōshū zensho 続曹洞宗全書 (ZSZ). Edited by Sōtōshū Zensho Kankōkai 曹洞宗全書刊行會. 10 vols. Tokyo: Sōtōshū Shūmuchō, 1973–1976.

Primary Sources

Anan kōshiki 阿難講式. 1829. Collection of the author.

Apidamo jushelun 阿毘達磨俱舍論. T 29, no. 1558.

Arakan 阿羅漢. Fascicle of *Shōbōgenzō*. DZO 1: 323–326; DZZ 1: 403–408; T 82: 152c–154a.

Ashikaga Tadayoshi kishin jōan 足利直義寄進状案. In *Yōkōji no meihō,* 88.

Ashikaga Tadayoshi migyōsho 足利直義御教書. In *Yōkōji no meihō,* 88.

Ayuwang jing 阿育王經. T 50, no. 2043.

Bendōwa 辦道話. DZO 1: 729–763; DZZ 2: 460–481.

Benzaiten kōshiki 弁財天講式. 1827. Dairyūji.

Bosatsukai fusatsushiki 菩薩戒布薩式. In the Manzan edition of the *Keizan shingi.* T 82: 431b–433b.

Buppō zenji kōshiki ryaku 佛法禅師講式略. Daitokuji. Facsimile available at Sōtōshū Bunkazai Chōsa Iinkai. Listed in Bunkazai 7: 82. See also *Dōgen zenji kōshiki.*

Busshō Nehan kōshiki 仏生涅槃講式. 1753. Yōkōji. Facsimile available at Sōtōshū Bunkazai Chōsa Iinkai. Listed in Bunkazai 7: 613.

Busshōe kōshiki 仏生会講式. 1751. Shōyōji. Facsimile available at Sōtōshū Bunkazai Chōsa Iinkai. Listed in Shūhō 2: 275.

———. 1865. Kadono Konzen Library Collection.

———. 1894. Research Institute for Japanese Music Historiography, Ueno Gakuen University.

Busshōe ryaku kōshiki 仏生会略講式. 1866. Tentokuin. Facsimile available at Sōtōshū Bunkazai Chōsa Iinkai. Listed in Bunkazai 7: 449.

———. n.d. Tentokuin. Facsimile available at Sōtōshū Bunkazai Chōsa Iinkai. Listed in Bunkazai 7: 449.

Butsuji kō kada narabini Shichisan 佛慈講伽陀並四智讃. 1694. Sōjiji Soin; Shōyōji; Kadono Konzen Library Collection. Facsimiles available at Sōtōshū Bunkazai Chōsa Iinkai. Listed in Bunkazai 7: 429 and Shūhō 2: 276.

Butsuji kōshiki 佛慈講式. ca. 1725. Yōkōji. Facsimile available at Sōtōshū Bunkazai Chōsa Iinkai. Listed in Bunkazai 7: 614. See also *Taiso Butsuji kōshiki.*

Butsuji kōshiki saimon 佛慈講式祭文. 1827. Yōkōji. Facsimile available at Sōtōshū Bunkazai Chōsa Iinkai. Listed in Bunkazai 7: 614.

Changshouwang jing 長壽王經. T 3, no. 161.

Chanyuan qinggui 禪苑清規. X 63, no. 1245.

Chion kōshiki 知恩講式. In *Shinshū seikyō zensho* 真宗聖教全書 5, edited by Shinshū Seikyō Zensho Hensanjo, 715–719. Kyoto: Ōyagi kōbundō, 1987.

Chixiu Baizhang qinggui 勅修百丈清規. T 48, no. 2025.

Daaluohan nantimiduoluo suoshuo fazhuji 大阿羅漢難提蜜多羅所説法住記. T 49, no. 2030.

Daban niepan jing 大般涅槃經. Translated by Dharmakṣema. T 12, no. 374.

Daban niepan jing 大般涅槃經. "Southern" version. T 12, no. 375.

Da fangguang Fo huayan jing 大方廣佛華嚴經. T 9, no. 278; T 10, no. 279.

Dafoding rulai miyin xiuzheng liaoyi zhupusa wanxing shoulengyan jing 大佛頂如來密因修證了義諸菩薩萬行首楞嚴經. T 19, no. 945.

Daigaku zenji Kenchō go kōshiki 大覺禅師建長五講式. 1862. Kenchōji.

Daihannya kōshiki 大般若講式. 1773. Research Institute for Japanese Music Historiography, Ueno Gakuen University.

———. 1893. ZSZ 2: 677–689. Reprint of 1773 edition.

Daruma kōshiki 達磨講式. ZSZ 2: 837–851.

———. 1877. Myōshinji edition. Research Institute for Japanese Music Historiography, Ueno Gakuen University; Komazawa University Library; collection of the author.

Dedao ticheng xizhang jing 得道梯橙錫杖經. T 17, no. 785.

Denkōroku 傳光録. T 82, no. 2585.

Dentō kōshiki 傳燈講式. See *Tōjō dentō kōshiki.*

Dentō kōshiki ino yō 傳燈講式 維那用. Sōjiji Soin.

Dentō kōshiki shikishi yō 傳燈講式 式師用. Sōjiji Soin.

Dōanryō kōmuchō 堂行寮公務帳. Eiheiji-chō: Daihonzan Eiheiji, n.d.

Dōgen zenji kōshiki 道元禪師講式. 1707. By Zuihō Daiki. Shōyōji (woodblock print). Komazawa University Library, Nukariya Bunko (manuscript). Facsimile of woodblock print edition available at Sōtōshū Bunkazai Chōsa Iinkai. Listed in Bunkazai 7: 276. See also *Buppō zenji kōshiki ryaku.*

Eihei kaisan Hōon kōshiki 永平開山報恩講式. Research Institute for Japanese Music Historiography, Ueno Gakuen University; Stanford University Library; collection of the author. See also *Jōyō daishi Hōon kōshiki.*

Eihei kōso gyōjō tekiyō 永平高祖行状摘要. 1878. Komazawa University Library.

———. 1885. National Diet Library Digital Collections, http://kindai.ndl.go.jp/info:ndljp/pid/822864. Reprint of 1878 edition.

Eihei shoso Dōgen zenji kōshiki 永平初祖道元禪師講式. 1707. By Zenzui Shōzen. Kōzenji. Research Institute for Japanese Music Historiography, Ueno Gakuen University. Facsimile available at Sōtōshū Bunkazai Chōsa Iinkai. Listed in Bunkazai 7: 698–699.

Eiheiji kaisan kigyō Hokke kōshiki 永平寺開山忌行法華講式. ZSZ 2: 819–836.

Fahua sanmei chanyi 法華三昧儀. T 46, no. 1941.

Fahua sanmei xingshi yunxiang fuzhuyi 法華三昧行事運想補助儀. T 46, no. 1942.

Fanwang jing 梵網經. T 24, no. 1484.

Fazhuji. See *Daaluohan nantimiduoluo suoshuo fazhuji*.

Flower Garland Sutra. See *Da fangguang Fo huayan jing*.

Foding zunsheng tuoluoni jing 佛頂尊勝陀羅尼經. T 19, no. 967.

Foshuo chichengguang daweide xiaozai jixiang tuoluoni jing 佛說熾盛光大威徳消災吉祥陀羅尼經. T 19, no. 963.

Fushuku hanpō 赴粥飯法. DZO 2: 348–357; DZZ 6: 46–73; T 82: 326–329.

Gasan kō kada 峨山講伽陀. In *Nehan kō kada narabini Shichisan* and *Hōyō*. Sōjiji Soin.

Genkōshakusho 元亨釈書. See Fujita 2011.

Gennin ron keimōshō 原人論啓蒙鈔. Komazawa University Library; National Diet Library Digital Collections, http://kindai.ndl.go.jp/info:ndljp/pid/818946, http://kindai.ndl.go.jp/info:ndljp/pid/818947.

Genpei jōsui ki 源平盛衰記. 7 vols. Tokyo: Miyai Shoten, 1991–2015.

Godaigo tennō rinji sha 後醍醐天皇綸旨写. Monzenshi 2: 13.

Godaigo tennō shusse dōjō gorinji 後醍醐天皇出世道場御綸旨. In *Tōkokusan Yōkōji shi*, 10–11.

Gomurakami tennō kuzenan 後村上天皇口宣案. Komonjo 1, no. 192. Also in *Tōkokusan Yōkōji shi*, 30–31.

Gomurakami tennō rinji sha 後村上天皇綸旨写. Monzenshi 2: 19.

Gotsuchimikado tennō rinji 後土御門天皇綸旨. Komonjo 1, no. 208. Also in *Yōkōji no meihō*, 99; *Tōkokusan Yōkōji shi*, 37–38.

Gyosan rokkan jō 魚山六巻帖. In *Zoku Tendaishū zensho Hōgi* 1 續天台宗全書 法儀 1, edited by Tendai Shūten Hensanjo, 110–265. Tokyo: Shunshūsha, 1996.

Gyosan shishō 魚山私鈔. T 84, no. 2713; National Diet Library Digital Collections, https://dl.ndl.go.jp/info:ndljp/pid/2543275.

Gyosan shōmyō shū 魚山声明集. T 84, no. 2712.

Hakusan kōshiki 白山講式. n.d. By Inoue Gishin. Tōshōji, Nagoya.

Heihanki 兵範記 [*Hyōhanki*]. 5 vols. In *Zōho shiryō taisei* 增補史料大成, edited by Zōho Shiryō Taisei Hankōkai. Kyoto: Rinsen shoten, 1965.

Hokke kōshiki 法華講式. See *Eiheiji kaisan kigyō Hokke kōshiki*.

Honchō monzui chūshaku 本朝文粋註釈. 2 vols. Edited by Kakimura Shigematsu. Tokyo: Fuzanbō, 1968.

Hōon kōshiki 報恩講式. By Kakunyo. T 83, no. 2665.

———. By Menzan. See *Eihei kaisan Hōon kōshiki* and *Jōyō daishi Hōon kōshiki*.

Hōyō 法要. 1694. Sōjiji Soin; Kadono Konzen Library Collection. Facsimile available at Sōtōshū Bunkazai Chōsa Iinkai. Listed in Bunkazai 7: 420.

Hōzan shukujiki 法山職事記. 1723–1724. Jissōji. Facsimile available at Sōtōshū Bunkazai Chōsa Iinkai. Listed in Shūhō 2: 116.

Huayan jing. See *Da fangguang Fo huayan jing*.

Jingde chuandeng lu 景徳傳燈録. T 51, no. 2076.

Jizō bosatsu kōshiki 地蔵菩薩講式. 1882. Research Institute for Japanese Music Historiography, Ueno Gakuen University.

———. 1885. Collection of the author.

Jizō kōshiki 地蔵講式. Tokyo: Yōshōji, 1982.

Jō tōshōgaku ron 成等正覺論 [*Engaku daishi kōki* 圓覺大師講記]. Kanazawa Bunkō. In *Kanazawa Bunko shiryō zensho* 1: 201–207.

Jōyō daishi Hōon kōshiki 承陽大師報恩講式. ZSZ 2: 717–733.

Jōyō daishi kōshiki 承陽大師講式. By Inoue Gishin. Nagoya: Tōshōji, 2002.

Jūnigatsu shōmyō kō yakusha hossoku 十二月聲明講役者法則. *Zōfukuin bunko zenpon shūsei* 3, no. 314.

Jūroku rakan fukuden senkōki 十六羅漢福田宣耕記. Stanford University Library.

Jūroku rakan genzui ki 十六羅漢現瑞記. DZO 2: 546; DZSK, 950; DZZ 7: 398.

Jūroku rakan kōshiki 十六羅漢講式. T 84: 900c17–902c12.

Jushelun. See *Apidamo jushelun*.

Jūshu chokumon 十種勅問. JDZ, 381–386; KZ 9: 263–325.

Jūshu gitai 十種疑滞. JDZ, 376–380; KZ 9: 227–261.

Kachō yōryaku 華頂要略. In *Dainihon bukkyō zenshō* 大日本佛教全書 128–130, edited by Bussho Hankōkai. Tokyo: Bussho Hankōkai, 1913.

Kada narabini hōyō 伽陀並法要. 1694. Sōjiji Soin; Kadono Konzen Library Collection. Facsimile available at Sōtōshū Bunkazai Chōsa Iinkai. Listed in Bunkazai 7: 419.

Kaisan kokushi Butsuji kōshiki 開山國師佛慈講式. 1806. Taineiji. Facsimile available at Sōtōshū Bunkazai Chōsa Iinkai. Listed in Bunkazai 5: 359.

Kaisei Rakan kōshiki 改正羅漢講式. Tōfukuji-ban 東福寺版. Collection of the author.

Kaiso kōshiki 開祖講式. 1715. Yōkōji. Facsimile available at Sōtōshū Bunkazai Chōsa Iinkai. Listed in Bunkazai 7: 614.

Kakuōzan Yōmeizenji nai shingi 覺皇山永明禪寺内清規. 1710. Yōmeiji. Facsimile available at Sōtōshū Bunkazai Chōsa Iinkai. Listed in *Sōtōshūhō* 曹洞宗報 2016, no. 11: 91.

Kannon kōshiki 觀音講式. T 84, no. 2728.

———. 1892. Komazawa University Library.

Kannon senbōhō 觀音懺摩法. ZSZ 2: 751–771.

Kannon Sutra. T 9: 56c02–58b07.

Kasekison nōke kōshiki 嘉石尊能化講式. 1864. Kadono Konzen Library Collection.

Kenchō go kōshiki 建長五講式. See *Daigaku zenji Kenchō go kōshiki*.

Keizan shingi 瑩山清規. Manzan edition. T 82, no. 2589.

———. 1501. Copied by Rinkō [*Rinkō shoshabon* 麟広書写本]. Yōkōji. Facsimile available at Sōtōshū Bunkazai Chōsa Iinkai. Listed in Bunkazai 7: 588.

Kenzeiki 建撕記. See *Shohon taikō Eihei kaizan Dōgen zenji gyōjō Kenzeiki*.

Kōgen jōkōin sen 光厳上皇院宣. In *Yōkōji no meihō*, 88.

Kōgon shūyō shū 講勤拾要集. *Zōfukuin bunko zenpon shūsei* 3, no. 301.

Kōsei sanchū Shōshitsu rokumon shū 校正纂註少室六門集. Komazawa University Library.

Kōso Jōyō daishi gyōjitsu zue 高祖承陽大師行實圖會. Komazawa University Library; National Diet Library Digital Collections, http://kindai.ndl.go.jp/info:ndljp/pid/822963.

Kōzanji Myōe shōnin gyōjō 高山寺明恵上人行状. *Kana gyōjō* 仮名行状. MSS 1: 10–80.

———. *Kanbun gyōjō* 漢文行状, *Hōon'inbon* 報恩院本. MSS 1: 156–231.

———. *Kanbun gyōjō* 漢文行状, *Jōzanbon* 上山本. MSS 1: 89–145.

Kōzen gokoku ron 興禪護國論. T 80, no. 2543.

Lengyan jing 楞嚴經. See *Dafoding rulai miyin xiuzheng liaoyi zhupusa wanxing shoulengyan jing*.

Lotus Sutra. See *Miaofa lianhua jing*.

Mahāprajñāpāramitā Sūtra. T 5–7, no. 220.

Meiji shinkoku Rakan kōshiki 明治新刻羅漢講式. Myōshinji-ban 妙心寺版. Collection of the author.

Meikyō shinshi 明教新誌. Osaka: Kobayashi, 2003, 13 CD-ROMs.

Miaofa lianhua jing 妙法蓮華経. T 9, no. 262.

Moriyoshi shinnō reisenan 護良親王令宣案. Komonjo 1, no. 174.

Morookadera Kannondō jiryōshikichi kishinjō 諸岳寺観音堂寺領敷地寄進状. Monzenshi 2: 12; Komonjo 3: no. 1965.

Myōken kōshikibon 妙見講式本. 1780. Dairyūji. Listed in *Sōtōshūhō* 曹洞宗報 2011, no. 11, 83.

Myōken kōshikibon zen 妙見講式本全. n.d. Dairyūji.

Myōkōan shingi 妙高庵清規. See *Nōshū shogakuzan nai Myōkōan shingi*.

Myōkōji rekishi nenpyō 明光寺歴史年表. Myōkōji. Facsimile available at Sōtōshū Bunkazai Chōsa Iinkai.

Nehan kō kada narabini Shichisan 涅槃講伽陀並四智讃. 1694. Sōjiji Soin. Facsimile available at Sōtōshū Bunkazai Chōsa Iinkai. Listed in Bunkazai 7: 420.

Nehan kōshiki 涅槃講式. ZSZ 2: 735–750.

———. 1692. Shōbōji. Facsimile available at Sōtōshū Bunkazai Chōsa Iinkai. Listed in Shūhō 2: 168.

———. 1696. Saifukuji. Facsimile available at Sōtōshū Bunkazai Chōsa Iinkai. Listed in Bunkazai 7: 261.

———. 1725. Shugetsuji. Facsimile available at Sōtōshū Bunkazai Chōsa Iinkai. Listed in Bunkazai 7: 489.

———. By Genshin. In *Dainihon bukkyō zensho* 大日本佛教全書 33, edited by Bussho Hankōkai, 183–185. Tokyo: Bussho Hankōkai, 1916.

Nianfo sanmei baowang lun 念佛三昧寶王論. T 47, no. 1967.

Nichiiki tōjō shosoden 日域洞上諸祖傳. SZ 16: 33–86.

Nihon tōjō rentōroku 日本洞上聯燈錄. SZ 16: 191–522.

Nijūgo zanmai shiki 二十五三昧式. NKS 4: 246–255.

Nikkan 日鑑. 1763. Yōkōji. Facsimile available at Sōtōshū Bunkazai Chōsa Iinkai. Listed in Bunkazai 7: 612.

Nirvāṇa Sutra. See *Daban niepan jing*.

Nōshū shogakuzan nai Myōkōan shingi 能州諸嶽山内妙高庵清規. 1798. ZSZ 2: 343–351.

Nōshū Tōkokusan Yōkōji gyōji shidai 能州洞谷山永光寺行事次第. 1501. See *Keizan shingi, Rinkō shoshabon*.

Ōjō kōshiki 往生講式. T 84, no. 2725.

Ōjō yōshū 往生要集. T 84, no. 2682.

Qianshou qianyan guanshiyin pusa guangda yuanman wuai dabeixin tuoluoni jing 千手千眼觀世音菩薩廣大圓滿無礙大悲心陀羅尼經. T 20, no. 1060.

Qing guanshiyin pusa xiaofu duhai tuoluoni zhou jing 請觀世音菩薩消伏毒害陀羅尼呪經. T 20, no. 1043.

Qixinlun shubi xiaoji 起信論疏筆削記. T 44, no. 1848.

Rakan kanjō sahō narabini saimon 羅漢勧請作法並祭文. Ninnaji. Facsimile available at the Research Institute for Japanese Music Historiography, Ueno Gakuen University.

Rakan kō hossoku 羅漢講法則. Kadono Konzen Library Collection; Komazawa University Library; Research Institute for Japanese Music Historiography, Ueno Gakuen University; Stanford University Library.

Rakan kō kada narabini Shichisan 羅漢講伽陀並四智讃. 1694. Sōjiji Soin; Kadono Konzen Library Collection. Facsimile available at Sōtōshū Bunkazai Chōsa Iinkai. Listed in Bunkazai 7: 420.

Rakan kōshiki 羅漢講式. 1779. Collection of the author.

———.1816. By Lanxi Daolong. Komazawa University Library.

———.1856. By Lanxi Daolong. Komazawa University Library.

———. n.d. By Lanxi Daolong. Reprint of 1856 edition. Engakuji.

Rakan ku 羅漢供. Ninnaji. Facsimile available at the Research Institute for Japanese Music Historiography, Ueno Gakuen University.

Rakan ku sahō 羅漢供作法. Hōryūji 法隆寺. Komazawa University Library.

Rakan ku saimon 羅漢供祭文. JDZ, 457–458; KZ 9: 35.

Rakan kushiki 羅漢供式. MSS 5: 327–366.

Rakan kuyō shikimon 羅漢供養式文. Manuscript attributed to Dōgen. DZSK, 225–237; DZSS, 91–94; DZO 2: 402–404; DZZ 7: 288–295; ZSZ 1: 23–29.

Rakan kuyōshiki 羅漢供養式. ZSZ 2: 787–803; Kadono Konzen Library Collection.

Rakan ōgenden 羅漢應驗傳. Komazawa University Library.

Rakan wasan 羅漢和讃. NKS 4: 46–48.

Record of the Perpetuity of the Dharma. See *Daaluohan nantimiduoluo suoshuo fazhuji*.

Rentōroku 聯燈錄. See *Nihon tōjō rentōroku*.

Ruizhou Dongshan Liangjie chanshi yulu 瑞州洞山良价禪師語録. T 47, no. 1986b.

Ryaku kōshiki (*Daijō shōin*) 略講式（大乘唱引）. Sōjiji Soin; Kadono Konzen Library Collection; Research Institute for Japanese Music Historiography, Ueno Gakuen University; collection of the author.

Ryōson shōki tō sajōchō 両尊征忌等差定帳. 1871. Sōjiji.

Sakujitsu Rakan kōshiki 朔日羅漢講式. In *Kōyasan kōshikishū* 高野山講式集, CD-ROM 1: 四1, 四2, 四3, 四4, 四5, 四6, 四49, 四53.

San kōshiki narabini hōyō 三講式並法要. 1813. Sōjiji Soin; Kadono Konzen Library Collection. Facsimile available at Sōtōshū Bunkazai Chōsa Iinkai. Listed in Bunkazai 7: 420.

Sansō yuiseki teradera okibumiki 山僧遺跡寺々置文記. JDZ, 416–418; KZ 8: 171–179.

Sekkyō hitsukei: Shurin tekiyō shitoku shō 説教必携　珠林摘要秖犢鈔. Komazawa University Library; National Diet Library Digital Collections, http://kindai.ndl.go.jp/info:ndljp/pid/818418, http://kindai.ndl.go.jp/info:ndljp/pid/818419.

Sekkyō rakusōdan 説教落草談. 14 vols. Komazawa University Library; National Diet Library Digital Collections, http://kindai.ndl.go.jp/info:ndljp/pid/818513 to http://kindai.ndl.go.jp/info:ndljp/pid/818526 inclusive.

Shaoshi liumen ji 少室六門集. T 48, no. 2009.

Shari sōdenki 舎利相傳記. DZO 2: 395–396.

Shengman shizi hou yisheng da fangbian fangguang jing 勝鬘師子吼一乘大方便方廣經. T 12, no. 353.

Shi kōshiki 四講式. 1686. By Kankai. Collection of Ozaki Shōzen.

Shiza kōshiki 四座講式. T 84, no. 2731; Kindaichi 1973: 491–527.

Shōbōgenzō 正法眼藏. DZO 1; DZZ 1–2; T 82, no. 2582.

Shogaku kaisan Keizan Butsuji zenji gyōjitsu 諸嶽開山瑩山佛慈禪師行實. SZ 16: 21–22.

Shogaku kokushi zenji kōshikibon 諸嶽國師禅師講式本. 1849. Untōan. Facsimile available at Sōtōshū Bunkazai Chōsa Iinkai. Listed in Bunkazai 7: 808.

Shogakuzan rinban nikkan 諸嶽山輪番日鑑. Keijuji. In Itō R. 2003b.

Shogakuzan rinbanchū nikki 諸嶽山輪番中日記. Shōyūji. In Itō R. 2001b.

Shogakuzan Sōjiji nikka shokyōyō shū 諸嶽山摠持寺日課諸経要集. Tsurumi: Daihonzan Sōjiji Sōdō kōryūkai, 2005.

Shogakuzan Sōjizenji shogyōji 諸嶽山総持禅寺諸行事. In Muromine 1965: 243–246.

Shōketsu sho 聲决書. *Zōfukuin bunko zenpon shūsei* 3, no. 323.

Shokō sahō shū 諸講作法集. 1661. Research Institute for Japanese Music Historiography, Ueno Gakuen University.

Shōmyō kihan 声明軌範. See *Shōwa kaitei Shōmyō kihan.*

Shōmyō zenshū 声明全集. Compiled by Taki Dōnin. Kyoto: Baiyōshoin, 1924. National Diet Library Digital Collections, https://dl.ndl.go.jp/info:ndljp/pid/915404.

Shōmyōshū 声明集. 1472. Kōyasan. Research Institute for Japanese Music Historiography, Ueno Gakuen University. Facsimile in Fukushima 1995, 9–52; and Fukushima, Arai, and Nelson 2018, 7–50.

Shōsai kichijō kyō jikisetsu 消災吉祥經直說. 1769. Komazawa University Library.

Shosaimon 諸祭文. 1624–1645. Research Institute for Japanese Music Historiography, Ueno Gakuen University.

———. 1673–1681. Research Institute for Japanese Music Historiography, Ueno Gakuen University.

Shōwa kaitei Rakan kōshiki 昭和改訂羅漢講式. See *Shōwa kaitei Shōmyō kihan.*

Shōwa kaitei Shōmyō kihan: Tanbutsue hosshiki, Rakan kōshiki, Daifusatsu shiki, Kannon senbō, furoku 昭和改訂声明軌範 歎佛会法式 羅漢講式 大布薩式 観音懺法 付録. 5 vols. Tokyo: Sōtōshū Shūmuchō, 1966.

Shōwa kaitei Sōtōshū gyōji kihan 昭和改訂曹洞宗行持軌範. 2nd ed. Edited by Sōtōshū Shūmuchō Kyōgakubu. Tokyo: Sōtōshū Shūmuchō, 2004.

Shōyūki 小右記. 3 vols. In *Zōho shiryō taisei* 增補史料大成, edited by Zōho Shiryō Taisei Hankōkai. Kyoto: Rinsen shoten, 1968.

Shūi Ōjōden 拾遺往生伝. In *Nihon shisō taikei* 日本思想大系 7, 277–392. Tokyo: Iwanami Shoten, 1974.

Sōji dainise Gasan oshō gyōjō 總持第二世峨山和尚行狀. SZ 17: 263–264.

Sōji kaisan Taiso ryakuden 摠持開山太祖略傳. 1879. Komazawa University Library; National Diet Library Digital Collections, http://kindai.ndl.go.jp/info:ndljp/pid/823275.

———. 1897. National Diet Library Digital Collections, http://kindai.ndl.go.jp/info:ndljp/pid/823276.

Sōji nidai oshō shōtō 總持二代和尚抄劄. ZSZ 2: 19–23.

Sōjiji chūkō engi 総持寺中興縁起. Monzenshi 2: 11–12.

Sōjiji kaibyaku no engi 総持寺開闢之縁起. Monzenshi 2: 13.

Sōjiji monto keiyakujō 摠持寺門徒契約狀. Komonjo 1, no. 86.

Sōjiji shohatto 総持寺諸法度. Monzenshi 2: 95.

Sōtō roku kōshiki 曹洞六講式. Research Institute for Japanese Music Historiography, Ueno Gakuen University.

Sōtōshū gyōji kihan 曹洞宗行持軌範. See *Shōwa kaitei Sōtōshū gyōji kihan.*

Sōtōshū ryōhonzan futatsu zensho 曹洞宗両本山布達全書. 6 vols. Komazawa University Library.

Sōtōshū ryōso denryaku 曹洞宗兩祖傳畧. Komazawa University Library; National Diet Library Digital Collections, http://kindai.ndl.go.jp/info:ndljp/pid/823326.

Sōtōzen mezame: Dōgen Zenji gotanjō 800 nen keisan, 750 kai daionki hōshū kinen; Daihonzan Sōjiji goiten 90 nen 曹洞禅覚: 道元禅師ご生誕800年慶讃750回大遠忌奉修記念, 大本山總持寺ご移転90年. [2000–2001]. Book, 10 videocassettes (VHS), 25 compact discs. Produced by Sōtōshū Shūmuchō, Daihonzan Eiheiji, and Daihonzan Sōjiji.

Sozan gyōhō shinan: Hattō butsuden hen 祖山行法指南 法堂佛殿篇. Eiheiji-chō: Daihonzan Eiheiji, 1975.

Śrīmālā Sūtra. T 12, no. 353.

Taiso Butsuji kōshiki 太祖佛慈講式. 1892. By Kohō Hakugan. Kanazawa Shiritsu Tamagawa Toshokan Kinsei Shiryōkan.

———. 1924. Yōkōji; Kanazawa Shiritsu Tamagawa Toshokan Kinsei Shiryōkan; Kadono Konzen Library Collection. *Kōshiki database,* no. 361.

Taiso Kōtoku enmyō kokushi gyōjitsu zue 大祖弘徳圓明國師行實圖會. Komazawa University Library.

Taiso kokushi goden 太祖國師御傳. See *Sōtōshū ryōso denryaku.*

Taiso ryakuden 太祖略伝. See *Sōji kaisan Taiso ryakuden.*

Tanbutsue hosshiki 歎佛會法式. ZSZ 2: 691–703.

Teiho Kenzeiki zue 訂補建撕記圖會. SZ 17: 33–162; Stanford University Library, 2 vols.

Tenzō kyōkun 典座教訓. DZO 2: 295–303; DZZ 6: 2–25; T 82: 320a02–323a15.

Tōdaiji yōroku 東大寺要録. Edited by Tsutsuki Eishun. Osaka: Zenkoku shobō, 1944.

Tōji jūgejō no kikyō 当寺十箇条之亀鏡. Monzenshi 2: 14.

Tōjō daifusatsuhō 洞上大布薩法. ZSZ 2: 805–818.

Tōjō dentō kōshiki 洞上傳燈講式. ZSZ 2: 853–869. Sōjiji Soin; Kadono Konzen Library Collection; collection of the author.

Tōjō go kōshiki 洞上五講式. Komazawa University Library; Research Institute for Japanese Music Historiography, Ueno Gakuen University.

Tōjō Rakan kōshiki 洞上羅漢講式. 1756. By Menzan. Kadono Konzen Library Collection.

Tōjō shōraihō 洞上唱禮法. ZSZ 2: 705–716.

Tōjō sōdō shingi gyōhōshō 洞上僧堂清規行法鈔. SZ 4: 29–208.

Tōjō sōdō shingi kōtei betsuroku 洞上 堂清規考訂別錄. SZ 4: 209–330.

Tōkoku goso gyōjitsu 洞谷五祖行實. SZ 16: 595–599.

Tōkokuki 洞谷記. JDZ, 392–463; KZ 8.

Tōkokusan jinmiraisai okibumi 洞谷山尽未来際置文. JDZ, 419–420; KZ 8: 182–194. In Azuma 2002, 20–21; *Yōkōji no meihō,* 30, 76–77.

Tōkokusan Yōkōji shi 洞谷山永光寺誌. 1924. Komazawa University Library.

Wenshu suoshuo zuisheng mingyi jing 文殊所説最勝名義經. T 20, no. 1188.

Wumenguan 無門關. T 48, no. 2005.

Yakushi kōshiki ryakuhon 薬師講式略本. n.d. Yōmeiji. Listed in *Sōtōshūhō* 曹洞宗報 2016, no. 11.

Yaoshi yigui yiju 藥師儀軌一具. T 19, no. 924.
Yiyao jing 遺教経. T 12, no. 389.
Yōhō Renpō keifu 鷹峰聯芳系譜. ZSZ 10: 319–398.
Yōkō Hakugan zenji gyōjō 永光白巖禪師行狀. In *Yōkō Hakugan zenji iroku,* 77–80.
Yōkō Hakugan zenji iroku 永光白巖禪師遺録. 1913. Komazawa University Library.
Yoshimi Yoritaka hōnō jō 吉見頼隆奉納状. In *Yōkōji no meihō,* 89.
Yuanren lun 原人論. T 45, no. 1886.
Zenkai danju yōketsushū 禪海探珠要訣集. Komazawa University Library; National Diet Library Digital Collections, http://kindai.ndl.go.jp/info:ndljp/pid/823185.
Zenrin shōkisen 禪林象器箋. By Mujaku Dōchū. Tokyo: Seishin Shobō, 1963.

Audio and Video Recordings

Anan kōshiki: Aichi Senmon Nisodō sōritsu hyakushūnen kinen 阿難講式: 愛知専門尼僧堂創立百周年記念. Performed at Aichi Senmon Nisodō. Produced by BBS Terebi, 2003, videocassette (VHS). Booklet.
Dōgen zenji nanahyakugojukkai daionki hōsan: Shinpen Hōon kōshiki 道元禅師七百五十回大遠忌奉賛　新編報恩講式. Performed at Daihonzan Eiheiji Betsuin Chōkokuji 大本山永平寺別院長谷寺. SonTech D00EM04702, 2002, compact disc. Booklet with liner notes.
Goitō hachijūnen kinen; Sōtōzen: Kōshiki no sekai. 御移東八十年記念　曹洞禅　講式の世界. Daihonzan Sōjiji Hōyō Jimukyoku, 1990, 2 audiocassettes. Booklet with liner notes.
Jizō kōshiki 地蔵講式. Performed at Sōjiji by the nuns of Aichi Senmen Nisōdō. In *Sōtōzen mezame,* videocassette 6, produced by Tōkai Terebi and Universal Music.
Kobutsu no manebi: Hosshiki shōmyō 古仏のまねび: 法式声明. Performed by Maekawa Hakuhō 前川博邦. Recorded in 1988–1989. Tōkai Bijon Kabushiki Kaisha, 3 DVDs.
Rakan kōshiki 羅漢講式. Performed at Sōjiji, 2004–2011. Video recordings by M. Mross. Online supplement to *Memory, Music, Manuscripts,* Stanford Digital Repository, https://searchworks.stanford.edu/view/dq109wp7548.
Shōmyō no tebiki 声明の手引き. Zenkoku Sōtōshū Seinenkai, Hōshiki Iinkai, [2009], 2 DVDs.
Shōmyō taikei 声明体系. Vol. 6 (of 8), *Zen* 禅, edited by Yokomichi Mario 横道萬理雄 et al. Hōzōkan, 1984, 4 LP records. Booklet with extensive liner notes.
Sōtōshū hosshiki shinan: Ino dōan kōshū 曹洞宗法式指南: 維那堂行講習. Recorded in 2010. Tokyo: Shikisha, 2 DVDs.
Sōtōshū hosshiki shōmyō kōza 曹洞宗法式声明講座. Performed by Maekawa Hakuhō 前川博邦. Bideo Monitā Kabushiki Kaisha, [1989], 10 videocassettes (VHS). Booklet with liner notes.
Sōtō-Zen: Chōka, senbō, narashimono 曹洞禅: 朝課 懺法 鳴物. Tōshiba EMI THX–90055, 1980, 6 LP records. Booklet by Watarai Shōjun 渡井正純 and Sawada Atsuko 澤田篤子.
Sōtō-Zen: Kōshiki, Tanbutsu, Fusatsu 曹洞禅: 講式 歎仏 布薩. Tōshiba EMI THX–90146–51, 1982, 6 LP records. Booklet by Watarai Shōjun 渡井正純 and Sawada Atsuko 澤田篤子.

Sōtō-Zen: Tange, Kitō, Kuyō 曹洞禅: 歎偈 祈祷 供養. Tōshiba EMI THX–90175–181, 1983, 6 LP records. Booklet by Watarai Shōjun 渡井正純 and Tsukamoto Atsuko 塚本篤子.

Tōjō dentō kōshiki 洞上傳燈講式. Performed at Sōjiji, 2018. Video recordings by M. Mross. Online supplement to *Memory, Music, Manuscripts,* Stanford Digital Repository, https://searchworks.stanford.edu/view/dq109wp7548.

Secondary Sources

Abe Shunshō 阿部俊正. 2019. "Butsuji kōshiki" 仏慈講式. *Sōtōshū sōgō kenkyū sentā gakujutsu taikai kiyō* 20: 85–90.

Amano Denchū 天納傳中. 2000. *Tendai shōmyō: Amano Denchū chosakushū* 天台声明: 天納傳中著作集. Kyoto: Hōzōkan.

Ambros, Barbara. 2016a. "A Rite of Their Own: Japanese Buddhist Nuns and the *Anan kōshiki.*" In Ambros, Ford, and Mross 2016, 207–250.

———. 2016b. "*Anan kōshiki:* An Annotated Translation." In Ambros, Ford, and Mross 2016, online supplement 3: 1–24.

Ambros, Barbara R., James L. Ford, and Michaela Mross, eds. 2016. *Kōshiki in Japanese Buddhism.* Special issue, *Japanese Journal of Religious Studies* 43, no. 1.

Aoyama Shundō 青山俊董. 2003. *Anan sama* 阿難さま. In *Anan kōshiki: Aichi Senmon Nisodō sōritsu hyakushūnen kinen.*

Arai Kōjun 新井弘順. 1986. *Musik und Zeichen: Notationen buddhistischer Gesänge Japans, Schriftquellen des 11.–19. Jahrhunderts.* Köln: Museum für Ostasiatische Kunst.

———. 1995. "The Historical Development of Music Notation for *shōmyō* (Japanese Buddhist Chant): Centering on *hakase* Graphs." In *Lux Oriente: Begegnungen der Kulturen in der Musikforschung,* edited by Klaus Wolfgang Niemöller and Chung Kyo-chul, 1–30. Kassel: Gustav Bosse.

———. 1996. "The Historical Development of Music Notation for shoomyoo (Japanese Buddhist chant): Centering on *hakase* Graphs." *Nihon ongakushi kenkyuu* 1: vii–xxxix.

———. 1999. "Concerning *shōmyō,* the Buddhist Chant of Japan." In *The Buddhist Chant in Its Cultural Context,* 295–337. Seoul: National Center for Korean Traditional Performing Arts.

———. 2008. *Jōrakue Shizakō hossoku to Shiza kōshiki no kenkyū* 常楽会『四座講法則』と『四座講式』の研究. Tokyo: Nishogakusha Daigaku.

Arai, Paula. 1999. *Women Living Zen: Japanese Sōtō Buddhist Nuns.* New York: Oxford University Press.

———. 2000. "Japanese Buddhist Nuns' Ritual of Gratitude and Empowerment." In *Women's Buddhism, Buddhism's Women: Tradition, Revision, Renewal,* edited by Ellison Findley, 119–130. Boston: Wisdom Publications.

———. 2008. "Women and Dōgen: Rituals of Empowerment and Healing." In *Zen Ritual: Studies of Zen Theory in Practice,* edited by Steven Heine and Dale S. Wright, 185–204. Oxford: Oxford University Press.

Assmann, Jan. 1992. *Das kulturelle Gedächtnis: Schrift, Erinnerung und politische Identität in frühen Hochkulturen.* Munich: C. H. Beck.

———. 2000. *Religion und kulturelles Gedächtnis: Zehn Studien Taschenbuch*. Munich: C. H. Beck.

Azuma Ryūshin 東隆真. 1974a. *Keizan zenji no kenkyu* 瑩山禅師の研究. Tokyo: Shunjusha.

———. 1974b. "Keizan zenji kenkyū no dōkō" 瑩山禅師研究の同行. In *Keizan zenji kenkyū: Keizan zenji roppyakugojukkai daionki kinen ronbunshū* 瑩山禅師研究: 瑩山禅師六百五十回大遠忌記念論文集, edited by Keizan Zenji Hōsan Kankōkai, 1113–1134. Tokyo: Keizan Zenji Hōsan Kankōkai.

———. 1974c. "Keizan zenji kankei bunken mokuroku" 瑩山禅師関係文献目録. In *Keizan zenji kenkyū: Keizan zenji roppyakugojukkai daionki kinen ronbunshū* 瑩山禅師研究：瑩山禅師六百五十回大遠忌記念論文集, edited by Keizan Zenji Hōsan Kankōkai, 1135–1182. Tokyo: Keizan Zenji Hōsan Kankōkai.

———. 1983. "Dōgen zenji to Rakan kōshiki ni tsuite" 道元禅師と羅漢講式について. *Indogaku bukkyōgaku kenkyū* 31: 76–83.

———. 1996. *Taiso Keizan Zenji* 太祖瑩山禅師. Tokyo: Kokusho Kankōkai.

———. 2000. "Shinshiryō Tōkokusan Yōkōji zō den Keizan zenji kunten Busshi hatsu nehan ryakusetsu kyōkyai kyō" 新資料洞谷山永光寺蔵伝瑩山禅師訓点仏垂般涅槃略説教誡経. *Komazawa joshi daigaku kenkyū kiyō* 7: 1–49.

———. 2002. *Yōkōji monogatari: Rekishi to bunkazai* 永光寺ものがたり一歴史と文化財一. Hakui: Yōkōji.

Baikaryū Eisanka Kenkyū Purojekuto 梅花流詠讃歌研究プロジェクト. 2019. *Sōtōshū kyōdanshi ni okeru Baikaryū* 曹洞宗教団史における梅花流. Tokyo: Sōtōshū Sōgō Kenkyū Sentā.

Bateson, Gregory. 1987. *Steps to an Ecology of Mind: Collected Essays in Anthropology, Psychiatry, Evolution, and Epistemology*. Northvale, NJ: Aronson. First published 1972.

Bell, Catherine. 1997. *Ritual: Perspectives and Dimensions*. New York: Oxford University Press.

Bellah, Robert N., Richard Madsen, William M. Sullivan, Ann Swidler, and Steven M. Tipton. 1985. *Habits of the Heart: Individualism and Commitment in American Life*. Berkeley: University of California Press.

Berry, Mary Elizabeth. 2006. *Japan in Print: Information and Nation in the Early Modern Period*. Berkeley: University of California Press.

Blacking, John. 1973. *How Musical Is Man?* Seattle: University of Washington Press.

Bodiford, William M. 1993. *Sōtō Zen in Medieval Japan*. Honolulu: University of Hawai'i Press.

———. 1994. "Sōtō Zen in a Japanese Town: Field Notes on a Once-Every-Thirty-Three-Years Kannon Festival." *Japanese Journal of Religious Studies* 21, no. 1: 3–36.

———. 1996. "Zen and the Art of Religious Prejudice: Efforts to Reform a Tradition of Social Discrimination." *Japanese Journal of Religious Studies* 23, nos. 1–2: 1–27.

———. 2012. "Remembering Dōgen: Eiheiji and Dōgen." In *Dōgen: Textual and Historical Studies,* edited by Steven Heine, 207–222. New York: Oxford University Press.

———. 2015. "Keizan's *Denkōroku:* A Textual and Contextual Overview." In *Dōgen and Sōtō Zen,* edited by Steven Heine, 167–187. New York: Oxford University Press.

———. 2017. "Introduction." In Foulk 2017, 2: 1–91.

Borup, Jørn. 2008. *Japanese Rinzai Zen Buddhism: Myoshinji, a Living Religion.* Leiden: Brill.

Braak, André van der. 2015. "The Practice of Zazen as Ritual Performance." In *Ritual Participation and Interreligious Dialogue: Boundaries, Transgressions and Innovations,* edited by Marianne Moyaert and Joris Geldof, 156–165. New York: Bloomsbury.

Breugem, Vincent Michaël Nicolaas. 2012. "From Prominence to Obscurity: A Study of the Darumashū, Japan's First Zen School." PhD diss., Leiden University.

Bumke, Joachim. 2010. "Der unfeste Text: Überlegungen zur Überlieferungsgeschichte und Textkritik der höfischen Epik im 13. Jahrhundert." In *Texte zur modernen Philologie,* edited by Uwe Wirth and Kai Bremer, 269–286. Stuttgart: Reclam.

Buswell, Robert E., Jr. 1995. "Hagiographies of the Korean Monk Wonhyo." In *Buddhism in Practice,* edited by Donald S. Lopez, 553–562. Princeton, NJ: Princeton University Press.

Callahan, Christopher T. 2011. "Kakunyo and the Making of Shinran and Shin Buddhism." PhD diss., Harvard University.

———. 2016. "Recognizing the Founder, Seeing Amida Buddha: Kakunyo's *Hōon kōshiki.*" In Ambros, Ford, and Mross 2016, 177–205.

Cerquiglini, Bernard. 1999. *In Praise of the Variant: A Critical History of Philology.* Translated by Betsy Wing. Baltimore: Johns Hopkins University Press.

Chen Ruixuan. 2018. "The *Nandimitrāvadāna:* A Living Text from the Buddhist Tradition." PhD diss., Leiden University. https://openaccess.leidenuniv.nl/handle/1887/66261.

Chibbett, David G. 1977. *The History of Japanese Printing and Book Illustration.* Tokyo: Kodansha International.

Cleary, Thomas, trans. 1990. *Transmission of Light: Zen in the Art of Enlightenment.* San Francisco: North Point Press.

Collcutt, Martin. 1981. *Five Mountains: The Rinzai Zen Monastic Institution in Medieval Japan.* Cambridge, MA: Harvard University Press.

———. 1983. "The Early Ch'an Monastic Rule: *Ch'ing kuei* and the Shaping of Ch'an Community Life." In *Early Chan in China and Tibet,* edited by Whalen Lai and R. Lancaster Lewis, 165–184. Berkeley, CA: Asian Humanities Press.

Cook, Francis Dojun. 1983. "Enlightenment in Dōgen's Zen." *Journal of the International Association of Buddhist Studies* 6, no. 1: 7–30.

———, trans. 2003. *The Record of Transmitting the Light: Zen Master Keizan's Denkōroku.* Boston: Wisdom Publications.

Copp, Paul F. 2005. "Voice, Dust, Shadow, Stone: The Makings of Spells in Medieval Chinese Buddhism." PhD diss., Princeton University.

Deegalle, Mahinda. 2006. *Popularizing Buddhism: Preaching as Performance in Sri Lanka.* Albany: State University of New York Press.

Demieville, Paul. 1929–1930. "Bombai." In *Hôbôgirin: Dictionnaire encyclopédique du bouddhisme d'après les sources chinoises et japonaises,* 93–113. Tokyo: Maison Franco-Japonaise.

Douglas, Gavin. 2015. "Buddhist Music." Oxford Bibliographies Online. https://www.oxfordbibliographies.com.

Ebie Gimyō 海老江義明. 2010. "Anan kōshiki" 阿難講式. In Suzuki Bunmei 2010, 309–325.

Eckel, Malcolm David. 1990. "The Power of the Buddha's Absence: On the Foundations of Mahāyāna Buddhist Ritual." *Journal of Ritual Studies* 4, no. 2: 61–95.

Eubanks, Charlotte D. 2011. *Miracles of Book and Body: Buddhist Textual Culture and Medieval Japan.* Berkeley: University of California Press.

Faure, Bernard. 1987. "The Daramu-shū, Dōgen, and Sōtō Zen." *Monumenta Nipponica* 42, no. 1: 25–55.

———. 1991. *The Rhetoric of Immediacy: A Cultural Critique of Chan / Zen Buddhism.* Princeton: Princeton University Press.

———. 1995. "Quand l'habit fait le moine: The Symbolism of the *kāsāya* in Sōtō Zen." *Cahiers d'Extrême-Asie* 8: 335–369.

———. 1996. *Visions of Power: Imagining Medieval Japanese Buddhism.* Princeton, NJ: Princeton University Press.

———, ed. 2003. *Chan Buddhism in Ritual Context.* London: Routledge.

———. 2016. *Gods of Medieval Japan. Vol. 1, The Fluid Pantheon.* Honolulu: University of Hawai'i Press.

Flood, Gavin. 2004. *The Ascetic Self: Subjectivity, Memory and Tradition.* Cambridge: Cambridge University Press.

Födermayr, Franz. 1982. "*Shichi-no-san:* Die Obertontiefstimme in Japan?" In *Festschrift Othmar Wessely zum 60. Geburtstag,* edited by Manfred Angerer, 151–205. Tutzing: Schneider.

Födermayr, Franz, and Werner A. Deutsch. 1995. "Zur Bedeutung klanganalytischer Techniken für die Untersuchung buddhistischer Gesänge." In *Lux Oriente: Begegnungen der Kulturen in der Musikforschung,* edited by Klaus Wolfgang Niemöller and Chung Kyo-chul, 349–361. Kassel: Gustav Bosse.

Fong, Wen. 1958. "Five Hundred Lohans at the Daitokuji." PhD diss., Princeton University.

Ford, James L. 2005. "Competing with Amida: A Study and Translation of Jōkei's *Miroku Kōshiki.*" *Monumenta Nipponica* 60, no. 1: 43–79.

———. 2006a. *Jōkei and Buddhist Devotion in Early Medieval Japan.* New York: Oxford University Press.

———. 2006b. "Buddhist Ceremonials (*kōshiki*) and the Ideological Discourse of Established Buddhism in Early Medieval Japan." In *Discourse and Ideology in Medieval Japanese Buddhism,* edited by Richard K. Payne and Taigen Daniel, 97–125. New York: Routledge.

Foulk, Theodore Griffith. 1987. "The Ch'an School and its Place in the Buddhist Monastic Tradition." PhD diss., University of Michigan.

———. 1993. "Myth, Ritual, and Monastic Practice in Sung Ch'an Buddhism." In *Religion and Society in T'ang and Sung China,* edited by Patricia Buckley Ebrey and Peter N. Gregory, 147–208. Honolulu: University of Hawai'i Press.

———, trans. 2001. "Instructions for the Cook." In *Nothing Is Hidden: Essays on Zen Master Dogen's Instructions for the Cook,* edited by Jisho Warner, Shōhaku Okumura, John McRae, and Taigen Dan Leighten, 21–40. New York: Weatherhill.

———. 2004. "*Chanyuan qinggui* and Other 'Rules of Purity' in Chinese Buddhism."

In *The Zen Canon: Understanding the Classic Texts,* edited by Steven Heine and Dale S. Wright, 275–312. Oxford: Oxford University Press.

———. 2006. " 'Rules of Purity' in Japanese Zen." In *Zen Classics,* edited by Steven Heine and Dale S. Wright, 137–170. Oxford: Oxford University Press.

———. 2008. "Ritual in Japanese Zen Buddhism." In *Zen Ritual: Studies of Zen Buddhist Theory in Practice,* edited by Steven Heine and Dale S. Wright, 21–82. Oxford: Oxford University Press.

———, trans. 2010a. *Standard Observances of the Soto Zen School. Vol. 1, Translation.* Tokyo: Sōtōshū Shūmuchō.

———, 2010b. *Standard Observances of the Soto Zen School. Vol. 2, Introduction, Glossaries, and Index.* Tokyo: Sōtōshū Shūmuchō.

———. 2012. " 'Just sitting' "? Dōgen's Take on Zazen, Sutra Reading, and Other Conventional Buddhist Practices." In *Dōgen: Textual and Historical Studies,* edited by Steven Heine, 75–106. New York: Oxford University Press.

———. 2015. "Dōgen's Use of Rujing's 'Just Sit' (*shikan taza*) and Other Kōans." In *Dōgen and Sōtō Zen,* edited by Steven Heine, 23–45. New York: Oxford University Press.

———, ed. and trans. 2017. *Record of the Transmission of Illumination by the Great Ancestor, Zen Master Keizan.* 2 vols. Tokyo: Sōtōshū Shūmuchō.

Foulk, Theodore Griffith, and Robert H. Sharf. 1993. "On the Ritual Use of Ch'an Portraiture in Medieval China." *Cahiers d'Extrême-Asie* 7: 149–219.

Friedrich, Michael. 1982. "Die Opfergebete (*saibun*) im Honchō-monzui." *NOAG* 131–132: 47–62.

Fujita Takuji 藤田琢司, ed. 2011. *Kundoku Genkō shakusho* 訓読元亨釈書. 2 vols. Kyoto: Zenbunka Kenkyūjo.

Fukushima Kazuo 福島和夫, ed. 1995. *Nihon ongaku shiryō shūsei 1: Gohan shōmyō fu* 日本音楽史料集成 1: 古版声明譜. Tokyo: Tōkyō Bijutsu.

Fukushima Kazuo 福島和夫, Arai Kōjun 新井弘順, and Steven Nelson. 2018. *Nihon no insatsu gakufu: Muromachi jidai hen* 日本の印刷楽譜: 室町時代篇. Tokyo: Bensei Shuppan.

Gane, Roy E. 2004. *Ritual Dynamic Structure.* Piscataway, NJ: Gorgias Press.

Germano, David, and Kevin Trainor. 2004. *Embodying the Dharma: Buddhist Relic Veneration in Asia.* Albany: State University of New York Press.

Giesen, Walter. 1977. *Zur Geschichte des buddhistischen Ritualgesangs in Japan: Traktate des 9. bis 14. Jahrhunderts zum shōmyō der Tendai-Sekte.* Kassel: Bärenreiter.

———. 1990. "Buddhistische Musik." In *Japan-Handbuch,* edited by Horst Hammitzsch, 1203–1208. 3rd ed. Stuttgart: Franz Steiner Verlag.

Girard, Frédéric. 1990. *Un moine de la secte Kegon à l'époque de Kamakura: Myōe (1173–1232) et le 'Journal des ses rêves.'* Paris: Ecole française d'Extrême-Orient.

Gladigow, Burkhard. 2004. "Sequenzierung von Riten und die Ordnung der Rituale." In *Zoroastrian Rituals in Context,* edited by Michael Stausberg, 57–76. Leiden: Brill.

———. 2008. "Complexity." In *Theorizing Rituals: Issues, Topics, Approaches, Concepts,* edited by Jens Kreinath, Jan Snoek, and Michael Stausberg, 483–494. Leiden: Brill.

Glassman, Hank. 2012. *The Face of Jizō: Image and Cult in Medieval Japanese Buddhism.* Honolulu: University of Hawai'i Press.

Goffman, Erving. 1974. *Frame Analysis: An Essay on the Organization of Experience.* Cambridge, MA: Harvard University Press.

Graf, Tim. 2017. "Brands of Zen: Kitō jiin in Contemporary Japanese Sōtō Zen Buddhism." PhD diss., Heidelberg University. http://archiv.ub.uni-heidelberg.de/volltextserver/23728/1/Dissertation%20Tim%20Graf.pdf.

Greene, Paul D., Keith Howard, Terry E. Miller, Phong T. Nguyen, and Hwee-San Tan. 2002. "Buddhism and the Musical Cultures of Asia: A Critical Literature Survey." In *Body and Ritual in Buddhist Musical Cultures.* Special issue, *The World of Music* 44, no. 2: 135–175.

Gregory, Peter N. 1991. *Tsung-mi and the Sinification of Buddhism.* Princeton, NJ: Princeton University Press.

———. 1995. *Inquiry into the Origin of Humanity: An Annotated Translation of Tsung-mi's Yüan jen lun with a Modern Commentary.* Honolulu: University of Hawai'i Press.

Grimes, Ronald L. 2010. *Beginnings in Ritual Studies.* 3rd ed. Waterloo: Ritual Studies International.

———. 2014. *The Craft of Ritual Studies.* Oxford: Oxford University Press.

———. 2017. "Bridging Rituals: A Daughter's Song." *Liminalities: A Journal of Performance Studies* 13, no. 2: 1–16.

Gülberg, Niels. 1993. "Buddhist Ceremonials (kōshiki) of Medieval Japan and Their Impact on Literature." *Taishō daigaku sōgō bukkyō kenkyūjo nenpō* 15: 67–81.

———. 1995. "Myōe saku *Busshōe kōshiki* ni tsuite" 明恵作『仏生会講式』について. *Taishō daigaku sōgō bukkyō kenkyūjo nenpō* 17: 1–29.

———. 1999. *Buddhistische Zeremoniale (kōshiki) und ihre Bedeutung für die Literatur des japanischen Mittelalters.* Stuttgart: Steiner.

———. 2006. "Kōshiki to wa nanika" 講式とは何か. In *Nihon kanbun shiryō, Gakusho-hen: Shōmyō shiryō shū* 日本漢文資料　楽書編: 声明資料集, edited by Tanaka Yukie, 30–40. Tokyo: Nishōgakusha Daigaku.

———. 2016. "*Jingi Kōshiki:* A Neglected Field of Study." In Ambros, Ford, and Mross 2016, 153–175.

———. 2018. "Hōe to kōshiki: Nanto Hokurei no kōshiki o chūshin toshite" 法会と講式ー南都・北嶺の講式を中心としてー. In *Nantogaku Hokureigaku no sekai: Hōe to butsudō* 南都学・北嶺学の世界: 法会と仏道, edited by Kusunoki Junshō, 51–72. Kyoto: Hōzōkan.

Handelman, Don. 2004. "Re-Framing Ritual." In *Dynamics of Changing Rituals,* edited by Jens Kreinath et al., 9–20. New York: Peter Lang.

———. 2005. "Bureaucratic Logic, Bureaucratic Aesthetics: The Opening Event of Holocaust Martyrs and Heroes Remembrance Day in Israel." In *Aesthetics in Performance: Formations of Symbolic Construction and Experience,* edited by Angela Hobart and Bruce Kapferer, 196–215. New York: Berghahn Books.

———. 2012. "Postlude: Framing Hierarchically, Framing Moebiusly." *Journal of Ritual Studies* 26, no. 2: 65–77.

Harada Kōdō 原田弘道. 1980. "Rakan kōshiki kō" 羅漢講式考. *Komazawa daigaku bukkyōgakubu ronshū* 11: 60–74.

Harich-Schneider, Eta. 1973. *A History of Japanese Music.* London: Oxford University Press.

Hayes, Matthew. 2018. "Faith, Devotion, and Doctrinal Knowledge: Interpretative Strategies in Shingon Liturgical Exegesis." *Journal of Religion in Japan* 7: 27–56.

Heine, Steven. 2003. "Abbreviation or Aberration? The Role of the *Shushōgi* in Modern Sōtō Zen Buddhism." In *Buddhism in the Modern World: Adaptations of an Ancient Tradition,* edited by Steven Heine and Charles S. Prebish, 169–192. New York: Oxford University Press.

———. 2014. *Like Cats and Dogs: Contesting The Mu Koan in Zen Buddhism.* Oxford: Oxford University Press.

———. 2017. "Thy Rod and Thy Staff, They Discomfort Me: Zen Staffs as Implements of Instruction." In Winfield and Heine 2017, 102–136.

———. 2020. *Readings of Dōgen's Treasury of the True Dharma Eye.* New York: Columbia University Press.

Heine, Steven, and Dale S. Wright, eds. 2008. *Zen Ritual: Studies of Zen Buddhist Theory in Practice.* Oxford: Oxford University Press.

Hirose Ryōkō 広瀬良弘. 1988. *Zenshū chihō tenkai shi no kenkyū* 禅宗地方展開史の研究. Tokyo: Yoshikawa Kōbunkan.

Ho Chi Chien. 2010. "The Śūraṃgama Dhāraṇī in Sinitic Buddhist Context: From the Tang Dynasty through the Contemporary Period." PhD diss., University of California, Los Angeles.

Ho Li-Hua. 2006. "Dharma Instruments (*Faqi*) in Chinese Han Buddhist Rituals." *The Galpin Society Journal* 59: 217–228.

Hornborg, Anne-Christine. 2017. "Interrituality as a Means to Perform the Art of Building New Rituals." *Journal of Ritual Studies* 31, no. 2: 17–27.

Horton, Sarah Johanna. 2001. "The Role of Genshin and Religious Associations in the Mid-Heian Spread of Pure Land Buddhism." PhD diss., Yale University.

———. 2008. "*Mukaekō:* Practice for the Deathbed." In *Death and the Afterlife in Japanese Buddhism,* edited by Jacqueline I. Stone and Mariko Namba Walter, 27–60. Honolulu: University of Hawai'i Press.

Ichimura Shohei, trans. 1994. *Zen Master Keizan's Monastic Regulations.* North American Institute of Zen and Buddhist Studies 2. Yokohama: Sōjiji.

———, trans. 2006. *The Baizhang Zen Monastic Regulations.* Taishō Vol. 48, No. 2025. Berkeley, CA: Numata Center for Buddhist Translation and Research.

Ikeda Rosan 池田魯参. 2001. "*Kennon senbō* no seiritsu haikei to Sōtōshū shi" 『観音懺法』の成立背景と曹洞宗旨. *Shūgaku kenkyū* 43: 203–208.

———. 2010. "Keizan zen no Makakasha sonja tashitō zen fuzoku setsu no igi" 瑩山禅の摩訶迦葉尊者多子塔前付嘱説の意義. *Sōtōshū sōgō kenkyū sentā gakujitsu taikai kiyō* 11: 345–350.

Imamura Genshū 今村源宗. 2002. "Senbun yowa" 撰文余話. Liner notes in *Dōgen zenji nanahyakugojukkai daionki hōsan: Shinpen Hōon kōshiki,* 19–20.

Inoue Gishin 井上義臣. 2000. *Kōshiki kankai* 講式簡解. Nagoya: Tōshōji.

———. 2002. *Jōyō daishi kōshiki* 承陽大師講式. Nagoya: Tōshōji.

———. 2005. *Onko chiyō: Tōmon gyōhō* 温故知要: 洞門行法. 3 vols. Nagoya: Daihonzan Eiheiji Nagoya Betsuin.

———. 2016. *Fushigina hanashi* ふしぎな話. Ashikaga-shi: Tekizenkai.

Irizarry, Joshua Aaron. 2011. "A Forest for a Thousand Years: Cultivating Life and Disciplining Death at Daihonzan Sōjiji: A Japanese Sōtō Zen Temple." PhD diss., University of Michigan.

Ishida Tetsuya 石田哲彌. 2006. "Rakan shinkō to minzoku shinkō fukyū no hikaku kenkyū" 羅漢信仰と民俗信仰普及の比較研究. *Shūgaku kenkyu* 48: 241–246.

Ishihara Jōmyō 石原成明. 2020. " 'Igi soku buppō' no dentō keisei ni tsuite" 「威儀即仏法」の伝統形成について. *Sōtōshū sōgō kenkyū sentā gakujutsu taikai kiyō* 21: 177–182.

Ishii Shūdō 石井修道. 1991. *Dōgen zen no seiritsushiteki kenkyū* 道元禅の成立史的研究. Tokyo: Daizō Shuppan.

Ishikawa Rikizan 石川力山. 2001. *Zenshū sōden shiryō no kenkyū* 禅宗相伝資料の研究. 2 vols. Kyoto: Hōzōkan.

Itō Ryōkyū 伊藤良久. 1998a. "Sōjiji rinjū seido seiritsu no ichikōsatsu" 總持寺輪住制度成立の一考察. *Indogaku bukkyōgaku kenkyū* 47, no. 1: 158–160.

———. 1998b. "Sojiji goin no kaisō jiki" 總持寺五院の開創時期. *Shūgaku kenkyū* 40: 145–150.

———. 1999. "Yōkōji Sōjiji ryōkyōdan seiriki no shōchō" 永光寺・總持寺、両教団勢力の消長. *Komazawa daigaku bukkyō gakubu ronshū* 30: 311–330.

———. 2001a. "Kinsei ni okeru Sōjiji goin rinjū seidō no kōsatsu (1): Yamagata-ken Shōyōji shozō bunsho kara" 近世における總持寺五院輪住制度の考察(一)ー山形県照陽寺所蔵文書からー. *Shūgaku kenkyū* 43: 167–172.

———. 2001b. "Kinsei ni okeru Sōjiji goin rinjū seidō no kōsatsu (2): Yamagata-ken Shōyōji shozō *Shogakuzan rinbanchū nikki* ni tsuite" 近世における總持寺五院輪住制度の考察(二)ー山形県照陽寺所蔵『諸嶽山輪番中日記』についてー. *Sōtōshū kenkyūin kenkyū kiyō* 31: 29–60.

———. 2002a. "Kinsei ni okeru Sōjiji goin rinjū seidō no kōsatsu (3): Rinjūzen no goin rinbanchi no shosō" 近世における總持寺五院輪住制度の考察(三)ー輪住前の五院輪番地の諸相ー. *Shūgaku kenkyū* 44: 139–144.

———. 2002b. "Kinsei ni okeru Sōjiji goin rinjū seidō no kōsatsu (4): gen goin rinbanchi shozō shiryō no shōkai" 近世における總持寺五院輪住制度の考察（四）ー元五院輪番地所蔵資料の紹介ー. *Shūgaku kenkyū kiyō* 15: 129–152.

———. 2003a. "Kinsei ni okeru Sōjiji goin rinjū seidō no kōsatsu (5): Ehime-ken Keijuji shozō bunsho kara" 近世における總持寺五院輪住制度の考察(五) ー愛媛県渓寿寺所蔵文書からー. *Shūgaku kenkyū* 45: 121–126.

———. 2003b. "Shiryō shōkai Ehime-ken Keijūji zō *Shogakuzan rinban nikkan*" 資料紹介・愛媛県渓寿寺蔵『諸嶽山輪番日鑑』. *Shugaku kenkyū kiyō* 16: 133–181.

———. 2005a. "Sōjiji goin rinjū seido no tenkai to igi" 總持寺五院輪住制度の展開と意義. *Tsurumi daigaku bukkyō bunka kenkyūjo kiyō* 10: 45–83.

———. 2005b. "Sōjiji rinban jūshoku no ichinen" 總持寺輪番住職の一年. In *Zen to shinri to jissen: Azuma Ryūshin hakashi goki kinen ronshū* 禅の真理と実践ー東隆眞博士古稀記念論集ー, 281–306. Tokyo: Shinshusha.

Itō Shintetsu 伊藤真徹. 1975. *Nihon jōdokyō bunkashi kenkyū* 日本浄土教文化史研究. Kyoto: Ryūbunkan.

Iwahara Taishin 岩原諦信. 1932. *Nanzan shinryū shōmyō no kenkyū* 南山進流声明の研究. Kyoto: Fujii Sahei.

Iwata Sōichi 岩田宗一. 1999. *Shōmyō no kenkyū* 声明の研究. Kyoto: Hōzōkan.

Joo, Bong Seok. 2007. "The Arhat Cult in China from the Seventh through Thirteenth Centuries: Narrative, Art, Space and Ritual." PhD diss., Princeton University.

———. 2009. "The Ritual of Arhat Invitation During the Song Dynasty: Why Did Mahāyānists Venerate the Arhat?" *Journal of the International Association of Buddhist Studies* 30, nos. 1–2: 81–116.

Joskovich, Erez. 2019. "Relying on Words and Letters: Scripture Recitation in the Japanese Rinzai Tradition." *Japanese Journal of Religious Studies* 46, no. 1: 53–78.

Jungaberle, Henrik, and Jan Weinhold, eds. 2006. *Rituale in Bewegung. Rahmungs- und Reflexivitätsprozesse in Kulturen der Gegenwart.* Berlin: LIT.

Kanazawa Bunko 金沢文庫. 2006. *Jiin ni hibiku myōon: Kikakuten* 寺院に響く妙音: 企画展. Yokohama: Kanagawa Kenritsu Kanazawa Bunko.

Kasai Kōyū 葛西好雄. 2003. "Shinshutsu shiryō *Eihei Dōgen zenji kōshiki: Hōon kōshiki* senku shiryō no hitotsu to shite" 新出資料『永平道元禅師講式』—『報恩講式』先駆資料の一つとして—. *Shūgaku kenkyū* 45: 97–102.

Kataoka Gidō 片岡義道. 1981. *Eishō Ronkō: Bukkyōgaku, ongakugaku ronbunshū* 叡聲論攷: 仏教学・音楽学論文集. Tokyo: Kokusho Kankōkai.

Katō Shōken 加藤正賢. 2011. "Sōtōshū ni okeru *Rakan kōshiki* no shikishidai to seiritsu" 曹洞宗における『羅漢講式』の式次第と成立. *Sōtōshū kenkyūin kenkyū kiyō* 41: 21–38.

Katsuura Noriko 勝浦令子. 2008. "*Sanbōe* Saiin Anan keka: Amadera butsuji no keifu" 『三宝会』西院阿難悔過—尼寺仏事の系譜—. In *Sanbōe o yomu* 三宝会を読む, edited by Kojima Takayuki, Kobayashi Mayumi, and Komine Kazuaki, 99–125. Tokyo: Yoshikawa Kōbunkan.

Kattago, Siobhan, ed. 2015. *The Ashgate Research Companion to Memory Studies.* Farham, Surrey: Ashgate.

Kawaguchi Kōfū 川口高風. 1981. "*Kannon senbō* hankōshijō ni okeru Hakuchō Teizan bon no tokuchō" 『観音懺法』刊行史上における白鳥鼎三本の特徴. *Zenkenkyūjo kiyō* 10: 171–186.

———. 2002. *Meiji zenki Sōtōshū no kenkyū* 明治前期曹洞宗の研究. Kyoto: Hōzōkan.

Kawai Taikō 河合泰弘. 1999. "*Tōkokuki* nishu taishō 2" 『洞谷記』二種対照(二). *Zenkenkyūjo kiyō* 27: 193–216.

———. 2002: "*Tōkukoki* nishu taishō 2–1" 『洞谷記』二種対照 二-(一). *Zenkenkyūjo kiyō* 30: 199–251.

Kendall, Laurel. 2009. *Shamans, Nostalgias, and the IMF: South Korean Popular Religion in Motion.* Honolulu: University of Hawai'i Press.

Kent, Richard Kellogg. 1995. "The Sixteen Lohans in the Pai-Miao Style: From Sung to Early Ch'ing." PhD diss., Princeton University.

Ketelaar, James Edward. 1993. *Of Heretics and Martyrs in Meiji Japan.* Princeton, NJ: Princeton University Press.

Kieschnick, John. 2003. *The Impact of Buddhism on Chinese Material Culture.* Princeton, NJ: Princeton University Press.

Kindaichi Haruhiko 金田一春彦. 1973. *Shiza kōshiki no kenkyū* 四座講式の研究. Tokyo: Sanseidō. First published in 1964.

Kinnard, Jacob N. 2004. "The Field of the Buddha's Presence." In *Embodying the Dharma: Buddhist Relic Veneration in Asia,* edited by David Germano and Kevin Trainor, 117–143. Albany: State University of New York Press.

Kirino Kōgaku 桐野好学. 2001. "Dōgen zenji to Shakason no reiseki" 道元禅師と釈尊の霊蹟. *Shūgaku kenkyū* 43: 77–82.

———. 2002. "Dōgen zenji to Rakan kuyō: Dōgen zenji sen *Rakan kuyō shikimon* saikō" 道元禅師と羅漢供養ー道元禅師撰『羅漢供養式文』再考ー. *Shūgaku kenkyū kiyō* 15: 61–95.

Köpping, Klaus-Peter. 2004. "Ritual und Theater im Licht ethnologischer Theorien: Interperformativität in Japan." In *Ritualdynamik: Kulturübergreifende Studien zur Theorie und Geschichte rituellen Handelns,* edited by Dietrich Harth and Gerrit Jasper Schenk, 339–361. Heidelberg: Synchron.

Kornicki, Peter Francis. 1998. *The Book in Japan: A Cultural History from the Beginnings to the Nineteenth Century.* Leiden: Brill.

———. 2006. "Manuscript, not Print: Scribal Culture in the Edo Period." *Journal of Japanese Studies* 31, no. 1: 23–52.

———. 2018. *Languages, Scripts, and Chinese Texts in East Asia.* Oxford: Oxford University Press.

Kōshiki Kenkyūkai 講式研究会. 1990. "Junji ōjō kōshiki" 順次往生講式. *Taishō daigaku sōgō bukkyō kenkyūjo nenpō* 12: 185–262.

———. 1991. "Jōkei no kōshiki sandai" 貞慶の講式三題. *Taishō daigaku sōgō bukkyō kenkyūjo nenpō* 13: 185–262.

———. 1993. "Kannon kōshiki to Hokke kōshiki" 観音講式と法華講式. *Taishō daigaku sōgō bukkyō kenkyūjo nenpō* 15: 179–238.

———. 2000. *Jōkei kōshiki shū* 貞慶講式集. Tokyo: Sankibō Busshorin.

Kreinath, Jens. 2012. "Naven, Moebius Strip, and Random Fractal Dynamics: Reframing Bateson's Play Frame and the Use of Mathematical Models for the Study of Ritual." *Journal of Ritual Studies* 26, no. 2: 39–64.

———. 2016. "Intertextualität und Interritualität als Mimesis: Zur Ästhetik interreligiöser Beziehungen unter Juden, Christen und Muslimen in Hatay." *Zeitschrift für Religionswissenschaft* 24, no. 2: 153–184.

———. 2017. "Interrituality as a New Approach for Studying Interreligious Relations and Ritual Dynamics at Shared Pilgrimage Sites in Hatay, Turkey." *Interreligious Studies and Intercultural Theology* 1, no. 2: 257–284.

Krueger, Derek. 2000. "Writing and the Liturgy of Memory in Gregory of Nyssa's Life of Macrina." *Journal of Early Christian Studies* 8, no. 4: 483–510.

———. 2004. *Writing and Holiness: The Practice of Authorship in the Early Christian East.* Philadelphia: University of Pennsylvania Press.

———. 2014. *Liturgical Subjects: Christian Ritual, Biblical Narrative, and the Formation of the Self in Byzantium.* Philadelphia: University of Pennsylvania Press.

Kubo Tsugunari and Yuyama Akira, trans. 2007. *The Lotus Sūtra.* 2nd ed. Berkeley, CA: Numata Center for Buddhist Translation and Research.

Kubovčáková, Zuzana. 2018. "Believe It or Not: Dōgen on the Question of Faith." *Studia Orientalia Slovaca* 17, no. 2: 193–215.

Kurebayashi Kōdō 榑林皓堂. 1960. "Nenge fuhō to Keizan Denkōroku: Dōgen zenji no sore to no taihi ni oite" 拈華付法と瑩山伝光録ー道元禅師のそれとの対比においてー. *Shūgaku kenkyū* 2: 5–13.

Kushida Ryōkō 櫛田良洪. 1965. "Shinhakken no Hōnen denki: *Chion kōshiki*" 新発見の法然伝記ー「知恩講私記」ー. *Nihon rekishi* 200: 217–220.

———. 1976. "Shiryō shōkai: Chion kōshiki" 史料紹介: 知恩講私記. *Bukkyōshi kenkyū* 10: 98–104.

Ledderose, Lothar. 2000. *Ten Thousand Things: Module and Mass Production in Chinese Art.* Princeton, NJ: Princeton University Press.

Leighton, Taigen Daniel. 2008. "Zazen as an Enactment Ritual." In *Zen Ritual: Studies of Zen Theory in Practice,* edited by Steven Heine and Dale S. Wright, 167–184. Oxford: Oxford University Press.

Lévi, Sylvain, and Édouard Chavannes. 1916. "Les seize Arhat protecteurs de la Loi." *Journal Asiatique* 8: 5–50, 189–304.

Little, Stephen. 1992. "The Arhats in China and Tibet." *Artibus Asiae* 52, nos. 3–4: 255–281.

Liu, Cuilan. 2018. "Reciting, Chanting, and Singing: The Codification of Vocal Music in Buddhist Canon Law." *Journal of Indian Philosophy* 46: 713–752.

LoBreglio, John. 2009. "Orthodox, Heterodox, Heretical: Defining Doctrinal Boundaries in Meiji-period Soto Zen." *Bochumer Jahrbuch zur Ostasienforschung* 33: 77–102.

Lu Wei-Yu. 2012. "The Performance Practice of Buddhist *Baiqi* in Contemporary Taiwan." PhD diss., University of Maryland.

Maegawa Ken'ichi 前川健一. 2012. *Myōe no shisō shiteki kenkyū: Shisō kōzō to shojissen no tenkai* 明恵の思想史的研究ー思想構造と諸実践の展開ー. Kyoto: Hōzōkan.

Maekawa Bokushō 前川睦生. [1989]. "Hōsshiki shōmyō kōza sōsetsu" 法式声明講座総説. In *Sōtōshū hosshiki shōmyō kōza,* 29–47.

———. [2000–2001]. "Girei to shōmyō" 儀礼と声明. In *Sōtōzen mezame,* 47–53.

———. n.d. "Kōso Dōgen zenji to shūkyō girei" 高祖道元禅師と宗教儀礼. Unpublished manuscript.

Matsuda Bun'yū 松田文雄. 1974. "Keizan zenji seju 58 sai setsu ni taisuru shiron" 瑩山禅師世寿58歳説に対する試論. *Shūgaku kenkyū* 16: 65–70.

Matsuoka Shinpei 松岡心平. 1991. "Ashikaga Yoshimochi to Kannon senbō soshite Tomonaga" 足利義持と観音懺法そして「朝長」. *Tōkyō daigaku kyōikugakubu jinbunkagakka kiyō* 94: 41–52.

Matsuura Shūkō 松浦秀光. 1976. "Tanbutsueshiki ni tsuite" 歎仏会式について. *Shūgaku kenkyū* 18: 73–78.

Meeks, Lori Rachelle. 2010. *Hokkeji and the Reemergence of Female Monastic Orders in Premodern Japan.* Honolulu: University of Hawai'i Press.

———. 2016. "Imagining Rāhula in Medieval Japan: The *Raun Kōshiki.*" In Ambros, Ford, and Mross 2016, 131–151.

Meshel, Naphtali S. 2014. *The "Grammar" of Sacrifice: A Generativist Study of the Israelite Sacrificial System in the Priestly Writings with The "Grammar" of* Σ. Oxford: Oxford University Press.

Michaels, Axel. 2005. "Rituelle Klangräume." In *Musik und Raum: Dimensionen im Gespräch,* edited by Annette Landau and Claudia Emmenegger, 33–44. Zürich: Chronos.

———. 2010. "The Grammar of Rituals." In *Grammars and Morphologies of Ritual Practices in Asia,* edited by Axel Michaels and Anand Mishra, 7–28. Sec. 1 of *Grammar and Morphology of Ritual.* Vol. 1, *Ritual Dynamics and the Science of Ritual.* Wiesbaden: Harrassowitz Verlag.

———. 2016. *Homo Ritualis: Hindu Ritual and Its Significance For Ritual Theory.* New York: Oxford University Press.

Michihata Ryōshū 道端良秀. 1983. *Rakan shinkō shi* 羅漢信仰史. Tokyo: Daitō Shuppansha.

Monhart, Michael. 1992–1993. "The Use of *shōmyō* in Shingon Ritual." *Studies in Central and East Asian Religions* 5–6: 139–144.

———. 1994. "A Fusion of Horizons: *Shōmyō* in Kogi Shingon Ritual." *Studies in Central and East Asian Religions* 7: 1–26.

Moyaert, Marianne, ed. 2019. *Interreligious Relations and the Negotiation of Ritual Boundaries: Explorations in Interrituality.* Cham, Switzerland: Palgrave Macmillan.

Mross, Michaela. 2007. "Das *Rakan kōshiki* der Sōtō-Schule: Übersetzung und Analyze eines liturgischen Textes." MA thesis, University of Hamburg.

———. 2009. "A Survey of the Literature on *shōmyō* in Europe and America." In *Bukkyō seigaku ni kiku kanjion: Bonbai ni koin wo saguru* 仏教声楽に聴く漢字音ー梵唄に古韻を探るー, 206–214. Tokyo: Nishogakusha Daigaku.

———. 2010. "Sōtōshū no hōon kōshiki ni kansuru kōsatsu: *Butsuji kōshiki* to *Tōjō dentō kōshiki* ni tsuite" 曹洞宗の報恩講式に関する考察ー佛慈講式と洞上傳燈講式についてー. *Indogaku Bukkyōgaku Kenkyū* 58, no. 2: 166–169.

———. 2011. "Sōtōshū ni okeru *Rakan kōshiki* no hensen" 曹洞宗における羅漢講式の変遷. *Sōtōshū sōgō kenkyū sentā gakujutsu taikai kiyō* 12: 479–484.

———. 2012a. "Rankei Dōryū *Rakan kōshiki* ni tsuite: Sono seiritsu to denpa o chūshin ni" 蘭渓道隆『羅漢講式』についてーその成立と伝播を中心にー. *Indogaku Bukkyōgaku Kenkyū* 60, no. 2: 682–687.

———. 2012b. "Noto Sōjiji to *Gasan kōshiki* ni tsuite" 能登總持寺と「峨山講式」について. *Sōtōshū sōgō kenkyū sentā gakujutsu taikai kiyō* 13: 315–320.

———. 2012c. "Buddhistische Rezitationskunst in den Shingon-Schulen am Beispiel des *Shiza kōshiki.*" In *Mittel und Wege religiöser Tradierung in Japan,* edited by Katja Triplett, 17–53. Halle: Universitätsverlag Halle-Wittenberg.

———. 2012d. "Keizan to *Butsuji kōshiki:* Sōjijikei to Yōkōjikei no sōiten ni tsuite" 瑩山紹瑾と「仏慈講式」ー總持寺系と永光寺系の相違点についてー. *Indogaku Bukkyōgaku Kenkyū* 61, no. 1: 26–30.

———. 2013a. "Sōjiji no nisoki ni kansuru kōsatsu: Jissōji shozō *Gasan kōshiki saimon* to *shikimon* o chūshin ni" 總持寺の二祖忌に関する考察ー実相寺所蔵「峨山講式祭文」と「式文」を中心にー. *Shūkyōgaku ronshū* 32: 107–136.

———. 2013b. "Noto Sōjiji to Gasan kōshiki ni tsuite 2: *Gasan kō kada* to *Ryōson shōki tō sajōchō* o chūshin ni" 能登總持寺と峨山講式について（二）ー「峨山講伽陀」と『両尊征忌等差定帳』を中心にー. *Sōtōshū kenkyūin kenkyū kiyō* 43: 163–187.

———. 2013c. "Kōyasan zō *Sakujitsu Rakan kōshiki* ni tsuite: Sōtōshū no *Rakan kōshiki* to no hikaku" 高野山蔵『朔日羅漢講式』についてー曹洞宗の『羅漢講式』との比較ー. In *Ronshū Bungaku to ongakushi: Shiika kangen no sekai* 論集 文学と音楽史ー詩歌管絃の世界ー, edited by Iso Mizue, 317–340. Osaka: Izumi Shoin.

———. 2014a. "A Local History of Buddhist Rituals in Japan: *Kōshiki* at the Sōtō Zen Temple Sōjiji from the Seventeenth through Nineteenth Centuries." PhD diss., LMU Munich.

———. 2014b. "The Independence Movement of Sōjiji: A Milestone in the Formation of Modern Sōtō Zen." Paper presented at the Annual Conference of the Association for Asian Studies, March 30.

———. 2015. "Vocalizing the Remembrance of Dōgen: A Study of the *Shinpen hōon kōshiki*." In *Dōgen and Sōtō Zen*, edited by Steven Heine, 210–234. Oxford: Oxford University Press.

———. 2016a. "Vocalizing the Lament over the Buddha's Passing: A Study of Myōe's *Shiza kōshiki*." In Ambros, Ford, and Mross 2016, 89–130.

———. 2016b. "Myōe's *Nehan kōshiki:* An Annotated Translation." In Ambros, Ford, and Mross 2016, online supplement 2: 1–20.

Muromine Baiitsu 室峰梅逸, ed. 1965. *Sōjiji shi* 総持寺誌. Yokohama: Daihonzan Sōjiji.

Nakano Tōzen 中野東禅. 1984. "Sōtōshū no shōmyō: Sono rekishi to tokushitsu" 曹洞宗の声明 その歴史と特質. In *Shōmyō taikei roku zen kaimei* 声明体系 六禅解明, edited by Yokomichi Mario 横道萬理雄 et al., 4–8. Kyoto: Hōzōkan.

Nakano Tōzen 中野東禅 et al. 2002. *Kanyaku Sōtōshū kōshiki* 簡訳曹洞宗講式. Tokyo: Shikisha.

Nelson, Steven G. 1998. "Buddhist Chant of Shingi-Shingon: A Guide for Readers and Listeners." In *Shingi shingon shyōmyō shūsei Volume 2* 新義真言声明集成 第二巻, edited by Shingonshū Buzanha Bukkyō Seinenkai, 458–503. Tokyo: Shingonshū Buzanha Bukkyo Seinenkai.

———. 2001a. "Fujiwara Takamichi sō: *Shiki hossoku yōi jōjō* ni okeru kōshiki no ongaku kōseihō" 藤原孝道草『式法則用意条々』における講式の音楽構成法. In *Chūsei ongakushi ronsō* 中世音楽史論叢, edited by Fukushima Kuzuo. Ōsaka: Izumi Shoin.

———. 2001b. "Improvisatory Vocal Realization of Written Texts in Early Medieval Japan: *Kōshiki* Lecture-Ritual Performance and Narration of the Tale of the Heike." Paper presented at the Annual Conference of the Association of Asian Studies, March 24.

———. 2003. "*Shōmyō:* The Buddhist Chant of Japan." In *Buddhist Ritual Chant from Korea and Japan*, 12–23. New York: Japan Society.

———. 2008a. "Court and Religious Music (1): History of *gagaku* and *shōmyō*." In *The Ashgate Research Companion to Japanese Music*, edited by Alison McQueen Tokita and David W. Hughes, 35–48. Hampshire: Ashgate.

———. 2008b. "Court and Religious Music (2): Music of *gagaku* and *shōmyō*." In *The Ashgate Research Companion to Japanese Music*, edited by Alison McQueen Tokita and David W. Hughes, 49–76. Hampshire: Ashgate.

———. 2009. "The History of the Musical Realization of *Kōshiki* Texts: From Planned Improvisation to Standardized Sectarian Versions." Paper presented at the Asian Studies Conference Japan, Tokyo, June 21.

Nettl, Bruno. 2015. *The Study of Ethnomusicology: Thirty-three Discussions*. Urbana: University of Illinois Press.

Nichols, Stephen G. 1990. "Introduction: Philology in a Manuscript Culture." Special issue, *Speculum* 65, no. 1: 1–10.

———. 1997. “Why Material Philology? Some Thoughts.” Beiheft, *Philologie als Textwissenschaft: Alte und neue Horizonte, Zeitschrift für deutsche Philologie* 116: 10–30.

Nodomi Jōten 納冨常天. 2007. “Sōjiji no konseki: Tsurumi goiten zengo o chūshin ni” 總持寺の今昔一鶴見御移転前後を中心に一. *Kyōdo tsurumi* 63: 1–22.

———. 2011. “Sōjiji goin no seiritsu to tenkai (2)” 總持寺五院の成立と展開（二）. *Tsurumi daigaku bukkyō bunka kenkyūjo kiyō* 16: 59–107.

Nomura Takumi 野村卓美. 2002. *Myōe Shōnin no kenkyū* 明恵上人の研究. Osaka: Izumi Shoin.

Okumura Shohaku. 2012. *Living by Vow: A Practical Introduction to Eight Essential Zen Chants and Texts*. Somerville: Wisdom Publications.

Olick, Jeffrey K., Vered Vinitzky-Seroussi, and Daniel Levy, eds. 2011. *The Collective Memory Reader*. New York: Oxford University Press.

Oppitz, Michael. 1999. “Montageplan von Ritualen.” In *Rituale heute: Theorien—Kontroversen—Entwürfe*, edited by Corinna Caduff and Joanna Pfaff-Czarnecka, 73–95. Berlin: Reimer.

Orzech, Charles D. 1998. *Politics and Transcendent Wisdom: The Scripture for Humane Kings in the Creation of Chinese Buddhism*. University Park: Pennsylvania State University Press.

Ōuchi Fumi 大内典. 2009. “The Lotus Repentance Liturgy of Shugendō: Identification from Vocal Arts.” *Cahiers d'Extrême-Asie* 18: 169–193.

———. 2016. *Bukkyō no koe no waza: Satori no shintaisei* 仏教の声の技: 悟りの身体性. Kyoto: Hōzōkan.

Ōyama Kōjun 大山公淳. 1969. *Bukkyō ongaku to shōmyō: Rekishi, Onritsu* 仏教音楽と声明: 歴史・音律. Wakayama-ken: Ōyama Kyōju Kinen Shuppankai.

Ozaki Shōzen 尾崎正善. 1995: “Honkoku Daianji zō *Ekō narabini shikihō*” 翻刻・大安寺蔵「回向并式法」. *Sōtōshū shūgaku kenkyūjo kiyō* 9: 73–118.

———. 1997. “Rinkō shoshabon *Keizan shingi* no Nehan kōshiki ni tsuite” 麟広書写本『瑩山清規』の涅槃講式について. *Sōtōshū shūgaku kenkyūjo kiyō* 11: 43–67.

———. 1998a. “Sōtōshū ni okeru Nehan kōshiki ni tsuite” 曹洞宗における涅槃講式について. *Shūgaku kenkyū* 40: 211–216.

———. 1998b. “Sōtōshū ni okeru Nehan kōshiki ni tsuite 2: Shohon no kōi to shingi shiryō ni okeru ichizuke” 曹洞宗における涅槃講式について（二）一諸本の校異と清規資料における位置づけ一. *Sōtōshū kenkyūin kenkyū kiyō* 29: 153–171.

———. 1998c. “Honkoku *Butsuji kōshiki*” 翻刻『仏慈講式』. *Sōtōshū shūgaku kenkyū kiyō* 12: 55–67.

———. 1999a. “*Butsuji kōshiki* ni tsuite”「仏慈講式」について. *Shūgaku kenkyū* 41: 115–120.

———. 1999b. “Honkoku *Enichi Tōfukuzenji gyōrei kihō*” 翻刻・『慧日山東福禅寺行令規法』. *Tsurumi daigaku bukkyō bunka kenkyūjo kiyō* 4: 55–75.

———. 2000. “Honkoku Kishizawa bunko zō *Kichijōzan Eiheiji nenchū teiki*” 翻刻・岸沢文庫蔵『吉祥山永平寺年中定規』. *Tsurumi daigaku kiyō dai yon bu jinbun shakai shizen kagaku hen* 37: 87–118.

———. 2010. *Watashitachi no gyōji: Shūmon girei o kangaeru* 私たちの行事一宗門儀礼を考える一. Tokyo: Sōtōshū Shūmuchō.

———. 2011. “Honkoku Kyōto Daigaku Bungakubu Toshokan zō *Tōfukuji Shingi* 1”

翻刻・京都大学文学部図書館蔵『東福寺清規』(1). *Tsurumi daigaku bukkyō bunka kenkyūjo kiyō* 16: 109–196.

———. 2012. "Honkoku Kyōto Daigaku Bungakubu Toshokan zō *Tōfukuji Shingi* 2" 翻刻・京都大学文学部図書館蔵『東福寺清規』(2). *Tsurumi daigaku bukkyō bunka kenkyūjo kiyō* 17: 111–176.

———. 2013. "Zenshū girei no kenkyū: Girei no hensen katei to sono haikei" 禅宗儀礼の研究ー儀礼の変遷過程とその背景ー. *Zenkenkyūjō Kiyō* 42: 1–20.

———. 2014a. "Sōtōshū *Fusatsu kōshiki* no hensen: Jyōkyōbon no shōkai o chūshin toshite" 曹洞宗『布薩講式』の変遷ー貞享本の紹介を中心としてー. *Tsurumi daigaku bukkyō bunka kenkyūjo kiyō* 19: 127–163.

———. 2014b. "Ryōdaihonzan no dōkō 両大本山の動向." *Sōtōshū sōgō kenkyū sentā gakujutsu taikai kiyō* 15: 15–20.

———. 2018. "*Shōbō shingi* saikō 1: *Zokusōzen* honkou no mondaiten to shohon to no kankei" 『正法清規』再考(1)ー『続曹全』翻刻の問題点と諸本との関係ー. *Sōtōshū sōgō kenkyū sentā gakujutsu taikai kiyō* 19: 139–144.

———. 2020. "Daihonzan Sōjiji Soin zō 'Bunri dokuritsu undō kankei shiryō' no shōkai" 大本山總持寺祖院蔵「分離独立運動関係史料」の紹介. *Sōtōshū sōgō kenkyū sentā gakujutsu daikai kiyō* 21: 117–122.

Paul, Diana Y. 2004. *The Sutra of Queen Śrīmālā of the Lion's Roar.* Berkeley, CA: Numata Center for Buddhist Translation and Research.

Payne, Richard Karl. 1991. *The Tantric Ritual of Japan: Feeding the Gods, the Shingon Fire Ritual.* Delhi: International Academy of Indian Culture and Aditya Prakashan.

———. 1999. "The Shingon *Ajikan:* Diagrammatic Analysis of Ritual Syntax." *Religion* 29, no. 3: 215–229.

———. 2004. "Ritual Syntax and Cognitive Theory." *Pacific World: Journal of the Institute of Buddhist Studies,* 3rd ser., no. 6: 195–227.

———. 2012. "Conversions of Tantric Buddhist Ritual: The Yoshida Shintō Jūhachi-shintō Ritual." In *Transformations and Transfer of Tantra in Asia and Beyond,* edited by István Keul, 365–398. Berlin: De Gruyter.

Poceski, Mario. 2008. "Chan Rituals of Abbots' Ascending the Dharma Hall to Preach." In *Zen Ritual: Studies of Zen Theory in Practice,* edited by Steven Heine and Dale S. Wright, 299–304. Oxford: Oxford University Press.

———. 2015. *The Records of Mazu and the Making of Classical Chan Literature.* Oxford: Oxford University Press.

———, ed. 2018. *Communities of Memory and Interpretation: Reimagining and Reinventing the Past in East Asian Buddhism.* Bochum: Projektverlag.

Pradel, Chari. 2016. *Fabricating the "Tenjukoku Shūchō Mandara" and Prince Shōtoku's Afterlives.* Leiden: Brill.

Quenzer, Jörg B. 2000. *Buddhistische Traum-Praxis im japanischen Mittelalter (11.–15. Jahrhundert).* Hamburg: O.A.G.

Quinter, David. 2006. "The Shingon Ritsu School and the Mañjuśrī Cult in the Kamakura Period: From Eison To Monkan." PhD diss., Stanford University.

———. 2011. "Invoking the Mother of Awakening: An Investigation of Jōkei's and Eison's *Monju kōshiki.*" *Japanese Journal of Religious Studies* 38, no. 2: 263–302.

———. 2014a. "Localizing Strategies: Eison and the Shōtoku Taishi Cult." *Monumenta Nipponica* 69, no. 2: 153–198.

———. 2014b. "Prince Shōtoku Ceremonial: Eison's *Shōtoku Taishi kōshiki.*" *Monumenta Nipponica* 69, no. 2: 199–219.

———. 2016. "Materializing and Performing Prajñā: Jōkei's Mañjuśrī Faith and the Kasagidera Restoration." In Ambros, Ford, and Mross 2016, 17–54.

Rambelli, Fabio. 2007. *Buddhist Materiality: A Cultural History of Objects in Japanese Buddhism.* Stanford, CA: Stanford University Press.

———. 2021. "The Dharma of Music: *Gagaku* and Buddhist Salvation in Medieval Japan." *Japanese Journal of Religious Studies* 48, no. 1: 45–71.

Rankin, Susan. 2011. "On the Treatment of Pitch in Early Music Writing." *Early Music History* 30: 105–175.

Rappaport, Roy A. 1999. *Ritual and Religion in the Making of Humanity.* Cambridge: Cambridge University Press.

Reader, Ian. 1986. "Zazenless Zen? The Position of Zazen in Institutional Zen Buddhism." *Japanese Religions* 14, no. 3: 7–27.

Riggs, David E. 2008. "Meditation in Motion: Textual Exegesis in the Creation of Ritual." In *Zen Ritual: Studies of Zen Theory in Practice,* edited by Steven Heine and Dale S. Wright, 223–260. Oxford: Oxford University Press.

Riggs, Diane E. 2004. "Fukudenkai: Sewing the Buddha's Robe in Contemporary Japanese Buddhist Practice." *Japanese Journal of Religious Studies* 31, no. 2: 311–356.

———. 2010. "The Cultural and Religious Significance of Japanese Buddhist Vestments." PhD diss., University of California, Los Angeles.

———. 2017. "Golden Robe or Rubbish Robe? Interpretations of the Transmitted Robe in Tokugawa Period Zen Buddhist Thought." In Winfield and Heine 2017, 197–228.

Ruppert, Brian D. 2000. *Jewel in the Ashes: Buddha Relics and Power in Early Medieval Japan.* Cambridge, MA: Harvard University Asia Center.

Sakauchi Tatsuo 坂内龍雄. 1973. "Tōjō dentō kōshiki no kaisetsu" 洞上伝灯講式の解説. In *Daihonzan Sōjiji goshōkie kinen* 大本山総持寺御征忌會記念. Unpublished manuscript.

———. 2010a: "Dentō kōshiki" 伝灯講式. In Suzuki Bunmei 2010, 256–280.

———. 2010b: "Hokke kōshiki" 法華講式. In Suzuki Bunmei 2010, 344–359.

Sakurai Shūyū 桜井秀雄. 1981. "Kaidai" 解題. In *Sōtōshū sensho daisankan, Kyōgihen: Shoki shūdan kyōri 3* 曹洞宗選書 第三巻 教義篇: 初期宗団教理 3, edited by Sōtōshū Sensho Hankōkai, 265–266. Kyoto: Dōhōsha.

Satō Mie 齋藤美枝. 2011. *Tsurumi Sōjiji monogatari* 鶴見總持寺物語. Yokohama: Tsurumi-ku Bunka Kyōkai.

Satō Shin'yū 佐藤信雄. 1973. *Gojikimatsu moto rinbanchi jiin meikan* 御直末・元輪番地寺院名鑑. Yokohama: Daihonzan Sōjiji Keizan Zenji 650-kai Daionki Kinen Hōsan Hankōkai.

Satō Shūkō 佐藤秀孝. 1999. "Kyōō Unryō, Kohō Kakumyō to shoki Sōtōshū kyōdan" 恭翁運良・孤峰覚明と初期曹洞宗教団. *Hanazono daigaku zengaku kenkyū* 77: 1–37.

Satō Tetsuei 佐藤哲英. 1979. *Eizan Jōdokyō no kenkyū* 叡山浄土教の研究. Kyoto: Hyakkaen.

Sawada Atsuko 澤田篤子. 2002. "Buddhist Music in Japan." In *East Asia: China, Japan, and Korea,* edited by Robert C. Provine, Yosihiko Tokumaru, and J. Lawrence

Witzleben, 611–618. Vol. 7, *Garland Encyclopedia of World Music.* New York: Routledge.

Seaquist, Carl Andrew. 2004. "Ritual Syntax." PhD diss., University of Pennsylvania.

Sekiguchi Dōjun 関口道潤, ed. 1995. *Sōtōshū Daihonzan Sōjiji Soin* 曹洞宗大本山総持寺祖院. 2nd ed. Kanazawa: Yoshida insatsu.

Sharf, Robert. 1993. "The Zen of Japanese Nationalism." *History of Religions* 33, no. 1: 1–43.

———. 1995. "Buddhist Modernism and the Rhetoric of Meditative Experience." *Numen* 42, no. 3: 228–283.

———. 2003. "Thinking through Shingon Ritual." *Journal of the International Association of Buddhist Studies* 26, no. 1: 51–96.

Shibata Dōken 柴田道賢. 1979. *Dōgen zenji no zaike kyōke* 道元禅師の在家教化. Tokyo: Shunjūsha.

Shih, Jen Lang. 2002. "The Perpetuity of the Dharma." PhD diss., University of California, Berkeley.

Shiina Kōyū 椎名宏雄. 2010a. "Nehan kōshiki" 涅槃講式. In Suzuki Bunmei 2010, 152–163.

———. 2010b. "Daruma daishi kōshiki" 達磨大師講式. In Suzuki Bunmei 2010, 326–333.

Shiina Kōyū 椎名宏雄 and Sakauchi Ryūyū 坂内龍雄. 2010. "Daihannya kōshiki" 大般若講式. In Suzuki Bunmei 2010, 360–373.

Shimizu Kunihiko 清水邦彦. 1995. "Jōkei no Jizō shinkō" 貞慶の地蔵信仰. *Rinrigaku* 12: 29–40.

———. 2008. "Chūsei Sōtōshū no Jizō shinkō" 中世曹洞宗の地蔵信仰. *Nihon shūkyō bunkashi kenkyū* 12, no. 2: 53–69.

———. 2009. "Chūsei goki Sōtōshū no Jizō shinkō" 中世後期曹洞宗の地蔵信仰. *Shūkyō kenkyū* 82, no. 4: 1200–1201.

Shiraishi Hōryū (Kogetsu) 白石芳留(虎月). 1930. *Tōfukuji shi* 東福寺誌. Kyoto: Daihonzan Tōfuku zenji.

Slottow, Stephen P. 2019. *The Americanization of Zen Chanting.* Hillsdale, NY: Pendragon Press.

Snoek, Jan A. M. 2006. "Some Thoughts about Handelman's Moebius Framing Theory." In *Rituale in Bewegung. Rahmungs- und Reflexivitätsprozesse in Kulturen der Gegenwart,* edited by Henrik Jungaberle and Jan Weinhold, 33–36. Berlin: LIT.

Sōtōshū Nisōshi Hensankai 曹洞宗尼僧史編纂会, ed. 1955. *Sōtōshū nisō shi* 曹洞宗尼僧史. Tokyo: Sōtōshū Nisōdan Honbu.

Sōtōshū Sensho Hankōkai 曹洞宗選書刊行会, ed. 1981a. *Sōtōshū sensho dainikan, Kyōgihen: Shoki shūdan kyōri* 2 曹洞宗選書 第二巻 教義篇: 初期宗団教理 2. Kyoto: Dōhōsha Shuppan.

———, ed. 1981b. *Sōtōshū sensho daisankan, Kyōgihen: Shoki shūdan kyōri* 3 曹洞宗選書 第三巻 教義篇: 初期宗団教理 3. Kyoto: Dōhōsha Shuppan.

Staal, Frits. 1979a."The Meaninglessness of Ritual." *Numen* 26: 2–22.

———. 1979b. "Ritual Syntax." In *Sanskrit and Indian Studies: Essays in Honor of Daniel H. H. Ingalls,* edited by M. Nagatomi, Bimal K. Matilal, and J. Moussaie Masson, 119–142. Dordrecht: Reidel.

———. 1989. *Rules without Meaning. Ritual, Mantras and the Human Sciences.* New York: Peter Lang.

Stausberg, Michael. 2014. "Ritual Orders and Ritologiques: A Terminological Quest for Some Neglected Fields of Study." *Scripta Instituti Donneriani Aboensis* 18: 221–242.

Steininger, Brian. 2017. *Chinese Literary Forms in Heian Japan: Poetics and Practice.* Cambridge, MA: Harvard University Asia Center.

Stevenson, Daniel F. 2015. "Buddhist Ritual in the Song." In *Modern Chinese Religion 1,* edited by John Lagerwey and Pierre Marsone, 328–448. Leiden: Brill.

Stewart, Pamela J., and Andrew J. Strathern, eds. 2012. "Ritual Framing: Gregory Bateson." Special issue, *Journal of Ritual Studies* 26, no. 2.

Stone, Jacqueline I. 1999. "Priest Nisshin's Ordeals." In *Religions of Japan in Practice,* edited by George J. Tanabe, Jr., 384–397. Princeton, NJ: Princeton University Press.

———. 2016. *Right Thoughts at the Last Moment: Buddhism and Deathbed Practices in Early Medieval Japan.* Honolulu: University of Hawai'i Press.

Strong, John S. 2004: *Relics of the Buddha.* Princeton, NJ: Princeton University Press.

Sugano Fumi 菅野扶美. 1987. "*Ongaku kōshiki* ni tsuite"『音楽講式』について. *Kokugo to kokubungaku* 64, no. 8: 39–55.

Suzuki Bunmei 鈴木文明, ed. 2010. *Shinpen Sōtōshū jissen sōsho* 3 新編曹洞宗実践叢書 3. Tokyo: Dōhōsha.

Suzuki Haruko 鈴木治子. 1991. "*Yokawa Kaidaiin geikō kiroku:* Kaisetsu narabini honkoku"『横川花臺院迎講記録』解説ならびに翻刻. *Kokubungaku tōsa* 16: 115–135.

Szczepanski, Beth. 2014. "Buddhism and Music." Oxford Bibliographies Online. https://www.oxfordbibliographies.com.

Takeuchi Kōdō 竹内弘道. 1998. "Gasan no Butsuji zenji-gō henjō ni tsuite" 峨山の仏慈禅師号返上について. *Shūgaku kenkyū* 40: 133–138.

Takeuchi Michio 竹内道雄. 1981. *Sōjiji no rekishi* 総持寺の歴史. Yokohama: Sōjiji.

Tamamuro Fumio 圭室文雄. 2008. *Sōjiji Soin komonjo o yomitoku: Kinsei Sōtōshū kyōdan no tenkai* 總持寺祖院古文書を読み解く一近世曹洞宗教団の展開一. Tokyo: Sōtōshū Shūmuchō.

Tambiah, Stanley J. 1979. "A Performative Approach to Ritual." *Proceedings of the British Academy* 65: 113–169.

Tanabe, George J., Jr. 1992. *Myōe the Dreamkeeper: Fantasy and Knowledge in Early Kamakura Buddhism.* Cambridge, MA: Harvard University Press.

———. 2004. "Chanting and Liturgy." In *Encyclopedia of Buddhism,* edited by Robert E. Buswell, Jr., 137–139. New York: Macmillan Reference.

Tokita, Alison McQueen. 2015. *Japanese Singers of Tales: Ten Centuries of Performed Narrative.* Burlington: Ashgate.

Tokiwa Gishin, trans. 2005. "A Treatise on Letting Zen Flourish to Protect the State (Taishō Volume 80, Number 2543)." In *Zen Texts,* 59–238. Berkeley, CA: Numata Center for Buddhist Translation and Research.

Tomabechi Seiichi 苫米地誠一. 1997. "Jōkei saku *Kannon kōshiki* yakuchū" 貞慶作『観音講式』訳注. *Taishō daigaku sōgō bukkyō kenkyūjo nenpō* 19: 59–86.

Tōyō Ongaku Gakkai 東洋音楽学会, ed. 1972. *Bukkyō ongaku* 仏教音楽. Tokyo: Ongaku no Tomosha.

Triplett, Katja. 2010. "Gründungslegenden in der Erinnerungspflege japanisch-buddhistischer Tempel am Beispiel des Tsubosakasan Minami Hokkeji." In *Geschichten und Geschichte: Historiographie und Hagiographie in der asiatischen Religionsgeschichte,* edited by Peter Schalk, 140–180. Uppsala: Almqvist & Wiksell.

Tsunoda Haruo 角田春雄. 2010. "Eihei kaisan hōon kōshiki no kaisetsu" 永平開山報恩講式の解説. In Suzuki Bunmei 2010, 230–253.

Tsunoda Tairyū 角田泰隆. 1997. "Tashitō zen fuhō setsu to ryōzen fuhō setsu: Nyojō, Dōgen, Keizan, san zenji no tachiba" 多子塔前付法説と霊山付法説一如浄・道元・瑩山、三禅師の立場一. *Komazawa tanki daigaku kenkyū kiyō* 25: 221–235.

Tsuruoka Hakuhō 鶴岡白鳳. 2010. "Dai isshō shōmyō 第一章 声明." In Suzuki Bunmei 2010, 43–57.

Turner, Victor W. 1973. "Symbols in African Ritual." *Science* 179: 1100–1105.

Uemura Takayoshi 植村高義. 1979. "Tanbutsue to rizumu" 歎仏会とリズム. *Shūkyō kenkyū* 21: 111–113.

Umeda Shinryū 梅田信隆. 1990. "Sanshōkaku hōyō goaisatsu" 三松閣落慶法要御挨拶. *Chōryū* 跳龍, June: 2–3.

Visser, Marinus Willem de. 1923. *The Arhats in China and Japan.* Berlin: Oesterheld.

———. 1935. *Ancient Buddhism in Japan: Sutras and Ceremonies in Use in the Seventh and Eighth Centuries A.D. and Their History in Later Times.* 2 vols. Leiden: Brill.

Waddell, Norman, and Masao Abe, trans. 2002. *The Heart of Dōgen's Shōbōgenzō.* Albany: State University of New York Press.

Watarai Shōjun 渡井正純. 1982. "Daijōji zō *Busshōe kōshiki* ni tsuite" 大乗寺蔵、「仏生会講式」について. *Sōtōshū kenkyūin kenkyūsei kenkyū kiyō* 14: 107–112.

———. 1983. "*Ryaku kōshiki* no shishō ni tsuite"「略講式」の詞章について. *Sōtōshū kenkyūin kenkyūsei kenkyū kiyō* 15: 75–78.

———. 1986. "*Kannon kōshiki* no shishō ni tsuite"「観音講式」の詞章について. *Sōtōshū kenkyūin kenkyūsei kenkyū kiyō* 17: 20–27.

Watarai Shōjun 渡井正純 and Sawada Atsuko 澤田篤子. 1980. Booklet in *Sōtō-Zen: Chōka, senbō, narashimono.*

———. 1982. Booklet in *Sōtō-Zen: Kōshiki, tanbutsu, fusatsu.*

Watarai Shōjun 渡井正純 and Tsukamoto Atsuko 塚本篤子. 1983. Booklet in *Sōtō-Zen: Tange, kitō, kuyō.*

Wei Li. 1992. "The Duality of the Sacred and the Secular in Chinese Buddhist Music: An Introduction." *Yearbook for Traditional Music* 24: 81–90.

Williams, Duncan Ryūken. 2005. *The Other Side of Zen: A Social History of Sōtō Zen Buddhism in Tokugawa Japan.* Princeton, NJ: Princeton University Press.

———. 2009. "The Purple Robe Incident and the Formation of the Early Modern Sōtō Zen Institution." *Japanese Journal of Religious Studies* 36, no. 1: 27–43.

Winfield, Pamela D., and Steven Heine, ed. 2017. *Zen and Material Culture.* Oxford: Oxford University Press.

Yamada Shōzen 山田昭全. 1995. "Kōshiki: Sono seiritsu to tenkai" 講式その成立と展開. In *Bukkyō bungaku kōza 8: Shōdō no bungaku* 仏教文学講座 8: 唱導の文学, edited by Ito Hiroyuki 伊藤博之 et al., 11–53. Tokyo: Benseisha.

Yamaguchi Masaaki 山口正章. 2012. *Chikujaku katsujaku* 築著磕著. Fukui: Ryūsenji.

Yamahata Shōdō 山端昭道. 1974. "Keizan zenji go renrei kōshi ron" 瑩山禅師御年齢考試論. In *Keizan zenji kenkyū: Keizan zenji roppyakugojukkai daionki kinen ronbunshū* 瑩山禅師研究: 瑩山禅師六百五十回大遠忌記念論文集, edited by Keizan Zenji Hōsan Kankōkai 瑩山禅師奉讃刊行会, 999–1057. Tokyo: Keizan Zenji Hōsan Kankōkai.

Yamamoto Sohō 山本素鳳. 2010a: "Daifusatsu kōshiki (furyaku fusatsu)" 大布薩講式（附略布薩）. In Suzuki Bunmei 2010, 89–141.

———. 2010b: "Rakan kōshiki" 羅漢講式. In Suzuki Bunmei 2010, 281–308.

Yifa. 2002. *The Origins of Buddhist Monastic Codes in China: An Annotated Translation and Study of the Chanyuan qinggui.* Honolulu: University of Hawai'i Press.

Yokoi Kakudō 横井覚道. 1967. "Nihon Sōtōshū denshō shōmyō kōshiki ni tsuite" 日本曹洞宗伝承声明講式について. *Shūgaku kenkyū* 9: 58–75.

Yōkōji no meihō 永光寺の名宝. 2000. Kanazawa: Ishikawaken Rekishi Hakubutsukan.

Yokoyama Hideo 横山秀哉. 1974. "Yōkōji sōritsu no igi to sono garan nit suite" 永光寺創立の意義とその伽藍について. *Shūgaku kenkyū* 16: 15–20.

Yokozeki Ryōin 横関了胤. 1970. *Sōtōshū hyakunen no ayumi* 曹洞宗百年のあゆみ. Tokyo: Sōtōshū Shūmuchō.

Yoshioka Hakudō 吉岡博道. 1982. "Meijiki no Eiheiji" 明治期の永平寺. In *Eiheijishi* 2 永平寺下巻, edited by Sakurai Shūyū, 1323–1408. Fukui: Daihonzan Eiheiji.

Index

Page numbers in **bold** refer to figures or tables.

acoustic modules, 103, 107, 121. *See also* music; soundscapes

address of invitation (*kanjōmon*): for arhats, 77–81, **78**, 93, 94, 95; musical instruments, 124; in Shingon school, 110n107, 112; vocalization, 23, 119, 129

Aichi Senmon Nisōdō, 52, 154

Akiba Tairyū, viii

Ambros, Barbara, 45

Amida's Pure Land, 24, 25, 29, 30, 235. *See also* Tendai school

Ānanda, 44, 78, 186, 187

Anan kōshiki, 44–45, 52, 59

Antaiji, 157n68

Aoyama Shundō, 52

Arai, Paula, 45

arhats: address of invitation (*kanjōmon*), 77–81, **78**, 93, 94, 95; definition, 63; Five Hundred, 64, 77–78, 79; images, 64–65, 69; *Rakan kuyō* (Offering for the arhats), 35; rituals, 107n100; Sixteen, 33, 63–64, 65, 66–67, 69, 79, 87–91, 105; veneration of, 63–66, 67. See also *Rakan kōshiki*

Ashikaga Tadayoshi, 209

Ashikaga Tadayoshi kishin jōan (Donation proposal by Ashikaga Tadayoshi), 208–209

Ashikaga Takauji, 209

Assmann, Aleida, 174n3

Assmann, Jan, 174n3, 229–230

aural dimension of rituals, 5–6, 12, 103, 116–117. *See also* acoustic modules; chants; music; soundscapes

Ayuwang jing (Sutra of King Aśoka), 30

Azegami Baisen, 203, 213–215, 261

Azuma Ryūshin, 212, 212n41

Baba Gijitsu, 152, 153, 162, 168

Baiyōshoin, 107

Bannan Eiju. See *Daruma kōshiki*

Bateson, Gregory, 62, 63

bells: *kanshō,* 122; large temple, 122; in monasteries, 120, 123; musical notation, **147**; *shukei* (handbell), 122, 123, **123**, 130, 145, 148; small (*rei*), 127, **127**, 130; *tenshō,* 121–122, **122**, 128. *See also* musical instruments

Bendōwa (Talk on pursuing the way), 156, 165

biographies: of Buddha, 188; of Dōgen, 202, 211, 212, 213; of Gasan, 188; of Keizan, 202, 211–212, 213, 218, 219, 226, 227, 230–231; of monks, 174, 175n8, 188, 211

Bodhidharma: *kōshiki* for, 11, 45; lineage, 186, 187; memorial services, vii–viii, 11, 46, 179; *Shaoshi liumen ji,* 213. See also *Daruma kōshiki*

bodhisattvas: directional, 76–77; Jizō, 19, 45, 222; Kannon, 44, 45, 176, 179n27, 188, 191, 197, 197n67, 198, 218–219, 222, 232; Myōken (Skt. Sudarśana), 40

Bodiford, William M., 230
Bonnon no ge. See *Gāthā of Sanskrit Sound*
Buddha: biography, 188; Jātaka stories, 188; memorial day, 26, 30; memorial services, 9, 37, 182; relics, 66–67, 91, 208. See also *Busshōe kōshiki*
Buddhist music (*bukkyō ongaku*), 6–10
Bukkan Bonjō, 47, 210–211, 212–213, 226. See also *Tōjō dentō kōshiki*
Bukkokuji, 157n68
Busshōe kōshiki (*Kōshiki* for the ceremony of the Buddha's birth), 43, 43n82, 46, 50, 59, **99–101**
Buswell, Robert E., Jr., 229
Butsuji kō kada narabini Shichisan, **138**, 184n42
Butsuji kōshiki (*Kōshiki* on Zen Master Butsuji): audiences, 182; collective memory of Keizan, 183, 200; composition, 38, 184, 184n39; origins, 184; performances, 38, 40, 46, 49, 174, 178, 182, 200; ritual frame, 184, 200; ritual manuals, 206–207; *shōmyō,* 184; significance, 183; vocalization, 137, 182. See also *Taiso Butsuji kōshiki*
Butsuji kōshiki manuscripts: list of extant, 239–242; musical notation, 137, **138**; at Sōjiji, 178, 184, 184nn37, 184n39; Taineiji, 185n44, 239–240, 243, 293–301; at Yōkōji, 178, 185n43, 239, 243, 281–291
Butsuji kōshiki shikimon: compared to *Dentō kōshiki,* 226; composition, 184; contents, 182, 218; monks reciting, 183; ritual frame, 184–185; Sōjiji version, 184, 196–200; sources, 184; translation, 243–258; verses used in other *kōshiki,* 216, 217; Yōkōji version, 184, 185–196, 198–199
Butsuji kōshiki transmission lineages: changes in Meiji era, 201; differences, 183–185, 196–200; Sōjiji, 173–174, 184–185, 196–200, 239–241; Yōkōji, 173–174, 184, 185–196, 198–199, 206–207, 239, 240
Byzantine Christianity, 174
Ceremony of Praising the Buddhas. See *Tanbutsue*
Chan patriarchs, 1, 67n33, 96, 186–187, 224
chants: Buddhist, 6, 9; *goeika* (Buddhist devotional hymns), 7n13, 47–48, 232; memorizing, 132; styles, 6n10, 28; sutra-chanting services (*fugin*), 11, 12, 96, 148; terms for, 7. See also *shōmyō*
Chixiu Baizhang qinggui (Imperial revision of Baizhang's rules of purity), 120–121, 126–127
Chōe, *Gyosan shishō,* **144**
Chōfukuji, 41
Chōgen, 64
Chōnen, 64
Christianity: Byzantine, 174; chants, 132; liturgical "we," 174
collective memory: expressed in *shikimon,* 233; of Keizan, 174, 183, 200, 201, 229–230; *kōshiki* performances as affirmation, 4–5, 59, 174, 201, 233
communal obeisance (*sōrai*): in *Butsuji kōshiki,* 184; in *Dentō kōshiki,* 215, 215n58; musical instruments, 124; in *Rakan kōshiki,* 82–83, 95; vocalization, 23, 118, 129
cymbals (*hatsu* or *hachi*), 107, 119, 124–125, **124**, 145, **147**

Dabeixin tuoluoni. See *Dhāraṇī of the Mind of Great Compassion*
Daifusatsu bosatsu shiki (Grand precepts meeting), 11, 32, 32nn47–48, 52n102, 58n115
Daihannya kōshiki, 41–42, 46n92, 51, 59, 97n81, 98, **99–101**
Daijōji: abbots, 39, 44, 222; Keizan and, 190, 192, 192n56, 196–197, 209, 220, 222; *kōshiki* performances, 43n82; proximity to Hakusan, 47; ritual handbooks, 57
Dainichi Nōnin, 43, 193n59
Daini Sōryū, *Myōken kōshiki* (*Kōshiki* for Myōken), 40–41, **41**
Dairyūji, 40
daishindoku ("grand true" reading style), 180, 180n29, 181, 182

Daruma kōshiki (*Kōshiki* on Bodhidharma): authors, 43; at Eiheiji, vii–viii, 43, 46, 51; multivolume editions, 57; performances, 43n78, 46, 97–98; *shikimon,* 213
Daruma school, 43, 67n33, 193n59
Deegalle, Mahinda, 21n4
denjū (transmission from master to disciple), 152. *See also* Dharma transmission
Denkōroku (Record of the transmission of the light), 190, 214, 222
Dentōin, 215, 224
Dentō kōshiki. See *Tōjō dentō kōshiki*
Dhāraṇī of the Jubilant Corona (*Foding zunsheng tuoluoni*), 180n28
Dhāraṇī of the Mind of Great Compassion (*Dabeixin tuoluoni*), 180, 180n28, 182, 215
Dharma transmission: *denjū,* 152; light or lamp metaphor, 214; narration in *Dentō kōshiki,* 1, 217, 221–223; Zen lineages, 185, 186–187
dōanryō (office of *ino* assistants), 148
Dōgen: ancestry, 48; anniversaries of death, 19, 39, 47–48; arhat cult and, 64–65; *Bendōwa* (Talk on pursuing the way), 156, 165; biographies, 202, 211, 212, 213; bone fragment, 193; collective memory of, 66, 230; compared to Keizan, 225, 230; disciples, 189; as founder of Sōtō school, 14, 59, 217; founding of Eiheiji, 177n18, 230; Great Master title, 206; *Kenzeiki,* 188; *kōshiki* performed by, viii, 32–33; *kōshiki* performed for, 19, 37, 39, 47–48, 49–50; lineage, 186, 187; memorial services, 37, 235; as patriarch, 202, 230; posthumous title, 202, 230; purple robe, 181n30; *Rakan kōshiki,* 31n45; *Rakan kuyō shikimon,* 33–35, **34**, 64–65, 66; relics and, 67n33; as Sōtō founder, 195; *Tenzō kyōkun* (Instructions for the cook), 156; on zazen, 156. See also *Dōgen zenji kōshiki; Eihei kaisan Hōon kōshiki; Eihei shoso Dōgen zenji kōshiki; Jōyō daishi kōshiki; Shōbōgenzō*
Dōgen zenji kōshiki (*Kōshiki* on Zen Master Dōgen), 39, 50, 96n79
Donge Zenzui, 173
Dongyang Dehui, *Chixiu Baizhang qinggui* (Imperial revision of Baizhang's rules of purity), 120–121, 126–127
dreams: monks' lives, 191n53; mothers', 188, 188n47, 211, 218; rituals, 65n25, 179n27; temple founding, 35n59, 192, 197, 198, 222
drums: accompanying sutra reading, vii; large, 127–128, **128**; *mokugyo* (wooden fish), 12, 121, 128, 128n28, **129**; use in *kōshiki,* 127–128, 129. *See also* musical instruments

Eckel, David, 67n35
Eiheiji: abbots, 37, 37n63, 181n30, 202, 204, 211, 212; arhats protecting, 65; as Dōgen's temple, 33, 177n18, 230; fieldwork at, vii, 13; *ino,* 149–150, 152; Keizan at, 219; memorial services, 235; novices, 27; ritual manuals, 43; rituals, 11, 114; rivalry with Sōjiji, 176–177, 177n18, 196, 201, 202–203, 223; satellite temples, 13, 19, 47, 48, 166–167, 234, 235; *shōmyō* teachers, 13, 168; as Sōtō head temple, 176–177, 202; Yōkōji and, 192
Eiheiji, *kōshiki* performances: *Busshōe kōshiki,* 43; contemporary, 11, 19, 47–48, 51, **52**, 235; *Daruma kōshiki,* vii–viii; by Dōgen, 33; for Dōgen, 19, 47–48; *Rakan kōshiki,* 86n66; in Tokugawa period, 46, 46n92, **46**
Eihei kaisan Hōon kōshiki (*Kōshiki* to repay benevolence received from the founder of Eihei[ji]): composition, 39; performances, 46n92, 48, 51; recent revision, 48, 232; replacement, 50; *shikimon,* 188, 208, 216; as source for *Dentō kōshiki,* 215, 215n58, 216–217, 226–227, 230; structure, **99–101**; sutra readings, 97, 97n82; use of Great Master title, 206
Eihei shoso Dōgen zenji kōshiki (*Kōshiki* on Zen Master Eihei Dōgen), 39

eisanka (Buddhist hymns), 6n10
Ejō, 189, 193, 219, 220
Engakuji, 31n45
Ennin, 7, 44n84, 215n58

Faure, Bernard, 64, 187n45, 193n59
Final Praise (*Gobai*), 97, 97nn83–84
Five Hundred Arhats, 64, 77–78, 79. *See also* arhats
Five Kōshiki of the Sōtō School (*Tōjō go kōshiki*), 57
Flood, Gavin, 174
Ford, James L., 26
Four Kōshiki, 136
Four Part Vinaya, 126
Four Shōmyō Melodies (*Shika hōyō*), 23, 83–86, 93, 95, 96, 184–185, 207
frames, 62–63. *See also* ritual frames
Fuekō. See *Universal Transfer of Merit*
fugin. See sutra-chanting services
Fujiwara family, 64
funerals: invocations of Jizō, 45; *kōshiki* performances, 151n56, 175, 235; for lay devotees, 10–12; training, 152. *See also* memorial services
fushi, 136, 137, **138**, 139–141, 161. *See also* musical notation

gagaku (court music), 9n18, 28–29, 29n35, 235–236
Gasan Jōseki: biography, 188; disciples, 183n33, 225; Keizan and, 194, 198, 222, 224; memorial services, 1–2, 39, 46, 46n93, 50, 178n21, 227; protection of Yōkōji, 193; as Sōjiji abbot, 173n2, 198, 224; as Yōkōji abbot, 176, 184
Gasan kōshiki, 39–40, 39n70, **40**, 188, 215
Gāthā of Falling Flowers (*Sange no ge*), 83, 85–86, **132**
Gāthā of Praising Incense (*Kōsan no ge*), 98
Gāthā of Sanskrit Sound (*Bonnon no ge*), 83, 85–86
Gāthā of the Sounding Staff (*Shakujō no ge*), 83, 85–86, 93, 127
Gāthā to Scattering Flowers (*Sange no ge*): in *Butsuji kōshiki,* 184; musical instruments, 123–124; musical notation, **146**, **147**; in *Rakan kōshiki,* 74, 83, 93, 95; vocalization, 74, 118, 128–129
Genkō shakusho, 190
Genpei jōsui ki (Record of the rise and fall of the Minamoto and Taira), 29
Genshin, 24, 24n16, 37, 37n61, 45, 215n58
Gidō, 43
Gien, 189
Giun, *Hokke kōshiki* (*Kōshiki* on the *Lotus* [*Sutra*]), 37, 46, 50
Gladigow, Burkhard, 60, 62n8
Godaigo, Emperor: memorial services, 203, 205; recognition of Sōjiji, 203, 223; ten questions sent to Keizan, 192–193, 198, 208, 212, 214, 223
godō, 69, 69n41, 72n42, 86, 154, 161, 166, 212
goeika (Buddhist devotional hymns), 7n13, 47–48, 232
Goffman, Erving, 62
Gomurakami, Emperor, 208, 223
Gotsuchimikado, Emperor, 208
Grand Precepts Meeting. See *Daifusatsu bosatsu shiki*
"grand true" reading style. See *daishindoku*
Great Sutra on the Perfection of Wisdom (*Mahāprajñāpāramitā Sūtra*), vii, 11, 41–42, 98, 109, 179, 181
guest-host paradigm, 95–96
Gülberg, Niels, 12, 20, 21n3, 22, 24n16, 26–27, 37
Gyōki, 198
Gyosan shishō, **144**

Haga Jōmyō, 47
hagiographies, 229. *See also* biographies
hakase. See musical notation
Hakusan (White Mountain), 19, 47
Hakusan kōshiki, 47, 53, 96n79
Hakuun Ekyō, 220
Halbwachs, Maurice, 174n3
Handelman, Don, 61n6, 63, 63n11
Haruki Shōshū, 13, 149, 150, 150n54, 151n59, 153
Hasegawa Ten'ei, 207
head temples: agreement between, 202; monastic training, 27, 69n41, 148;

novices, 27, 156–157; in Tokugawa period, 46, 176–177; "two head temples, one essence" (*ryōzan ittai funi*) doctrine, 177, 203. *See also* Eiheiji; Sōjiji
Heart Sutra, vii, 66n31, 98
Heroic March Dhāraṇī (*Lengyan zhou*), 179, 179n27, 180, 180n29, 181, 182
Hiei, Mt., 220
Hōenji, 136
Hokke kōshiki (*Kōshiki* on the *Lotus* [*Sutra*]), 37, 46, 50
Hōkōji, vii
Hōkyōji, 47, 152, 248n38
Hōnen, 175
Hōonji, 152
Hōon kōshiki. See *Eihei kaisan Hōon kōshiki*
hōon kōshiki (*kōshiki* to repay benevolence received), 38–40, 47, 175, 188
Hornborg, Anne-Christine, 60
Horton, Sarah Johanna, 24n16
Hōshōji, 39, 192n56
hosshiki (ritual procedures), 116–117
hosshiki kōshiki (ritual procedures and *kōshiki*), 117
hosshiki shōmyō (ritual procedures and Buddhist chant), 117, 155–156, 157, 158–159
Hōyō, **56**
hōyō (ceremonies), 163–164. *See also* rituals
human rights movement, Sōtō school, 48, 48n98, 232
Hymn of the Four Wisdoms (*Shichisan*): in *Butsuji kōshiki,* 184; in *kōshiki,* 23; musical instruments, 123, 124–125; omitted from *kōshiki* performances, 98; in *Rakan kōshiki,* 69, 74–77, **75**, 93, 95; in Shingon school, 110n109; text, 120; vocalization, 119, 129
hymns. See *eisanka; goeika; wasan*
hyōbyaku. See pronouncement of intention

Imai Gen'yū, 152, 153
Imamura Genshū, 19, 48, 232
ino, 72, 72n43, 148, 149–150, 154, 165
Inoue Gishin: *Hakusan kōshiki,* 47, 53, 96n79; on *Hymn of the Four Wisdoms,* 77; *Jōyō daishi kōshiki* (*Kōshiki* for Great Master Jōyō), 19, 47–48, 96n79; *kōshiki* by, 26, 232; on *kōshiki,* 32n49, 53, 59, 116, 167, 234; on postures, 104; on *shikimon* reading, 118, 118n6
instrumental music, 28–29, 30, 123–124. *See also* musical instruments
interrituality, 60, 60n3, 102, 103, 114, 233
intertextuality: interrituality as extension of, 60; of *kōshiki,* 103, 200, 210–211, 226–227, 233; of *shikimon,* 23, 207
invitation (*kanjō*), 23, 66n31, **111**. *See also* address of invitation
Itō Ryōkō, ix

Jakuen, 189, 220
Jakushū Kankō, 44
Jātaka stories, 188
Jien, 25
Jigenji, 45
Jizō, 19, 45, 222
Jizō kōshiki, 26, 45, 53, 59
Jōjin, 64
Jōjūji, 207, 209, 222, 224
Jōkei: *Jizō kōshiki,* 26, 45; *Kannon kōshiki,* 26, 44; *Shari kōshiki,* 29
Jōken, 176, 192, 197–198, 209, 222
Jōmanji, 205n17, 221
Jōyō daishi kōshiki (*Kōshiki* for Great Master Jōyō), 19, 47–48, 96n79
Jūmujin'in shari kōshiki (*Kōshiki* on the relics of Jūmujin'in), 30
Junji ōjō kōshiki (*Kōshiki* on rebirth in the Pure Land), 29
Jūroku Rakan kōshiki (*Kōshiki* on the Sixteen Arhats), 26n26, 35. See also *Shiza kōshiki*

Kada narabini hōyō, **143**, **147**, 184n42
Kaisan kokushi Butsuji kōshiki (Taineiji manuscript), 185n44, 239–240, 243, 257–258, 293–301
Kakua, 43
Kakuban, 25, 235
Kakumyō, 197, 198

Kakunyo, 175

kami: kōshiki written for, 20, 49; mountain, 47, 195, 198; separation from buddhas, 202

kangen kō (lit. assembly of wind and string instruments), 28–29, 30

kangen kōshiki, 29–30, 235–236

kangyō (practicing in the cold), 152–153, 153n61

Kankai, 136

Kannon, 44, 45, 176, 179n27, 188, 191, 197, 197n67, 198, 218–219, 222, 232

Kannon kōshiki (*Kōshiki* on Kannon): of Jōkei, 26, 44; performances, 53, 59, 235; structure, 98, **99–101**; use of title, 20

Kannon senbō (Kannon repentance ceremony): composition, 44n84; instrumental music, 75n48; *kōshiki* term used for, 32; performances, 9, 44n84, 53, 151n56, 167; replacement by *Kannon kōshiki,* 44; ritual handbooks, 58n115

Kannon Sutra, 188, 218

kanshō bells, 122

karaoke, 153, 165, 168

Kasekison nōke kōshiki, 41, **42**, 50, 59, **99–101**

Kasuisai, 13, 145, 149, 161

Kawase Genkō, 155

Keijūji, 173

Keizan Jōkin: arhat cult and, 35n59, 65, 65n25; biographies, 202, 211–212, 213, 218, 219, 226, 227, 230–231; collective memory of, 174, 183, 200, 201, 229–230; death, 193, 193n60, 224; disciples, 176, 194–195, 198, 222, 225; enlightenment experience, 189–190, 220; as founder of Sōtō school, 203, 214–215, 217; *kōshiki* performed by, viii, 35–36, 37n62; *kōshiki* performed for, viii, 1–2, 49–50, 177, 227–229; life story, 187–191, 193, 193n60, 211, 216, 218–219, 220, 221–222, 224–225; lineage, 185, 186, 187, 189, 193n59, 214, 224, 225; mausoleum, 215, 224; memorial services for, 1–2, 46, 50, 173, 178–183, 209–210, 227–229, 235; as patriarch, 201, 202, 216–217, 221, 230; posthumous names and titles, 173n2, 184n37, 202, 206, 210, 225, 230; previous lives, 65n25, 188; relics buried by, 67n33; *Sansō yuiseki teradera okibumiki* (Will on the temples I leave behind), 209; temples founded by, 40, 175–176, 190–192, 192n56, 196–198, 205n17, 209; *Tōkokuki* (Record of Tōkoku[san]), 35n59, 37, 65n25, 191–192, 191n53, 193nn59–60, 211; *Tōkokusan jinmiraisai okibumi* (Will on the future of Tōkokusan), 193n59, 209; writings, 224. See also *Butsuji kōshiki; Tōjō dentō kōshiki*

Keizan shingi (Pure rules of Master Keizan), Rinkō manuscript: musical notation, 130, **132**, 133, **134**, **144**, 145; *Nehan kōshiki,* 36, 37, 37n62; *Rakan kōshiki,* 36–37, **36**, 66; use of *kōshiki* term, 31n46

Kenchōji, 31n45

Kendall, Laura, 151n60

Kenzeiki, 33, 188

Keta shrine, 190, 191

Kimura Bunmei, 211

kinetic modules, 103–105, 106–107, 150–151

Kishigami Kōjun, 155

Koan Shikan, 176, 184, 193, 194, 198, 224

Kohō Chisan, 204

Kohō Hakugan, 177, 201, 203, 204, 212. See also *Taiso Butsuji kōshiki*

Kojima Shōin, 166–167

Kokan Shiren, *Genkō shakusho,* 190

Kōkōji, 222, 224

kōkyō kō, 37

Komazawa University, 96

Kōmyō, Emperor, 208

Kōsan no ge. See *Gāthā of Praising Incense*

Kōsen Mujaku, 44

kōshiki: adopted from other schools, 42–46, 60–61, 232–233; composition, 60–61, 102, 115, 233; contemporary, 26, 47–48, 232; cultural influence, 20, 30; definition (broad and narrow senses), 21–24, 31,

31n46, 154; English translations, 21; history in Sōtō school, 31, 32–47, 48–50, **49**, 58–59, 232; invention and development of genre, 3, 9, 20, 21, 24–27; as living tradition, 232; localized, 38, 40–41, 46, 58, 232; in Meiji era, 201, 231; number composed, 20; objects of veneration, 20, 22, 26, 29, 48–49, **50**, **51**; scholarship on, viii, 3–4, 5, 235–236; standardization, 54, 57; use of term in Sōtō school, 31–32

kōshiki performances: actors, 27, 68, 69, 72–73, 92–93, 148; before images, 29; as collective memory affirmation, 4–5, 59, 174, 201, 233; in concert, 54; contemporary, 19, 27, 50, 51–54, **51**, **52**, 234, 235; diversity, 30, 45, 235; dress rehearsals, viii, 149; at funerals, 151n56, 235; before images, 29; implements, 74, 74n45, 106, 106n98; instrumental music, 28–29, 30, 123–124; lengths, 118; in medieval period, 20, 28–29, 32–37; in Meiji era, 47, 50; as monastic rituals, 2, 59, 182, 235; movements, 30, 92–93, 103–105, 106–107, 150–151, 234; multidimensionality, 102–107, 115, 233, 234; by nuns, 52–53, 59; officiants (*dōshi* or *shikishi*), 69, 72; recordings, 13, 53, 234; ritual implements, 106, 106n98; sites, 29–30; soteriological function, 234; soundscape, 9, 117, 128–130, **131**, 233–234; standardization, 30, 232; theater techniques and dance, 30; in Tokugawa period, 31n45, 38, 40, 43, 45–46, **46**, 97, 178, 184n42, 232; at training temples, 51, 53, 148–149; in vernacular language, 22–23. *See also* Eiheiji; musical instruments; Sōjiji; vocalization; *and individual titles*

kōshiki structure: intertextuality, 103, 200, 210–211, 226–227, 233; ritual elements, 21, 23–24; variations, 21, 22, 23, 96–98, **99–101**, 102. *See also* modules; ritual frames

kōshiki texts: amendments, 55; archives, viii–ix, 12–13; authors, 25–26, 45; influence on literature in other genres, 20; languages, 22–23, 41; manuscripts, 54–55, **56**; as material objects, 105; in medieval period, 25–26; in Meiji era, 26, 47; multivolume editions, 57–58; number of, 20, 26, 235; in Tokugawa period, 26–27, 37, 38–46, 54; transmission, 27, 54; woodblock print editions, 38, 54, 55, 136, 206, 215. *See also* musical notation; *and individual* kōshiki

Kōya Kennin, 149, 150, 153, 165

Kōya, Mt., 8, 27, 30, 109–112, 130. *See also* Shingon school

Kōzanji, 44

Kreinath, Jens, 63n11

Krueger, Derek, 174, 174n5, 200

Kūkai, 7, 24n16, 35, 88, 110n107

Kuonjōin Nisshin, 153n61

Lanxi Daolong (J. Rankei Doryū), 31n45, 43

lay devotees: chanting and hymn singing, 7n13, 9; in *kōshiki* audiences, 27, 59, 68, 69, 118n6, 120, 182, 235; memorial services, 11–12, 43; participation in *kōshiki,* 27, 27n29; rituals performed for, 167; texts written for, 226

Ledderose, Lothar, 61

Li Longmin, 64

literature, influence of *kōshiki,* 20

liturgy: Chinese, 7; development in Japan, 7, 9, 26; fluidity, 5; of memory, 174; songs of edification (*kyōke*), 23, 23n11; use of term, 10n19; vocalization, 116, 117–118; Zen, 3, 10

Lotus Sutra, 97n82, 153n61, 179, 188, 189–190, 220, 223, 226. See also *Hokke kōshiki*

Machida Muneo, 48n98

Maekawa Bokushō: on *bonnon,* 158n70; field research and, vii, viii, 13; musical notation system, 145, **146**; rituals performed, 157; students, 161; teaching activities and methods, vii, 52, 149, 150, 154; training, 152, 153, 155; views of *shōmyō* practice, 116, 154–161, 162–163, 164, 168–169, 234; "Zen Master Dōgen and Religious Rituals" (*Kōso Dōgen zenji to shūkyō girei*), 155–161

Maekawa Hakuhō: influence, 155; recordings, 151; students, 58, 152, 154, 161, 164; teaching activities, 58; view of *shōmyō* practice, 161, 162

Maitreya, 67, 89

Manshōji, 44

Manzan Dōhaku, 36, 39

Marvelously Beneficial Disaster-Preventing Dhāraṇī (*Xiaozai miao jixiang tuoluoni*), 180n28

material modules, 105–106

Matsuda Bun'yū, 193n60

medieval period: *kōshiki* performances, 20, 28–29, 32–37; *kōshiki* texts, 25–26; socio-political changes, 26

Meeks, Lori Rochelle, 21

Meihō Sotetsu, 176, 184, 193, 194, 198, 222, 224, 225

Meiji emperor, 210, 225

Meiji era: Buddhist music, 8; Keizan biographies, 211–212, 231; *kōshiki,* 26, 47, 50, 201, 231; religious policies, 201–202, 203; Sōtō school, 201–203, 204, 210; Zen Buddhism, 2. See also *Tōjō dentō kōshiki*

Meiji shinkoku Rakan kōshiki, **108**

Meiken, 25

Meishū Shushin, 39

memorial services: for Bodhidharma, vii–viii, 46, 179; for Buddha, 9, 37, 182; for Dōgen, 37, 235; at Eiheiji, 235; for Gasan, 1–2, 39, 46, 46n93, 50, 178n21, 227; for Godaigo, 203, 205; for Keizan, 1–2, 46, 50, 173, 178–183, 209–210, 227–229, 235; for lay devotees, 11–12, 43; for monks, 39, 175; for patriarchs, 11, 38, 50, 96; ritual forms, 175; at Sōjiji, 11–12, 173, 178–183, 178n21, 235; at Yōkōji, 173, 178. *See also* funerals; *kōshiki* performances

memory. *See* collective memory

Menzan Zuihō: arhat cult and, 65, 65n25; on authorship of *Daruma kōshiki,* 43; *Daihannya kōshiki,* 41–42, 46n92, 51, 59, 97n81, 98, **99–101**; on Dōgen's authorship of *Rakan kōshiki,* 35; *Hokke kōshiki* edited by, 37n63; *Tōjō Rakan kōshiki,* 66; *Tōjō sōdō shingi kōtei betsuroku,* 128n28. See also *Eihei kaisan Hōon kōshiki*

merit: produced in rituals, 12, 163; transfer of, 24, 24n14, 92, 93–94, 102; *Universal Transfer of Merit* (*Fuekō*), 92, 118, 124, 130, 184

Ministry of Cultural Affairs, 234

modularity: of ritual frames, 61–62, 63, 96–97, 102–103, 184, 233; of rituals, 98, 102, 114–115, 210–211

modules: acoustic, 103, 107, 121; kinetic, 103–105, 106–107, 150–151; material, 105–106; textual, 102–103

mokugyo (wooden fish), 12, 121, 128, 128n28, **129**

monasteries, Zen: bells, 120, 123; funerals and memorial services, 11–12; soundscapes, vii, 6, 120

monastic training: in etiquette, 103–104; at head temples, 27, 69n41, 148; in ritual expertise, 10, 152; in *shōmyō,* viii, 5–6, 10, 28, 51, 148–152, 153, 154. See also *godō; ino*

monks, Sōtō: annual rituals, 11; biographies, 211; changing robes, 177; as head priests, 53; memorial services, 39. *See also* monastic training; *shōmyō* specialists

monks, Zen: biographies, 174, 175n8, 188; dreams, 191n53; lineages, 174, 175; memorial services, 175; novices, 10–12

Morita Shōkō, 86, 87, 88, 90, 91

Moriyoshi shinnō reisen'an (Order by Prince Moriyoshi), 209

Mugai Chikō, 176, 184, 193, 194, 198, 222, 224

Mugaku Guzen, 44

Mūlasarvāstivāda Vinaya, 126

Munakata Gihō, 149–150, 152, 168

music: Buddhist (*bukkyō ongaku*), 6–10;

court (*gagaku*), 9n18, 28–29, 29n35, 235–236; instrumental, 28–29, 30, 123–124; in *kōshiki* performances, 28–29, 30; melodic change, 137; rhythm, 103; in rituals, 5–6, 7–10, 12, 109, 112, 114, 116–117; traditional Japanese, 20; as Ur-sound, 158; use of term, 6; vocal, 103; Western, 8, 145
musical instruments: cymbals (*hatsu* or *hachi*), 107, 119, 124–125, **124**, 145, **147**; drums, 12, 121, 127–128, **128**, **129**; functions in *kōshiki* performances, 6, 121, 123–124; in *Genpei jōsui ki,* 29; gongs (*shōgo*), 29; gongs, small (*nyō*), 119, 124, 125, **125**, 145; *kangen kō,* 28–29; monks' use of, 120–121; musical notation for, 145, **146**, **147**, 148; quality, 121; singing bowls (*daikei, keisu*), 74, 121, 123–124, **124**, 130, 145, **147**; sounding staff (*shakujō*), 85–86, 125–127, **126**, 148; sounds, 103, 107; use in rituals, 6, 7, 103. *See also* bells; soundscapes
musical notation: in Rinzai ritual handbooks, 109; Western, 141, 145
musical notation (*hakase*): development in Japan, 7–8; earliest examples, 8, 36–37, 130; functions, 132–133; *fushi,* 136, 137, **138**, 139–141, 161; for instruments, 145, **146**, **147**, 148; learning to read, viii, 132, 151; melodic organization, 137–139; new style of Sōtō notation, 133, **135**, 136–137, **137**; old style of Sōtō notation, **132**, 133, **134**, **135**, 136; in ritual handbooks, 36–37, 130–133, **134**, **135**, 136–137, **137**, 145; Shingon school notation, 8, 130, 141, **143**; standardization, 160–161; systems, 7–8, 130, 133, 133n36, 136–137, 145; Tendai school notation, 133, 141, **142**
musicians, professional, 28–29
Myōe: *Busshōe kōshiki,* 43, 43n82, 46, 50, 59, **99–101**; dreams, 191n53; *Jūmujin'in shari kōshiki,* 30; *Jūroku Rakan kōshiki,* 35; *kōshiki* by, 24n13, 26, 43, 44, 45, 48n100; *Rakan kōshiki,* 66, 67n34; *Rakan wasan,* 67n34; *Shiza kōshiki,* 26, 26n26, 27, 27n29, 35, 48n100, 67n34, 114n117; temple, 44
Myōgenji, 157n68
Myōken (Skt. Sudarśana), 40
Myōken kōshiki (*Kōshiki* for Myōken), 40–41, **41**, 50, 59, 97n81, **99–101**
Myōkōji, 212, 212n43
Myōshinji: *Daruma kōshiki,* 43n78; *Rakan kōshiki* performances, 107; ritual handbook, 107, 108, **108**

Nandimitrā, 66–67, 67n33. See also *Record of the Perpetuity of the Dharma*
Nanzan Shin school, 109
Nehan kō kada narabini Shichisan, **134**, **135**, **138**
Nehan kōshiki (*Kōshiki* on the Buddha's passing): attribution to Genshin, 37, 37n61; images used in, 105; of Lanxi Daolong, 31n45; manuscripts, 31n46, 36, 37, 37n62, 54, **134**, **135**, 136, **137**; multivolume editions, 57; performances, 37, 37n62, 46, 51, 97–98, 97n82, 105; *shikimon,* 31n46, **137**; verses used in other *kōshiki,* 199. See also *Shiza kōshiki*
Nelson, Steven G., 21, 118
New Kamakura schools, 235
New Year's celebrations, 11
Nihon tōjō rentōroku (Transmission of the lamp in the Japanese Sōtō school), 211, 220, 222, 226
Nijūgo zanmai shiki (Ceremony of the twenty-five samādhi), 24–25, 24n16, 235
Nittaiji Senmon Sōdō, 13, 148–149, 152, 161
novices: at head temples, 27, 156–157; young monks' associations, 51, 151, 168; Zen, 10–12. *See also* monastic training; training temples
Nozaki Taiyū, 165
nuns: disciples of Sawaki Kōdō, 155; *kōshiki* performances, 52–53, 59; rituals for Ānanda, 44–45; *shōmyō* training, 52, 154
Nyoraibai. See *Praise of the Thus Come One*

Nyoraibaimon. See *Verse of the Praise of the Thus Come One*

Ōbaku school, 7, 8
objects of veneration: images, 29, 40, 105; of *kōshiki*, 20, 22, 26, 29, 48–49, **50**, **51**. *See also* address of invitation; arhats; communal obeisance
offertory declaration (*saimon*): in *Butsuji kōshiki*, 184; in *Dentō kōshiki*, 215; posture of monks, 104; in *Rakan kōshiki*, 81–82, **81**, 95; in *Taiso Butsuji kōshiki*, 207; texts, 24n13, 69n39; vocalization, 23–24, 117–118, 129
Ōjō kōshiki (*Kōshiki* on rebirth [in Amida's Pure Land]), 25, 27, 29, 30
Okamura Kōbun, 155
Ongaku kōshiki (*Kōshiki* on music), 29
Oppitz, Michael, 62
Orzech, Charles D., 61n6
Ōuchi Seiran: *Sōtōshū ryōso denryaku* (Short biographies of the two patriarchs of the Sōtō school), 212, 218, 226, 227; *Tōjō zaike shushōgi* (The meaning of practice-realization for lay members of the Sōtō school), 212n42
Ozaki Shōzen, 184n39

patriarchs: biographies narrated in *kōshiki*, 5; Chan, 1, 67n33, 96, 186–187, 224; memorial services, 11, 38, 50, 96; Sōtō, 201, 202, 212, 230; sutra-chanting services, 11. *See also* Dōgen; Keizan Jōkin
percussion instruments. *See* drums; musical instruments
postures, 104
Praise of the Relics (*Shari rai*), 111, 111n114, 112, 113
Praise of the Thus Come One (*Nyoraibai*): importance, 96; length, 119n9; musical instruments, 145; musical notation, 141, **142**, **143**, **144**; omitted from *kōshiki* performances, 98; performances, 7, 83–85, **84**, 106; posture of monks, 104; text, 84n65; vocalization, 96, 119, 129
pronouncement of intention (*hyōbyaku*), 9, 21, 22, 24, 24n15, 26, 31n46, 117–118, 185–187
proselytization, *kōshiki* for, 25
Pure Land. *See* Amida's Pure Land
pure sound (*bonnon*), 158, 158n70
"pure Zen" practices, 2, 10

Raihai no ge, 215n58
Rakan kō hossoku, 110–112, **111**
Rakan kō kada narabini Shichisan, **139**
Rakan kōshiki (*Kōshiki* on the arhats): attributed to Dōgen, 33–35, 59, 64–65, 66; of Dōgen, 31n45; *Keizan shingi* manuscript, 36–37, **36**, 66; of Lanxi Daolong, 31n45; as model, 61, 63, 96–97, 194, 199, 207; multivolume editions, 57; musical notation, **139**, **142**; Myōe's version, 66, 67n34; popularity, 66; in Rinzai school, 107–109, 112–113, **113**; ritual handbooks, 68, 97, 105, 106–107, 110–112; *shikimon*, 93, 207; in Shingon school, 109–112, 113–114, **113**; sources, 66; by Yōsai, 33–35
Rakan kōshiki performances: actors, 68, 69, 72–73, 92–93; address of invitation (*kanjōmon*), 77–81, **78**, **80**, 93, 94, 95; ceremonial space, 68–69, **70**, **71**, 106; communal obeisance, 82–83, 95; contemporary, 51–52, **52**, 53, 68–93, 96; at Eiheiji, 86n66; *Four Shōmyō Melodies* (*Shika hōyō*), 83–86, 93, 95, 96; *Hymn of the Four Wisdoms*, 69, 74–77, **75**, 95; images used in, 69, 105; instrumental music, 123–124; motives, 59, 66; offertory declaration, 81–82, **81**, 95; reading of Dharma words, 79, **80**, 95; rehearsals, viii; ritual space purification, 73–77, 93, 94; *San-Bon-Shaku*, 83, 85–86, **85**; seating order, 69, **72**, 73, 94–95; *shikimon* reading, 86–91, 86n66, **87**, 93, 95, 96; in Tokugawa period, 46; transfer of merit, 92, 93–94
Rakan kōshiki structure: compared to other *kōshiki*, **99–101**; comparison

among schools, 111–114, **113**; modules, 102–107; ritual frame, 93–96, 107–108; ritual handbooks, 68
Rakan kushiki, 66, 67n34
Rakan kuyō (Offering for the arhats), 31n46, 35
Rakan kuyō shiki, **55**
Rakan kuyō shikimon, 33–35, **34**, 64–65, 66
Rakan pai, 66, 66n31
Rankin, Susan, 132
Rappoport, Roy A., 102
Reader, Ian, 11
reading (*yomu shōmyō*), 8, 28, 116–118
recitation (*kataru shōmyō*), 8, 28
Record of the Perpetuity of the Dharma, Narrated by the Great Arhat Nandimitrā (Skt. *Nandimitrāvadāna,* Ch. *Daaluohan nantimiduoluo suoshuo fazhuji*), 33, 64, 66–67, 67n33, 90
Reinan Shūjo, 211n39. See also *Nihon tōjō rentōroku*
relics: of Buddha, 66–67, 91, 208; in Daruma school, 193n59; *Shari kōshiki,* 26n26, 29, 35, 48n100, 67n33; veneration, 67n33; of Zen masters, 193
Rentōroku. See *Nihon tōjō rentōroku*
Rinzai school: founder, 33–35; Hōtō branch, 220; *kōshiki,* 31n45, 43, 43n78, 61; *Rakan kōshiki,* 35n55, 107–109, 112–113, **113**; ritual handbooks, 107–109, **108**; rituals, 109, 114; *shōmyō,* 114
ritual frames: building, 61; of *Butsuji kōshiki,* 184, 200; of *Dentō kōshiki,* 215; of *kōshiki,* 61, 63, 102–103, 115, 184, 233; modularity, 61–62, 63, 96–97, 102–103, 184, 233; nested, 94–95, 115; of *Rakan kōshiki,* 93–96, 107–108; of *shikimon,* 93–95, **94**, 102–103, 115
ritual manuals. See *kōshiki* texts
ritual procedures. See *hosshiki*
rituals: for Ānanda, 44–45; annual, 9, 11, 12; aural dimension, 5–6, 12, 103, 116–117; changing of robe (*tenne*), 177; collective memory and, 4–5, 174; daily, 11; definition, 5, 5n8; evolution, 5, 75n48; guest-host paradigm, 95–96; interrituality, 60, 60n3, 102, 103, 114, 233; *kōshiki* term used for, 32; modularity, 98, 102, 114–115, 210–211; monthly, 11; movements during, 104–105, 106–107, 150–151; *shinsanshiki,* 53; sutra-chanting services (*fugin*), 11, 12, 96, 148; theatrical elements, 30; at training temples, 11, 148; variations, 60; in vernacular language, 20, 22–23; Zen, 4, 9, 157, 158, 163–164. *See also* chants; funerals; *kōshiki;* liturgy; memorial services; merit; *and specific rituals*
ritual space purification, 73–77, 93, 94, 128–129
ritual spaces, 23, 69, 163–164
ritual specialists, 154. See also *shōmyō* specialists
robe, 155, 177, 181n30, 186, 197, 205, 221, 225
Rokudō kōshiki (*Kōshiki* on the six realms), 24–25
rolling reading. See *tendoku*
Ryaku kōshiki (*Daijō shōin*), 57, 57n114, **57**, **135**
Ryūkan, 175

Saichō, 7, 24n16, 35, 88
Saifukuji, 136
saimon. See offertory declaration
Sakai Tokugen, 155
Sakauchi Ryūyū, 77
Sakujitsu Rakan kōshiki (*Kōshiki* for the arhats on the first day of the year), 109–110
San-Bon-Shaku: handbell cues, 123; omitted from *kōshiki* performances, 98; posture of monks, 104; in *Rakan kōshiki,* 83, 85–86, **85**; vocalization, 118–119, 118n8, 129
Sange no ge. See *Gāthā of Falling Flowers; Gāthā to Scattering Flowers*
San kōshiki narabini hōyō, 97n82, 184n42
Sansō yuiseki teradera okibumiki (Will on the temples I leave behind), 209
Sawada Atsuko, vii, 120
Sawaki Kōdō, 155, 157n68

Seigan kōshiki (*Kōshiki* on [Amida's] vow), 25
Sengcan, 224
Shakujō no ge. See *Gāthā of the Sounding Staff*
Shari kōshiki (*Kōshiki* on relics), 26n26, 29, 35, 48n100, 67n33
Shichisan. See *Hymn of the Four Wisdoms*
shikan taza (just sitting), 165–166
shikimon (central text of ceremony): abbreviated readings, 86, 96, 102, 118, 234; collective memory expressed in, 233; composition, 102; in *Daruma kōshiki*, 213; in *Dentō kōshiki*, 1, 215, 216–226, **228**, 265–280; in *Eihei kaisan Hōon kōshiki*, 188, 208, 216; functions, 93; included in ritual manuals, 54, 206–207; intertextuality, 23, 207; *kōshiki* genre defined by, 102; languages, 227; musical instruments, 124, 127, 130; in *Nehan kōshiki*, 31n46, **137**; in *Rakan kōshiki*, 86–91, 86n66, **87**, 93, 95, 96, 207; reading speeds, 118, 118n6, 234; ritual frames, 93–95, **94**, 102–103, 115; structure, 22; sutra quotations, 23; in *Taiso Butsuji kōshiki*, 205, 206, 207–209, 217; vocalization, 28, 28n34, 117–118, 118n4, 129–130. See also *Butsuji kōshiki shikimon*
Shinchi Kakushin, 220
Shingen, 29
shingi (rules of purity), 120
Shingon school: *kōshiki* performances, 25, 61, 112; musical notation, 141, **143**; *Rakan kōshiki*, 109–112, 113–114, **113**; ritual handbooks, 110–112; rituals, 9, 95, 112, 114, 114n117; *shikimon* vocalization, 28, 118n4; Shingi branch, 25; *shōmyō*, 7–8, 109, 112, 114; use of *kōshiki* term, 22
Shinran, 175
Shinryū, 133, 136
Shintō, 202
Shiza kōshiki (*Kōshiki* in four sessions), 26, 26n26, 27, 27n29, 35, 114n117. See also *Nehan kōshiki*; *Shari kōshiki*
Shōbōgenzō (Dōgen): *Arakan*, 33n52, 65n23; on etiquette, 103n91; influence, 39, 155, 165n88; publication, 230; on zazen, 166
Shōbōji, 136
shōmyō (Japanese Buddhist chant): as artistic expression, 161, 162, 169; concert performances, 8–9; development in Japan, 7–9; *Four Shōmyō Melodies* (*Shika hōyō*), 83–86, 93, 95, 96, 184–185, 207; genres, 9, 117; individual interpretations, 235; languages, 9, 117–118, 119–120; meanings of texts, 165; melodies, **140**, 145; monastic training, viii, 51, 52, 148–152, 153, 154; musical notation, 130–133, 136–141, 145; oral transmission, 132–133, 149, 152, 161; popularity among monks, 96, 167–168, 234; reading (*yomu shōmyō*), 8, 116–118; recitation (*kataru shōmyō*), 8; recordings, 8, 150n54, 151, 151n59, 159, 234; religious meanings, 161–162, 166; Rinzai school, 114; ritual manuals, 58, **144**; Shingon school, 7–8, 109, 112, 114; song (*utau shōmyō*), 9, 117, 118–119; soteriological function, 159, 161, 164, 234; Sōtō school, 12, 114; use of term, 7; vocal training, viii, 5–6, 10, 28, 152–153, 234; as Zen practice, 153–167, 234. See also *Tanbutsue*
Shōmyō kihan. See *Shōwa kaitei Shōmyō kihan*
shōmyō specialists: musical backgrounds, 168; recordings, 151; ritual manuals, 58; on singing *goeika*, 47–48; teaching activities, 51, 58, 151; views of practice, 154–168, 234–235; vocal training, 152–153, 234
shōmyō teachers: need for, 132, 148, 149; notation systems, 145; private instruction, 152; recordings, 149–150, 151; solo performances, 53; teaching methods, 149–150, 151. *See also* Baba Gijitsu; Haruki Shōshū; Imai Gen'yū; *ino;* Kōya Kennin; Maekawa Bokushō;

Maekawa Hakuhō; Munakata Gihō; Nozaki Taiyū; Suzuki Bunmei; Terakura Shōyū; training temples
Shōmyō zenshū, **142**
Shōun Setsugan, 209–210
Shōwakai, 47
Shōwa kaitei Rakan kōshiki, 74n47, 119n9, **147**
Shōwa kaitei Shōmyō kihan (Regulations for *shōmyō,* revised in the Shōwa era): appendix with Western musical notation, 141, 145; diagram of setup and seating order, **70**; musical instruments instructions, 120n14; musical notation, 139, **140**, 160–161; publication, 58; *Rakan kōshiki,* 66; use of, 58, 74n47
Shunkō, 178–181, 182
Six Kōshiki of the Sōtō School (*Sōtō roku kōshiki*), 57
Sixteen Arhats, 33, 63–64, 65, 66–67, 69, 79, 87–91, 105. *See also* arhats
Snoek, Jan A. M., 63n11
Sōgenji, 53
Sōjiji: abbot rotation system, 176, 182–183; abbots, 39–40, 173, 176, 181n30, 203; branch temples, 176, 177, 178, 183; fieldwork at, viii, 13; *godō,* 212; Hall of the Great Ancestors (Daisodō), 1–2, 68–69, **71**, 73–74, 106, 121, **122**; as head temple, 176–177, 202; history, 176–177, 196–198, 205, 222; independence, 203; *ino,* 72, 154, 165; *kōshiki* manuscripts, 55, **56**; lay parishioners, 11–12; in Meiji era, 202–203; memorial services held, 1–2, 11–12, 173, 178–183, 178n21, 235; novices, 27, 69, 93, 149, 152, 164; rituals, 11, 66, 114; rivalry with Eiheiji, 176–177, 177n18, 196, 201, 202–203, 223; rivalry with Yōkōji, 176, 183–184, 192–193, 196, 205, 210, 223, 229; Sanshōkaku, 53; *shōmyō* training, 149, 150; singing bowls, 123, 123n18; status, 209, 214, 222, 223–224; subtemples, 183, 183n33
Sōjiji, *kōshiki* performances: *Butsuji kōshiki,* 173–174; ceremonial space, 68–69, **70**, **71**, 106; contemporary, 1–2, 19, 51–52, 53; *Dentō kōshiki,* 1–2, 69n39, **71**, 227, **228**; dress rehearsals, 149; group photos, 92; *Rakan kōshiki,* viii, 68–93; ritual handbooks, 184–185n42; sutra readings, 97n82; in Tokugawa period, 38, 40, 46, 46n93, **46**, 97n82, 184n42. See also *Rakan kōshiki* performances
Sōjiji Soin, ix, 13, 28n34, 39, 166, 177
Sōji kaisan Taiso ryakuden (Brief biography of the Great Ancestor, founder of Sōji[ji]): audience, 226; author, 211; influence, 211, 231; in Japanese, 227; Keizan's life story, 218, 219, 220, 222; purpose, 212; sources, 211–212, 223
song (*utau shōmyō*), 9, 28, 117, 118–119
songs of edification (*kyōke*), 23, 23n11
sōrai. See communal obeisance
Sōtō nuns' association, 19
Sōtō school: Dōgen as founder, 14, 59, 217; etiquette, 103–104, 114, 234; head temples, 27; human rights movement, 48, 48n98, 232; Keizan as founder, 203, 214–215, 217; lineages, 186, 187, 189, 194–195; in Meiji era, 201–203, 204, 210; nuns, 44–45, 52–53, 59, 154, 155; outreach movement, 213; practices, 234; reform movement, 39, 54, 211; rituals, 32, 32nn48–49, 102, 166–167, 234; *shikan taza* (just sitting), 165–166; spread in Japan, 194–195, 225; unity of practice and realization (*shushō ittō*), 156, 234. See also *kōshiki;* monks, Sōtō; patriarchs
Sōtōshū ryōso denryaku (Short biographies of the two patriarchs of the Sōtō school), 212, 218, 226, 227
sounding staff (*shakujō*), 85–86, 125–127, **126**, 148
soundscapes: of *kōshiki,* 9, 117, 128–130, **131**, 233–234; of monasteries, vii, 6, 120; of rituals, 9, 12, 116, 233–234; silence, 128. *See also* acoustic modules; aural dimension of

rituals; music; musical instruments; vocalization
Sri Lanka, *bana* ritual, 21n4
Stevenson, Daniel F., 61n6
Sugawara Shigehiro, 43
sutra-chanting services (*fugin*), 11, 12, 96, 148
Sutra of the Teachings Left by the Buddha (*Yiyao jing*), 179, 182
sutra readings: in cold weather, 153n61; drum accompaniment, 128; in *kōshiki* performances, 97, 97n82; rolling, vii, 11, 41–42, 98, 109, 128n29, 179, 181; as Zen practice, 155
sutras: enacting scenes from, 30; verses used in *kōshiki*, 227
Suzuki Bunmei: musical notation system, 145, **146**; as novice, 148–149; teaching activities, 13; views of *shōmyō* practice, 161–164, 168–169, 235
Suzuki Eiichi, 28n34, 86n66, 118n4, 166
Suzuki Kakuzen, 155

Taineiji manuscript. See *Kaisan kokushi Butsuji kōshiki*
Taiso Butsuji kōshiki: collective memory expressed in, 201; contents, 206–207; explanatory notes, 205–206, 207; intentions, 204–206, 210, 229, 230; models, 206–207; offertory declaration, 207; performances, 203–204; postscript, 207; preface, 204–205, 207, 229, 259–260; printed text, 205, 206, 213, 215; reprint by Shōun Setsugan, 209–210; *shikimon,* 205, 206, 207–209, 217; structure, 207; writing of, 231
Taiso ryakuden. See *Sōji kaisan Taiso ryakuden*
Taki Dōnin, *Shōmyō zenshū,* **142**
Takiya Takushū. See *Sōji kaisan Taiso ryakuden*
Tamamuro Fumio, ix
Tanabe, George J., Jr., 119–120
Tanbutsue (Ceremony of praising the Buddhas), 11, 32, 52n102, 150, 150n55, 151n56, 167
tantō (head of training), 47, 69, 72, 72n42, 152, 154
tea ceremonies, 53
Teiho Kenzeiki zue, **65**
Tendai school: founding, 7; *kōshiki,* 20, 24–25, 27, 29; musical notation, 133, 141, **142**; rituals, 9; *shikimon* vocalization, 28, 118n4; *shōmyō,* 7–8. *See also* Twenty-Five Samādhi Society
tendoku (rolling reading), vii, 11, 41–42, 98, 109, 128n29, 179, 181
Ten Great Vows [*of Kannon*] (*Jū daigan-mon*), 98
tenshō bells, 121–122, **122**, 128
Tenzō kyōkun (Instructions for the cook), 156
Terakura Shōyū, 53, 152, 164–166, 169
Tettsū Gikai, 67n33, 189, 189n50, 193, 193n59, 214, 219, 220–221, 222
textual modules, 102–103. See also *kōshiki* texts
theater techniques and dance, 30
Three Dhāraṇī (*san darani*), 180, 180n28
Tōdaiji, 7, 25, 29, 64, 83
Tōfukuji, 107–109, 107n100
Tōjō dentō kōshiki (*Kōshiki* on the transmission of the light in the Sōtō school): audience, 226; collective memory expressed in, 201; commissioning, 213–214; communal obeisance, 215, 215n58; composition, 47; contents, 215–226; intentions, 216, 226, 230, 231; intertextuality, 226–227; as monastic ritual, 218, 226, 227; offertory declaration, 215; performances, 1–2, 52, 69n39, **71**, 226, 227, **228**; postscript, 213–214, 263–264; preface, 213–214, 261; printed text, 215, 215n59, 303–316; purpose, 218, 229; as replacement for *Butsuji kōshiki,* 49; ritual frame, 215; ritual manual, 215; *shikimon,* 1, 215, 216–226, **228**, 265–280; sources, 215, 216–217, 218, 219, 220, 226–227; title, 213–215; writing of, 201, 210–211, 213, 231
Tōjō Rakan kōshiki, 66

Tōkōji, ix
Tōkoku goso gyōjitsu, 184, 189–190, 193n60
Tōkokuki (Record of Tōkoku[san]), 35n59, 37, 65n25, 191–192, 191n53, 193nn59–60, 211
Tōkokusan jinmiraisai okibumi (Will on the future of Tōkokusan), 193n59, 209
Tōkokusan Yōkōji shi, 209n35
Tokugawa period: head and branch temples, 46, 176–177; *kōshiki* performances, 31n45, 38, 40, 43, 45–46, **46**, 97, 178, 184n42, 232; *kōshiki* texts, 26–27, 37, 38–46, 54; musical notation system, 133, 136, 141; religious regulations, 177
Tōshōji, 47
Tōunji, 41
Tōzan Tanshō, 220
training temples: contemporary, 10, 13; *kōshiki* performances, 51, 53, 148–149; rituals, 11, 148; *shōmyō* training, 148–151, 152; soundscapes, 120; zazen training, 157n68. *See also* monastic training; *shōmyō* teachers
Triplett, Katja, 229
Tsubosakasan Minami Hokkeji, 229
Tsuruoka Hakuhō, 166
Turner, Victor W., 60
Twenty-Five Samādhi Society (*Nijūgo zanmai e*), 21, 24

Uchiyama Kōchō, 157n68
Universal Transfer of Merit (*Fuekō*), 92, 118, 124, 130, 184

Verse of the Praise of the Thus Come One (*Nyoraibaimon*), 84n65, 98, 118, 118n7, 119n9
vocalization: of *dhāraṇīs,* 182; history in Buddhism, 7n12; in *kōshiki,* 23, 27–28, 96, 117–120, 129, 137, 182, 234; of *shikimon,* 28, 28n34, 117–118, 118n4, 129–130; of *shōmyō,* 159–161; styles, 9, 117–119. *See also* musical notation
vocal training, viii, 5–6, 10, 28, 152–153, 234

wasan (Japanese hymns), 7n13, 9, 23, 23n12, 26
Watarai Sōjun, 120
Wenshu suoshuo zuisheng mingyi jing (Sutra spoken by Mañjuśrī on the supreme meaning), 221
Western music, 8
Western musical notation, 141, 145

Xiaozai miao jixiang tuoluoni. See *Marvelously Beneficial Disaster-Preventing Dhāraṇī*
Xuanzang, 64

Yakushi kōshiki, 45, 50, 59
Yamada Shōzen, 24n16, 25, 29, 30
Yamahata Shōdō, 193n60
Yinyuan Longqi (J. Ingen Ryōki), 8, 128n28
Yōkan (or Eikan), 25, 29, 30
Yokawa kadaiin geikō kiroku (Record of the *mukae kō* at Yokawa's Kadaiin), 30
Yōkōji: abbots, 40, 176, 177–178, 184, 201, 203, 204, 209, 224; buildings, 192, 204; *Butsuji kōshiki* and, 173–174, 178, 184, 185–196, 185n43, 243; Eiheiji and, 192; history, 175–176, 177–178, 190–193, 205, 208–209, 209n35; Keizan as abbot, 176, 222, 230; *kōshiki* performances, 37, 38, 40, 173–174, 210; in Meiji era, 201, 203, 204; memorial services for Keizan, 173, 178; naming, 191–192; rivalry with Sōjiji, 176, 183–184, 192–193, 196, 205, 210, 223, 229; status, 192–193, 205, 208, 222. See also *Tōjō dentō kōshiki; Taiso Butsuji kōshiki*
Yōmeiji, 45, 97–98
Yōsai (or Eisai), 33–35, 35nn54–55, 44n84, 64, 107, 181n30
young monks' associations, 51, 151, 168
Yuiseki kōshiki (*Kōshiki* on the remaining traces), 26n26, 35. See also *Shiza kōshiki*

zazen: breathing method, 160; Dōgen on, 156; practice of, 10, 12, 14, 155–157, 157n68; relationship to

shōmyō, 160, 165–166, 234; *shikan taza* (just sitting), 165–166; teachers, 154, 155, 157n68
Zen Buddhism: collective memory, 174; lineages, 185, 186–187; liturgies, 3, 10; in Meiji era, 2; Ōbaku school, 7, 8; practices, 156–157; "pure Zen" practices, 2, 10; rituals, 4, 9, 157, 158, 163–164; as silent tradition, 6; temples, 10–11; transmission, 152; Western scholarship on, 2–4. *See also* patriarchs; Rinzai school; Sōtō school
Zen-Kūge Ryūgin Kai, ix
Zenzui Shōzen, *Eihei shoso Dōgen zenji kōshiki* (*Kōshiki* on Zen Master Eihei Dōgen), 39
Zhaozhou (J. Jōshū), 220
Zhiyi, 44n84
Zongmi, 213
Zuihō Daiki, *Dōgen zenji kōshiki* (*Kōshiki* on Zen Master Dōgen), 39, 50, 96n79
Zuiryūji, 204
Zunshi. See *Kannon senbō*

About the Author

Michaela Mross is assistant professor in the Department of Religious Studies at Stanford University. She specializes in Sōtō Zen, Buddhist rituals, sacred music, and manuscript and print culture in premodern Japan. She has published numerous articles on Buddhist rituals and co-edited a special issue of the *Japanese Journal of Religious Studies* on *kōshiki.*

Kuroda Institute
Studies in East Asian Buddhism

Studies in Ch'an and Hua-yen
Robert M. Gimello and Peter N. Gregory, editors

Dōgen Studies
William R. LaFleur, editor

The Northern School and the Formation of Early Ch'an Buddhism
John R. McRae

Traditions of Meditation in Chinese Buddhism
Peter N. Gregory, editor

Sudden and Gradual: Approaches to Enlightenment in Chinese Thought
Peter N. Gregory, editor

Buddhist Hermeneutics
Donald S. Lopez, Jr., editor

Paths to Liberation: The Margā and Its Transformations in Buddhist Thought
Robert E. Buswell, Jr., and Robert M. Gimello, editors

Sōtō Zen in Medieval Japan
William M. Bodiford

The Scripture on the Ten Kings and the Making of Purgatory in Medieval Chinese Buddhism
Stephen F. Teiser

The Eminent Monk: Buddhist Ideals in Medieval Chinese Hagiography
John Kieschnick

Re-Visioning "Kamakura" Buddhism
Richard K. Payne, editor

Original Enlightenment and the Transformation of Medieval Japanese Buddhism
Jacqueline I. Stone

Buddhism in the Sung
Peter N. Gregory and Daniel A. Getz, Jr., editors

Coming to Terms with Chinese Buddhism: A Reading of The Treasure Store Treatise
Robert H. Sharf

Ryōgen and Mount Hiei: Japanese Tendai in the Tenth Century
Paul Groner

Tsung-mi and the Sinification of Buddhism
Peter N. Gregory

Approaching the Land of Bliss: Religious Praxis in the Cult of Amitābha
Richard K. Payne and Kenneth K. Tanaka, editors

Going Forth: Visions of Buddhist Vinaya
William M. Bodiford, editor

Burning for the Buddha: Self-Immolation in Chinese Buddhism
James A. Benn

The Buddhist Dead: Practices, Discourses, Representations
Bryan J. Cuevas and Jacqueline I. Stone, editors

The Making of a Savior Bodhisattva: Dizang in Medieval China
Zhiru

How Zen Became Zen: The Dispute over Enlightenment and the Formation of Chan Buddhism in Song-Dynasty China
Morten Schlütter

Hokkeji and the Reemergence of Female Monasticism in Premodern Japan
Lori Meeks

Conceiving the Indian Buddhist Patriarchs in China
Stuart H. Young

Patrons and Patriarchs: Chan Monks and Regional Rulers during the Five Dynasties and Ten Kingdoms
Benjamin Brose

Right Thoughts at the Last Moment: Buddhism and Deathbed Practices in Early Medieval Japan
Jacqueline I. Stone

Ritualized Writing: Buddhist Practice and Scriptural Cultures in Ancient Japan
Bryan D. Lowe

Chan Before Chan: Meditation, Repentance, and Visionary Experience in Chinese Buddhism
Eric M. Greene

The Poetry Demon: Song-Dynasty Monks on Poetry and the Way
Jason Protass

Memory, Music, Manuscripts: The Ritual Dynamics of Kōshiki *in Japanese Sōtō Zen*
Michaela Mross